THE LAW OF CONTRACT DAMAGES

This is the first work to concentrate solely on damages for breach of contract and provides the most comprehensive and detailed treatment of the subject to date. Written by a commercial barrister and academic for both practitioners and scholars, this text explores the familiar principles and the more recent developments of those principles. To assist understanding and practicality, much of the book is arranged by reference to the type of the complaint (such as the mis-provision of services, the non-payment of money, or the temporary loss of use of property), rather than by the more traditional subject-matter specialisms (eg sale of goods, charterparties, surveyor's negligence). Tort decisions are drawn on to the extent that the applicable principles are the same as or usefully similar to those in contract, and there is also detailed coverage of many practically important but often neglected areas, such as damages for lost management time and the proper evidential approach to proving lost profits.

The Law of Contract Damages

Adam Kramer

·HART·
PUBLISHING
OXFORD AND PORTLAND, OREGON
2014

Published in the United Kingdom by Hart Publishing Ltd
16C Worcester Place, Oxford, OX1 2JW
Telephone: +44 (0)1865 517530
Fax: +44 (0)1865 510710
E-mail: mail@hartpub.co.uk
Website: http://www.hartpub.co.uk

Published in North America (US and Canada) by
Hart Publishing
c/o International Specialized Book Services
920 NE 58th Avenue, Suite 300
Portland, OR 97213-3786
USA
Tel: +1 503 287 3093 or toll-free: (1) 800 944 6190
Fax: +1 503 280 8832
E-mail: orders@isbs.com
Website: http://www.isbs.com

British Library Cataloguing in Publication Data
Data Available

ISBN: 978-1-84946-407-9

Typeset by Compuscript Ltd, Shannon
Printed and bound in Great Britain by
CPI Group (UK) Ltd, Croydon CR0 4YY

Foreword

The law of contract is a system of rules for enforcing promises or, more usually, requiring the payment of compensation for breaking them, and for shifting the risk of future or unknown events. In England the judges have developed this branch of the law over several centuries in a multitude of precedents which have worked out the ramifications of its various principles in great detail. As a result, English contract law has a clarity and predictability which makes it the system of choice for countless commercial transactions, many of which have nothing to do with England. It is a national asset, the jewel in the crown of the common law.

It is, however, neither perfect nor static. It is in the nature of judge-made law that it avoids what Jean-Étienne-Marie Portalis, the principal draftsman of the Code Napoleon, described as the 'the dangerous ambition of wanting to regulate everything and foresee everything.' It adapts to changes in the practices of trade and commerce. And it is subject to constant reconsideration and refinement by generations of judges with a view to removing obscurities and inconsistencies. This process is essential because it is a reproach to any system of commercial law if lawyers have to tell their clients that although the facts are clear, it is anyone's guess how a judge will apply the law to them.

In making these adaptations and improvements to the law of contract, English judges have a long tradition, going back to Lord Mansfield, of drawing upon the work of systematic writers on the law. In the 18th and 19th centuries these tended to be continental writers, as the homegrown practitioner's text book was anything but systematic, rather resembling a miscellaneous collection of precedents such as would today be thrown up by a computer search. But since the middle of the last century there has been a growing recognition in appellate courts of the value of writings by academics or members of the profession who have had the opportunity to consider the principles of the law as a whole rather than merely the fragment under consideration in a particular case.

The ability to stand back and analyse principles is a necessary corrective to two tendencies to which the common law system of judge-made law tends to be prone. The first is what in modern management-speak would be called a silo mentality, that is, a failure to see the connections between one branch (or twig) of the law and another. A system of precedent encourages lawyers to look for resemblances between their case and some earlier reported decision, but sometimes those resemblances, like Fluellen's comparison of Henry V with Alexander the Great ('There is a river in Macedon; and there is also moreover a river at Monmouth and there is salmons in both') are not the most relevant for the purpose in hand. Analysis is necessary to show that cases which were previously thought in some relevant respect to be different, actually exemplify applications of the same principle. Lord Atkin's analysis of the law of negligence in *Donoghue v Stevenson* is a celebrated example.

A second source of confusion in the law is the opposite, namely, a tendency to want to explain all cases as manifestations of a single principle when in fact there is more than one in play. Adam Smith, in his *Theory of Moral Sentiments*, noted 'a propensity, which is natural to all men, but which philosophers in particular are apt to cultivate with a peculiar fondness, as the great means of displaying their ingenuity, the propensity to account for all appearances from as few principles as possible.' The same is true of lawyers; not perhaps to display ingenuity but from a misguided belief that life should be simpler than it is. For example, it caused general astonishment and admiration when Lord Diplock pointed out in *Hong Kong Fir Shipping Co Ltd v Kawasaki Kishen Kaisha Ltd* [1962] 2 QB 26 that the concepts of conditions and warranties were inadequate for determining in every case whether a breach of contract entitled the other party to rescind. Many terms—probably most—are 'innominate'. A breach of such a term may or may not give rise to a right of rescission, depending upon how serious it is. How did judges manage before Lord Diplock pointed this out? They did what judges usually do when the law requires them to apply a rule based upon an inadequate analysis of the issues: they cheated. If the breach was sufficiently serious, they declared the term to have been a condition and if not, they said it had been a warranty. Of course that made it difficult to explain why much the same term should be a condition in one case and a warranty in another. The actual grounds for such decisions, as opposed to the formal grounds, were opaque. But until the *Hong Kong Fir* case, the full explanation had to be suppressed. As Lord Diplock acidly remarked in *Ilkiw v Samuels* [1963] 1 WLR 991, 1004, 'the law is nearly always most obscure in those fields in which judges say that the principle is plain, but the difficulty lies in its application to particular facts.'

The law of damages, a substantial and important part of the law contract, contains examples of both deficiencies of analysis: the fragmentation of single principles and the reductionism which tries to make do with one principle when more are required. If I may mention an example in which I was personally involved, the majority decision of the House of Lords in the *Achilleas* [2009] 1 AC 61 was an attempt to release judges from the difficulties of having to decided whether losses resulting from a breach of contract were too remote by means of the single criterion of whether they were foreseeable at the time of the contract. These difficulties had been foreseen by Lord Penzance in *Gee v Lancashire and Yorkshire Rlwy Co* (1860) 6 H & N 211, 221, only six years after *Hadley v Baxendale* (1854) 9 Exch 341. The efforts of judges to decide every case on the sole basis of foreseeability has resulted in either fine linguistic distinctions about degrees of foreseeability (as in *The Heron II* [1969] 1 AC 350) or the kind of opaque reasoning which makes the distinction between foreseeable and unforeseeable damage seem entirely arbitrary.

I mention this case because it was an article by Adam Kramer, the author of this book, which contributed to the adoption of a new approach by the House of Lords in the *Achilleas*. The kind of analysis contained in that article is now displayed on the wider canvas of the whole law of contractual damages. It is exactly the kind of systematic discussion of a legal topic by which writers can assist judges in the development of the common law. It provides a detailed examination of all the rules on the subject, their relationship to each other and occasionally the difficulties arising out of the way they have been formulated in some of the authorities. This is a subject that, in the standard works on the law of contract as a whole, is necessarily discussed at a more superficial level. But I expect this book to become a prime source for anyone who has a practical problem or needs to formulate an argument concerning contractual damages.

Leonard Hoffmann, autumn 2013

Preface

Most contract disputes, in common with legal disputes generally, turn primarily on facts and not law. That said, there are two areas of English and Welsh contract law that are most often important to disputes. The first is the law governing the interpretation of contracts. The second is the law governing the calculation of contract damages. The interpretation of contracts is now well served by a handful of detailed practitioner textbooks. Contract damages, however, although incisively covered in more general works such as *McGregor on Damages* and *Chitty on Contracts*, have no detailed treatment devoted to them.

And there is a lot to say. Although the principles of contract damages were first fixed in the nineteenth century, and we still routinely cite *Robinson v Harman* and *Hadley v Baxendale* from 1848 and 1854 respectively, the last 20 years have seen a process of rapid development of case law and rationalisation of principle in and around contract damages. Conspicuous examples from the House of Lords include *Ruxley Electronics v Forsyth* on cost of cure and non-pecuniary loss (1995), *SAAMCo* on the scope of duty and valuer's negligence (1996), *Attorney General v Blake* on restitutionary damages (2001), *Alfred McAlpine v Panatown* on third party loss (2001), *Farley v Skinner* on non-pecuniary loss (2001), *Lagden v O'Connor* on impecuniosity (2003), *Sempra Metals* on loss of use of money (2007), *The Golden Victory* on mitigation and the date of assessment (2007), and *The Achilleas* on remoteness (2008). Important cases from the lower courts include *Bence Graphics* in the Court of Appeal on the difference in value and consequential loss in goods cases (1996), the *WWF* dispute in the Court of Appeal on *Wrotham Park* damages (2007), *Durham Tees Valley Airport* in the Court of Appeal on the minimum obligation rule (2010), *Giedo Van der Garde v Force India Formula One* in the High Court on difference in value in service cases (2010), and *Omak Maritime v Mamola Challenger* in the High Court on reliance loss (2010).

As well as the big questions, there are numerous fairly confined issues that arise in practice but as to which it has been (until now) difficult to locate clear commentary and case authority. (When can a claimant claim for lost management time? When must a claimant give credit for the value of a debt or right it has against a third party? Are hedging costs too remote? How is the date of assessment fixed in a share sale case?) The aim of this book is to provide the student and practitioner with at once both a clearly structured explanation of the bigger principles, and a detailed coverage of the more confined issues and the case law.

I have limited the book to contract damages, excluding tort claims, for a few reasons. First, the law of tort damages is less coherent than contract damages, because different torts have different rules. Secondly, any work covering tort damages necessarily must include a detailed coverage of personal injury damages and ship collisions, which carries the danger of making such a book a little unwieldy for the commercial practitioners and others who do not deal with these areas, and for contract lawyers and students. Thirdly, I don't know as much about tort law. That said, a large portion of the questions raised by a contract law damages inquiry are identical or nearly identical to those in tort, particularly negligence. Examples that spring to mind include the scope of duty in professional negligence, loss upon damage to property, mitigation and the date of assessment, and breaks in the chain of causation. Tort cases, accordingly, are present in numbers in some sections of this book.

In introducing this book, I must thank Richard Hart and his team at Hart Publishing. The free rein he has provided is what has kept this book fun to write, particularly during the last six months when I've wanted to devote my time instead to my wife, Kathryn, and our little daughter, Megan. Thanks and apologies go in equal measure to them. And I am also grateful to McGill University in Montreal, where I wrote a large portion of this book while a visiting scholar during the summer of 2012, and to my chambers 3 Verulam Buildings and my clerks, who have helped me to fit my writing in amongst the commitments of my barrister's practice.

This book is long and my eyes can no longer focus on it. Fortunately, I have a number of friends and colleagues—among them, academics, fellow barristers, and instructing solicitors—who have kindly read and commented on different sections. This has helped me to avoid some of the clumsiness and errors that otherwise would be present. For such editorial work, as well as the editing team at Hart, my thanks go to Andrew Dyson, Ed Fiddick, Ian Higgins, Simon McLoughlin, Natalie Moore, Niki Newbegin, Scott Ralson, Sarah Rees-Leonard, Kate Shipton, Steve Smith, and Stephen Whinder.

Finally, I'd like to thank Lord Hoffmann. I admire and agree with almost everything he said while making his considerable mark on contract law. Also, he was the first, and so far the only, judge to cite my work in our highest court. Last of all, he has kindly agreed to write the foreword to this book.

London, December 2013

Contents

Subject-matter Table of Contents

This alternative table of contents is arranged by traditional contract subject-matter categorisation, to assist those practising or studying in one area to find sections that may be of particular relevance to them (although it remains the thesis of this book that the applicable damages principles are almost always universal and not subject-specific).

Table of Cases

Table of Legislation

Part 1

Introduction

1

A Brief Introduction to the Contract Damages Award

About the award of damages; an introduction to the basic principles of damages and the theory behind the remedy; damages awards in foreign currencies.

1.1 Summary

THIS BOOK DEALS with what is probably the principal remedy granted by courts for breach of contract, and certainly the most commonly disputed, the award of damages.[1] This encompasses all pecuniary awards that are not made pursuant to an action for an agreed sum/action for a debt, which is a form of specific relief ordering performance of a promise to pay money, and is not covered by this book.[2]

The vast majority of contract damages awards are compensatory, and so the majority of this book is about how that compensation is calculated. Contract damages awards may also be made on a restitutionary, nominal or punitive/exemplary basis, and these bases are also discussed below in chapter twenty-three.[3]

---

[1] Damages for torts and breaches of equitable obligations (especially trust, fiduciary duty and confidence) are not considered here, although the principles applicable to such claims and contract claims are largely the same and many tort and equity cases are considered here where useful.

[2] However, the quasi-mitigation aspects of the action for an agreed sum from *White and Carter v McGregor* [1962] AC 413 (HL) are discussed below in chapter sixteen, section 16.3B.

[3] Restitutionary awards for breach of contract—restitutionary damages—are covered by this book, but restitutionary awards made under the law of unjust enrichment, albeit sometimes after the contract has been terminated for repudiatory breach, are not damages and not covered by this book.

1.2 The Damages Remedy

A. Damages and Other Remedies

(i) Damages are a Remedy for Breach

The contract damages award is a remedy for breach of contract. If there has been no breach of contract there can be no award of contract damages. The question of breach, however, falls outside the scope of this work.

(ii) Breach of Contract is a Wrong per se

Breach of contract is actionable per se. Unlike the tort of negligence, for example, the cause of action for breach of contract does not require any damage to have been suffered. Breach alone is enough. This means that limitation starts to run against a contract claim (including for breach of a contractual duty of care) on the date of breach (the date on which the cause of action arises), whereas on a tortious negligence claim it runs from the date of damage (the date on which that cause of action arises).

For no particularly good reason, the remedy available for breach of contract when no damage has been suffered (and when restitutionary damages and punitive damages are also not available) is not a declaration of breach, but rather an award of damages: 'nominal damages'. Such an award is, as its name indicates, not compensatory, and is not subject to any of the damages principles discussed in this book. Its purpose and effect is very similar to that of a declaration. The nominal damages award is briefly discussed below in chapter twenty-three, section 23.1.

(iii) Damages are the Principal Remedy for Breach of Contract

In English law, damages are the primary remedy for breach of contract.

Most of the 'specific' remedies of specific performance, the injunction and the action for an agreed sum, so called because they result in delivery of the very thing (*specie*) that was promised, play second fiddle to the award of contract damages. This is most apparent in the case of specific performance, which is only awarded where the claimant is able to demonstrate that damages would be inadequate.[4] Awards of specific performance are rare, particularly in commercial cases. Prohibitory injunctions are a little more common, but of necessity primarily only arise where the promise is a negative one.[5]

(iv) The Action for an Agreed Sum

Awards of the specific remedy of an agreed sum are far more common than specific performance, although probably rarer than the award of compensation, if only

---

[4] *Beswick v Beswick* [1968] AC 58 (HL).
[5] Particular types of negative obligation are discussed below in chapter ten.

because the action for an agreed sum is only available where there is a promise to pay a sum of money, whereas damages are available for breach of any contractual obligation.[6]

Because the award of a debt/agreed sum is an award of money, it can be confused with damages, the other award of money for breach. The differences between the two are basic. The agreed sum is simply the award of the sum promised in the obligation. There is no measurement of loss or anything else, no rules of mitigation,[7] remoteness or causation. Accordingly, it will usually be a preferable remedy for the claimant, where available. Thus, for example, where there are periodic payments due to the claimant under a contract and the claimant is terminated, the claimant will usually claim under the action for an agreed sum for historic payments (plus interest), but will have to claim damages in respect of future payments (the compensatory measure of which requires discounting to allow for the acceleration in receipt, quite apart from the rules of mitigation and causation).

Accordingly, once it is established that the claimant is entitled to an award of an agreed sum, there are few or no legal principles that need to be considered. This is in sharp contrast with the claim for damages.

B. Sources of the Remedy

(i) Common Law

Contract damages are a common law remedy, both in the sense of being primarily a creature of case law rather than statute, and in the sense of being a creature of the Common Law rather than Equity.[8]

Lord Diplock, in the House of Lords decision in *Photo Production Ltd v Securicor Transport Ltd*, explained the mechanism by which the damages award arises.[9] As he put it,

> breaches of primary obligations give rise to substituted or secondary obligations on the part of the party in default … These secondary obligations of the contract breaker … arise by implication of law—generally common law, but sometimes statute, as in the case of codifying statutes passed at the turn of the century, notably the Sale of Goods Act 1893. The contract, however, is just as much the source of secondary obligations as it is of primary obligations; and like primary obligations that are implied by law, secondary obligations too can be modified by agreement between the parties … Every failure to perform a primary obligation is a breach of contract. The secondary obligation on the part of the contract breaker to which it gives rise by implication of the common law is to pay

---

[6] For further discussion of the action for an agreed sum see below in chapter sixteen, section 16.3B.

[7] Subject to the rule from *White and Carter v McGregor* [1962] AC 413 (HL), discussed below in chapter sixteen, section 16.3B.

[8] Equity's version of damages is known as 'equitable compensation'.

[9] *Photo Production Ltd v Securicor Transport Ltd* [1980] AC 827 (HL) at 848–89. This followed his earlier analysis in *Moschi v Lep Air Services Ltd* [1973] AC 331 (HL) at 350.

monetary compensation to the other party for the loss sustained by him in consequence of the breach.[10]

This makes clear the basic features of the award, namely: (i) the obligation to pay damages arises by operation of law and not by any promise in the contract, but (ii) the obligation to pay damages can be modified by agreement. The latter point is discussed below at sub-section (v).

(ii) The Common Law and Damages on Termination

The right to damages that arises upon termination for repudiatory breach is slightly different from the right that arises upon breach (repudiatory or otherwise) without termination. That right to damages upon termination includes not merely the 'general secondary obligation' to pay damages compensating for the breach that has occurred,[11] but also

> there is substituted by implication of law for the primary obligations of the party in default which remain unperformed a secondary obligation to pay monetary compensation to the other party for the loss sustained by him in consequence of their non-performance in the future.[12]

Lord Diplock called this the 'anticipatory secondary obligation', and confirmed that this too could be modified by express clauses just like the 'general secondary obligation'.[13] This obligation arises when the primary obligations come to an end on termination. It means that a claim for damages following repudiatory breach is in effect a claim for breach not only of the obligation already breached, but also for breach of all future obligations the defendant had (which are 'anticipated' by the award). The net effect of this (given the savings the claimant makes by being excused its own future obligations) is a claim against the defendant for loss sustained by the coming to an end and so non-performance of the entire remainder of the contract, eg a claim for the net lost profit on the entire contract.

(iii) Lord Cairns' Act

Section 2 of the Chancery Amendment Act 1858, passed before the Courts of Law and Courts of Equity (Chancery) were fused by the Judicature Acts, provides for the Courts of Chancery to make an award of damages in lieu of specific performance 'in addition to or in substitution for ... specific performance, and such damages may be assessed in such manner as the court shall direct'. Despite repeal of the 1858 Act, the jurisdiction of the court to award such damages continued,[14] and is now found in section 50 of the Senior Courts Act 1981.[15]

---

[10] Ibid at 848–49. See also *C Czarnikow Ltd v Koufos (The Heron II)* [1966] 2 QB 695 (CA) Diplock LJ at 730–31.

[11] *Photo Production Ltd v Securicor Transport Ltd* [1980] AC 827 (HL) at 848–49.

[12] Ibid.

[13] Ibid.

[14] *Leeds Industrial Co-operative Society Ltd v Slack* [1924] AC 851 (HL).

[15] Section 50 reads: 'Where the Court of Appeal or the High Court has jurisdiction to entertain an application for an injunction or specific performance, it may award damages in addition to, or in substitution for, an injunction or specific performance'. Originally called the Supreme Court Act 1981.

The House of Lords confirmed in *Johnson v Agnew*,[16] however, that the measure of damages in lieu of specific performance is the same as at common law.[17] This is not always appreciated, and some cases use the fact of the award being in place of specific performance to seek to justify a measure believed by the judge to be not wholly based on compensation and loss in the way that ordinary contract damages are.[18]

The possible disparity arises because specific performance will often deliver the claimant into a different position than damages will (even allowing for the fact that damages only give the monetary equivalent of performance). For example, specific performance of an obligation to deliver property always gives, at trial, the property itself. Damages for breach of the same obligation may not give the value of the property at trial (for example where the claimant could have been expected to obtain a replacement at an earlier date); or may require the claimant to give credit for costs the claimant would have incurred but for the breach but did not, or benefits the claimant received as a result of the breach.[19]

A particular measure of contract damages, so-called *Wrotham Park* or hypothetical bargain damages, grew up out of the Lord Cairns' Act power although it is now seen as part of the general common law of contract and not restricted to the situation where specific performance or an injunction has been sought.[20]

Although not a question of the measure of damages, one difference between the two awards may be that damages in lieu of specific performance are technically available when no breach has occurred but specific performance is available.[21] Damages in lieu may also be awarded in respect of future wrongs, whereas ordinary contract damages may not.[22]

(iv) The Sale of Goods Act

As is discussed further below,[23] the Sale of Goods Act 1979 (in sections 50, 51 and 53) provides statutory actions enabling the buyer or seller to claim damages. These sections lay down the measure of damages but do so in terms ('estimated loss directly and naturally resulting, in the ordinary course of events, from the

---

[16] *Johnson v Agnew* [1980] 1 AC 367 (HL).

[17] Ibid at 400 (Lord Wilberforce). See also *Attorney General v Blake* [2001] AC 268 (HL) Lord Nicholls at 281.

[18] For example in *Semelhago v Paramadevan* [1996] 2 SCR 415 (SC of Canada) the Supreme Court of Canada seems to rely both on the flexibility of the common law date of assessment rule (which is legitimate) and the need to ensure that damages are a 'true substitute for' and 'true equivalent of specific performance' (which is illegitimate), Sopinka J at paras 16 and 19. Likewise *Lunn Poly Ltd v Liverpool & Lancashire Properties Ltd* [2006] EWCA Civ 430 Neuberger LJ at paras 21–24, where the Court of Appeal took the view that a partial account of profits would be available as damages in lieu (although did not award one) and that additional flexibility arose when applying the *Wrotham Park* measure as damages in lieu.

[19] Thus in *Semelhago v Paramadevan*, ibid, such benefits were ignored, and the Supreme Court only reluctantly allowed the deduction of costs.

[20] See below in chapter twenty-two, section 22.3.

[21] *Oakacre Ltd v Claire Cleaners (Holdings) Ltd* [1982] Ch 197 (Davies QC).

[22] See the comments of Millett LJ in *Jaggard v Sawyer* [1995] 1 WLR 269 (CA) at 290–91 and of Lord Nicholls in *Attorney General v Blake* [2001] AC 268 (HL) at 281.

[23] See chapters four and five.

breach') that do no more than record the common law measure.[24] As discussed below,[25] the only real difference between the Sale of Goods Act 1979 damages remedy and the common law remedy is that in certain circumstances the 1979 Act provides for a rebuttable presumption that the award is to be measured by reference to the market at the date of delivery,[26] whereas there is no such presumption at common law.

(v) The Effect of the Contract on the Damages Award

As explained above in sub-section (i), although the obligation to pay damages does not arise by agreement, it can be modified and affected by agreement. Indeed, the parties' agreement affects the measure of damages in the following ways:

First, the parties may by an exclusion or limitation clause or similar delineate the scope of the defendant's responsibility, for example excluding liability for lost profits, or restricting liability for lost profits to a certain sum.

Secondly, the parties may impliedly allocate responsibility for certain consequences of breach. A party is only liable for types of loss for which the contract-breaker impliedly accepted responsibility.[27]

Thirdly, the parties may set down by a figure or formula the amount of damages payable upon a certain breach, by a liquidated damages clause.

Fourthly, the parties may contractually agree a certain factual or legal matter that impacts on damages. Thus they may agree that a party has not relied on certain advice or information, and such a non-reliance clause may estop the parties from alleging reliance.[28] Conversely the parties may agree (warrant) that there has been reliance, which would prevent the need for it to be proven.

The parties are free to do the above, subject to the common law doctrine of penalties (which governs whether liquidated damages clauses are enforceable), and the statutory provisions in the Unfair Contract Terms Act 1977 and the Unfair Terms in Consumer Contracts Regulations 1999.[29]

Only the second of the above list of four is covered by this book. The others are questions of express contract terms and not of damages rules.

---

[24] And s 54 expressly preserves the right to recover interest or special damages where ordinarily recoverable 'by law'.

[25] See chapter four, section 4.2C, and chapter five, section 5.1A.

[26] In sub-ss 50(3), 51(3) and 53(3).

[27] *Transfield Shipping Inc v Mercator Shipping Inc (The Achilleas)* [2009] AC 61 (HL). This is the modern formulation of the rule of remoteness, which is discussed below in chapter fourteen, sections 14.2 and 14.5–14.6.

[28] This is the doctrine developed in *Peekay Intermark Ltd v Australia and New Zealand Banking Group Ltd* [2006] 2 Lloyd's Rep 511 (CA) and *Springwell Navigation Corp v JP Morgan Chase Bank* [2010] EWCA Civ 122.

[29] There is no longer a common law doctrine of fundamental breach preventing a certain type of exclusion clause. This was abolished by *Suisse Atlantique Société d'Armement Maritime SA v NV Rotterdamsche Kolen Centrale* [1967] 1 AC 361 (HL) and *Photo Production Ltd v Securicor Transport Ltd* [1980] AC 827 (HL).

C. The Nature of the Damages Award

(i) No Obligation to Pay Damages Prior to Judgment

Prior to judgment, there is no legal obligation to pay damages.[30] The payment of damages prior to judgment is no defence to a claim for damages, and damages are not recoverable for the non-payment of damages.[31]

(ii) Assessment Once and For All at Trial

Damages for all loss caused by a single breach must be recovered once and for all at the trial of that cause of action.[32] Where events have not yet happened, the court will very rarely adopt a policy of waiting and seeing or of requiring the claimant to come back to court when it has been proven that (eg) the claimant has not died in the time a contract of employment was due to run.[33] As Schiemann LJ has observed,

> in many cases judgment will be before the wrongful act ceases to have a deleterious effect on the plaintiff. In those cases, the court has to look into the future and award a figure which includes the value as at the time of judgment of best estimates of future loss or damage. The putting of a present figure on future loss, which exercise will often involve making judgments as to possible future events rather than waiting to see what happens, is the price that has to be paid for early finality in litigation and certainty for the parties.[34]

Nevertheless, the court's case management powers do allow the splitting of a trial into two trials, one of liability and another of quantum, which is common. More rarely, however, these powers are exercised to allow the court to split up quantum into different trials or to defer an award in relation to a particular head of loss. In *Deeny v Gooda Walker (No 3)*,[35] Phillips J agreed to award damages for past losses to Lloyd's names suing their managing agents for negligence, but to defer

---

[30] Despite the suggestion by Lord Diplock that the obligation arises immediately: see above at text to n 10. This is explored by S Smith, 'The Law of Damages: Rules for Citizens or Rules for Courts?' in D Saidov and R Cunnington (eds), *Contract Damages: Domestic and International Perspectives* (Oxford, Hart Publishing, 2008) and 'Duties, Liabilities and Damages' (2011–12) 125 *Harvard L Rev* 1727.

[31] *President of India v Lips Maritime Corp* [1988] 1 AC 395 (HL).

[32] *Rowntree & Sons Ltd v Allen & Sons (Poplar) Ltd* (1935) 41 Com Cas 90; *Patel v Hooper & Jackson* [1999] 1 WLR 1792 (CA) Nourse LJ at 1800. The position is different where there are continuing breaches of an obligation in a contract that has not been terminated. The concept of the continuing breach of contract is discussed in *National Coal Board v Galley* [1958] 1 WLR 16 (CA) at 26, and is of importance where limitation periods are being applied.

[33] *Richardson v Mellish* (1824) 2 Bing 229, 130 ER 294.

[34] *Kennedy v KB Van Emden & Co* [1997] 2 EGLR 137 (CA) at 141. This is a problem the law of personal injury awards has long since reconciled itself to. See eg Lord Lloyd in *Page v Sheerness Steel plc* [1999] 1 AC 345 (HL) at 363–64: 'It is of the nature of a lump sum payment that it may, in respect of future pecuniary loss, prove to be either too little or too much. So far as the multiplier is concerned, the plaintiff may die the next day, or he may live beyond his normal expectation of life. So far as the multiplicand is concerned, the cost of future care may exceed everyone's best estimate. Or a new cure or less expensive form of treatment may be discovered. But these uncertainties do not affect the basic principle'. In relation to quantifying damages as to future losses, see further chapter twelve, section 12.2, and chapter thirteen, section 13.6 below.

[35] *Deeny v Gooda Walker (No 3)* [1995] 1 WLR 1206 (Phillips J).

adjudication as to the future losses (the claims the claimants would face from third parties but had not yet faced) to another day. The reasons given were that the third party loss was uncertain, and there was a risk that the recovery would be dissipated before the third party claims were brought. The judge did reaffirm, however, that: 'The desirability of bringing an end to litigation will normally make it appropriate for the court to make a single award of damages which includes the best assessment possible of future loss'.

Where (as in *Deeny*) the loss consists of future liability to third parties, the court may seek to quantify the loss as best it can.[36] Alternatively, and rather than guessing the amount of the liability, the court may grant an indemnity, which provides that the claimant is entitled to reimbursement from the defendant only if, when and to the extent that the claimant has to make payment to third parties[37] or is found to have suffered the relevant loss.[38]

Such a deferral of assessment of future losses is more common in personal injury cases, where it is uncertain whether a disease or deterioration will occur in the future, in which case an award of 'provisional damages' may be made with 'further damages' awarded later.[39] It is also an option, rarely exercised, in cases where there was insufficient evidence at trial to prove a particular head of loss.[40]

(iii) Single Lump Sum

The award of damages must be a single lump sum.[41] (There is an exception in personal injury cases, where it is possible to order interim payments,[42] and also periodical payments into the future, the latter designed to avoid the problem of a claimant imprudently prematurely spending a lump sum that was designed to compensate for an income long into the future.[43])

(iv) Unconditional

An award of damages must be unconditional. Thus the court cannot award damages on the condition that the claimant transfer securities to the defendant,[44] or

---

[36] *Pennant Hills Restaurants Pty Ltd v Barrell Insurances Pty Ltd* (1981) 55 ALJR 258 (HC of Australia); *Total Liban SA v Vitol Energy SA* [2001] QB 643 (Gross QC).

[37] *Trans Trust SPRL v Danubian Trading Co Ltd* [1952] 2 QB 297 (CA) at 303 and 307; *Markel International Insurance v Surety Guarantee Consultants* [2008] EWHC 3087 (Teare J) at para 8. See also the discussion in *Deeny v Gooda Walker (No 3)* [1995] 1 WLR 1206 (Phillips J).

[38] *The Board of Trustees of National Museums and Galleries on Merseyside v AEW Architects and Designers Ltd* [2013] EWHC 2403 (TCC) (Akenhead J) at para 115.

[39] Rule 41 of the Civil Procedure Rules, implementing s 31A of the Senior Courts Act 1981 and s 51 of the County Courts Act 1984.

[40] *The Board of Trustees of National Museums and Galleries on Merseyside v AEW Architects and Designers Ltd* [2013] EWHC 2403 (TCC) (Akenhead J) at para 115.

[41] *Fournier v Canadian National Rly* [1927] AC 167 (PC).

[42] Rule 25.6 of the Civil Procedure Rules, giving effect to s 31 of the Senior Courts Act 1981.

[43] Rules 41.4 and following of the Civil Procedure Rules, giving effect to the Damages Act 1996 as amended by the Courts Act 2003.

[44] *Banbury v Bank of Montreal* [1918] AC 626 (HL).

order that part of the damages are not to be paid if the claimant elects to adopt an endowment policy.[45]

(v) Accelerated Receipt

One consequence of an award covering losses not yet suffered is that the claimant is being compensated at an earlier time than it will suffer the loss (ie an earlier time than it would have received the future benefit or will suffer the future harm). In the opposite situation of pre-trial losses, the court awards interest on damages to allow for the time between suffering the loss and the award. Conversely, where damages are awarded for post-trial (ie future) losses, it is often necessary to discount the award to allow for accelerated receipt, ie to allow for the benefit the claimant gets by receiving the money early and being able to use it (such as to earn interest) for the intervening breach, whereas but for the breach it would have only received the benefit or suffered the loss later.[46] This reduction for accelerated receipt should allow for two elements: the first is the interest that the claimant will be able to earn on the money during the intervening period (which points towards a discount on the sum), and the second is the inflation that the money will be subject to in the intervening period, reducing its buying power (which also points towards a decrease in the sum).[47]

(vi) Appeals

The presumption is that on appeal a court will not admit evidence that was not before the first instance court.[48] This general practice preserves finality of the trial, and should not be departed from merely where future events that were uncertain at trial have become more certain or have taken place.[49]

(vii) After Judgment

Once judgment has been given, the all or nothing nature of civil litigation means that no further damages can be claimed from the same breach. The cause of action is lost, or merged, into the judgment, which is calculated to include all damages

---

[45] *Patel v Hooper & Jackson* [1999] 1 WLR 1792 (CA).

[46] Eg *Interoffice Telephones Ltd v Robert Freeman Co Ltd* [1958] 1 QB 190 (CA); *Robophone Facilities Ltd v Blank* [1966] 1 WLR 1428 (CA); *Lavarack v Woods of Colchester Ltd* [1967] 1 QB 278 (CA) at 291; *Pennant Hills Restaurants Pty Ltd v Barrell Insurances Pty Ltd* (1981) 55 ALJR 258 (HC of Australia); *Pugh v Cantor Fitzgerald International Ltd* [2001] EWCA Civ 307 at para 3; *Seatbooker Sales Ltd v Southend United Football Club Ltd* [2008] EWHC 157 (QB) (Seymour QC) at para 116; *Zodiac Maritime Agencies Ltd v Fortescue Metals Group Ltd (The Kildare)* [2011] 2 Lloyd's Rep 360 (Steel J) at para 73.

[47] In personal injury cases, awards of future loss of earnings are made on the basis of a lump sum that can be invested in a low-risk way to provide for periodical payments equivalent to the earnings lost, and this will usually be by assuming an investment in index-linked government securities (rather than equities), as these automatically deal with inflation as they are linked to the retail price index: *Wells v Wells* [1999] AC 345 (HL); *Patel v Beenessreesingh* [2012] UKPC 18 (PC).

[48] Rule 52.11(2)(b) of the Civil Procedure Rules.

[49] *Mulholland v Mitchell* [1971] AC 666 (HL).

(including interest) as if payment is made at the date of judgment. Thereafter, any late payment must be compensated for by interest at the judgment rate (arising under the obligation to pay interest on a judgment), if at all.[50]

(vii) Tax

Usually damages will be taxed as income received by an individual or corporation. As explained below, the basic rule is that where it makes a difference the law will adjust the damages award to allow both for the tax that the claimant has avoided because of the breach and the tax the claimant will have to pay on the damages award, although where the tax is identical in both cases no adjustment needs to be made as the two effectively cancel each other out.[51]

1.3 The Principles of Compensation

A. Compensation and the 'But For' Test

The basic measure of contract damages is as set out by Baron Parke in *Robinson v Harman* in 1848:[52]

> [W]here a party sustains loss by reason of a breach of contract, he is, so far as money can do it to be placed in the same situation, with respect to damages, as if the contract had been performed.

This dictum has been cited and approved countless times.[53] For a useful recent reformulation, the reader is directed to article 9:502 of the Principles of European Law:

> The general measure of damages is such sum as will put the aggrieved party as nearly as possible into the position in which it would have been if the contract had been duly performed. Such damages cover the loss which the aggrieved party has suffered and the gain of which it has been deprived.

---

[50] The right to post-judgment interest arises under the Judgments Act 1838 only; it is not available at common law: *Chubb v Dean*, 24 April 2013 (Cooke J). Contractual interest may be available post-judgment: *Standard Chartered Bank v Ceylon Petroleum Corp* [2011] EWHC 2094 (Comm) (Hamblen J) at para 12. Where a judgment is in a foreign currency, the rate of judgment interest is at the court's discretion under section 44A of the Administration of Justice Act 1970 (see *Standard Chartered Bank v Ceylon Petroleum Corp* [2011] EWHC 2094 (Comm) (Hamblen J) at paras 16–18).

[51] See below in chapter thirteen, section 13.7.

[52] *Robinson v Harman* (1848) 1 Ex Rep 850.

[53] For examples taken only from House of Lords decisions see *Bain v Fothergill* (1874) LR 7 HL 158 (HL) Lord Chelmsford at 85; *Watts, Watts and Co v Mitsui and Co* [1917] AC 227 (HL) Lord Dunedin at 241; *C Czarnikow Ltd v Koufos (The Heron II)* [1969] 1 AC 350 (HL) Lord Pearce at 413; *Swingcastle Ltd v Alastair Gibson* [1991] 2 AC 223 (HL) Lord Lowry at 237; *Ruxley Electronics and Construction Ltd v Forsyth* [1996] AC 344 (HL) Lord Jauncey at 355; *Alfred McAlpine Construction Ltd v Panatown Ltd* [2001] 1 AC 518 Lord Jauncey at 562; *Golden Strait Corp v Nippon Yusen Kubishika Kaisha (The Golden Victory)* [2007] 2 AC 353 (HL) Lord Scott at para 29. It also worth noting that Baron Alderson, who formulated the classic contract remoteness test in *Hadley v Baxendale* six years later, was part of the court in *Robinson v Harman* (1854) 9 Exch 341.

(i) Compensatory

The key feature of the damages award is that it is compensatory. As Lord Nicholls observed, 'Leaving aside the anomalous exception of punitive damages, damages are compensatory. That is axiomatic'.[54] The aim of the award is not to deter or punish, nor to strip the defendant of any gain (which would be a restitutionary award), but rather to measure the loss to the claimant, that loss being the difference between the situation the claimant is in and that it would have been in.

(ii) The 'But For' Test

A crucial built-in feature of the damages award is the requirement of factual causation. Only if the claimant would not have suffered a detriment or achieved a gain 'but for' the breach (which is in Latinate form the *sine qua non* test) is the loss recoverable, as is inherent in Parke B's test that the situation to be measured is that 'as if the contract had been performed'.

(iii) The 'Expectation' Measure

This award is often called the 'expectation' measure (mainly by academic commentators) because the promisee is entitled to be put by an award of damages in the same position as it 'expected' to be in if the promisor had performed the contract.[55] The award is in this respect forward-looking. Thus, because of the damages award, a promise takes effect as a guarantee of the position the promisee will be in if the promise is performed: the promisor will either put the promisee in that position by performing (or being made to perform), or will do so by being made to pay damages. The promisee can therefore build on that promise in planning its affairs.

Traditionally the expectation measure has been contrasted with the 'reliance' or tort measure. This is often said to be a separate measure of loss based on the claimant's expenditure rather than the expectation principle.[56] In truth such thinking is unhelpful. The basic principle is as stated by Parke B in *Robinson v Harman*. Where but for the breach the claimant would not have entered into a transaction, the claimant can recover all the losses suffered in that transaction (as well as lost profits that would have been made in an alternative transaction). But this is not because any different measure applies to the expectation measure, putting the claimant in the position it would have been in but for the breach. It is merely because the expectation—what would have happened but for the breach—was that the defendant would have (eg) taken care in giving advice, and had it done so the transaction would not have been entered into at all. The claimant is entitled by damages to be put in that position. Thus the damages in a contract or tort duty of care case, like those in a strict liability contract case, are

---

[54] *Attorney General v Blake* [2001] AC 268 (HL) Lord Nicholls at 282. See also *Johnson v Agnew* [1980] 1 AC 367 (HL) Lord Wilberforce at 400 (also echoing Parke B in *Robinson v Harman*): 'The general principle for the assessment of damages is compensatory, ie, that the innocent party is to be placed, so far as money can do so, in the same position as if the contract had been performed'.

[55] From L Fuller and W Perdue, 'The Reliance Interest in Contract Damages' (1936) 46 *Yale LJ* 52.

[56] Ibid.

explained by the single principle that requires undoing the breach and putting the claimant in the position as if it had not happened. It is just that sometimes that position but for the breach is one after a successful transaction, and sometimes it is merely the position after not having engaged in an unsuccessful transaction.[57]

In contract law the claimant cannot recover damages measured by the expenditure incurred in entering into the contract that was breached by the defendant, ie damages to put the claimant in the position as if it had never contracted with the defendant. This may be the measure for tortious pre-contractual misrepresentation (where but for the wrong the claimant would not have contracted with the defendant) or restitution for unjust enrichment following termination of the contract (giving back what the claimant conveyed under the contract), but cannot be the award for breach of the contract itself. Thus, for example, in *Quirk v Thomas* the damages for breach of a promise to marry could not include the profits of the business the claimant forewent for the marriage, because had the contract been performed the claimant would not have earned the profits.[58] However, as discussed below, where the position that would have arisen but for the breach is uncertain, the courts may rely on a presumption that the claimant would have broken even, and therefore would have earned revenue (the expectation measure) equal to the expenditure in the transaction. Such an award is not an award of a reliance measure; rather a conventional expectation award but under which the measurement is assisted by a rebuttable presumption.[59]

B. The Breach Position and the Non-Breach Position

As a result of the expectation measure, the but for test, and the basic compensatory aspect of damages, the fundamental comparison at the heart of contract damages is between what happened following the breach (what I have called 'the breach position') and what would have happened but for the breach (what I have called 'the non-breach position').[60] As Hicks QC has explained with admirable clarity:

> I take the governing principle to be that damages should be such as will restore the plaintiff, so far as a monetary award can do so, to the position which it would have occupied had the breaches found to have been committed by the defendants not occurred. On that basis an inquiry into damages should therefore normally take the form of a comparison, in financial terms, between the events which have actually happened, [*which I refer to in this book as the breach position*] and those which would have happen[ed] had the relevant breach not occurred, [*which I refer to in this book as the non-breach position*] the former being susceptible of direct evidence, but the latter being necessarily hypothetical.[61]

---

[57] See D Friedmann, 'The Performance Interest in Contract Damages' (1995) 111 *LQR* 628 and 'Rights and Remedies' (1997) 113 *LQR* 628 and SA Smith, 'Rights, Remedies and the Normal Expectancies in Tort and Contract' (1997) 113 *LQR* 426.

[58] *Quirk v Thomas* [1916] 1 KB 516 (CA) at 534–35.

[59] See below in chapter eighteen, section 18.3.

[60] These terms came from Andrew Dyson. See further A Dyson and A Kramer, 'There is No "Breach Date Rule": Mitigation, Difference in Value and Date of Assessment' (2014) *LQR* forthcoming.

[61] *Stephenson Blake (Holdings) Ltd v Streets Heaver Ltd* [2001] Lloyd's Rep PN 44 (Hicks QC) at para 159. And see *Infiniteland Ltd v Artisan Contracting Ltd* [2004] EWHC 955 (Ch) (Park J) at para 125, where the judge adopted counsel's terminology for the two valuations in the share purchase agreement dispute of the 'actual valuation' and the 'but for valuation'.

The breach position is a matter of working out what happened after the breach, although the principles of legal causation and mitigation alter that somewhat.

The non-breach position is a matter of working out what would have happened had the breach not occurred, although this is sometimes modified by the concepts of loss of chance or the defendant's minimum obligation rule.

The essence of the contract damages enquiry is to find the net difference between the breach and non-breach positions. It is only by doing this that one can work out what loss was caused by the breach, ie what the claimant does not have but would have had but for the breach, and what the claimant has but would not have had but for the breach. A post-breach detriment is nothing to do with the defendant if it would have happened anyway (ie if the detriment also forms part of the non-breach position), and the same is true of a gain.

This can be illustrated by a simple diagram:

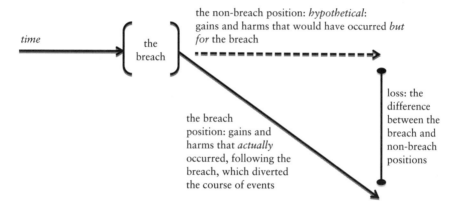

Because the essence of working out the breach position and the non-breach position so different, and because legal rules operate on them differently, they are unpacked separately in different parts of this book, especially chapter twelve for the breach position, and chapter thirteen for the non-breach position.

C. What is Not Covered by Baron Parke's Dictum

Parke B's dictum in *Robinson v Harman*[62] covers the basic compensatory principle and the 'but for' test of factual causation. It omits, however, the following two important principles (as well as some other less important rules):

— Some actions, omissions and events are treated as robbing the breach of responsibility for their consequences, and thus losses and gains caused by such actions, omissions and events are deemed not to have occurred. This is the principle of legal causation, and incorporates the important principle that

---

[62] Text to n 52 above.

a claimant is deemed to have acted reasonably to avoid losses, known as the mitigation principle.[63]

— Losses falling outside the scope of the defendant's responsibility are unrecoverable. This encompasses the remoteness and scope of duty principles, as well as the rule limiting recovery of mental distress/loss of amenity damages.[64]

D. Other Measures of Contract Damages

More than 99.9 per cent of contract damages awards are on the basic compensatory principles discussed above and covered in detail in the majority of this book. There are, however, a small minority of cases where a non-compensatory award of restitutionary damages is made, and in theory there may in extreme circumstances be an award of punitive damages. These are discussed below in chapter twenty-three.

1.4 The Theory of Contract Damages

The theory of contract damages, and of contract law generally, is a separate subject that requires and justifies its own exploration elsewhere,[65] and moreover is of minimal importance to the practising lawyer. The following is a very basic introduction to the relevant topics.

A. Economic Efficiency

Oliver Wendell Holmes Junior has observed that, at least in the majority of cases when specific performance is unavailable and leaving purely moral considerations aside, 'The duty to keep a contract at common law means a prediction that you must pay damages if you do not keep it—and nothing else'.[66] What this highlights is that it will sometimes be more efficient for the defendant to breach a contract and pay damages than for it to perform the contract, because it will cost the defendant more to perform than the amount of damages it must pay upon breach. Whether or not this is true depends upon the way damages are measured, but given the essentially compensatory measure that English law imposes, and the rarity of specific performance, it is certainly true that it will often be cheaper for the defendant to, in effect, buy itself out of the contract by breaching and paying damages. This is most obviously the case where the defendant's business is loss-making, or where the defendant has a limited supply of its goods or services and has a buyer who values the goods or services more than the defendant. If D has contracted to supply goods to A for £100, and B is willing to pay £150, and there is no available market

---

[63] See below in chapter fifteen.

[64] See below in chapter fourteen.

[65] For a summary, see SA Smith, *Contract Theory* (Oxford, OUP, 2004) section 11.3, also 3.2.2, 4.1.2–4.1.3 and 4.3.3–4.3.4.

[66] OW Holmes Jnr, 'The Path of the Law' (1897) 10 *Harvard L Rev* 457. See also OW Holmes Jnr, *The Common Law* (1881) 301 ff.

(as seems likely; otherwise it is hard to explain the difference in price that A and B are willing to pay), then providing A's loss from non-supply is less than £50, D will profit from breaching the contract with A, compensating it for its loss, and supplying B instead.

The above is an economic analysis of the way contracts operate. However, there is a school of theorists, largely American,[67] who advocate setting and adjusting as well as justifying legal contractual rules in a way that encourages efficient breach, and that encourages economic efficiency generally (for example by setting a remoteness rule that encourages that loss falls on the party who can most efficiently bear or insure it). Such economic theories show no signs of purchase on the English judiciary, however, who remain, like the English law of contract, almost entirely uninterested in how efficient or inefficient a particular rule or outcome will be. In my view, this is as it should be.

B. Promissory Theories

The prevailing theory of contract law sees it as upholding the practice of promising.[68] Such an approach helps to explain the general expectation measure of damages, which focuses on the value of the promised performance to the claimant. Moreover, it helps to explain the primacy in contract law of the terms of the contract, the otherwise surprisingly marginal role that rules of policy play, and the for the most part unavailability of punitive damages. Thus the modern approach to interpretation and implication of terms focuses on the meaning of what was expressly or impliedly agreed between the parties.[69] So too do the scope of duty and remoteness principles.[70] So too, arguably, does the rule that determines when damages for non-pecuniary loss are recoverable.[71]

There nevertheless remain rules that are not, at least currently, explicable solely on the basis of the parties' agreement. In contract damages, the principal of these is the rule of mitigation, alongside the rule of legal causation/*res inter alios acta*/collateral acts. These are rules that exculpate the claimant because something between the breach and the loss or gain, or something about the loss or gain, means that the loss or gain (or the events that led to it) should be disregarded and not attributed to the breach of the defendant. These rules are not, however, inconsistent with the promissory theory: upholding a promise by compensating for the difference between the position the claimant is in and that it would have been in but for the

---

[67] Especially Richard Posner: RA Posner, *Economic Analysis of Law*, 8th edn (Aspen Casebooks, Wolters Kluwer, 2010).

[68] The first account in time and impact being that of C Fried, *Contract as Promise* (Cambridge, MA, Harvard University Press, 1981).

[69] See especially the judgments of Lord Hoffmann in *Investors Compensation Scheme v West Bromwich Building Society* [1998] 1 WLR 896 (HL) (construction) and *Attorney General of Belize v Belize Telecom Ltd* [2009] 1 WLR 1988 (PC) (implied terms).

[70] See the judgments of Lord Hoffmann in *South Australia Asset Management v York Montague* [1997] 1 AC 191 (HL) (scope of duty) and *Transfield Shipping Inc v Mercator Shipping Inc (The Achilleas)* [2009] AC 61 (HL) (remoteness).

[71] See below in chapter nineteen.

breach does not require the defendant to compensate all aspects of the claimant's position, even where that position is primarily the responsibility of the claimant or something else other than the defendant.

C. Reliance Theories

There remains a strain of theory that contends that contract law really protects the reliance of the claimant upon the promise, and the harm that results from that reliance, rather than upholding the promise itself (or its value). Atiyah in England and Fuller and Perdue in America wrote the most influential works in this vein.[72] For them, damages should and do lean towards a tort-like measure, compensating the claimant for having relied upon the promise, rather than putting the claimant in the position it expected to be in had the contract been performed (save, these theorists would say, where an award of expectation damages is a useful proxy for the reliance loss). The most important impact of this for practice is on the question of whether there is an independent reliance measure of damages that can be awarded even where reliance is greater than the expectation interest, most obviously where the claimant has made a bad bargain. As regards English law, this battle has been lost by the reliance theorists, and it is now clear that there is no reliance measure, and the case law on the topic goes no further than establishing a rebuttable presumption that had the contract been performed the claimant would have broken even.[73]

D. Default Rule Theories

A final theoretical concept that is useful for the reader to be aware of is that of the default rule. This explains legal rules that the parties are able to contract out of (most rules in the contract sphere) as merely 'default rules', ie rules that apply in default of the agreement of the parties, to fill gaps where the parties have not agreed. In the damages context, the parties are free to expressly allocate responsibility by exclusion and limitation clauses, but in default of them doing so the common law remoteness rule applies. Whether one is an economic or a promissory theorist, seeing the remoteness rule (or the presumptive market measure in sale of goods cases, for example) as a default rule around which the parties can expressly contract may assist in understanding its operation.[74]

---

[72] PS Atiyah, *The Rise and Fall of Freedom of Contract* (Oxford, Clarendon Press, 1979) and *Promises, Morals and Law* (Oxford, Clarendon Press, 1981), and LL Fuller and WR Perdue, 'The Reliance Interest in Contract Damages' (1936) 46 *Yale LJ* 52.

[73] See further chapter eighteen, section 18.3, below.

[74] For some key examples of the huge literature on default rules see CJ Goetz and RE Scott, 'The Limits of Expanded Choice: An Analysis of the Interactions Between Express and Implied Contract Terms' (1985) 73 *California L Rev* 261; I Ayres and R Gertner, 'Filling Gaps in Incomplete Contracts: An Economic Theory of Default Rules' (1989) 99 *Yale LJ* 87; RE Scott, 'A Relational Theory of Default Rules for Commercial Contracts' (1990) 19 *J Legal Stud* 597; R Barnett, 'The Sound of Silence: Default Rules and Contractual Consent' (1992) 78 *Virginia L Rev* 821; and '… And Contractual Consent' (1994) 3 *South California Interdisciplinary LJ* 421.

1.5 The Currency of the Award

Since 1975, English courts have been able to give judgments in a foreign currency, with the conversion to Sterling applied if necessary on enforcement, applying the rate prevailing at the date of that enforcement.[75] Although initially applied in cases of actions for a debt,[76] this principle was then applied by the House of Lords in *The Folias and The Despina R* to claims for tort damages (the claim in relation to *The Despina R* was a collision claim) and contract damages (*The Folias* claim was a charterparty case of damaged goods).[77]

The general rule is in two stages: First, does the contract provide for a currency to govern contract damages? Secondly, if not, what is the appropriate currency out of those in the contemplation of the parties?

A. The First Stage: The Currency of the Contract

The first rule is one of contract law and conflict of laws/private international law:

> If from the terms of the contract it appears that the parties have accepted a currency as the currency of account and payment in respect of all transactions arising under the contract, then it would be proper to give a judgment for damages in that currency ... But there may be cases in which, although obligations under the contract are to be met in a specified currency, or currencies, the right conclusion may be that there is no intention shown that damages for breach of the contract should be given in that currency or currencies.[78]

In *The Folias*, although the charter provided for hire and other contractual payments to be made in US dollars, that did not mean that the parties had impliedly provided for all damages awards to be paid in that currency. However, where a charterparty expressed that demurrage was to be paid in US dollars then an award of demurrage was awarded in that currency.[79]

B. The Second Stage/General Rule: The Truest Expression of Loss, if Not Too Remote

If there is no contractually agreed currency, the courts are free to decide upon the currency:

> in which the loss was felt by the plaintiff or 'which most truly expresses his loss' ... In ascertaining which this currency is, the court must ask what is the currency, payment in

---

[75] *Miliangos v Frank (Textiles) Ltd* [1976] AC 443 (HL). The date of enforcement has, however, been found to be the date of the charging order before it is made final, not the date of the receipt of proceeds thereunder, thereby creating a currency exchange risk between the date of execution and the receipt of proceeds: *Carnegie v Giessen* [2005] 2 WLR 2510 (CA).

[76] *Miliangos v Frank (Textiles) Ltd* [1976] AC 443 (HL).

[77] *Services Europe Atlantique Sud v Stockholms Rederiaktiebolag SVEA (The Folias and The Despina R)* [1979] AC 685 (HL).

[78] *The Folias and The Despina R* [1979] AC 685 (HL) Lord Wilberforce at 700.

[79] *Federal Commerce and Navigation Co Ltd v Tradax Export SA* [1977] 1 QB 324 (CA), explained by *The Folias and The Despina R* [1979] AC 685 (HL) Lord Wilberforce at 701.

which will as nearly as possible compensate the plaintiff in accordance with the principle of restitution, and whether the parties must be taken reasonably to have had this in contemplation...[80]

In some cases the 'immediate loss' currency may be appropriate, in others the currency in which it was borne by the plaintiff. There will be still others in which the appropriate currency is the currency of the contract.[81]

The question therefore combines the evaluation of in what currency the claimant feels the loss with the remoteness question of whether it was in the reasonable contemplation of the parties that this would be the case.

Where tungsten rods bought by the claimant Dutch company in Brighton were warehoused with the defendant in England, it was not foreseeable that loss upon theft of the goods would be suffered in anything other than Sterling (and so it did not matter in what currency the owner in fact felt the loss, eg by purchasing a replacement).[82]

In contrast, in cases of international sale or carriage of goods, the suffering of a loss in a foreign currency will rarely be too remote.[83] The appropriate currency will prima facie be the currency of the port of discharge, and therefore a cargo owner will recover in Cuban pesos if the goods should have been delivered to Cuba.[84] It is for the parties to show that the currency in which the claimant felt its loss was a different currency.[85]

Often, however, the currency in which the loss is suffered is not the currency that might reasonably have been expected. The loss will often be felt in the currency the claimant had, and therefore spent to buy a replacement (or would have if, as must be assumed, it had mitigated its loss), and the prima facie port of discharge rule will in such cases be displaced. In *The Folias*, the Swedish ship owner was liable to a charterer (under a charterparty in which payments were in US dollars) for damage to goods, and the French charterer satisfied the Brazilian cargo owner's claim against it in French francs converted at that date into Brazilian cruzeiros.[86] The loss was suffered by the payment of French francs and it was in the parties' contemplation that the French charterer would have to use French francs, and so the judgment for damages was given in French francs.

In *The Federal Huron*, where soya beans were delivered damaged to a French company in France and always purchased and insured in US dollars, the loss was felt in dollars. (This was true even of the expenses incurred in France, as they were

---

[80] *The Folias and the Despina R* [1979] AC 685 (HL) Lord Wilberforce at 701.
[81] Ibid at 703.
[82] *Metalhaandel JA Magnus BV v Ardfields Transport Ltd and Eastfell Ltd* [1988] 1 Lloyd's Rep 197 (Gatehouse J).
[83] *The Folias and The Despina R* [1979] AC 685 (HL).
[84] *Empresa Cubana Importada de Alimentos v Octavia Shipping Co SA (The Kefalonia Wind)* [1986] 1 Lloyd's Rep 273 (Bingham J) at 291.
[85] Ibid.
[86] *The Folias and the Despina R* [1979] AC 685 (HL), Lord Wilberforce at 702. See also *The Food Corp of India v Carras (Hellas) Ltd (The Dione)* [1980] 2 Lloyd's Rep 577 (Lloyd J).

handled through the claimant's US dollar account.) Further, the parties must have expected this.[87]

Likewise in *The Texaco Melbourne* it was shown that the claimant (the Ghana Ministry of Fuel and Energy) only used Ghana cedis, and would therefore have had to use cedis to purchase foreign currency to purchase replacement oil.[88] The appropriate currency must be determined at the date of suffering of the loss, and the fact that the currency had appreciated or depreciated between that date and date of judgment (nine years of heavy deprecation of the Ghana cedi in the *Texaco Melbourne* case) was not to be taken into account in determining the currency of the award, with the period of delay to be compensated in interest only.[89] Although it has been criticised, this decision seems correct, since if the claimant had bought replacement oil it would have been put in the position as if the contract had been performed and suffered its loss in cedis.[90] The real problem is whether an award of interest adequately compensates for the period without cedis that would have been insulated from depreciation by being continuously converted into and out of dollars (through oil trading), which is a matter for the calculation of the interest award.

Finally, it should be noted that non-pecuniary loss will always be appropriately measured in Sterling (or, more's the point, never inappropriately measured in Sterling), since it is not suffered in any currency.[91]

---

[87] *Société Française Bunge SA v Belcan NV (The Federal Huron)* [1985] 2 Lloyd's Rep 189 (Bingham J) at 192. See also *Virani Ltd v Marcel Revert y Compagnia SA* [2003] EWCA (Civ) 1651.

[88] *Attorney General of the Republic of Ghana v Texaco Overseas Tankships Ltd (The Texaco Melbourne)* [1994] 1 Lloyd's Rep 473 (HL) Lord Goff at 476ff.

[89] *The Texaco Melbourne* [1994] 1 Lloyd's Rep 473 (HL) Lord Goff at 476ff.

[90] C Proctor, 'Changes in Monetary Value and the Assessment of Damages' in D Saidov & R Cunnington, *Contract Damages: Domestic and International Perspectives* (Oxford, Hart Publishing, 2008) at 480–82.

[91] Cf *Hoffman v Sofaer* [1982] 1 WLR 1350 (Talbot J) as regards pain, suffering and loss of amenity in a personal injury award.

Part 2

Types of Complaint

2

Pure Services: Non-Supply/Defective Supply/Delayed Supply

Damages for breach of contracts to supply services not related to property, such as cleaning, teaching, carriage, administration, and information technology. Includes: services to commercial claimants, services to public bodies, services to consumers. Also covers damages for lost management time.[1]

2.1. Introduction
2.2. Services to Commercial Claimants
2.3. Services to Public Bodies
2.4. Services to Consumers

2.1 Introduction

A. 'Pure' Services and What This Chapter Covers

WHEN CONSIDERING SERVICES, it is it useful to borrow from unjust enrichment law a distinction between pure services and other services. Pure services are those that do not provide the promisee with a marketable residue, which would most typically be a piece of property or an increase in the value of property. The 'impure' service, in this sense, is typified by the construction contract, where the purpose of the service is the creation or improvement to a piece of property. Insofar as a service provides or alters property in this way the claimant's complaint, and therefore the measure of damages, is similar to that in the case of non-supply of property or supply of defective property (such as in sale of goods cases), or damage to property. Accordingly, for such cases the reader is referred to chapter four.[2]

This chapter, in contrast, deals solely with non-provision or defective provision of pure services, such as teaching, entertainment and leisure. (Advice is discussed

---

[1] This chapter excludes misadvice and professional negligence claims, for which see chapter three.

[2] The relevance of this distinction in unjust enrichment cases is as to the nature of the enrichment by the recipient of the service (eg for the purposes of establishing a *quantum meruit* or similar case against that recipient). In impure service cases the property or other marketable end product is the enrichment (and often an incontrovertible benefit). In pure service cases the enrichment, where the law recognises one, is less easy to quantify because not tradeable.

in the immediately succeeding chapter.) Such services are ubiquitous in practice but, apart from employment, carriage and professional advice, under-examined in the textbooks and literature, which focus on those few pure service areas and on the sale of goods and construction. The chapter also covers pretty much anything that does not fall within the other chapters, ie not merely services engaged for money, but also promises to do or abstain that form part of commercial or other contracts.

B. The General Approach

Damages in services cases are assessed according to the ordinary principles of contract law. The cost of cure (in cases of defective services) or replacement (in cases of non-delivery of services) is awarded where all reasonable claimants would have taken it or where it has in fact been expended or is intended and is reasonable. Often the cost of cure or replacement is inappropriate or unreasonable, for example in time-sensitive cases[3] or where the service is ultimately supplied but is supplied late. In such cases, and in the usual way, the claimant is entitled to recover its unavoided and unavoidable loss, which will include non-pecuniary loss, lost profits, costs, and compensation for damage to property or personal injury.

C. Late Delivery by a Carrier

A typical case of defective service provision arises in carriage cases, where the carrier delivers its passengers or cargo but does so late. Damages for temporary loss of use of property (such as in late delivery of goods by a carrier or seller) are covered in chapter six. Carriage of persons is covered in the present chapter.[4] There can be other carriage cases not falling into either category. For example, in one Canadian case a carrier was told that contract tender documentation had to be delivered by 12 noon on 2 October 1973, but in breach it was delivered at 3.17pm and so lawfully disregarded by the tender recipient. The claimant recovered for the lost profit on the lost contract of CAN$70,000.[5]

---

[3] Eg failure to provide a driving practice test booked for the night before the driving test, an example from *Giedo Van der Garde BV v Force India Formula One Team Ltd* [2010] EWHC 2373 (QB) (Stadlen J) at para 458, and see also paras 484–85. See further chapter four, n 221.

[4] Eg *Hobbs v London and South Western Railway Co* (1875) LR 10 QB 111 as to awards for non-pecuniary loss and *Le Blanche v London and North Western Railway Co* (1876) 1 CPD 286 as to awards for reasonable consequential expenses. As to the particular difficulties of remoteness in relation to lost profits resulting from delayed carriage of persons, see the discussion below in chapter fourteen, section 14.3.

[5] *Cornwall Gravel Co Ltd v Purolator Courier Ltd* (1978) 83 DLR (3d) 267 (Ontario HC), affirmed (1979) 115 DLR (3d) 511 (Ontario CA) and [1980] 2 SCR 118 (SC of Canada).

D. Types of Loss

The same types of harm arise in service cases as in other contract cases. This may include lost profits, lost increase in the value of property,[6] damage to property,[7] liability to third parties,[8] and non-pecuniary loss.[9]

E. The Importance of the Type of Claimant

The types of loss suffered, and so the general pattern of the damages award, vary according to whether the service was (or should have been) provided to a commercial claimant or to a consumer. Most obviously, commercial claimants largely feel their loss in financial terms, whereas non-commercial claimants may not. The remainder of this chapter is therefore divided according to the type of claimant, although the majority of the decisions and working out of principles relate to commercial claims.

2.2 Services to Commercial Claimants

A. Direct Proof of Financial Loss

(i) Cost of Replacement

Where a replacement employee or service provider is enlisted as a result of the defendant's breach,[10] or it would be reasonable to engage one,[11] then that cost of cure is the measure of loss.

(ii) Liability to Third Parties

Where the defendant's breach caused the claimant to have liability to third parties, the claimant can recover an indemnity for its liability and costs in the usual way.[12] Thus where a Greek hotel owner provided unsafe rooms to a tour operator, leading

---

[6] Eg construction cases such as *Applegate v Moss* [1971] 1 QB 406 (CA) at 414 (and see chapter four on property); tenant's failure to repair cases, which are governed by s 18(1) of the Landlord and Tenant Act 1927 and discussed below in chapter four, section 4.3(iii)(d); landlord's failure to repair cases, eg *Calabar Properties Ltd v Stitcher* [1984] 1 WLR 287 (CA) Griffiths LJ at 297–98.

[7] Eg *Logical Computer Supplies Ltd v Euro Car Parks Ltd* [2002] IP & T 233 [2001] All ER (D) 197 (Richard Fernyhough QC) (IT services damage to hard disk). There are also many cases of damage to cargo by a carrier, eg *The St Cloud* (1863) B & L 4, 166 ER 269.

[8] See below chapter twenty.

[9] See below chapter nineteen.

[10] Eg *National Coal Board v Galley* [1958] 1 WLR 16 (CA). In the lease context in relation to replacement accommodation see chapter eight, nn 39 and 40, below.

[11] *De Beers UK Ltd v Atos Origin IT Services UK Ltd* [2010] 134 Con LR 151 (Edwards-Stuart J) at para 345.

[12] See below chapter twenty.

to the death of the operator's customer's two children by carbon monoxide poisoning, the operator recovered an indemnity from the hotel owner.[13]

(iii) Direct Proof of Financial Loss

The claimant may in some cases be able to prove lost profits in the ordinary way.

In one Scottish case the defendant manufactured and distributed the claimant's brand of cardboard under a licence from the claimant, for a period after the claimant acquired the brand and before the claimant became sole manufacturer and distributor. The defendant distributed defective board and adopted an antagonistic attitude to customers which damaged the claimant's brand and led to the claimant earning lower profits after it became sole distributor, and £4.25m in damages were awarded.[14]

In another case the defendant electricity supplier breached its contract by interrupting the power supply, causing a partially completed concrete pour to be wasted, although the losses were found to be too remote.[15]

And in *Giedo Van der Garde BV v Force India Formula One Team Ltd*,[16] the defendant's failure to provide the paid-for Formula One test driving practice was thought to have ended the claimant's chances of a Formula One career, permitting an award of lost chance of earnings in such a career (assessed at only US$100,000,[17] given how speculative such a career was).[18]

(iv) Difficulties of Proof

In many business cases it will be difficult to prove a particular loss of custom or profit. As Lord Templeman put it in *Miles v Wakefield*, 'A strike may involve the employer in a loss of profits but it is impossible to show that any particular proportion of the loss is attributable to the industrial action of an individual worker'.[19] In some cases the problem of proof will arise because the services are simply not sufficiently directly linked to the profit-making activity, for example the loss of secretarial, cleaning, training or IT services, or the services of a chauffeur,[20] as well as a variety of back-office (non-client-facing) functions in most businesses.

---

[13] *Thomas Cook Tour Operations Ltd v Tourmajor Ltd* [2013] EWHC 2139 (QB) (Swift J).

[14] *Tullis Russell Papermakers Ltd v Inveresk Ltd* [2010] CSOH 148 (Court of Session, Outer House).

[15] *Balfour Beatty Construction (Scotland) Ltd v Scottish Power plc* (1994) 71 BLR 20 (HL).

[16] *Giedo Van der Garde BV v Force India Formula One Team Ltd* [2010] EWHC 2373 (QB) (Stadlen J) at 496.

[17] Although the court ultimately awarded much more than this on the alternative basis not of profits lost but of the value of the services not provided, or the non-pecuniary loss suffered. See the discussion at section 2.2C in this chapter.

[18] With hindsight it appears that the judge was right to award a low sum for the loss of chance, not because the chances of succeeding but for the breach were so low, but because the breach did not impair those chances as much as was thought: in 2013, subsequent to the judgment, Mr Van der Garde commenced driving in the Caterham Formula One team, so it appears that he may not have lost much.

[19] *Miles v Wakefield Metropolitan District Council* [1987] AC 539 (HL) at 560.

[20] An example of Lord Templeman in *Miles v Wakefield MDC* [1987] AC 539 (HL) at 560.

However, the starting point is that, as Lord Templeman explained in *Miles v Wakefield*, 'An employer always suffers damage from the industrial action of an individual worker. The employer suffers the loss of the services of the worker'.[21] Roche LJ explained in *Ebbw Vale Steel, Iron and Coal Co v Tew* the court's approach in such cases:

> In the case of a hewer [in a coal mine] such as Tew, the application of these principles [measuring lost profit] is not difficult. It may be more difficult with another class of work-man not so directly concerned in getting coal from the seam. But with another class of workman, a tribunal must do its best either to assess the contribution of the workman in question to output and arrive at a figure representing his notional output during the period of default, or if it cannot do that, it must decide upon the evidence what would have been the value to the employer of the services he did not give.[22]

The difficulty comes in fairly assessing and quantifying the loss in such cases.

B. The Presumption of Breaking Even

In service cases it will often be difficult to prove lost profits, and in these circumstances the claimant will often be able to rely on the presumption that it would at least have broken even, an important principle discussed below in chapter eighteen.[23] In essence, the court will rebuttably presume that the claimant would have broken even on its venture, but for the breach, and if the claimant cannot prove it would have made a profit and the defendant cannot prove the claimant would have made a loss, damages are measured by this unrebutted presumption.

(i) The Costs of the Venture Generally

Applying the presumption of breaking even is simplest where the services were critical, such that the breach actually caused a venture to be aborted or wholly interrupted. The abortion of the venture, with no revenue being earned from it, simplifies the calculation that leads from the unrebutted presumption of breaking even. For example, when the American actor defendant in *Anglia TV Ltd v Reed*[24] breached his contract, the entire film was cancelled. The claimant was entitled to recover the lost revenue, the outcome of the film was impossible to prove, and so the presumption that the claimant would have broken even was unrebutted and the lost revenue was presumed to be the same as the expenditure wasted on the film venture.[25] And in the Court of Appeal decision of *Dataliner Ltd v Vehicle Builders & Repairers Association*,[26] the damages for breach by the providers of a defective trade show (the defects being failure to organise and advertise it properly) were measured on the presumption that but for the breach the claimant would have earned enough

---

[21] Lord Templeman in *Miles v Wakefield MDC* [1987] AC 539 (HL) at 560.
[22] Roche LJ in *Ebbw Vale Steel, Iron and Coal Co v Tew* [1935] 1 LJNCCA 284.
[23] This principle is discussed below in chapter eighteen, section 18.3.
[24] *Anglia TV Ltd v Reed* [1972] 1 QB 60 (CA).
[25] Discussed further below in chapter eighteen, section 18.3.
[26] *Dataliner Ltd v Vehicle Builders & Repairers Association* (CA) 27 August 1995.

new business to recoup its expenditure on attending the show. Here the venture (the trade show) was not actually aborted, but the approach was the same, as the show was totally ineffective for the purpose of profit-making.[27]

(ii) The Price Paid to the Defendant

A key element in the costs that it is presumed would have been recouped will be (where paid or owed) the price paid to the defendant itself for the services. Thus, had Mr Reed's fee of £1,050 plus expenses been paid at the date of breach, that too would have been recoverable from him in damages in *Anglia TV Ltd v Reed*, discussed in the previous section, as an expense wasted that (it was presumed) would have been recouped through revenue.

Sometimes the defendant's fee will be the entire cost that it is presumed would have been recouped. In *Playup Interactive Entertainment (UK) Pty Ltd v Givemefootball Ltd*[28] the organiser of the Professional Footballers' Association Fans Awards failed to provide contact details for around a million football fans (and some other benefits) to the claimant sponsor of the awards, who was a provider of interactive games based on predicting the outcome of football matches and would have marketed its games to the fans. Walker J agreed with the claimant's approach of starting the damages calculation with the sum arrived at by apportioning the price between the contact details and other benefits that were provided and those that were promised, on the basis that it saved having to have expert evidence as to the realisable value of what was promised and the realisable value of what was delivered and 'proceeds upon the assumption that the Sponsorship Agreement was worth what PlayUp paid for it' and that assumption was not challenged.[29]

Another example is *White Arrow Express Ltd v Lamey's Distribution Ltd*,[30] where the defendant skimped on the delivery and related services it provided to the claimant's mail order business. The award in that case is best understood as using the difference in market value of the services promised and those provided as a proxy or presumptive indicator of the amount of profits, but the reasoning in that particular case is discussed further below.[31]

(iii) 'Lost Management Time' Claims: Where the Defendant's Breach
       Diverted the Claimant's Staff

The same approach is applied to cases where the defendant caused the loss of a service that was to be provided by a third party, ie the defendant is not the service provider. Thus, where the defendant's breach significantly disrupts the claimant's

---

[27] See also *Bowlay Logging Ltd v Domtar Ltd* (1978) 87 DLR (3d) 325 (British Columbia SC), aff'd (1982) 135 DLR (3d) 179; *Ampurius Nu Homes Holdings Ltd v Telford Homes (Creekside) Ltd* [2012] 144 Con LR 72 (Roth J) app allowed on repudiation [2013] 4 All ER 371 (CA).

[28] *Playup Interactive Entertainment (UK) Pty Ltd v Givemefootball Ltd* [2011] EWHC 1980 (Comm) (Walker J).

[29] Ibid at para 272.

[30] *White Arrow Express Ltd v Lamey's Distribution Ltd* [1995] CLC 251, (1995) 15 Tr LR 69 (CA).

[31] See section 2.2C in this chapter.

business so as to take up time of the claimant's employees, the claimant can recover for lost employee time (often inaccurately called a 'lost management time' claim) in the amount of the relevant employees' wages for the lost time. This is true even if no extra employees were taken on and so the claimant demonstrably suffered no extra cost because even but for the breach of contract (or duty of care; many of the cases are tort cases) the wages would still have been paid,[32] and even if the claimant suffered no directly provable loss of profit.

The position was authoritatively summarised by Wilson LJ in the Court of Appeal decision in the statutory tort case of *Aerospace Publishing v Thames Water Utilities*:[33]

I consider that the authorities establish the following propositions.

(a) The fact and, if so, the extent of the diversion of staff time have to be properly established and, if in that regard evidence which it would have been reasonable for the claimant to adduce is not adduced, he is at risk of a finding that they have not been established.

(b) The claimant also has to establish that the diversion caused significant disruption to its business.

(c) Even though it may well be that strictly the claim should be cast in terms of a loss of revenue attributable to the diversion of staff time, nevertheless in the ordinary case, and unless the defendant can establish the contrary, it is reasonable for the court to infer from the disruption that, had their time not been thus diverted, staff would have applied it to activities which would, directly or indirectly, have generated revenue for the claimant in an amount at least equal to the costs of employing them during that time.

Dealing with and expanding upon the three points in turn:

First, it is important that the diversion of staff time from ordinary duties is properly proven,[34] although it need not necessarily be by detailed records if unavailable.[35]

Secondly, the staff diversion must involve 'significant disruption' to the claimant's revenue-generating business.[36] This may be inferred from the sheer scale and time of the work done by the staff in relation to the breach and its consequences.[37]

---

[32] Of course, if there were additional employees or contractors engaged as a result of the breach, their costs would be recoverable on ordinary principles.

[33] *Aerospace Publishing Ltd v Thames Water Utilities Ltd* [2007] EWCA Civ 3 (CA) Wilson LJ at para 86, the rest of the Court agreeing. This dictum has been quoted with approval in: *Al Rawas v Pegasus Energy Ltd* [2009] 1 All ER 346 (Jack J) (damages under freezing order cross-undertaking); *Borealis AB v Geogas Trading SA* [2011] 1 Lloyd's Rep 482 (Gross LJ) (contract of gas supply); *Tinseltime Ltd v Roberts* [2011] EWHC 1199 (TCC) (HHJ Stephen Davies) (nuisance).

[34] See also *Bridge UK.com Ltd v Abbey Pynford plc* [2007] EWHC 728 (TCC) (Ramsey J) (contract) at paras 123–35, and the tort cases of *Tate and Lyle Food and Distribution Ltd v Greater London Council* [1982] 1 WLR 149 (Forbes J) at 152 and *R+V Versicherung AG v Risk Insurance and Reinsurance Solutions SA* [2006] EWHC 42 (Comm) (Gloster J) at para 77 (conspiracy to defraud).

[35] *Horace Holman Group Ltd v Sherwood International Group Ltd* [2001] All ER (D) 83 (Nov) (Bowsher QC) at para 73. There was inadequate evidence in *Peregrine Systems Ltd v Steria Ltd* [2004] EWHC 275 (TCC) (Seymour QC) at paras 185–86.

[36] Note that it is not necessary that the claimant is a profit-making business, providing it is a revenue-generating (even if not-for-profit) business: *The Salvage Association v Cap Financial Services Ltd* [1995] FSR 654 (HHJ Thayne Forbes).

[37] *Al Rawas v Pegasus Energy Ltd* [2009] 1 All ER 346 (Jack J) at para 23 (damages under freezing order cross-undertaking).

The recovery is still available in relation to 'back office' employees, and not only 'profit makers',[38] as long as the relevant staff are directly or indirectly involved in 'revenue-generating activities'.[39] In one case a bank employee having to spend several months in Vietnam did not disrupt the bank's business in any way.[40] Likewise, where a company's engineers spent time working on faults in the defendant's telecoms handsets that was not a disruption to revenue-generating activities because it was their usual support function.[41] However, the time of several employees trying to get to grips with defective or inadequate computer software has been held to be recoverable,[42] as has additional time spent by building contractors,[43] or the time spent investigating the defendant's fraud, plus the overheads attributable to that employee's time.[44] In one case a claim for diversion of executive time dealing with the defendant landlord's breaches of the covenant to repair was refused without discussion, although there was no real evidence that the claimant corporate tenant of a residential property had profit-making activities that were disrupted.[45]

Thirdly, as a matter of ordinary principles, the claim is not and cannot be one for the wages of the employees, as but for the contract breach or tort the employees would still have been paid. The claim is rather for the loss of revenue or other benefit that the employees would have generated if doing the jobs for which they were employed.[46] As the quotation of Wilson LJ shows (particularly 'unless the Defendant can establish the contrary' and 'infer'[47]), what arises is a rebuttable presumption that the staff would have generated as much revenue as they cost.[48] As Birss QC explained in the *Azzurri Communications Ltd* case,

> if the breach can be said to have caused diversion of staff to an extent substantial enough to lead to a significant disruption of the business then it is reasonable to draw the inference of a loss of revenue equal to the cost of employing the staff.[49]

Thus the claim is for that lost revenue, not for the cost itself. The basis of the presumption is that, as the accountancy expert observed in the case of *Horace Holman*

---

[38] *Horace Holman Group Ltd v Sherwood International Group Ltd* [2001] All ER (D) 83 (Nov) (Bowsher QC) at paras 75–78.

[39] Wilson LJ in *Aerospace Publishing Ltd v Thames Water Utilities Ltd* [2007] EWCA Civ 3 (CA) at para 87.

[40] *Standard Chartered Bank v Pakistan National Shipping Corp* [2001] EWCA Civ 55 (CA) (deceit).

[41] *Azzurri Communications Ltd v International Telecommunications Equipment Ltd* [2013] EWPCC 17 (Birss QC) at para 93.

[42] *Horace Holman Group Ltd v Sherwood International Group Ltd* [2001] All ER (D) 83 (Nov) (Bowsher QC) and obiter in *Sam Business Systems Ltd v Hedley and Co* [2002] EWHC 2733 (Bowsher QC).

[43] Obiter in *Standard Chartered Bank v Pakistan National Shipping Corp* [2001] EWCA Civ 55 (CA) Potter LJ at para 49.

[44] *Nationwide Building Society v Dunlop Haywards (DHL) Ltd* [2010] 1 WLR 258 (Clarke J) (fraud).

[45] *City and Metropolitan Properties Ltd v Greycroft Ltd* [1987] 1 WLR 1085 (Mowbray QC) at 1088 and 1090.

[46] Thus lost time of employees whose jobs are to deal with just the sorts of problems the defendant has caused may not give rise to a claim as they were not diverted from anything else.

[47] Above, text to n 33, at (c).

[48] As well as the cases at n 33 above, see also at *4 Eng Ltd v Harper* [2009] Ch 91 (David Richards J) at para 40.

[49] *Azzurri Communications Ltd v International Telecommunications Equipment Ltd (t/a SOS Communications)* [2013] EWPCC 17 (Birss QC) at para 92, also para 94.

Group Ltd v Sherwood International Group Ltd, 'every employer values each employee at more than the employee is paid, otherwise there is no point in employing him'.[50] Or as Lord Templeman has observed, 'The value of those services to the employer cannot be less than the salary payable for those services, otherwise most employers would become insolvent'.[51] Even with back-office time, 'the claimants were paying for time which was to be a benefit to them and they lost the benefit of that time' (and that staff's diversion would have had a knock-on effect on front-office staff).[52] As one judge observed, the cost of employee time is taken as an 'approximation for the loss of revenue'.[53]

The award is therefore of inferred lost revenue equal to the amount the employees are paid. Any higher value (such as their external charge-out rate) can only be recovered if the claimant actually proves that it lost revenue of that amount (whether by charging out the staff to third parties or otherwise).[54]

This approach is closely analogous to that in more general wasted expenditure/reliance damages cases where it is assumed that, had a venture not been aborted, the claimant would have earned revenue so as to recoup the expenditure of a venture, ie would have broken even, and therefore (if the presumption is not rebutted) the claimant recovers damages in the amount of the wasted expenditure. Here the same approach is applied but merely to the single expenditure of the relevant services: it is presumed that the revenue (or other recoverable benefit or obviation of harm) that would have been provided by the employee or other service-provider (the services of which the claimant was deprived by the defendant) would have been equal to the wages or other price of that employee or other service-provider.

Thus if the claimant separately advances a particularised lost profit claim, the lost management time claim would be duplicatory.[55]

(iv) Lost Overheads

Similarly, building contractors who have been delayed can often claim for office or other off-site overheads on the basis that they would have been reimbursed by revenue earned on other projects but for the delay.[56] The same principles as apply to lost management time must logically apply here too.

---

[50] *Horace Holman Group Ltd v Sherwood International Group Ltd* [2001] All ER (D) 83 (Nov) (Bowsher QC) at para 75, quoted by Wilson LJ in *Aerospace Publishing Ltd v Thames Water Utilities Ltd* [2007] EWCA Civ 3 (CA) at para 82.

[51] *Miles v Wakefield MDC* [1987] AC 539 (HL) at 560.

[52] *Horace Holman Group Ltd v Sherwood International Group Ltd* [2001] All ER (D) 83 (Nov) (Bowsher QC) at para 78.

[53] Stanley Burnton J's view in *Admiral Management Services Ltd v Para-Protect Europe Ltd* [2002] 1 WLR 2722 at 2745–46 (breach of confidentiality).

[54] *Azzurri Communications Ltd v International Telecommunications Equipment Ltd (t/a SOS Communications)* [2013] EWPCC 17 (Birss QC) at para 94.

[55] *Tinseltime Ltd v Roberts* [2011] EWHC 1199 (TCC) (HHJ Stephen Davies) at para 73.

[56] *Try Build Ltd v Invicta Leisure Tennis Ltd* (1997) 71 Con LR 140 (Bowsher QC) at paras 107–8, applying *JF Finnigan Ltd v Sheffield City Council* (1988) 43 BLR 124 (Stabb QC) at 134; *Walter Lilly & Co Ltd v Mackay* [2012] EWHC 1773 (TCC) (Akenhead J). See also *Nationwide Building Society v Dunlop Haywards (DHL) Ltd* [2010] 1 WLR 258 (Clarke J) (fraud) as to overheads.

(v) Loss of the Claimant's Own Work Time

In *Haysman v Mrs Rogers Films Ltd*,[57] the claimant was managing director and majority owner of a company and his own time was diverted by having to deal with the damage to his home caused by the defendant's breaches. The court awarded a pro-rated amount of the claimant's annual net dividend and other income, on the basis that a certain number of days' profitable work (a smaller number than claimed for) had been unavoidably lost, and that this was a reasonable way of quantifying a relatively small loss. Similarly in the solicitor's negligence case of *Gold v Mincoff Science & Gold*, a dentist was held in principle entitled to recover for the profits lost while he diverted his time to a substantial claim he faced from a third party as a result of the defendant's negligence.[58]

C. No Separate Claim for Difference in Market Value

(i) Support for a Difference in Market Value of the Service Claim

The question of how the value of services to the employer should be measured arose in *White Arrow Express Ltd v Lamey's Distribution Ltd*.[59] In that case the supplier promised to provide an enhanced delivery service for the claimant's mail order business (the delivery to include, among other things, the giving of advance notice to customers, the removal of packaging, and the delivery staff wearing a particular uniform). Instead, the defendant provided only a basic service, but the claimant was unable to prove that it had thereby incurred liability to any of its customers or lost any custom. Although there was no recovery because the claimant had not properly pleaded and evidenced its loss (instead formulating the claim as being for a part of the price paid by the claimant), Lord Bingham MR explained, obiter, that a claimant can only recover if it can prove loss, specifically that the defendant has 'injured his financial position', by demonstrating 'specific heads of loss, or persuade the court to draw an inference of loss', but also commented that:

> It is, on the other hand, obvious that in the ordinary way a party who contracts and pays for a superior service or superior goods and receives a substantially inferior service or inferior goods has suffered loss. If A hires and pays in advance for a 4-door saloon at £200 per day and receives delivery of a 2-door saloon available for £100 per day, he has suffered loss. If B orders and pays in advance for a 5-course meal costing £50 and is served a 3-course meal costing £30, he has suffered loss. If C agrees and pays in advance to be taught the violin by a world famous celebrity at £500 per hour, and is in the event taught by a musical nonentity whose charging rate is £25 per hour, he has suffered loss. It is irrelevant whether A, B or C would be entitled to reject the goods or services tendered if they in fact accept them. It would defy common sense to suggest that A, B or C have suffered

---

[57] *Haysman v Mrs Rogers Films Ltd* [2008] EWHC 2494 (QB) (Derek Sweeting QC) paras 18–19. See also the construction case of *The Board of Governors of the Hospitals for Sick Children v McLaughlin & Harvey plc* (1987) 19 Con LR 25 (Newey QC) at 97.

[58] *Gold v Mincoff Science & Gold* (21 December 2000), (Neuberger J) at paras 159–64.

[59] *White Arrow Express Ltd v Lamey's Distribution Ltd* [1995] CLC 1251, (1996) 15 Tr LR 69 (CA).

no loss, and are not financially disadvantaged by the breach. *The measure of damages in all of these cases is the difference between the price paid (or, if it is lower, the market value of what was contracted for) and the market value of what was obtained ...*

It is not the law that an innocent party who contracts for a de luxe service and receives a sub-standard service is in principle denied a claim to more than nominal damages ... an innocent party in such a position must quantify, or at least provide evidence from which the court may draw an inference as to, *the difference between the value (usually the market value) of what was contracted for and the value (again, usually the market value) of what was provided.* (Emphasis added)[60]

Bingham MR went on to explain his view that in the holiday cases where a holiday of a lesser standard than promised was provided, the claimant would have a claim for the difference in value between the two holidays 'irrespective of any claim for loss of enjoyment, disappointed expectation or inconvenience'.[61] Bingham MR's clear view was, therefore, that the claimant is entitled to the difference in the market value between the service provided and that promised, although this must be treated with caution as the point was obiter and agreed by the parties (the defendant instead focussing its attack, successfully, on the claimant not having led any such market evidence). The same view was expressed, obiter and in passing, by Lord Nicholls in *Attorney General v Blake*:[62]

If a shopkeeper supplies inferior and cheaper goods than those ordered and paid for, he has to refund the difference in price. That would be the outcome of a claim for damages for breach of contract. That would be so, irrespective of whether the goods in fact served the intended purpose. There must be scope for a similar approach, without any straining of principle, in cases where the defendant provided inferior and cheaper services than those contracted for.

The most extensive discussion of the point then came in the 2010 first instance decision of Stadlen J in *Giedo Van der Garde BV v Force India Formula One Team Ltd*.[63] In that case the claimant (and his corporate entity) had paid for 6,000 km of test driving with attendant benefits, and only been provided with around a third of that. Stadlen J carefully reviewed the various authorities at some length, and awarded damages of US$1,865,000—essentially a proportion of the price paid on the presumption that this represented the value of the laps to the driver.

In this case the ultimate goal of Mr Van der Garde was to become a professional Formula One driver, and the lost earnings from that career, on a loss of chance basis, were assessed by the judge at US$100,000.[64] The difficult question arising

---

[60] At 1255–56.
[61] See further especially *Milner v Carnival plc* [2010] 3 All ER 701 (CA) at paras 29–43, discussed below at section 2.4A in this chapter.
[62] *Attorney General v Blake* [2001] AC 268 (HL) at 286.
[63] *Giedo Van der Garde BV v Force India Formula One Team Ltd* [2010] EWHC 2373 (QB) (Stadlen J) at para 496. See also R Stevens, 'Damages and the Right to Performance: A *Golden Victory* or Not?' in J Neyers, R Bronaugh and S Pitel (eds), *Exploring Contract Law* (Oxford, Hart Publishing, 2009) and 'Rights and Other Things' in A Robertson and D Nolan (eds), *Rights and Private Law* (Oxford, Hart Publishing, 2011), whose theory supports a difference in market value award for both goods and services cases, with a consequential loss award on top of that, and only the latter award being subject to reduction by causation, mitigation and remoteness principles.
[64] [2010] EWHC 2373 (QB) para 412.

here is whether that loss exhausts the claimant's right to recovery, or whether there might be some further recovery (as ultimately there was in this case) and if so on what basis.

The approach taken by the judge, following that of the Court of Appeal in *White Arrow*, was to find that the claimant was entitled to a free-standing claim for the difference in market value between the service promised and that provided, quite independently of the claim for the consequential lost profit.

The first essential point is that this was seen as a recovery of damages for 'loss', but independently of the consequential loss of profit. Thus as the judge noted:

> In Sir Thomas Bingham's hypothetical example in *White Arrow Express* of the person who agrees and pays in advance to be taught to play the violin by a world famous celebrity for £500 per hour and is in the event taught by a musical non-entity whose charging rate is £25 per hour there was no suggestion that the measure of loss, namely the difference between the price paid for (or if lower, the market value of what was contracted for) and the market value of what was obtained, was dependent on proof that the Claimant had suffered consequential financial loss in the form of the loss of opportunities of himself earning money as a professional violinist. *Loss of the enhanced service was itself a loss measurable by the difference between the value of the celebrity lesson and the value of a musical non-entity lesson.*[65]

And further:

> the Claimants are entitled to be compensated by an award of damages for the loss suffered by them by reason of the failure of Spyker to provide 4,000-odd kilometres of test driving and the associated paddock pass and sponsorship benefits. *That loss is to be assessed by reference to the value of the kilometres and associated benefits which should have been but were not provided. The assessment of that value is a matter of evidence.* (Emphasis added)[66]

For Stadlen J, the market value (of the laps, celebrity violin lessons, etc) was the key. The price may provide evidence of the market value, but it is the market value which governs. If the claimant had a good deal and underpaid then the damages for non-supply would be greater than the price, and the reverse if a bad deal.[67] For the judge this US$1.865m award was an alternative, not an addition, to the award of US$100,000 for the lost chance of financial profits.[68] Stadlen J's approach is consistent with the obiter comments of the Court of Appeal in *White Arrow*, and the dictum of Lord Nicholls in *Attorney General v Blake*.

(ii) Why the 'Difference in Market Value' Approach is Wrong

However, although the result may be correct, the judge's explanation (and the obiter comments in *White Arrow* and *Attorney General v Blake*) are unworkable and wrong. It departs too far from the ordinary concept of loss, and would have a profoundly unsettling effect on the law. In sale of goods cases (from which the

---

[65] Ibid para 438.
[66] Para 487.
[67] Paras 438 and 487.
[68] Para 560.

analogy is drawn explicitly by Lord Nicholls in his dictum in *Blake*[69]) the market measure makes sense because the goods will be tradeable and often replaceable on the market, so the market is the means of identifying an actual pecuniary loss, being the additional cost of purchasing a replacement, or lost revenue from selling the promised goods. This is not true of a service, which cannot be traded. As Walker J observed in the *Playup* case,[70] this is only an orthodox approach 'in cases where there is a market for a commodity or where the court is in a position to identify both the realisable value of what was promised and the realisable value of what was delivered'.

Moreover, if the market value measure is an independent measure, then it would mean that in *every* contract case the claimant can, as an alternative to any lost profit (of which there may not be any) or non-pecuniary loss, recover the difference in market value of the services. Does this mean that where a carrier is a week late in delivering goods (cf *Hadley v Baxendale*), it is necessary to lead evidence as to what the market value of carriage arriving a week late is as compared with the faster carriage promised? If Mr Van der Garde had proven that he certainly lost US$1.5m of Formula One earnings would he still be entitled to the difference in market value of US$1.865m in the alternative? If a professional provides bad advice, can the claimant recover the difference in the market value of the good advice and the bad advice?

The confusion arises because of two particular features of the *Van der Garde* case. The first is that the contract was about both financial and non-pecuniary benefit. The second is that the financial loss was established by a loss of chance. If the service had been construction or carriage provided to a claimant operating for profit, and it could have been demonstrated that the claimant would have made a loss if the defendant's service had been performed, then the cases show that the claimant could not have recovered damages, as it would be no worse off by the defendant having refused to perform its services.[71] In such a case it does not matter that the defendant's services had a market value, because the sole type of loss contemplated (ie within the defendant's assumed responsibility) is loss of profit. If there is a net loss of revenue it is recoverable. If not, no damages are payable even if the defendant fails to provide part of its service and for some reason the service has already been paid for. Accordingly, wasted expenditure is unrecoverable where it is greater than the lost revenue such that the award would put the claimant in a better position than it would have been in but for the breach,[72] and *Wrotham Park* reasonable fee damages cannot be recovered if they would put the claimant in a better position than it would have been but for the breach.[73]

---

[69] This reasoning was adopted by Stadlen J at para 435.

[70] *Playup Interactive Entertainment (UK) Pty Ltd v Givemefootball Ltd* [2011] EWHC 1980 (Comm) (Walker J) at paras 269 and 272.

[71] *Bowlay Logging Ltd v Domtar Ltd* (1978) 87 DLR (3d) 325 (British Columbia SC), aff'd (1982) 135 DLR (3d) 179 and *Ampurius Nu Homes Holdings Ltd v Telford Homes (Creekside) Ltd* [2012] 144 Con LR 72 (Roth J) app allowed on repudiation [2013] 4 All ER 377 (CA).

[72] See below in chapter eighteen, section 18.3.

[73] *BGC Capital Markets (Switzerland) LLC v Rees* [2011] EWHC 2009 (QB) (Sir Jack) at para 97: 'The intended function of the claim here is to avoid BGC's problem that it cannot show that it has suffered any loss because it has not in fact done so. In my judgment the award of release payment

However, *Van der Garde* was not merely a case of a commercial entity losing a profitable opportunity. Mr Van der Garde was an individual and what was at stake was his future lifestyle and career. In that situation, there may be non-pecuniary value in the lifestyle and enjoyment during the period of training denied him, and in the improvements to his driving abilities. More importantly, Mr Van der Garde did not only lose a relatively small chance of earning money if the Formula One career had occurred (which, so the judge in that case assessed, came to US$100,000 when the chance was multiplied by the amount of earnings), but also the same chance of receiving during his career all the non-pecuniary benefits of a career as a racing driver, including the celebrity, prestige and fun, the attendant lifestyle, and the satisfaction of being able to repay the confidence of his main backer, his girlfriend's father. (Such a non-pecuniary value ascribed to satisfaction gained from a particular career or vocation is recognised in personal injury and employment discrimination cases by an award for loss of 'congenial employment', which is quantified separately from an award of loss of amenity or injury to feelings, and there is no reason why it should not also be recoverable in contract law where it is part of the contemplated non-pecuniary loss.[74])

Finally, it may be said that there is a non-pecuniary value to self-esteem and sense of self in being given the opportunity to succeed or fail by ones own abilities, even though the chance of success was small, and so the mathematical loss of chance calculation seems particularly inadequate. Loss of chance cases throw up particular difficulties, especially where non-pecuniary losses are involved, because most people value a chance of a big win at higher than its mathematical value; damages for a lost lottery ticket would otherwise be de minimis.[75]

(iii) The Objectives of the Service, and Means to Ends

The better view, therefore, is that *Van der Garde* is not a purely commercial case and not a good example against which to develop principles applicable to commercial disputes (and note that all the examples used by Stadlen J are non-commercial), as the award in *Van de Garde* is an award of non-pecuniary loss, and the market value measure provides at most some evidence of that loss.[76] Stadlen J is right to emphasise that what is important is not merely value but value *to the claimant*,[77] as to which the market value has little to say. Despite the emphasis on market value,

---

damages is not available as a substitute for conventional damages to compensate a claimant for damage he has not suffered. Nor should it be used to award a larger sum than a conventional calculation of loss provides'.

[74] See eg *Ministry of Defence v Cannock* [1995] 2 All ER 449 (EAT). The award is rarely much more than £10,000.

[75] It is clear from the reasoning in *Van der Garde* [2010] EWHC 2373 at para 437 that the judge thought the loss of chance aspect of the calculation in particular made the award of a mere US$100,000 unfair, ie although US$100,000 was a proper award for lost profits as a matter of law and arithmetic, that did not change the fact that the laps 'might have led to very significant earnings possibly running into millions of pounds' but now never will.

[76] See below in chapter nineteen, section 19.2C(ii) for discussion of the use of proxies in measuring non-pecuniary loss.

[77] [2010] EWHC 2373 at paras 424, 425, 428, 435, 437 and 458.

Stadlen J crucially and correctly accepts that it is only a proxy: 'The loss is assessed by the value of those lessons. The best evidence of that value is likely to be the market price of driving lessons at the date of breach'.[78] Thus, the market value of a service is irrelevant in cases where the service is merely intended to serve the bottom line, although the price may be a useful proxy for the lost revenue by means of the presumption of breaking even. Similarly, where non-pecuniary loss is suffered and not too remote, market value is relevant only as evidence of the amount of non-pecuniary loss.[79]

In the case of driving lessons (or Formula One practice laps), it is a matter of interpretation whether the defendant assumes responsibility only for the effect on the end result (ie loss through failing the test/not becoming a Formula One driver), treating the service only as a means to that end, or whether there is further non-pecuniary benefit in having the lesson, improving abilities, and feeling that one has maximised one's chances, even if ultimately the result is not altered. Stadlen J is right that, if the latter is the correct interpretation in a particular case, a claimant has suffered a loss if it pays for 20 driving lessons and is only given six but was bound to fail the test anyway (having failed ten times before).[80] However, that loss is not necessarily anything to do with the market value of the lessons.

Moreover, in some cases only the end result is contemplated as the value of the service to the claimant, such as the profit in a purely financial case, or (possibly) passing the driving test in the non-financial example being discussed. In such cases, as Stadlen J correctly observes, if what is provided was 'no less effective in securing the objective which the superior (or larger number of) services contracted for were intended to achieve' then there is no loss suffered if the breach does not cause a failure of the contemplated goal. This applies in the driving test example whether the claimant would have failed anyway, or whether the claimant passes despite the breach.[81] In these cases, again, market value has nothing to do with recovery.

This is exactly the problem that arose in the *City of New Orleans v Firemen's Charitable Association*[82] case, where the fire service had contracted to have available on call a certain number of engines and personnel etc. If the only contemplated value to the claimant of the fire-fighting service was the result of putting out all fires occurring in New Orleans, then the defendant's breach in providing too few fire fighters is irrelevant save to the extent that as a result fires were not put out.[83] If, however, it is contemplated that the City of New Orleans had some non-pecuniary value (eg peace of mind of citizens, or public relations of the City, eg if it had told the citizens how many fire-fighters it had procured) in having and knowing it had the right number of fire fighters on standby at any one time, then even if all the fires

---

[78] Ibid para 458. That Stadlen J did not see market value as determinative is also clear from his discussion of the *City of New Orleans* case at para 435; clearly the market value of the services provided in that case was lower than the market value of the services promised. And see also para 436 which does not seem to be focusing on market value.

[79] For the discussion of remoteness of non-pecuniary loss see below in chapter nineteen, section 19.1E.

[80] *Van de Garde* (Stadlen J) [2010] EWHC 2373 at para 438.

[81] Ibid para 436.

[82] *City of New Orleans v Firemen's Charitable Association* 9 So 486 (1891).

[83] As Stadlen J correctly observes in *Van der Garde* [2010] EWHC 2373 at para 435.

were put out the City may have suffered non-pecuniary loss. Stadlen J in *Van der Garde* clearly thought that Mr van der Garde was in this latter category of there being additional value quite apart from the result (of a profitable career), as can be seen from his explanation of the City of New Orleans case and his distinguishing it in the *Van der Garde* case.[84] Security and safety cases such as *City of New Orleans* provide a particular test of this distinction between result (the goal is merely related to how many incidents there were) and process (the goal involves having the safety mechanism in place).[85]

And, similarly, in the context of non-pure service cases, choices made in specifications for a building or other property can be ignored with impunity by builders if they make no difference to the financial value of the resulting property and the only contemplated objective of the service is the financial bottom line of the property, but not if it is contemplated that the claimant ascribes aesthetic (non-pecuniary) value to the preference quite apart from the financial bottom line, as in such cases the ignoring of the specification causes the claimant loss.[86] All turns on what types of value *to the claimant*, and therefore loss, are within the risk and responsibility impliedly assumed by the defendant: ie all turns on remoteness.

(iv) Market Value as a Proxy for Loss

We have seen above that a presumption that the claimant would have broken even, and therefore that the revenue or value that would have been earned from a service would at least equal the price of the service, is (quite properly) employed in assessing damages where lost profits cannot directly be proven.[87]

Similarly, as is explained below in relation to non-pecuniary loss,[88] the value of the service to third parties (ie market value, as awarded in *Van der Garde* and discussed in *White Arrow*) may also provide useful evidence of the value of the services.

D. Conclusion

In summary of the above, the better view is that:

(1) In claims for non- or defective provision of services to a business, the claimant can prove that it suffered financial loss.

(2) Further, it is rebuttably presumed that the claimant would have earned from the service revenue equal to the cost of the services. (This could have explained *Van der Garde*, save that the presumption was rebutted in that case as the court was able to quantify the lost profits at a loss of chance

---

[84] Ibid paras 435–37.
[85] Cf goods case *The Alecos M* [1991] 1 Lloyd's Rep 120, where substantial damages were refused on failure to provide a spare propeller. See chapter four text to nn 10 and 478 below.
[86] As in *Ruxley Electronics and Construction Ltd v Forsyth* [1996] AC 344 (HL), discussed below in chapter nineteen, section 19.1C.
[87] See section 2.2B in this chapter.
[88] Chapter nineteen, section 19.2C.

award of US$100,000.)[89] It is also rebuttably presumed that the claimant would have earned revenue equal to the wages or other costs from third party employees or service-providers whose efforts were diverted by the defendant's breach.

(3) The courts should be astute to recognise which cases are not purely commercial cases, such that the contemplated interests protected include interests other than the bottom line and so can give rise to recovery for non-pecuniary loss. Such awards are discussed below in relation to commercial public bodies and consumers in sections 2.3 and 2.4 in this chapter. *Van der Garde* is such a case, as explained above. Non-pecuniary loss is discussed generally below in chapter nineteen.

(4) There is no generally available award for the difference between the market value of the service provided and that promised.

2.3 Services to Public Bodies

Where an employee or independent contractor provides services to a public body or private non-profit-making body it will often be the case that the purpose of engaging the services is not profit-related. In such cases it is not only impossible in a particular case to show a financial loss from the non-provision or defective provision of the service (unless additional costs, such as by engaging a replacement, were incurred), but also to address financial loss in this way is entirely to disregard what the claimant and the contract for services were all about.

Thus in *Miles v Wakefield MDC*, the Council was permitted to withhold a proportion of a marriage Registrar's wages (3/37) when he refused to officiate on Saturdays, therefore being unavailable for three out of his weekly 37 hours. The House of Lords held that the employer had suffered damage by not getting services from the Registrar, and 'A man who pays something for nothing truly incurs loss. The value of the lost services cannot be less than the value attributable to the lost hours of work'.[90] The House therefore valued those services as being the same as the price the Council was paying the Registrar.[91]

Similarly, damages have been awarded for a schoolteacher's refusal to take an extra five pupils on top of his existing class of 31, the damages being measured as 5/36 of his salary.[92] Similar examples might include a third party contractor engaged by a public body to provide waste collection services, repair roads, fix gas leaks, build a leisure centre etc.

---

[89] Cf claims by commercial tenants for non-repair where no direct loss of profits can be proven, discussed below in chapter eight, section 8.3.

[90] *Miles v Wakefield MDC* [1987] AC 539 (Lord Templeman) at 560.

[91] See eg the discussions in *Giedo Van der Garde BV v Force India Formula One Team Ltd* [2010] EWHC 2373 (QB) (Stadlen J) at para 421 and *Re Home & Office Fire Extinguishers Ltd, Rodliffe v Rodliffe* [2012] EWHC 917 (Ch) (Strauss QC) at para 68: 'It was held that the Council could withhold a proportionate amount of his salary, on the simple basis that it had lost the value of his services, quantifying the loss by taking that proportion of his salary'.

[92] *Royle v Trafford Borough Council* [1984] IRLR 184 (Park J).

Such public service contracts therefore share many features with consumer contracts, and in such cases the value of the service must be non-pecuniary (although the label 'enjoyment' is not appropriate in these cases, unlike many consumer cases). The price paid, or the relevant portion of it, can be used as a rebuttably presumed proxy for the loss, because it must be presumed that the service was worth to the claimant what the claimant was willing to pay for it.[93]

2.4 Services to Consumers

Consumers pay for a myriad of services in their lives. A major category is professional advice or assistance, especially in purchasing or selling a residence or preparing a will. Residential leases may be the most expensive service a consumer pays for. Domestic building works and healthcare are other major categories of consumer contract, as are insurance (although it is debatable whether this is properly characterised as a service) and holidays. The majority of other service contracts entered into by consumers are for relatively small sums of money and are rarely litigated (at least to the level of a reported decision), for example restaurant meals, entertainment, cleaning services, car or other repairs, and public or private transport. Examples discussed in the case law (often as illustrations) include delivery of an inferior rental car,[94] service of an inferior meal in a restaurant,[95] music lessons provided by a musical non-entity instead of by a world famous celebrity,[96] or the provision of only six out of a block booking of 20 driving lessons.[97]

No special principles apply to consumer cases, save that damages for non-pecuniary loss, discussed in some detail in chapter nineteen below, are far more readily available than in non-consumer cases and may be the primary measure of damages where no replacement is available. (The most commonly considered example is that of the holiday.)

A. Difference in Market Value?

It has been suggested that a consumer claimant is entitled to recover the difference in market value between the service promised and that provided. In *Jackson v Horizon Holidays*, Lord Denning MR suggested that the true principle from *Jarvis v Swan's*

---

[93] See below in chapter nineteen, section 19.2C, and see the discussion of awards to consumers in the next section.

[94] *White Arrow Express Ltd v Lamey's Distribution Ltd* (1995) 15 Tr LR 69 (CA); *Giedo van der Garde BV v Force India Formula One Team Ltd* [2010] EWHC 2373 (QB) (Stadlen J) at para 458. Quoted above at text to n 149.

[95] Ibid.

[96] Ibid.

[97] *Giedo Van der Garde BV v Force India Formula One Team Ltd* [2010] EWHC 2373 (QB) (Stadlen J) at para 458. The actual facts of that case concerned Formula One test laps, and it is discussed above in some detail at section 2.2C(i). The issue discussed there, where the education was for both non-pecuniary reasons (self-improvement, enjoyment, satisfaction etc) and pecuniary reasons (ultimately increasing employability or profitability), will arise in many education cases.

Tours[98] permitted recovery of 'not only the difference in value between what was promised and what was obtained, but also damages for mental distress, inconvenience, upset, disappointment and frustration caused by the loss of the holiday',[99] and this has been interpreted by Bingham MR, commenting obiter in a later (commercial) case, as permitting recovery of the difference between the market value of the service provided and the market value of the service promised, whether the service be a holiday, a meal or a violin lesson.[100] In the *Jackson* case itself, the Court approved the judge's award on the basis that it was made up of £600 for diminution in value of the service and £500 for mental distress.

More recently, in *Milner v Carnival plc* the claimants went on a world cruise that involved noisy vibrations, were moved to an inferior cabin, and reasonably disembarked 28 days into a 106-day cruise.[101] As well as an award of £8,500 each for physical discomfort, distress and inconvenience, and after a refund for the unused days, the Court of Appeal awarded £3,500 for

> pecuniary loss—the diminution in value: the loss here is the monetary difference between what was bought and what was supplied. The task is to assess the amount by which the advertised holiday turned out to be less in money terms than the customer had paid for it.[102]

In *Giedo Van der Garde BV v Force India Formula One Team Ltd*[103] some of these and various other consumer services (eg driving lessons) were discussed as leading to such an award.

This issue is discussed above at section 2.2C in the context of services to commercial entities. The conclusion reached there is that there can in law be no award for the difference in market value of a service, only an award for loss. It is quite proper to consider the value of a service *to the claimant*, and distress caused to the claimant, but both are ways of assessing non-pecuniary and not pecuniary loss.[104] Accordingly, the entire awards in *Jarvis* and *Jackson* are best understood as non-pecuniary loss awards, albeit that some of the loss may be 'mental distress' and other aspects of the loss may be other types of non-pecuniary loss. The difference in market value may, however, be a good starting point or proxy for the non-pecuniary loss, as discussed in the residential lease context in the next sub-section and more generally in non-pecuniary loss cases in chapter nineteen, section 19.2C(ii).

---

[98] *Jarvis v Swans Tours Ltd* [1973] QB 233 (CA).

[99] *Jackson v Horizon Holidays Ltd* [1975] 1 WLR 1468 (CA) at 1472.

[100] *White Arrow Express Ltd v Lamey's Distribution Ltd* (1995) 15 Tr LR 69 (CA). See further the extensive quotation above at text to n60.

[101] *Milner v Carnival plc* [2010] 3 All ER 701 (CA).

[102] Ibid, [2010] EWCA 389 (Ward LJ) at para 29, also para 43.

[103] *Giedo Van der Garde BV v Force India Formula One Team Ltd* [2010] EWHC 2373 (QB) (Stadlen J) at 496.

[104] Contra *Milner v Carnival plc* [2010] 3 All ER 701 (CA) Ward LJ at paras 29 and 43, although Ward LJ noted at para 43 that it would be duplicatory to award difference in value of a non-pecuniary service and non-pecuniary loss, which demonstrates that, as in landlord breach cases, the true principle is that of loss, and the difference in market or other value is just a proxy for or measure of the non-pecuniary loss.

3

Misadvice (Especially Professional Negligence) and Contractual Misstatement

Damages for misadvice and contractual misstatement, most frequently in the professional negligence context

3.1 Introduction to the Breach and Non-Breach Positions in Advice and Similar Cases[1]

A. Introduction

A particular type of complaint arises mainly (but not only) in relation to negligent advice cases or cases of breaches of collateral warranties as to pre-contractual statements. This type of complaint is different from the usual service case in the following respects.

— First, it usually (at least where the case concerns misadvice rather than war-ranties as to pre-contractual statements) involves the claimant focusing on a transaction or course of conduct—be it a contract, purchase or piece of litigation—that the claimant embarked upon *with a third party*, as a result of the defendant's breach.
— Secondly, in a lot of such cases the main thrust of the claimant's complaint is simply that the defendant caused the claimant to enter into the transaction and it would not have done so but for the defendant. The emphasis in such cases,

---

[1] For explanation of the term 'non-breach position' see the diagram in this section, and the discussion above in chapter one, section 1.3B.

like in tort claims for misstatements inducing a transaction,[2] is therefore on the defendant having made the claimant's position worse from the pre-transaction starting point, rather than failing to make the claimant's position better.

B. Introduction to the Non-Breach Position: What Would the Claimant Otherwise Have Done?

It is for the claimant to prove on the balance of probabilities what it would have done but for the misadvice. If it cannot show that it would not have done anything different, then the breach has caused no loss and it can only recover nominal damages.[3]

The point made in the introduction to this section concerns the non-breach position. The specific pattern of the damages award depends upon what the claimant would have done but for the breach (ie if it had not been given the bad advice, or if it had had the relevant issue pointed out to it). As mentioned, in many cases the complaint goes no further than that the claimant would not have entered into the transaction, and so the non-breach position is unusually simple. In such cases, it appears that the claimant is merely seeking to be put into the status quo ante the transaction. Of course, the claimant is not entitled to that, as even but for the breach time would have run and things would have happened, but where the claimant would have done nothing for that time, the non-breach position is little more than the status quo ante plus damages for loss of interest on money for the intervening time. The pattern of the damages award feels very much, therefore, like *undoing* the transaction.

(i) 'No Transaction' and 'Successful-Transaction' Cases

For some time the terms 'no transaction' and 'successful-transaction', coined by Staughton LJ in *Hayes v James and Charles Dodd*,[4] and used subsequently,[5] were used to distinguish between types of non-breach position, ie different types of situation that (the claimant claims) would have come about but for the breach. The 'no transaction' fact pattern involves the claimant alleging that but for the breach it would not have entered into the transaction it did, or anything like it. The 'successful-transaction' fact pattern resolves that but for the breach the claimant would have entered into the transaction with the same third party (bought the house, lent the money, etc) but involves an allegation that it would have done so on more favourable terms (paying less, lending less, with better contractual protections, with a greater security etc).

---

[2] At common law, by the negligent misstatement principle of *Hedley Byrne & Co Ltd v Heller & Partners Ltd* [1964] AC 465 (HL) and the tort of deceit, and by the statutory tort in section 2(1) of the Misrepresentation Act 1967. Some of the cases in this section are tort cases or concurrent contract/tort cases

[3] See below chapter thirteen, section 13.2B.

[4] *Hayes v James and Charles Dodd* [1990] 2 All ER 815 (CA) at 818–19.

[5] Eg *Brown v Cuff Roberts* (CA), 12 February 1996; *Banque Bruxelles Lambert SA v Eagle Star Insurance Co Ltd* [1995] QB 375 (CA) Bingham MR at 404–5 and 407–8; *Downs v Chappell* [1997] 1 WLR 426 (CA) Hobhouse LJ at 440.

Indeed in some cases the measure will have to balance both of the 'successful-transaction' and 'no transaction' bases using a loss of chance calculation, where whether a transaction would have gone ahead on different terms or not gone ahead at all is dependent upon a third party.[6]

Lord Hoffmann in *South Australia Asset Management v York Montague ('SAAMCo')* disapproved of the use of these terms on general grounds.[7] He correctly pointed out that in every case the claimant is entitled to point to an alternative transaction that it would have entered into. This is of course correct. The basic loss calculation compares the breach and non-breach positions. There is a range of non-breach positions in misadvice cases—the claimant would not have entered into any such transaction and just kept its money on deposit; the claimant would have entered into a completely different transaction with a completely different counterparty; the claimant would have entered into a similar transaction with the same counterparty but on different terms—and there is no difference of principle between them. Even a claimant who would have held its money on deposit but for the misadvice, and so claims damages to undo the transaction and give it deposit interest instead, has a claim as to a sort of alternative transaction. The terms 'no transaction' and 'successful-transaction' are therefore less used than previously.

That said, there remains a certain practical utility to the terms. Where the case is a successful-transaction case, the claimant will rarely reasonably extricate itself entirely from the transaction (which, in broad terms, it would have entered into anyway), and so it will not be necessary for the claimant to make the basic comparison between the price that was paid and the value of the property or business acquired at the relevant date of extrication. Instead, the inquiry is more usually into the specific differences between the transaction as was and that as it would have been: the amount by which the price would have been lower, or costs would not have needed to be incurred, etc. The non-breach position, and the alternative transaction represented by it, is therefore not very different from the breach position.

In a no transaction case, it will almost always be reasonable for the claimant to look to extricate itself from the transaction, and any decision not to do so will be treated as breaking the chain of causation, ie a sale will be deemed even if it does not take place. Accordingly, the value of the property or business acquired will come into play as something to credit against the price paid. Such cases come much closer to the tort model of restoring the claimant to the status quo ante.[8]

Nevertheless, as Lord Hoffmann pointed out, in no transaction cases too, the claimant often (although certainly not always) would not have stood still and would have done something else instead of the transaction complained of. Where that is the case, the alternative transaction must be brought into play (if either of the parties relies upon it). Yet even then, the alternative transaction will not merely be the actual transaction tweaked, but will usually be an identified general type of transaction that would have been entered into with a different counterparty.

---

[6] *Joyce v Bowman Law Ltd* [2010] EWHC 251 (Ch) (Vos J). This was discussed in detail in *Kelleher v O'Connor* [2010] IEHC 313 (Irish High Court) at paras 9.5–9.9, where the judge called such cases 'intermediate cases'.

[7] *South Australia Asset Management Corp v York Montague Ltd* [1997] 1 AC 191 (HL) at 218.

[8] As discussed above in section 3.1A.

To adapt the basic diagram above at chapter one, section 1.3B

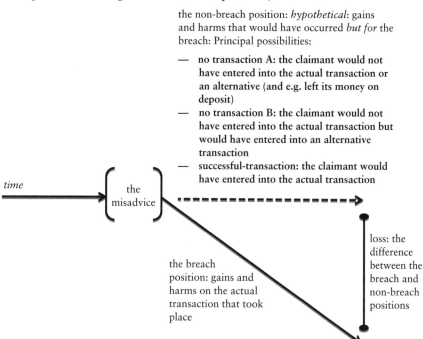

(ii) The Scope of Duty Qualification

In professional negligence cases, the recovery is frequently modified by the scope of duty principle. Although the defendant's negligence may have caused certain losses, and in particular in a no transaction case may have meant that but for the breach the claimant would not have entered into the relevant transaction (buying a house, lending money, etc) at all, nevertheless the defendant may not be liable for all the consequences of having entered into the transaction. The detail of when the defendant will have a limited duty—often when the defendant's role is characterised as one of providing information rather than advising or procuring—is discussed below in section 14.5B, where the principle is considered generally. That principle must be kept in mind when reading the present section. This is most especially true in lender claims against valuers, where the no transaction/successful-transaction factual causation question ultimately makes little difference: although it affects the basic measure of loss, which must still be worked out as a first step, that loss will usually be capped by the amount of the overvaluation, as was explained in the valuer case of *SAAMCo* itself. In summary 'one must compare the loss actually suffered with what the position would have been if it had not entered into the transaction, and [*and this is the scope of duty point:*] ask what element was attributable to the inaccuracy of the information'.[9]

---

[9] *Portman Building Society v Bevan Ashford* [2000] 1 EGLR 81 (CA) Otton LJ at 85.

(iii) The Breach Position: Causation, Mitigation, Extrication and Adoption

In advice cases, the most important principles when assessing the breach position (with which position the non-breach position will be compared to calculate recoverable loss)[10] are the principles of legal causation and mitigation. The way the loss calculation works will very much depend upon whether the claimant has or should have extricated itself from the transaction (eg sold the property it was induced to buy), and if so when. If the case is an extrication case (as most no transaction cases and few successful-transaction cases are[11]), the claimant's loss will often be calculated by reference to an actual or hypothetical sale of the acquired asset, often (although not always) shortly after the acquisition, with most of the claimant's losses thereby being avoided. If the case is one in which it was reasonable for the claimant not to extricate itself from the transaction until much later or indeed never to do so, the recoverable losses will include many continuing harms or foregone gains arising from being involved with the transaction over time, as well as, possibly, costs of cures by which the claimant reasonably attempts to make the best of the situation it has reasonably adopted or become stuck with.

C. Concurrent Contract and Tort Liability

Professional negligence disputes are the most common concurrent tort and contract disputes, because the process of engaging a professional usually involves both the making of an express or implied contract that the professional will take reasonable care, and the express or implied assumption of responsibility such as founds a tortious duty of care.[12]

That need not concern the readers of this book, who might otherwise be worried that they were getting only half of the picture by reading a contract damages book when answering a professional negligence question. The tortious principles add nothing to the contract damages principles. The measure of loss is in these circumstances the same, because the content of the duty of care is the same, and so the position the claimant would have been in if there had been no breach of duty (the damages test in both contract and tort) is the same. The causational principles (see chapter fifteen below) are the same, the scope of duty principle (see chapter fourteen, section 14.5B below) is the same, and in all likelihood the remoteness test is the same and follows the contract principles (as discussed at chapter fourteen, section 14.5C below). The main difference between the two causes of action for practical purposes is the differing principles of limitation of actions, a subject which falls outside the scope of this work.

---

[10] See above in chapter one, section 1.3 for an explanation of these terms.
[11] See above in section 3.1B(i).
[12] As established in *Henderson v Merrett Syndicates Ltd* [1995] 2 AC 145 (HL), also *South Australia Asset Management Corp v York Montague Ltd* [1997] 1 AC 191 (HL).

D. This Chapter

In the light of the foregoing explanation, this chapter is divided as follows:

— Section 3.2 deals with the specific issues arising in extrication cases. Most no transaction cases raise these issues.
— Section 3.3 deals with the issues arising in non-extrication/adoption cases. Many successful-transaction cases raise these issues.
— Section 3.4 then deals with issues arising out of the variety of non-breach positions and alternative transactions. These issues arise in both no transaction and successful-transaction cases, although the actual transaction will be more different to the alternative transaction in the former than the latter case.

3.2 Extrication Cases

A. The Measure of Loss

(i) The Price Less Value Measure, and Comparison with the Warranty Measure

In no transaction cases, the prima facie measure of damage (often inaccurately called the 'diminution in value') is the difference between the amount spent—including, in property purchase cases, the price, stamp duty and other costs paid (which the claimant would have kept but for the breach)—and the value of anything acquired in the transaction (for which the claimant must give credit). As Lord Nicholls has put it:[13]

> Frequently, but not always, the plaintiff would not have entered into the relevant transaction had the defendant fulfilled his duty of care and advised the plaintiff, for instance, of the true value of the property. When this is so, a professional negligence claim calls for a comparison between the plaintiff's position had he not entered into the transaction in question and his position under the transaction.

This is the same measure as in claims for the tort of negligent misrepresentation or deceit;[14] in such cases, too, the claimant's complaint is that but for the wrong the claimant would not have entered into the transaction—'They would have bought no property, spent no money and borrowed none from the bank'[15]—and it is that non-breach position the damages must seek to put the claimant in.

This is different to the breach of warranty measure. Thus if a defendant values the property or advises that a business has a certain profitability, where the complaint is that the defendant breached a duty of care the defendant is *not* obliged to put the claimant in the position as if what the defendant advised were true. Surveyors and other advisers do not usually *warrant* that the building or transaction is free from defect, worth a certain sum, profitable, etc. Rather the complaint

---

[13] *Nykredit Mortgage Bank plc v Edward Erdman Group Ltd (No 2)* [1997] WLR 1627 (HL) at 1631.
[14] Subject to differences in relation to causation and remoteness.
[15] *Hayes v James and Charles Dodd* [1990] 2 All ER 815 (CA) Staughton LJ at 818.

is that the defendant's negligent valuation or advice induced the claimant to enter the transaction and but for the negligence the claimant would not have bought the property or business, at least on the terms it did.[16]

In these cases, the warranty measure will often be similar to the advice/tort measure, because the value of the property/business as promised will often be the same as the price paid. The advice/tort measure will, however, be better for the claimant where the claimant made a bad bargain, and the warranty measure will be better where the claimant made a good bargain. To take a simple example given in *Ford v White & Co*:

> A sees a picture on sale at £100. He consults an art expert, who negligently advises him that the picture is an old master worth £50,000. A buys the picture, but cannot in fact find a purchaser willingly to pay more than £5 for it. Is his measure of damage £95, or £49,995? I should have thought obviously the former.[17]

This is correct. But for the breach the claimant would have had his £100 and not the £5 picture. He would never have had a £50,000 picture. However, if there had been a warranty that the picture was an old master, the loss would be the difference between the actual value and the warranted value. Similarly, if an agent purchases the wrong sort of opium for the principal, but the right sort is not available, it is liable for the consequences of the unwanted purchase but not liable to put the principal into the position as if the opium had been as requested (given that such opium was not available, so would not but for the breach have been purchased).[18]

As will be seen, focusing on the true measure also emphasises that (unlike in a warranty case) the claimant can recover the costs of entering the transaction, and that the value of the property for which credit must be given is the value that can be released on a sale to the market, whenever that could be expected to take place.

Early surveyor cases incorrectly suggested that the warranty measure applied,[19] but the Court of Appeal confirmed the correct measure in *Ford v White & Co* (quoted above), where negligent advice by a solicitor induced the claimant to buy a property it would not otherwise have bought, but the property was in fact worth the price paid.[20] Accordingly, the claimant was entitled to nominal damages only. Likewise this correct measure was set out in the surveyor case of *Perry v Sidney Phillips & Son*[21] as being the 'the difference between the price paid by the plaintiff and the value at the date of its acquisition',[22] and the Court of Appeal reconfirmed this in subsequent surveyor and other decisions.[23]

---

[16] See especially *Smith and Smith v Peter North* (2001) 82 Con LR 126 (CA) Parker LJ at para 52; *South Parklands Hockey and Tennis Centre Inc v Brown Falconer Group Pty Ltd* [2004] SASC 81 (SC of South Australia); *Kelleher v O'Connor* [2010] IEHC 313 (Irish High Court) at paras 9.1–9.2.

[17] *Ford v White & Co* [1964] 1 WLR 885 (Pennycuick J).

[18] *Cassaboglou v Gibb* (1883) 11 QBD 797.

[19] *Philips v Ward* [1956] 1 WLR 471 (CA) and subsequent cases.

[20] *Ford v White & Co* [1964] 1 WLR 885 (Pennycuick J).

[21] *Perry v Sidney Phillips & Son* [1982] 1 WLR 1297 (CA).

[22] Ibid, Oliver LJ at 1303. However, see below as to a qualification as to the date of the valuation.

[23] See further *Watts v Morrow* [1991] 1 WLR 1421 (CA) at 1430; *Hayes v James and Charles Dodd* [1990] 2 All ER 815 (CA); *Patel v Hooper & Jackson* [1999] 1 WLR 1792 (CA); *Gardner v Marsh & Parsons* [1997] 1 WLR 489 (CA); *Smith and Smith v Peter North* (2001) 82 Con LR 126 (CA) Parker LJ at para 52.

The same applies to lender claims. In *Swingcastle Ltd v Alastair Gibson*[24] a lender that would not have lent but for the defendant surveyor's valuation of the security property was entitled to recover the amount loaned, plus interest for loss of use of the loaned money, plus the solicitor's and valuer's costs of the transaction, but less the sums paid by the borrower on the loan plus any sum recovered on sale of the security property.[25]

(ii) The First Thing Wrong with the 'Price Less Value' Measure: It Omits the Alternative Transaction

The 'price less value obtained' formulation tells only half of the damages story; the half that turns on the fact that but for the defendant's breach the claimant would not have entered into the transaction it entered into. The other half of the story is revealed when the full non-breach position is explored: what would the claimant have done instead? In what used to be called 'successful-transaction' cases,[26] the answer is that the claimant would have entered into a similar transaction with the same third party. In such cases it is quite wrong to award the basic measure of 'the difference between the price paid by the plaintiff and the value at the date of its acquisition'[27] because the claimant would but for the breach have acquired the property anyway. Instead, the measure is the difference between the price paid by the claimant and the price that would have been paid, and between the value of the property acquired and that which would have been acquired.

Even in 'no transaction' cases, where the claimant would not have entered into the transaction with the third party, either party may wish to prove what the claimant would have done instead, rather than assume that the claimant would have just held the money it would not have spent on the unwanted transaction and earned interest on it.

Particular issues in relation to alternative transactions are discussed below in section 3.4.

---

[24] *Swingcastle Ltd v Alastair Gibson* [1991] 2 AC 223 (HL). See also *Nykredit Mortgage Bank plc v Edward Erdman Group Ltd (No 2)* [1997] WLR 1627 (HL) Lord Nicholls at 1631 as to the basic measure in such cases, and *Omega Trust Co v Wright Son & Pepper (No 2)* [1998] PNLR 337 (Douglas Brown J).

[25] As explained in section 3.1B(ii), such lender claims must always be read subject to the scope of duty rules. Furthermore, the case law indicates that the lender actually first suffers loss (for the purposes of the calculation of interest) when the amount of the loan plus interest for loss of use of that money (as opposed to the interest promised under the contract of loan) exceeds the 'value of the rights acquired, namely the borrower's covenant and the true value of the over-valued property [in which the lender has a mortgage]': *Nykredit Mortgage Bank plc v Edward Erdman Group Ltd (No 2)* [1997] WLR 1627 (HL) at 1631. As is explained in that case, the lender does not necessarily suffer loss at the date of the loan (as the market value of the covenant and security rights may exceed the loan), nor is the loss only suffered on the date of realisation of the security, but is a fluctuating loss that may arise in between the two. See further chapter sixteen, section 16.6A(i).

[26] See above in section 3.1B(i).

[27] *Perry v Sidney Phillips & Son* [1982] 1 WLR 1297 (CA) Lord Oliver at 1303.

(iii) The Second Thing Wrong with the 'Price Less Value' Measure: It Assumes an Assessment at the Date of Acquisition

The second modification that needs to be made to 'the difference between the price paid by the plaintiff and the value at the date of its acquisition'[28] formulation is that whether the claimant must give credit for the value 'at the date of its acquisition' depends upon the principle of mitigation. In other words, when the claimant must give credit for the value of the property depends upon when the claimant could reasonably have expected to sell or when it adopts the property, if at all.

The case law has confirmed that the date on which credit must be given for the property value depends upon the date on which the claimant should have sold it. Thus if the defendant induces the claimant to purchase property with a latent defect which at the date of acquisition is (even allowing for the defect) worth the price paid, but which by the time the defect is discovered is worth much less, the claimant is not barred from recovery by the unrealistic argument that it has suffered no loss because it paid no more than the property was worth. Instead, and subject to scope of duty arguments and other refinements to the causation principle, the claimant's loss is quantified at the date when the claimant should have sold the property. Any prior market movement therefore will affect the loss, although any subsequent market movement should or could have been avoided by prompt sale and is therefore caused by the claimant's unreasonableness or market speculation and not the defendant's breach.[29]

Thus it was abundantly clear in the Court of Appeal in *Patel v Hooper & Jackson*,[30] where, for reasons including the defect being hidden, the date on which the claimant should have sold property, and therefore the date on which the value of the property is taken into account as a deduction from the loss, was September 1993, four years after acquisition, with costs of alternative accommodation and inconvenience in the meantime being compensable. In fact the claimant had not sold the property prior to the trial in 1996, but by the rules of mitigation the claimant was nevertheless deemed to have sold it in September 1993.[31]

A similar approach to the date of valuation of the property was applied in the Court of Appeal decision in *Hayes v James and Charles Dodd*, where the claimant recovered the costs of financing the purchase up to the date of the sale but also had to give credit for the rise in the property value to that date (ie for the amount realised by the sale).[32] Thus in another case Bingham LJ explained that the 'diminution in value date of breach rule should not be "mechanistically applied in circumstances in circumstances where it may be appropriate"'.[33] And Lord Hoffmann in *SAAMCo*

---

[28] Ibid.

[29] As to retention of property beyond a particular date being speculation and not for the defendant's account, see further chapter sixteen, section 16.5 below.

[30] *Patel v Hooper & Jackson* [1999] 1 WLR 1792 (CA).

[31] But see chapter seventeen n 101 as to the date on which the diminution in value was taken.

[32] *Hayes v James and Charles Dodd* [1990] 2 All ER 815 (CA), esp at 822. Likewise the cost of life insurance was recoverable but had a claim been made the claimant would probably have had to give credit for the insurance payout: Staughton LJ at 822.

[33] *County Personnel (Employment Agency) Ltd v Pulver & Co* [1987] 1 WLR 916 (CA) at 925.

confirmed the principle that a post-acquisition date for selling property is taken where 'the claimant had reacted reasonably to his predicament'.[34]

The senselessness of an unthinking application of the diminution in value rule is shown by cases in which the claimant acquired a lease not a freehold. In such cases, especially commercial lease cases, it may make no sense to talk of the diminution in the value of the property acquired. Indeed, the lease may in fact be not only worthless but onerous, and the true loss is found in the costs of extrication from the transaction, which may take some time, and are not measured at the date of acquisition.[35]

Moreover, there are the cases where it was reasonable for the claimant to adopt the transaction (discussed in section 3.3 below). In the House of Lords' decision in *Farley v Skinner*,[36] because it was not reasonable to expect the claimant to sell the property at all, and therefore it was reasonable for the claimant to adopt the unwanted transaction, the Lords ruled that although the claimant must give credit for the value of the property received, it may also recover for post-acquisition losses including inconvenience and sometimes the cost of curing defects. Thus in that case Lord Hutton expressly rejected the argument that the above quotation of Bingham LJ in *County Personnel* restricted the damages to assessment based on a sale at a date when the claimant could have sold the property (one year after acquisition), because:

> I consider that in the circumstances of this case where the plaintiff had expended a considerable sum of money in improving the house before he was aware of the defendant's failure to inform him of aircraft noise, and where he would have had to incur very considerable expense in selling and buying a new house and moving to it, it was reasonable for him to decide to stay in the house, even though that involved putting up with the noise, and I think that the trial judge was right to reject the defendant's argument on this point.[37]

In that case Lord Hutton expressly confirmed that damages were not restricted to an assessment at an earlier date as suggested by Bingham LJ's comments in *Watts v Morrow*, namely that

> If, on learning of the defects which should have been but were not reported, a purchaser decides, for whatever reason, to retain the house and not move out and sell, I would question whether any loss he thereafter suffers, at least in the ordinary case, can be laid at the door of the contract-breaker.[38]

The true position is that it depends whether the 'reason' for retaining the house is an independent one by which the claimant should be taken to have broken the chain of causation.[39]

---

[34] *South Australia Asset Management Corp v York Montague Ltd* [1997] 1 AC 191 (HL) at 219 and 222.

[35] *County Personnel (Employment Agency) Ltd v Pulver & Co* [1987] 1 WLR 916 (CA), esp at 926: 'On the facts of the present case the diminution in value rule would involve a somewhat speculative and unreal valuation exercise intended to reflect the substantial negative value of this underlease. It would also seem likely to lead to a total claim well above the figure the plaintiff claims'. Also *Zeneca Ltd v King Sturges & Co*, 19 September 1996 (Jackson QC).

[36] *Farley v Skinner* [2002] 2 AC 732 (HL).

[37] Ibid at 762.

[38] *Watts v Morrow* [1991] 1 WLR 1421 (CA) at 1445. Similarly Ralph Gibson LJ at 1436.

[39] See further below in chapter sixteen, section 16.5, and chapter seventeen.

One key case is worth dealing with at this point, as an illustration of the approach, properly understood. In the tort of misrepresentation case of *Hussey v Eels*,[40] a residential land purchaser who could not afford to cure subsidence the vendor had hidden, managed to secure planning permission to rebuild (after three attempts and two and a half years), and then sold the land to developers at about twice the purchase price. On a proper analysis, there were only two reasonable courses available to the claimant upon acquisition. The first was to sell immediately upon learning of the subsidence, which was very shortly after purchase. The second was to adopt the transaction and repair the property at a cost of £17,000. The planning permission solution occurred around two years later and was not something the claimants could have been expected to do, ie was beyond the call of the duty of mitigation. The proper analysis is that as the claimants could not afford to pay for the repairs at the date of discovery of the subsidence, they must be deemed to have sold the property (the only reasonable course open to them) and any subsequent conduct is speculation by them.[41] Had the property then dropped in value, the defendant would not have to compensate the increased loss, and so the consequences of retaining and later developing are also irrelevant to the claim. In any event (and this is the way the court analysed the claim) the Court of Appeal was of the view that retention of the land and obtaining of planning permission were 'not part of a continuous transaction of which the purchase of land and bungalow was the inception' and therefore not 'caused' by the breach.[42]

Perhaps it is more accurate to say that, as Staughton LJ put it, the claimant purchaser can recover: 'all the money which they spent, less anything which they subsequently recovered, provided always that they acted reasonably [*and did not speculate at their own risk*] in mitigating their loss'.[43] Or as Gibson LJ put it, the claimant is entitled to 'all the losses incurred as a result of entering into the transaction where he would not have entered into the transaction if properly advised and the losses are caused by entry into the transaction and by extrication from it'.[44]

(iv) Successful-Transaction Cases and Extrication

There may also be cases where although but for the breach the claimant would have entered into the transaction on other terms, still a reasonable (or the only reasonable) response of a claimant to the transaction is to extricate itself, in which case the costs of extrication and the losses on the transaction will be recoverable as they would in a 'no transaction' case, but with the alternative situation the claimant

---

[40] *Hussey v Eels* [1990] 2 QB 227 (CA).

[41] Mustill LJ (ibid at 233) confirmed that the claimants were not unreasonable and acted legitimately in staying in the property but that fails to grapple with the point. It may not be unreasonable, but it is an act of speculation the results of which should not be for the defendant's account. See further below in chapter sixteen, section 16.5.

[42] Mustill LJ (ibid) at 233 and 240–41.

[43] *Hayes v James and Charles Dodd* [1990] 2 All ER 815 (CA) at 820. For the discussion of the causative significance of speculation, see below in chapter sixteen, section 16.5.

[44] *Watts v Morrow* [1991] 1 WLR 1421 (CA) at 1438.

would have been in (the non-breach position) being the same transaction but on the better terms that would have been achieved but for the defendant's negligence.[45]

B. The Date of Extrication

As explained above, the date of extrication is crucial in these cases. The claimant must give credit for the value of the property or business received in the transaction. This value is assessed on the date of extrication. It is on that date that the measure is taken of the sum received on extrication (typically sale of the property), or, more often, that would have been received if the claimant had extricated itself at the appropriate moment. It is up to but not beyond that date that continuing losses, including costs and non-pecuniary losses, are recoverable, because the actual or deemed extrication will stop them arising.[46] The date on which the extrication must be taken to occur is the date on which the claimant reasonably did or reasonably could have been expected to sell, and this will post-date the date of acquisition if the claimant did not know of the defect, if the claimant was locked into the transaction, or if for any other reason it was reasonable to delay. This is discussed in more detail below in chapter seventeen, in relation to the general damages question of the date of assessment.

C. Heads of Recovery in Extrication Cases, Ignoring the Alternative Transaction

As set out below in section 3.4C, sometimes the alternative transaction the claimant would have entered into means that some of the expenses incurred under the breach position would also have been incurred under the non-breach position. In such cases the expense cannot be recovered as it was not caused by the breach since it would have been incurred anyway, even without the breach. For example a claimant who would have bought the property anyway cannot recover the price as a loss, only any part of the price that would not have been incurred (if but for the breach the price would have been lower).

The losses in this section are discussed without regard for the alternative transaction, working from the basic assumption that neither party raises the alternative transaction and therefore, as occurs in many cases, damages are awarded to put the claimant in the position it would have been in if it had not entered into the transaction and had merely left any money earning interest for the period of the

---

[45] *Funnell v Adams and Remer* [2007] EWHC 2166 (QB) (Wilkie J) seems to be such a case, although it is not completely clear whether but for the breach the claimant would have entered the lease on better terms rather than not entering that lease at all. And see *Murray v Lloyd* [1989] 1 WLR 1960 (Mummery J), where the claimant did not have to extricate itself from the lease acquired, but did have to purchase a replacement to follow it, and the costs of doing so were recovered.

[46] The cut off at the date when the claimant should have sold is shown by *Naughton v O'Callaghan* [1990] 3 All ER 191 (Waller J) at 198 (but see the discussion of that case above at text to n 172 and surrounding); *Patel v Hooper & Jackson* [1999] 1 WLR 1792 (CA); *Kelleher v O'Connor* [2010] IEHC 313 (Irish High Court).

transaction. To put it another way, the alternative transaction of merely putting money on deposit is assumed where no other is raised.

The following are the types of harm the claimant can claim in the extrication cases, allowing for credit to be given for the value of the property (as discussed above) and any gains made while holding it.

(i) The Price and Transaction Costs

As set out above,[47] one of the primary elements of the recovery is the price paid in the transaction that would not have been paid but for the breach: the price of the property or stake in the investment, advance under the loan (in lender claims), or premium for the insurance (where the claimant took out insurance), etc.

In addition to the price, the claimant will also be able to recover the transaction costs, including legal costs,[48] the costs of financing a purchase,[49] stamp duty,[50] and any premium on life insurance that was required as a condition of the transaction.[51] (As to whether the defendant can evade such costs by showing that they would have been incurred anyway, see below.[52])

(ii) Financial Losses under the Transaction before Extrication

The claimant will be able to recover on-going financial losses suffered whilst tied into the transaction, before the date (if any) on which the claimant should have extricated itself, including the costs of alternative accommodation prior to the sale where the property was uninhabitable,[53] providing they were reasonably incurred and would not have been incurred in any case;[54] the cost of improvements made to try to make the business profitable;[55] the cost of expenditure incurred to try to make a development viable despite undisclosed archaeological restrictions;[56] the cost of mortgage payments on the property;[57] overdrafts and other business liabilities;[58]

---

[47] See sections 3.1B(i) and 3.2A(i).

[48] *Manorgate Ltd v First Scottish Property Services Ltd* [2013] CSOH 108 (Court of Session, Outer House) at paras 76–79.

[49] *Waddell v Blockey* (1879) 4 QBD 678 (CA) Bramwell LJ at 681 (deceit); *East v Maurer* [1991] 1 WLR 461 (CA) (deceit); *Hayes v James and Charles Dodd* [1990] 2 All ER 815 (CA); *4 Eng Ltd v Harper* [2009] Ch 91 (Richards J) at para 110 (deceit); *Butler-Creagh v Hersham* [2011] EWHC 2525 (QB) (Eady J) at para 125 (deceit). While the costs of selling the property were allowed in *Hardy v Wamsley-Lewis* (1967) 203 EG 1039 (Paull J) but the costs of purchasing it in the first place were, erroneously, disallowed.

[50] This was not disputed in *Patel v Hooper & Jackson* [1999] 1 WLR 1792 (CA). See also *Butler-Creagh v Hersham* [2011] EWHC 2525 (QB) (Eady J) at para 125 (deceit).

[51] *Hayes v James and Charles Dodd* [1990] 2 All ER 815 (CA) Staughton LJ at 822.

[52] See section 3.4C.

[53] *Patel v Hooper & Jackson* [1999] 1 WLR 1792 (CA).

[54] See below in section 3.4C.

[55] *East v Maurer* [1991] 1 WLR 461 (CA) (deceit).

[56] *Manorgate Ltd v First Scottish Property Services Ltd* [2013] CSOH 108 (Court of Session, Outer House) at paras 80–81.

[57] *Scullion v Colleys* [2010] EWHC 2253 (Ch) (Snowden QC): negligent surveyor liable for shortfall between rental income and mortgage payments on overvalued buy-to-let flat.

[58] *Esso Petroleum Co Ltd v Mardon* [1976] 1 QB 801 (CA).

general trading losses;[59] bad debts or liability on a guarantee;[60] 'the costs of investigating the defendant's fraud'[61] or the costs of working out what replacement computer system to acquire.[62]

Thus in the surveyor negligence case of *Hayes v James and Charles Dodd*,[63] the claimant recovered the entire costs of running the business for five years before it was possible to sell it, including rent, interest paid to the bank, rates, insurance, plant, and redundancy payments. In the solicitor negligence case of *Scott v Vertex Law*,[64] the claimant recovered around £245,000 of investment in purchasing the business and around £140,000 of capital invested in the business after purchase but prior to selling it five years later, less the proceeds of sale. This award apparently included the costs of seeking (unsuccessfully) to resolve the planning issue, which was the defect of which the defendant failed to warn. And in *Havenledge Ltd v Graeme John & Partners*,[65] the claimants were permitted to claim for the £500,000 spent on developing a nursing home on the acquired property before discovering it was on top of a mine, as well as the profits that would have been made on an alternative transaction.[66] The property was, despite the mine, not worth any less at the date of acquisition than the price paid for it, but the latency of the defect meant that the claimant had suffered a recoverable loss in terms of its expenditure, although it entirely recouped the price paid (which would otherwise be a loss) by virtue of the value of the land acquired.

Sometimes there will be no extrication to speak of. In *Aneco*,[67] the claimant reinsurer recovered the full US$35m of loss it had suffered by entering into the treaty reinsurance arrangements that the defendant broker induced. The reinsurer could not extricate itself, and had simply to pay the claims under the reinsurance when they arose.

(iii) Liability to Third Parties Arising under the Transaction before Extrication

Similarly, a claimant can recover damages indemnifying it for liability it has incurred to a third party as a result of the defendant's negligence, and the costs of such a dispute with the third party.[68] This is common in construction and other professional negligence disputes. See further chapter twenty.

---

[59] *East v Maurer* [1991] 1 WLR 461 (CA) (deceit).

[60] *Woods v Martins Bank Ltd* [1959] 1 QB 255 (Salmon J).

[61] *4 Eng Ltd v Harper* [2009] Ch 91 (Richards J) at para 110 (deceit).

[62] *Stephenson Blake (Holdings) Ltd v Streets Heaver Ltd* [2001] Lloyd's Rep PN 44 (Hicks QC) at para 167.

[63] *Hayes v James and Charles Dodd* [1990] 2 All ER 815 (CA).

[64] *Scott & Scott v Kennedys Law LLP and Vertex Law LLP* [2011] EWHC 3808 (Ch) (Vos J).

[65] *Havenledge Ltd v Graeme John & Partners* (CA) 18 December 2000.

[66] And see *Dent v Davis Blank Furniss* [2001] Lloyd's Rep PN 534 (Blackburne J).

[67] *Aneco Reinsurance Underwriting Ltd v Johnson & Higgins Ltd* [2002] 1 Lloyd's Rep 156 (HL).

[68] Alternatively, although usually less usefully, if the defendant is also liable to the third party directly (usually in tort), the claimant may be able to sue the defendant for a contribution under the Civil Liability (Contribution) Act 1978.

In the solicitor's negligence case of *Allied Maples v Simmons and Simmons*,[69] the claimant was entitled to damages measuring the lost chance that but for negligent drafting constituting the breach, the contract with the third party would have included a warranty that reduced the claimant's liabilities to third parties.

(iv) Non-Pecuniary Loss

A claimant can recover damages for the physical inconvenience suffered which would not have been suffered but for the breach, including under any alternative transaction.[70]

(v) The Cost of Extrication from an Unwanted Transaction[71]

The claimant will be able to recover the costs of reasonably extricating itself from the transaction, most typically by selling any property acquired in the transaction.[72] Obiter comments suggest that these costs are only recoverable if incurred, eg if the claimant does decide to sell the property,[73] but the Court of Appeal has confirmed the correct position that they are recoverable anyway if the claimant should reasonably have extricated itself, as the claimant is deemed to have made the sale in mitigation of its loss whether or not it in fact did so.[74]

The costs of extrication other than sale will also be recoverable where applicable.[75]

---

[69] *Allied Maples v Simmons and Simmons* [1995] 1 WLR 1602 (CA).

[70] *Ezekiel v McDade* (1994) 37 Con LR 140 (CA).

[71] The phrase 'costs of extrication' is used by the judiciary, see eg *County Personnel (Employment Agency) Ltd v Pulver & Co* [1987] 1 WLR 916 (CA) at 926; *Patel v Hooper & Jackson*, 8 August 1996 (Reese QC); *Greymalkin Ltd v Copleys* [2004] EWHC 1155 (Ch) (Collins J) throughout but discussed at para 81; *Fulham Leisure Holdings Ltd v Nicholson Graham & Jones* [2006] EWHC 2017 (Ch) (Mann J) at para 260; *Funnell v Adams and Remer* [2007] EWHC 2166 (QB) (Wilkie J) at paras 16 and 20.

[72] *Waddell v Blockey* (1879) 4 QBD 678 (CA) Bramwell LJ at 681 (deceit, claimant can recover the commission on resale); *Hardy v Wamsley-Lewis* (1967) 203 EG 1039 (Paull J); *East v Maurer* [1991] 1 WLR 461 (CA) (deceit); *Davis v Churchward Brook Haye & Co* (CA) 6 May 1993 (deceit); *Patel v Hooper & Jackson* [1999] 1 WLR 1792 (CA): negligent surveyor liable for costs of extrication from purchase of uninhabitable house (including costs of alternative accommodation in the meantime).

[73] *Ford v White & Co* [1964] 1 WLR 885 (Pennycuick J) at 888; *Philips v Ward* [1956] 1 WLR 471 (CA) Romer LJ at 478; and especially *Watts v Morrow* [1991] 1 WLR 1421 (CA) Gibson LJ at 1436 point 4 and Bingham LJ at 1445.

[74] *Patel v Hooper & Jackson* [1999] 1 WLR 1792 (CA) Nourse LJ at 1001; also *Kelleher v O'Connor* [2010] IEHC 313 (Irish High Court). See further below in relation to mitigation and deeming in chapter fifteen, sections 15.2B(ii) and 15.3B(iv)(a).

[75] *County Personnel (Employment Agency) Ltd v Pulver & Co* [1987] 1 WLR 916 (CA): negligent solicitor liable for costs of extrication from an onerous and problematic under-lease; *Hayes v James and Charles Dodd* [1990] 2 All ER 815 (CA): negligent solicitor liable for costs of extrication from business; considered obiter by Bingham MR in *Reeves v Thrings & Long* (CA) 19 November 1993; dictum of Lord Scott in *Farley v Skinner* [2002] 2 AC 732 (HL) at para 108. Not awarded in *Oates v Anthony Pitman & Co* (CA) 7 May 1998 (solicitor inducing purchase of holiday let property) because not properly formulated and proved.

(vi) The Cost of Curing Defects to Make Property Saleable

In *Gregory v Shepherds*,[76] because of the defendant solicitor's negligence the claimant bought a property subject to a charge where but for the breach it would have been free of the charge. The charge prevented the claimant from selling the property until its belated removal after nine years. The claimant recovered the £1,219 costs of procuring its removal, as well as damages for the eight and a half years of loss of use of the £50,000 that would have been received in 1991 from a resale if there had been no charge but which was instead received on resale in 2000. Similarly the finance costs during the period of delay while the problem is being sorted out may be recoverable.[77]

Likewise, the costs of emergency works to property or repairs to make the property saleable and enable extrication will be recoverable,[78] as will the costs of investigating defects prior to a sale.[79]

(vii) The Cost of Repairs and Inconvenience During the Repairs

Otherwise, in extrication cases the costs of repairing the property to put it into the condition it was believed (as a result of the defendant's negligence) to be in are not recoverable, nor therefore are damages for the costs of alternative accommodation and inconvenience during those works.[80] (Cases where the claimant reasonably adopted the transaction, in which case the repairs were caused by the breach or were an act of mitigation, are different. See below in section 3.3A.)

The first reason is that in extrication cases the claimant will usually reasonably be expected to sell the property upon discovering the relevant defect, and any later repair costs will therefore be deemed avoided and be unreasonable.[81]

A further reason arises in many successful-transaction cases, namely that frequently the complaint is not that the defendant caused the defect, but that the defendant failed to warn the claimant of it. Accordingly, the claimant cannot recover the cost of repairs or the inconvenience or costs of accommodation suffered during such repairs, since they would have been suffered anyway, the complaint being that

---

[76] *Gregory v Shepherds* (CA) 16 June 2000. In relation to losses caused by such delay see also *G + K Ladenbau (UK) Ltd v Crawley & de Reya* [1978] 1 WLR 266 (Mocatta J); and *McElroy Milne v Commercial Electronics Ltd* [1993] 1 NZLR 39 (NZCA), cited with approval by Lord Hoffmann in *South Australia Asset Management Corp v York Montague Ltd* [1997] 1 AC 191 (HL) at 219 and 222; and *John Grimes Partnership Ltd v Gubbins* [2013] EWCA Civ 37.

[77] *Kirkton Investments Ltd v VMH LLP* [2011] CSOH 200 (Court of Session, Outer House).

[78] *Treml v Ernest W Gibson & Partners* [1984] EGLR 162 (Popplewell J); *Broadoak Properties Ltd v Young & White* [1989] EGLR 263 (Fox-Andrews QC).

[79] *Morgan v Perry* (1974) 229 EG 1737 (Jones); *Broadoak Properties Ltd v Young & White* [1989] EGLR 263 (Fox-Andrews QC).

[80] *Cross v Martin & Mortimer* [1989] 1 EGLR 154 (Phillips J), decided before the case law had clearly established the correct measure in these cases, and without a decision that the claimant reasonably held on to the property or had adopted it, is to be doubted in relation to the award of the costs of alternative accommodation and inconvenience during the repair works.

[81] *Holder v Countrywide Surveyors Ltd*, 11 March 2002 (Harvey QC), where the diminution in value at the date of acquisition (the date of discovery was approved by the judge but there was no evidence as to values) was higher than the repair costs at that date, but lower than the costs at the later date of trial, and the claimant was confined to the diminution in value at the earlier date.

claimant would have paid less for the property but not that the property would not have been defective.[82] Nevertheless, and contrary to principle, there is authority in favour of an award of damages for physical inconvenience caused by repairs and for the costs of accommodation, the judges in those cases recognising the illogicality of the position.[83]

Further, the cost of repairs plus attendant costs and losses is a useful indicator of the amount by which the claimant's purchase price would have been lower, because a purchaser will often be able to negotiate a reduction in price that matches the cost to which the purchaser will be put in fixing a known defect.[84] This may not be an accurate indicator: some purchasers will need an extra deduction to entice them to bother or because it will be more difficult to obtain finance to purchase a defective property,[85] or conversely there may be no need to deduct the entire cost of cure because the cure may improve the value of the property when carried out.[86]

3.3 Adoption/Non-Extriction Cases

In a few no transaction cases and many successful-transaction cases it is reasonable for the claimant to adopt the transaction and not extricate itself at all. Although the claimant would not have entered into the transaction but for the misadvice, nevertheless the transaction may be something that can be made to satisfy the claimant at less cost than extrication would require, particularly if the case is a successful-transaction case and the transaction is broadly as the claimant wanted, or the claimant has expended considerable post-acquisition costs before discovering the defect.

---

[82] *Bigg v Howard Son & Gooch* [1990] 1 EGLR 173 (Hicks QC). Damages for inconvenience but not the cost of repairs would be recoverable if, for example, the defendant's breach caused the claimant to move into the property before doing the works where otherwise it would have done the works before moving in. Similarly they would be recoverable, if not too remote, if the distress/inconvenience was caused simply by not knowing in advance of the defects: *Perry v Sidney Phillips* [1982] 1 WLR 1297 (CA) Denning MR at 1302. (Oliver and Kerr LJJ justified them on a broader basis, but that is because they, apparently correctly, viewed the case as a 'no transaction' case. Accordingly Hicks QC in *Bigg v Howard Son & Gooch* [1990] 1 EGLR 173 at 175 was probably wrong to find that he was bound by *Perry* to find that compensation for inconvenience during repair is recoverable.) Likewise part of the costs of repairs would be recoverable if the defendant's breach delayed the repairs and therefore led to them costing more.

[83] *Hooberman v Salter Rex* [1985] EGLR 144 (Smout QC); *Bigg v Howard Son & Gooch* [1990] 1 EGLR 173 (Hicks QC) at 175; *Holder v Countrywide Surveyors Ltd*, 11 March 2002 (Harvey QC) at paras 71 and 88.

[84] *Cross v Martin & Mortimer* [1989] 1 EGLR 154 (Phillips J); *Steward v Rapley* [1989] 1 EGLR 159 (CA); *Bigg v Howard Son & Gooch* [1990] 1 EGLR 173 (Hicks QC); *Watts v Morrow* [1991] 1 WLR 1421 (CA) Gibson LJ at 1435; *Oswald v Countrywide Surveyors Ltd* [1996] 2 EGLR 104 (CA); *Hoadley v Edwards* [2001] PNLR 964 (Evans-Lombe J); *Holder v Countrywide Surveyors Ltd*, 11 March 2002 (Harvey QC) at paras 24, 35–36 and 47. And as to landlord and tenant cases in relation to the cost of repairs as an indicator of the diminution in value of the reversion, see the cases at chapter four nn 308 to 310 and accompanying text.

[85] *Holder v Countrywide Surveyors Ltd*, 11 March 2002 (Harvey QC) at para 72. But as to whether inconvenience is ever taken into account by a valuer, see *Perry v Sidney Phillips* [1982] 1 WLR 1297 (CA) Oliver LJ at 1305–6.

[86] *Oswald v Countrywide Surveyors Ltd* [1996] 2 EGLR 104 (CA) Kennedy LJ at 105. And see *Hood v Shaw* (1960) 200 EG 777 (Paull J): 'probably a bit more, on the ground that people do not like having to spend money on doing a major operation to a house and not knowing what they may find when they do that major operation'.

Thus, as Lord Hutton observed in *Farley v Skinner* 'it was reasonable for him to decide to stay in the house, even though that involved putting up with the noise'.[87] Other adoption cases are discussed below in section 17.3B(vii).

In such cases it is wrong to assess the difference in value at the date of acquisition, as the property was not and could not have been expected to be sold then or at all, and instead the claimant can recover the costs of repairs and other on-going financial and non-pecuniary losses that would not have been incurred, and must give credit for the value of the property after such repairs or at trial.

It is failure properly to recognise this category of cases where adoption of the transaction was necessary or reasonable, and to distinguish it from the usual category where extrication at a particular date could be expected, that has led to confusion in some of the cases, in particular as to whether the cost of curing a defect should be recovered.

A. Costs of Cure Generally

Where but for the breach the claimant would still have entered into the transaction, just on different terms (ie successful-transaction cases), it will often be more reasonable to pay for a cure of the defect (the difference between the transaction as is and as it would have been) than for the claimant to extricate itself from the transaction altogether, and in such cases the cost of that cure will be recoverable as a reasonable cost caused by the breach.

The same may be true in no transaction cases, although less frequently. In the ordinary no transaction case the damages calculation will be premised on the claimant extricating itself from the transaction. In such extrication cases, unless the cost of cure is needed to make extrication possible (ie to get a good price for the property), such a cost is not reasonably incurred and so is irrecoverable.[88]

The present section deals with the non-extrication/adoption cases, where the claimant does not sell up and is not expected (by the principle of mitigation) to do so. In such cases, providing the cost of cure is reasonable, it will be recoverable, given that it was caused by the defendant (in that, but for the breach, the claimant would not have incurred it). As with other service or goods cases, the question is often whether the cost of cure is proportionate to the loss that will remain if the cure is not effected.

B. Defects in Title and Similar in Adoption Cases

Frequently the defendant's professional's negligence in carrying out an acquisition means that the claimant acquires what it wants (ie the case is a successful-transaction case) but with a defect in title or other legal or similar problem.

---

[87] *Farley v Skinner* [2002] 2 AC 732 (HL) at 762, discussed and quoted more fully above at text to n 37.

[88] See above in section 3.2C(vi) and (vii).

There may be a relatively simple defect in title that can be cured by incurring an expense, which is then recoverable.[89] The same may be true even where the defect is more serious. In *Dent v Davis Blank Furniss*,[90] discussed below,[91] the claimants reasonably remained in their property and procured its removal from the commons register (that registration being the matter the defendant should have warned the claimants of). Similarly in *Herrmann v Withers LLP*,[92] the lack of access to a communal garden (as to which the defendant solicitors misadvised) meant that the claimant overpaid by around £350,000, but most of that difference in value could have been eliminated by negotiating an 80-year assignable licence at a cost of £25,000 plus negotiating costs. The claimant recovered those smaller costs that it should have incurred, plus the £65,000 residual difference between the price paid and the value of the property had those steps been taken, and £2,000 for loss of amenity. In this decision the roles were reversed as it was the defendant who successfully contended that the claimant should have incurred these costs. Accordingly there was no contention that the claimant should have sold the property rather than negotiating the licence, and it was therefore agreed that in the circumstances of a £6.8m purchase it was reasonable for the claimant to adopt the property and deal with the defect (the stamp duty on a replacement property would alone have exceeded the costs of the cure, ignoring the difference in value award of around £350,000 which the claimant would also have been entitled to).

And in *Murray v Lloyd*, the claimant acquired a 15-year tenancy but, due to the solicitor's negligence (in advising her to have it granted into a corporate name without obtaining the landlord's consent to assign into her personal name), without a right to a succeeding statutory tenancy.[93] There was no need for extrication here—the claimant would have entered into the tenancy even but for the breach, and for the first 15 years there was no difference between it and what the claimant would have had. Instead, the award was measured by the cost (£110,000) of purchasing an alternative lease to replace the statutory tenancy that the claimant would have had but for the breach.

In *Fulham Leisure Holdings Ltd v Nicholson Graham & Jones*, in principle the purchaser of the holding company of Fulham Football Club might recover the costs of getting to the position it would have been in if its solicitors had taken reasonable care to ensure that the minority shareholders could be diluted or squeezed out of the company, although the £7.75m actually spent in buying them out put the claimant beyond the position it would have been in, and was an unreasonable expense.[94]

---

[89] *Kelleher v O'Connor* [2010] IEHC 313 (Irish High Court) obiter at para 9.7.
[90] *Dent v Davis Blank Furniss* [2001] Lloyd's Rep PN 534 (Blackburne J).
[91] Text to chapter seventeen n 112.
[92] *Herrmann v Withers LLP* [2012] EWHC 1492 (Ch) (Newey J). The facts are discussed further in chapter nineteen at text to n 65.
[93] *Murray v Lloyd* [1989] 1 WLR 1060 (Mummery J).
[94] *Fulham Leisure Holdings Ltd v Nicholson Graham & Jones* [2006] EWHC 2017 (Ch) (Mann J). Reversed on grounds of liability, the cross-appeal on quantum therefore not being considered: [2008] EWCA Civ 84.

C. Costs of Physical Repair

In adoption cases, the costs of physical repair will be recoverable where the defendant is responsible for the defect which is being repaired, or responsible for the claimant rather than a third party being liable to pay for them.[95]

Moreover, even in the typical surveyor case where the defendant is not responsible for the defect, only for failing to warn the claimant about it, where the case is a no transaction case, the claimant may be able to recover the costs of repairing the defect, once it is accepted that adopting the transaction is reasonable. This is not an illegitimate application of the warranty measure of damages (ie an award falsely treating the breached obligation as a promise that the property was not defective). It merely applies the ordinary rules of causation and mitigation, and recognises the costs of repairs as a reasonable consequential cost that was caused by the breach, because it caused the claimant to buy a property it would not have bought and this reasonably resulted in repair costs once the claimant reasonably adopted the property.[96] The justifiable opposition to the warranty measure, which is inapplicable on the correct analysis, should not be allowed to prevent the award of the costs of repairs where it is correct to do so for these reasons.[97]

The key is in identifying whether the claimant has been locked into the transaction or reasonably adopted it, and whether repair costs reasonably follow from that.

First, it is necessary to deal with an extrication/non-adoption case where the costs of repair were rightly rejected. In *Smith and Smith v Peter North*, the dwelling and farm bought by the claimant was, despite the surveyor's report failing to point out various defects, in fact worth more than the claimant paid.[98] The claimant argued that it was reasonable for it to stay in the property given its ideal location and facilities for show-jumping.[99] The first point of note is that it is not at all clear that but for the breach the claimant would not have bought the property anyway for the same (below market) price,[100] in which case no loss has been caused. Assuming, however, that the claimant would not have bought the property but for the breach, the suitability of the property cannot be a reason for now sticking with it. That does not lock the claimant in, and it is still reasonable to expect the claimant to extricate itself from the deal (at no cost) and accordingly the cost of repairs and alternative accommodation following the claimant deciding to keep the property is an avoidable loss and/or one properly treated as caused by the claimant's own decision to

---

[95] The argument that the vendor would have covered the repairs failed in *Gardner v Marsh & Parsons* [1997] 1 WLR 489 (CA).

[96] The same does not apply in successful-transaction cases. There the adoption of the transaction is unsurprising—anything else would likely be unreasonable—and the repair costs would have been suffered in any case (although eg the price paid may have been lower if the claimant had known of the defect, and so that extra price paid is recoverable).

[97] See especially the reasoning in *Watts v Morrow* [1991] 1 WLR 1421 (CA), where the efforts not to apply the warranty measure did lead to failure to recognise that such costs could be awarded on the true measure.

[98] *Smith and Smith v Peter North* (2001) 82 Con LR 126 (CA).

[99] See ibid, para 18.

[100] The point was not directly discussed but cf Parker LJ at para 39 and Judge LJ at para 61, and note how keen the claimant was on the premises at para 18.

keep the property. The claims for those costs were rightly struck out, and this was rightly upheld by the Court of Appeal.

The situation was different in *Hipkins v Jack Cotton*[101] and *Syrett v Carr &* *Neave*.[102] In *Hipkins* the £14,000 repair costs were awarded as the claimant had reasonably stuck with the property. In *Syrett* the cost at trial of repairs (over £88,000 including ancillary costs) was awarded, it being found reasonable of the claimant to retain the property as she was so involved in it by the time the defects were discovered. Both decisions may be criticised on their facts, on the basis that it might be said to have been reasonably expected that the claimants would sell the properties, although there are indications that the repairs were cheaper. However, it cannot be denied that there will be situations where a claimant reasonably retains the property indefinitely (even after discovering the defect), most obviously in cases where the costs of repairs and other losses (including on-going inconvenience) will be lower than the claim (including for all expenses incurred on the property before a defect was discovered) if the claimant extricates itself from the transaction. And in *Zeneca Ltd v King Sturges & Co*[103] the tenant was also locked in as it had a 20-year lease and had already commenced works when the defects the defendant surveyor had failed to warn of were discovered. This was reasonable and repairs were ordered.

Both *Hipkins* and *Syrett* were (wrongly) doubted by Gibson LJ in *Watts v Morrow* in the Court of Appeal.[104] Bingham LJ was less trenchant, observing that the costs of repair exceeded the difference in value (and so perhaps suggesting it was disproportionate).[105] It is clear, however, that the *Watts v Morrow* approach to taking the difference between price and value at the date of acquisition is only a prima facie approach.[106] It has been confirmed since *Watts v Morrow*, and contrary to the tenor of the judgments in that decision, that the award is based on whether the claimant reasonably extricated itself from the transaction or could have been expected to do so and at whatever date that sale would have taken place.[107] The House of Lords' decision in *Farley v Skinner*[108] makes it plain that sometimes it is reasonable not to sell the property.

Thus the correct position requires the court to work out, in the light of the full cost of extrication (including all expenses to date, including stamp duty and improvements reasonably carried out before discovering the defect,[109] and inconvenience from the upheaval of moving), whether it is reasonable for the claimant to have stuck with the property rather than selling it, and if so whether costs of

---

[101] *Hipkins v Jack Cotton* [1989] 2 EGLR 157 (Baker J).
[102] *Syrett v Carr & Neave* [1990] 2 EGLR 161 (Bowsher QC).
[103] *Zeneca Ltd v King Sturges & Co*, 19 September 1996 (Jackson QC).
[104] *Watts v Morrow* [1991] 1 WLR 1421 (CA) at 1434–38.
[105] Ibid at 1444–45. And note that it is not even clear that but for the breach the purchase would not have gone ahead.
[106] Eg *Smith and Smith v Peter North* (2001) 82 Con LR 126 (CA) Parker LJ at paras 32 and 53.
[107] *Patel v Hooper & Jackson* [1999] 1 WLR 1792 (CA).
[108] *Farley v Skinner* [2002] 2 AC 732 (HL).
[109] Arguments as to the real costs of the acquisition and resale were important to the trial judge but fell on deaf ears in *Watts v Morrow* itself [1991] 1 WLR 1421 (CA) at 1428.

repairs and inconvenience and other on-going losses are too remote or avoidable or whether they are recoverable.

Indeed on its facts, *Watts v Morrow* is itself problematic. It is not clear that but for the breach the transaction would not have gone ahead, ie that this is a no trans-action case at all.[110] If it would have gone ahead with a price reduction then the cost of repair, which the Wattses had incurred, was clearly irrecoverable as but for the breach it would have been suffered anyway. Assuming this was a no transac-tion case, the substantial defects not spotted by the surveyor were only discovered after the Wattses had moved in. Although the house was only worth £15,000 less than the Wattses paid for it, the first instance judge and counsel for the claimant rightly pointed out that there would be substantial costs of resale and purchase of a replacement including stamp duty and agents' and solicitors' fees, a large time and inconvenience cost, an increase in the cost of a replacement property due to a year's market rise, the thrown away mortgage costs, and there was uncertainty as to what price the property would fetch when it did sell.[111] Gibson LJ noted that the costs on reselling had apparently not been pleaded,[112] and but for that the judge's finding that it was reasonable to adopt the property and perform the repairs seems right, in which case the Court of Appeal was wrong to disregard all that and hold the claimant to the amount by which the price exceeded the market value at the date of acquisition. Gibson LJ held that 'If, however, the cost of repairs would exceed the diminution in value, then the ruling in *Philips v Ward*, where it is applicable, prohibits recovery of the excess because it would give to the plaintiff more than his loss',[113] which is only partially right. First, as Gibson LJ himself observes,[114] the relevant comparator is not merely the diminution in value but 'all the losses incurred as a result of entering into the transaction where he would not have entered into the transaction if properly advised and the losses are caused by entry into the transac-tion and by extrication from it'. Bingham LJ stated that the cost of repairs exceeded the diminution in value[115] but it appears likely that they did not exceed the total losses on a resale which were avoided by the adoption and repairs. Secondly, if it is reasonable to expect the claimant to sell then any losses above those suffered on such a sale are indeed unrecoverable as being avoidable, but only if it is reasonable to expect the claimant to sell.

Finally, in *Hussey v Eels*, a case of a misrepresentation by a vendor of land as to there not being a history of subsidence, it is clear that had the claimants been able to afford the £17,000 to repair the property they would have recovered that as a reasonable cost of mitigation.[116]

---

[110] Gibson LJ records (ibid at 1425–26) that Mrs Watts would not have wanted it to go ahead but Mr Watts would. But at 1435 Gibson LJ seems to indicate that this is a no transaction case.

[111] The judge is quoted by Gibson LJ [1991] 1 WLR 1421 at 1428 and counsel's figures recited at 1434.

[112] Gibson LJ (ibid at 1428).

[113] At 1435.

[114] At 1438.

[115] At 1444.

[116] *Hussey v Eels* [1990] 2 QB 227 (CA).

D. Lost Amenity on an Alternative Transaction

A claimant can recover lost amenity suffered on the transaction that was adopted (where not cured).[117]

3.4 The Non-Breach Position: The Alternative Transaction the Claimant Would Have Entered Into

As explained above, the harms suffered on the actual transaction are only the beginning of the story. The calculation of loss requires the proof that these harms would not have been suffered under any alternative transaction the claimant would have entered into (see below at section 3.4C), and proof of what gains would have been made under the alternative transaction (see below at section 3.4B).

A. Where Costs on the Alternative Transaction Would Have Been Lower

There is a loss where the claimant would have incurred costs on an alternative transaction but they would have been lower. This arises most typically in cases where the alternative transaction would have been with the same third party but on different terms (ie 'successful-transaction' cases).[118]

(i) Lower Price or Advance

In cases where but for the breach the claimant would have paid a lower price, the amount by which the price would have been lower is recoverable in damages[119] along with any amount by which the stamp duty would have been lower.[120] This typically arises in lender claims because 'in practice the alternative transaction which a defendant is most likely to be able to establish is that the lender would have lent a lesser amount to the same borrower on the same security',[121] and so the lender often

---

[117] *Herrmann v Withers LLP* [2012] EWHC 1492 (Ch) (Newey J) at para 125. Given that the claimant was deemed to have mitigated and acquired an 80-year licence of access to the garden, the £2,000 award must be understood as the loss for the period when the claimant was without access (before it should have successfully negotiated the licence) plus any loss of amenity from knowing it only had a licence and was (as a mere licensee) a second-class user of the gardens as compared with some other users and the position the claimant was expecting to be in.

[118] If the transaction would have been different but no worse, then no loss has been suffered: *BDG Roof-Bond Ltd v Douglas* [2000] 1 BCLC 401 (Park J) (solicitor negligence).

[119] *Perry v Sidney Phillips* [1982] 1 WLR 1297 (CA); *Bigg v Howard Son & Gooch* [1990] 1 EGLR 173 (Hicks QC); *Howard v Horne & Sons* [1990] 1 EGLR 272 (Bowsher QC); *Holder v Countrywide Surveyors Ltd*, 11 March 2002 (Harvey QC); *Capita Alternative Fund Services (Guernsey) Ltd v DriverJonas* [2011] EWHC 2336 (Comm) (Eder J).

[120] *Holder v Countrywide Surveyors Ltd*, 11 March 2002 (Harvey QC) at para 64, although the point was conceded and it is not clear that this was in fact a successful-transaction rather than a no transaction case on the facts.

[121] *South Australia Asset Management Corp v York Montague Ltd* [1997] 1 AC 191 (HL) Lord Hoffmann at 218.

claims only the difference between the amount it lent and the amount it would have lent (which difference is often the product of the loan-to-value ratio and the amount of the overvaluation).[122] The cost of repairs will sometimes be a good indication of the amount of the price reduction that could have been obtained.[123]

Sometimes in cases where the claimant would have entered into a transaction with the same third party but on different terms, judges talk in terms of the difference between the price paid and the true market value of the property,[124] failing to realise that this is not the basic measure where the claimant would have bought the property even but for the breach. It is clear (including from the results in most of these cases) that although the market value is a good indication of the price the claimant would have paid, it is the latter measure that should be used: if the claimant would have bought anyway, the claimant can recover the amount by which it would have paid less. As Hicks QC explained of surveyor's negligence cases in *Bigg v Howard Son & Gooch*:[125]

> It is common ground between the parties, and I agree, that the measure of damages is that established by the Court of Appeal in the case of *Perry v Sidney Phillips & Son* [1982] 1 WLR 1297, which is, in my understanding, best expressed as the difference between the price which the plaintiffs actually paid for the house and the price which a purchaser properly advised by competent surveyors would have paid at the date of the purchase. It is fundamental to this measure of damages that the consequence of the surveyors' negligence has not been to leave the plaintiffs with a less valuable building than he would otherwise have obtained (there never was a sound building to acquire), but to cause him to pay more than the actual building was worth, and if a shorthand phrase is desired it is therefore best described not as 'loss of value' or even 'diminution in price' but rather as something like 'excess cost', 'price inflation' or 'overpayment'. That is why the cost of remedial work is not as such an appropriate measure of damage.

Thus in *Howard v Horne & Sons*,[126] although the claimant had bought the property for below the market value, he was awarded damages for the lost opportunity to negotiate the price down still further below the market value, since the proper measure of loss was the amount by which he paid more than he would otherwise have paid (not the difference between the amount he paid and the value of what he obtained).

Perry v Sidney Phillips & Son[127] is usually considered to be the leading case on this measure,[128] but in fact it was a no transaction case, ie but for the breach

---

[122] *Singer & Friedlander v John D Wood & Co* [1977] 2 EGLR 84 (Watkins J); *Corisand Investments Ltd v Druce & Co* [1978] EGLR 86 (Gibson J); *The Mortgage Corp v Halifax (SW)* [1999] Lloyd's Rep PN 159 (Hutton J); *Scotlife Homeloans (No 2) Ltd v Kenneth James & Co* [1995] EGCS 70 (Crawford QC).

[123] See text to n 84 above.

[124] *Philips v Ward* [1956] 1 WLR 471 (CA) at 473; *Hooberman v Salter Rex* [1985] EGLR 144 (Smout QC) at 147 (which talks about the rule requiring a comparison with the market value but then measures the reduction the claimant could have obtained); *Howard v Horne & Sons* [1990] 1 EGLR 272 (Bowsher QC).

[125] *Bigg v Howard Son & Gooch* [1990] 1 EGLR 173 (Hicks QC) at 174.

[126] *Howard v Horne & Sons* [1990] 1 EGLR 272 (Bowsher QC).

[127] *Perry v Sidney Phillips & Son* [1982] 1 WLR 1297 (CA).

[128] Eg *Hayes v James and Charles Dodd* [1990] 2 All ER 815 (CA) Staughton LJ at 819.

the claimant would not have bought the property at all.[129] This can be seen from Denning MR's judgment, which seems to treat the transaction as one that would have gone ahead but for the breach, and on that assumption his formulation of the measure of loss as 'the difference in price which the buyer would have given if the report had been carefully made from that which he in fact gave owing to the negligence of the surveyor'.[130]

No issue of date of assessment arises here, because the question is the additional price that would have been paid at the date of acquisition,[131] and there is no reasonable extrication measure as the defendant cannot be blamed for the transaction, only its particular terms.

(ii) Lower Costs

The perfect illustration of the situation in which the claimant would have contracted with the same party but with lower costs is provided by the deceit case of *Clef Aquitaine SARL v Laporte Materials (Barrow) Ltd*.[132] In that case the claimant entered into a 20-year agreement to purchase the defendant manufacturer's building materials at prices fixed by reference to an agreed price list and to distribute them in France at a 300–400 per cent mark-up. The agreement was induced by the defendant's fraudulent misstatements that the price list contained the minimum prices the defendant charged to other customers. Even on the terms on which it was entered into, the distribution agreement was profitable to the claimant. They did not seek to rescind, nor did they suffer any net loss during the term of the agreement, indeed quite the contrary. The novelty of this case, therefore, was that the fraud had induced a profitable transaction. However, had the statements not been made, it was found that the claimant would still have entered into the distribution agreement but on cheaper terms for the claimant, who would have made a higher margin on the goods as they would still have charged the same prices to its customers in France.[133] The Court of Appeal rightly upheld an award of the amount by which the claimant had overpaid (as compared with what it would have paid),[134] correctly applying the principle that the claimant is entitled to any benefits it would

---

[129] This is clearest from the report of the first instance decision: [1982] 1 All ER 1005 (Bennett QC) at 1008.

[130] *Perry v Sidney Phillips & Son* [1982] 1 WLR 1297 (CA) at 1302 Denning MR. Oliver and Kerr LJJ's judgments seem to be based on the case being a no transaction case and hence do not talk about a difference between the price paid and the price that would have been paid. Further, in the commercial survey case of *Prudential Assurance Co Ltd v McBains Cooper*, 27 June 2000 (Havery QC), the parties and court all agreed that the award should be the difference between the value as incorrectly indicated in the report and the actual value, which is incorrect as a matter of law but probably accurately reflects the amount of the overpayment given that the price was fixed by reference to the valuations and the valuation discussion in that case referred to what price reductions a purchaser would procure.

[131] *Perry v Sidney Phillips & Son* [1982] 1 WLR 1297 (CA) Denning MR at 1302.

[132] *Clef Aquitaine SARL v Laporte Materials (Barrow) Ltd* [2001] QB 488 (CA). And cf the European law claim dispute in *Crehan v Inntrepreneur Pub Co (CPC)* [2004] EWCA Civ 637 as regards the difference between purchasing beer at higher tied pub rates and purchasing beer at lower free house rates.

[133] At the bottom of 492.

[134] Simon Brown LJ and Sedley LJ. Ward LJ reached the same conclusion but on the artificial basis that the goods bought were worth less than paid by the amount of the overcharging.

have had on an alternative transaction (but for the wrong) but did not have on the actual transaction.

Likewise, where the defendant accountant's negligence caused the claimant to operate its business on a particular basis, the claimant recovered the tax that would have been saved if it had been properly advised.[135] Or where the claimant's repairs liability was greater under a 20-year lease than it would have been under a five-year tenancy, the extra liability was recovered.[136]

B. Greater Revenue/Profits on the Alternative Transaction

The claimant is entitled to claim the lost profits it would have made if it had not entered into the transaction that the defendant induced.

(i) Being Clear about What is Being Claimed: No Claim for Lost Profits on the Unwanted Transaction Itself

It is clear that in a no transaction case, ie where the claimant would not have entered into the transaction at all but for the wrong, the claimant cannot recover for lost profits on the transaction that was entered into, because the complaint is not (as in a warranty case) that the claimant's transaction was not as profitable as hoped (or as indicated by the defendant), but rather that the claimant would not have entered into the transaction at all had the defendant not breached its contract. Accordingly, it is clear that lost profits cannot be claimed on the transaction that the claimant did enter into because but for the breach those profits would still not have been earned. The relevant revenue does not form part of the non-breach position. As Bingham LJ observed:

> It must, however, be accepted on the findings of the deputy judge that if they had not been negligently advised the plaintiffs would not have entered into this underlease at all. This being so, damage cannot be assessed with reference to a specific gain which the plaintiffs could only have made if they had entered into this underlease.[137]

In the lender context, this means that in a no transaction case the lender cannot claim the interest or other payments that the borrower promised but did not pay, because but for the breach there would have been no loan (although credit must be given for all payments actually received from the borrower).[138]

(ii) Lost Profits on the Alternative Transaction with a Different Third Party

The claimant is entitled to claim profits on an alternative transaction that would have been entered into, but for the breach, in place of the unwanted transaction.

---

[135] *Slattery v Moore Stephens* [2003] STC 1379 (Englehart QC). And see *In re Thomas Gerrard & Son Ltd* [1968] 1 Ch 455 (Pennycuick J).

[136] *Plummer v Tibsco Ltd*, 9 March 2001 (Neuberger J).

[137] *County Personnel (Employment Agency) Ltd v Pulver & Co* [1987] 1 WLR 916 (CA) Bingham LJ at 926 pt 6. See also eg *Oates v Anthony Pitman & Co* (CA) 7 May 1998.

[138] *Swingcastle Ltd v Alastair Gibson* [1991] 2 AC 223 (HL).

This is essentially a claim for loss of use of the money that the claimant expended on the unwanted transaction, and was described in the deceit case of *Smith New Court Securities* by Lord Steyn as 'classic consequential loss'.[139] Thus, in one case it was explained that the claimant was entitled to recover 'not the loss of the income stream from the Property [that it purchased] itself but the loss of a similar alternative income stream'.[140]

A typical category of such claims is that of the lost profits on a business, such as where professional negligence caused the claimant to purchase a business and diverted the claimant from buying a more profitable business,[141] or commercial or development property.[142]

A common situation is where the defendant caused the claimant to sell something at a lower price than it would, but for the breach, have achieved. Where a defendant valuer undervalued a rugby ground for English rugby club Wasps, the recoverable loss was the amount by which Wasps then undersold the property, ie the difference between the price it received and the price it would have received if it had had a careful valuation.[143] Where a solicitor procured that a lease was in a company name rather than the claimant's name, the claimant could recover the difference between the value of the lease as it was and the higher value it would have had in her own name.[144] In another case, the breach led to the claimant locking itself into a sale of shares to the defendant at a price many millions of pounds lower than that it would have achieved earlier to a specific other buyer.[145] And where a claimant would, but for the breach by the solicitor, have sold its property sooner, it can recover as damages against the solicitor or other professional the interest on the profits of that sale that it would have received earlier than it in fact did,[146] as well (in suitable cases) as the difference in price caused by a market drop during that period.[147] In other cases,

[139] *Smith New Court Securities Ltd v Scrimgeour Vickers (Asset Management) Ltd* [1997] AC 254 (HL) at 282.

[140] *Keydon Estate Ltd v Eversheds LLP* [2005] EWHC 972 (Ch) (Evans-Lombe J) at para 31.

[141] Eg *Havenledge Ltd v Graeme John & Partners* [2001] PNLR 17 (CA) (although time-barred). However, the case law consists mainly of misrepresentation and deceit cases. See below in chapter eighteen, section 18.4.

[142] *Jenmain Builders v Steed & Steed* (CA), 20 February 2000; *Keydon Estate Ltd v Eversheds LLP* [2005] EWHC 972 (Ch) (Evans-Lombe J); *Joyce v Bowman Law Ltd* [2010] EWHC 251 (Ch) (Vos J).

[143] *Trustees of WASPS Football Club v Lambert Smith Hampton Group Ltd* [2004] EWHC 938 (Comm) (Langley J). A plea of a more complicated alternative transaction that would have released a greater profit was not accepted. See also *Johnson v Bingley Dyson & Finney*, 13 February 1995 (Hytner QC); *John D Wood & Co (Residential and Agricultural) v Knatchbull* [2004] 1 EGLR 33 (Heppel QC); *Tom Hoskins plc v EMW Law* [2010] EWHC 479 (Ch) (Floyd J).

[144] *Powell v Whitman Breed Abbott & Morgan* [2003] EWHC 1279 (QB) (Tugenhat J).

[145] *British & Commonwealth Holdings plc v Quadrex Holdings Inc* (CA), 10 April 1995.

[146] *G + K Ladenbau (UK) Ltd v Crawley & de Reya* [1978] 1 WLR 266 (Mocatta J); *McElroy Milne v Commercial Electronics Ltd* [1993] 1 NZLR 39 (NZCA) cited with approval by Lord Hoffmann in *South Australia Asset Management Corp v York Montague Ltd* [1997] 1 AC 191 (HL) at 219 and 222; *Gregory v Shepherds* (CA), 16 June 2000.

[147] *R and S Contractors v Architectural Design Associates*, 16 October 1992 (HHJ Rich); *McElroy Milne v Commercial Electronics Ltd* [1993] 1 NZLR 39 (NZCA) cited with approval by Lord Hoffmann in *South Australia Asset Management Corp v York Montague Ltd* [1997] 1 AC 191 (HL) at 219 and 222; *Kirkton Investments Ltd v VMH LLP* [2011] CSOH 200 (Court of Session, Outer House); *John Grimes Partnership Ltd v Gubbins* [2013] EWCA Civ 37.

a claimant may be able to prove that it lost out because the defendant prevented it from selling to a better (more creditworthy) buyer.[148]

Turning to lender claims, in the *Swingcastle* case the House of Lords explained that where the defendant causes the claimant lender to lend: 'What the lenders lost, in addition to their other damages, was the use of the £10,000 while it was perforce locked up in the loan'.[149] In such lender claims, although 'the lender is entitled to prove that, even though he would not have lent to that borrower on that security, he would have done something more advantageous than keep his money on deposit',[150] in practice a general award for interest is made on a rough quantification, rather than following proof of loss on a specific lending or other transaction the bank would have made.[151]

Where recoverable, and like an award of interest for loss of use of money, such lost profits will be recoverable for the entire period up until the date of trial, not only until the date when the claimant discovered the wrong and could have extricated itself from the transaction it did enter into,[152] save where there has been a failure to mitigate.[153] However, it has been said that the courts should approach such claims in a 'cautious and conservative manner'.[154]

If the claimant cannot prove a particular lost profit then the court may be willing to assume a certain return. Thus in one case where negligent solicitors failed to point out a planning problem that would have deterred the claimants from buying a particular business, the judge refused to require the claimants to give credit for around £115,000 that the claimants had taken out of the business for expenses and living costs (ie profit) on the basis that he was willing to assume that

> [h]ad there been no transaction, it is perfectly clear that both the Scotts would have worked at something else and earned enough to live with their family. They would either have bought another guest house or they would have carried on as a teacher and caterer respectively.[155]

As the judge also awarded the net capital expenditure but without this deduction, in effect the judge inferred that the claimants would not only have broken even but also made at least as much profit as they in fact did make.[156] In another case the

---

[148] *Matlaszek v Bloom Camillin (a firm)* [2003] EWHC 2728 (Ch) (Park J). See chapter eighteen text to n 89 below.

[149] *Swingcastle Ltd v Alastair Gibson* [1991] 2 AC 223 (HL) Lord Lowry at 237.

[150] *South Australia Asset Management Corp (SAAMCo) v York Montague Ltd* [1997] 1 AC 191 (HL) Lord Hoffmann at 218.

[151] See chapter seven, section 7.2C below.

[152] *Parabola Investments Ltd v Browallia Cal Ltd* [2011] 1 QB 477 (CA).

[153] *Esso Petroleum Co Ltd v Mardon* [1976] 1 QB 801 (CA) Denning LJ at 821–22; *Parabola Investments Ltd v Browallia Cal Ltd* [2011] 1 QB 477 (CA) Toulson LJ at paras 45 and 58.

[154] *County Personnel (Employment Agency) Ltd v Pulver & Co* [1987] 1 WLR 916 (CA) (solicitor's negligence) Bingham LJ at 926 pt 7.

[155] *Scott & Scott v Kennedys Law LLP and Vertex Law LLP* [2011] EWHC 3808 (Ch) (Vos J) at para 70.

[156] See also *Hussey v Eels* [1990] 2 QB 227 (CA) where one reason for not giving credit for profit made by keeping the property was that an alternative property would have made a similar profit thorugh a market rise which offset the profit actually made: see Mustill LJ at 233.

court found that the claimant would have broken even but no more, and so awarded capital losses but no lost profit.[157]

The default claim, absent any proof of a particular alternative transaction by either party, is for interest on the money that was spent on the transaction induced by the defendant. The effective presumption is that the claimant would have invested its money, or had borrowed its money, and the compensation is by an ordinary rate of interest.[158]

(iii) Lost Profits on an Alternative Transaction with the Same Third Party

Where the complaint is that the transaction would have been different if the claimant had advised, it may include a complaint that the claimant would have made more profit.[159]

In *Joyce v Bowman Law Ltd*,[160] the defendant solicitor's negligence led to the claimant purchaser of a dilapidated cottage and land not also acquiring an advertised option for the claimant to purchase neighbouring development land for £20,000. Damages were recovered for the lost 29 per cent chance of profitably developing the land, those losses not being too remote, less the profit that would have been made if the claimant had mitigated by proceeding with a smaller development. In another development case, the defendant solicitor's negligence slowed down a development project leading to a reduced profit, which was recoverable,[161] as may be increased finance costs,[162] or the entire development profit where the solicitor's breach led to the claimant failing to acquire the property at all.[163] And in another case, a £1.8m award was made for the lost chance of negotiating an agreement to provide the claimant with royalties and other profits from construction of the Eden Project in Cornwall.[164]

(iv) Lost Litigation

The recovery in lost litigation cases is of the lost profit that would have been made from the litigation (or the reduced liability that would have been incurred). See below in section 13.5. Similarly, in negligent advice cases the claimant may lose the opportunity to purchase property. In such cases, subject to remoteness, the claimant

---

[157] *Davis v Churchward Brook Haye & Co* (CA), 6 May 1993 (deceit).

[158] See chapter seven on loss of use of money and awards of interest.

[159] Dictum of Bingham LJ in *County Personnel (Employment Agency) Ltd v Pulver & Co* [1987] 1 WLR 916 (CA) at 926 pt 6. And cf the discussion above in sections 3.4A(ii) and 3.4B of cases such as *Clef Aquitaine SARL v Laporte Materials (Barrow) Ltd* [2001] QB 488 (CA) where the complaint is that the costs would have been lower.

[160] *Joyce v Bowman Law Ltd* [2010] EWHC 251 (Ch) (Vos J).

[161] *Marshall v Mackintosh* (1898) 14 TLR 458 (Kennedy J); *Finley v Connell Associates*, 27 July 2001 (Ouseley J); *Kirkton Investments Ltd v VMH LLP* [2011] CSOH 200 (Court of Session, Outer House).

[162] *Kirkton Investments Ltd v VMH LLP* [2011] CSOH 200 (Court of Session, Outer House).

[163] *Watts v Bell & Scott WS* [2007] CSOH 108 (Court of Session, Outer House).

[164] *Ball v Druces & Attlee (No 2)* [2004] EWHC 1402 (QB) (Nelson J).

can claim lost profits from the purchase[165] or, where it is not certain the purchase would have been made, damages for the loss of a chance of such a purchase.[166]

(v) Insurance Brokers and Non-Responding Insurance

Where a defendant insurance broker's negligence leads to the claimant's insurance policy being voidable by the insurer when but for the negligence it would have been valid, or not covering a particular event when but for the negligence it would have done so, the claimant's loss is the money it would or might (the loss of chance measure) have received from the insurer but did not receive, as well as any consequential damage to the claimant's business.[167]

C. Where the *Defendant* Relies on the Alternative Transaction: Costs that Would Have Been Incurred Anyway

The general principle, as a matter of ordinary causation, must be that the claimant cannot recover for any costs or losses that would have been suffered on an alternative transaction because in that case they were not as a matter of fact caused by the breach.

Thus Bingham MR obiter (and dissenting on liability) in *Reeves v Thrings & Long*[168] was inclined to disallow the net losses on a development transaction for the following reason:

> I accept that had the true position been explained he would not have entered into this transaction at all, but I incline to think that he would be over-compensated by this measure, since whatever he had invested in on the eve of the current recessionary cycle might well have led to loss.

Similarly, in *Patel v Hooper & Jackson*,[169] the Court of Appeal disallowed a claim for mortgage interest and endowment policy and house insurance premiums because the claimants would have incurred them in any event on an alternative similar house, had the defendant's breach not induced them to purchase the unwanted property. Likewise, where costs were incurred on a 20-year lease but would also have been incurred on an alternative five-year tenancy they are to that extent not recoverable.[170]

---

[165] *Jenmain Builders v Steed & Steed* (CA), 20 February 2000, although the development profit was held to be built into the capital value of the property lost and any further loss avoidable had the claimant pursued an alternative development.

[166] *Thomas Eggar Verrall Bowles v Rice*, 21 December 1999 (Rimer J).

[167] *Arbory Group Ltd v West Craven Insurance Services* [2007] PNLR 23 (Grenfell J). Also *Everett v Hogg Robinson* [1973] 2 Lloyd's Rep 217 (CA); *Dunbar v A & B Painters* [1986] 2 Lloyd's Rep 38 (CA); *Unity Insurance Brokers Pty Ltd v Rocco Pezzano Pty Ltd* (1998) 192 CLR 603 (HC of Australia); *O & R Jewellers v Terry and Jardine Insurance Brokers* [1999] Lloyd's Rep IR 436 (Le Quesne QC).

[168] *Reeves v Thrings & Long* (CA), 19 November 1993. See also *South Australia Asset Management Corp v York Montague Ltd* [1997] 1 AC 191 (HL) Lord Hoffmann at 217–18 (as to a lender's losses).

[169] *Patel v Hooper & Jackson* [1999] 1 WLR 1792 (CA) Nourse LJ at 1803.

[170] *Plummer v Tibsco Ltd*, 9 March 2001 (Neuberger J).

This is a perfectly legitimate approach, although it is important to ensure that if one part of an alternative transaction is taken into account then all of it is. It is not enough for a defendant merely to demonstrate that stamp duty or mortgage interest costs that were incurred by the claimant (as part of the breach position) would have been incurred anyway under an alternative transaction (the non-breach position), if the claimant would have recouped the costs by revenue on the alternative transaction that was not earned on the actual transaction, or even made a profit. In that case, the claimant has suffered a net loss: not the costs, which would have been incurred anyway, but the lost revenues, which would have been earned but for the breach. It is therefore necessary, if the inquiry is to take in the alternative transaction so as to negate certain costs that would have been incurred, to ask what revenue would have been earned (by an increase in value of the alternative property, revenue from the business, etc). And if the lost profit on the alternative transaction is claimed, but not the net *revenue*, then the costs have already been deducted from the claim on the alternative transaction and there is no need to give credit for them a second time by deducting the costs incurred on the actual transaction as being costs that would have been incurred anyway.[171]

(i) Temporary Confusion in the Case Law

Despite these cases, there is a strain of dicta in the misrepresentation and deceit cases to the effect that the courts must not look to what would have taken place in an alternative transaction. As Waller J put it in *Naughton v O'Callaghan*:

> the plaintiffs are entitled to ask the court to look simply at the contract they made in reliance on the representation which induced them to enter into that bargain. They are entitled to say that there must be no speculation one way or the other about what would have happened if they had not purchased this horse and if no misrepresentation had been made to them.[172]

In that case Waller J agreed to apply what he appropriately called 'blinkers' and rejected the defendant's argument that various expenses would have been incurred in any event on an alternative horse.[173] However, this must be understood as a judgment on the particular case and not a statement of principle; in *Naughton* the alternative transaction would have been pure 'speculation' and the claimant was able to respond to the defendant's argument that 'that may be so, but if they bought the horse described by the defendant it might have paid for its keep and reaped for them rich rewards'. Accordingly, the true principle is that if the alternative transaction is taken into account then the entire transaction must be taken into account, as explained above, and in *Naughton* there was simply not enough evidence, or it must be presumed that the alternative transaction would have broken even, and so any costs that would have been incurred anyway would but for the breach have been recouped, and so should not be deducted from the claim. Other dicta suggesting that

---

[171] *4 Eng Ltd v Harper* [2009] Ch 91 (Richards J) at para 110 (deceit).
[172] *Naughton v O'Callaghan* [1990] 3 All ER 191 (Waller J) at 198.
[173] Ibid.

losses on an alternative transaction should be ignored can be similarly explained on the facts.[174]

However, in the deceit case of *Downs v Chappell* it was held that a market drop that the claimant suffered prior to the date of extrication but would have suffered on an alternative transaction was nevertheless recoverable as a loss,[175] and this was followed by May J in the deceit case of *Slough Estates*.[176] May J explained in *Slough Estates* that in *Downs*, Hobhouse LJ had become confused by asking what would have happened if the representations had been true, which as Lord Hoffmann explained in *SAAMCo*, is broadly the correct approach where there is a limited scope of duty but not correct in a deceit case.[177]

However, that does not mean that where the evidence is before the court it is wrong to look at what alternative transaction would have taken place but for the deceit, and plainly the court does do so when addressing profits the claimant would have made (see the next section). In the deceit case of *Parabola Investments Ltd v Browallia Cal Ltd*,[178] Toulson LJ appeared to confirm, obiter, an asymmetry in deceit cases such that in a case of an unwanted transaction, although the claimant may prove that it would have made profits on an alternative transaction, the defendant will not be allowed to prove that the claimant would have lost the money anyway,[179] but observed

> That head of loss is recoverable regardless of what Tangent [the claimant] would otherwise have done with its trading fund. It would not matter, for example, if Mr Gill [of the claimant] would otherwise have given the entire amount to charity. He was entitled to use his money as he chose and to have the fund restored.

This statement is correct because giving the money to charity, like using it to buy food, is *res inter alios acta*,[180] but if the claimant would have traded the money and lost it and the defendant can prove that (which it could not in *Parabola* itself) then this should properly be taken into account.

What is most important for the purposes of contract damages is to note, however, that any such limitation in deceit cases does not apply to the usual negligence and contract cases. Lord Hoffmann in *SAAMCo* was explicit about this: 'If for example the lender would have lost the same money on some other transaction, then the valuer's negligence has caused him no loss' and 'in principle there is no reason why the valuer should not be entitled to prove that the lender has suffered no loss

---

[174] *United Motor Finance Co v Addison & Co Ltd* [1937] 1 All ER 425 (PC) Sir George Rankin at 429, where it was not proven what would have happened; likewise *Royscot Trust Ltd v Rogerson* [1991] 2 QB 297 (CA) Balcolme LJ at 303, where the judge also confirmed that there was no evidence of the alternative transaction.

[175] *Downs v Chappell* [1996] 1 WLR 426 (CA) Hobhouse LJ at 438, 441 and 444.

[176] *Slough Estates plc v Welwyn Hatfield District Council* [1996] 2 EGLR 219 (May J) at 243–46.

[177] See further chapter fourteen, section 14.5B(i).

[178] *Parabola Investments Ltd v Browallia Cal Ltd* [2011] 1 QB 477 (CA) at para 55.

[179] Although the ordinary approach taking into account all aspects of the alternative transaction appears to have been applied in the deceit case of *4 Eng Ltd v Harper* [2009] Ch 91 (Richards J) at para 110.

[180] See further the discussion below in chapter eleven, section 11.2D.

because he would have used his money in some altogether different but equally disastrous venture'.[181]

Most recently, the asymmetry has been expressly considered and found not to exist in the High Court contract and misrepresentation decision in *Yam Seng Pte Ltd v International Trade Corp Ltd*.[182] An approach by which the claimant can recover a profit it would have made but for the breach but the defendant cannot reduce damages by proof that the claimant would have made a loss would be 'not merely difficult but impossible to defend' as there is 'no difference in principle' between the two types of alternative transaction.[183]

This returns us to the starting point: it is open to both the claimant and defendant to point to an alternative transaction to show that a gain that was not made would have been made, or that a loss that was made would have been made anyway, respectively. The whole transaction must be considered. Any cases to the contrary are explicable on their facts but do not reflect any legal principle modifying the basic comparison between what happened and what would have happened.

---

[181] *South Australia Asset Management Corp v York Montague Ltd* [1997] 1 AC 191 (HL) at 217–18 (the latter quotation was cited in *Slough Estates* [1996] 2 EGLR 219 at 244 but May J appears not to have focused on that part of the quotation). This was not, however, the reason for the result in the *SAAMCo* case itself. As Lord Hoffmann explained in *Nykredit Mortgage Bank plc v Edward Erdman Group Ltd (No 2)* [1997] WLR 1627 (HL) at 1638: 'There was, for example, no evidence that if the lender had not made the advance in question he would have lost his money in some other way'.

[182] *Yam Seng Pte Ltd v International Trade Corp Ltd* [2013] 1 Lloyd's Rep 526 (Leggatt J) at paras 209–17.

[183] *Yam Seng Pte Ltd v International Trade Corp Ltd* [2013] 1 Lloyd's Rep 526 (Leggatt J) at para 217.

4

Property Non-Delivery, Destruction and Defects (Damage, Sale, Construction, Misrepair)

Damages in property cases, including sale (non-delivery and defects), construction, defective property under charters or leases, and other cases of damage or destruction to property. Focuses in turn on damages in cases of replacement, damages in cases of repair, and damages in other cases.

4.1. Introduction to the Different Measures of Loss
4.2. The First Cure: Replacement on the Market
4.3. The Second Cure: Repair
4.4. Further Issues in Repair and Replacement Cases
4.5. The Measure When there is No Market Replacement and No Repair

THIS CHAPTER IS concerned with all cases in which, as a result of breach, the claimant's existing property is damaged or destroyed, or the property the claimant was promised is not delivered (or is delivered but lawfully rejected) or is defective.[1] The key situations in which these cases arise are: (i) breach of a contract for the sale of goods or land by the defendant to the claimant; (ii) breach by the defendant of the obligation to re-deliver the claimant's goods or land after hire, lease or charter; (iii) breach of an obligation to build or improve the claimant's goods or land (ie in construction or repair contracts); and (iv) damage to or destruction of the claimant's property (including by a carrier or other service-provider).

4.1 Introduction to the Different Measures of Loss

A. The Measures in Destruction and Non-Delivery Cases

(i) The Importance of Market Replacement

The basic measure of damages is the same in all contract cases: such damages as put the claimant in the position it would have been in had the breach not taken place. In

---

[1] Receiving property on hire, rather than as owner, is discussed separately in chapter eight.

destruction and non-delivery cases, that becomes such damages as put the claimant in the position it would have been in had the property not been destroyed/had the property been delivered.

However, because property can often be replaced, in many destruction and non-delivery cases the damages measure becomes much simpler than measuring all the losses resulting from not having the property. In many such cases the property can be replaced on the market. Where such a replacement is reasonably obtained, or would reasonably be expected to be obtained (and so is deemed by the mitigatory principle to have been obtained whether or not it actually was), the complicated and bespoke on-going losses resulting from not having the property are eliminated from the damages enquiry. The claimant can do with the replacement whatever it would have done with the original property, ie use it, live on it, sell it, incorporate it into a manufacturing process etc, and so the losses that would have resulted from the claimant's inability to put the property to those intended uses have been successfully avoided.

(ii) The Loss of Use of Money Following Market Replacement

Although eliminating on-going losses of use of the property from the date of replacement,[2] the mitigatory act of purchasing a replacement does usually introduce a new on-going loss, that of loss of use of money.

The recourse to the market for a replacement converts the loss of use of property into a loss of use of money. In destruction cases it will be loss of use of the entire cost of the replacement from the date of replacement, which money the claimant would have had but for the breach. The same will be true in non-delivery cases, but only if the claimant has already paid for the non-delivered property (and only up until recovery of the price that was paid for nothing). More usually in non-delivery cases, the claim for loss of use of money will only be for the amount by which the replacement property cost more than the contract price, ie the amount the claimant would have paid the defendant but for the breach.

The market replacement nevertheless simplifies things greatly, because loss of use of money claims are much simpler and more homogenous than loss of use of property claims, and in eliminating the loss of use of property and replacing it with loss of use of money, the claimant usually reduces its loss to a simple interest calculation. Claims for loss of use of money (which can be more complex than this) are discussed in chapter seven.

B. The Measures in Damage, Defect and Incomplete Construction/Repair Cases

(i) Market Replacement

These situations are similar to those in destruction or non-delivery cases, discussed in the previous section. Again, in many cases the claimant will replace its on-going

---

[2] There may still be a claim for damage resulting from temporary loss of use of the property during the time prior to the replacement, as discussed in chapter six below.

losses from the damage or defect with a mere loss of use of money by replacing the property. This time, though, the claimant will also usually be expected to sell the damaged/defective property and thereby further reduce its loss. Thus the usual method of mitigation will involve a sale to the market as well as a purchase of a replacement from it.

(ii) Repair

However, in these cases, unlike in destruction or non-delivery cases, there is a common alternative means of avoiding losses: repair rather than replacement. Again, repairing the property leaves the claimant only with a loss of use of money claim (for the cost of repairs, from the date on which they were paid for), as well as any residual claim for temporary loss of use of property during the period until the repairs were completed.

(iii) Which Approach—Repair or Replacement or Neither?

Deciding between the different measures depends upon reasonableness. Did the claimant make a reasonable choice (if the choice has been made or will be made)? Is there a choice that all reasonable claimants would have made and which the claimant will therefore be deemed to have made (by the principle of mitigation)? These questions depend upon a variety of factual circumstances.

Thus the tax and other transactional costs of buying land or ships will often mean that repair of such property is much more reasonable than replacement, especially with relatively minor damage/defects/incomplete construction, but often even with more major problems. It is therefore not surprising that a large proportion of the repair cases concern land (typically damage to or incomplete construction of buildings) and ships (typically damage by tortious collision).

Similarly if a car is scratched it will be unreasonable to sell the car and buy an unscratched replacement, and the only reasonable approach will be to have a re-spray or similar.

Conversely, with mis-described commodities (eg one type of oil, not another) there is often no cure or 'repair' available, and even if there were it still would be cheaper to sell the property and purchase a replacement than to seek to cure it.

Both options are not always available. If there is no market for replacement then that measure cannot apply. If the claimant could not reasonably have been expected to repair or replace before it sold the property (eg where a defect is latent), then neither measure will apply.

(iv) Sub-Sales

The practical application of these rules can be complicated, especially in the context of breach by sellers. In most cases sub-sales or other intended uses by buyers are legally irrelevant to the calculation of the buyer's loss because the losses are avoidable by a purchase of a replacement. The principle of mitigation therefore prevents recovery of any loss related to such sub-sales or other uses. But that only applies where a replacement is available (ie there is a market) and where that replacement could be expected to have been purchased to avoid the losses (so not in cases of latent defects where the claimant did not know there was a problem, nor in cases where there is a sub-sale that requires the originally promised goods and cannot be satisfied by any replacement). Thus there is no rule that sub-sales are to be ignored, although they often are. Nor is there a rule that damages are assessed at the date of breach and by reference to the market price, although it often is. There are only the legal principles of remoteness, mitigation and causation.

(v) This Chapter

This chapter is divided up as follows:

First, in section 4.2, the option of replacing property on the market is discussed, including the questions of when it is appropriate and how it is measured.

Secondly, in section 4.3, the option of repairing property or completing incomplete works is discussed, again including discussion of when this measure applies.

Thirdly, in section 4.4, some issues arising in both replacement and repair cases are discussed, including residual losses (in addition to the cost of replacement or repair) that arise under those measures, and the question of betterment. Damages for temporary loss of use of property, one of these residual losses often not avoided by replacement or repair, are covered by chapter six. Damages for loss of use of money, the loss that follows replacement or repair,[3] are covered by chapter seven.

Fourthly, in section 4.5, the ordinary or default measure of loss, where no replacement or repair applies, is discussed. This is the usual compensation for the on-going losses resulting from not having the relevant property. This category is not really a 'measure' of loss; rather it is the application of all the ordinary rules in the absence of the easy simplification that comes with the two main types of loss avoidance (recourse to the market and repair). This measure is often referred to as the 'diminution in value' because where there is damage or destruction, defect or non-delivery, or mis-construction, and no replacement or repair, the claimant is merely stuck with the damaged or defective property and/or without the desired property, and the court has to calculate how much less the property the claimant has is worth than the property the claimant should have had. However, 'diminution in value' is only one part of the rules that apply to determine what losses the claimant has suffered if it has not been able to replace or repair the property, and these may include losses through use or non-use over time, and liabilities to third parties.

4.2 The First Cure: Replacement on the Market

The market replacement measure is the measure of loss based upon the obtaining by the claimant of a replacement on the market. It is a cure that can apply both to cases where the property is destroyed or not delivered (where a replacement is bought on the market) and cases where the property is merely damaged or defective (where a replacement is bought from and the faulty property is sold to the market).

---

[3] As discussed above in section 4.1A(ii).

This is in contrast with the other major property-related cure, that of repair, which of course only applies to damaged or defective property and not to destroyed or non-delivered property.

A. In What Situations Does the Market Replacement Measure Apply?

Whether the market replacement measure applies is purely a question of mitigation and/or legal causation. The principle of mitigation deems a claimant to have done what all reasonable people in its position would have done, but only if it has not itself done it.

These principles are summarised below, under the discussion of mitigation in chapter 15 section 15.3, and in relation to sale of goods in section 4.2C.

In short:

— If the claimant goes to the market, and does so within the range of reasonable possibilities (in terms of time and which market), then the actual market price will be used to measure the damages. The claimant acted reasonably, and there was therefore no omission that broke the chain of causation and invokes the causation/mitigation principle. The actual losses are recoverable.
— If the claimant does not go to the market at all, then the law will, applying the mitigatory principle, select a reasonable market price and deem that to have been achieved, contrary to fact.
— If the claimant goes to the market but does so outside the range of reasonable times/markets, then the law will ignore the actual market price and select a reasonable market price and deem that to have been achieved, contrary to fact. In practice, it is only in the case of volatile markets or other rare circumstances that a defendant will argue that that although the claimant did go to the market, the actual market price should be ignored.

Thus in the majority of cases, as Devlin J has explained:

> Whether that is put as the price which the buyer actually gets for the [defective] goods, or whether it is put as the market price obtainable for the goods on the day when the buyer should sell them, I do not think matters very much … If he chooses not to sell the goods he is not to be put in any better or worse position by delaying for his own purposes, so that, in substance, it is the price which he actually gets on selling them, or the price which he actually could get if he did sell them.[4]

B. Situations in Which the Market Replacement Measure Does Not Apply

As explained in the previous section, the market replacement measure applies where the principles of mitigation and legal causation so provide. Nevertheless, the types of situation in which it does not apply, by application of the ordinary mitigation

---

[4] *Kwei Tek Chao v British Traders and Shippers* [1954] 2 QB 459 (Devlin J) at 494.

principle, can be identified and explained. Thus (i) below provides that the market replacement measure does not apply where market replacement is impossible. (ii) to (iv) provide that the market replacement measure does not apply where there is a cheaper or better alternative. (v), the most common in practice, arises where the claimant did not know there was anything wrong with the property until it was already too late to go to the market. And (vi) applies where a replacement would be no use because the intended use of the property requires the specific goods and where that use (a chain sub-sale) is not too remote. (vii) merely identifies the special position arising in consumer cases because of the statutory remedies available there.

(i) There is No Replacement Available on the Market or Otherwise

There are numerous cases in which there is no replacement available.[5] This arises where the property is unique, which is most common in land cases but can arise in other cases too.[6] Any presumption that damages should be measured by the market at the date of breach (which presumption applies in sale of goods cases, as discussed below) is rebutted in these cases:

> The rationale for assessing the damages at the date of breach in the case of breach of contract for the sale of goods is that if the innocent purchaser is compensated on the basis of the value of the goods as of the date of breach, the purchaser can turn around and purchase identical or equivalent goods. The purchaser is therefore placed in the same financial situation as if the contract had been kept.

> Different considerations apply where the thing which is to be purchased is unique ... The rationale that the innocent purchaser is fully compensated, if provided with the amount of money that would purchase an asset of the same value on the date of the breach, no longer applies.[7]

Similarly there is no replacement reasonably available where there are regulations restricting supply,[8] or where the property consists of internationally shipped goods needed for immediate use (which therefore cannot be replaced at the place where needed in a reasonable time).[9]

---

[5] The following are all non-delivery cases: *Grébert-Borgnis v J & W Nugent* (1885) 15 QBD 85 (CA); *Duff & Co v The Iron and Steel Fencing and Buildings Co* (1891) 19 R 199 (Court of Session, 1st Division); *Patrick v Russo-British Grain Export Co Ltd* [1927] 2 KB 535 (Salter J); *Foaminol Laboratories Ltd v British Artid Plastics Ltd* [1941] 2 All ER 393 (Hallett J); *Household Machines Ltd v Cosmos Exporters Ltd* [1947] KB 217 (Lewis J); *Lesters Leather & Skin Co Ltd v Home and Overseas Brokers Ltd* (1948) 82 Ll L Rep 202 (CA); *Coastal (Bermuda) Petroleum Ltd v VTT Vulcan Petroleum SA (No 2) (The Marine Star)* [1994] 2 Lloyd's Rep 629 (Mance J), appeal allowed on other grounds: [1996] 2 Lloyd's Rep 383 (CA); *M&J Marine Engineering Services Co Ltd v Shipshore Ltd* [2009] EWHC 2031 (Comm) (Field J).

[6] *O'Grady v Westminster Scaffolding Ltd* [1962] 2 Lloyd's Rep 238 (Edmund Davies J) as explained in *Darbishire v Warran* [1963] 1 WLR 1067 (CA); *Vanda Compania Ltda of Costa Rica v Société Maritime Nationale of Paris (The Ile Aux Moines)* [1974] 2 Lloyd's Rep 502 (Mocatta J) (specialised ship, although the issue was wrapped up in pleading points); *Zakrzewski v Chas J Odhams & Sons* [1981] 2 EGLR 15 (Rougier QC) (the availability of the market had not yet been decided at the date of the hearing);.

[7] *Semelhago v Paramadevan* [1996] 2 SCR 415 (SC of Canada) Sopinka J at paras 13–14.

[8] *J Leavey & Co Ltd v George H Hirst & Co Ltd* [1944] KB 24 (CA).

[9] Eg *Duff & Co v The Iron and Steel Fencing and Buildings Co* (1891) 19 R 199 (Court of Session, 1st Division); *Montevideo Gas and Drydock Co Ltd v Clan Line Steamers Ltd* (1921) 6 Ll L Rep 539

(ii) Replacement is Unreasonably Expensive or Onerous (Including Where Repair is Cheaper)

Occasionally the replacement will be held to be unreasonably expensive or difficult. This was found by the Court of Appeal, overturning Steyn J, in the non-delivery case of *The Alecos M*, where there was no market for spare propellers and although the claimant could have had one manufactured, the £150,000 cost of so doing was disproportionate to the value to the claimant of the spare propeller; the claimant had no genuine intention of manufacturing one; and spare propellers were not generally considered necessary.[10] Only the propeller's scrap value was awarded. The same issue arose in *Robot Arenas Ltd v Waterfield*, where the former set of the television series 'Robot Wars' had only scrap value and was unreasonable to replace.[11] Similarly, in *Cullinane v British 'Rema' Manufacturing Co Ltd* it would have been too much to expect the purchaser of a machine which worked but operated at below the warranted rate to replace it, given that it would require large dismantling costs, enlargement of the building, and a long delay.[12] And in another case, the impecuniosity of the claimant and effects of inflation may have made it unreasonable to expect the claimant to purchase replacement land.[13] Further, in some cases replacement may be unreasonable because the property was already about to be replaced.[14]

One might contrast the unusual case of *Diamond Cutting Works Federation Ltd v Triefus & Co*,[15] where the financial bottom line was not the only factor. In that case the claimant was an Israeli non-profit-making trade body which purchased diamonds and sold them on to its members at cost price. Although the claimant buyer therefore would have suffered no loss of profit as a result of the non-supply (because it sold the diamonds at cost), it was still entitled to recover the extra cost of purchasing replacement diamonds (for its members) on the market. This must be because it was reasonable to replace the goods for reasons other than profit. The same result was reached in the High Court of Australia's decision in *Clark v Macourt*.[16] It was reasonable for a doctor who had bought a reproductive services practice with unusable sperm (because they did not have the appropriate accompanying records) to purchase replacement sperm at a price of over $1m, even though for ethical and regulatory reasons she only ever sold the sperm on at a little less than cost price. Here it was reasonable for the claimant to replace the sperm so that she could continue to provide her assisted reproduction services. (The more difficult

---

(Roche J) affirmed (1921) 8 Ll L Rep 192 (CA); *Frank Mott & Co Ltd v Wm H Muller & Co (London) Ltd* (1922) 13 Ll L Rep 492 (Rowlatt J).

[10] *Sealace Shipping Co Ltd v Oceanvoice Ltd (The Alecos M)* [1991] 1 Lloyd's Rep 120 (CA), approved by Lord Lloyd in *Ruxley Electronics and Construction Ltd v Forsyth* [1996] AC 344 (HL) at 371.

[11] *Robot Arenas Ltd v Waterfield.* [2010] EWHC 115 (QB) (Edelman QC) at paras 99–100.

[12] *Cullinane v British 'Rema' Manufacturing Co Ltd* [1954] 1 QB 292 (CA) at 314.

[13] *Zakrzewski v Chas J Odhams & Sons* [1981] 2 EGLR 15 (Rougier QC) at 17.

[14] See the tort case of *Southampton Container Terminals Ltd v Schiffarhts-Gesellshcaft 'Hansa Australia' mbH & Co (The Maersk Colombo)* [2001] 2 Lloyd's Rep 275 (CA).

[15] *Diamond Cutting Works Federation Ltd v Triefus & Co Ltd* [1956] 1 Lloyd's Rep 216 (Barry J) at 227.

[16] *Clark v Macourt* [2013] HCA 56 (HC of Australia).

question in these cases was why the courts found that the claimants had suffered any loss, given that they recouped the majority of their costs of the replacements from their onward buyers.[17])

In damaged or defective land cases and defective building works cases the transactional costs, including stamp duty land tax, will often make it unreasonably expensive to cure a defect by selling the land and purchasing a replacement that does not have the defect, even when such a replacement is available. The usual measure in such cases will be the cost of repair, as in cases of damage to ships.[18] The more minor the defect compared with the value of the property, the more likely it is that repair will be more reasonable than complete replacement.[19] The test for reasonableness of repair is discussed below in section 4.3B. Where the repair cost is unreasonable and the replacement cost is also unreasonable the ordinary difference in value and other losses measure (section 4.5 below) applies.[20]

Despite the above, the court is not usually concerned with what the claimant does with its damages, and where replacement is reasonable it will not necessarily matter that the claimant is not in fact going to replace the property (for example because it has decided to move part of its facility elsewhere for its own reasons).[21]

(iii) *The Goods are Intended for a Sale to the Market and the Selling Price is Lower than the Buying Price*

Logically, although replacement will be the normal measure where the goods are intended for practical use,[22] where the contemplated employment of the property is simply a sale to the market for profit, and the cost of purchasing a replacement on the market is greater than the cost of selling to the market, the market replacement measure should not be applied, as it would be unreasonable to purchase goods only to sell them to the market at a lower price than they were just purchased. Instead damages based on the lost profit from the market selling price should be awarded.

---

[17] See the discussion below at text to n 388.

[18] See the discussion below in section 4.2D(iii).

[19] *Parsons (Livestock) Ltd v Uttley Ingham & Co Ltd* [1978] QB 791 (CA) is a vivid example: the only defect in the food hopper was that its ventilator had not been open at the time of delivery. Opening that ventilator was the only cure needed, and clearly selling the hopper and purchasing a replacement with an open ventilator would be ludicrously unreasonable (and unsurprisingly the point did not arise; the only dispute was as to the harm caused before the ventilator was opened). And see *Whitecap Leisure Ltd v John H Rundle Ltd* [2007] EWHC 1352 (QB) (Foster J) at para 95, where the cost of replacement was only available if the 'system was beyond economic repair to render it of satisfactory quality and fit for its purpose'. This was overturned on the issue of rejection: [2008] EWCA Civ 429. Or it may be that the defect makes no difference at all to value and so no replacement or repair is needed: eg *Taylor & Sons Ltd v Bank of Athens* (1922) 91 LJKB 776 (McCardie J), where the defect in the documents for a documentary sale of locust beans, namely that the goods had been shipped and the documents signed late, made no difference to their value at the date of delivery.

[20] Eg *Tito v Waddell (No 2)* [1977] Ch 106 (Megarry V-C) (damages reserved for later assessment); *Ruxley Electronics and Construction Ltd v Forsyth* [1996] AC 344 (HL) (damages for £2,500 lost amenity, zero financial difference in value).

[21] See *Mueller Europe Ltd v Central Roofing (South Wales) Ltd* [2013] EWHC 237 (TCC) (Stuart-Smith J) at para 148.

[22] Eg the dredger in *Owners of Dredger Liesbosch v Owners of SS Edison (The Liesbosch)* [1933] AC 449 (HL).

The case law is not entirely consistent on this point: see the discussion below in section 4.5A(ii)(a).

(iv) It is More Reasonable to Re-contract with the Seller

In contract of sale cases, it may be reasonable for the buyer to re-negotiate with the seller and ultimately re-contract. If that is the case, the loss will be measured in the light of that replacement contract, rather than by the market measure.[23] If the renegotiations fall through, the market (or other appropriate) price will be taken at the later date when the buyer should have gone to the market.[24]

(v) Latent Defects that Have Caused Loss before Discovery

Latent defects (or damage) provide a specific problem because the claimant does not know about the defect until the property has been employed. In those circumstances, and depending upon what the employment of the property entails, the claimant usually cannot be expected to mitigate the loss by repair or market replacement because it was unaware of the need for any mitigation until it was too late.

In contrast, in *patent* defect cases the loss will usually be reasonably avoidable by repair or by replacement on the market, rather than using the defective goods or selling them on without disclosing the defect, which actions can lead to further losses. (Where the defect was always patent, the relevant market replacement would be expected to take place at or shortly after the date of delivery. Where the defect was initially latent but was discovered before the property had been on-sold or modified, the relevant market replacement will be expected to take place at or shortly after the date of discovery of the defect.[25])

The unavoidable losses that arise will depend upon the use to which the property was put.[26] If the goods were on-sold (either before or after processing) before the defect was discovered, the losses will consist of lost profits on the sub-sale and liability to the sub-buyer. If the goods were employed in use (eg a machine employed in an industrial process) the loss may again be in profits, or damage to other property.

The problem of the latent defect in property is almost exclusively one arising in contracts for supply, as it is very rare that property will be latently *damaged*, ie damaged in the course of contractual performance without the claimant knowing about it.

(a) Introduction to Remoteness and Latent Defects

It is very important when considering latent damage cases to understand that the remoteness and mitigation principles operate very differently in the context of sub-sales

---

[23] *R Pagnan & Fratelli v Corbisa Industrial Agropacuaria Limitada* [1970] 1 WLR 1306 (CA). See further below in chapter sixteen, section 16.9C.
[24] See above in section 17.2B (i).
[25] See section 4.2(B)(v)(f) below.
[26] See further below in section 4.5.

of latently defective property to their operation in the context of sub-sales where property is not delivered or is patently defective.

By way of contrast, in the non-delivery situation, when it is being asked whether damages should be measured by reference to the lost profits or the liabilities on a sub-sale, the question is whether it is within the scope of the defendant's responsibility not only that the claimant would sell the goods (which will almost never be too remote), and not only that the claimant would *pre*-sell the goods (which will usually be too remote), but that the claimant would pre-sell the goods on a string contract which could only be satisfied by the contractual goods (which will almost always be too remote). Without the last of these being true and within contemplation, the loss on the sub-sale would have been avoidable by market replacement and therefore irrecoverable.

In a latent damage case, liability to the sub-buyer arises simply from the defect being latent and the buyer having sold the goods before discovering the defect. This loss arises on all sales, whether forward sales agreed prior to delivery by the defendant or ordinary market sales entered into after delivery. It cannot have been expected to be avoided by market replacement, because the claimant could not have known of the need to replace. It is not dependent upon what price the sub-sale was made at or with whom, and does not depend upon the sub-sale being part of a chain contract. It merely depends on the sub-sale including a similar description or warranty to the head contract, as will usually be the case, such that the (latent) breach of the head contract leads to a breach of the sub-contract.[27] The point is clearly made by Lord Goddard CJ in *Hammond v Bussey*:

> At the time when the defendant sold the coal, he knew that the plaintiffs were buying the coal in order to sell it again to the owners of steamers calling at Dover to be used as steam-coal on such steamers; and he therefore knew that the plaintiffs would enter into contracts with others similar to the contract he himself had made with the plaintiffs, that is to say, into contracts for the sale of steam-coal, which would amount to a warranty that the coal was reasonably fit to be used for the purposes of steam-coal on board steamers. He did not know, it is true, with what specific persons the plaintiffs would make such contracts, but that seems to me immaterial. The defendant supplied under the contract coal that was not reasonably fit to be used as such steam-coal, that is to say, something different from that which he had contracted to supply. The fact that this was so was not a fact which would be patent to the plaintiffs on inspection of the coal; it could only be found out when it came to be used, which was not by the plaintiffs but by their sub-vendees. Such a breach of such a contract with regard to such a subject-matter necessarily made the plaintiffs liable to an action by their sub-vendees, and the result was the plaintiffs were sued for damages by their sub-vendees.[28]

In contrast with the claim in relation to the claimant's liability to the sub-buyer, the lost profits claim in a latent damage case, where the sub-buyer rejects the goods for the defect, is a different type of loss and a different matter. That loss will depend upon the price at which the sub-sale was made, and therefore whether the sub-sale was a forward contract (entered into before the defendant delivered or should have

---

[27] Confusion on just this point can be seen for example in the obiter discussion in *Choil Trading SA v Sahara Energy Resources Ltd* [2010] EWHC 374 (Comm) (Clarke J) at paras 123–30.
[28] *Hammond v Bussey* (1887) 20 QBD 79 (CA) at 86. See also Bowen LJ at 94–95.

delivered the goods) or not. Although the loss was still unavoidable, even without a string sub-contract (one that requires exactly the same goods as were bought under the head sale) it will still depend upon whether the buyer pre-sold the goods and if so when and at what price. Such a pre-sale will often not be within the seller's responsibility, or in some cases a lost profit of a market sale will be, but not the lost profit on a forward sale (as the defendant could have expected the ordinary prompt market sale but not to be exposed to a forward sale at an uncertain time in advance of the date of delivery).

(b) Straight Sub-Sale of Latent Property without Modification of the Property

Where property is merely on-sold with the defect still latent, the losses on the sub-sale will usually be within the parties' contemplation, and could not reasonably have been avoided. As has been observed in a late delivery case, 'everybody who sells to a merchant knows that he has bought for re-sale'.[29]

The classic example is the case of seeds. A defect in seeds will usually only be discovered after the seeds have been planted by the sub-buyer. In *Randall v Raper*[30] there was a sale of seed barley warranted to be chevalier seed barley, although in fact of inferior quality. The buyer claimant resold to four sub-buyers with the same warranty, and they brought claims for lost profits after the defect came to light. The claimant recovered damages measured by his liability to the sub-buyers. As Lord Campbell CJ observed: 'It was a probable, natural, even a necessary consequence of this seed not being chevalier barley that that it did not produce the expected quantity of grain'.[31] Similarly where mink food was made up and sold but did not meet the required formula, the buyer could claim for an indemnity for its liability on on-sale,[32] also where a fur was sub-sold for use and caused dermatitis and a claim for personal injury.[33]

In *Biggin v Permanite*,[34] some latently defective roofing adhesive was on-sold for use in repairing Dutch roofs after WWII, leading to claims by the users. The measure of loss was found by Devlin J to be the purchaser's liability to its on-buyers. Devlin J observed:

> It has often been held—I have already referred to the authorities—that the profit actually made on a subsale which is outside the contemplation of the parties cannot be used to reduce the damages measured by a notional loss in market value. If, however, a subsale is within the contemplation of the parties, I think that the damages must be assessed by reference to it, whether the plaintiff likes it or not. Suppose that the only fault in the compound was its incompatibility with bitumen felt, the chance that it might produce bad

---

[29] *Kwei Tek Chao v British Traders and Shippers Ltd* [1954] 2 QB 459 (Devlin J) at 489.

[30] *Randall v Raper* (1858) EB & E 84.

[31] Likewise where seed is being used by the defendant rather than sold: see text to n 42 below.

[32] *Ashington Piggeries Ltd v Christopher Hill Ltd* [1972] AC 441 (HL). See also *Pinnock Bros v Lewis & Peat Ltd* [1923] 1 KB 690 (Roche J) where the sale of copra cake for ultimate use as cattle food was contemplated; *Butterworth v Kingsway Motors Ltd* [1954] 2 All ER 694 (Pearson J) where resale of a car was contemplated (this was a case of breach of warranty of title but the title was ultimately fed and the sales affirmed, save for the final sale in the chain to the claimant, so the case was in effect one of a latent defect later discovered and cured).

[33] *Sidney Bennett Ltd v Kreeger* (1925) 41 TLR 609 (Branson J).

[34] *Biggin & Co Ltd v Permanite Ltd* [1951] 1 KB 422 (Devlin J) at 435–36.

results would certainly reduce its market value before use. But if it is the plaintiff's liability to the ultimate user that is contemplated as the measure of damage and if in fact it is used without injurious results so that no such liability arises, the plaintiff could not claim the difference in market value, and say that the subsale must be disregarded. I say this so as to make it clear, that although I have come to the conclusion that, if the plaintiffs' basic claim fails, they can to some extent rely on the alternative of difference in market value, it is not because I think the plaintiffs have an option in the matter.

... Liability for physical damage remains the criterion of loss ... The liability for physical damage remains the primary measure of liability contemplated by the parties. The result is that in respect of compound sold after September 30, from whose use no physical damage resulted, the plaintiffs can claim nothing: in the case of any quantity from whose use physical damage has resulted, the plaintiffs may obtain (subject to the next point) the cost of making good, etc., or the difference in market value, whichever is the less.

One of the important points Devlin J makes here is that where it is contemplated that goods would be sold with the defect still latent, and they were so sold, market value is irrelevant, whether the difference in market value at the date of delivery would provide a greater or smaller loss than the actual loss on the sub-sale. The actual loss was on the sub-sale, this was not too remote, and so this is the measure of loss.[35]

As Devlin J explained: 'It is, no doubt, true that [the finding that a loss is not too remote] generally operates in favour of a plaintiff rather than against him, but I think that it is capable of doing either'.[36] This approach was applied in the New Zealand decision in *McSherry v Coopers Creek Vineyard Ltd*.[37] The claimant purchased wine for resale, but the wine did not match and was inferior to its label and its description. This was not discovered (or discoverable) until after the sale to the consumers. None of the customers complained and so the claimant got away with it. Although the market value of the wine as delivered was less than the market value as promised, the claimant actually sold the wine and this was a not too remote use of the wine. Accordingly, the loss had to be measured by the sub-sale for better or worse. In that case it was, from the claimant's point of view, for worse, and only nominal damages were awarded. Similarly, in another case where the claimant bought from the defendant and on-sold contaminated alcoholic fizzy drinks (called Bacardi Breezer), the claimant recovered the costs of an expensive product recall.[38] Here the loss had to be measured by the sub-sale, but unlike in *McSherry* and *Bence Graphics*, there was a significant loss. And similarly in a case where the claimant

---

[35] In fact, in *Biggin* there had been a reasonable compromise between the claimant and sub-buyers at £43,000, and the Court of Appeal allowed the appeal, holding that this should be the measure of loss and not Devlin J's assessment of the claimant's liability to the sub-buyers, ignoring the compromise. Thus the Court of Appeal awarded the actual loss, rather than Devlin J's deemed loss (which was the actual loss after the settlement was deemed not to have taken place). However, no doubt was cast on the remainder of Devlin J's judgment and principles, nor did the Court of Appeal ever suggest that the market value should be the measure of recovery: [1951] 2 KB 314 (CA).

[36] *Biggin & Co Ltd v Permanite Ltd* [1951] 1 KB 422 at 436.

[37] *McSherry v Coopers Creek Vineyard Ltd* (2005) 8 NZBLC 101 (Panckhurst J).

[38] *Bacardi-Martini Beverages Ltd v Thomas Hardy Packaging Ltd* [2002] 1 Lloyd's Rep 62 (Tomlinson J) affirmed [2002] 2 Lloyd's Rep 379 (CA). The damages between the claimant and defendant were agreed on the second day of trial: see [2002] 1 Lloyd's Rep 62 at para 13. See also *Garside v Black Horse Ltd* [2010] EWHC 190 (QB) (King J) (car rejected by hire purchaser as a result of defect).

had used unsafe carbon dioxide in its fizzy drinks the costs of the product recall and destruction were recoverable.[39]

It should be noted that the recoverability from the defendant of the sub-sale liability depends not only upon the fact of the sub-sale being not too remote but also upon the breached terms of the sub-sale not being too remote[40] (otherwise recovery may be limited to what it would have been on more ordinary sub-sale terms[41]).

(c) Where the Latently Defective Property was to be Processed then Sub-Sold

Remoteness issues may arise where the goods are not merely on-sold but are modified, processed or incorporated into a particular product before use. The sale of latently defective animal food provides a good example. Remoteness will rarely be a problem in such a case because, as was observed in one case (about computer capacitors) 'one cannot in good conscience say that one is buying or selling animal feed and yet claim to be oblivious to what it is used for'.[42] Thus, where the incorporation of groundnut extractions into cattle and poultry food compounds was contemplated, and it was also known that poultry food might be fed to young pheasants, the amount of the liability of the buyer of the groundnut extractions to the buyers of the food compounds whose pheasants died was recoverable.[43]

Seed cases, again, provide good examples. Thus in one case lost profits for potato crops were recovered where the defect in the seeds (they were described as 'Early Don Regents' but also had some 'Bastard' seeds mixed in) was not discoverable by reasonably intermediate examination prior to the crop being harvested; ie the defect was latent.[44]

Remoteness will frequently not be a problem in cases of processed latently defective goods. In *Kasler & Cohen v Slavouski*,[45] the supplier of dyed rabbit skins knew the claimant buyer was a furrier who was using them to make coat fur collars. The coat was sold to a coat-buyer, on to a sub-buyer, on to a draper, and then on to the consumer, who claimed against the draper who passed the claim up the chain. The

---

[39] *Britvic Soft Drinks Ltd v Messer UK Ltd* [2002] 1 Lloyd's Rep 20 (Tomlinson J), affirmed [2002] 2 Lloyd's Rep 368 (CA).

[40] See Devlin J in *Biggin & Co Ltd v Permanite Ltd* [1951] 1 KB 422 at 433: 'If the variation to a description is such that it is impossible to say whether the injury that ultimately results would have flowed from the breach of the original warranty, the parties must as reasonable men be presumed to have put the liability for the injury outside their contemplation as a measure of compensation ... Suppose that all the Dutch government did in their subsales was to add to the original warranties given to them by the plaintiffs a guarantee that the compound could be used at any time within two years, whereas in fact it was usable only for one year after manufacture. Looked at generally, that is a material addition, but if, in fact, it had been used within one year with injurious results, the additional warranty ought not, I apprehend, to bar the claim ... When the terms of each Dutch contract and the nature of the physical damage are known, I think that the test will be whether the Dutch government could show that the whole of its liabilities to the contractor arose from the failure of the compound to behave as warranted by the plaintiffs'. Contrast *Dexters Ltd v Hill Crest Oil Co (Bradford) Ltd* [1926] 1 KB 348 (CA).

[41] See below in chapter fourteen, section 14.4.

[42] *Britestone Pte Ltd v Smith & Associates Far East Ltd* [2007] SGCA 47 (Singapore CA) Rajah JA at para 23.

[43] *Henry Kendall & Sons v William Lillico & Sons Ltd* [1969] 2 AC 31 (HL).

[44] *Wagstaff v Short-horn Dairy Co* (1884) Cab & El 324. See also *George Mitchell (Chesterhall) Ltd v Finney Lock Seeds Ltd* [1983] 2 AC 803 (HL) (cabbage seed producing 60 acres of unmerchantable cabbage, although the lost profits were irrecoverable due to a limitation clause that was upheld).

[45] *Kasler & Cohen v Slavouski* [1928] 1 KB 78 (Branson J).

claimant recovered for its liability to the buyer of the coat (including costs), and the liability was accordingly passed up the chain from the ultimate consumer through to the claimant and on to the defendant supplier.

And in a Canadian case on the supply of defective fabric used by the claimant in swimming pool covers, Cory J had no problems in finding that lost profits would naturally result from the breach:

> Most commercial contracts pertaining to the sale and delivery of material or goods must, of necessity, be entered into with a view to making a profit in the future. To say otherwise would amount to a denial of the profit motive in the free enterprise system. The case at bar is a prime example. The plaintiff made known to the defendant that it wished to manufacture and sell a specific type of pool cover. It had determined that there was a profit to be made. It was to secure such a profit that it entered into the contract with Thiokol to supply the material for the manufacture of the pool covers.

> Let us consider the unlikely scenario wherein the executive or board of directors of Thiokol sat down and discussed what was likely to happen if they supplied defective material to Tarpoly (the plaintiff) …The Thiokol executives would have foreseen or contemplated the very effects that befell Tarpoly.[46]

The same applied where latently defective mortar led to the costs of having to demolish and rebuild a building and a loss of ground rent profits, given that the claimant could not by reasonable diligence have discovered the defects in the mortar before using it;[47] likewise where defective steel damaged the claimant's machine and required repair.[48]

The leading case on latent defects is the controversial but correct decision of the Court of Appeal in *Bence Graphics International Ltd v Fasson UK Ltd*,[49] which is typically contrasted with the Court of Appeal decision in *Slater v Hoyle*, discussed below.[50] In *Bence Graphics* some vinyl film bought for £564,328 was not as durable as warranted, and the trial judge found as a fact that (perhaps somewhat surprisingly) the film actually delivered was worthless. The film had been bought as a raw material for the claimant's manufacture of decals (shipping container labels). The vast majority of the film, all but about £22,000-worth, was processed in this way and sold on as decals before the claimant became aware (or could have become aware) of the defect.

In fact, very few purchasers of those labels complained or claimed against the claimant. Following *Slater* and applying the prima facie measure in section 53(3) of the Sale of Goods Act 1979, the trial judge awarded £564,328, being the difference between the price paid (this figure) and the market value of the goods delivered (zero). The Court of Appeal reduced the award to £22,000, the difference between the price paid and market value of the small amount of film that had not been sold on and would not now be sold on, plus the amount of consequential loss suffered by

---

[46] *Canlin Ltd v Thiokol Fibres Canada Ltd* (1983) 142 DLR (3d) 450 (Ont CA) Cory J at paras 12–13.
[47] *Smith v Johnson* (1899) 15 TLR 179.
[48] *Bacon v Cooper (Metals) Ltd* [1982] 1 All ER 397 (Cantley J).
[49] *Bence Graphics International Ltd v Fasson UK Ltd* [1998] QB 87 (CA).
[50] See section 4.2(B)(v)(g).

reason of claims by label purchasers against the claimants (such a sum to be assessed but unlikely to be large) in relation to the film that had been sold on. The majority of the Court of Appeal,[51] disagreeing with the trial judge, found that the use of the vinyl to make decals was within the parties' contemplation.[52] This follows the result, mentioned in the previous section on sub-sale of unprocessed latently defective goods and *Biggin v Permanite* and *McSherry v Cooper's Creek*, that where a use is not too remote, and the loss could not reasonably have been avoided by recourse to the market (because the defect was latent), then the *actual* loss by that use is the correct measure, whether greater or smaller than the market measure.[53] As Otton LJ observed in *Bence Graphics*,

> If the buyer uses the goods to make some product out of them the value of the goods is not taken [as the measure of loss]

and

> the damages must be assessed by reference to the sub-sale 'whether the plaintiff likes it or not.' Thus the plaintiff does not have the option to choose which outcome is most favourable to him. It is for the court to determine the correct measure of damage, not the aggrieved party. Where the court determines the proper measure the effect of the choice may reduce the amount of damages claimed or increase it.[54]

The decision in *Bence Graphics* has been said by Christopher Clarke J in a later decision to have recognised the following:

> (a) that the principle in Hadley v Baxendale is one of 'recovery of true loss and no more (or less), namely to put the complaining party, so far as money can do it, in the position he would have been if the contract [had] been performed'; (b) that 'the ... loss directly and naturally resulting, in the ordinary course of events, from the breach of warranty' includes loss that the parties, in their state of knowledge, must be taken to have contemplated; (c) that the application of that test may mean that a difference in value test is inapplicable; (d) the importance of principle over practicality and (e) the potential significance of seeing what the buyer has done with the goods in determining the damages to which he is to be entitled.[55]

This is a perceptive commentary on remoteness in this sort of case. Point (c) deserves emphasising: where what the buyer has done with the goods (point (e)) falls within the remoteness test (points (a) and (b)) then the difference in value test is not applicable and damages are measured by the actual losses. As per point (d), these principles must prevail over the practicality of a 'difference in value at the date of delivery' test.

Similarly, in a Singapore case, capacitors were resold on a sub-sale and the sub-buyer incorporated them into circuit boards, at which time the defect in the

---

[51] *Bence Graphics International Ltd v Fasson UK Ltd* [1998] QB 87, Thorpe LJ dissenting.
[52] Ibid Otton LJ at 100, Auld LJ at 106–7.
[53] See above in section 4.2(B)(v)(b).
[54] *Bence Graphics International Ltd v Fasson UK Ltd* [1998] QB 87 (CA). [1998] QB 87 (CA) at 98 and 100.
[55] *Transfield Shipping Inc v Mercator Shipping Inc (The Achilleas)* [2006] EWHC 3030 (Comm) at para 88 (ultimately overturned on application of the remoteness test by the House of Lords at [2009] AC 61 (HL)).

capacitors (that they were counterfeit) was discovered and the sub-buyer performed an expensive purging exercise to recall and replace the counterfeit capacitors, and sought to pass that cost up the chain of sales to the defendant vendor. There was no problem with remoteness, as capacitors are only ever used in circuit boards so the seller must have known that they would be so used by a sub-buyer, and further the defect was latent. *Bence Graphics* was applied and the sub-sale measured the loss.[56]

In *GKN Centrax Gears Ltd v Matbro Ltd*[57] some defective axles were sold to the claimant, who incorporated them into its fork lift trucks, which broke down because the axles could not take the necessary load. There was no remoteness issue as 'Centrax knew as well as anybody the purpose for which these axles were required',[58] and the claimant recovered not only for the cost of settling a claim from a sub-buyer and the costs of modifying some of the sold trucks and repairing others, ie the losses on the sub-sales, but also for lost profits on future sales that would have been made to the particular sub-buyers who ceased to order from the claimant.

(d) Where the Latently Defective Property was to be Used in Some
    Other Way: Commercial Use

The same rules apply even where the property was not immediately sold on or processed for sub-sale, but used in some other way. The number of commercial uses of property is almost limitless. The question of whether or not the use, and therefore the damage from the latent defect, was too remote will be tested on a case by case basis, but where not too remote the actual loss from that use is the true measure of loss; any difference in market value of the goods is totally irrelevant: but for the breach the claimant would not have realised the higher value by a straight market sale, so that is not its loss.

In one case the defendant supplied chains which were used to pull conveyor belts that were involved in the manufacture in ovens of fibreglass insulation products. Defects in the chains were discovered about fourteen months after installation, and the chains were replaced. The claimant recovered the cost of the replacement plus lost profits.[59] In the famous case of *Parsons (Livestock) Ltd v Uttley Ingham & Co Ltd*,[60] the claimant recovered for the damage caused to its pigs as a result of the feeding to them of mouldy pignuts. The mouldiness was caused during the period before the 'defect' in the food hopper supplied by the defendant was than cured by the opening of its ventilator. In *Zakrzewski v Chas J Odhams & Sons*, the defect in

---

[56] *Britestone Pte Ltd v Smith & Associates Far East Ltd* [2007] SGCA 47 (Singapore CA).

[57] *GKN Centrax Gears Ltd v Matbro Ltd* [1976] 2 Lloyd's Rep 555 (CA).

[58] Ibid at 574 (Denning LJ) also 577 (Stephenson LJ).

[59] *Renold Australia Pty Ltd v Fletcher Insulation (Vic) Pty Ltd* [2007] VSCA 294 (Victoria CA). See also *Harbutt's 'Plasticine' Ltd v Wayne Tank & Pump Co Ltd* [1970] 1 QB 447 (CA); *RG McLean Ltd v Canadian Vickers Ltd* (1970) 15 DLR (3d) 15 (Ontario CA) (sale of defective printing press led to lost profits); *Sunnyside Greenhouses Ltd v Golden West Seeds Ltd* (1972) 27 DLR (3d) 434 (Alberta CA), affirmed (1973) 33 DLR (3d) 384 (sale of defective greenhouse panels which caused lost profit from crops); *Burns v MAN Automotive (Aust) Pty Ltd* (1986) 161 CLR 653 (HC of Australia) (defective diesel prime mover locomotive).

[60] *Parsons (Livestock) Ltd v Uttley Ingham & Co Ltd* [1978] QB 791 (CA). But see the discussion below at chapter sixteen, text to n 27.

an income-producing piece of real property meant that damages were to be assessed after the defect was discovered, and would not be assessed on the basis of a market replacement, if there wasn't a market (that factual point had not yet been decided) or inflation made it too expensive for the claimant to go to the market.[61]

The 2002 decision in *Great Future International v Sealand Housing Corp*,[62] however, provides some cause for concern. The claimant entered a subscription agreement in 1997 for purchase for US$49m of shares from the defendant as a long-term investment. In other words, the shares were bought for resale to the market, but after a period of time rather than immediately. There were breaches of contractual warranties and the purchase was induced by tortious misstatements and deceit. On discovery of the deceit in 1999, the claimant reasonably elected to 'adopt' the purchase (rather than selling out)[63] and fought the defendant for control of the company, funded a receivership of the company at a cost of US$3.4m, and sought performance of its contracts in the face of harassment and opposition.[64] These efforts were largely successful and by the date of assessment the shares had recovered much of their value. Further, Lightman J rejected the defendant's arguments that the claimant had failed to mitigate by not doing a particular deal in 2001–02, not least because the shares had been bought as a long-term investment[65] and the claimant was willing to sell but a serious and good faith offer never came forward.[66]

Lightman J found (as was not disputed) that the claimant had to give credit for sale of approximately US$3m of the shares the day after acquisition in 1997, and also found the claimant had to give credit for the US$1 received on sale of further shares in 2001 as part of a deal to pass on the costs of funding the disputes with the defendant. Otherwise, the judge ordered that damages be assessed after deduction of the actual value of the shares at the date of acquisition in 1997. The motivation for this seems to have been that otherwise the postponement of the date of valuation would have benefited the wrongdoer defendant.[67]

As a matter of principle, this is not without difficulties. If the correct date of assessment was 1997 because the claimant could be assumed to have sold the shares then, then there should have been no investigation into any subsequently credits (the deal in 2001 producing US$1) or subsequent failure to mitigate by not doing a deal in 2001–02 (such failure investigated but ultimately not found). Moreover, given that the shares were bought as a long-term investment and the fraud not discovered until 1999, that date (not contended for by either side) should prima facie be the appropriate date for assessment: the claimant could not be expected to sell the shares earlier (and was in effect locked-in by having purchased for a long-term investment as in *Smith New Court Securities*)[68] and was free to sell the shares in

---

[61] *Zakrzewski v Chas J Odhams & Sons* [1981] 2 EGLR 15 (Rougier QC) at 17.
[62] *Great Future International Ltd v Sealand Housing Corp* [2002] EWHC 2454 (Ch) (Lightman J), appeal allowed on an evidential point [2002] EWCA Civ 1183.
[63] Ibid Lightman J at paras 27(b), 29, 147 and 174.
[64] Ibid para 149.
[65] See para 147.
[66] Ibid paras 149–51.
[67] Ibid para 29.
[68] See below in chapter seventeen, section 17.3B(vi).

1999, and indeed failure to sell then would be speculation on its part and at its own risk. If, however, retaining the shares beyond that date and pursuing the defendants were reasonable means of mitigating loss (and not steps that were above and beyond the call of duty and not legally caused by the breach)—because there was no real market for the shares (there was some evidence to support that) and/or the shares were a long-term investment—then the date of assessment should have been the date of trial, as the defendant contended. However, the claimant should have recovered the costs of pursuing the defendant through receivership and other means (which costs were apparently not sought by the claimant).[69]

Overall there is in fact no problem with the decision because the issue was already *res judicata* as a result of an earlier consent order agreeing to the date of acquisition as the date for the assessment,[70] but there remain concerns about the obiter reasoning of Lightman J in which he considered the above points despite the existence of the consent order.

A similar lack of clarity arose in *Naughton v Callaghan*, also a case of both breach of warranty and misrepresentation.[71] The decision is discussed below, but one clear factual feature there, and the important one for the purposes of this discussion of latent defects, was that the claimant was not expected to sell the defective horse until the defect was discovered.

(e) Where the Latently Defective Property was to be Used in Some Other Way: Consumer Use

Perhaps the most obvious examples of non-remote damage caused by use of latently defective goods are cases of personal injury caused by products used as intended by claimant consumer buyers. Reported examples include beer containing arsenic,[72] woollen underwear containing sulphites and so causing dermatitis,[73] and a toy catapult causing a child to lose his eye.[74] Recovery may also include costs resulting from personal injury to or death of the claimant's family member,[75] the loss caused by physical damage to the claimant's property as a result of the defect,[76] or liability to third parties.[77]

---

[69] And it should not matter that the increased value of the shares was a result of these efforts—Lightman J at para 27(e)—since that is to say no more than that the mitigation was successful. Had the efforts been wasted the claimant could still have recovered their cost.

[70] Ibid paras 31–37.

[71] See chapter seventeen, section 17.3B(i).

[72] *Wren v Holt* [1903] 1 KB 610 (CA).

[73] *Grant v Australian Knitting Mills* [1936] AC 85 (PC).

[74] *Godley v Perry* [1960] 1 WLR 9 (Edmund Davies J).

[75] *Preist v Last* [1903] 2 KB 148 (CA) (costs of treatment of the claimant's wife when a hot water bottle burst and scalded her); *Frost v Aylesbury Dairy Co* [1905] 1 KB 608 (CA) (costs and expenses caused by claimant's wife's illness and death from typhoid caused by the defendant's infected milk); *Jackson v Watson & Sons* [1909] 2 KB 193 (CA) (costs of a housekeeper to replace the claimant's wife who died after eating the defendant's tinned salmon).

[76] Eg *Wilson v Rickett, Cockerell & Co Ltd* [1954] 1 QB 598 (CA) (explosive coal, liability for damage to furniture and other property).

[77] Eg *Lexmead (Basingstoke) Ltd v Lewis* [1982] AC 225 (HL), although liability was not found in that case, as the claimant had continued to use the defective coupling after discovery of the defect and so had broken the chain of causation.

(f) Contrast Patent Defect Cases

As explained above,[78] in cases of patent defects, the usual measure is the difference between the price and the market value as, in the usual way, the claimant can be expected to avoid most of its losses by selling the defective property on the market and buying a non-defective replacement. This mitigatory step is available to the claimant because the claimant knows about the defect. (Moreover, if the claimant did continue to use the defective property in the knowledge of its defect that would ordinarily break the chain of causation between the breach and the harm.[79])

Thus in *Jones v Just*[80] the sea water damage to the purchased Manilla hemp was discovered on delivery. The recovery was the difference between the value of the hemp as promised and the value at the date of delivery, and not the earlier date of the sale.

Where a defect was initially latent, ie not discovered on delivery, but was discovered before the property had been sold on, modified or used, the market value will be taken at the date on which the claimant discovered the defect and should have replaced the property.[81] Thus in *Applegate v Moss* the claimant buyer of a house did not, because of the defendant's concealment, discover the defect until eight years after purchase.[82] The difference between actual value (by then, zero) and market value was taken at that later date. Another good example is *Bominflot Bunkergesellschaft für Mineralöle mbH & Co v Petroplus Marketing AG*.[83] There, Hamblen J confirmed that in a case of a latent defect that did not become patent until after delivery, where on discovery of the defect the buyer acted reasonably in seeking to minimise its loss:

> the starting point should be the date on which the Buyer discovered the problem. Moreover, where, as here, the Buyer was unable (despite its efforts) to sell the unsound cargo immediately on discovering the problem, the relevant date should be the date of the eventual sale (in order to give full effect to s 53(2)).

It did not matter (and the court did not ask) whether the goods had or would have been worth more or less at the date of delivery: the market measure replaced the 'diminution in value at the date of acquisition' measure because there was mitigation by resort to the market.

Likewise in *Kwei Tek Chao v British Traders and Shippers*,[84] the market measure was applied to goods afloat on the date on which it was discovered that the

---

[78] See above text to n 23.

[79] See further below at text to n 89 and chapter sixteen, section 16.5A.

[80] *Jones v Just* (1868) LR 3 QB 197. See also eg *Marimpex Mineralöl Handelsgesellschaft mbH v Louis Dreyfus et Compagnie Menralöl GmbH* [1995] 1 Lloyd's Rep 167 (Clarke J).

[81] If the goods have already been supplied to the buyer while the defect was latent, but the defect is then discovered, the claimant may be expected to pass that knowledge to the sub-buyer and so minimise the liability to that buyer: *Biggin Co Ltd v Permanite Ltd* [1951] 1 KB 422 (Devlin J) at 435.

[82] *Applegate v Moss* [1971] 1 QB 406 (CA). Also *King v Victor Parsons Ltd* [1972] 1 WLR 801 (CA); *Naughton v O'Callaghan* [1990] 3 All ER 191 (Waller J).

[83] *KG Bominflot Bunkergesellschaft für Mineralöle mbH & Co v Petroplus Marketing AG (The Mercini Lady)* [2012] EWHC 3009 (Comm) (Hamblen J) at paras 59–60.

[84] *Kwei Tek Chao v British Traders and Shippers Ltd* [1954] 2 QB 459 (Devlin J) at 494.

documents were forged and replacement goods were needed, not the earlier date on which the documents were tendered. As Devlin J explained:

> As to the consequences of a wrong which deceives the aggrieved party, whether it be a tort or a breach of contract, the aggrieved party cannot be expected to act in such a manner as to compensate himself until he has ascertained the fact. It seems to me quite fictitious to talk of the buyers having to be treated as if they had gone out into the market and bought goods on November 10, when, in fact, they had supposed that they had already taken up goods which were in accordance with the contract, and they had no notion, and could have had no notion, that they had any rights with regard to the contract.[85]

In *Van den Hurk v R Martens & Co Ltd*[86] the drums of sodium sulphide were (reasonably) only opened when they reached the end user sub-buyer, and the market replacement measure was applied at that date when they were rejected by the sub-buyer some months after the initial delivery date, by which time the market had risen. In such cases it should also be open to the claimant to recover any liability to the sub-buyer on the rejection on ordinary principles, as for those purposes the defect was latent and the loss unavoidable but ordinary. Similarly, the costs of transporting the goods to and from the sub-buyer (before and after rejection) should be available.[87]

In accordance with the ordinary application of the mitigation principle, losses after the date on which the defect should have been discovered and the property sold will usually be unrecoverable because the claimant is deemed to have avoided them by recourse to the market.[88] The simple point is that 'Once the injured party learns of the breach, he can minimize the loss for which the other will be required to compensate by immediately purchasing a replacement'.[89] The claimant who nevertheless supplies defective goods acts unreasonably and cannot recover the losses resulting.[90]

It is only if there is a string contract of specific goods, in which case replacement goods are not available, that further losses (on the sub-sale) are unavoidable even in a patent defect case. In such a case, the further losses are recoverable, but only if not too remote, as discussed below in section 4.2B(vi), and if the chain of causation is not broken.

Even where there is no available market eg because there is a string contract, and so lost profits on a sub-sale are unavoidable and recoverable if not too remote, liability to the sub-buyer for losses caused by the patent defect are usually not recoverable because it would not usually be reasonable, after discovery of the defect, to

---

[85] Ibid at 495–96. Also at 494: 'as soon as he knows of his rights he must sell the goods. He cannot do so before he does know his rights' and 497: 'the relevant date is not the date of breach, but the date when the plaintiffs could, acting with reasonable diligence, and after they knew of their rights, have resold the goods on the market and obtained the best price they could for them'.

[86] *Van den Hurk v R Martens & Co Ltd* [1920] 1 KB 850 (Bailhache J). Also *Obaseki Bros v Reif & Son Ltd* [1952] 2 Lloyd's Rep 364 (HL) (Lord Goddard).

[87] See eg *Molling and Co v Dean and Son (Ltd)* (1901) 18 TLR 217.

[88] *Salford City Council v Torkington* [2004] EWCA Civ 1546, discussed below in chapter eighteen, section 18.4D.

[89] *Johnson v Perez* (1988) 166 CLR 351 (HC of Australia) at para 8.

[90] *Dobell (GC) & Co Ltd v Barger and Garratt* [1931] 1 KB 219 (CA) at 238; *Biggin & Co Ltd v Permanite Ltd* [1951] 1 KB 422 (Devlin J) at 435.

nevertheless supply them under the a sub-sale, and any attempt so to do is usually a speculation by the claimant and not a reasonable act of mitigation. If it goes wrong, the claimant could not recover the additional losses (presumably liability to the sub-buyer and lost profits), and conversely, as Scrutton LJ observed:

> If the buyer is lucky enough, for reasons with which the seller has nothing to do, to get his goods through on the sub-contract without a claim against him, this on principle cannot affect his claim against the seller any more than the fact that he had to pay very large damages on his sub-contract would affect his original seller.[91]

Again, the reader should contrast the situation of latent defects, where it is entirely reasonable to supply the defective goods on the sub-sale because even if they would have been replaceable on the market if the claimant had known of the defect, the claimant cannot be blamed for not knowing and so not replacing them.

However, in *The Cisco*, the claimant sugar refiner bought sugar which was damaged by seawater by the defendant carrier. Had the sugar been sold, it would have had only 25 per cent of its value as the damaged sugar was only of use to animal feed processors, meaning that it had diminished in market value by around CAN\$226,000.[92] The claimant was able to and did reasonably mix the wet sugar with dry sugar and then refine it, and thereby create a satisfactory product for human consumption. The claimant was therefore restricted to recovery of around CAN\$76,000 for the additional costs of processing and unloading:

> where the damaged goods have been repaired without any option being considered, the ... market value ... does not exist since no market was looked for. To apply the formula [of difference in market price at the date of delivery] in this case would be to give it an air of unreality.[93]

(g) *Slater v Hoyle & Smith Ltd*

Much confusion has been caused by the Court of Appeal decision in *Slater v Hoyle & Smith Ltd*,[94] which pre-dated *Bence Graphics*.[95] In *Slater* the claimant bought in

---

[91] *Slater v Hoyle & Smith Ltd* [1920] 2 KB 11 (CA) at 22–23. If the sub-contract is clearly in terms such that the defect did not matter and there was no risk of a complaint, it may be that the principle of mitigation would require the claimant to offload the defective goods to a buyer who did not mind (this being an alternative market in which a higher-than-ordinary-market price can be achieved). In that case the supply of the goods under the sub-sale (whether that entered into before the head contract or that entered into later) would be taken into account as reasonable mitigation, and no loss would have been suffered, given that the claimant had to supply under the sub-sales at the sub-sale prices in any event, whether the cloth had been defective or not. Clearly, as the latent defect cases such as *Bence Graphics International Ltd v Fasson UK Ltd* [1998] QB 87 (CA) and *McSherry v Coopers Creek Vineyard Ltd* (2005) 8 NZBLC 101 (Panckhurst J) show, sometimes a defect may make no difference to a buyer. Similarly where the sub-sale is not too remote and includes a right in the buyer to cancel without liability, the mitigatory principle may deem the buyer to have exercised that right. There was such a right in *Rodocanachi Sons & Co v Milburn Bros* (1887) 18 QBD 67 (CA) but, as explained below at n 136, the sub-sale was too remote so the non-liability to the sub-buyer was irrelevant (just as liability to the sub-buyer would have been).

[92] *Redpath Industries Ltd v The Cisco* (1993) 110 DLR (4th) 583.

[93] Ibid Desjardins JA at 590. A similar mixing was found to be unrealistic and not expected in the mouldy corn case of *CHS Inc Iberica SL v Far East Marine SA (MV Devon)* [2012] EWHC 3747 (Comm) (Cooke J).

[94] *Slater v Hoyle & Smith Ltd* [1920] 2 KB 11 (CA).

[95] *Bence Graphics International Ltd v Fasson UK Ltd* [1998] QB 87 (CA) is the key case on latent defects, and is discussed above at 4.2(B)(v)(c).

June 1918 1,625 136-yard pieces of unbleached grey cotton cloth at around 11d per yard for delivery in December 1918. However, unknown to the defendant supplier, the claimant had in December 1917, six months prior to contracting with the defendant, entered into a contract to sell to a third party bleached cloth for a lower price than 11d per yard, and had also in June 1918, shortly after entering the contract with the defendant, entered into another contract to sell bleached cloth to the same third party at a higher price than 11d per yard. The cloth delivered was not of contractual quality, and (an important point often overlooked) this defect was patent at the time of delivery.[96]

The claimant nevertheless bleached 691 pieces of the cloth and used it to part-fulfil the earlier sub-sale to the third party, the one at a price lower than the 11d per yard head contract price. The third party used the cloth to make shirts, and although it complained as to quality, it had not by the time of trial made any claim and probably had a different test of merchantability than under the head contract of sale and so claims were unlikely.[97] At first sight, at least, there was no actual loss.

The Court of Appeal nevertheless upheld the award of the difference between the market value of the promised goods (1 shilling/yard) and the value of the delivered goods (7½ pence per yard) on the date of delivery, ignoring the sub-sale and the fact that it appeared to have eliminated any actual loss of the claimant for the 691 pieces to which it related. The reasoning of the Court of Appeal was not entirely consistent. Bankes LJ seemed to think that as the sub-sale was not of identical goods to the goods under the main contract, it could not be taken into account as mitigation of the loss.[98] Warrington LJ thought that the non-delivery cases of *Rodocanachi v Milburn* and *Williams v Agius*[99] had determined that sub-sales had as a matter of law to be ignored, and observed that given that the goods sold were not the same as those bought and the claimant could have supplied other replacement goods on the sub-sale, the reduction of the loss by the sub-sale is 'good fortune, with which the plaintiffs have nothing to do'.[100] Scrutton LJ appeared to base his reasoning on the sub-sale not being within the parties' contemplation,[101] and on the claimant having the option of using other goods for the sub-contract,[102] and also supported the reasoning in *Rodocanachi v Milburn* and *Williams v Agius*.[103]

The decision is often seen as irreconcilable with the later *Bence Graphics*,[104] but actually it is not. In *Bence Graphics* it was clear that the use of the vinyl film in decals was within the parties' contemplation, and, more importantly, the defect was

---

[96] This is clear from the fact that at the time of accepting the goods the claimant refused further deliveries on the grounds of the defect: see the headnote in the Law Reports and Warrington LJ [1920] 2 KB 11 (CA) at 16. This point, that *Slater* is explicable as a patent defect case, was made first, to this author's knowledge at least, by Andrew Dyson in an unpublished conference paper in 2012.

[97] See [1920] 2 KB 11 (CA) Scrutton LJ at 19.

[98] Ibid at 15.

[99] Discussed below at text to n 125.

[100] Ibid at 17–18.

[101] Ibid at 20 and 24.

[102] Ibid at 20.

[103] Ibid at 21–24.

[104] Auld LJ in *Bence Graphics International Ltd v Fasson UK Ltd* could not distinguish them and doubted *Slater*: [1998] QB 87 (CA) at 102. See also *Bear Stearns Bank plc v Forum Global Equity* [2007] EWHC 1576 (Comm) (Andrew Smith J) at para 204.

latent and so could not have been avoided by a replacement purchase. Accordingly, mitigation and remoteness principles not being engaged, the actual loss, and no more, was quite rightly recoverable.

In *Slater* the position was very different. The defect in *Slater* was patent[105] and there was no string contract (which was also true of *Bence* but is only important where a defect is patent), ie the sub-contracts did not require the specific cloth sold by the defendant.[106] This meant that, unlike in *Bence Graphics*, the claimant in *Slater* had the choice as to whether to supply the goods bleached on the sub-sales or to supply them unbleached to the market and use replacement goods for the sub-sale. Although the claimant in fact used the contract goods on the sub-contract, that was a free choice the claimant had (as both Warrington and Scrutton LJJ observed) and therefore was res inter alios acta and akin to speculation (as Scrutton LJ expressly noted[107]). The step *might* have been a reasonable act of mitigation, if there was no risk of breach on the sub-contract because eg the bleaching eradicated the defect, but the reports do not disclose sufficient facts to take the point any further and their Lordships in the Court of Appeal did not appear to think that the act should be viewed in this light. If, however, there was any risk that supplying the defective (albeit processed) goods on the sub-sale would lead to liability, and there does appear to have been such a risk, the step (although ultimately successful) was clearly unreasonable and to be disregarded,[108] and so the claimant should be deemed to have instead sold the goods on the market and bought a replacement to supply on the sub-sale or otherwise use, as any prudent claimant would.[109]

Some observers also seek to explain *Slater* on the basis of remoteness, ie on the basis that the bleaching and then selling of the cotton was too remote.[110] It is correct that there was no finding that this was in the parties' contemplation in *Slater*, and certainly remoteness seems to have been in the minds of the judges,[111] but it does not seem likely that bleaching and on-sale were too remote,[112] and moreover on a proper understanding of remoteness it should act as a cap, preventing

---

[105] See above at n 95.

[106] *Slater v Hoyle & Smith Ltd* [1920] 2 KB 11 (CA) Bankes LJ at 17, Warrington LJ at 17, Scrutton LJ at 20. This was a point on *Slater* that was emphasised in *Louis Dreyfus Trading Ltd v Reliance Trading Ltd* [2004] 2 Lloyd's Rep 243 (Andrew Smith J) at paras 21–22.

[107] [1920] 2 KB 11 at 23.

[108] *Dobell (GC) & Co Ltd v Barger and Garratt* [1931] 1 KB 219 (CA) at 238.

[109] See further text to n 90 above.

[110] The remoteness explanation of *Slater* is preferred by Otton LJ in *Bence Graphics* [1998] QB 87 (CA) at 99. See also *Interallianz Finanz AG v Independent Insurance Co Ltd*, 18 December 1997 (Thomas J) and *Renold Australia Pty Ltd v Fletcher Insulation (Vic) Pty Ltd* [2007] VSCA 294 (Victoria CA) Chernov JA at para 22.

[111] Scrutton LJ shows that remoteness was at least partly in his mind in *Slater* [1920] 2 KB 11 (CA) at 20 and 24. The House of Lords decision in *Re Hall (R and H) Ltd and WH Pim Junior & Co's Arbitration* [1928] All ER Rep 763 (HL), confirming that despite *Rodocanachi Sons & Co v Milburn Bros* (1887) 18 QBD 67 and *Williams Bros v Ed T Agius Ltd* [1914] AC 510 (HL) sub-sales are properly taken into account where not too remote, was still a few years away.

[112] Auld LJ in *Bence Graphics* [1998] QB 87 (CA) at 103 emphasised that the seller in *Slater* knew that the cotton was to be sold on, and found the remoteness explanation unconvincing: 'there can be no doubt that, in contracting to sell 3,000 pieces of unbleached cloth of a certain quality, the seller knew that he was dealing with a commercial buyer who would sell them on either unprocessed or processed to some degree'.

recovery exceeding the ordinary non-remote market trading losses (eg if the sub-buyers of the bleached cotton had made a huge claim against the claimant in *Slater*) but not permitting the recovery, as in *Slater*, of *more* than the actual loss of zero.[113]

(vi) Non-Remote Chain Sub-Sales Requiring the Exact Contract Goods

Leaving latent defects, and returning to non-delivery and patent defect disputes, whether or not there is an available market, losses on the sub-sale may well be unavoidable because the 'the sale is of specific goods, and the buyer has resold [in the sub-sale] the same goods' (and so market replacement cannot assist),[114] or alternatively the sub-sale would allow for replacement goods but there is no time to acquire them eg because 'the contract of resale has the same delivery date as the contract of sale'.[115] As Devlin J explained in *Kwei Tek Chao*:

> it may very well be that in the case of string contracts, if the seller knows that the merchant is not buying merely for re-sale generally but on a string contract where he will re-sell those specific goods and where he could only honour his contract by delivering those goods and no others, the measure of loss or profit on the re-sale is the right measure.[116]

As Devlin J points out here, there are two key aspects to the situation: first, that there is a string contract which the claimant cannot satisfy by replacement goods, thus preventing the rule of mitigation from making the sub-sale irrelevant as it ordinarily would be; secondly, that the string contract is not too remote. As he also points out, in these circumstances the losses on the sub-sale, ie the actual losses, are the right measure. The market measure is irrelevant, as the claimant did not go to the market (so it is not relevant to the actual loss) and was not reasonably expected to have done so (so it is not relevant by the rule of mitigation). We have seen this simple recovery of actual unavoidable losses in defective delivery cases[117] and in late delivery cases[118] and it is no less true of non-delivery cases.

(a) Pre-Arranged Sub-Sales will Usually be Too Remote

In the vast majority of cases, losses on specific sub-sales will be avoidable on the market. Even where they are not, for example because the sub-sale is on a string and requires the very goods to which the defendant's breach relates, in most cases specific sub-sales will be too remote.[119] Although the lost profits of a sale to the market are dependent upon market movements between the date of contract and the date of delivery, such losses are still recoverable, but specific sub-sales engaged prior to the date of contracting or after that date but prior to the date of delivery are usually too remote as providing a further order of uncertainty. This was explained

---

[113] See below in chapter fourteen, section 14.4.
[114] *Patrick v Russo-British Grain Export Co Ltd* [1927] 2 KB 535 (Salter J) at 541 (non-delivery).
[115] Ibid at 541. See for example *Williams v Reynolds* (1865) 34 LJQB 221.
[116] *Kwei Tek Chao v British Traders and Shippers Ltd* [1954] 2 QB 459 (Devlin J) at 489–90.
[117] *Bence Graphics International Ltd v Fasson UK Ltd* [1998] QB 87 (CA).
[118] *Wertheim v Chicoutimi Pulp Company* [1911] 1 AC 301 (HL).
[119] A different test probably applies to torts, eg *France v Gaudet* (1871) LR 6 QB 199 (trover).

eloquently and fully by the Court of Queen's Bench in *Williams v Reynolds* in 1865.[120] Although it may be quite common for a buyer to arrange a sub-sale before his goods arrive, the losses on that sub-sale are outside the parties' contemplation (or, in the modern formulation, outside the seller's implied assumption of responsibility) for the same reason the losses in the charterparty case of *The Achilleas*[121] were. As the Court in *Williams v Reynolds* put it:

> The reason is that such a profit is utterly incapable of valuation. It may depend upon change of weather, a scientific discovery, an outbreak of war, a workmen's strike. It will depend upon the energy and sagacity of the person who purchases the goods, and the solvency of the person to whom he sells them again. In short, [if the sub-sale profits were recoverable], no one could contract to sell goods which were not actually in his possession without charging an additional premium commensurate to the profits which the vendee might possibly make, and for which he himself would have to pay, if prevented from carrying out his agreement ... The seller contracts on a speculation of what the price may be at the time of delivery, and not with reference to five or six bargains which the buyer may make in the mean time, about which he knows nothing.[122]

In that case the buyer of cotton was limited to the difference between the market price and the contract price, and the higher price of the sub-sale was ignored.

Greer LJ observed similarly in *The Arpad*, a case of destruction/non-delivery by a carrier:

> [I]t seems to me unreasonable to hold that a shipowner contracting with the shipper on the terms of a bill of lading should be held liable to pay damages occasioned to an unknown assignee of the bill of lading,[123] measured by the loss sustained by reason of the latter's inability to comply with a [sub-sale] contract made two months before the shipment by such unknown assignee, the shipowner having no notice of such contract and no opportunity of refusing to carry goods on the terms that he should be so liable.[124]

In the important decision of *Williams v Agius*,[125] the original contract for 4,500 tons of coal was at 16s 3d per ton, the price on the sub-sale (already entered into by the date of non-delivery) was 19s per ton, and the market price at the date of delivery was 23s 6d per ton. Had the contract been performed the buyer would have made a profit of 2s 9d per ton, and yet the court awarded the 7s 3d per ton difference between the original contract price and the market (not the sub-sale). In so doing, the House, purporting to follow the carrier non-delivery case of *Rodocanachi v Milburn*,[126] and the sale case of *Williams v Reynolds* having been cited in argument,[127] claimed to disregard the sub-sale. There was no explicit discussion

---

[120] *Williams v Reynolds* (1865) 34 LJQB 221; 6 B & S 495.
[121] *Transfield Shipping Inc v Mercator Shipping Inc (The Achilleas)* [2009] AC 61 (HL), discussed in chapter six, section 6.4B(i).
[122] Compton J at 222–23. See further *Aryeh v Lawrence Kostoris Son Ltd* [1967] Lloyd's Rep 63 (CA).
[123] The shipper's rights under the contract of carriage passing by automatic assignment with the bill of lading to one purchasing the goods from the shipper.
[124] *The Arpad* [1934] P 189, [1934] All ER Rep 326 (CA) at 320. See also *Heskell v Continental Express Ltd* [1950] 1 All ER 1033 (Devlin J) at 1049, a carriage late delivery case.
[125] *Williams Bros v Ed T Agius Ltd* [1914] AC 510 (HL).
[126] *Rodocanachi Sons & Co v Milburn Bros* (1886) 18 QBD 67 (CA).
[127] *Williams v Reynolds* (1865) 34 LJQB 221.

of remoteness in this case (like in *Rodocanachi v Milburn*[128] but unlike in the later House of Lords' decision in *Hall v Pim*[129]), although Viscount Haldane emphasised that the sub-sale transaction was 'independent' of the breach.[130]

The first point to make is that a little thought shows that the claimant was awarded its actual loss on the sub-sale: unlike in some cases where the claimant has 'got away with it' on the sub-sale, here there was every indication that the claimant would suffer loss equal to the market measure in any case, once one adds together the lost profit on the sub-sale (only 2s 9d per ton) and the liability to the sub-buyer (4s 6d per ton, being the difference between the sub-sale contract price and the market price which the sub-buyer will have to pay for a replacement). Accordingly, neither remoteness nor mitigation are needed to justify the amount of the award.

In any event, both can justify it. As this was not a string contract,[131] the claimant could reasonably have been expected to purchase a replacement on the market, thus making the market measure the correct measure of loss. Alternatively, in the light of the House of Lords' decision in *Hall v Pim* in 1928,[132] the losses on the non-string sub-sale were (as will usually be the case) outside the seller's contemplation and too remote.[133]

In keeping with this approach to remoteness of sub-sales in non-delivery cases, in *Seven Seas Properties Ltd v Al-Essa (No 2)*,[134] the vendor of some flats in need of refurbishment understood incorrectly from the purchaser that the latter intended to refurbish them and then sell them on, as most purchasers would intend. In fact, the purchaser had found a sub-buyer willing to buy them at a higher price, producing a profit on a back-to-back sale without the need to refurbish them. The loss sustained on the re-sale was held to be too remote. It was not enough that the securing of a particular immediate sub-buyer was an available possibility; the vendor defendant needed more to be taken to have assumed the risk of loss on such a sub-contract.

An additional feature that makes losses on a specific sub-sale too remote is that, where there is a market for replacement goods (and save in latent defect cases), such losses on a specific sub-sale will in any event usually be avoidable. Thus the mere fact that back-to-back contracts (eg forward-selling goods promised by the defendant) are a common way of avoiding risk and doing business is unlikely to bring losses on a sub-sale within the seller's contemplation, because the missing ingredient that gives rise to the lost profit on the sub-sale which the parties do not

---

[128] In that case, although there was no explicit discussion of remoteness, Lord Esher confirmed that 'barring special circumstances' the sub-sale would be disregarded, whether it caused greater or less damages than the market measure, as it consisted of 'circumstances peculiar to the plaintiff' and that were 'accidental'.

[129] *Re Hall (R and H) Ltd and WH Pim Junior & Co's Arbitration* [1928] All ER Rep 763 (HL), discussed below at text to n 138.

[130] *Williams Bros v Ed T Agius Ltd* [1914] AC 510 at 520, citing *British Westinghouse Co v Underground Electric Railways Co of London* [1912] 3 KB 128.

[131] [1914] AC 510, Lord Dunedin at 523.

[132] Although *Williams v Agius* was not referred to in that judgment, Viscount Haldane and Viscount Dunedin sat on both panels. Further, *Rodocanachi v Milburn* was referred to in the Court of Appeal decision, reported at [1927] All ER Rep 227, which the House will have read with care.

[133] Cf Viscount Haldane LC [1914] AC 510 at 520, Lord Dunedin at 523. See also *The Arpad* [1934] All ER Rep 326 (CA).

[134] *Seven Seas Properties Ltd v Al-Essa (No 2)* [1993] 1 WLR 1083 (Lightman QC).

contemplate is that the forward contract cannot be satisfied by replacement goods if necessary, ie that the forward contract requires exactly the goods which, because of the defendant's breach, are no longer available.[135]

There are almost no cases of destruction or damage to goods that were subject to a chain contract (in contrast with non-delivery or delivery of defective goods). However, it can be predicted with some confidence that where the damage or destruction is by a carrier, the losses on chain sub-sales are likely to be too remote. As is explained below, it is often the defendant's knowledge of the buyer's business or the terms of the sale contract that renders a sub-sale not too remote, and a carrier is unlikely to have sufficient knowledge to bring losses on chain sub-sales within the scope of the defendant's responsibility.[136]

(b) Consequences of a Finding of Remoteness

Where a sub-sale is too remote the law ignores it (sometimes calling it '*res inter alios acta*', although that term is best kept for legal causation), capping loss at the level that was not too remote, which in these cases would be the additional cost of purchasing a replacement on the market or the lost profit from selling the non-delivered or defective goods on the market. As Andrew Smith J has put it in a case of breach of warranty (which was equivalent to late delivery, given the nature of the breach of warranty):

> Profit or loss made by a buyer on a sub-sale is generally irrelevant to the assessment of his damages for breach by a seller of a warranty of quality or a failure to deliver (except, it may be, as evidence of market price). This is an application of general principles governing remoteness of damage, and not an exception to them. If a particular sub-sale is not within the contemplation of the parties when the contract of sale is made, damages are to be assessed without regard to it, and it makes no difference that the parties were aware that the buyer was a merchant dealing in and re-selling such goods.[137]

(c) When a Sub-Sale will not be Too Remote

The leading case on this point is the inter-war House of Lords decision of *Re Hall (R and H) Ltd and WH Pim Junior & Co's Arbitration*,[138] which concerned a contract for the sale of a type of Australian corn known as 'cheat' at 51s 9d per quarter ton. Between the date of the original contract and delivery, the buyer sub-sold the corn at 56s 9d per quarter, and before delivery the sub-buyer later sub-sub-sold the same corn at 59s 3d per quarter (in fact to the original seller as agent for another). The market price then dropped to 53s 9d per quarter by the date on which the defendant should have but did not deliver the corn.

---

[135] *Bear Stearns Bank plc v Forum Global Equity* [2007] EWHC 1576 (Comm) (Andrew Smith J) at para 203.

[136] See *The Arpad* [1934] All ER Rep 326 (CA) at 336 and *Rodocanachi Sons & Co v Milburn Bros* (1887) 18 QBD 67 (CA), in both of which cases the sub-sale was too remote. On the difference between carriers and sellers and the effect this has on remoteness, see the discussion in chapter six, text to nn 92–94. (But compare the trover case of *France v Gaudet* (1871) LR 6 QB 199.)

[137] *Louis Dreyfus Trading Ltd v Reliance Trading Ltd* [2004] 2 Lloyd's Rep 243 (Andrew Smith J) at para 17 (a breach of warranty case).

[138] *Re Hall (R and H) Ltd and WH Pim Junior & Co's Arbitration* [1928] All ER Rep 763 (HL).

Not only were such string contracts common in the industry, but the contract itself, like many modern standard form commodities contracts, expressly contemplated sale of specific goods by a string contract while the goods were still in transit. The House of Lords, allowing the appeal, found the string contract to have been within the parties' contemplation, and awarded damages for the 5s per quarter lost profit on the sub-sale rather than the 2s per quarter difference between the head contract price and the market price at delivery. The claimant also recovered for its liability to its sub-buyer (who presumably had a similar lost profits claim for 2s 6d per quarter).

As to the concern of the indeterminacy of the supplier's liability, Viscount Dunedin observed:

> It was stated that this opened an interminable vista of successive contracts and successive damages. That is not so. There is a practical chock in two ways. The contracts must have been entered into before the time of delivery, and they must be contracts in accordance with the market, not extravagant and unusual bargains.[139]

The first instance judge in *The Achilleas*, Clarke J, correctly explained *Hall v Pim* in the following clear terms:

> Hall v Pim was an application of Hadley v Baxendale [ie of the remoteness test]. The case plainly decides that loss of profits on a sub sale can be recovered if the contract itself contemplates that the buyers will sub sell the very cargo without possibility of substitution and, at the time of beach, the sub contract price exceeds the contract ... price.[140]

As to the circumstances in which the sub-sales will not be found too remote, the relevant features mentioned in *Hall v Pim* were the market practice and that the contract of sale expressly contemplated the possibility of pre-delivery sub-sale.[141] Loss on a sub-sale may also be found not to be too remote where the goods are dealt on a commodity market for which sale of specific loads while afloat is common,[142] or the original seller otherwise knows that the goods are on a string contract[143] or, if not, at least that the practical effect of the arrangements is that the same

---

[139] Ibid at 767. If they were extravagant and unusual, the damages would be capped at the level as if they had been ordinary sub-sales: see chapter fourteen, section 14.4, below.

[140] *Transfield Shipping Inc v Mercator Shipping Inc (The Achilleas)* [2006] EWHC 3030 (Comm) at para 80. See also *James Finlay & Co Ltd v NV Kwik Hoo Tong Handel Maatschappij* [1929] 1 KB 400 (CA) Scrutton LJ at 411 and Sankey LJ at 417; *Heskell v Continental Express Ltd* [1950] 1 All ER 1033 (Devlin J) at 1049.

[141] See also *Allied Canners & Packers Inc v Victor Packing Co* (1985) 162 Cal App 3d 905 (California CA).

[142] Diplock LJ, obiter, in *Aryeh v Lawrence Kostoris Son Ltd* [1967] Lloyd's Rep 63 (CA) (non-delivery) at 72. Also *JL Lyon & Co Ltd v Fuchs* [1920] 2 Ll L Rep 333 (Rowlatt J) (non-delivery); *Heskell v Continental Express Ltd* [1950] 1 All ER 1033 (Devlin J) (delay by warehousing agent) obiter at 1049.

[143] *Borries v Hutchinson* (1865) 18 CB (NS) 445 (late delivery, where lost profit on the sub-sale was not too remote, but liability on the sub-sale resulting from the sub-seller's sub-sub-sale was too remote); *Grébert-Borgnis v J & W Nugent* (1885) 15 QBD 85 (CA) (non-delivery); *Frank Mott & Co Ltd v Wm H Muller & Co (London) Ltd* (1922) 13 Ll L Rep 492 (Rowlatt J) (non-delivery); *Household Machines Ltd v Cosmos Exporters Ltd* [1947] KB 217 (Lewis J) (non-delivery); *Coastal International Trading Ltd v Maroil AG* [1988] 1 Lloyd's Rep 92 (Leggatt J) (non-delivery).

goods will or will probably be subject to the sub-sale.[144] Similarly, where the seller arranges a sale to the claimant knowing that the claimant will then let out the same property on hire purchase, the lost profit on the hire purchase if the hire purchaser then rejects the property because of the seller's breach (the car being defective) is recoverable.[145]

Even if the sub-sale is not too remote, some terms of it may be, in which case the ordinary sub-sale loss will be a cap on recovery.[146]

(d) The Sub-Sale also Limits the Recovery

It is therefore clear that actual losses on a sub-sale are recoverable in non-delivery and patent defect cases where the sub-sale losses cannot reasonably be avoided (usually because there is a string contract) and the sub-sale is not too remote, even where those losses exceed the prima facie market measure as applied by the Sale of Goods Act 1979 sections 51(3) and 53(3). This was the result in the House of Lords' decision in *Hall v Pim* discussed in the previous section.

Nevertheless, there remain judges and commentators who argue that if the actual losses on the sub-sale, even though not too remote, are *less* than the market measure under sections 51(3) and 53(3), the greater market measure nevertheless applies. This is a consequence of ascribing to the market measure more force than its rebuttably presumptive nature allows, as discussed generally above.[147]

We have seen elsewhere (following the Court of Appeal decision in *Bence*) that in latent defect cases the presumption in favour of the market measure in 53(3) is rebutted where (as is usually the case) the losses on sub-sale or other use of the defective property are not too remote, and that accordingly the actual losses are awarded whether greater or less than the market measure.[148] The same is true of late delivery cases, where the difference in value on the dates of promised and actual delivery is only relevant if the claimant would have sold the goods on delivery (actual loss) and/ or the claimant did or should have bought replacement goods when the defendant breached by being late (the mitigation principle). The reader is referred to the body of cases and dicta in section 4.5A(ii)(a) to the effect that the claimant's actual loss is the true measure unless remoteness or mitigation alter that.

And, logically, the same is true of non-delivery and patent defect cases. The actual loss is the true measure unless remoteness or mitigation provide otherwise. Where the losses were not reasonably avoidable by purchasing a replacement (because there is a string contract or no available market), and the use by sale on a sub-sale is not too remote, the losses are recoverable and the market measure irrelevant. There is no principle by which although actual losses greater than the market measure

---

[144] *Hinde v Liddell* (1875) LR 10 QB 265 (non-delivery); *Coastal (Bermuda) Petroleum Ltd v VTT Vulcan Petroleum SA (No 2) (The Marine Star)* [1994] 2 Lloyd's Rep 629 (Mance J) (non-delivery), appeal allowed on other grounds: [1996] 2 Lloyd's Rep 383 (CA); *Bear Stearns Bank plc v Forum Global Equity* [2007] EWHC 1576 (Comm) (Andrew Smith J) (non-delivery) obiter at para 206. See also *M&J Marine Engineering Services Ltd v Shipshore Ltd* [2009] EWHC 2031 (Comm) (Field J), although the remoteness issue was not discussed in the judgment.

[145] *Garside v Black Horse Ltd* [2010] EWHC 190 (QB) (King J).

[146] See below in chapter fourteen, section 14.4 and accompanying text.

[147] Chapter fourteen, section 14.2C, and also the immediately following sub-section to this one.

[148] See section 4.2B(v)(b). And for patent defect cases, see *The Cisco* at text to n 92 above.

are recoverable (as *Hall v Pim* unarguably demonstrates), the market measure nevertheless provides a minimum or floor measure,[149] and that is not the true legal position. Where not too remote, the actual losses (by sub-sale or otherwise) replace the market as the measure of loss in these cases (or, more accurately, the rule of mitigation does not require the market measure to replace the actual loss as the measure of loss in these cases).

Nevertheless, the supporters of the supposed rule that the market measure provides for a minimum recovery gain some support from some of the early decisions of the appellate courts in which sub-sales were apparently ignored (eg *Rodocanachi v Milburn, Williams v Agius*). But in addition to being illogical, such cases clearly prove too much because they suggest that the market measure applies irrespective of sub-sales, whereas the House of Lords decision in *Hall v Pim* puts beyond doubt that this is incorrect. See further, however, the discussion under the immediately following heading.

(e) Inconsistencies in the Sub-Sales Rules?

There is often said to be an inconsistency between cases in which a sub-sale was taken into account and cases in which it was not.[150] The sub-sale was ignored for the purposes of the damages calculation in *Rodocanachi v Milburn* (1886, Court of Appeal)[151] and *Williams v Agius* (1914, House of Lords)[152] on non-delivery (carriage and sale respectively), although in the latter it probably made no difference to the damages measure; and in *Slater v Hoyle & Smith* (1919, Court of Appeal)[153] on defective goods. The sub-sale formed the basis of the damages measure in *Hall v Pim* (1928, House of Lords)[154] on non-delivery, *Bence Graphics International Ltd v Fasson UK Ltd* (1996, Court of Appeal)[155] on defective delivery, and *Wertheim v Chicoutimi Pulp Co* (1910, Privy Council)[156] on delay.

Questions have been raised as to how, within the non-delivery cases, *Williams v Agius* can be consistent with *Hall v Pim*.[157] Because in *Hall v Pim* the non-remote sub-sale allowed damages to be *increased* beyond the market measure, but there is no English non-delivery case confirming that the non-remote sub-sale can *reduce* damages below the market measure (as *Wertheim* confirms for late delivery and *Bence Graphics* for defective delivery),[158] there have been first instance comments suggesting that different principles must therefore apply to non-delivery cases and

---

149 See the discussion in the next section.
150 The late delivery sub-sale cases considered here are discussed below in chapter six, section 6.3C(ii).
151 *Rodocanachi Sons & Co v Milburn Bros* (1887) 18 QBD 67 (CA).
152 *Williams Bros v Ed T Agius Ltd* [1914] AC 510 (HL).
153 *Slater v Hoyle & Smith Ltd* [1920] 2 KB 11 (CA).
154 *Re Hall (R and H) Ltd and WH Pim Junior & Co's Arbitration* [1928] All ER Rep 763 (HL).
155 *Bence Graphics International Ltd v Fasson UK Ltd* [1998] QB 87 (CA).
156 *Wertheim v Chicoutimi Pulp Company* [1911] 1 AC 301 (HL).
157 *James Finlay & Co Ltd v NV Kwik Hoo Tong Handel Maatschappij* [1929] 1 KB 400 (CA) Scrutton LJ at 409–12, Greer LJ at 416.
158 Although this point was upheld in the Californian Court of Appeal in *Allied Canners & Packers Inc v Victor Packing Co* (1985) 162 Cal App 3d 905 (California CA).

defective delivery cases.[159] Indeed the House of Lords in *Williams v Agius* said that non-delivery was different to delay.[160] Some commentators suggest that the market measure is an irreducible minimum award and that sub-sales cannot decrease the amount of damages and *Bence Graphics* is therefore wrong.[161]

However, in truth, Lord Upjohn was correct in the remoteness decision of the House of Lords of *The Heron II* when he said (although not focusing on sub-sale issues) that 'the same general principles apply' to non-delivery, defective goods and delay cases.[162] It would be irrational to have a hard and fast rule in cases of non-delivery or defective delivery and not delay, disapplying the remoteness/*res inter alios acta* tests, and to do so would be inconsistent with the cases. In none of *Rodocanachi*, *Williams* or *Wertheim* was the remoteness rule explicitly considered, and only Scrutton LJ referred to it in *Slater*. Yet the House of Lords decision in *Hall v Pim* made it absolutely clear that an actual sub-sale, where not too remote, would be taken into account in a non-delivery case. That case only concerned a sub-sale increasing loss beyond the market measure, but numerous dicta in all categories of case confirm that the remoteness test in this context is double-sided, and that taking the special circumstances of a sufficiently proximate sub-sale into account may increase losses (as in *Hall v Pim*) or decrease them (as in *Bence Graphics*), in either situation displacing the general market measure. Moreover, in countless more cases the court simply looks to the sub-sale or other post-breach use of the property (in a manufacturing process etc) and does not ask whether the actual non-remote loss was smaller than the difference in value at the date of breach, and therefore whether, as these commentators would have it, the larger market measure loss should nevertheless be awarded. This is not because the actual losses are in all these cases clearly greater than any market measure (as indeed they usually are), but because the market measure is simply irrelevant where the claimant could not have been expected to purchase a replacement and had a non-remote use other than immediate sale. Indeed, counsel would be given short shrift if they tried in such cases (of non-remote post-delivery uses, or latent defects) to take a judge to the difference in market value at the date of delivery. Sub-sales measure the actual loss and therefore are the starting point in the damages calculation, but are disregarded if too remote (or at least losses are capped at the non-remote amount) or if their losses are not caused by the breach. They should not be disregarded if this rule does not apply.

This, then, is the applicable rule in all cases, although what it is reasonable to do and whether a sub-sale will be too remote may vary from non-delivery cases to

---

[159] *Bear Stearns Bank plc v Forum Global Equity* [2007] EWHC 1576 (Comm) (Andrew Smith J) obiter (the sub-sale of specific goods was too remote in any case).

[160] [1914] AC 510 (HL) Lord Dunedin at 523, Lord Atkinson at 529. See also Scrutton LJ in *Slater v Hoyle & Smith Ltd* [1920] 2 KB 11 (CA) at 24.

[161] See Stevens above chapter two n 63 and GH Treitel, 'Damages for Breach of Warranty of Quality' (1997) 113 *LQR* 188.

[162] *C Czarnikow Ltd v Koufos (The Heron II)* [1969] 1 AC 350 (HL) at 427. As His Lordship observed, there are 'substantial differences in practice between late delivery and non-delivery' because '[w]here marketable goods are lost it is almost axiomatic that the market price measures the damage; the same cannot be said of delay; it all depends on circumstances'. This is because in delay cases it is less frequently reasonable to buy a replacement and so the market price will only measure loss if the reasonably contemplated intended use was to *sell* the goods on delivery.

delay cases, carriage cases to sale cases, and indeed within these categories. The best explanation of these decisions is therefore on the facts, as set out above where each case is discussed. The sub-sale was too remote in *Rodocanachi* and *Williams*, but not in *Hall v Pim*, *Bence* and *Wertheim*. And in *Slater*, the loss (or avoidance of loss) on the sub-sale by trying to get patently defective goods through was *res inter alios acta*, ie not legally caused by the breach.

(vii) Consumer Goods

In consumer sale of goods cases the market measure does not necessarily apply,[163] not as a result of the ordinary principles of mitigation and remoteness, rather because of statutory provisions in Part 5A of the Sale of Goods Act 1979 providing for other remedies.[164] Further, ordinary principles may make repair more reasonable than replacement where damaged or defective property has sentimental value[165] or particular suitability to the claimant[166] (or alternatively, it might be said that in these situations the property is unique and no replacement is available on the market[167]).

C. The Presumption of a Market Replacement Measure and the Sale of Goods Act 1979

The Sale of Goods Act 1979 sets out the measure of recovery in cases of non-delivery and defective goods as follows:

Section 51 Damages for non-delivery.

(1) Where the seller wrongfully neglects or refuses to deliver the goods to the buyer, the buyer may maintain an action against the seller for damages for non-delivery.

(2) The measure of damages is the estimated loss directly and naturally resulting, in the ordinary course of events, from the seller's breach of contract.

(3) Where there is an available market for the goods in question the measure of damages is prima facie to be ascertained by the difference between the contract price and the market or current price of the goods at the time or times when they ought to have been delivered or (if no time was fixed) at the time of the refusal to deliver.

---

[163] Although it often will. See for example *Ashworth v Wells* (1898) 78 LT 136 (CA), showing that ordinarily damages will be available for the cost of a replacement.

[164] By those statutory provisions the buyer may choose to require repair or replacement or reduction in the price of the goods, provided such remedy is not disproportionate, in the alternative to an award of damages.

[165] *O'Grady v Westminster Scaffolding Ltd* [1962] 2 Lloyd's Rep 238 (Edmund Davies J) (tort).

[166] *Algeiba v Australind* (1921) 8 Ll L Rep 210.

[167] *Darbishire v Warran* [1963] 1 WLR 1067 (CA) (tort).

Section 53 Remedy for breach of warranty.

(1) Where there is a breach of warranty by the seller, or where the buyer elects (or is compelled) to treat any breach of a condition on the part of the seller as a breach of warranty, the buyer is not by reason only of such breach of warranty entitled to reject the goods; but he may—

    (a) set up against the seller the breach of warranty in diminution or extinction of the price, or

    (b) maintain an action against the seller for damages for the breach of warranty.

(2) The measure of damages for breach of warranty is the estimated loss directly and naturally resulting, in the ordinary course of events, from the breach of warranty.

(3) In the case of breach of warranty of quality such loss is prima facie the difference between the value of the goods at the time of delivery to the buyer and the value they would have had if they had fulfilled the warranty.

(4) The fact that the buyer has set up the breach of warranty in diminution or extinction of the price does not prevent him from maintaining an action for the same breach of warranty if he has suffered further damage.

What is clear from these sections is that the basic rule is that the ordinary common law rules of damages apply. This is shown by sections 51(2) and 53(2), which set out the 'measure of damages' as being the 'estimated loss directly and naturally resulting, in the ordinary course of events, from the breach of warranty'. It is confirmed by section 62(2) which confirms that the common law rules continue to apply except where inconsistent with the provisions of the Act, and by section 54 which confirms that special damages are recoverable where available in law.

The main contribution of these sections is, therefore, the expressly prima facie (ie rebuttable) rules in section 51(3) and 53(3) that measure damages by reference to the market at the date of delivery.

In section 53(3), which applies to defective goods claims, the prima facie measure is the difference between the market value of the goods as delivered and the value as promised, and is put forward as a prima facie measure of 'such loss', ie of the loss recoverable under ordinary rules by section 53(2). Auld LJ has adverted in *Bence* to 'the danger of giving it a primacy in the code of section 53 that it does not deserve' and emphasised that the primary measure is that in section 53(2), which merely applies the ordinary remoteness rules.[168] Otton LJ confirmed a point that is unsurprising in relation to a prima facie rule, namely that either party can rebut the presumption in section 53(3).[169]

In non-delivery cases, but only where there is an 'available market', by section 51(3) the award is prima facie the difference between the market and contract price at the time of delivery, but with no reference back to section 51(2) and the ordinary measure. Still, although sometimes forgotten, it is plain that as Goff J observed 'the

---

[168] *Bence Graphics International Ltd v Fasson UK Ltd* [1998] 1 QB 87 (CA) at 102.
[169] Ibid at 97.

principle set out in sub-s (3) of the Act is only a prima facie rule. The principle set out in sub-s (2) remains the governing principle'.[170]

As Lloyd J has also observed in *The Caloric*:

[t]he difference between contract and market price, as appears from s. 51(3) itself, is only the prima facie measure of damages. No doubt it represents a convenient rule in the great majority of cases. But if it does not correspond to the plaintiff's true loss in accordance with s. 51(2) of the Act, then he may recover either more or less depending on the circumstances.[171]

Moreover, as Mance J explained in *The Marine Star*, 'An available market is a means of mitigating any loss otherwise contemplated which has become incorporated into the general measure of recovery',[172] and that the market measure in section 51(3) is merely an application of the mitigation principle.[173] Mustill J similarly described section 51(3) as 'founded on a presumed mitigation'.[174] Thus in non-delivery cases it is rebuttably presumed by this prima facie rule that the buyer will be able to avoid and is expected to have avoided all losses by purchasing a replacement on the market. If there is no available market this is impossible and section 51(3) is not engaged. If there is an available market the loss may still not be avoidable and so the presumption in section 51(3) will be rebutted and the ordinary measure in section 51(2) applicable. As Erle CJ observed in 1865 (some time before the first Sale of Goods Act was enacted in 1893):

As a general rule, a vendor who fails to deliver goods according to his contract, must pay as damages to the vendee the difference between the value of the goods at the time of breach of contract as compared with the contract-price: or, in other words, if the vendee can go into the market and get the article contracted for, the vendor must reimburse him the difference between that which he has been compelled to pay for it and the price at which the vendor had contracted to deliver for it. But, where the article is not one of constant demand and supply, so that there is no market which can be resorted to for the purpose of obtaining it, another principle must be had recourse to in order to determine the measure of damages which the vendee is to recover: and that principle has been adopted here, in accordance with the rule in Hadley v Baxendale, 9 Exch 341 … The vendor is to pay to the vendee such damages as he may fairly and reasonably be supposed to have considered that he would be liable to pay in the event of his failure to perform his contract.[175]

Lord M'Laren clearly explained the point in 1891 in a Scottish decision:

The rule which is most usually applies is, that the damage is the difference between the contract price and the market price at the time when the breach of contract is ascertained—that is generally on the arrival and examination of the goods. The rule certainly presupposes

---

[170] *Koch Marine Inc v D'Amica Societa Di Navigazione ARL (The Elena D'Amico)* [1980] 1 Lloyd's Rep 75 (Goff J) at 87.

[171] *R Pagnan & F Lli v Lebanese Organisation for International Commerce (The Caloric)* [1981] 2 Lloyd's Rep 675 (Lloyd J) at 678.

[172] *Coastal (Bermuda) Petroleum Ltd v VTT Vulcan Petroleum SA (No 2) (The Marine Star)* [1994] 2 Lloyd's Rep 629 (Mance J) at 635, appeal allowed on other grounds: [1996] 2 Lloyd's Rep 383 (CA).

[173] See also *Deutsche Bank AG v Total Global Steel Ltd* [2012] EWHC 1201 (Comm) (Andrew Smith J) at para 166.

[174] *Industria Azucarera Nacional SA v Empresa Exportadora de Azucar (Cubazucar)*, 29 February 1980 (Mustill J), affirmed [1983] 2 Lloyd's Rep 171 (CA).

[175] *Borries v Hutchinson* (1865) 18 CB (NS) 445.

that a purchaser for resale is not to lose his profit on the adventure, because if he acts upon the rule—that is, if he supplies himself with goods at the market price of the day, he is able to make the same profit on the substituted goods that he would have made on the goods to be supplied under the contract, only his profit is paid to him in two portions, so much by the subvendee, and the balance by the seller who is liable in damages. The principle seems to be this, that the first purchaser has a duty to do what is within his power to lessen the loss to the seller by replacing the goods at the current price of the day, and that if he fails in doing so he will only recover from the seller the same sum which the seller would have had to pay in case the purchaser had supplied himself elsewhere.

If huts could have been obtained in the colony [of South Africa, the place of delivery] at wholesale prices, it would have been the pursuers' duty to supply themselves so as to lessen the loss to the defendants, but as this could not be done, I am afraid the consequence is that the whole loss must fall on the defenders.[176]

And as Lord Hoffmann has explained of section 51(3) in *SAAMCo*:

But the purpose of this prima facie rule is not to ensure that the damages will always be the same irrespective of the date of trial. It is because where there is an available market, any additional loss which the buyer suffers through not having immediately bought equivalent goods at the market price is prima facie caused by his own change of mind about wanting the goods which he ordered: compare Waddell v. Blockey (1879) 4 Q.B.D. 678. The breach date rule is thus no more than a prima facie rule of causation. It is not concerned with the extent of the vendor's liability for loss which the breach has admittedly caused.[177]

These lengthy quotations were necessary because the presumptive market measure in non-delivery and defective goods cases is frequently misunderstood. Only if it is appreciated that it is a *presumption* that losses can be avoided by a particular type of mitigation, which presumption is rebutted where that mitigation is impossible (eg no available market) or will in any case not avoid the losses (eg string contract or latent defect), will it be understood when the presumption is rebutted and why. As Lloyd LJ has observed, 'the breach date is the right date for assessment of damages only where there is an immediately available market for the sale of the relevant asset or, in the converse case, for the purchase of an equivalent asset'.[178]

That the Sale of Goods Act 1979 measure is a presumption based on mitigation can be seen not only from the cases in which the presumption of the market measure is rebutted entirely, but also those where the market measure is applied, in the decisions as to what amounts to a relevant market, and whether the market measure should be applied but on a date after the date of delivery, as discussed in

---

[176] *Duff & Co v The Iron and Steel Fencing and Buildings Co* (1891) 19 R 199 (Court of Session, 1st Division).

[177] *South Australia Asset Management Corp v York Montague Ltd* [1997] 1 AC 191 (HL) at 221. For further dicta also explaining the Sale of Goods Act presumptive market measure as an application of the mitigatory principle, see also *Melachrino v Nickoll and Knight* [1920] 1 KB 693 (Bailhache J) at 697; *Lesters Leather & Skin Co Ltd v Home and Overseas Brokers Ltd* (1948) 82 Ll L Rep 202 (CA) Lord Goddard CJ at 205; *Radford v De Froberville* [1977] 1 WLR 1262 (Oliver J) at 1285; *Gardner v Marsh & Parsons (a firm)* [1997] 1 WLR 489 (CA) Gibson LJ at 507; *BP Plc v Aon Ltd* [2006] EWHC 424 (Comm) (Colman J) at para 312; *Golden Strait Corp v Nippon Yusen Kubishika Kaisha (The Golden Victory)* [2007] 2 AC 353 (HL) Lord Brown at para 79; *Transfield Shipping Inc v Mercator Shipping Inc (The Achilleas)* [2007] 2 Lloyd's Rep 555 (CA) Rix LJ at para 102.

[178] *Hooper v Oates* [2013] 3 All ER 211 (CA) Lloyd LJ at para 38.

the next section. The so-called date of assessment issue is discussed below in chapter seventeen and the conclusion is the same: there is no rule as to date of assessment any more than there is a rule as to market measure; there are only the basic rules (especially of mitigation) and useful rebuttable presumptions assisting in their application.

D. The Measure in Cases of Market Replacement

Market replacement is a way of avoiding most on-going losses by replacement of property on the market. Where this cure applies, the measure of damages is the net cost of acquiring the replacement (whether or not a replacement was actually acquired[179]). In destruction or non-supply cases this is the price of replacement property.[180] In damage or defect cases it is the price of replacing undamaged/non-defective property on the market, less the price obtainable for the damaged or defective property.[181] As regards the price that can be obtained on the market, the existence of special interest buyers who will pay more must be taken into account if not too remote.[182]

Once this cure has been performed, most loss (financial or non-financial) will have been avoided, as the claimant will have the property it would have had but for the breach, and can do with it exactly what it would have done if the contract had been performed. Any sub-sale or other contract or purpose the claimant had for the property will usually become irrelevant, as it can be fulfilled and so any loss under it has been avoided. There may, however, be additional losses resulting from the delay or other losses that are unavoidable in this way (for example liabilities on sub-sales that required the specific goods supplied by the promisor and cannot be satisfied by replacement goods). However, in many cases the claimant will have swapped the continuing losses from not having the property that it would have suffered for a much simpler loss of use of money spent on the replacement. In this way the replacement crystallises the loss, because it reduces it to a much more easily

---

[179] Eg *Air Studios (Lyndhurst) Ltd v Lombard North Central plc* [2012] EWHC 3162 (QB) (Males J), where purchase of a replacement was the reasonable thing to do to mitigate losses of profits. Although this was not in fact undertaken, it was nevertheless the measure of loss because deemed by the mitigatory principle to have taken place.

[180] The difference between the cost of purchasing on the market and the price obtainable by selling to the market is discussed further below in section 4.5A(ii)(a). If an exact replacement is unavailable it may be reasonable to expect the claimant to purchase an approximate replacement that fulfils its needs: *Uctkos v Mazzetta* [1956] 1 Lloyd's Rep 209 (Ormerod J) (tort).

[181] On the unusual facts of *Empresa Cubana Importada de Alimentos v Octavia Shipping Co SA (The Kefalonia Wind)* [1986] 1 Lloyd's Rep 273 (Bingham J), the damage to the goods (maize intended for cattle and chickens) led to their being confiscated by a public authority and compulsorily sold at a mandatory (low) price to the pig market. In such circumstances the claimant had behaved reasonably and there was no break in the chain of causation and so the credit the claimant had to give was of the actual low price received, not the market price of the maize: Bingham J at 289 and 291. In that case some of the *undamaged* maize was also confiscated and condemned, but that broke the chain of causation and the defendant was not responsible for it: Bingham J at 288.

[182] *AW Group Ltd v Taylor Walton* [2013] EWHC 2610 (Ch) (Hodge QC) obiter at para 233, and the cases cited therein.

quantifiable sum, albeit that it does not eliminate it, as the loss of use of money will continue to accrue until judgment.

The losses that are not avoided by the replacement are discussed in section 4.4A below.

(i) Sale of Goods and the Market Replacement Measure

(a) Is There a Market? Which Market?

There cannot be a market replacement where there is no available market.[183] Whether there is an 'available market', whether the price should be taken at the date of delivery (as set out in sections 51(3) and 53(3)) or later, and whether the market price rule applies at all, all depend upon what is reasonable in the circumstances— specifically on what the reasonable buyer would have done to avoid his loss.[184] The crucial factor is whether the market can provide a reasonable replacement for the property (ie property matching the same specification or sufficiently similar or equivalent that the claimant can be expected to make do with it or reasonably use it as a replacement)[185] and at the place where the goods were wanted.[186] The market may even be a black market (operated in breach of price control covenants).[187] However, the market has to be a market in the relevant goods, and the claimant is not expected to go unreasonably far in seeking out an alternative supplier.[188] In line with the cases on repair,[189] a claimant is entitled to a true replacement and is not required to take something worse, or to buy more cheaply at auction where that is more risky (due to lack of warranties) and not the market the claimant is accustomed to.[190] Thus in one (non-goods) case a claimant was entitled to buy serialisation rights to a book directly from the copyright holder when the defendant failed to deliver, even though the cost was more than twice the price under the breached contract with the defendant.[191]

---

[183] See section 4.2B(i) above.

[184] When this is forgotten there are often arid discussions about whether a market for equivalent goods a few months later or in another location is a market such that the presumptive measure in section 51(3) is engaged or is applicable instead as the proper measure under section 51(2), section 51(3) not applying for lack of an available market. See eg *Air Studios (Lyndhurst) Ltd v Lombard North Central plc* [2012] EWHC 3162 (QB) (Males J). The same question—what should the claimant reasonably have been expected to do—applies in both cases, and the route chosen to navigate the particular sub-sections is of no real importance.

[185] See eg *Hinde v Liddell* (1875) LR 10 QB 265 (more expensive replacement); *Coastal (Bermuda) Petroleum Ltd v VTT Vulcan Petroleum SA (No 2) (The Marine Star)* [1994] 2 Lloyd's Rep 629 (Mance J), appeal allowed on other grounds: [1996] 2 Lloyd's Rep 383 (CA).

[186] *Obaseki Bros v Reif & Sons Ltd* [1952] 2 Lloyd's Rep 364 (Lord Goddard).

[187] *Mouat v Betts Motors Ltd* [1959] AC 71 (HL).

[188] *Lesters Leather & Skin Co Ltd v Home and Overseas Brokers Ltd* (1948) 82 Ll L Rep 202 (CA).

[189] Below at nn 256–57.

[190] *Ferngold Plant Hire Ltd v Weham* (CA), 13 March 2000 (a case of failure to redeliver after hire).

[191] *Times Newspapers Ltd v George Weidenfeld & Nicolson Ltd*, 28 March 2001 (Bell J).

(b) Timing of the Market Price

Although sections 51(3) and 53(3) talk of the date of delivery, the justification for the presumption that this is the date of assessment is the mitigation principle. Accordingly, the appropriate date for taking the market price is either (i) the date on which the buyer without unreasonable delay in fact goes to the market to buy a replacement, or (ii) the date on which all reasonable buyers would have gone or could have been expected to go to the market, even if earlier or later than the date of delivery.[192]

There are many reasons why it may be reasonable for the claimant not to have resorted to the market for a replacement immediately on delivery (or to have done so prior to the date of delivery, in cases of termination for anticipatory breach), and they are discussed below at chapter seventeen, section 17.2. In all such cases the market value at the date of delivery is irrelevant, although the market value at a later date *is* relevant. Key examples of the reasons that displace and delay the date when a reasonable replacement should be obtained, and that are discussed in that section, include: latency of the defect, reasonably pressing the defendant for performance for a time, and not being able to afford to go to the market.

The non-delivery case of *Garnac Grain Co v Faure & Fairclough*,[193] as subsequently explained,[194] is authority for the proposition that where a large volume of goods can only be purchased at a reasonable price over a period of time, the court may measure the market replacement price as 'the price at which a buyer could obtain the goods over a period of days rather than the price that he would have to pay if required to make an immediate purchase' and 'may, or possibly should, adopt the price which would produce the lower of two alternative awards'.[195]

(ii) Destruction of Goods and the Market Replacement Measure

The market replacement cost is the normal measure in destruction of property cases.[196] Most destruction cases are tort cases, but contractual examples include carrier cases,[197] and sale of goods cases where the supplied goods destroy other property of the claimant.[198] The principles are essentially the same as in sale of goods

---

[192] In such a situation, strictly speaking, the prima facie rule in section 51(3) is disapplied in favour of the common law rules, which apply exactly the same measure but on a different date.

[193] *Garnac Grain Co Inc v HMF Faure & Fairclough Ltd* [1968] AC 1130 (HL).

[194] *Shearson Lehman Hutton Inc v Maclaine Watson & Co Ltd (No 2)* [1990] 3 All ER 723 (Webster J), obiter (*Shearson* was a non-acceptance case not a non-delivery case).

[195] Ibid Webster J at 730. See also the approach in relation to the gradual purchase of a large quantity of shares in *Asamera Oil Corp Ltd v Sea Oil & General Corp* [1979] 1 SCR 633 (SC of Canada), with a view to minimising the market effect that a large purchase or sale in one go would have. And as to non-acceptance cases, see chapter five n 30 below and surrounding text.

[196] See *Owners of Dredger Liesbosch v Owners of SS Edison (The Liesbosch)* [1933] AC 449 (HL); *Voaden v Champion (The Baltic Surveyor and Timbuktu)* [2001] 1 Lloyd's Rep 739 (Colman J) at para 23, appeal allowed in part [2002] 1 Lloyd's Rep 623 (CA).

[197] *Rodocanachi Sons & Co v Milburn Bros* (1887) 18 QBD 67 (CA); *The Arpad* [1934] P 189, [1934] All ER Rep 326 (CA).

[198] *Smith v Green* (1875) 1 CPD 92: a cow with foot and mouth disease effectively rendered worthless the other cows. Also *Parsons v Uttley Ingham & Co Ltd* [1978] QB 791 (CA). And see *Voaden v Champion (The Baltic Surveyor and Timbuktu)* [2002] 1 Lloyd's Rep 623 (CA), Rix LJ at para 83, confirming that the same measure applies in tort and contract.

cases, save that the Sale of Goods Act presumption in favour of the market measure that applies in such cases does not apply to non-sale of goods destruction or damage cases, because the Act does not apply to such cases.

In most destruction or damage cases the courts fail to focus on the distinction between the *cost* of purchasing a replacement on the market and the market *selling price* of the property, merely awarding the market 'value' of the property.[199] This rarely matters, of course, as usually the two are the same.[200] See further the discussion above in section 4.5 A(ii)(a).

One (tort) case where that distinction *was* made was *The Maersk Colombo*, where the market replacement measure was disapplied because it was not reasonable for the claimant to purchase a £2.4m replacement for its dock crane, which would have had to be completed in the US and shipped to Southampton.[201] The claimant had no intention of purchasing such a replacement because it had already ordered one at the date of the destruction, and so was correctly confined to the market *selling* price of the crane, some £665,000, as that was its actual loss. Similarly in *Ali Reza-Delta Transport Co Ltd v United Arab Shipping Co*,[202] the market re-sale value of the goods at the time and place of their destruction was awarded, there being no evidence that the claimant intended to replace the goods (although that point was not decisive in this case). In both of these Court of Appeal decisions[203] the following dictum of Holland J (set out in the judgment of Clarke LJ) in *The Maersk Colombo* was approved:

(1) On proof of the tortious destruction of a chattel, the owner is prima facie entitled to damages reflecting the market value of the chattel 'as is'.
(2) He is so entitled whether or not he intends to obtain a replacement.
(3) The market or resale value is to be assessed on the evidence, there being no standard measure applicable to all circumstances.
(4) If the claimant intends to replace the chattel, and if the market or resale value as assessed is inadequate for that purpose, then the higher replacement value may, in the event, be the appropriate measure of damages.
(5) When and if replacement value is claimed, the claimant can only succeed to the extent that the claim is reasonable; that is, that it reflects reasonable mitigation of its loss.
(6) The claim will ordinarily be reasonable if it is reasonable to replace the chattel and the cost of replacement is reasonable.

Thus, as is clear from that dictum and the two Court of Appeal decisions, in destruction cases the claimant is entitled to the market selling price, and is only entitled to displace that by the market replacement measure if it *does* intend to purchase a replacement and such a replacement is reasonable. The intention test forms part of

---

[199] Eg *The Llanover* [1947] P 80 (Pilcher J).

[200] Although confusion is caused where apparently what's awarded is the loss of profits on a particular fixture and the market value of the vessel before or after that fixture: *The Philadelphia* [1917] P 101 (CA). Where a replacement is available, the measure should be the cost of replacement plus any interim lost profits pre-dating the replacement.

[201] *Southampton Container Terminals Ltd v Schiffahrts-Gesellschaft 'Hansa Australia' mbH & Co (The Maersk Colombo)* [2001] 2 Lloyd's Rep 275 (CA).

[202] *Ali Reza-Delta Transport Co Ltd v United Arab Shipping Co* [2003] 2 Lloyd's Rep 450 (CA).

[203] *The Maersk Colombo* Clarke LJ at paras 71 to 72; *Ali Reza-Delta Transport Co Ltd* Tuckey LJ at paras 11–12.

the general reasonableness test which determines whether a market replacement is to be applied, especially where the market resale price (ie the value of the goods) plus consequential losses are lower than the replacement cost. This is broadly the same test as applies to determine whether a cost of cure by repair is recoverable, as discussed in detail below in section 4.3B.

The timing of the replacement, like in goods cases, will be the time at which the claimant could reasonably be expected to purchase the replacement. In *The Liesbosch* that date was some time after the collision because 'some substantial period was necessary to procure at Patras a substituted dredger'.[204] Likewise in *The Fortunity* no suitable vessel (to replace one of a fleet of 13 similar vessels) was available until next season.[205]

Further, in destruction cases impecuniosity of the claimant will more frequently be a problem than in cases of non-delivery under a sale of goods contract (where the claimant will usually have in hand the money that had been intended for the seller). In *The Liesbosch* itself the claimant's money was all tied up in the vessel and the particular contract with the port authority and it had to hire a replacement at a high price and then purchase it on finance with the help of the port authority itself.[206] In that case the delay caused by those steps was not brought into account but nowadays it would be (and the legal effect of impecuniosity in *The Liesbosch* was disapproved of by the House of Lords in *Lagden v O'Connor*[207]).

As the High Court of Australia observed in relation to the differing timing of the replacement and sale measures, whereas the date of trial may be appropriate for valuing the price of a replacement for destroyed goods, if (in contrast) '[i]t was to be *sold* immediately [then] the damages should reflect the price the injured party would have obtained on the intended date of sale' (emphasis added) and any price rise after that date is irrelevant to the loss.[208]

The replacement must be the same as or equivalent to what is being replaced. If the replacement is the same price but eg a different colour, the cost is recoverable.[209] If it is more expensive than an equivalent, only the cost of the equivalent is recoverable.

(iii) Damage to Property or Failure to Improve Property and the Market Replacement Measure

(a) Usually Cheaper to Repair Land and Ships

Many of the cases of damage to property (often tort cases) or failure to improve property (especially in the construction context) concern ships or land and buildings,

---

[204] *The Liesbosch* [1933] AC 449 (HL) Lord Wright at 465.

[205] *Owners of M/C Four Hearts v Owners of M/V Fortunity (The Fortunity)* [1961] 1 WLR 351 (Hewson J).

[206] *The Liesbosch* [1933] AC 449 (HL).

[207] *Lagden v O'Connor* [2004] 1 AC 1067 (HL). See the discussion of impecuniosity below in chapter sixteen, section 16.7.

[208] *Johnson v Perez* (1988) 166 CLR 351 (HC of Australia) at para 12, also para 15.

[209] *Gagner Pty Ltd v Canturi Corporation Pty Ltd* [2009] NSWCA 413 (CA of New South Wales) at para 105.

where repair is usually more economic than replacement. The frequent uniqueness of such property, often high transactional costs (commissions, fees and stamp duty land taxes), and the sheer trouble of trading it, will often mean that it is entirely unrealistic to expect the claimant to sell it when damaged or incomplete and purchase a replacement, in contrast with the usual situation with more fungible goods.[210]

In such cases where replacement is not reasonable, the claimant will have to either repair the property it has (see below in section 4.3), or live with it in a defective state (see below in section 4.5). As Lord Lloyd observed in *Ruxley*: 'Nobody in their senses would move house merely in order to have the pleasure of diving into a deeper swimming pool. The analogy with defective chattels, such as a motor car, for which there is a ready market, is very strained'.[211] Although in theory, in *Ruxley* the house with a 7 ft 6 ins deep swimming pool (what the promisee would have had in that case if there had been no breach) had the same market value as an identical with a 6 ft 9 ins swimming pool (what the promisee actually got), it would be impossible to find the same house but with the deeper pool, and stamp duty costs would make the move more expensive than rebuilding the swimming pool. Similarly, in most construction cases it is cheaper or more reasonable to repair the work than sell the land and buy a replacement, as is demonstrated by the fact that the promisee engaged builders in the first place, rather than merely trading on the market.

(b) Where it is Cheaper to Replace

Where damaged property is unusable in its current state and it is cheaper to replace than to repair, property is said to be a 'constructive total loss' (especially ships) or a 'write off' (especially cars), in which cases the claimant can recover the cost of replacement less any salvage value remaining in the property.[212]

Even if the property is still usable, it may still be cheaper to replace. In *Dominion Mosaics v Trafalgar Trucking*, given the loss of profits that would have been suffered during rebuilding and the cost of so doing, it was reasonable to purchase replacement premises rather than rebuild the existing premises after they burned down due to the defendant's tortiously caused fire.[213]

The same principles apply in relation to damage to goods. As Widgery LJ observed of such cases in *Harbutt's Plasticine Ltd v Wayne Tank & Pump Co Ltd* (a case that concerned damage to a building in breach of contract): 'If the article damaged is a motor car of popular make, the plaintiff cannot charge the defendant with the cost of repair when it is cheaper to buy a similar car on the market'.[214] Thus in one case of negligent advice and installation of a defective computer system, the claimant recovered the cost of a replacement system.[215]

---

[210] See section 4.2B(ii) above.

[211] Lord Lloyd in *Ruxley Electronics and Construction Ltd v Forsyth* [1996] AC 344 (HL) at 371. See also *Hollebone v Midhurst and Fernhurst Builders Ltd* [1968] 1 Lloyd's Rep 38 (HHJ Richards) at 39.

[212] Eg *The Fortunity* [1961] 1 WLR 351 (Hewson J) (ship); *Darbishire v Warran* [1963] 1 WLR 1067 (CA) and *Mason v British Railway Board* (CA), 6 October 1992 (cars).

[213] *Dominion Mosaics Ltd v Trafalgar Trucking Co Ltd* [1990] 2 All ER 246 (CA).

[214] *Harbutt's 'Plasticine' Ltd v Wayne Tank & Pump Co Ltd* [1970] 1 QB 447 (CA) at 473.

[215] *Stephenson Blake (Holdings) Ltd v Streets Heaver Ltd* [2001] Lloyd's Rep PN 44 (Hicks QC) at para 159. The reasonableness of the replacement was demonstrated by the fact that the defendant itself supported the decision to purchase that replacement.

An unusual set of facts arose in *Strutt v Whitnell*, where the seller offered himself to repurchase the defective land (it had a warranty of vacant possession but there was a tenant who wouldn't leave) for the purchase price, thus eliminating all loss; it was not contended that the property with vacant possession was worth any more than the sum that the claimant had paid and that the seller was offering to repay.[216] Given that it appears that, as the parties knew, the buyer did not want the house, which he had initially sold to the seller then rebought only so that he could use his right against the builder to claim for structural defects, the buyer's conduct in refusing to resell seems unreasonable, although the decision is justifiable on the facts by the judge not being convinced that the seller had made a firm offer or that the buyer did not have a good commercial reason for wanting the house.

(iv) Failure to Redeliver after Lease, Hire or Charter, and the Market Replacement Measure

The same principles allowing an award of the market replacement measure in appropriate cases apply in cases of redelivery of goods in a damaged state at the end of a lease, hire or charter,[217] although the sorts of goods that are leased, hired or chartered and litigated upon are often more valuable goods where the more economically sensible (and so reasonable) cure is typically repair rather than replacement. A tenant who is obliged to replace something is not required to upgrade it to bring it into line with current standards, unless legislation requires that.[218]

4.3 The Second Cure: Repair

A. Introduction

The principal alternative cure to market replacement in defective or damaged property cases, and the most common measure in land/construction/ship cases (where resorting to a market replacement is rarely realistic or reasonable), is that of employing a third party to repair the property or otherwise cure the defect.[219]

---

[216] *Strutt v Whitnell* [1975] 1 WLR 870 (CA).

[217] *Ferngold Plant Hire Ltd v Wenham* (CA) [2000] *Commercial Lawyer* 1424.

[218] *Sunlife Europe Properties Ltd v Tiger Aspect Holdings Ltd* [2013] EWHC 463 (TCC) (Edwards-Stuart J) at para 46(4).

[219] The key here is that the claimant has property that needs repairing. It therefore applies in cases of *services* that should have improved or repaired property as much as to property cases. Of course, where a defendant has promised to provide a 'pure' service (see the discussion above in chapter two at section 2.1A and n 3), with no property aspect, the claimant can then also sometimes obtain the cost of a replacement service provider as a reasonable cost caused by the breach, although frequently where property is not involved it will not be possible to obtain an alternative service, often because the time during which the service would have been useful has passed. There is no point in getting replacement exam tuition after the exam, or replacement cleaning after the relevant month when the cleaning should have been provided. In other cases the claimant will have been locked into the consequences of the service, and no replacement service can save him from that. This is typically the case with advice: if I make loss-making investments on bad advice, paying for good advice will not cure the problem of

Where such a cure is reasonable, the cost of it is recoverable. Thus Oliver J observed in the case of *Radford v De Froberville*,[220] which concerned a purchaser's covenant with the vendor to build a wall on the purchased land, that:

> If [the claimant] contracts for the supply of that which he thinks serves his interest—be they commercial, aesthetic or merely eccentric—then if that which is contracted for is not supplied by the other contracting party, I do not see why in principle he should not be compensated with the cost of supplying it through someone else or in a different way, subject to the proviso, of course, that he is seeking compensation for a genuine loss and not merely using a technical breach to secure an uncovenanted profit.

This 'cost of supplying it through someone else' is the cost of repair discussed in this section.

As with the cost of cure by market replacement, whether the cost of cure by a third party's repair or similar is recoverable, or whether the claimant is confined to other damages measures (primarily the diminution in value of the defective or damaged property it is left with, discussed below in section 4.5), largely turns on the question of what is reasonable in the same sense used in the mitigation principle.

Indeed, the mitigation principle provides that where the repair is cheaper than the loss thereby avoided, it may be that all reasonable claimants would pay for the repair and in those situations the law will in fact deem the claimant to have done the same at the relevant time, even if it in fact did not do so.[221] Where the cure has already been incurred the question is whether it was a reasonable expense that therefore flows from the breach rather than being an independent or collateral decision (the causation principle). Otherwise, where the cure has not been performed but not all claimants would perform it, the question is whether the cure is intended and whether, given that intention and the question of proportionality, the not-yet-incurred cure can be said to be the true measure of loss as a future reasonable cost caused by the breach (the causation test again).

(i) Relationship with Other Measures

If the damage is rectified by a process that is not too remote or unreasonable, most usually cure/repair, then that cost of cure (plus any loss of use) replaces the diminution in value as the measure of loss: 'If the loss has only been avoided by incurring a substituted expense, it is that substituted expense which becomes the measure of that head of loss'.[222] The cost of repair results from and mitigates the diminution in value.[223]

Where the cost of repair is awarded, it will eliminate most other losses because the repair will put the property in the position it would have been in but for

---

the losses I have incurred. In property cases, however, the long-term effects of the breach can often be eliminated by repair.

[220] *Radford v De Froberville* [1977] 1 WLR 1262 (Oliver J) at 1270.

[221] See further section 4.3B(i)(c) below.

[222] *Jones v Stroud District Council* [1986] 1 WLR 1141 (CA); *Dimond v Lovell* [2002] 1 AC 384 (HL) Lord Hobhouse at 406; *Burdis v Livsey* [2003] QB 36 (CA).

[223] Eg *Dimond v Lovell* [2002] 1 AC 384 (HL) Lord Hoffmann at 401.

the breach. However, the claimant will be able to claim for any losses that are not avoided where not too remote, such as the costs of financing the repair,[224] damages for loss of use of the property during the period of repair,[225] and any inconvenience arising from the repairs. Such additional losses are discussed below in section 4.4 A.

B. The Reasonableness Test

(i) Introduction

Where, as is usual, the cost of repair or another cure is greater than the diminution in value and other losses that would be avoided by the cure, the court must ask whether the cure is nevertheless a reasonable cost to incur.

Although long-standing, and fundamental to the principles of mitigation and legal causation, the reasonableness test was authoritatively re-confirmed in the cost of cure context by the House of Lords in 1995 in the defective construction case of *Ruxley Electronics and Construction Ltd v Forsyth*.[226] It was there held that the £21,560 proposed cost of turning the 6 feet 9 inches deep pool (as built) into a 7 feet 6 inches deep pool (as contracted for) was out of proportion to the claimant's loss, including difference in property value, and it would not be reasonable for the claimant to incur it. Accordingly, the claimant was confined to recovery of its loss absent such a cure (the general measure discussed below in section 4.5), which in that case was £2,500 loss of amenity plus zero diminution in property value.

This expressly adopted[227] the approach of the famous American judge Cardozo J in *Jacob & Youngs v Kent* in 1921:[228]

> It is true that in most cases the cost of replacement is the measure ... The owner is entitled to the money which will permit him to complete, unless the cost of completion is grossly and unfairly out of proportion to the good to be attained. When that is true, the measure is the difference in value.

In that case the specifications for a residential house provided for pipework to be in pipes manufactured by a Reading company, whereas only two fifths of the pipes were so sourced, the remainder having been manufactured by various other companies. This was no difference in quality, appearance or value, and the pipes were mostly encased within the walls and so invisible. The very substantial cost of ripping out and replacing the piping was refused by the majority.[229]

---

[224] *FG Minter Ltd v Welsh Health Technical Services Organisation* (1980) 13 BLR 1 (CA).

[225] See chapter six.

[226] *Ruxley Electronics and Construction Ltd v Forsyth* [1996] AC 344 (HL). See also references to reasonableness in the many cases discussed in *Ruxley*, including *East Ham Corp v Bernard Sunley* [1966] AC 406 (HL) and *Radford v De Froberville* [1977] 1 WLR 1262 (Oliver J).

[227] [1996] AC 344 (HL) Lord Lloyd at 366. See also Lord Jauncey at 357.

[228] *Jacob & Youngs v Kent* (1921) 230 NY 239 (NYCA).

[229] The decision was by bare 4:3 majority. Cardozo J also gave this striking example: 'Specifications call, let us say, for a foundation built of granite quarried in Vermont. On the completion of the building, the owner learns that through the blunder of a subcontractor part of the foundation has been built of

(a) The Broad Application of this Test beyond Construction Cases

The reasonableness test for determining whether the cost of repairs are recoverable, as exemplified by *Ruxley Electronics*, applies wherever there is damaged or defective property (not only in construction cases), and in both contract and tort. Notably, the test applies to: cases of damage to goods, whether in contract[230] or tort;[231] cases of damage to buildings and land, whether in contract[232] or tort;[233] cases of damage to ships or aircraft, whether in contract[234] or tort; cases of supply of defective goods (although with all but the most expensive and unusual goods the market replacement measure will usually govern);[235] cases of defective construction;[236] cases of breach upon redelivery of chartered vessels,[237] leased aircraft[238] or rented land and buildings in an unsatisfactory state at the end of the hire period.[239]

(b) The Burden of Proof

The authorities do not speak with one voice as to where the burden lies in relation to reasonableness. The close connection between this test and the test of mitigation would suggest that the burden lies on the defendant to show that works are unreasonable. Thus it has been said that a claimant will 'ordinarily' be entitled to the cure[240] and that the cost of rectification will be 'prima facie' recoverable in defective construction cases.[241] However, there is authority that there is no presumption

---

granite of the same quality quarried in New Hampshire. The measure of allowance [*against the price due*] is not the cost of reconstruction'.

[230] *Stow (George) & Co Ltd v Walter Lawrence Construction Ltd* (1992) 40 Con LR 57 (Hicks QC); *Logical Computer Supplies Ltd v Euro Car Parks Ltd* [2002] IP & T 233 (Richard Fernyhough QC).

[231] *Italian State Railways v Minnehaha* (1921) 6 Ll L Rep 12 (CA); *Darbishire v Warran* [1963] 1 WLR 1067 (CA); *Southampton Container Terminals Ltd v Schiffahrts-Gesellschaft 'Hansa Australia' mbH & Co (The Maersk Colombo)* [2001] 2 Lloyd's Rep 275 (CA) Clarke LJ at paras 38 and 55, confirming that the test applies to tortious damage cases generally; *Aerospace Publishing Ltd v Thames Water Utilities Ltd* [2007] EWCA Civ 3 (CA). But as discussed below in section 4.5B(vi), there is sometimes confusion as to the true role of repair awards in damage cases.

[232] *Harbutt's 'Plasticine' Ltd v Wayne Tank & Pump Co Ltd* [1970] 1 QB 447 (CA) where the defendant's installation of unsuitable wax storage and dispensing equipment led to the claimant's factory burning down.

[233] *Farmer Giles Ltd v Wessex Water Authority* [1990] 1 EGLR 177 (CA); *Scutt v Lomax* (2000) 79 P & CR D31 (CA); *Bryant v Macklin* [2005] EWCA Civ 762.

[234] *Meredith Jones & Co Ltd v Vangemar Shipping Co Ltd (The Apostolis) (No 2)* [1999] 2 Lloyd's Rep 292 (Longmore J) at 301, [2000] 2 Lloyd's Rep 337 (CA) obiter at 348 (the cargo owner's liability for damage to the vessel was overturned); *Transafrik International Ltd v Venus Corporation Ltd* (2008) 121 Con LR 78 (Akenhead J) (the aircraft consultant's failure to repair the leased aircraft rendered repair uneconomic).

[235] See section 4.2 above.

[236] Such as *Ruxley* itself (above n 226).

[237] *Tharros Shipping Co Ltd v Bias Shipping Ltd (The Griparion (No 2)* [1994] 1 Lloyd's Rep 533 (Rix J); *Channel Island Ferries Ltd v Cenargo Navigation Ltd (The Rozel)* [1994] 2 Lloyd's Rep 161 (Phillips J).

[238] *Sunrock Aircraft Corp Ltd v Scandinavian Airlines System (SAS)* [2007] 2 Lloyd's Rep 612 (CA) at paras 28–35.

[239] See below in section 4.3B(iii)(d).

[240] *Southampton Container Terminals Ltd v Schiffahrts-Gesellschaft 'Hansa Australia' mbH & Co (The Maersk Colombo)* [2001] 2 Lloyd's Rep 275 (CA) Clarke LJ at para 30 principles 2 and 3.

[241] *Ruxley Electronics and Construction Ltd v Forsyth* [1996] AC 344 (HL) Lord Jauncey at 358.

in favour of the cost of cure and that the burden falls on the claimant to show that such cost is reasonable.[242]

The better view is that the burden of proof is to fall on the defendant as regards a cost of cure that has already been incurred or an argument that another step not taken should have been taken (such as market replacement), as an ordinary application of the causation and mitigation principles, but that the burden falls on the claimant in cases where the cost of cure has not yet been incurred, where the intention of the claimant to perform the cure is important and a matter that only the claimant can prove.

(c) No Reasonableness Test if the Cost of Repair is Less than the Diminution in Value

The reasonableness test only applies where the cost of repair is *greater than* the difference in value and other losses, ie than the compensable losses the claimant will be left with if the property is not repaired. In such cases, the question is whether it is reasonable to incur the cost of cure despite it being the more expensive solution.

If the repair is actually *cheaper* than the diminution loss (and market replacement is unavailable or also more expensive), then the repair clearly is reasonable and indeed will usually be deemed to have been effected by the duty to mitigate, whether or not the repair is in fact purchased.[243] No issue of reasonableness or intention to do the work arises.

Sometimes the cost of repair will be *the same as* the diminution in value. This is typical where the property cannot realistically be used without effecting the repairs, as any purchaser will have to effect the repair to use the property and so will deduct from the price it will pay the cost of that repair. In such cases the difference in value can be inferred from the cost of repair (whether or not the repairs are effected),[244] the two measures are the same, no issue of reasonableness arises, and the cost of repair is usually the proper award.[245] Of course, there are good reasons why in some cases the difference in value will not match the cost of repair exactly.[246]

---

[242] *Pegler Ltd v Wang (UK) Ltd* (2000) 70 Con LR 68 (Bowsher QC) at paras 228–30.

[243] Lord Lloyd in *Ruxley Electronics and Construction Ltd v Forsyth* [1996] AC 344 (HL) at 366. *Southampton Container Terminals Ltd v Schiffahrts-Gesellschaft 'Hansa Australia' mbH & Co (The Maersk Colombo)* [2001] 2 Lloyd's Rep 275 (CA) Clarke LJ at para 30 principle 1, quoted above at text to n 205. See for example *Culworth Estates Ltd v Society of Licensed Victuallers* [1991] 2 EGLR 54 (CA); *Redpath Industries Ltd v The Cisco* (1993) 110 DLR (4th) 583 (damage by carrier); *Douglas v Glenvarigill Co Ltd* [2010] CSOH 14 (Court of Session, Outer House) (defective delivery).

[244] *Jones v Herxheimer* [1950] 2 QB 106 (CA) at 117–18 confirmed in *Latimer v Carney* [2006] EWCA Civ 1417. See also the comments of Greer LJ in *The London Corporation* [1935] P 70 (CA) at 77: 'prima facie, the value of a damaged vessel is less by the cost of repairs than the value it would have if undamaged'; *Tharros Shipping Co Ltd v Bias Shipping Ltd (The Griparion (No 2)* [1994] 1 Lloyd's Rep 533 (Rix J) (although lost profits were awarded instead as repair was uneconomic); and *Clegg v Andersson (t/a Nordic Marine)* [2002] EWHC 943 (QB) (Seymour QC) at para 60, appeal allowed as the goods had been rejected [2004] Lloyd's Rep 32 (CA).

[245] In relation to a merchant vessel see *Channel Island Ferries Ltd v Cenargo Navigation Ltd (The Rozel)* [1994] 2 Lloyd's Rep 161 (Philips J) obiter at 167, and in relation to rented residential accommodation see *Jones v Herxheimer* [1950] 2 QB 106 (CA) at 117–18 confirmed in *Latimer v Carney* [2006] EWCA Civ 1417 (CA). See also *Drummond v S & U Stores* (1980) 258 EG 1293 (Glidewell J). See also the surveyor and related cases above in chapter three n 84 and accompanying text.

[246] See above in chapter three nn 85 to 86 and accompanying text.

(ii) Prompt and No More Than Necessary

It must be reasonable not only to pay for *a* cure, but to pay for *the* cure for which the claimant claims. Thus the cure must be:

— the cheapest necessary to cure the defect or damage;[247]
— performed within a reasonable time (which will usually be not until the defect was discovered, but then reasonably promptly after that[248]), although it will sometimes be commercially reasonable to await the outcome of litigation where the defendant denies liability[249] and/or where the clamant cannot afford the cure otherwise,[250] or because it is necessary to let the property settle before rectification is performed,[251] in which case the cost of repairs must be assessed at the date of judgment;[252] and
— such as will achieve as closely as possible the result promised by the defendant (although sometimes the cure can only give the next best thing[253]). The question is not whether the repair or replacement was performed reasonably, but whether it goes no further than necessary to make good the breaches.[254] A defendant cannot argue (for example) that a claimant should make do with a fence instead of the more expensive wall the defendant had himself promised to build and not built,[255] although where more expensive a 'complete and meticulous' job may be unreasonable where a slightly less meticulous job would not be.[256] A good example is that in cases of destroyed trees it is often reasonable to replace with young trees but not with far more expensive mature trees.[257] Where the cure gives more than the claimant would have had but for the

---

[247] *Dean v Ainley* [1987] 1 WLR 1729 (CA).

[248] *East Ham Corp v Bernard Sunley & Sons Ltd* [1966] AC 406 (HL) at 445. In that case the defect was discovered six years after the construction completed.

[249] *Dodd Properties (Kent) Ltd v Canterbury City Council* [1980] 1 WLR 433 (CA); *Bevan Investments Ltd v Blackhall and Struthers (No. 2)* [1978] 2 NZLR 97 (NZCA); *Cory & Son v Wingate Investments* (1980) 17 BLR 104 (CA); *South Parklands Hockey and Tennis Centre Inc v Brown Falconer Group Pty Ltd* [2004] SASC 81 (SC of South Australia); *Aldgate Construction Co Ltd v Unibar Plumbing & Heating Ltd* (2010) 130 Con LR 190 (Akenhead J).

[250] See the discussion of impecuniosity, below in chapter sixteen, section 16.7.

[251] *South Parklands Hockey and Tennis Centre Inc v Brown Falconer Group Pty Ltd* [2004] SASC 81 (SC of South Australia).

[252] See eg *The Board of Trustees of National Museums and Galleries on Merseyside v AEW Architects and Designers Ltd* [2013] EWHC 2403 (TCC) (Akenhead J) at para 108, where the cost of repairs was updated to the date of trial/judgment by an 'adjustment for inflation'.

[253] In *Radford v De Froberville* the covenant was to build a boundary wall on the defendant's land but the cure was to build a wall on the claimant's land (the defendant having since sold the land).

[254] *Sunlife Europe Properties Ltd v Tiger Aspect Holdings Ltd* [2013] EWHC 463 (TCC) (Edwards-Stuart J) at para 45.

[255] Oliver J in *Radford v De Froberville* [1977] 1 WLR 1262 at 1284. See also *William Cory & Son v Wingate Investments (London Colney) Ltd* (1980) 17 BLR 104 (CA), especially Walton J, speaking metaphorically at 117: 'Can it really be that the Court can substitute margarine for butter in this manner, even though many people cannot tell the difference?'

[256] *Dodd Properties (Kent) Ltd v Canterbury City Council* [1980] 1 WLR 433 (CA) Cantley J at 441 (appeal allowed, same report at 447, on different grounds).

[257] *Scutt v Lomax* (2000) 79 P & CR D31 (CA); *Bryant v Macklin* [2005] EWCA Civ 762.

breach, there may be a reduction in damages for betterment, which principle is discussed below.[258]

Thus where the work is yet to be done, the court will measure the award by the cheaper remedial scheme.[259] This is said to be part of the rule of mitigation.

Where work has been done at excessive cost, reasonable costs only are recoverable.[260] However, 'the actual costs will almost always be the starting point of any assessment of the reasonable costs of reinstatement'.[261] Usually if a claimant happens to be able to perform the repairs more cheaply than they would cost others, that fact is to be disregarded as *res inter alios acta* and the market cost is recoverable.[262]

(a) The Relevance of the Claimant Having Advice as to the Cure

The court will be slow to find that a remedial scheme adopted on (non-negligent) advice[263] or under scrutiny of a loss adjuster or similar oversight[264] was unreasonably expensive or unnecessary, although having taken such advice is not conclusive as to reasonableness. A stark example of such work being unreasonable, even where taken on advice, can be found in *McGlinn v Waltham Contractors Ltd*.[265] There the reasonable response to the defendant construction contractor's breaches would have been to incur the considerable costs of repair, but instead (and partly for reasons unrelated to the breaches) the claimant demolished the whole building with a view to rebuilding, although it never did rebuild. The claimant recovered the costs of repair which it should have incurred but now never would incur, as valued at the date when they should have been incurred, plus interest from that date, the court deeming the claimant to have done that which it would be reasonable to expect it to do.[266]

(iii) Proportionality and the Weighing Exercise

The key factor in the reasonableness test will be how the cost of cure compares with the loss suffered if the cure is not effected, ie the remaining difference in financial value, loss of amenity, and losses of profit (which losses are discussed below in

---

[258] See section 4.4B.
[259] *George Fischer Holding Ltd v Multi Design Consultants Ltd* (1998) 61 Con LR 85 (HHJ Hicks) at para 194.
[260] McKelvie M in *The Pactolus* (1856) Swa 173, 166 ER 1079; *The Pacific Concord* [1961] 1 WLR 873 (Lord Merriman P); *The Naxos* [1972] 1 Lloyd's Rep 149 (Brandon J) obiter; *Gagner Pty Ltd v Canturi Corporation Pty Ltd* [2009] NSWCA 413 (CA of New South Wales) at paras 105–7; *Sunlife Europe Properties Ltd v Tiger Aspect Holdings Ltd* [2013] EWHC 463 (TCC) (Edwards-Stuart J) at para 46(6).
[261] *Brit Inns Ltd v BDW Trading Ltd* [2012] EWHC 2143 (TCC) (Coulson J) at para 54.
[262] See chapter sixteen, section 16.7A.
[263] *The Pactolus* (1856) Swa 173, 166 ER 1079; *The Board of Governs of the Hospitals for Sick Children v McLaughlin & Harvey plc* (1987) 19 Con LR 25 (Newey QC) at 96. See further the discussions in *McGlinn v Waltham Contractors Ltd* [2007] EWHC 149 (TCC) (Coulson QC) at paras 795–98 and *Brit Inns Ltd v BDW Trading Ltd* [2012] EWHC 2143 (TCC) (Coulson J) at para 55 and the cases cited therein. In the tort property damage context see also *Lodge Holes Colliery Co Ltd v Wednesbury Corp* [1908] AC 323 (HL) Lord Loreburn CJ at 325.
[264] *Brit Inns Ltd v BDW Trading Ltd* [2012] EWHC 2143 (TCC) (Coulson J) at para 56.
[265] *McGlinn v Waltham Contractors Ltd* [2007] EWHC 149 (TCC) (Coulson QC) at paras 827–29.
[266] Ibid. See also *Tomlinson v Wilson* (Langan) 11 October 2007.

section 4.5). The courts will only award the cost of cure where it is 'proportionate' (or, perhaps more accurately, where it is not disproportionate). The centrality of whether the loss is 'proportionate' is now firmly established in the case law.[267]

The fact that the cost of cure exceeds the difference in value does not make cure disproportionate and so unreasonable; however if the cost of cure exceeds the difference in value by a dramatic margin then it is likely to be disproportionate.[268] In *Harrison v Shepherd Homes*,[269] some new residential homes had foundational problems which led to cracking, but the cost of 'repiling' the homes would be more than the value of the homes once repiled. The judge awarded the difference in value between the houses with and without the problems, which turned in particular on whether each home was mortgageable or not, plus an award to allow for the chance that some limited remedial work would be needed to fix the cracking at some time in the future (rather than merely optional, as it was at the date of trial). This was upheld by the Court of Appeal.

Similarly, the cost of repair may be disproportionate,[270] eg where a defective building is not worth repairing,[271] where a £1.1m repair would avoid a £15,000 diminution in value,[272] where after repair a vessel will be worth half the cost of the repairs,[273] or where replacement is cheaper and so repair uneconomic.[274]

The financial losses to be weighed against the cost of cure must include not only the financial difference in value of the property but also (where not built into that value) any lost profits. However, in a case where the market is such that after repair the revenue earnable on the profit-making property would not be enough to justify the repair, the cost of repair will not be awarded.[275] Conversely, where the claimant may get planning permission to develop the land, it may be reasonable to incur the

---

[267] *Channel Island Ferries Ltd v Cenargo Navigation Ltd (The Rozel)* [1994] 2 Lloyd's Rep 161 (Philips J); *Darlington Borough Council v Wiltshier Northern Ltd* [1995] 1 WLR 68 (CA) Steyn LJ at 79; *Ruxley Electronics and Construction Ltd v Forsyth* [1996] AC 344 (HL) Lord Bridge at 353, Lord Mustill at 361, and Lord Lloyd at 367 and 369; *Latimer v Carney* [2006] EWCA Civ 1417 at para 24. The US Restatement (Second) of Contracts applies a test of 'clearly disproportionate': §348(2)(b).

[268] This may be based on a principle described in the US Restatement (Second) of Contracts, under a section dealing only with construction contracts, as 'economic waste' §346(1). See also *Peevyhouse v Garland Coal & Mining Co* 382 P 2d 109 (1962) (SC of Oklahoma).

[269] *Harrison v Shepherd Homes* [2012] EWCA Civ 904.

[270] Eg *Ruxley Electronics and Construction Ltd v Forsyth* [1996] AC 344 (HL) itself; *Stow (George) & Co Ltd v Walter Lawrence Construction Ltd* (1992) 40 Con LR 57 (Hicks QC); *Channel Island Ferries Ltd v Cenargo Navigation Ltd (The Rozel)* [1994] 2 Lloyd's Rep 161 (Phillips J); *Meredith Jones & Co Ltd v Vangemar Shipping Co Ltd (The Apostolis) (No 2)* [2000] 2 Lloyd's Rep 337 (CA), obiter at 348; *Logical Computer Supplies Ltd v Euro Car Parks Ltd* [2002] IP & T 233 (Richard Fernyhough QC), where although damage to a computer hard disk led to loss of data, it would be unreasonable to go to the £45,000 expense of re-entering all the lost data as it was historical and of little (and decreasing) usefulness, and instead £15,000 was awarded for diminution in value of the computer system as a management tool.

[271] *Applegate v Moss* [1971] 1 QB 406 (CA) at 414.

[272] *Stow (George) & Co Ltd v Walter Lawrence Construction Ltd* (1992) 40 Con LR 57 (Hicks QC).

[273] *Attica Sea Carriers Corp v Ferrostaal Poseidon Bulk Reederei (The Puerto Buitrago)* [1976] 1 Lloyd's Rep 250 (CA) at 255.

[274] See text to nn 290 and following.

[275] *Tharros Shipping Co Ltd v Bias Shipping Ltd (The Griparion) (No 2)* [1994] 1 Lloyd's Rep 533 (Rix J).

heavy cost of cure rather than suffer the otherwise small diminution in value in the undeveloped land.[276]

(a) The Relevance of Personal Preference and Non-Financial Loss

Before *Ruxley Electronics*, it was said that the only recoverable loss was financial loss, and so a repair or other cure was reasonable in consumer cases or cases of personal preference because damages would be inadequate if the cost of cure were refused.[277] Thus in one case, reinstatement by rebuilding a collapsed house was reasonable where the land had 'special and particular value' to the claimant and in particular satisfied his inclination to keep horses and other livestock as part of his 'chosen way of life', which he would be unlikely to be able to do elsewhere.[278] In another, it was reasonable to repair a car that had great sentimental value for the claimant, even though it would have been cheaper to replace it.[279]

After *Ruxley Electronics*, as discussed below in chapter nineteen section 19.1C(i), personal preferences, eg as to a particular colour or type of brick, will now be taken into account more directly. This is because after *Ruxley* it is clear that the damages award absent a cure can take account of non-pecuniary loss (by an award of loss of amenity or similar).[280] Accordingly, the inadequacy of damages should play less of a part: if there is a non-pecuniary loss that is not too remote then it will sound in damages for non-pecuniary loss, and if there is a personal preference not amounting to such a recoverable non-pecuniary loss then arguably it should be irrelevant. Instead of arguments that damages are inadequate, the balance considered in the proportionality question is altered. The balance is now between the cost of cure and the financial value *and non-pecuniary loss* that would be suffered if cure is not ordered. In *Ruxley* itself the cost of rebuilding the pool at the time of trial was £21,560, and this had to be compared not merely with the financial loss suffered absent a cure (zero), but the total recoverable losses suffered absent a cure (the £2,500 of loss of amenity).[281]

The extent of the defect/omission is important to these figures. In *Ruxley* the 'contractual objective' of the contract had been achieved 'to a substantial extent',[282] and so the loss of amenity was fairly modest. As it was put in a later case, the swimming pool was 'fully functional'.[283] However, had the swimming pool in *Ruxley* which should have been 7 feet 6 inches deep, been only 4 feet deep rather than 6 feet 9 inches deep as was the case, and therefore too shallow for diving and not great for

---

[276] *Minscombe Properties Ltd v Sir Alfred McAlpine & Son Ltd* [1986] 2 EGLR 15 (CA).

[277] This is similar to the pattern of argument in specific performance cases, where an explicit justification of the award of specific performance is the inadequacy of damages.

[278] *Ward v Cannock Chase District Council* [1986] Ch 546 (Scott J) at 574 and 577 (tort).

[279] *O'Grady v Westminster Scaffolding Ltd* [1962] 2 Lloyd's Rep 238 (Edmund Davies J). But see '*Algeiba*' v '*Australind*' (1921) 8 Ll L Rep 210 (Hill J). Contrast *O'Grady* with *Darbishire v Warran* [1963] 1 WLR 1067 (CA), where the claimant's preference for the existing car, given that the claimant knew its reliability and history, was not enough to justify repair instead of cheaper replacement.

[280] Emphasised in *Ruxley Electronics and Construction Ltd v Forsyth* [1996] AC 344 (HL) by Lord Jauncey at 358 and Lord Lloyd at 370.

[281] See especially Lord Lloyd at 363, 367 and 369.

[282] Lord Jauncey in *Ruxley* at 358.

[283] *Melhuish & Saunders Ltd v Hurden* [2012] EWHC 3119 (TCC) (Havelock-Allen QC) at paras 63–64.

swimming, it might be conjectured that the house's financial value would have been affected and the loss of amenity would have been far greater than £2,500. In those circumstances the comparison would have been between the cost of cure of £21,560 (assuming the cost of rebuilding would have been the same) on the one hand, and a substantial difference in financial value and loss of amenity which together would be far in excess of £2,500. In those circumstances the cost of cure would be less likely to be disproportionate.

In many cases the calculus is not performed so explicitly. Sometimes the difference in financial value is not quantified, but it is nevertheless clear to the court that it is significant in amount, as in one case where the wall ties were not fully functional and might pose a danger of future physical damage and make it difficult to get buildings insurance.[284] In other cases it may not be possible accurately to estimate the difference in financial value if a cure is not effected, and in such cases it will usually be reasonable to effect the cure, particularly where it is not a matter of repairing defective work but instead performing work that the defendant promised to do and has simply refused to do.[285]

In other cases, similarly it is the loss of amenity that the courts will omit to explicitly quantify, while they nevertheless emphasise such non-pecuniary loss as a reason for justifying awarding the cost of cure or replacement, just as they did in cases prior to the *Ruxley* decision. Thus in one case it was reasonable to rebuild the claimants' bungalow built to their specifications on countryside land at a cost of around £284,000, and not confine the claimants to the difference in financial value of £108,000, in part because the property had been designed for the comfort of the claimants' autistic son and there was no evidence of close comparables, and that son typically took time to get used to anywhere new but had by the time of trial got used to the particular property.[286] Similarly, in a trespass case of damage to a memorial ground for the claimant's daughter, 'regard must be had to the special value to the claimant of the particular property damaged by the trespass, its use, position, features, seclusion, locality, uniqueness or rarity', although in that case the cost of replacement by exactly the same mature trees as had been destroyed was too high and a lower sum awarded for cure (along with a sum for loss of amenity).[287]

(b) Comparing the Cost of Replacement

Part of the assessment of reasonableness involves not only comparing the cost of repair with the diminution in value, but also comparing the cost of repair with (where realistic) the cost of replacement, although in practice the two comparisons are often the same exercise. Where replacement is much cheaper it will often be unreasonable to repair,[288] eg where the cost of repair 'greatly exceeds' the cost

---

[284] Ibid.

[285] See *Sunshine Exploration Ltd v Dolly Varden Mines Ltd* [1970] SCR 2 (SC of Canada).

[286] *Cox v Sloane*, 19 July 2000 (Seymour QC).

[287] *Scutt v Lomax* (2000) 79 P & CR D31 (CA) Clarke LJ.

[288] See the dictum in the construction contract case of *Mueller Europe Ltd v Central Roofing (South Wales) Ltd* [2013] EWHC 237 (TCC) (Stuart-Smith J) at para 142. In tort damage cases *Italian State Railways (The Legnano) v Owners of SS Minnehaha* (1921) 6 Ll L Rep 12 (CA) and *Darbishire v Warran* [1963] 1 WLR 1067 (CA) the market replacement was cheaper and the claimants had failed to mitigate by paying for repairs to the ship and car respectively. In the *Minnehaha* case Lord Sterndale MR at 13

of market replacement[289] or property is in any case 'commercially not worth repairing'.[290]

However, where there is sentimental value or similar the repair may still be reasonable even though more expensive than replacement,[291] and likewise if replacement is not readily available or any replacement would be less suitable than the repaired vessel.[292]

Further, the lost profits that would result during repair may mean that it is more reasonable to cure the loss in other ways, such as by replacing the premises.[293] In other words, the cost of repair must be added to the other losses that will be suffered during repair, when this is compared with the cost of replacement (or the losses that remain absent repair or replacement).

Conversely, repair will often be cheaper than replacement,[294] and so more reasonable.

(c) Is the Contract Price Relevant?

The case law rightly focuses on proportionality of the cost of cure as against the losses suffered if no cure is effected. However, it is arguable that the original contract price is also relevant to reasonableness. Although this was not mentioned by their Lordships in *Ruxley Electronics v Forsyth*,[295] it is not difficult to imagine that the £21,560 cost of cure of the shallow swimming pool would have seemed more reasonable (even when compared with an alternative £2,500 loss of amenity) if the contract price had been, say, £177,000, rather than the actual contract price of £17,707.40. The reason for the arguable difference in reasonableness in the two cases may be that with a higher contract price relative to the cost of cure, there would appear to be less hardship to the supplier and more room for the supplier still to make profit, as well as more reason for the claimant to exact a demanding standard (albeit that this may also play out in a larger measure of loss of amenity).[296]

---

referred to the question as being whether (as in that case) the repaired value 'is very much less' than the cost of repair. See also tort damage case *Derby Resources AG v Blue Corinth Marine Co Ltd (The Athenian Harmony)* [1998] 2 Lloyd's Rep 410 (Colman J), where treatment of the contaminated oil was unrealistic.

[289] *Darbishire v Warran* [1963] 1 WLR 1067 (CA) (tort car damage) Harman J at 1071, who noted that 'This arises out of the plaintiff's duty to minimise his damages. Were it otherwise it would be more profitable to destroy the plaintiff's article than to damage it'. This has been re-explained (wrongly) in *Coles v Hetherton* [2013] EWCA Civ 1704 (CA) at paras 30–32.

[290] *Mason v British Railways Board* (CA), 6 October 1992 (tort car damage, car was worth £600 before the accident and repairs would cost £2,085 so it was a 'write-off'); *Dimond v Lovell* [2002] 1 AC 384 (HL) (tort car damage) obiter Lord Hobhouse at 406. See also *Applegate v Moss* [1971] 1 QB 406 (CA) at 414 (contract of construction) and *Transafrik International Ltd v Venus Corporation Ltd* (2008) 121 Con LR 78 (Akenhead J) (contract with an aircraft consultant).

[291] See nn 279 and following above and accompanying text.

[292] *Algeiba v Australind* (1921) 8 Ll L Rep 210 (Hill J) (tort).

[293] *Dominion Mosaics & Tile Co Ltd v Trafalgar Trucking Co Ltd* [1990] 2 All ER 246 (CA).

[294] See text to nn 18–19 above.

[295] *Ruxley Electronics and Construction Ltd v Forsyth* [1996] AC 344 (HL).

[296] But see eg *Rowlands v Collow* [1992] 1 NZLR 178 (NZ HC) where the court awarded damages of NZ$41,000 for the cost of cure plus NZ$16,000 for professional costs plus NZ$18,000 for distress when awarding the cost of cure of a defective driveway that had cost around NZ$26,000 only six years earlier.

(d) The Statutory Cap in Cases of Redelivery of Land in Poor
    Condition after a Lease

In claims by landlords against tenants for disrepair or (as it is called in commercial cases) 'dilapidations', the common law rules of damages including remoteness apply,[297] also including the *Ruxley* test of reasonableness as regards the cost of cure.[298]

However, this is subject to a statutory cap that does not apply at common law, enacted by section 18(1) of the Landlord and Tenant Act 1927, which provides that the diminution in value of the landlord's reversion provides a cap on recovery: the damages for a tenant's breach of a leasehold covenant to keep or put premises in repair 'shall in no case exceed the amount (if any) by which the value of the reversion (whether immediate or not) is diminished owing to the breach'. Thus, although the usual common law inquiry must be carried out, where the cost of the works (including loss during the works) is greater than the diminution in value, the loss is capped even if the full cost of cure would have been awarded at common law as a reasonable cost. The typical case in which this will be important is one in which the landlord's reversion is ripe for redevelopment that would obliterate the relevant dilapidations, in which that this is the way the most competitive purchasers would see the property, and therefore the dilapidations have little or no effect on the sale value of the reversion.[299]

Further, a second element of section 18(1) of the 1927 Act provides that no damages for the cost of curing the tenant's redelivery in disrepair are recoverable if the premises 'in whatever state of repair they might be' would, at or shortly after the termination of the tenancy, 'have been or [will] be pulled down or such structural alterations made therein as would have rendered valueless the repairs covered by the covenant'.[300] The key point to note here is that the bar only operates where the landlord has already 'made up his mind' at the date of termination of the lease, and irrespective of the state of repair or disrepair of the property,[301] to perform the post-breach works that will obliterate the damage.[302] This is called the 'doctrine of

---

[297] *Ebbetts v Conquest* [1895] 2 Ch 377 (CA), affirmed [1896] AC 490 (HL).

[298] *Latimer v Carney* [2006] EWCA Civ 1417 Arden LJ at para 24; *PGF II SA v Royal and Sun Alliance Insurance plc* [2010] EWHC 1459 (TCC) (HHJ Toulmin) at paras 12–70.

[299] Eg *Ravengate Estates Ltd v Horizon Housing Group Ltd* [2007] EWCA Civ 1368. See also *Hammersmatch Properties (Welwyn) Ltd v Saint-Gobain Ceramics & Plastics Ltd* [2013] EWHC 1161 (TCC) (Ramsey J).

[300] Both aspects of the statutory section were a response to *Joyner v Weeks* [1891] 2 QB 31 (CA), in which the cost of cure was held by the Court of Appeal to be the normal, and possibly only, measure of damages for breach of a tenant's obligation to return property in good repair, even if (for example) the property was to be demolished upon surrender of the property and the landlord had no intention of repairing the property, and even if the property was let to a third party by a follow-on lease and would not be repaired beforehand. That position was modified even before the 1927 Act by *Ebbetts v Conquest* [1895] 2 Ch 377 (CA), affirmed [1896] AC 490 (HL).

[301] Hence the section specifying that the destruction would have taken place 'in whatever state of repair [the premises] might be'.

[302] *Cunliffe v Goodman* [1950] 2 KB 237 (CA); *PGF II SA v Royal and Sun Alliance Insurance plc* [2010] EWHC 1459 (TCC) (HHJ Toulmin) at paras 41–46.

supercession',[303] or the doctrine of 'negation', and in such cases claims can only be made for those aspects of the disrepair which survive the refurbishment.[304]

When valuing the diminution, the costs of repair will often nevertheless be awarded, it being often inferred by the courts that the value of the reversion was diminished by the amount of the costs of repair (because anyone buying the reversion would have to incur that cost, and indeed a period of disruption on top[305]) and therefore that this award complied with the cap in section 18(1).[306] Where the repairs are to be carried out the cost of repairs is prima facie the measure of the diminution in value.[307] However, it has been repeatedly confirmed that where the landlord (and/or a purchaser of the reversion) would be unlikely to perform the repairs, the cost of repairs may be little or no guide as to the diminution in value, which is, it must always be remembered, the true measure, and at the very least the amount of cost of repairs may need to be discounted to give an estimate of the diminution in value.[308]

In other cases, where the diminution in value of the reversion was zero, only nominal damages were available.[309] And in one pre-1927 Act case the lessor recovered an indemnity of its liability to the head lessor under the head-lease, that liability satisfying the test of remoteness.[310] That award is still available as a matter of law, but the total award is subject to the section 18(1) cap. A more common alternative measure of the diminution in value will be the market rate, or a capitalisation of the difference in the rates of return on the reversion.

In two mining lease cases (to which the statutory cap does not apply) the mining company failed to perform the restoration works it had promised, and in both the cost of cure measure was refused;[311] likewise in the case of a leased shop-front not restored by the lessee to its original state, where such restoration would not have affected the value of the shop in any way.[312] However, in *Haviland v Long* the cost of repairs were awarded, as a measure of the diminution in value.[313]

---

[303] Discussed in *PGF II SA v Royal & Sun Alliance Insurance plc* [2010] EWHC 1459 (TCC) (HHJ Toulmin) at para 54 and surrounding. See also *Sunlife Europe Properties Ltd v Tiger Aspect Holdings Ltd* [2013] EWHC 463 (TCC) (Edwards-Stuart J) at para 41.

[304] *Firle Investments Ltd v Datapoint International Ltd*, 9 May 2000 (Reese QC); *Ravengate Estates Ltd v Horizon Housing Group Ltd* [2007] EWCA Civ 1368.

[305] *Lintott Property Developments Ltd v Bower*, 27 May 2005 (Reddihough J).

[306] *Jones v Herxheimer* [1950] 2 KB 106 (CA); *Haviland v Long* [1952] 2 QB 80 (CA); *Latimer v Carney* [2006] EWCA Civ 1417.

[307] *Mather v Barclays Bank* [1987] 2 EGLR 254 (Baker QC) at 255. In that case more extensive renovations were carried out, so the costs could not be used to evidence the diminution in value.

[308] *Smiley v Townshend* [1950] 2 KB 311 (CA), Denning LJ at 322–23. Approved by Dillon LJ in *Culworth Estates Ltd v Society of Licensed Victuallers* [1991] 2 EGLR 54 (CA) at 56; *Crewe Services & Investment Corp v Silk* [1998] 2 EGLR 1 (CA) Robert Walker LJ at 4.

[309] *London County Freehold & Leasehold Properties Ltd v Wallis-Whiddett* [1950] WN 180 (Humpreys J); *Landeau v Marchbank* [1949] 2 All ER 172 (Lynskey J); *Ultraworth Ltd v General Accident Fire & Life Assurance Corp* [2000] 2 EGLR 115 (Havery QC).

[310] *Ebbetts v Conquest* [1895] 2 Ch 377 (CA).

[311] *Peevyhouse v Garland Coal & Mining Co* 382 P 2d 109 (1962) (SC of Oklahoma); *Tito v Waddell (No 2)* [1977] Ch 106 (Megarry V-C); and cf *Jordan v Norfolk County Council* [1994] 4 All ER 218 (Nicholls V-C) (tort). But contrast *Sunshine Exploration Ltd v Dolly Varden Mines Ltd* [1970] SCR 2 (SC of Canada).

[312] *James v Hutton and J Cook & Sons Ltd* [1950] 1 KB 9 (CA).

[313] *Haviland v Long* [1952] 2 QB 80 (CA).

(e) Repair by the Seller in Consumer Defect Cases

In consumer sale of defective goods cases there is an additional statutory right to repair of goods within a reasonable time if the buyer so requires and if it is not impossible or disproportionate, taking account of the value of the goods, the significance of the defect, the inconvenience to the buyer and the other remedies.[314] This is, of course, not the same as being awarded the costs of paying a third party to perform repairs.

(iv) A Genuine Intention to Incur the Cost of Cure if Awarded it

The following sections concern the importance of a genuine intention to effect repairs to the question of whether the cost of cure is reasonable.

(a) Where the Cost of Cure has Already been Incurred

One way of demonstrating a genuine intention to effect the cure is to pay for the cure before trial. This does not mean that the court will necessarily award the cost of that cure; the reasonableness test remains to be applied (as with any case of a claimant seeking to recover a mitigatory or other consequential expense that has been incurred). It does mean, however, that the genuineness of the intention to effect the cure, which is one part of the reasonableness test, is not in doubt. As the cure has already been effected, this factor, at least, weighs in the claimant's favour in the reasonableness balancing exercise.[315]

In practice the burden on the defendant seeking to prove unreasonableness (for example by showing disproportionality) in cases where the cost of cure has been incurred is a heavy one:

> The claimant who has in fact reinstated the property will ordinarily be entitled to recover the reasonable cost of doing so, even if the cost is greater than the diminution in value, unless he has acted unreasonably in reinstating the property.[316]

Further, the fact that the claimant has effected the cure and taken the risk of having to bear that cost itself (and not recoup it from the defendant) is also evidence of the loss of value or amenity suffered by the claimant, ie what it was worth to the claimant, and whether the repairs were reasonably necessary.[317] Thus, effecting the cure helps to show that significant pecuniary or non-pecuniary loss was expected to result absent the cure.

Occasionally, repairs will be found to have been unreasonable even though already carried out, especially where the claimant or its insurers carried them out with one eye on an expectation of reimbursement by the defendant.[318] Further, to

---

[314] Sections 48A and 48B of the Sale of Goods Act 1979.
[315] *Tito v Waddell (No 2)* [1977] Ch 106 (Megarry V-C) at 333.
[316] *Southampton Container Terminals Ltd v Schiffahrts-Gesellschaft 'Hansa Australia' mbH & Co (The Maersk Colombo)* [2001] 2 Lloyd's Rep 275 (CA) Clarke LJ at 281 para 30 principle 2. See further *Jones v Herxheimer* [1950] 2 QB 106 (CA). But see section 4.3B(i)(b) above and surrounding text as to the burden of proof.
[317] *Latimer v Carney* [2006] EWCA Civ 1417 Arden LJ at para 24.
[318] *Stow (George) & Co Ltd v Walter Lawrence Construction Ltd* (1992) 40 Con LR 57 (Hicks QC).

embark on the works while the dispute is part-heard is a high-risk strategy as it removes evidence that would have been available and leads to an unusually stringent application of the reasonableness test.[319]

(b) The Relevance of Intention

In the normal case the court has no concern with the use to which a plaintiff puts an award of damages.[320] It has been said that if a cost of cure is reasonable then that is the loss suffered[321] and 'intention as to the subsequent use of the damages ceases to be relevant'.[322]

However, where the cost of cure has not yet been incurred, it is not yet a loss, and if it is never incurred it will never be a loss,[323] meaning that the only loss suffered by the claimant is the ordinary measure of the difference in value plus consequential losses.[324] In these circumstances (save where the cure is the cheapest solution and deemed to take place by the mitigatory principle, or is used merely as a proxy to prove the diminution in value), it is necessary that the claimant prove that it intends to effect the cure. As a matter of conventional damages principles, this can be put in terms of the claimant needing to prove on the balance of probability that it will incur the expense so as to prove that the cost of cure is an actual future loss, in the same way that all other future losses must be proven on the balance of probabilities (where dependent upon the claimant). The usual way to address this question, however, is to look at the genuineness of intention as part of the reasonableness test.[325]

Megarry V-C has usefully explained some of the ways a claimant might demonstrate such a genuine intention:[326]

> An action for specific performance is doubtless one way of manifesting a sufficient intention that the work shall be done: but there are others. Thus the plaintiff may be contractually bound to a third party to do the work himself, as in Conquest v. Ebbetts [1896] A.C. 490.[327] Other cases of what may be called extraneous coercion may easily be imagined, such as the enforcement by a local authority of some statutory obligation.

---

[319] *Tomlinson v Wilson (t/a Wilson & Chamberlain)*, 11 May 2007 (Langan J).

[320] *Ruxley Electronics and Construction Ltd v Forsyth* [1996] AC 344 (HL) Lord Jauncey at 359 and Lord Lloyd at 372.

[321] See also Megarry V-C in *Tito v Waddell (No 2)* [1977] Ch 106 at 332 and 334.

[322] Lord Jauncey in *Ruxley* [1996] AC 344 at 359, also 357. See also *Bellgrove v Eldridge* (1954) 90 CLR 613 (HC of Australia) at 620.

[323] The House of Lords in *Ruxley Electronics and Construction Ltd v Forsyth* [1996] AC 344 (HL), for example, was concerned that, given that the shallower pool gave rise to only £2,500 loss of amenity, if awarded the £21,560 cost of cure, Mr Forsyth would have chosen not to effect the cure and rebuild the pool, and instead kept the money for other things. See also the tort damage case of *The Kingsway* [1918] P 344 (CA).

[324] Lord Lloyd in *Ruxley* [1996] AC 344 at 373.

[325] Lord Jauncey in *Ruxley* at 359.

[326] *Tito v Waddell (No 2)* [1977] Ch 106 at 333–34. For an example of a case where a genuine intention was found and was important, see *Radford v De Froberville* [1977] 1 WLR 1262 (Oliver J) at 1283–84.

[327] See also *Newton Abbot Development Co Ltd v Stockman Bros* (1931) 47 TLR 616 (Roche J), where the genuineness of intention was supported by the fact that a claimant's purchasers under a sub-sale were asking for repairs to be carried out, even though the property had been sold at a profit and the claimant was not *obliged* to the purchasers to carry out these repairs.

Or the claimant may have plans for development that require the cure to be performed.[328]

Conversely, where the courts are not satisfied that the claimant genuinely intends to do the work, they do not award cost of cure damages.[329] There are many reasons why a claimant might fail to satisfy a court as to such a genuine intention. These include that the cure is now impossible because the property has been disposed of[330] or destroyed.[331] Planning permission for the work may be unobtainable.[332] The property may be intended as development land for resale[333] or may in any case be sold or intended to be sold in its current state.[334] The reason for the work may have ceased to apply.[335] The claimant may have failed to effect the cure where it could easily have done so and afforded to do so.[336] (However, in many cases, as a result of impecuniosity or otherwise, it will have been reasonable to wait until trial rather than paying for the cure and then seeking recovery of the incurred cost.[337]) Finally, on this topic, the fact that the claimant has received an insurance pay-out of the cost of reinstatement does not mean that in fact the claimant intends to carry out such a reinstatement.[338])

---

[328] *Minscombe Properties Ltd v Sir Alfred McAlpine & Son Ltd* [1986] 2 EGLR 15 (CA).

[329] *Wigsell v School for Indigent Blind* (1882) 8 QBD 357 (Div Ct); *James v Hutton and J Cook & Sons Ltd* [1950] 1 KB 9 (CA) at 17; *Tito v Waddell (No 2)* [1977] Ch 106 (Megarry V-C) at 332–36; *Ruxley* [1996] AC 344 at 372–73 Lord Lloyd; *Southampton Container Terminals Ltd v Schiffahrts-Gesellschaft 'Hansa Australia' mbH & Co (The Maersk Colombo)* [2001] 2 Lloyd's Rep 275 (CA); *Birse Construction Ltd v Eastern Telegraph Co Ltd* [2004] EWHC 2512 (TCC) (Humphrey Lloyd QC). See also the sale of goods case of *Sealace Shipping Co Ltd v Oceanvoice Ltd (The Alecos M)* [1991] 1 Lloyd's 120 (CA), where the question was as to the manufacture of replacement goods, not the carrying out of works. However, there is a strain of dicta doubting the importance of an actual intention to do the work: see *De Beers UK Ltd v Atos Origin IT Services UK Ltd* (2010) 134 Con LR 151, where Edwards-Stuart J at para 345 wrongly says that an intention to effect the cure is unimportant, misunderstanding *Giedo van der Garde BV v Force India Formula One Team Ltd* [2010] EWHC 2373 (QB) (Stadlen J) at para 484 (where that judge was discussing recovery of damages for the value of the services, not for the cost of cure).

[330] *Eldon Weiss Home Construction Ltd v Clark* (1982) 39 OR (2d) 129 (Ont Co Ct); cf *Calabar Properties Ltd v Stitcher* [1984] 1 WLR 287 (CA) at 299. This did not itself appear to be a bar to recovery of the cost of repairs in *Meredith Jones & Co Ltd v Vangemar Shipping Co Ltd (The Apostolis) (No 2)* [2000] 2 Lloyd's Rep 337 (CA), obiter at 348, although disproportionality was.

[331] *The Argonaftis* [1989] 2 Lloyd's Rep 487 (Sheen J) at 493–94 (tort). However, even if repair is impossible, the cost of repairs may still be available as a measure of the diminution in value of the property: see text to nn 246–248 above. And if the property was destroyed with a view to a more radical method of cure, namely rebuilding, then even if that were unreasonable the cost of repair would still be recoverable as the cost the claimant should have incurred if mitigating its loss: *McGlinn v Waltham Contractors Ltd* [2007] EWHC 149 (TCC) (Coulson QC).

[332] *Ward v Cannock Chase DC* [1986] Ch 546 (Scott J) at 576.

[333] *Taylor Wholesale Ltd v Hepworths Ltd* [1977] 1 WLR 659 (May J) at 669–70 (tort); *IJ Manufacturing v Riel* [2001] BCSC 32 (British Columbia SC).

[334] *Dodd Properties (Kent) Ltd v Canterbury City Council* [1980] 1 WLR 433 (CA) Donaldson J at 456–57; *Birse Construction Ltd v Eastern Telegraph Co Ltd* [2004] EWHC 2512 (TCC) (Humphrey Lloyd QC) at paras 52–53. However, such a sale will not prevent an award of the cost of cure if the sale is *res inter alios acta* and to be disregarded. See below in chapter sixteen, section 16.12B.

[335] *Wigsell v School for Indigent Blind* (1882) 8 QBD 357 (Div Ct).

[336] *Birse Construction Ltd v Eastern Telegraph Co Ltd* [2004] EWHC 2512 (TCC) (Humphrey Lloyd QC) at para 52.

[337] See chapter sixteen, n 164 below and accompanying text.

[338] *Taylor Wholesale Ltd v Hepworths Ltd* [1977] 1 WLR 659 (May J) at 669 (tort).

(c) Giving an Undertaking to Spend the Award on a Cure

The law has a somewhat inconsistent approach to the relevance of a claimant who has not yet effected a cure giving an undertaking to the court that if it is awarded cost of cure damages it will use them to effect a cure. As set out above, judges often repeat that a claimant is free to do what it wishes with his damages.[339] On the other hand, what better way to demonstrate the genuineness of an intention to effect the cure? Such an undertaking given at trial was of some importance in *Dean v Ainley*.[340] Indeed, it has been persuasively argued by one commentator that it should always be a condition of a court awarding cost of cure damages (at least where greater than the difference in value) that a claimant undertakes to use them for the purpose of effecting a cure.[341]

What is clear, however, is that genuineness of intention is only one factor going to reasonableness. Lack of a genuine intention will prevent the award of the cost of cure, but the fact of an intention does not guarantee one. Where, for example, the cure is disproportionate, offering an undertaking to effect the cure will not render the cure reasonable. As Lord Lloyd put it in *Ruxley*, a claimant 'cannot be allowed to create a loss, which does not exist, in order to punish the defendants for their breach of contract'.[342] In *Ruxley* itself, the cure was found to be disproportionate and so unreasonable, despite an undertaking being offered by Mr Forsyth.[343]

(d) Intention and Contracts for the Benefit of Third Parties

As discussed in chapter twenty-one, in some circumstances a claimant can recover damages on behalf of and for the benefit of a third party, under the *Albazero* principle, with a duty then to account to the third party for those damages. When it comes in such cases to establishing a genuine intention to effect a cure, it must be the intention of *the third party* to effect the cure (once the damages have been accounted for to it by the claimant) that is relevant. The claimant's own intention to effect the cure is clearly irrelevant. For example, the financier claimant in *Darlington Borough Council v Wiltshier Northern Ltd* would have no interest in completing construction itself.[344]

As is also explained below, in some cases, under what is sometimes called Lord Griffiths' broader ground, the claimant can recover damages on its own behalf even though the contractual service would, if performed properly, have benefited a third party and not the claimant.[345] In these cases, in the usual way, if the claimant

---

[339] See above text to nn 322 to 324.

[340] *Dean v Ainley* [1987] 1 WLR 1729 (CA) at 1735. Oliver J mentioned the possibility of an undertaking in *Radford v De Froberville* [1977] 1 WLR 1262 at 1284, and Megarry V-C discussed it in *Tito v Waddell (No 2)* [1977] Ch 106 at 333.

[341] C Webb, 'Performance and Compensation: An Analysis of Contract Damages and Contractual Obligation' (2006) 26 *Oxford Journal of Legal Studies* 41 at 62–63.

[342] [1996] AC 344 at 373.

[343] *Ruxley Electronics and Construction Ltd v Forsyth* [1996] AC 344 (HL) Lord Lloyd at 362–63. It may have been important in that case that (as Lord Lloyd recites) the undertaking was first offered to the Court of Appeal, with the aim of side-stepping the first instance judge's finding of fact that Mr Forsyth had no intention of building a new pool. An undertaking offered at a similarly late stage was unpersuasive in *Crewe Services & Investment Corp v Silk* [1998] 2 EGLR 1 (CA) at 5.

[344] See the discussion in *Darlington Borough Council v Wiltshier Northern Ltd* [1995] 1 WLR 68 (CA) Dillon LJ at 75.

[345] See chapter twenty-one, section 21.2, below.

wishes to recover the cost of cure it must show it has a genuine intention to effect the cure.[346] Where the third party has a direct right of action then that may help the defendant to show that the claimant does not intend to effect the cure.[347]

(v) An Overall Test of Fairness?

It has been said that

> [i]n assessing what is the reasonable cost of reasonable reinstatement, the court will consider whether the amount awarded is objectively fair; that is fair to both parties. In particular, the court will not award a sum which is out of proportion to the benefit conferred on the claimant.[348]

The last sentence is merely a reference to the proportionality test discussed above, but the first sentence suggests that some broader test of hardship, even beyond proportionality to the claimant's loss, must be applied.

The better view is not that there is some further test of policy, but merely that in asking whether it is reasonable to spend the defendant's money on a third party cure, the court and claimant should not be any freer with the money than if it had been the claimant's own money. Thus it is useful to ask whether incurring that cost is 'what a reasonable man would do with his own money, even if he had ample funds' and whether he would 'think expenditure at that level reasonable to achieve the benefit that would be achieved—having the other options in mind'.[349] In other words, it may be useful to consider reasonableness on the counterfactual assumption that the money being spent was the claimant's and not the defendant's, to reflect the claimant's duty not to be frivolous merely because it is someone else's money at stake.[350] It is another aspect of the point made above that a genuine intention to effect the cure is necessary, but not sufficient, to establish reasonableness.[351]

4.4 Further Issues in Repair and Replacement Cases

A. Losses Recoverable in Addition to the Cost of Repair or Replacement

(i) Additional Costs

Where there is repair or replacement there may be additional costs incurred, and these will be recoverable under ordinary principles.

---

[346] Lord Griffiths in *Linden Gardens Ltd v Lenesta Sludge Disposals Ltd* [1994] 1 AC 85 (HL) at 96–97; *Alfred McAlpine Construction Ltd v Panatown Ltd* [2001] 1 AC 518 (HL) Lord Goff at 556, Lord Jauncey at 574.

[347] *Alfred McAlpine Construction Ltd v Panatown Ltd* [2001] 1 AC 518 (HL) Lord Jauncey at 574.

[348] *Southampton Container Terminals Ltd v Schiffahrts-Gesellschaft 'Hansa Australia' mbH & Co (The Maersk Colombo)* [2001] 2 Lloyd's Rep 275 (CA) Clarke LJ at para 30 principle 4.

[349] *Bryant v Macklin* [2005] EWCA Civ 762 (trespass damage to trees) Chadwick LJ at para 24.

[350] See eg *Sharif v Garrett & Co (a firm)* [2002] 3 All ER 195 (CA) Tuckey LJ at para 29. See also chapter fifteen, text to n 63 below.

[351] See text to n 344 above.

In some cases the claimant may incur and recover the costs of testing the damaged or defective goods,[352] and storing them until repair.[353] Or there may be costs of storing goods while a building is being repaired.[354] In a case of goods damaged by a carrier, additional stevedoring costs and warehousing costs from segregating the damaged cargo, as well as the costs of arresting the vessel to obtain security for the dispute and the costs of a salvage sale, were all recoverable.[355] Sometimes, temporary repairs may be necessary to allow damaged property to continue to perform a task or to travel to the place of permanent repairs.[356] There may also be additional finance costs payable if construction work overruns, or to pay for the repairs, and they may be recoverable.[357]

In other cases there may be costs of commissioning a replacement,[358] adapting the replacement,[359] or transporting the replacement.[360]

(ii) Damages for Temporary Loss of Use or Costs or Inconvenience Pending Replacement or Repair

Subject to the ordinary rules, the claimant will be able to recover damages for the loss of use of property during the period while the replacement or repair was awaited. These may consist of general damages for inconvenience, specific lost profits or costs, or the cost of a temporary replacement. All of these matters are covered in chapter six. This problem arises most frequently in cases of latent defects, or where for other reasons it will take considerable time for the claimant to extricate itself from the property or transaction or to acquire a replacement.[361]

---

[352] *KG Bominflot Bunkergesellschaft für Mineralöle mbH & Co v Petroplus Marketing AG* [2012] EWHC 3009 (Comm) (Hamblen J) (sale of defective goods).

[353] *Douglas v Glenvarigill Co Ltd* [2010] CSOH 14 (Court of Session, Outer House) (sale of defective goods). The defendant's argument that the claimant had acted unreasonably and should have avoided the cost by storing the vehicle on the street was rejected.

[354] *Rushmer v Countrywide Surveyors (1994) Ltd* (1999) 29 LS Gaz 30 [2000] PNLR 529 (Aylen QC) (surveyor's negligence).

[355] *CHS Inc Iberica SL v Far East Marine SA (m/v Devon)* [2012] EWHC 3747 (Comm) (Cooke J) at para 93.

[356] Eg *The Kingsway* [1918] P 344 (CA).

[357] *FG Minter Ltd v Welsh Health Technical Services Organisation* (1980) 13 BLR 1 (CA); *Saigol v Cranley Mansion Ltd (No 3)* (2000) 72 Con LR 54 (CA).

[358] *KG Bominflot Bunkergesellschaft für Mineralöle mbH & Co v Petroplus Marketing AG* [2012] EWHC 3009 (Comm) (Hamblen J) (sale of defective goods).

[359] *The Liesbosch* [1933] AC 449 (HL) (tortious damage).

[360] Ibid; *KG Bominflot Bunkergesellschaft für Mineralöle mbH & Co v Petroplus Marketing AG* [2012] EWHC 3009 (Comm) (Hamblen J) (sale of defective goods).

[361] See above in section 4.2B(v), and *The Liesbosch* [1933] AC 449 (HL).

Similarly, non-pecuniary losses are recoverable where caused by the defects in the property. The cases mainly concern defective cars,[362] and residential property.[363] This is the same principle as commonly leads to an award for inconvenience where buildings are rendered less comfortable or uninhabitable for a time due to floods, building works etc.[364]

(iii) Residual Diminution in Value

Even after repair, there may be a residual diminution in value (for example due to the stigma of having had repairs and therefore there being residual concerns as to the property), for which the claimant may claim damages in addition to the cost of repair.[365]

B. Betterment

The rule of betterment is the flip side of the principle of mitigation. The mitigatory and causation principles provide that the reasonable cost of repair or replacement is recoverable from the defendant. The rule of betterment provides that the cost of repair or replacement is irrecoverable to the extent that it was not reasonably necessary, and further that credit must be given for any betterment to the claimant's property that results from repair or replacement unreasonably going too far.

---

[362] See below under the discussion of delay in chapter six, section 6.5. *Jackson v Chrysler Acceptances Ltd* [1978] RTR 474 (CA), where damages were awarded for a holiday partly spoiled by a car that kept breaking down (the vendor under the hire-purchase agreement having been told specifically what the car was for), approved by Lord Steyn in *Farley v Skinner* [2002] 2 AC 732 (HL) at para 19. Also *Bernstein v Pamson Motors (Golders Green) Ltd* [1987] 2 All ER 220 (Rougier J) at 231 where a car's defects led to a 'totally spoilt day'; *Douglas v Glenvarigill Co Ltd* [2010] CSOH 14 (Court of Session, Outer House) (defective delivery) at para 42, where a family's defective third car led to troublesome journeys and trips to the car repairers and £500 was awarded. See also *Lagden v O'Connor* [2004] 1 AC 1067 (HL) at para 27. But see *Alexander v Rolls Royce Motor Cars Ltd* [1996] RTR 95 (CA), where damages for distress were disallowed on a contract for repair of a domestic car, although as a matter of fact it does not appear that there was any distress so such a finding was probably obiter. Similarly, such damages were refused in the case of a boat used for personal use in *Voaden v Champion (The Baltic Surveyor and The Timbuktu)* [2002] 1 Lloyd's Rep 623 (CA).

[363] Eg *Harrison v Shepherd Homes Ltd* [2011] EWHC 1811 (TCC) (Ramsey J) at paras 326–27, although mental distress damages were disallowed in that same case of sale of a residence at paras 324–25. This last point should be doubted: a residential home is intended both for enjoyment and financial value, and the fact that there was a financial diminution in value should not prevent a recovery for loss of amenity. Also *Hunt v Optima (Cambridge) Ltd* [2013] EWHC 681 (TCC) (Akenhead J) at para 263. See also the non-residential case of *Dominion Mosaics & Tile Co Ltd v Trafalgar Trucking Co Ltd* [1990] 2 All ER 246 (CA), where such lost profits during repair meant that it was actually more reasonable to replace.

[364] See below chapter nineteen, section 19.3.

[365] *Hughes v Quentin* (1838) 8 Car & P 703 (tort); *The Georgiana v The Anglican* (1872) 21 WR 280 (tort); *Payton v Brooks* [1974] 1 Lloyd's Rep 241 (CA) (tort) obiter Edmund Davies LJ at 244; *Thomas v TA Phillips (Builders) Ltd & Taff Ely Borough Council* (1985) 9 Con LR 72 (John Davies QC) (construction); *Mooney v Irish Geotechnical Services Ltd* (Irish High Court), 24 February 1997 (tort); *Leahy v Rawson* [2004] 3 IR 1 (Irish High Court); *Shepherd Homes Limited v Encia Remediation Ltd* [2007] EWHC 1710 (TCC) (Jackson J) at paras 719 ff (construction contract).

The basic principle has been summarised by Lord Hope, in the context of paying for temporary car hire while the claimant's tortiously damaged car is being repaired:

> It is for the defendant who seeks a deduction from expenditure in mitigation on the ground of betterment to make out his case for doing so. It is not enough that an element of betterment can be identified. It has to be shown that the claimant had a choice, and that he would have been able to mitigate his loss at less cost. The wrongdoer is not entitled to demand of the injured party that he incur a loss, bear a burden or make unreasonable sacrifices in the mitigation of his damages. He is entitled to demand that, where there are choices to be made, the least expensive route which will achieve mitigation must be selected. So if the evidence shows that the claimant had a choice, and that the route to mitigation which he chose was more costly than an alternative that was open to him, then a case will have been made out for a deduction. But if it shows that the claimant had no other choice available to him, the betterment must be seen as incidental to the step which he was entitled to take in the mitigation of his loss and there will be no ground for it to be deducted.[366]

As Lord Hope indicates, often, the minimum necessary to replace or repair will still give the claimant better than it had before the breach. The archetypal example of this is where something old has to be replaced and, as is often the case, only a new replacement is available. Thus a claimant was entitled to a new for old factory without giving credit for betterment in the contract case of physical damage of *Harbutt's Plasticine*, where the claimant had no option but to rebuild anew, it was 'not in practice possible to rebuild and re-equip a factory with old and worn materials',[367] and the claimant had added no extras to the factory. The same applies to any such replacement of new for old where an equivalent second-hand version is not available, and no credit need be given for the extra lifespan of the new property as compared with that being replaced.[368] Or, to take an example from a different context:

> If a man who has taken a third class ticket from London to the north by one of the great companies is by the negligence of that company damaged by their breach of contract to convey him, and he, to reduce the damages, goes to another of the great companies and takes a ticket by the next train on that line, and is thus enabled to reach his destination by the contract time, but cannot travel by that train unless he takes a first class ticket, his

---

[366] *Lagden v O'Connor* [2004] 1 AC 1067 (HL) Lord Hope at para 34.
[367] *Harbutt's 'Plasticine' Ltd v Wayne Tank & Pump Co Ltd* [1970] 1 QB 447 (CA) Cross LJ at 476.
[368] *Hollebone v Midhurst and Fernhurst Builders Ltd* [1968] 1 Lloyd's Rep 38 (Richards QC) (beams and electric wiring in a house); *Bacon v Cooper (Metals) Ltd* [1982] 1 All ER 397 (Cantley J) (rotor in the claimant's fragmentiser machine, damaged by steel supplied by the defendant); *Pegler Ltd v Wang (UK) Ltd* (2000) 70 Con LR 68 (Bowsher QC) (computer system) at paras 243 and 249; *PGF II SA v Royal and Sun Alliance Insurance plc* [2010] EWHC 1459 (TCC) (HHJ Toulmin) (landlord's refurbishment). See also the tort ship damage cases of *The Gazelle* (1844) 2 Wm Rob 279 and *The Pactolus* (1856) Swa 173,166 ER 1079, and the land damage case of *Dominion Mosaics v Trafalgar Trucking* [1990] 2 All ER 246 (CA). Cf *Haysman v Mrs Rogers Films Ltd* [2008] EWHC 2494 (QB) (Derek Sweeting QC) paras 18–19, where the defendant had promised to restore the claimant's home after use and no credit needed to be given for the inevitable improvements that this would involve. See also the construction case of *The Board of Governors of the Hospitals for Sick Children v McLaughlin & Harvey plc* (1987) 19 Con LR 25 (Newey QC) at 97.

damages may well be the whole of the sum he has to pay for that ticket, although the result is that he has enjoyed a greater luxury of travel.[369]

Where the defendant is able to show that the claimant did more than the minimum,[370] the extra—the betterment—won't be recoverable[371] but the reasonable cost will.[372] Thus in cases of tortiously damaged cars where the cost of temporary replacements are claimed, it has been held that although it is reasonable to engage a specialist accident hire company to deal with the replacement, part of the cost (including the credit aspect unless the claimant is impecunious) may be unrecoverable as relating to further services additional to the replacement car.[373]

An alternative approach to betterment has been suggested by the Court of Appeal in *Voaden v Champion*, in the judgment of Rix LJ.[374] Rix LJ sought to explain the earlier cases of betterment on the basis that in truth there was no betterment in those cases because a new part in an old machine and a new building do not really give an advantage, or else they were exceptions (the two exceptions specified by that judge consisting of repair of chattels, and the destruction of buildings where the building is needed to prevent the collapse of a building or loss of profits[375]). Rix LJ then indicated that a claimant must give credit even for betterment that was unavoidable, ie even where the claimant did not have a choice to take a lesser but still reasonable repair or replacement, if the repair or replacement provided a genuine added benefit. New for old would, he said, over-compensate the defendant. Thus in that case, only 8/30 of the £60,000 cost of a replacement pontoon (plus the £900 cost of deploying the pontoon) were awarded for the destroyed pontoon to allow for the fact that it had eight years of life left but the new pontoon would have had 30 years.[376]

The difficulty here is one that has already fallen for consideration by the law of unjust enrichment in relation to proof of enrichment.[377] The law of unjust enrichment recognises that ordering restitution will unjustifiably infringe the defendant's

---

[369] *British Westinghouse Electric & Engineering Co Ltd v Underground Electric Railways Co of London* [1912] 3 KB 128 (CA) at 147 (appeal allowed [1912] AC 673 (HL)).

[370] The burden is on the defendant: *Pegler Ltd v Wang (UK) Ltd* (2000) 70 Con LR 68 (HHJ Bowsher) at para 246; *Lagden v O'Connor* [2004] 1 AC 1067 (HL) Lord Hope at para 34; *Stellarbridge Management Inc v Magna International (Canada) Inc* (2004) 71 OR (3d) 263 (Ontario CA); *Kuwait Airways Corp v Iraqi Airways Co (No 6)* [2004] EWHC 2603 (Comm) (Cresswell J) at para 251.

[371] *Harbutt's 'Plasticine' Ltd v Wayne Tank & Pump Co Ltd* [1970] 1 QB 447 (CA) at 476 and *Axa Insurance UK plc v Cunningham Lindsey United Kingdom* [2007] EWHC 3023 (TCC) (Akenhead J). Cf the discussion above at text to n 256 and following.

[372] See the cases above at nn 261–62.

[373] *Dimond v Lovell* [2002] 1 AC 384 (HL) obiter Lords Browne-Wilkinson, Hoffmann and Hobhouse; Lords Nicholls disagreeing on the point and Lord Saville expressing no view; *Burdis v Livsey* [2003] QB 36 (CA); *Pattni v First Leicester Buses Ltd* [2011] EWCA Civ 1384, where the process of separating out the additional benefits from the 'basic hire rate' (as Aikens LJ called it) was dealt with in some detail. On the separate issue of when it is reasonable to use credit where impecunious, see *Lagden v O'Connor* [2004] 1 AC 1067 (HL).

[374] *Voaden v Champion (The Baltic Surveyor and The Timbuktu)* [2002] 1 Lloyd's Rep 623 (CA).

[375] Ibid, para 85.

[376] Distinguished in *Re-Source America International Ltd v Platt Site Services Ltd* [2004] EWHC 1405 (TCC) (Thornton QC) at para 51 (construction), appeal allowed (2005) 105 Con LR 30 (CA) although this point was approved at para 12; followed in *Kuwait Airways Corp v Iraqi Airways Co (No 6)* [2004] EWHC 2603 (Comm) (Cresswell J) especially at para 368 (tort).

[377] Readers are referred to specialist texts on unjust enrichment.

right to choose how allocate its resources unless the defendant freely accepted the benefit on the understanding that it would pay for it, or the defendant was incontrovertibly benefited (ie acquired a benefit that was already measured in money, such as cash itself, or made a direct saving of an expense the defendant would definitely have incurred). Otherwise, the defendant is being forced to pay for something that, although it may value it, it would not otherwise pay for, at least at that time, and unjust enrichment is refused for lack of actionable enrichment.

If a claimant's property is damaged or mis-repaired, and in repairing it the claimant necessarily improves the property, then the claimant's position has indeed been bettered if no credit is given for the improvement. The property may be worth more, or may last longer. But if the claimant does not sell the property and thereby realise the benefit, and does not intend to do so,[378] to require the claimant to give credit for that betterment, by a deduction from the cost of repair, is to force the claimant to pay for an improvement that it received but that it did not at that time choose to buy. The repair was not chosen by the claimant, the betterment (having new rather than old) was not chosen by the claimant, and if the claimant does not recover the full cost of the repair then it is being wrongly forced pay to improve its property. As a general principle, *Voaden v Champion* must be wrong.

The situation is entirely different where the betterment has by the date of trial being turned into money, ie the claimant has sold the property and got more money than it would but for the breach, or has run the property for more profit (due to higher efficiency or a longer life-span) than it would have but for the breach (as in *British Westinghouse*, one of the cases relied on by Rix LJ in *Voaden*), or the betterment will in the future be turned into money. Thus in the Australian case of *Hoad v Scone Motors Pty Ltd*, the claimants replaced their old tractor with a new one which would give them more money when they sold their farm 18 months later, which they had already planned to do.[379] The same is true where the claimant is recovering lost profits for a future period and as part of that must give credit for the savings it makes.[380]

In *Voaden*, the trial judge, who did not mention the word 'betterment', distinguished damage cases, with awards based on the costs of reasonable mitigation, from destruction cases like *Voaden* itself where the damages were (the judge said) measured by the value of the property lost.[381] (Rix LJ in the Court of Appeal doubted the relevance of the damage/destruction distinction.[382]) There was also some doubt as to whether the claimant truly would purchase a replacement.[383] On reflection, therefore, it may be that the decision is justified on its facts on the basis that the replacement was not a reasonable expense and/or not intended, and the

---

[378] This problem is particularly acute in the law of unjust enrichment in the cases on unwanted works on land or other property that is not to be immediately sold. See the discussion in *Cressman v Coys of Kensington (Sales) Ltd* [2004] 1 WLR 2774 (CA) per Mance LJ at paras 33–36.

[379] *Hoad v Scone Motors Pty Ltd* [1977] 1 NSWLR 88 (New South Wales CA).

[380] *Re-Source America International Ltd v Platt Site Services Ltd* [2005] 2 Lloyd's Rep 50 (CA).

[381] *Voaden v Champion (The Baltic Surveyor and The Timbuktu)* [2001] 1 Lloyd's Rep 739 (Colman J) at para 106.

[382] Ibid [2002] 1 Lloyd's Rep 623 (CA) at para 85.

[383] Ibid at para 91, although the trial judge said he assumed she would replace it: [2001] 1 Lloyd's Rep 739 (Colman J) at para 106.

market value of the vessel was therefore all that was recoverable. This would not be a matter of betterment, only of establishing the market value on a sale (which is significantly less than the cost of a new replacement). The same point arose in *Robot Arenas Ltd v Waterfield*.[384] There the set from television programme 'Robot Wars' was not a profit-earning chattel but rather was commercially useless and therefore unreasonable to replace, and so (had liability been found) no substantial damages would have been awarded.

C. Credit for Additional Revenue Where Goods Sold at Cost Price

Usually, where goods are replaced on the market with an equivalent the claimant will then be able to sell the replacement at the same price or use the replacement in the same way as the original. Occasionally, however, special features mean that the claimant sells the replacement at its cost price, with no profit, and further that the market will bear the cost of the replacement even if higher than the price that would have been payable if the contractual price that would have been payable if the defendant had not breached. The upshot of such a set of circumstances is that the more the claimant pays, the more revenue it will receive, although with no change to its profits. This is not betterment as such, as the claimant has bought a reasonable replacement at a reasonable price, but it is a case where the replacement property yields greater revenue than the original.

This arose in two cases discussed above in section 4.2B(ii). In both cases the court awarded substantial damages despite the fact that the claimant was able to pass on its costs to its buyers without any ill effects. If these decisions are right, it must be because the circumstances that meant that the claimant would not be making any profit from the profitable goods, and that the claimant's sub-buyers would take the goods on even at a higher price caused by the breach, are *res inter alios acta* and to be disregarded. Thus the fact that the claimant in *Diamond Cutting Works Federation Ltd v Triefus & Co*[385] did not want the diamonds for profitable sale but rather for sale at cost to its members was *res inter alios acta*. Likewise the fact that in *Clark v Macourt*[386] the valuable sperm could only (due to various regulations) be sold at cost price or less was also *res inter alios acta*. This explanation is more problematic for the second case, where the seller and buyer (both Australian doctors in this field) both knew that as a result of the regulatory regime in Australia the sperm were destined for sale without profit,[387] and in which such an explanation was not employed by the majority to explain their decision.[388] There is a lot to be said for Gageler J's dissent in the High Court of Australia and the Court of Appeal's decision below that no loss was suffered: the claimant did not have much

---

[384] *Robot Arenas Ltd v Waterfield* [2010] EWHC 115 (QB) (Edelman QC).
[385] *Diamond Cutting Works Federation Ltd v Triefus & Co* [1956] 1 Lloyd's Rep 216 (Barry J).
[386] *Clark v Macourt* [2013] HCA 56 (HC of Australia), facts discussed above at n 16.
[387] See para 42.
[388] The *res inter alios acta* reasoning does seem to have been at the back of the majority's minds at paras 22, 28 and 129, although their primary reasoning is based on the incorrect understanding that it is legitimate to claim the difference in value at the date of acquisition and thereby debar the court from looking at what happened later.

or any increased irrecoverable costs,[389] she was never going to make profit on the sperm, there was no clear evidence that she made less profit on the services that accompanied the sperm,[390] and the charging of the additional expense to the sperm customers appears to have arisen directly out of the breach and so not to be collateral or *res inter alios acta* or break the chain of causation, but rather to be successful mitigation.[391] That being the case, the decision is doubtful.

4.5 The Measure When there is No Market Replacement and No Repair

In most cases, either of the market replacement or repair measures will apply because one of those two methods of mitigation will be available.[392] Where neither of those cures is available, the court is simply left with the ordinary principles. The claimant can recover all not too remote unavoidable losses resulting from the destruction, non-delivery, damage or defectiveness of the property, up to and beyond trial.[393] As always with contract damages, the claimant must be put in the position in which it would have been but for the breach, subject to the remoteness, causation and mitigation principles.

A. Lost Profits

(i) Profits from a Lost Pre-Arranged Sub-Sale

Where a pre-arranged sub-sale is not too remote (see above section 4.2Bvi(c)) and the market measure does not apply (eg because there is no available market on which to buy a replacement or the sub-sale requires the specific goods), the claimant's recovery will be measured by the losses on the specific sub-sale, whether the sub-sale price is greater or less than the market price at the same time. (Where the sale is arranged after delivery, the matter is slightly different and dealt with under the next section.) Such losses will most frequently include the claimant's liability to the third party sub-buyer (below in chapter twenty) but will also include lost profits

---

[389] Unless the 'buffer' between what the claimant paid for the sperm and what she charged (see paras 34 and 46 and [2012] NSWCA 367 (NSW CA) at paras 39 and 121) was proportionate and so she retained more of a loss for the more expensive sperm. It does seem that there was some increase in irrecoverable costs of sourcing the alternative sperm: see Gageler J in the HCA at paras 71–2 and see the NSW CA at paras 129–30, but it appears that this was not pursued as part of the claim and the claimant asserted that she was completely indemnified as to those costs by her on sale: see the NSW CA decision at paras 36 and 131.

[390] Although Keane J suggested this might be the case in the HCA at para 129.

[391] See the NSW CA decision at paras 112 and 127.

[392] In most sale of goods cases, the market measure applies or, if not, the cost of repair measure. In most construction cases, the cost of repair measure applies.

[393] As set out, for sale of goods cases, in sections 51(2) and 53(2) of the Sale of Goods Act 1979. See further *Foaminol Laboratories Ltd v British Artid Plastics Ltd* [1941] 2 All ER 393 (Hallett J).

where such lost profits were caused by the non-delivery/destruction[394] or defect/damage.[395]

In cases of latent defects, the claimant will often have sold the goods under a specific sale on the market. The lost profit recoverable will be measured by the lost profit on the particular sub-sale entered into,[396] provided it is not so unusual as to be out of the parties' contemplation as a possible sub-sale (which it won't be if it was made on the market).

(a) Avoiding Losses through Pre-Arranged Sub-Sales

Where the sub-sale is not too remote, there may be options the sub-sale affords the claimant which will allow it to mitigate loss. The claimant may have a cancellation clause in the sub-sale contract enabling it to get out of the contract without any liability.[397] In such a case it may be reasonable to expect the claimant to cancel the sub-sale and merely claim lost profits against the buyer (rather than the cost of the replacement). Equally, however, it may be that (by the mitigation rule) not all buyers could be expected to take that step, given that there may be commercial relationship benefits to satisfying a sub-sale rather than cancelling it, even though it is profit-neutral (because the defendant is satisfying any lost profits claim).[398]

Still more difficult is the case where the claimant has liability to the sub-buyer and no cancellation clause, but still has the option of merely breaching the contract with the sub-buyer and paying damages. In many cases this will in fact not reduce the claimant's loss.[399] Even if it would, it will often not be reasonable for relationship

---

[394] *Engell v Fitch* (1868) LR 3 QB 314 at 334, affirmed in qualified terms (1869) LR 4 QB 659 at 665–68 (land); *Grébert-Borgnis v J & W Nugent* (1885) 15 QBD 85 (CA) (non-delivery); *Re Hall (R and H) Ltd and WH Pim Junior & Co's Arbitration* [1928] All ER Rep 763 (HL) (non-delivery); *Household Machines Ltd v Cosmos Exporters Ltd* [1947] KB 217 (Lewis J) (non-delivery); *A/S D/S Heimdal v Questier & Co Ltd* (1949) 82 Ll L Rep 452 (Morris J) (goods perished after failure to load); *MV Pyramid Sound NV v Briese Schiffahrts GmbH and Co (The Ines)* [1995] 2 Lloyd's Rep 144 (Clarke J) at 157–58 (carrier non-delivery; recovery was the sum lost on the sub-sale not the larger amount claimed as the market value). The loss was too remote in *Seven Seas Properties Ltd v Al-Essa (No 2)* [1993] 1 WLR 1083 (Lightman QC).

[395] *Garside v Black Horse Ltd* [2010] EWHC 190 (QB) (King J); *Louis Dreyfus Trading Ltd v Reliance Trading Ltd* [2004] 2 Lloyd's Rep 243 (Andrew Smith J).

[396] *Butterworth v Kingsway Motors Ltd* [1954] 2 All ER 694 (Pearson J) (lack of title discovered after sub-sale, which was then undone, so equivalent to a latent defect case; defendant's lost profit from sale to the claimant was recoverable against the third party and further up the chain); *Garside v Black Horse Ltd* [2010] EWHC 190 (QB) (King J).

[397] There apparently was such a clause in the *Williams v Agius* contract, although as explained above, the sub-sale was too remote in that case. As for the cancellation clause: the umpire and majority of the Court of Appeal found that the term was not incorporated; the first instance judge, Hamilton LJ dissenting in the Court of Appeal, and at least Lord Atkinson and Lord Moulton in the House of Lords, found that the term was incorporated. See Viscount Haldane LC [1914] AC 510 at 516–18, Lord Atkinson at 525–26 and 528, and Lord Moulton at 531–32.

[398] Cf *James Finlay & Co Ltd v NV Kwik Hoo Tong Handel Maatschappij* [1929] 1 KB 400 (CA), where it was held that the mitigation rule did not require a buyer to rely on a conclusive evidence clause to force goods with an incorrectly dated bill of lading through onto his sub-buyers because it would damage the buyer's commercial reputation to do so.

[399] To take *Williams v Agius* as an example: If the sub-sale is performed by purchase of a replacement, the claimant's loss is the difference between the contract price of the goods (16s 3d per ton) and the market price of a replacement (23s 6d per ton), giving 7s 3d per ton. If the sub-sale is breached the claimant's loss is the profit the claimant would have made on the contract (the sub-sale price of 19s per

or reputation reasons to require the claimant to do so, and further damages on a sub-sale may (for all the reasons being discussed here) be unpredictable.[400]

(ii) Profits from a Lost Sale to the Market on Delivery

(a) Buying Price or Selling Price?

Where there is no available market for buying a replacement, and the property would have been sold, the measure of recovery is the lost profit from such a sale. This applies to non-delivery/destruction cases[401] and cases of patent (or discovered latent) defects.[402] Thus if a seaport was closed and so the claimant would have had to wait at port incurring hire charges, that had to be taken into account in assessing lost profit.[403] Properly understood, in this situation the claim should be for the market selling price, as the claimant is not buying a replacement but merely selling its goods.

Even where there is an available market on which a replacement could have been purchased, if the claimant was intending to sell the property to the market and this is not too remote a purpose (and it rarely *will* be too remote), the proper measure of recovery should be the lost profits from the market selling price (as compared with the contract price), not the cost of purchasing a replacement by the market replacement price (as compared with the contract price).

In most cases this is a distinction without a difference because 'the difference between buying and selling prices in a market may be expected to be marginal',[404] but where there *is* such a difference the loss should still be measured by the market selling price and not the market replacement price, since it will often be unreasonable to avoid that loss by purchasing a replacement from the market at a higher cost only to resell it immediately at a lower cost, thereby increasing the losses.[405]

The majority of the case law is consistent with this approach, but it does not speak with one voice.

---

ton less the contract price of 16s 3d per ton) plus the damages on the sub-sale (the market value of 23s 6d per ton, less the sub-sale contract price of 19s per ton), still giving 7s 3d per ton.

[400] Lord Dunedin [1914] AC 510 at 523 in *Williams v Agius.*

[401] *Duff & Co v The Iron and Steel Fencing and Buildings* Co (1891) 19 R 199 (Court of Session, 1st Division) (non-delivery of sheds); *J Leavey & Co Ltd v George H Hirst & Co Ltd* [1944] KB 24 (CA) (non-delivery of overcoats); *Lesters Leather & Skin Co Ltd v Home and Overseas Brokers Ltd* (1948) 82 Ll L Rep 202 (CA) (non-delivery): a small reduction was made to allow for the uncertainty that the profits would have been earned; *Duncombe v Porter* (1953) 90 CLR 295 (HC of Australia) (defective delivery); *Coastal (Bermuda) Petroleum Ltd v VTT Vulcan Petroleum SA (No 2) (The Marine Star)* [1994] 2 Lloyd's Rep 629 (Mance J), appeal allowed on other grounds: [1996] 2 Lloyd's Rep 383 (CA); *Truk (UK) Ltd v Tokmakidis GmbH* [2000] 1 Lloyd's Rep 543 (Jack QC).

[402] See above in section 4.2B(v)(f).

[403] *R Pagnan & F Lli v Lebanese Organisation for International Commerce (The Caloric)* [1981] 2 Lloyd's Rep 675 (Lloyd J).

[404] *Attorney General of the Republic of Ghana v Texaco Overseas Tankships Ltd (The Texaco Melbourne)* [1993] 1 Lloyd's Rep 471 (CA) Leggatt LJ at 475. Also *Kwei Tek Chao v British Traders and Shippers Ltd* [1954] 2 QB 459 (Devlin J) at 497.

[405] The situation is different where the claimant has pre-sold the goods and so doing was not too remote. In that situation it would be reasonable to purchase a market replacement so as to satisfy the sub-sale, rather than to breach that sub-sale.

In *The Texaco Melbourne*, where there was little available market in Ghana from which to purchase replacement oil but a market of Ghanaian buyers who would buy oil (the sale to which was the intention of the claimant importer), the Court of Appeal rightly applied the selling price, rather than looking to an alternative market in Italy from which oil could have been purchased (but was not).[406] Similarly in the defective goods case of *Jones v Just*,[407] the Manilla hemp was imported for sale on the local market. A panel of the Court of Exchequer upheld an award by a jury upon Blackburn J's direction that they find the difference between

> the rate which the hemp was worth when it arrived [which was the amount realised by auction of the defective hemp] compared with the rate which the same hemp would have realised had it been shipped in the state in which it ought to have been shipped,

ie the difference between the market selling prices.[408] In contrast, in *St Ströms Bruks Aktie Bolag v Hutchison*[409] the claimant had imported wood-pulp and already entered into an on-sale contract, and therefore the House of Lords correctly confirmed that the market replacement cost was the applicable measure: whether there was a difference between the buying and selling prices or not, the claimant would reasonably have to buy a replacement to fulfil the on-sale.

The approach outlined follows that of Devlin J in *Kwei Tek Chao v British Traders and Shippers*,[410] which was a late delivery case where the buying and selling prices were significantly different. Devlin J rightly held that 'the buying price has nothing to do with the calculation which I have to make' and

> a calculation which supposes, incorrectly and notionally, that he should go out and buy another quantity of the same goods, has nothing to do with the reality of the matter. What he wishes to do in those circumstances, in order to put himself in the same position, is to sell the goods, not to buy them.[411]

It is therefore completely clear in late delivery cases that it is the effect of the delay on the market sale profit that is to be measured.[412]

Devlin J in *Kwei Tek Chao* contrasted the position in delay cases with that in non-delivery cases where

> the buyer, if he had wanted to provide himself with similar goods for the purpose of fulfilling his contract of resale, could have gone out in the market as on the day of the rejection and bought them, and the difference between the contract price and the lower buying price would have been the profit which he made by virtue of the rejection, and which in one sense he has lost because he did not reject. It is also true that if a buyer rejected and wanted

---

[406] *Attorney General of the Republic of Ghana v Texaco Overseas Tankships Ltd (The Texaco Melbourne)* [1993] 1 Lloyd's Rep 471 (CA).

[407] *Jones v Just* (1868) LR 3 QB 197.

[408] See also *Kliger v Sadwick* [1947] 1 All ER 840 (Hilbery J) where the claimant in a non-delivery of clothing cases recovered the 'price which the plaintiff could have obtained for each of the types of coat', ie the selling price.

[409] *St Ströms Bruks Aktie Bolag v John & Peter Hutchison (a firm)* [1905] AC 515 (HL).

[410] *Kwei Tek Chao v British Traders and Shippers Ltd* [1954] 2 QB 459 (Devlin J).

[411] Ibid at 497–98.

[412] See eg *Czarnikow Ltd v Koufos (The Heron II)* [1969] 1 AC 350 (HL) (carriage), *Kwei Tek Chao v British Traders and Shippers Ltd* [1954] 2 QB 459 (Devlin J) (sale), and the discussion of such cases in chapter six. The Sale of Goods Act 1979 does not contain a provision on this.

to claim damages against the seller, the measure of damages, which could only arise at all if the market had risen and not fallen, would be the price at which he bought goods in order to put himself in the same position. But those calculations, and the relevance of the buying price, depend upon the fact that the buyer has not got the goods. He has returned them, and is putting himself in the same position, so far as he can, as if the contract goods had been delivered. Therefore he has to buy.[413]

These comments are correct provided the claimant has to fulfil a contract of resale, as Devlin J observed. In that situation the loss must be measured by the cost of replacement, whether higher than the market selling price or not. Where, however, the claimant has no contract of resale and was merely intending to sell the non-delivered/destroyed/defective/damaged goods to the market, the loss should be measured by the market selling price.

However, it was the buying market price that was applied in the non-delivery case of *Oxus Gold plc v Oxus Resources Corporation*.[414] In that case the buyer had a warrant entitling it to purchase shares in a gold-mining company at 15¼p per share. It sought to exercise the warrant on 30 December 2003 with a view, the buyer said, to selling the shares immediately. The latest date on which the seller could lawfully have given effect to the warrant and delivered the shares was 13 January 2004. Although the point wasn't resolved, the evidence indicated that the sale price on that date may well have been far higher than the purchase price, and so it would have been 'commercially irrational' for the buyer to have purchased a replacement on the market (given that it wanted them only to sell).[415] Despite this finding, and the fact that the buyer did not have any onward sale arranged, Langley J reluctantly held that he was bound by a principle from *Williams Bros v Ed T Agius Ltd*,[416] and that authority at the highest level obliged him to award the market replacement price and not the market selling price.

In this respect, *Oxus* is wrong. *Williams v Agius* did not deal with the situation where the buying and selling market prices differed. The Court of Appeal decisions in *Texaco Melbourne* (not referred to in *Oxus*), and general principle, show that the position that Langley J would have preferred if he did not believe himself bound by contrary authority is the correct one. Plainly the measure in section 51(3) of the Sale of Goods Act 1979 is only the prima facie measure, and in any event it refers to the 'market or current price of the goods' (which could refer to the market selling price as well as the market replacement price). Where the actual use of property is not too remote the market replacement measure is displaced (eg the latent defect cases such as *Bence Graphics*,[417] or cases where there is a sub-sale that is not too remote, such as *Hall v Pim*,[418] or cases where other mitigation should have been performed such as *Payzu v Saunders*,[419]) and the same approach should be taken where the intended

[413] [1954] 2 QB 459 at 497.
[414] *Oxus Gold plc v Oxus Resources Corporation* [2007] EWHC 770 (Comm) (Langley J) at paras 79–83.
[415] Ibid Langley J at para 80.
[416] *Williams Bros v Ed T Agius Ltd* [1914] AC 510 (HL): see above at text to n 125.
[417] *Bence Graphics International Ltd v Fasson UK Ltd* [1998] QB 87 (CA).
[418] *Re Hall (R and H) Ltd and WH Pim Junior & Co's Arbitration* [1928] All ER Rep 763 (HL).
[419] *Payzu Ltd v Saunders* [1919] 2 KB 581 (CA).

use is merely a sale to the market and where equally a purchase from the market is not expected and does not take place.

(b) Identifying the Market Price

A specific sub-sale price obtained by the claimant (and which is, of course, fixed on the market) will often be good evidence of the selling price that could have been achieved on the market. In *Sony Computer Entertainment UK Ltd v Cinram Logistics UK Ltd*, the claimant only claimed its sub-sale price for the computer memory cards the defendant had lost, and the defendant did not argue the point as that figure was lower than the market selling price (because the sub-sale price included a discount as a part of a major trading relationship).[420] In other cases, too, the actual sub-sale price is accepted as good evidence of the market price.[421]

In other cases, where it is not easy to show the market price, the court will (as in other areas of contract damages) rebuttably presume that the property was worth the agreed price plus expenses, under the presumption that the claimant would have broken even.[422] This may be the best explanation of *Wallington v Townsend*,[423] where damages in an aborted sale of land case were awarded in the amount of the wasted conveyancing costs and non-returned deposit where the claimant could not prove the value of the property that would have been conveyed.[424] If, for example, the property is worth the price paid but no more, the claimant should not recover any additional wasted expenditure, as it would have been incurred even if the property had been supplied; in other words, the claimant would have made a loss on the transaction in the amount of the wasted expenditure.[425]

This same presumption of breaking even, leading to an award of the total expenditure, obtains in goods cases.[426]

The cost of repairs, even if not actually incurred (or deemed to have been incurred), will often be a useful prima facie measure of the diminution in market value, where the property is economical to repair, but is no more than a prima facie

---

[420] *Sony Computer Entertainment UK Ltd v Cinram Logistics UK Ltd* [2008] EWCA Civ 955.

[421] *A/S D/S Heimdal v Questier & Co Ltd* [1948–49] 82 Ll L Rep 452 (Morris J) at 472–73; *The Argonaftis* [1989] 2 Lloyd's Rep 487 (Sheen J); *KG Bominflot Bunkergesellschaft für Mineralöle mbH & Co v Petroplus Marketing AG* [2012] EWHC 3009 (Comm) (Hamblen J) at para 74; *CHS Inc Iberica SL v Far East Marine SA* [2012] EWHC 3747 (Comm) (Cooke J) at para 92. This may be the best explanation for *M&J Marine Engineering Services Ltd v Shipshore Ltd* [2009] EWHC 2031 (Comm) (Field J), where the remoteness or otherwise of the sub-sale was not considered.

[422] See chapter eighteen, section 18.3.

[423] *Wallington v Townsend* [1939] 1 Ch 588 (Morton J).

[424] See also *Lloyd v Stanbury* [1971] 2 All ER 267 (Brightman J).

[425] *Wallington v Townsend* [1939] 1 Ch 588 (Morton J) at 592.

[426] *McRae v Commonwealth Disposals Commission* (1951) 84 CLR 377 (HC of Australia). See also *CCC Films (London) Ltd v Impact Quadrant Films Ltd* [1985] QB 16 (Hutchinson J) in a carriage case of lost goods. Cf *Cullinane v British 'Rema' Manufacturing Co Ltd* [1954] 1 QB 292 (CA). Costs of improvements made before the contract was finalised may, however, not be recoverable as being too remote and being solely at the risk of the purchaser: *Lloyd v Stanbury* [1971] 2 All ER 267 (Brightman J). That decision was made at a time when reliance loss was incorrectly thought to be an independent measure, and may best be explained on the basis that it would go too far to presume on those facts that the claimant would have broken even when those particular pre-contractual costs are included.

measure.[427] In some cases the diminution in value will be found to be less than the cost of repairs, however, in which case the cost of repair will, on ordinary principles, only be recoverable if reasonable,[428] and otherwise only the smaller diminution figure will be recoverable.[429]

(c) Lost Profits from a Later Sale

In *Mallon v Halliwells LLP* the defendant solicitors' negligence prevented the claimant acquiring in 2005 a right to the proceeds of sale of a development, but the development was (and would but for the breach have been) only sold in 2008.[430] As there had been no failure to mitigate by selling earlier, the value of the right the claimant lost had to be taken at trial rather than as at 2005, and such an assessment would take into account the facts known at trial. By that date, the development was in negative equity and although some investors might have bought the right to proceeds, the claimant failed to prove it had any real market value.

(d) Lost Profits from Repeat Orders

Where not too remote, recovery can be made for lost profits from repeat orders lost as a result of the claimant breaching its contract with sub-buyers.[431] However, in one case a loss of appointment as school uniform outfitters to a particular convent school was held too remote a loss from the late delivery by the defendant cloth supplier.[432]

---

[427] *Coles v Hetherton* [2013] EWCA Civ 1704 (CA). *The Glenfinlas* [1918] P 363 (Roscoe R); *The London Corporation* [1935] P 70 (CA) Greer LJ at 77; *Meredith Jones & Co Ltd v Vangemar Shipping Co Ltd (The Apostolis) (No 2)* [1999] 2 Lloyd's Rep 292 (Longmore J) at 301, appeal allowed on liability [2000] 2 Lloyd's Rep 337 (CA) at 348 (contract); *Dimond v Lovell* [2000] QB 216 (CA) Scott V-C at para 100, affirmed [2002] 1 AC 384 (HL); *Southampton Container Terminals Ltd v Schiffahrts-Gesellschaft 'Hansa Australia' mbH & Co (The Maersk Colombo)* [2001] 2 Lloyd's Rep 275 (CA) Clarke LJ at paras 76–77. As to the cost of repairs being a prima facie measure for diminution in value in other contexts, see text to nn 308–10.

[428] See section 4.3B above.

[429] *The London Corporation* [1935] P 70 (CA) obiter Greer LJ at 77: 'evidence may establish that the value of the vessel undamaged is exactly the same as her value after she had been damaged'; *Darbishire v Warran* [1963] 1 WLR 1067 (CA); *The Argonaftis* [1989] 2 Lloyd's Rep 487 (Sheen J) at 493–94; *Stow (George) & Co Ltd v Walter Lawrence Construction Ltd* (1992) 40 Con LR 57 (Hicks QC) (contract). However, the current legal position is as discussed in sections 4.5B(v) and in *Coles v Hetherton* [2013] EWCA Civ 1704 (CA) (dismissing the appeal against Cooke J [2012] EWHC 1599 (Comm) and explaining *Darbishire v Warran* [1963] 1 WLR 1067 (CA) at paras 30–32), such that in physical damage cases the immediate diminution in value is not subject to the mitigatory principle. Of course, the relationship between the difference in market value and cost of cure measure is well understood in the construction context, where the latter is a specific expense to avoid the former and/or which is caused by the former. See further A Burrows, *Remedies for Torts and Breach of Contract*, 3rd edn (Oxford, OUP, 2009) at 242–43.

[430] *Mallon v Halliwells LLP* [2012] EWCA Civ 1212.

[431] *GKN Centrax Gears Ltd v Matbro Ltd* [1976] 2 Lloyd's Rep 555 (CA) (defective goods). See further below in chapter eighteen, section 18.2C(iv)(e).

[432] *Simon v Pawson and Leafs Ltd* [1932] All ER Rep 72 (CA).

(iii) Lost Profits from Use Other than Sale

Where non-delivered/destroyed/defective/damaged property would have been used for a different purpose than sale (eg employed in a business), lost profits may well be recoverable on ordinary principles.[433] This may include the lost profits on development of real property that has been damaged[434] or not delivered,[435] although in another case the lost development profits were held to be too remote from a defect in title.[436] Recovery may also include the lost income the non-delivered property would have produced,[437] such as through a charterparty,[438] or the lost profits where a machine does not operate at the warranted rate.[439]

Again, these actual losses, when not too remote, are the full extent of the award. This may be greater or less than the market selling price, although often we will never know which, because in such situations the courts, quite rightly, do not trouble to discuss the market value of the property which was never intended to be sold on (and cannot be replaced) and is therefore irrelevant.[440]

The loss in these cases is therefore primarily the damages resulting from loss of use, which is discussed in detail in chapter six. No award of the value of the property should be made in addition where the loss of use award covers the remaining useful life of the property, since an award for loss of use for the remaining life of the property fully compensates the claimant and gives all that the claimant would have had but for the breach.[441] Where, however, the loss of use is only awarded for part of the life of the property, the residual diminution in value of the property at the end of that period should also be awarded.[442]

---

[433] *Montevideo Gas and Drydock Co Ltd v Clan Line Steamers Ltd* (1921) 6 Ll L Rep 539 (Roche J), affirmed (1921) 8 Ll L Rep 192 (CA) (non-delivery, gas production); *The Liesbosch* [1933] AC 449 (HL) (tortious destruction, profits from using vessel for dredging); *The Llanover* [1947] P 80 (Pilcher J) (tortious destruction, income under the vessel's current charter); *RG McLean Ltd v Canadian Vickers Ltd* (1970) 15 DLR (3d) 15 (Ontario CA) (sale of defective printing press led to lost profits); *Sunnyside Greenhouses Ltd v Golden West Seeds Ltd* (1972) 27 DLR (3d) 434 (Alberta CA), affirmed (1973) 33 DLR (3d) 384 (sale of defective greenhouse panels which caused lost profit from crops).

[434] *Farmer Giles Ltd v Wessex Water Authority* [1990] 1 EGLR 177 (CA): contract of indemnity but treated as if tort damages for trespass.

[435] *Cottrill v Steyning and Littlehampton Building Society* [1966] 1 WLR 1083 (Elwes J); too remote in *Diamond v Campbell-Jones* [1961] Ch 22 (Buckley J). Also *Joyce v Bowman Law Ltd* [2010] EWHC 251 (Ch) (Vos J), a professional negligence case.

[436] *Upton Park Homes Ltd v Macdonalds* [2010] PNLR 12 (Court of Session, Outer House), although mitigation was not discussed and may also explain the result.

[437] *Wenham v Ella* (1972) 127 CLR 454 (HC of Australia).

[438] *The Racine* [1906] P 273 (CA).

[439] *Cullinane v British 'Rema' Manufacturing Co Ltd* [1954] 1 QB 292 (CA). Only three years of profits were claimed in that case.

[440] Eg *Foaminol Laboratories Ltd v British Artid Plastics Ltd* [1941] 2 All ER 393 (Hallett J).

[441] In *British Westinghouse Electric & Manufacturing Co Ltd v Underground Electric Railways Co of London* [1912] AC 673 (HL) the claimant avoided loss by purchasing replacement machinery some time after delivery of the defective machinery. However, even if it had not, the claimant's claim for the difference in value, pursued although with little vigour (see p 680), should never have been made (and was not granted) because the machines were for use and the arbitrator and courts rightly recognised that such losses sounded in the costs or lost profit through the lift of the machines.

[442] See the breach of trust decision *Tang Man Sit v Capacious Investments Ltd* [1996] AC 514 (PC). As to the interaction between capital value and revenue in assessing loss, see further chapter eighteen, section 18.1, below.

B. The Diminution in Value in Cases Where No Immediate Sale is Contemplated

Where an immediate sale is contemplated, the diminution in sale price will be the measure of the loss, as discussed in the previous section. However, in many cases property is not intended for an immediate sale to the market, but rather to be used for commercial or non-commercial purposes. There remain two reasons why the diminution in value, ie the difference between market selling prices, may nevertheless be awarded, instead of or as well as the lost profits or loss of amenity from the commercial or non-commercial purposes (also discussed in the previous section).

(i) Capital Value as a Measure of the Lost Income Stream

First, the capital value of property provides a good presumptive measure of the use value of the property for its life. That is what the market is valuing.[443]

(ii) Most Non-consumable Assets are Ultimately Tradeable/Traded

Secondly, most property is not only used but is also, at the right time for its owner, traded.

Thus houses are lived in but traded at the right opportunity;[444] cars too.[445] Commercial machinery and premises are used but sit as assets on the company's books and are also sold or traded up at the right time.[446] The tradeable value of such property must at all times be a contemplated loss of the property, alongside any loss from use. The specific future date of the sale, when the property will cease to be used and held and will instead be sold, may be capable of establishment by evidence, but is often merely a matter of speculation.

Moreover, in most cases the date on which the claimant would have sold the property is a matter of circumstance and choice particular to the claimant and unrelated to the defendant's breach or discovery or cure of it, and so should be disregarded by the court as *res inter alios acta* (ie it is not necessary or arguably relevant in each case to have evidence as to when the claimant would in fact have sold his house or machine). The better approach is to deem a sale on the date on which the claimant has a free choice to make such a sale, after (for example) any

---

[443] See below in chapter eighteen, section 18.2B for a discussion of capital value as a measure of an income stream, and the cases cited therein. See in particular *Cullinane v British 'Rema' Manufacturing Co Ltd* [1954] 1 QB 292 (CA) as regards defective property, and *The Liesbosch* [1933] AC 449 (HL) at 463 and *The Llanover* [1947] P 80 (Pilcher J) as regards damaged or destroyed property.

[444] See below in chapter nineteen, section 19.1C. Thus in *Jarvis v Richards & Co*, 30 July 1980 (Nourse J) it was within a solicitor's contemplation that a claimant would hold a house for 9 months and then sell it.

[445] This is illustrated by *Butterworth v Kingsway Motors Ltd* [1954] 2 All ER 694 (Pearson J) at 702, in which there was a chain of sales of a car with no title. On the sale to a motor dealer it was clearly contemplated that the car would be resold, but on the sale by the motor dealer to Mr Hayton it was expected that he would use the car and not, as in fact occurred, resell it to the defendant. Nevertheless the liability on the sub-sale to the defendant, and the costs of that dispute, were held not to be too remote in the earlier links in the chain.

[446] Cf H Street, 'Supervening Events and the Quantum of Damages' (1962) 78 *LQR* 70 at 71.

period of being locked in or reasonably holding for a minimum time to make the initial purchase work for the claimant. (A deemed sale of a residential house may be after five or 10 years).

(iii) Thus Two Types of Loss: On-going and Capital

This means that in many cases the claimant can be said to have suffered two alternative losses: the continuing loss of use of the property while the property is held or deemed to be held, and the capital loss when the property is or is deemed subsequently to be traded.

No damages for loss of use after the future date of a putative sale should be awarded, because they are inconsistent with that measure. It would be double recovery to award damages for loss of use after that date, but is entirely proper to award damages for loss of use up to any date of assessment of capital loss.

In the swimming pool case, *Ruxley*, there could have been (but was not on the facts) a diminution in capital value to be realised when the house was sold, in addition to a loss of enjoyment during use.[447] In such a case, the claimant should have recovered the loss of amenity for a reasonable period during which it would be normal and not a personal choice to hold the house, say 10 years, then also the depreciation in the sale price likely after that time on a putative sale as a result of the shallower pool. Even absent such a diminution in financial value, the loss of amenity should only really have been awarded for that (say) 10 years, rather than forever.

(iv) Assessing Value

Given the competing reasons for calculating and awarding diminution, the courts rightly will not slavishly adopt the market selling price (where the diminution in value is not taken on the basis solely of a deemed immediate market sale), but will instead sometimes assess the value of the property as a going concern to the claimant.[448]

Tito v Waddell (No 2) was a uniquely difficult case.[449] Breach of a contractual undertaking to replant trees after the completion of phosphate mining on Ocean Island in the Pacific Ocean sounded in damages for the (relatively small) diminution in the value of the land where the trees had originally stood, the amount being reserved to another hearing. This is so even though there was no suggestion that the land was to be sold by the islanders. Without knowing how the diminution in value was assessed, it is difficult to say more.

Sometimes there will be no diminution in value, and in that case damages may be nominal. In a tort case of destruction of a billiard hall, the fire had actually saved the claimant the cost of clearing the site for development purposes and so no damages were awarded.[450] A difficult damage case arose in the concurrent contract and tort

---

[447] *Ruxley Electronics and Construction Ltd v Forsyth* [1996] AC 344 (HL).
[448] *The Harmonides* [1903] P 1 (Gorell Barnes J).
[449] *Tito v Waddell (No 2)* [1977] Ch 106 (Megarry V-C).
[450] *Taylor Wholesale Ltd v Hepworths Ltd* [1977] 1 WLR 659 (May J) at 669–70. See also *The London Corporation* [1935] P 70 (CA) Greer LJ at 77.

dispute of *Texaco Ltd v Arco Technology Inc*,[451] where the defendant's negligence in mis-loading a catalyst into the claimant's oil refinery reactor led to damage to the catalyst. The reactor was then out of use for a period until a new catalyst could be inserted and the main claim related to pecuniary losses from that delay. The claimant in fact unreasonably attempted to re-use the damaged catalyst, which led to its having to be destroyed and broke the chain of causation to any further loss. As regards damages for the harm to the catalyst itself, although its useful life had been reduced there was no market for second-hand catalysts or sensible repair possible. Only nominal damages were allowed.

(v) Is Diminution in Value Automatic?

The not improper willingness to award the diminution in value whether or not the property was to be sold has led to some thought that the diminution in value is recoverable automatically and irrespective of the other rules of damages. It is not. This can be seen from the following: (1) where damages are measured by the non-remote consequences of use of the property (such as the damages on a sub-sale of latently damaged property) that measure governs the loss whether greater than or less than the diminution in value at some earlier date such as the date of breach.[452] (2) where damages are measured by the cost of replacement or repair, that measure governs the loss whether greater than or less than the diminution in value at some earlier date—'If the loss has only been avoided by incurring a substituted expense, it is that substituted expense which becomes the measure of that head of loss';[453] (3) where the loss is reduced by a post-breach repair or replacement or otherwise, the actual cost governs the loss whether greater than or less than the diminution in value;[454] (4) where the property was already damaged,[455] or already due to be destroyed,[456] no loss is recoverable.[457]

However, in damage and destruction cases the diminution in value is said to be recoverable separately from the loss of use or cost of repairs, and is suffered instantly at the point of the collision or other damage.[458] This may be in part

---

[451] *Texaco Ltd v Arco Technology Inc*, 31 July 1989 (Phillips J) and then 1 October 1989 (Phillips J).

[452] *Redpath Industries Ltd v The Cisco* (1993) 110 DLR (4th) 583, *Bence Graphics International Ltd v Fasson UK Ltd* [1998] 1 QB 87 (CA) and *McSherry t/a Mainland Wine Negociants v Coopers Creek Vineyard Ltd* (2005) 8 NZBLC 101 (Panckhurst J), where the claimant was able to sell the defective or damaged property without loss. See above sections 4.2B(v)(b)–(d) and 4.2B(vi)(d).

[453] *Jones v Stroud District Council* [1986] 1 WLR 1141 (CA); *Dimond v Lovell* [2002] 1 AC 384 (HL) Lord Hobhouse at 401 and 406; *Burdis v Livsey* [2003] QB 36 (CA). For cases in which the cost of repair was less than the diminution in market value, see the cases cited at n 245 above.

[454] See chapter sixteen, section 16.13D(i)(b) below. *Galbraith, Pembroke & Co Ltd v Regent Stevedoring Co Ltd* (1946) 79 Ll L Rep 292 (Atkinson J) where repairs were already due to take place and so there was no recovery; *Southampton Container Terminals Ltd v Schiffahrts-Gesellschaft Hansa Australia mbH & Co (The Maersk Colombo)* [2001] 2 Lloyd's Rep 275 (CA) where the property was already due to be replaced and so there was no recovery.

[455] *Performance Cars v Abraham* [1962] 1 QB 33 (CA). And see the cases cite at chapter sixteen, n section 16.13D(i)(a).

[456] *Taylor Wholesale Ltd v Hepworths Ltd* [1977] 1 WLR 659 (May J) at 669–70.

[457] See further chapter sixteen, section 16.13D (i)(b).

[458] *Dimond v Lovell* [2002] 1 AC 384 (HL) Lord Hobhouse at 406 who refers to it as a 'capital account loss'; *Burdis v Livsey* [2003] QB 36 (CA) Aldous LJ at para 84; *Coles v Hetherton* [2013] EWCA Civ 1704 (CA) at paras 27–9 and 41. See also *Salcon Ltd v United Cement Pte Ltd* [2004] 4 SLR 353

because frequently supervening events (such as post-breach destruction by a third party[459]) or the receipt of collateral benefits (such as insurance or other third party arrangements covering repair or losses of profit, or the claimant performing the work itself cheaply[460]) are deemed not to have occurred by the rules of legal causation, in which case the pattern of the award starts to look like and approximates to an award for the immediate diminution in value despite subsequent events.

(vi) Burdis v Livsey (CA) (2002) on Repair Costs

In car cases in particular, issues frequently arise as to whether the claimant may recover even though its repairs were paid for by an insurer or other third party. The usual principle applicable to costs of temporary replacement vehicles, for example, is that where the cost is paid for by insurance or benevolence or another *res inter alios acta*, that is to be disregarded and the claimant treated as having paid the cost and able to recover, but other third party payments (including under a post-collision credit hire agreement) *are* taken into account such that the claimant cannot recover against the defendant if such an agreement with a third party is unenforceable and so the claimant does not have to repay under it.[461]

A different view was taken by the Court of Appeal in *Burdis v Livsey*.[462] The Court there held, the reasoned judgment being that of Aldous LJ, that a 'fundamental' distinction had to be drawn between repair costs and hire costs, as repair costs 'measure' the diminution in value which is a 'direct' loss suffered instantly at the point of damage and only falls to be reduced by subsequent events that are not collateral or *res inter alios acta*, whereas hire costs are special damage, a potential consequential loss that must be actually suffered by the claimant to be recoverable, save for the limited exceptions by which avoidance of such expenses, insurance and benevolence are to be disregarded.[463]

This is somewhat confused. It is correct that the diminution in value is suffered immediately where the lack of value is a non-remote loss (because the property is considered tradeable). However, the cost of repairs is not the measure of this loss (although it provides prima facie evidence of the amount of the loss) but rather a consequence of it, usually a reasonable mitigation of it.[464] Moreover, there is only one set of rules governing supervening causes and collateral benefits. As Aldous LJ correctly identified, the 'diminution in value' loss can be reduced (or indeed increased) by supervening events, including mitigation, that are treated as sufficiently causatively connected with the breach. But the same is true of hire costs; the collaterality or otherwise of benefits is merely an application of this causation

---

(Singapore CA) where, although liability for the costs of repair had been conceded, the court confirmed that in principle a diminution in value claim may have been available in the alternative.

[459] See chapter sixteen, section 16.13D(ii) below.

[460] See chapter sixteen, sections 16.10 and 16.7A respectively, below.

[461] *Dimond v Lovell* [2002] 1 AC 384 (HL) and see the discussion below in chapter sixteen, section 16.10E.

[462] *Burdis v Livsey* [2003] QB 36 (CA). The impecuniosity point in this case was decided correctly and that decision affirmed in *Lagden v O'Connor* [2004] 1 AC 1067 (HL).

[463] [2003] QB 36 (CA) paras 84–95.

[464] See above in section 4.3A(i).

rule. Thus the reason why the temporary hire costs being covered for free by an unenforceable post-accident credit agreement prevented recovery in *Dimond v Lovell* was that it was held by the House of Lords to be neither collateral nor *res inter alios acta*, and for the same reason the cost of repairs should have been unrecoverable in *Burdis v Livsey*.[465]

C. Other Losses

(i) Indemnity of the Claimant's Liability to a Third Party

Damage or destruction of goods, and even more commonly breach of sale contracts, frequently give rise to liability to the sub-buyer.[466] Where the sub-sale is not too remote, the liability to the sub-buyer, along with any lost profit on the sub-sale, will be recoverable. This is discussed in chapter twenty. In such cases it is worth remembering that the claimant recovers the liability to the third party *instead* of any difference in market value claim; the claimant has been paid for the goods under a sub-sale and that sub-sale measures the loss.[467] To award the difference in market value (which assumes a purchase of a replacement on the market or a sale to the market) *and* a measure based on the particular sub-sale would be confused and liable to lead to double recovery.

(ii) Costs

The claimant may, alternatively, recover the costs of preventative action such as a product recall taken upon discovery of a latent defect,[468] or the issuing of a notice,[469] or conducting repairs to products that have failed,[470] providing the steps taken were reasonable. Thus as Hicks QC has observed:

> I use the phrase 'diminution in value' as a convenient shorthand for the alternative measure to cost of reinstatement, and because it is used in the authorities and was used in argument,

---

[465] A Burrows, *Remedies for Torts and Breach of Contract*, 3rd edn (Oxford, OUP, 2009) at 242–43. As Cooke J observed in *Coles v Hetherton* [2012] EWHC 1599 (Comm) (Cooke J) at para 41, *Burdis* seems to treat the hire agreement as *res inter alios acta*; however that finding was not open to the Court in *Burdis* given that it was bound by *Dimond v Lovell*.

[466] And see eg *Lloyds and Scottish Finance Ltd v Modern Cars and Caravans (Kingston) Ltd* [1966] 1 QB 764 (Edmund Davies J), a case of defective title where the claimant recovered the costs of interpleader litigation with the true owner of the property.

[467] Liability to the third party will often include a market value claim by the third party, not based on the difference between the value of the goods promised by the defendant and those delivered, but rather the difference between the market value of the goods promised by the claimant to the third party and those delivered to that third party (or alternatively a claim based on the third party's liability to its sub-buyer, or its loss of non-market profits if not too remote, etc).

[468] *Motium Pty Ltd v Arrow Electronics Australia Pty Ltd* [2011] WASCA 65 (Western Australia CA).

[469] *Holden Ltd v Bostock & Co Ltd* (1902) 50 WR 323 (CA).

[470] *GKN Centrax Gears Ltd v Matbro Ltd* [1976] 2 Lloyd's Rep 555 (CA). The claimant actually made some profits from selling spares as a result of the breach, but although it should in principle have given credit for these, the profit was offset by the claimant's general inconvenience and expense and so no deduction was made for it.

but in truth (as indeed will be apparent from the terms in which I have discussed the issue and is not in dispute) an award on this basis must include other elements, in particular what would have been the cost of commissioning one of the unused tanks.[471]

(iii) Damage to Other Property of the Claimant or a Third Party

Where there is a latent defect or damage, this may cause damage to other property of the claimant or a third party. In the former case the claimant can recover compensation for the value of that property or consequential losses including of profits,[472] in the latter case an indemnity for the liability to the third party,[473] subject always to the rules of remoteness.

(iv) Non-Pecuniary Loss

In most consumer goods cases the cost of replacement will be the proper measure, but there may be exceptional cases where that measure is not appropriate and so the non-pecuniary and pecuniary losses are recoverable.

The question of non-profitable use was raised in *Clydebank Engineering Co v Don Jose Ramos Ysquierdo y Castaneda*, where the defendant failed to supply the government with a warship, although the matter was resolved in that case by a liquidated damages clause.[474] The ship would not have been sold, so the sale price was not (for that reason, anyway) the correct measure. The ship would not have been used to make profit, so that could not be the measure. Nevertheless, the ship would have been used for non-financial purposes (albeit not comfortably described by the terms 'amenity' or 'freedom from distress') and the House of Lords made it clear that they would have awarded damages for such loss, although because of the liquidated damages clause they did not need to assess the value of such damages.[475] In *The Alecos M*, however, there was no award for the loss of use of a non-delivered spare propeller and merely a small award for scrap value,[476] although that decision came before the House of Lords' decision in *Ruxley v Forsyth* and even though in a commercial case there may be room for an award for non-pecuniary loss. But in a consumer non-delivery case where a lease did not include a roof terrace, an award for non-pecuniary loss was made.[477]

As in non-delivery or defective delivery cases, similarly non-pecuniary loss may be available upon destruction or damage to property or (more frequently) defective

---

[471] *Stow (George) & Co Ltd v Walter Lawrence Construction Ltd* (1992) 40 Con LR 57 (Hicks QC) at 149.

[472] *Parsons (Livestock) Ltd v Uttley Ingham & Co Ltd* [1978] QB 791 (CA); *Holden Ltd v Bostock & Co Ltd* (1902) 50 WR 323 (CA) (sugar contaminated with arsenic spoiled the beer it was brewed into).

[473] See chapter twenty.

[474] *Clydebank Engineering Co v Don Jose Ramos Ysquierdo y Castaneda* [1905] AC 6 (HL) at 11–12.

[475] However, as to the measure of such damages, given that the value depends upon the existence of profound peace or the imminence of war, see Lord Sumner's comments in *The Chekiang* [1926] AC 637 (HL).

[476] *Sealace Shipping Co Ltd v Oceanvoice Ltd (The Alecos M)* [1991] 1 Lloyd's 120 (CA).

[477] *Saunders v Edwards* [1987] 1 WLR 1116 (CA).

or incomplete domestic building works.[478] An example might be the supply of breast implants or other cosmetic surgery products: in such cases it may not be reasonable to require a cure by replacement (although it may be), and non-financial enjoyment was clearly the intended purpose of the purchase. And in one Arkansas case, a jewellery repairer lost the plaintiff's rings but, not knowing that they were of sentimental importance and not having impliedly accepted responsibility for that feature of them, the non-pecuniary loss was too remote.[479] Similar examples can be found in tort cases of conversion of a stamp collection (with accompanying loss of the hobby),[480] and trespass on (and damage to) a burial ground,[481] and bailment cases of loss of the claimant's parents' cremated remains[482] or the claimant's sperm, frozen for infertility reasons.[483]

D. Special Rules

(i) Common Law Abatement

By the doctrine of abatement, originating in *Mondel v Steel*,[484] a defendant to an action for the price by a construction professional may reduce the price it is obliged to pay by 'the amount by which the product of the contractor's endeavours has been diminished in value as a result of the defective performance',[485] setting up the abatement as a partial defence to the action for the price. The price cannot be abated by any amount for consequential losses (eg for delay), which must be pursued by a separate counterclaim if at all.[486]

The doctrine has a limited scope, which has been fixed mainly by accidents of historical development rather than logic. It has been said by Lord Diplock to be available 'for breaches of warranty in contracts for sale of goods and for work and labour' but to be 'restricted to contracts of these types'.[487] The balance of authority supports the view that abatement is unavailable in cases of legal or design professional services or carriage, and so is confined to sale and construction services cases.[488]

---

[478] Below in chapter nineteen, section 19.1C(i).

[479] *Stifft's Jewelers v Oliver* 678 SW 2d 372 (1984) (SC of Arkansas). And see *Campin v Capels* 461 NE 2d 712 (1984) (CA of Indiana) in relation to theft of some rings.

[480] *Graham v Voigt* (1989) 94 FLR 146 (SC of the Australian Capital Territory).

[481] *Scutt v Lomax* (2000) 79 P & CR D31 (CA), where a memorial ground was cleared by a trespassing JCB digger.

[482] *Mason v Westside Cemeteries Ltd* (1996) 135 DLR (4th) 361 (Ontario Ct).

[483] *Yearworth v North Bristol NHS Trust* [2010] QB 1 (CA).

[484] *Mondel v Steel* (1841) 8 M& W 858.

[485] *Multiplex Constructions (UK) Ltd v Cleveland Bridge UK Ltd* [2006] EWHC 1341 (TCC) (Jackson J) at para 652, summarising the prior authorities. See in particular *Modern Engineering v Gilbert-Ash* [1974] AC 689 (HL) Lord Diplock at 717; *Aries Tanker v Total Transport* [1977] 1 WLR 185 (HL) Lord Wilberforce at 190; *Mellowes Archital Ltd v Bell Projects Ltd* (1997) 58 Con LR 22 (CA).

[486] *Mellowes Archital Ltd v Bell Projects Ltd* (1997) 58 Con LR 22 (CA).

[487] *Modern Engineering v Gilbert-Ash* [1974] AC 689 (HL) at 717.

[488] *Hutchinson v Harris* (1978) 10 BLR 19 (CA) Stephenson LJ at 31; followed in *Foster Wheeler Group Engineering Limited v Chevron*, 29 February 1996 (Humphrey Lloyd QC); *Multiplex Constructions (UK) Ltd v Cleveland Bridge UK Ltd* [2006] EWHC 1341 (TCC) (Jackson J) at para 652. However, in *Turner Page Music Ltd v Torres Design Associates Ltd*, 12 March 1997 (Hicks QC),

In sale of goods cases, the doctrine is only of procedural importance, permitting common law abatement by the amount by which goods delivered are worth less than those promised.[489] Given that there also exists an equitable set-off of the counterclaim for damages in the same measure (ie diminution in value), many abatement cases arise where the set-off is excluded by a term in the contract,[490] as that is where abatement becomes important.

The doctrine is potentially more important in construction cases, where it permits recovery on the basis of the difference in market value of the services provided. This is significant when considering whether such a measure is available as damages at common law (as the law would be incoherent if a separate procedure, abatement, permitted a different measure of de facto recovery).[491] Alternatively, if that measure is not available in damages, abatement is significant as an alternative remedy to damages of which lawyers should be aware.

The better view is that the remedy of abatement is an anomaly that does permit a different measure of de facto recovery in construction cases (although the 'recovery' is not by damages but by deduction from the price due). The courts have shown an unwillingness to extend abatement beyond that sphere into professional services cases generally.[492] Further, the trend in practice has been towards measuring the abatement by the diminution in value of the product of the construction or the cost of remedial works (which measures are the usual measures of damages), albeit that these are said to be a proxy for the true abatement measure of difference in value of the work itself.[493] Although a form of damages,[494] the abatement remedy is something of a *sui generis* remedy that arose in construction law to allow a just result where the claimant had substantially performed (and so was entitled to the price), but before the Judicature Acts made equitable set-off available and before the Chancery Amendment Act 1858 made damages available in addition to specific performance.

---

considering *Hutchinson v Harris*, the judge held that the doctrine *did* apply to a contract for design and other professional services where a part of the work had not been done at all (rather than had been done defectively), although appeared to focus on abatement by the part of the price attributed to that work rather than by the value of the work per se. See also *DRL v Wincanton* [2010] EWHC 2896 (QB) (Davies) at para 234, supporting the view that a claim for damages for breach of a logistical services contract is not for abatement properly so called, appeal allowed on a different point [2011] EWCA Civ 839 with para 234 of the first instance decision commented upon but not disapproved at para 34 of the judgment of Lloyd LJ.

[489] *Topfell Ltd v Galley Properties Ltd* [1979] 1 WLR 446 (Templeman J); *Ezekiel v Kohali* [2009] EWCA Civ 35.

[490] *Modern Engineering v Gilbert-Ash* [1974] AC 689 (HL); *Acsim (Southern) v Danish Contracting and Development* (1989) 47 BLR 55 (CA); *Mellowes Archital Ltd v Bell Projects Ltd* (1997) 58 Con LR 22 (CA).

[491] And in this vein see the comments of Lord Millett in *Alfred McAlpine Construction Ltd v Panatown Ltd* [2001] AC 518 (HL) at 586.

[492] See text to nn 489–90 above.

[493] *CA Duquemin v Ramond Slater* (1993) 65 BLR 124 (Newey J) at 134; *Multiplex Constructions (UK) Ltd v Cleveland Bridge UK Ltd* [2006] EWHC 1341 (TCC) (Jackson J) at paras 652 and 654.

[494] *Alfred McAlpine Construction Ltd v Panatown Ltd* [2001] 1 AC 518 (HL) Lord Millett at 586.

(ii) Statutory Abatement in Consumer Cases

In consumer goods cases, the Sale of Goods Act 1979 as amended provides that a claimant can obtain a reduction in the purchase price as an alternative to a damages claim.[495] This is an adjustment of the contract as if the claimant had bought the defective goods in the first place, analogous to abatement, although the legal basis of calculation is not yet clear. (And readers should note that, as explained above, even in non-consumer cases, common law abatement of the price is available in cases of sale.[496])

(iii) Non-Delivery of Land

Until 1989 there was a special rule (known as 'the rule from *Bain v Fothergill*' after the case of that name[497]) that where a vendor failed to supply land due to the vendor's lack of title, the buyer's damages were limited to the cost of investigating the title.[498] This was abolished by section 3 of the Law Reform (Miscellaneous Provisions) Act 1989. Thus where replacement and repair are not applicable, the basis measure is the difference between the contract price and the market value, subject to usual principles as to lost profits, mitigation and remoteness.[499]

---

[495] Section 48A Sale of Goods Act 1979.

[496] See the immediately preceding sub-section of this book.

[497] *Bain v Fothergill* (1874) LR 7 HL 158; also *Flureau v Thornhill* (1776) 2 Wm Bl 778.

[498] There was an exception where the vendor knew his title was defective. Both the rule and the exception were applicable in the damages case from which the basic rule of contract damages is often said to be derived, *Robinson v Harman* (1848) 1 Exch 850.

[499] *Engell v Fitch* (1868) LR 3 QB 314 at 334, affirmed in qualified terms (1869) LR 4 QB 659 at 665–68; *Brading v F McNeill & Co* [1946] 1 Ch 145 (Evershed J); *Diamond v Campbell-Jones* [1961] Ch 22 (Buckley J); *Cottrill v Steyning and Littlehampton Building Society* [1966] 1 WLR 1083 (Elwes J); *Malhotra v Choudhury* [1980] Ch 52 (CA); *Homsy v Murphy* (1997) 73 P & CR 26 (CA).

5

Refusal/Failure to Accept Performance

Damages following a buyer's wrongful rejection or refusal to accept goods or services. Includes consideration of the issue of the lost volume sale.

5.1. Cure by Finding a Replacement Customer on the Market
5.2. Lost Volume Sales: Where Supply Outstrips Demand
5.3. No Replacement
5.4. Non-Financial Loss

Introduction

THIS CHAPTER CONCERNS cases where the defendant purchaser has refused to accept the claimant's supply of goods or services. This may be a direct refusal, which in practice is likely (unless specific performance is available) to lead to termination of the contract, or it may be repudiatory breach of another sort (for example where the purchaser wrongly purports to accept a repudiatory breach by the supplier where there wasn't one). The damages covered by this chapter arise where the contract is terminated.[1]

A. The Measure of Damages as Compared with Non-Supply Cases

The damages measure for non-acceptance is similar to that for non-supply, although adjusted for the parties' different roles. In the case of refusal to accept a supply the claimant must look for and sell to a replacement customer whereas in a non-supply case the claimant must find and buy from a replacement supplier. The unavoidable losses will usually be simpler in cases of non-acceptance than non-supply. A purchaser might have used its goods or services for a multitude of purposes, including for a specific sub-sale or profitable use or as a consumer with non-financial damage. A supplier, however, supplies in return for money and profit and the consequential loss from delay in obtaining that money is limited.[2] The exception is employment, where employees supply services for reasons other than money.[3]

---

[1] If the contract is affirmed and the supply goes ahead, there may be a more limited claim for delay in payment that is covered by chapter seven.
[2] See chapter seven.
[3] See below in section 5.4A.

B. Breach of Warranty of Authority

It should be added that the non-acceptance measure also applies to breach of warranty of authority cases where the sale or supply does not proceed because of the false warranty of authority. Although the defendant in such cases has not refused to accept the supply, which was never to be made to him, the lost profit on the sale is still claimable against the defendant as if it had been an intended purchaser refusing to accept.[4]

5.1 Cure by Finding a Replacement Customer on the Market

As in non-supply cases, in the usual non-acceptance case the market will provide means of mitigating loss, this time by finding an alternative customer. Where there is such a market, and providing supply does not outstrip demand,[5] the claimant supplier will usually be deemed to have had recourse to that market and found a replacement customer for its supply on that market. The primary measure of recoverable lost profit is then the difference between the market selling price at the time when the supplier could reasonably have been expected to supply the goods or services to an alternative customer found through the market (or otherwise), and the contract price.

If (although this is for obvious reasons relatively rare) the defendant breached on a rising market or in another circumstances where the contract price is lower than or the same as the price the claimant can obtain on the market, the seller will have suffered no loss of profit.

A. Sale

(i) The Sale of Goods Act 1979

Although the common law measure based upon finding a replacement customer on the market applies to all sale cases (including land cases as discussed below), it is repeated by section 50(3) Sale of Goods Act 1979:

> (2) The measure of damages is the estimated loss directly and naturally resulting, in the ordinary course of events, from the buyer's breach of contract.
> (3) Where there is an available market for the goods in question the measure of damages is prima facie to be ascertained by the difference between the contract price and the market or current price at the time or times when the goods ought to have been accepted or (if no time was fixed for acceptance) at the time of the refusal to accept.[6]

---

[4] Eg *Habton Farms (an unlimited company) v Nimmo* [2003] EWCA Civ 68.
[5] See the discussion below in section 5.2.
[6] Section 54 confirms that nothing in the Act affects the seller's right to recover interest or special damages where available at common law.

The prima facie rules in the Act are just presumptions as to what conduct is unreasonable; or more accurately what conduct it is presumed that all reasonable claimants would have taken. As explained by Rix J in one case,

> such prima facie rules are only, at bottom, rules of thumb relating to causation and mitigation. The underlying questions remain: what loss has this breach caused as its normal and direct consequence? and what conduct should be presumed to be unreasonable (eg failing to sell shares or a fungible commodity in an available market) in the absence of the displacement of that presumption?[7]

(ii) The Available Market

Section 5(3) of the 1979 Act specifies that the market measure applies where there is an 'available market'. As explained, the measure is based on the price that the claimant seller could reasonably be expected to have obtained on the market in replacement of the contract with the defendant, ie the market selling price. As to what counts as a market, there are various definitions in the case law, including 'sufficient traders who are in touch with each other to evidence a market'.[8] However, given that the essence of the rule is mitigation and the assumption that where reasonable a buyer will take a replacement customer in mitigation, *any* willing buyer, ie 'one actual buyer on that day at a fair price',[9] is relevant as a potential source of a mitigatory sale and so relevant to the measure of loss, whether that technically counts as a market sale under section 50(3) or simply as a non-market sale deemed to have taken place under the rule of mitigation by section 50(2). The Court of Appeal has explained that it is not necessary to identify a specific willing buyer that existed at the relevant time (eg by name), and the court may infer the existence of a market from any sufficient evidence including from earlier offers to buy or sell the goods.[10]

(iii) Actual Market Resale

As in the case of non-delivery by a seller,[11] where, following non-acceptance by the buyer, the seller does find a replacement buyer on the market and acts reasonably in so doing, the actual recoupment amount will be the amount deducted,[12] and the court will not be over-quick to determine that an actual resale was unreasonably

---

[7] *Tharros Shipping Co Ltd v Bias Shipping Ltd (The Griparion) (No 2)* [1994] 1 Lloyd's Rep 533 (Rix J) at 537. See also *Bem Dis A Turk Ticaret S/A Tr v International Agri Trade Co Ltd (The Selda)* [1999] 1 Lloyd's Rep 729 (CA) Hirst LJ at 732.

[8] *ABD (Metals and Waste) Ltd v Anglo Chemical and Ore Co Ltd* [1955] 2 Lloyd's Rep 456 (CA) Sellers J at 466.

[9] *Shearson Lehman Hutton Inc v Maclaine Watson & Co Ltd (No 2)* [1990] 3 All ER 723 (Webster J) at 730.

[10] *Bulkhaul Ltd v Rhodia Organique Fine Ltd* [2009] 1 Lloyd's Rep 353 (CA) Smith LJ at paras 29–35.

[11] See above in chapter four, section 4.1.

[12] Eg *McCandless Aircraft LC v Payne* [2010] EWHC 1835 (QB) (Tugenhat J); *Aercap Partners 1 Ltd v Avia Asset Management AB* [2010] EWHC 2431 (Comm) (Gross LJ) at para 108; *Hooper v Oates* [2013] 3 All ER 211 (CA) Lloyd LJ at para 38.

timed or at an unreasonable price. In such cases, because the seller has acted reasonably, the rule of mitigation does not cut in, and so (subject to remoteness) the actual loss is recoverable and 'If the property market has declined during that time, it is of no avail for the defaulting buyer to say that this should not be laid at his door'.[13]

(iv) Timing of the Deemed Market Sale

The features that may delay when a seller could reasonably be expected to have resort to the market are discussed below in chapter seventeen, section 17.3, below, and the reader is referred to that section.

The application of the mitigatory principle to the specific issue of the seller's resort to the market is exemplified by the Privy Council decision in *AKAS Jamal v Moolla Dawood Sons & Co.*[14] The seller of shares in British Burma Petroleum Company Ltd waited two months after the date of delivery and non-acceptance by the buyer, before selling them on the market at a higher price than the market price at the date of delivery, although lower than the contract price. The Privy Council measured recovery as if the claimant had sold on the market immediately after the date of delivery, and therefore awarded more than the actual loss and gave the claimant the benefit of the rise in the market during the two months after delivery.

The principle was briefly explained by Lord Wrenbury for the court as follows:

> If the seller retains the shares after the breach, the speculation as to the way the market will subsequently go is the speculation of the seller, not of the buyer; the seller cannot recover from the buyer the loss below the market price at the date of the breach if the market falls, nor is he liable to the purchaser for the profit if the market rises.[15]

Thus the claimant is deemed to have supplied promptly to the market and recovery is calculated on that basis, not on the basis of the actual loss including by a sale at a higher or lower price later.

His Lordship also cited cases on collateral advantages,[16] showing his understanding that any profit made from speculation was not part of a continuous transaction with the breach and must be ignored,[17] ie that it is the rule of legal causation that modifies the breach position to determine for what sale the claimant must give credit.

The Court of Appeal applied this approach in *Campbell Mostyn (Provisions) Ltd v Barnett Trading Co.*[18] The seller waited two weeks after the date of breach to sell the cargo of South African tinned ham, by which date the price had risen dramatically due to a government announcement that in future such goods would require a licence. The defendants argued that the claimant's wait was reasonable as there was little or no available market at the date of breach, and therefore the higher price should be taken into account and the seller's losses treated as reduced accordingly.

---

[13] *Hooper v Oates* [2013] 3 All ER 211 (CA) Lloyd LJ at para 38 (sale of land).
[14] *AKAS Jamal v Moolla Dawood Sons & Co* [1916] 1 AC 175 (PC).
[15] Ibid, Lord Wrenbury at 179.
[16] Ibid.
[17] See further chapter sixteen, section 16.5.
[18] *Campbell Mostyn (Provisions) Ltd v Barnett Trading Co* [1954] 1 Lloyd's Rep 65 (CA).

The judge rejected that contention and found as a matter of fact that there was an available market at the date of delivery, albeit that demand and therefore prices were low, and he assessed the damages as at the date of the breach. The Court of Appeal (on a second appeal) upheld this factual finding and agreed that damages must be awarded calculated by a sale at the date of the breach.[19]

The principle and outcome in these cases are sound. In *Jamal* there was no finding that the claimant acted reasonably in delaying for two months, and although the claimant had been negotiating with the defendant during that time, it had given notice very shortly after the date for delivery that it would be going to the market, but not done so.[20] Its actions in waiting were therefore a speculation; likewise in *Campbell Mostyn*. However, both decisions do betray some of the rigidness characteristic of the decisions of the nineteenth century and first-half of the twentieth century in assuming that the date for delivery would always be the date for assessment of the market selling price.[21] As later decisions have shown, where a claimant acted reasonably in delaying, not by way of speculation but, for example, because it was negotiating with the defendant in an attempt to secure performance, then the principles at play (particularly mitigation and causation) prescribe that the market selling price at a later date than breach must be used.

This point was put beyond doubt by the House of Lords decision in *Johnson v Agnew*,[22] a case of non-acceptance by a purchaser of land (which was therefore governed by the same principles as sale of goods cases, but not the 1979 Act itself). Upon non-acceptance the seller sought and obtained an order for specific performance; the buyer did not comply, and the seller had the order dissolved and sought damages. Lord Wilberforce, giving the only reasoned judgment, explained that the date of assessment depended upon the mitigatory rule, and that the claimant had acted reasonably in pursuing specific performance. He therefore awarded damages based on the lost profit as against the market price at the date upon which the specific performance was aborted due to non-compliance by the buyer, summarising the principle as follows:

> In cases where a breach of a contract for sale has occurred, and the innocent party reasonably continues to try to have the contract completed, it would to me appear more logical and just rather than tie him to the date of the original breach, to assess damages as at the date when (otherwise than by his default) the contract is lost.[23]

Similarly, the Court of Appeal decision in *Habton Farms v Nimmo* shows that if the seller of a horse, rather than going to the market for a replacement, reasonably pursues the buyer, and doing so was not independent from the wrong, then the market selling price should be taken at the later date of whenever the seller should

---

[19] See also *Bulkhaul Ltd v Rhodia Organique Fine Ltd* [2009] 1 Lloyd's Rep 353 (CA), especially at paras 24–25.

[20] [1916] 1 AC 175 at 177–78.

[21] Especially *Jamal v Moolla Dawood & Sons* at 179–80, citing *Rodocanachi v Milburn* (1886) 18 QBD 67 (CA) and *Williams Bros v Ed T Agius Ltd* [1914] AC 510 (HL).

[22] *Johnson v Agnew* [1980] AC 367 (HL).

[23] Ibid at 401–2.

be expected to have given up on the buyer.[24] In that case the horse had died of peritonitis, which (like a fall in the market) was held to be an ordinary consequence, and so the market value at the later date from which the loss was calculated was zero. Likewise, in the Privy Council case of *E Johnson & Co (Barbados) Ltd v NSR Ltd*, the seller reasonably gave up on the buyer when the land became Crown property and specific performance became impossible, and damages were assessed at that date.[25] The same will apply where the buyer leads the seller for a time to believe that it will perform, albeit late.[26]

However, if the mitigatory rule would have required the claimant to accept the repudiatory breach and terminate, the loss will be measured as if it had done so.[27]

In a New Zealand case not wholly unlike *Johnson v Agnew*, a land buyer who failed to complete on a contract to purchase for NZ$1.1m was liable for damages at the difference between the contract price and the value at the date on which completion should have taken place (NZ$700,000).[28] In this case the vendor sought for 19 months to negotiate with the purchaser, during which time the property rose significantly in value to NZ$1.2m, and then when the negotiations failed the vendor decided to adapt the property to its own use, after which time it rose even more dramatically in value to NZ$4m at the date of the hearing, which was three and a half years after the aborted completion. The vendor's retention of the property rather than offering it on the market was expected by the parties, as the vendor had always been a reluctant seller who had initially bought the property to use, not to sell. (The vendor had also bought a substitute building in the same street for NZ$510,000, and it went up in value to NZ$3m.)

This decision seems to be wrong, as the negotiations with the purchaser seem to have been have been reasonable attempts to mitigate that followed continuously from the breach, and so the measure of loss should have been taken at the date when the negotiations broke off, by which date the loss was zero (the market price having risen above the contract price). Although it was contemplated that the vendor might keep the property even after that date, its decision to do so, although not unreasonable, should probably still be treated as a collateral act by which the vendor took the risk of property movements: had it done so and the property decreased in value, the vendor could not have claimed for the additional loss.[29]

Following non-acceptance by the buyer in *Shearson Lehman Hutton Inc v Maclaine Watson & Co Ltd (No 2)*[30] the seller could have sold 7,755 tons of tin to merchants immediately, or at a better price to consumers over the course of a few days. Consistently with the non-delivery cases in which a large volume of

---

[24] *Habton Farms (an unlimited company) v Nimmo* [2003] EWCA Civ 68, a case of breach of warranty of authority of the buyer but where the same principles apply as to non-acceptance by a buyer. Also *Hickman v Haynes* (1875) LR 10 CP 598, where the seller reasonably pressed the buyer for a time until resorting to the market.

[25] *E Johnson & Co (Barbados) Ltd v NSR Ltd* [1997] AC 400 (PC) at 411–12.

[26] *Toprak Mahsulleri Ofisi v Finagrain Compagnie Commerciale Agricole et Financière* [1979] 2 Lloyd's Rep 98 (CA).

[27] See below in chapter sixteen, section 16.3.

[28] *Turner v Superannuation & Mutual Savings Ltd* [1987] 1 NZLR 218 (Smellie J in the Auckland HC).

[29] As to these points on the date of assessment, see further chapter sixteen, section 16.5, and chapter 17.

[30] *Shearson Lehman Hutton Inc v Maclaine Watson & Co Ltd (No 2)* [1990] 3 All ER 723 (Webster J).

replacement goods must be purchased over a period of time to achieve a reasonable price,[31] the judge awarded the price that would have been obtained through selling the tin over the course of a few days, which was lower than the market selling price at the date of breach.[32]

This is an application of the general principles, as per *Johnson v Agnew*, where the reasonable delay in selling to the market is not caused by negotiations with or pursuit of the defendant but by other factors. Likewise in *Aercap Partners 1 Ltd v Avia Asset Management AB* it reasonably took a year to find another buyer for an aircraft, and the damages were measured by reference to the value at the later date (under that resale).[33]

Finally, the proper date for the market price may be earlier than the date for performance if there is an anticipatory breach that was accepted by the seller, as there was in *Gebrüder Metelmann GmbH & Co KG v NBR (London) Ltd.*[34]

B. Charterparties and Leases

In contracts of sale, the refusal or failure to accept performance will usually occur at the start of the contract. In charterparties, leases and hire purchase agreements there may similarly be an in initial refusal to accept delivery, or the refusal to accept performance may take the form of a repudiation part way through the term of the contract. The same principles apply: the claimant can recover in damages the total amount of hire the claimant owner was entitled to under the contract, less the amount received (or which should have been received in mitigation), plus any additional costs or losses.

Thus the usual measure when a charterer repudiates a charterparty is the difference between the rate a shipowner can obtain by chartering the vessel on the market (in reasonable mitigation of its loss) and the contract rate. Thus, Goff J in *The Elena D'Amico* explained:

> [T]he damages will generally be assessed on the basis of the difference between the contract rate for the balance of the charter-party period and the market rate for the chartering in of a substitute vessel for that period. If however the time charterer decides not to take advantage of that market then, generally speaking, that will be his own business decision independent of the wrong; and the consequences of that decision are his. If he judges the market correctly, he reaps the benefit; if he judges it incorrectly, then the extra cost falls upon him.

It does not matter (and this was important in relation to the findings of the arbitrator in that case) that his decision was a reasonable one, or was a sensible business

---

[31] See above chapter four, n 197 and surrounding text.
[32] See also *Smith New Court Securities Ltd v Scrimgeour Vickers (Asset Management) Ltd* [1997] AC 254 (HL) as to the need for the gradual sale of shares.
[33] *Aercap Partners 1 Ltd v Avia Asset Management AB* [2010] EWHC 2431 (Comm) (Gross LJ).
[34] *Gebrüder Metelmann GmbH & Co KG v NBR (London) Ltd* [1984] 1 Lloyd's Rep 614 (CA). See further chapter fifteen, section 15.3B(ii).

decision, taken with a view to reducing the impact upon him of the legal wrong committed by the shipowners.[35]

Accordingly if the market charter rate is higher than the contract rate then the owner has suffered no recoverable loss.[36] Moreover, if the owner cannot show that it would have been able to supply the vessel and so earn the charter rate, likewise it has suffered no recoverable loss.[37]

The question of the relevant date of the market charter rate is the same as the question in relation to the market date for sale of goods discussed above (see chapter four, section 4.2D(i)(b)), ie it may be later than the date of breach if a replacement could not reasonably have been expected to be contracted immediately. Thus if it reasonably took a lessor some time to engage a replacement tenant, the actual rate received was taken as the correct measure, not the market rate at the date of breach.[38]

This basic measure was applied in *The Golden Victory*,[39] where it was explained as being based on the mitigatory principle,[40] however, the question that arose there was as to the duration for which this should be applied. As it was known that even but for the breach the charter would have been lawfully terminated in 2003 when war broke out,[41] only damages up to that time could be recovered. The damages were based on the difference between the contract rate and the replacement rate that could have been achieved on the market (which was a spot rate, and then a long-term fixture rate but including a profit share provision). It had been found and accepted that a replacement charter would have itself contained a war clause.[42] However, had this not been the case, the loss for the period would be the difference between the replacement charter rate and the market rate that would have prevailed in wartime.[43] Indeed it would be possible (although unlikely) for the replacement charter to actually be better than the wartime market rate that the shipowner would have received had the defendant not breached and instead terminated lawfully on the outbreak of war, in which case this benefit would have to be taken into account.

It may be reasonable, if a full replacement time charter is unavailable, to merely make what money the owner can by shorter spot charters or short time charters here and there, with those actual earnings being deducted from what would have been

---

[35] *Koch Marine Inc v D'Amica Societa di Navigazione Arl (The Elena D'Amico)* [1980] 1 Lloyd's Rep 75 (Goff J) at 89.

[36] *Staniforth v Lyall* (1830) 7 Bing 169, discussed in *British Westinghouse Electric & Manufacturing Co Ltd v Underground Electric Railways Co of London Ltd* [1912] AC 673 (HL) by Viscount Haldane LC at 689 to 690; *Omak Maritime Ltd v Mamola Challenger Shipping Co* [2010] EWHC 2026 (Comm) (Teare J).

[37] *Flame SA v Glory Wealth Shipping PTE Ltd* [2013] EWHC 3153 (Comm) (Teare J).

[38] *Techno Land Improvements Ltd v British Leyland (UK) Ltd* [1979] 2 EGLR 27 (Goulding J) in relation to land.

[39] *Golden Strait Corp v Nippon Yusen Kubishika Kaisha (The Golden Victory)* [2007] 2 AC 353 (HL).

[40] Lord Bingham at para 10. Also *Zodiac Maritime Agencies Ltd v Fortescue Metals Group Ltd (The Kildare)* [2011] 2 Lloyd's Rep 360 (Steel J) at para 65.

[41] See below in chapter thirteen, section 13.3B(iv).

[42] Lord Carswell [2007] 2 AC 353 (HL) at para 67.

[43] Lord Mance in the Court of Appeal in *The Golden Victory* [2006] 1 WLR 533 (CA) at para 27.

earned under the breached time charter, providing they form part of the continuous dealing and are sufficiently closely connected to the breach.[44] Moreover, the owner is not expected to go back to the time charter market at the completion of each spot charter, and it will be a question of fact whether an owner is treated as failing reasonably to have mitigated by failing to take up a time charter in circumstances where the time charter market revived some time after the breach but before the end of the balance period of the terminated charter.[45]

The same principles apply to hire and leases generally,[46] and to hire purchase agreements.[47]

Where there is no market to hire out the property (for example because it requires repair and the repair is at that time uneconomic or unaffordable) it may be reasonable for the owner merely to wait. In that case, the losses will be the full amount that the charterer would have paid under the time charter.[48] Alternatively, with unique goods, it may be reasonable to require the owner to sell the goods for as much as it can if they cannot be hired out again.[49]

C. Employment

In the context of dismissal claims, discussed in more detail below,[50] the main limiting factor on the claimant's damages had he or she not been unfairly dismissed will be the replacement wages the claimant actually made or should have made through such alternative job (the equivalent to an alternative customer in a goods supply case) as the claimant should reasonably have obtained in mitigation of loss.[51] If the employee takes up equivalent employment the very next day then the loss will be zero;[52] likewise if he or she secures a better-paid job.[53] It may be that the employee

---

[44] *Golden Strait Corp v Nippon Yusen Kubishika Kaisha (The Golden Victory)* [2007] 2 AC 353 (HL) Lord Brown at para 81; *Dalwood Marine Co v Nordana Line A/S (The Elbrus)* [2010] 2 Lloyd's Rep 315 (Teare J); *Zodiac Maritime Agencies Ltd v Fortescue Metals Group Ltd (The Kildare)* [2011] 2 Lloyd's Rep 360 (Steel J) at paras 63 and 67–72.

[45] *Zodiac Maritime Agencies Ltd v Fortescue Metals Group Ltd (The Kildare)* [2011] 2 Lloyd's Rep 360 (Steel J) at paras 65–66; *Glory Wealth Shipping Pte Ltd v Korea Line Corp (The Wren)* [2011] EWHC 1819 (Comm) (Blair J) at paras 27 and 31.

[46] See *Techno Land Improvements Ltd v British Leyland (UK) Ltd* [1979] 2 EGLR 27 (Goulding J) in relation to a lease of land. Also *Gray v Owen* [1910] 1 KB 622.

[47] Eg *Yeoman Credit Ltd v Waragowski* [1961] 1 WLR 1124 (CA); *Lombard North Central plc v Butterworth* [1987] QB 527 (CA).

[48] *Tharros Shipping Co Ltd v Bias Shipping Ltd (The Griparion) (No 2)* [1994] 1 Lloyd's Rep 533 (Rix J).

[49] *Bulkhaul Ltd v Rhodia Organique Fine Ltd* [2009] 1 Lloyd's Rep 353 (CA).

[50] See section 5.4A below and chapter thirteen, section 13.3(iv)(a)–(b).

[51] Eg *Lavarack v Woods of Colchester Ltd* [1967] 1 QB 278 (CA); *Red Deer College v Michaels* [1976] 2 SCR 324 (SC of Canada); *Secretary of State for Employment v Wilson* [1978] 3 All ER 137 (EAT); *Peara v Enderlin Ltd* [1980] ICR 804 (EAT); *Ministry of Defence v Wheeler* [1998] 1 All ER 790 (CA); *Société Générale, London Branch v Geys* [2013] 1 AC 523 (SC) Lord Wilson at para 79. For discussion of how the law deals with the question of whether the claimant would have earned bonuses etc, see below in chapter 13, section 13.3B(ii).

[52] *Secretary of State for Employment v Wilson* [1978] 3 All ER 137 (EAT).

[53] Eg *Rowley v Cerberus Software Ltd* [2001] IRLR 160 (CA).

could reasonably be expected to accept replacement employment with the original breaching employer, at least if it is on the same terms as before.[54] The employee may well not be expected to take the first job that comes along,[55] but should act as if it were not expecting any compensation from the previous employer.[56]

In slight modification of the ordinary rules, where compensation is provided for the sum that would have been paid during a proper notice period, frequently any sum earned in alternative employment need not be deducted from the award.[57] Properly understood, this is not in conflict with ordinary contract law principles, as the essence of the reasoning behind the principles is that, realistically, the breach was not in not giving proper notice but in not paying a proper sum in lieu of that notice, as it is good industrial practice to do. Such a sum is not repayable once paid even if the employee obtains proper employment, and so but for the breach the employee would have had the proper sum whatever employment it then obtained during the notice period.[58]

D. Additional Losses

Even where a replacement customer for the claimant's goods or services is available, the claimant will still be able to recover any additional losses not avoided, such as the reasonable costs of storing goods for a time[59] or of going to the market, or losses resulting from any delay in receiving the money from the supply.[60]

In many cases the supplier will have incurred costs in anticipation of the performance required of it, or part-performed. To the extent that those costs do not lead to savings on the replacement supply or otherwise, and so increase the total costs the claimant incurred beyond those it would have incurred but for the breach, the claimant is entitled to recover such costs. To be clear, the claimant is to be put in the position it would have been in but for the breach. This is not a recovery of wasted expenditure per se; it is a recovery of the net lost revenue, which is increased by any increase in actual costs.

Further, the defendant's breach may damage the claimant not only by a loss of profit on the immediate contract, but also by loss of future earnings prospects arising out of the inability to build the claimant's reputation or similar. These are discussed below.[61]

---

[54] See below in chapter 16, section 16.9C(ii).

[55] *AG Bracey Ltd v Iles* [1973] IRLR 210 (Sir Donaldson).

[56] *Archbold's (Freightage) Ltd v Wilson* [1974] IRLR 10 (National Industrial Relations Court). Cf text to chapter 15 n 63 below.

[57] This is the principle from *Norton Tool Co Ltd v Tewson* [1973] 1 WLR 45 (National Industrial Relations Court).

[58] *Babcock FATA Ltd v Addison* [1988] QB 280 (CA), especially Ralph Gibson LJ at 292. The principle does not apply in relation to constructive dismissal: *Stuart Peters Ltd v Bell* [2009] EWCA 938.

[59] *Harlow & Jones Ltd v Panex (International) Ltd* [1967] 2 Lloyd's Rep 509 (Roskill J).

[60] See chapter seven.

[61] See chapter eighteen, section 18.2C(iv).

5.2 Lost Volume Sales: Where Supply Outstrips Demand

A. Sale of Goods

Where the supplier's supply exceeds demand, either because the supplier can manufacture to order as many items as are needed, or because the supplier purchases its goods from a third party and the goods are not scarce, the buyer's failure to accept the goods means that the supplier has lost a sale that cannot be replaced. Even if the supplier sells the particular goods that were intended for the defendant to another buyer, had the defendant accepted those goods the supplier would still have made the sale to the other buyer using alternative goods, and overall has suffered a loss of profit of one sale. In other words, the supplier will have ended up making (say) 99 sales that year rather than 100.

In those circumstances the supplier is entitled to recover the lost profits of a sale, ie the contract price less the supplier's total costs (including, especially, the purchase or manufacturing costs of the item). This is exemplified by the case of *Thompson Ltd v Robinson (Gunmakers) Ltd*,[62] where the claimant sold one fewer Vanguard car than they would have done but for the breach. See similarly *Interoffice Telephones Ltd v Robert Freeman Co Ltd*, where the claimant's supply of office telephone systems on hire outstripped demand, so the claimant was entitled to lost profits for the remaining period of the defendant's hire contract without reduction for any income from other customers.[63]

Where, however, demand exceeds supply (ie overall the supplier has to turn some buyers away), then a supplier's total number of sales will not have been reduced by the defendant's breach in not accepting the goods, and there will be no loss other than the amount by which the defendant had agreed to pay more than the market price (if it had). In *Charter v Sullivan*,[64] only nominal damages were awarded where a car dealer managed, in successful mitigation of its loss, to sell the new Hillman Minx car to a replacement buyer and gave evidence that he could sell 'all the Hillman Minx we can get'. In those circumstances, the claimant 'sold the same number of

---

[62] *Thompson Ltd v Robinson (Gunmakers) Ltd* [1955] Ch 177 (Upjohn J). See also *Re Vic Mill Ltd* [1913] 1 Ch 465 (Ch); *Sony Computer Entertainment UK Ltd v Cinram Logistics UK Ltd* [2008] EWCA Civ 955 (a case of destruction of goods by a bailee, where it was held that the burden was on the bailee to show that the claimant's supply was greater than demand); *Neri v Retail Marine Corp* 285 NE 2d 311 (1972) (NYCA); *RE Davis Chemical Corp v Diasonics* 924 F 2d 709 (1991) (USCA 7th Cir). Cf the issue of loss caused by patent infringements, where sales by the defendant may cause the claimant loss of volume, but not if the claimant could not have effected the sale: *Watson Laidlaw & Co Ltd v Pott, Cassels and Williamson* (1914) 1 SLT 130 (HL).

[63] *Interoffice Telephones Ltd v Robert Freeman Co Ltd* [1958] 1 QB 190 (CA). See similarly the Canadian Supreme Court decision in *Apeco of Canada Ltd v Windmill Place* [1978] 2 SCR 385, where a tenant repudiated a commercial lease, the specific part of the warehouse was successfully re-let to another tenant, but overall the building was only half let and so if the defendant had not breached its lease the replacement tenant would merely have taken alternative space in the building and thus there was still a net loss of rent from the defendant's lease. The right decision was reached although the Court failed to spot the real issue and instead justified the decision on the basis that the re-letting was collateral/*res inter alios acta*.

[64] *Charter v Sullivan* [1957] 2 QB 117 (CA).

cars and made the same number of fixed profits as he would have sold and made if the defendant had duly carried out his bargain'[65] and so suffered no loss.

Similarly where goods are distinctive and were sold to a replacement purchaser in successful mitigation of loss, the seller will have difficulty in proving that the replacement purchaser would have bought different goods if the defendant had performed, ie that any volume of sales was lost. Accordingly, only nominal damages were awarded in *Lazenby Garages Ltd v Wright*,[66] where the seller managed to find a replacement buyer for a second-hand BMW, and at a higher price than that in the breached contract.[67] The same situation will arise where only a certain quota of goods are legally permitted to be sold.[68]

The overall question is whether the supplier would have made more money but for the breach.

B. Service Cases

The same principle applies in service cases. Often a service provider's supply is greater than its demand. Thus a cleaning company can work its staff harder or employ more staff to fulfil all the orders it has. In such situations the fact that the claimant picks up another customer for its services does not mean that it has not lost any profits.[69]

However, sometimes demand outstrips supply, as it does for a one-man building business or a printer's with a limited number of presses. If, say, the one-man builder's booking for a week's work in May is cancelled but he or she finds another job, or the printer's presses are all in use even after a cancellation, the builder and printer's cannot claim for any loss.[70] Of course, it is important to take care when analysing this situation: if the builder fills the week in May with work he or she would otherwise have done in June, and then has a period in June with no work, then overall he or she has still lost a profit and his supply outstripped demand. Similarly if the printer's uses all the presses at the time of the cancelled work with work that was not time sensitive and could have been done later, and still has spare capacity later, then it too has still suffered a loss of profit.[71]

---

[65] Ibid Jenkins LJ at 130. It was not proved that demand exceeded supply in *Acre 1127 Ltd v De Montford Fine Art Ltd* [2011] EWCA Civ 87 at paras 54–60. See also *Britvic Soft Drinks Ltd v Messer UK Ltd* [2002] 1 Lloyd's Rep 20 (Tomlinson J) at para 124(ii), affirmed [2002] 2 Lloyd's Rep 368 (CA), where the claimant supplier of fizzy drinks could not recover from the defendant seller of carbon dioxide the lost profits on replacement products supplied, as they would not have been sold in addition to the first supply (for which the price had been paid and the profit earned).

[66] *Lazenby Garages Ltd v Wright* [1976] 1 WLR 459 (CA).

[67] See also *Alton House Garages v Marleywood Marine*, 5 July 1983 (Webster J).

[68] Cf *SS Strathfillan (Owners) v SS Ikala (Owners) (The Ikala)* [1929] 1 AC 196 (HL).

[69] Cf *Karas v Rowlett* [1944] SCR 1 (SC of Canada), where the defendant repudiated a lease but the profits the claimant made on a new business were not taken into account to reduce the claim because it was not shown that the claimant could not have operated both, ie that the replacement was an alternative.

[70] See *Amsalem v Ravid* [2008] EWHC 3028 (TCC) (Akenhead J) at para 168.

[71] *Western Web Offset Printers Ltd v Independent Media Ltd* (CA) 4 October 1995. See also *Hill & Sons v Edwin Showell & Sons Ltd* (1918) 87 LJKB 1106 (HL), where the issue was identified but not resolved. And see *Dalwood Marine Co v Nordana Line A/S (The Elbrus)* [2010] 2 Lloyd's Rep 315 (Teare J), where the arbitrator found no loss where a shipowner, following repudiation by a charterer,

5.3 No Replacement

Where there is no replacement customer available on the market, or the market does not avoid loss because supply outstrips demand (see the previous section),[72] the measure of damages is simply the net lost profit on the transaction; in other words the total revenue that would have been earned but was not, less the saving of the costs that would have been incurred but have not been.[73]

This is illustrated by *Harlow & Jones Ltd v Panex (International) Ltd*.[74] The buyers of 10,000 tons of steel blooms repudiated and the sellers, who had themselves bought from Russian suppliers, looked for a buyer but there was none to be found. The Russian suppliers took back 1,500 tons without any claim, and the claimant, having escaped making expenditure in relation to that part of the shipment, recovered from the defendant the lost profit it would have made on that 1,500 tons, being the difference between the price it would have received from the defendant and the price it would have paid to the Russian sellers. Thus, as regards that 1,500 tons, the default difference in value measure was disapplied as not reflecting the actual loss. The other 8,500 tons were some months later sold for US$56/ton and the claimant was awarded the difference between that sum and the price it would have received from the defendant. The claimant also recovered storage charges incurred in the interim while looking for a buyer.

A similar measure was also awarded in *Trans Trust SPRL v Danubian Trading Co*.[75] In that case there was a string of sale contracts such that the buyer's failure to open a letter of credit on a rising market meant that the seller could not itself buy the goods and indeed was liable to its own seller for non-acceptance. Ordinarily on a rising market a seller would have sold the goods to the market at a higher than contract price and recovered only nominal damages.[76] However, in this case it was contemplated that what actually happened would happen, ie the breach would mean that the entire chain fell through (effectively due to the claimant's impecuniosity, ie inability to raise the letter of credit itself), and the seller did not get the goods and so could not mitigate by selling them to another.[77] In the circumstances, and these consequences not being too remote, the prima facie measure under the (previous equivalent) Sale of Goods Act was displaced and the actual loss of profit on the deal (ie the difference between the contract price and the seller's purchase contract price) was awarded, it being confirmed that this displacement of the market measure could in other circumstances have worked against the seller:

One can imagine cases in which the principle as applied by the judge would give him less. If the market price had fallen so that the prima facie measure gave a

---

started and finished a later charter early, but the Court confirmed that it might have been open to the arbitrator to find that there had been a net loss in total profits suffered after the date of notional redelivery as a result of accelerating work that would otherwise have been done later and so earning less later.

[72] Eg *Western Web Offset Printers Ltd v Independent Media Ltd* (CA) 4 October 1995.
[73] Any costs that have been incurred are not saved and so should not be deducted.
[74] *Harlow & Jones Ltd v Panex (International) Ltd* [1967] 2 Lloyd's Rep 509 (Roskill J).
[75] *Trans Trust SPRL v Danubian Trading Co Ltd* [1952] 2 QB 297 (CA).
[76] Ibid Somervell LJ at 300–301.
[77] And, as Denning LJ confirmed (ibid at 306), the claimant had not been shown to have unreasonably failed to find another buyer who would open a letter of credit and save the chain.

larger sum than the loss of profit, the seller might find himself restricted to his loss of profit on the deal if that was the loss contemplated in the circumstances by the parties.[78]

The liability of the seller to its head-seller was, however, too remote, it depending upon the head-seller's own impecuniosity and liability to its seller, the manufacturer.[79] This case shows the correct approach, and shows the confusion that the presumptions in the Sale of Goods Act can cause. The true approach is to work out what the actual loss was and then work out whether any of the actual events and loss should be disregarded and deemed to have been otherwise, by the rules of remoteness, mitigation and causation.

However, there was no substantial recovery in *North Sea Energy Holdings v Petroleum Authority of Thailand*.[80] The buyer repudiated a contract for a large quantity of crude oil. The seller had an arrangement with a supplier who was to acquire the oil from a Saudi Arabian prince and supply it to the seller at a huge discount of US$1.10 to the official price, as compared with a usual market discount available on the market of in the region of 2–6¢, which would mean it would make a huge profit on the sale to the defendant. It was found that the claimant would not in fact have been able to supply the oil, as on the balance of probabilities the Saudi prince would not have supplied it to the claimant's supplier.[81] Obiter, had the claimant been caused a loss of profit (ie had it been able to acquire the oil as it claimed), the extravagant profit the claimant would have made was too remote, and although it was agreed that under the *Cory v Thames Iron Works* principle[82] the normal non-remote measure of profit was still recoverable despite this extravagance, there was insufficient evidence to found such a 'market claim'.[83]

Finally, in *Bulkhaul Ltd v Rhodia Organique Fine Ltd*,[84] where the lessee of bespoke chemical storage tanks repudiated five years into a 10-year lease, the lessor recovered the profit that would have been made from leasing during the remaining five years (after which the tanks would have had no residual value), less the net profit (price, less costs) it should have received had it mitigated by selling the tanks, which it in fact did not do.

---

[78] [1952] 2 QB 297, Somervell LJ at 302.

[79] See similarly *Addax Ltd v Arcadia Ltd* [2000] 1 Lloyd's Rep 493 (Morison J) in relation to the effect of a late loading of crude oil caused by the buyer on the seller's profits, where the delay affected the price the seller paid to its seller. And see *Collins v Howard* [1949] 2 All ER 324 (CA), where a lender's having sourced money for a loan from sale of shares which, upon the defendant pulling out of the loan, the lender bought back at a higher price, was too remote.

[80] *North Sea Energy Holdings NV v Petroleum Authority of Thailand* [1997] 2 Lloyd's Rep 418 (Thomas J), affirmed [1999] 1 Lloyd's Rep 483 (CA).

[81] [1997] 2 Lloyd's Rep 418 at 436. There were two reasons for this. One was that the prince would not have been able to get the oil, which, depending upon a third party, should have been a finding on a loss of chance, as the Court of Appeal noted: [1999] 1 Lloyd's Rep 483 (CA) at 493–96. However, the other, independent, reason was that the defendant could and would not have specified in advance the destination to which it was taking the oil, a matter properly found on the balance of probabilities: [1999] 1 Lloyd's Rep 483 (CA) at 496, and this was a precondition to the Saudi prince providing the oil.

[82] See below in chapter fourteen, section 14.4.

[83] [1997] 2 Lloyd's Rep 418 at 438–39. These issues did not arise for consideration by the Court of Appeal, where an appeal was dismissed: [1999] 1 Lloyd's Rep 483 (CA).

[84] *Bulkhaul Ltd v Rhodia Organique Fine Ltd* [2009] 1 Lloyd's Rep 353 (CA).

Where the claimant cannot prove its lost profit, but the defendant cannot prove that the claimant would not have earned revenue, the damages may be measured on the basis of the presumption of breaking even, giving an award of wasted expenditure. This was the approach taken in the leading Australian authority on the point, *Commonwealth v Amann Aviation Pty Ltd*,[85] which concerned the Commonwealth repudiating the claimant's contract to provide coastline aerial surveillance services.

5.4 Non-Financial Loss

Although ordinary legal principals apply, non-financial loss will be rare in cases of non-acceptance by the consumer of the goods or services, because most suppliers supply goods and services in order to make money and for no other reason, and any other reason would in any event usually be too remote.

A. Employment and Dismissal[86]

The obvious exception is employment. Although employees also supply their services for money, they also gain satisfaction from it. Thus in personal injury cases, where a claimant can no longer pursue his or her preferred career, a separate award is made for the loss of that choice and enjoyment, and the same should be true in contract cases where the claimant is deprived of a career.[87] In employment cases, an employer can, by suspension or dismissal, cause significant distress and psychiatric injury to employees.

When determining whether a claim for non-pecuniary loss (or any other loss) may be brought for breach of a contract of employment, whether for breach of the common law implied obligation of mutual trust and confidence or otherwise,[88] it is necessary to determine whether the loss results from dismissal or not.

All claims for loss resulting from dismissal are governed by the statutory action for unfair dismissal, codified in the Employment Rights Act 1996 and other attendant legislation. This action has exclusive jurisdiction over dismissal claims. This is significant in this context because non-pecuniary loss (such as mental/psychiatric harm) is irrecoverable under such an action[89] but, because of the action's exclusive jurisdiction, irrecoverable outside the action too, where resulting from dismissal. This rule stems from the decision in *Johnson v Unisys Ltd*,[90] and the area in which the unfair dismissal action has exclusive jurisdiction is called 'the *Johnson* exclusion

---

[85] *Commonwealth of Australia v Amann Aviation Pty Ltd* (1992) 174 CLR 64 (HC of Australia). Discussed further below in chapter thirteen, section 13.3B(vii), and chapter eighteen, section 18.3B.

[86] See also D Brodie, 'A Fair Deal at Work' (1999) 19 *OJLS* 83.

[87] See chapter two n 74 above and surrounding text.

[88] *Malik and Mahmud v Bank of Credit and Commerce International SA* [1998] AC 20 (HL).

[89] *Norton Tool Co Ltd v Tewson* [1973] 1 WLR 45 (National Industrial Relations Court); *Dunnachie v Kingston upon Hull City Council* [2005] 1 AC 226 (HL).

[90] *Johnson v Unisys Ltd* [2003] 1 AC 518 (HL) (developing the law from *Addis v Gramophone Company Ltd* [1909] AC 488 (HL)). See also *Dunnachie v Kingston upon Hull City Council* [2005] 1 AC 226 (HL); *Eastwood and another v Magnox Electric plc* [2005] 1 AC 503 (HL).

area'.[91] Even where the rules relating to dismissal, such as codes of practice, are expressly set out or incorporated in an employment contract, their relevance is governed by statute (their breach may be reflected in the final award made by the Employment Tribunal) and therefore, as the Supreme Court has confirmed, breach of these express rules will also not give rise to a common law action for damages for loss resulting from the manner of dismissal.[92] As was summarised by Cranston J, 'It has been held that damages are not recoverable for a breach of either an express or implied term of the employment contract concerning the procedures leading to dismissal (the so-called Johnson exclusion)'.[93]

Where, however, the claim is not a claim relating to the manner or consequences of dismissal, but rather an anterior or separate breach of the employment contract (including the obligation to give notice of dismissal), the unfair dismissal action does not apply and the ordinary common law contract rules govern.[94] Thus an employer's repudiatory breach that gives rise, upon later acceptance, to a constructive dismissal, is nevertheless outside the *Johnson* exclusion area and subject to ordinary common law principles.[95] And a breach of the duty of trust and confidence that leads to a suspension but not a dismissal can sound in damages for psychiatric injury or mental distress.[96]

The Canadian courts, for example, permit awards for non-pecuniary and other loss arising out of the manner of dismissal.[97]

---

[91] Eg *Edwards v Chesterfield Royal Hospital NHS Foundation Trust* [2012] AC 22 (SC) passim. The approach by which the statutory action has exclusive jurisdiction over dismissal claims was criticised in Lady Hale's dissent in *Edwards*. The exclusionary jurisdiction approach is overlaid by an approach by which non-pecuniary loss or 'stigma damages' resulting from the *manner* of dismissal is arguably too remote: *Addis v Gramophone Company Ltd* [1909] AC 488 (HL), *Johnson v Unisys Ltd* [2003] 1 AC 518 (HL), and *Edwards* Lord Phillips.

[92] *Edwards v Chesterfield Royal Hospital NHS Foundation Trust* [2012] 2 AC 22 (SC).

[93] *Yapp v Foreign & Commonwealth Office* [2013] IRLR 616 (Cranston J) at para 96.

[94] Ibid at paras 96–97.

[95] *Eastwood and another v Magnox Electric plc* [2005] 1 AC 503 (HL); *GAB Robins (UK) Ltd v Triggs* [2008] IRLR 317 (CA). But as to the difficulties of categorising breaches as within and without the *Johnson* exclusion area, see *Monk v Cann Hall Primary School* [2013] IRLR 732 (CA).

[96] *Gogay v Hertfordshire County Council* [2000] IRLR 70 (CA); *Yapp v Foreign & Commonwealth Office* [2013] IRLR 616 (Cranston J). See also *Mahmud and Malik v BCCI SA* [1998] AC 20 (HL). See further the cases in chapter nineteen n 45 below.

[97] *Wallace v United Grain Growers Ltd* [1997] 3 SCR 70 (SC of Canada); *Honda Canada Inc v Keays* [2008] 2 SCR 362 (SC of Canada).

6

Temporary Loss of Use of the Claimant's Property

Damages for loss following the claimant being temporarily deprived of its property, including while awaiting replacement or repair, upon delayed delivery by a seller or carrier, or upon delayed redelivery by a tenant or charterer. The loss of use will sound in the cost of hiring a replacement, or lost profits from a sale to the market or use of the property, or non-pecuniary loss.

6.1. Introduction
6.2. The Cost of Hiring a Temporary Replacement
6.3. Lost Profits from Sale to the Market
6.4. Lost Profits from Employment of the Property
6.5. Loss of Use of Non-Profit-Earning Goods

6.1 Introduction

CONTRACT LAW TREATS compensation for being kept out of property in broadly the same way whatever the breach and however it caused the period without the property, the measure in both contract and the tort of negligence being compensation to put the claimant in the position it would have been in if the claimant had not lost the use of the property for the relevant period.[1]

This complaint, and therefore this measure, arises in cases of delay, for example late delivery by a seller or carrier, or late completion by a builder or repairer, or late delivery by a lessee or charterer after hire or use. The loss of use may also arise where the defendant carrier, tenant or other co-contractor damages or destroys property; or where a seller, lessor/shipowner fails to deliver property or delivers defective property, or a lessee or charterer fails to redeliver, and it takes some time to replace or repair the property.

---

[1] Damages in the torts of conversion and trespass are less straightforward and the measure adopted is not identical to the contract and negligence measure.

A. Compare Permanent Loss of Use

The quantification of damages for permanent loss of use, ie destruction or non-delivery where there is no replacement, gives rise to different issues. The damages recoverable in such cases are discussed above in chapter four.

B. Replacement and Repair

The assumption in this chapter is that the issue of mitigation has already been resolved, ie the particular loss of use of the property cannot reasonably be avoided by replacement or repair. (The reader is referred to chapter four on damage, destruction, non-delivery and defective goods as to these alternative measures based on replacement or repair.) In delayed delivery cases, the option of a permanent replacement does not arise for obvious reasons,[2] although a temporary replacement (as discussed below) may be reasonable.

C. Other Losses in Delay Cases

In addition to the losses set out below (the cost of a temporary replacement, lost profits on a sub-sale or use of the property, losses from deprivation of non-profit-making property), delayed delivery may cause other harms which, subject to remoteness, will be recoverable. This includes any additional costs resulting from the delay,[3] such as increased import duties,[4] costs of transhipment[5] or freight and insurance charges.[6] It also includes liability to third parties resulting from the delay.[7]

In some circumstances, the price payable under a contract may vary according to a formula dependent upon time (for example a clause that allows the price to be recalculated according to a particular exchange rate), such that a delay by the supplier may lead the recipient to have to pay an increased price to that supplier (in contrast with the cases below in which delay leads to the recipient earning less upon a resale of the property). Such an increase is recoverable in damages, even where it is a dramatic increase brought about by a revaluation of the purchase currency.[8]

---

[2] Exceptionally, there might be cases where the most reasonable thing to do is purchase replacement goods and then sell them upon the delayed delivery.

[3] Eg *Smeed v Foord* (1859) 1 E & E 602 (additional cost of stacking and drying wheat upon late delivery of a threshing machine); *Croudace Construction Ltd v Cawoods Concrete Products Ltd* [1978] 2 Lloyd's Rep 55 (Parker J) at 58 (obiter) as regards the costs of an idle building site if bricks are delivered late, affirmed [1978] 2 Lloyd's Rep 55 (CA).

[4] *SS Ardennes (Cargo Owners) v SS Ardennes (Owners)* [1951] 1 KB 55 (Goddard CJ).

[5] *Monarch Steamship Co Ltd v Karlshamns Oljefabriker (A/B)* [1949] AC 196 (HL).

[6] *Borries v Hutchinson* (1865) 18 CB (NS) 445.

[7] *Contigroup Companies Inc v Glencore AG* [2005] 1 Lloyd's Rep 241 (Glick QC) (late delivery by vendor of butane gas); *ASM Shipping Ltd of India v TTMI Ltd of England (The Amer Energy)* [2009] 1 Lloyd's Rep 293 (Flaux J) (late delivery of vessel by owner to charterer).

[8] *Aruna Mills Ltd v Dhanrajmal Gobindram (The Leipzig)* [1968] 1 QB 655 (Donaldson J).

6.2 The Cost of Hiring a Temporary Replacement

In many cases the claimant will be able to mitigate any temporary loss of use by paying for hire of a temporary replacement. This has been applied in contract cases in relation to temporary alternative accommodation during works necessitated by breaches by landlords,[9] surveyors[10] and other construction professionals.[11]

The majority of case law on the subject, however, concerns tort claims arising out of car collisions,[12] in which temporary car-hire costs are routinely claimed and awarded, and indeed an industry has arisen in relation to the financing of such costs.[13] In these cases the cost of hiring a temporary replacement is a cost incurred in mitigating the claimant's loss of use of the vehicle and 'The expense of doing so will then become the measure of the loss which he has sustained under this head of his claim. It will be substituted for his claim for loss of use by way of general damages' but it must be reasonable.[14] As Longmore LJ has observed, 'It would not follow that a claimant who never hired a replacement car (eg because he was out of the country at the time or already had a spare) would be entitled to the cost of so doing'.[15] The claimant, if able to prove that a replacement is reasonably required (because '[t]he need for a replacement car is not self-proving'[16]), may recover the cost of hiring an equivalent and no more.[17] The burden of showing that the amount

---

[9] *Calabar Properties Ltd v Stitcher* [1984] 1 WLR 287 (CA) (obiter, landlord's covenant to repair) approved in *Wallace v Manchester City Council* [1998] 3 EGLR 38 (CA). Cf *Axa Insurance UK plc v Cunningham Lindsey United Kingdom* [2007] EWHC 3023 (TCC) (Akenhead J).

[10] *Hooberman v Salter Rex* [1985] EGLR 144 (Smout QC); *Cross v Martin & Mortimer* [1989] 1 EGLR 154 (Phillips J); *Hipkins v Jack Cotton* [1989] 2 EGLR 157 (Baker J) (negligent surveyor inducing purchase); *Bigg v Howard Son & Gooch* [1990] 1 EGLR 173 (Hicks QC) at 175; *Holder v Countrywide Surveyors Ltd*, 11 March 2002 (Harvey QC). Although in principle there should be recovery in a limited range of surveyor cases, most of these decisions (other than *Hipkins*) should be doubted on this point for the reasons given above in chapter three, sections 3.2C(ii) and (vii) and 3.3C.

[11] *Cox v Sloane*, 19 July 2000 (Seymour QC); *Saigol v Cranley Mansion Ltd* (2000) 72 Con LR 54 (CA); *South Parklands Hockey and Tennis Centre Inc v Brown Falconer Group Pty Ltd* [2004] SASC 81 (Supreme Court of South Australia); *Iggleden v Fairview New Homes (Shooters Hill) Ltd* [2007] EWHC 1573 (TCC) (Coulson QC) at paras 102–3; *Melhuish & Saunders Ltd v Hurden* [2012] EWHC 3119 (TCC) (Havelock-Allen QC) at para 123.

[12] And in relation to ships see: *The Yorkshireman* (1826) 2 Hagg Adm 30n; *The Ikala* [1929] 1 AC 196 (HL); *Liesbosch Dredger (Owners) v SS Edison (Owners) (The Liesbosch)* [1933] AC 449 (HL), although the cost of hiring the replacement was disallowed in that case due to the old rule, since disapproved, as to disregarding the consequences of impecuniosity; *The World Beauty* [1970] P 144 (CA).

[13] For discussion of the much-litigated issues relating to whether the third party's paying for the temporary replacement on a finance or other scheme prevents the claimant's recovery, see below in chapter sixteen, section 16.10E.

[14] *Lagden v O'Connor* [2004] 1 AC 1067 (HL) Lord Hope at para 27. See also eg *The World Beauty* [1970] P 144 (CA) at 116 and 120. However, in *Lagden*, Lord Scott at paras 78–79 and Lord Walker at para 101 did not view the cost of a replacement in consumer cases as mitigating the inconvenience or loss of use damage; rather as simply a reasonable consequential expense recoverable if not too remote. The same result is reached but Lord Hope's analysis is to be preferred.

[15] *Bee v Jenson* [2007] 4 All ER 791 (CA) obiter at para 21.

[16] Lord Mustill in *Giles v Thompson* [1994] 1 AC 142 (HL) at 167.

[17] *O'Grady v Westminster Scaffolding Ltd* [1962] 2 Lloyd's Rep 238 (Edmund Davies J); *Watson Norie Ltd v Shaw* [1967] 1 Lloyd's Rep 515 (CA); *HL Motorworks (Willesden) v Alwahbi* [1977] RTR 276 (CA); *Daily Office Cleaning Contractors Ltd v Shefford* [1977] RTR 361 (Stabb QC); *Giles v Thompson* [1994] 1 AC 142 (HL); *Dimond v Lovell* [2002] 1 AC 384 (HL); *Bee v Jenson* [2007] 4 All ER 791 (CA); *Singh v Yaqubi* [2013] EWCA Civ 23 (CA). All of these are tort cases concerning car damage.

of the hire was excessive is on the defendant.[18] Costs attributable to any additional benefits procured through the particular funding mechanism for the temporary replacement will be irrecoverable.[19]

6.3 Lost Profits from Sale to the Market

The primary recoverable loss in cases of loss of use of tradeable goods will be the lost profit that would have been made selling the property to the market. Remoteness will often not be a problem. As Devlin J observed, 'everybody who sells to a merchant knows that he has bought for re-sale'.[20] And as Lord Morris explained in the leading case of late delivery by a carrier, *The Heron II*:

> When he contracted with the respondents to carry their sugar to Basrah, though he did not know what were the actual plans of the respondent, he had all the information to enable him to appreciate that a delay in arrival might in the ordinary course of things result in their suffering some loss. He must have known that the price in a market may fluctuate. He must have known that if a price goes down someone whose goods are late in arrival may be caused loss.[21]

Where the property or a replacement is obtained late (whether due to a late delivery, the need to await repair of defective goods, or for some other reason) the measure of loss is prima facie the difference between the selling price that would have been obtained and the selling price that is in fact obtained at the later date (or would have been if the claimant had acted reasonably and promptly in selling the late obtained property).[22]

A. The Relevant Market Prices are the Selling Prices

In these cases of late delivery the market replacement price (relevant where replacement is assumed or carried out) is irrelevant and the relevant market price is the market selling price, ie the price that can be obtained on a sale to the market.[23] Devlin J has confirmed in a case of late delivery of goods by a seller that the relevant price is the 'selling price' and that 'the buying price has nothing to do with the calculation which I have to make' and

> a calculation which supposes, incorrectly and notionally, that he should go out and buy another quantity of the same goods, has nothing to do with the reality of the matter. What

---

And see *Moore v DER Ltd* [1971] 1 WLR 1476 (CA), where the temporary replacement was hired pending permanent replacement rather than repair.

[18] *Dickinson v Tesco plc* [2013] EWCA Civ 36 (CA) Aikens LJ at para 93.

[19] See below in chapter four, section 4.4B, where this is discussed in the context of betterment.

[20] *Kwei Tek Chao v British Traders and Shippers Ltd* [1954] 2 QB 459 (Devlin J) at 489.

[21] *Czarnikow Ltd v Koufos (The Heron II)* [1969] 1 AC 350 (HL) at 400.

[22] Note that, unlike in cases of non-delivery and defective delivery, there is no Sale of Goods Act 1979 provision setting out the measure of recovery by a buyer in cases of late delivery. But see eg *Czarnikow Ltd v Koufos (The Heron II)* [1969] 1 AC 350 (HL) Lord Morris at 400 as to this being the prima facie measure.

[23] See the discussion above in chapter four, section 4.5A(ii)(a).

he wishes to do in those circumstances, in order to put himself in the same position, is to sell the goods, not to buy them.[24]

As for the relevant date, that is the 'the date when the plaintiffs could, acting with reasonable diligence, and after they knew of their rights, have resold the goods on the market and obtained the best price they could for them'.[25]

B. Application of this Measure

(i) Sale of Goods: Late Delivery

This measure, awarding the loss due to a market fall, has been applied to cases of late delivery by a seller.[26]

(ii) Carriage of Goods: Late Delivery

This same measure has been applied to cases of late delivery of goods by a carrier by land,[27] sea[28] or air.[29]

(iii) Construction: Late Completion

The same measure has been applied to late completion of construction cases where the property is to be sold,[30] although the matter will often be dealt with by a liquidated damages clause. However, lost profits resulting from a drop in the market will sometimes be too remote and/or outside the scope of duty of the defendant.[31]

---

[24] *Kwei Tek Chao v British Traders and Shippers Ltd* [1954] 2 QB 459 (Devlin J) at 497–98.

[25] Ibid.

[26] *Wertheim v Chicoutimi Pulp Co* [1911] 1 AC 301 (PC); *Kwei Tek Chao v British Traders and Shippers Ltd* [1954] 2 QB 459 (Devlin J) at 497. See also *Gatoil International Inc v Tradax Petroleum Ltd (The Rio Sun)* [1985] 1 Lloyd's Rep 350 (Bingham J), where the judge seemed to think this was the only measure, irrespective of what the claimant was going to do with the goods even if that use was not too remote.

[27] Obiter in *Horne v Midland Railway Co* (1873) LR 8 CP 131 where the principle was confirmed but no drop in the market was proven; also (although less clearly) *Elbinger Aktiengesellschaft v Armstrong* (1874) LR 9 QB 473.

[28] *Czarnikow Ltd v Koufos (The Heron II)* [1969] 1 AC 350 (HL): a voyage charterparty claim with a decline in the sugar market at Basra during the nine days of delay by the shipowner. The House in *The Heron II* declined to follow *The Parana* (1877) 2 PD 118 (CA) where, in part due to the uncertainty of carriage by sea in the 'golden age of sail', the market loss was held to be too remote, and confirmed that *The Parana* had been a decision on the facts and had not laid down a general rule of law.

[29] *Panalpina International Transport Ltd v Densil Underwear Ltd* [1981] 1 Lloyd's Rep 187 (HHJ Edgar Fay).

[30] *T&S Contractor Limited v Architectural Design Associates*, 16 October 1992 (Rich QC). In that case the market drop up to the date when the claimant should have sold the property was taken as the measure of loss, and the subsequent period, during which the claimant failed to sell due to unreasonable marketing, was disregarded.

[31] Eg *Earl's Terrace Properties Ltd v Nilsson Design Ltd* [2004] EWHC 136 (TCC) (Thornton QC) at paras 102ff, obiter. But see also below in chapter sixteen, section 16.13C.

(iv) Property Damage: Delay During Repair

Likewise, the same applies to property damage cases. In the tort case of *Blue Circle Industries v Ministry of Defence*,[32] the claimant recovered the difference in value between the date when the claimant would have sold its estate and the date when it was able to sell it after it had been decontaminated of radioactivity caused by the defendant. The claimant did not have to give credit for the increase in the value of the property after the date on which it could reasonably have been expected to sell, because any speculation after that date was at its own risk and therefore a collateral benefit to be ignored. Similarly had the value dropped after that date, the claimant's additional loss would have been unrecoverable as being avoidable loss. As Simon Brown LJ put it, these two questions (whether credit must be given if the value rises and whether a claim can be made if the value drops) 'must be answered the same way' and in this case on that date 'the risk [should] be regarded as switching back to [the claimant]'.[33]

(v) Charterparty: Late Redelivery by a Charterer[34]

In one case the charterer under a five-year term redelivered an aircraft late to the owner. The owner had in fact entered into a contract to sell (rather than re-charter) the aircraft, but the loss on that contract was too remote (following *The Achilleas* where it was held that follow-on charters would have been too remote).[35]

C. Sub-Sales of the Property Entered Prior to the Date of Delivery

(i) The Remoteness Issue[36]

As in the case of non-delivery and defective delivery, a pre-arranged sub-sale in a delay case may increase or decrease the loss of the claimant. It may increase it by giving the claimant a lost profit and/or liability on the sub-sale, and it may decrease it where the delay causes the claimant a lesser loss in profit on the sub-sale than it would have suffered on the market. The governing principle is remoteness, and the major types of recoverable loss will be lost profit on the sub-sale[37] and liability to the sub-seller.[38]

---

[32] *Blue Circle Industries plc v Ministry of Defence* [1999] Ch 289 (CA).

[33] Ibid at 321.

[34] Often a charterer of a ship who redelivers late will be contractually liable to pay the contract hire rate for the overrun period, and not common law damages.

[35] *A Pindell Ltd v AirAsia Berhad* [2010] EWHC 2516 (Comm) (Tomlinson J). See below at n 55 for discussion of *The Achilleas*.

[36] See also the discussion in relation to non-delivery and defective goods in section 4.2A(v)(a) (latent defects) and section 4.2A(vi) (non-delivery and patent defects).

[37] *Dreyfus Trading Ltd v Reliance Trading Ltd* [2004] 2 Lloyd's Rep 243 (Andrew Smith J).

[38] *Contigroup Companies Inc v Glencore AG* [2005] 1 Lloyd's Rep 241 (Glick QC). As to the principles applicable to measuring the quantum of liability to a sub-buyer and determining whether the sum paid or payable under a settlement with a sub-buyer is reasonable and so recoverable see below in chapter twenty, section 20.1D. See also *Elbinger Aktiengesellschaft v Armstrong* (1874) LR 9 QB 473.

(ii) Sale

The Privy Council's decision in *Wertheim v Chicoutimi Pulp Company*[39] is the leading authority on delay in delivery to deal with remoteness and pre-arranged sub-sales. Here 5s per ton of goods was recovered, far less than if the sub-sale had been ignored and it had been assumed that the claimant were selling on the market.

The buyer had pre-sold the wood pulp to a specific sub-buyer for 65s/ton and the late delivery did not prevent fulfilment of the sub-sale. The buyer could not claim for a drop in the market (in that case a drop from 70s at the due date to 42s 6d at the actual delivery date) because had the contract been performed the buyer would have been in exactly the same position as that it in fact found itself (ie still supplying the goods to the same sub-buyer for the same price), and the resale could not be ignored as collateral or irrelevant.[40] The best explanation of *Wertheim* is that the 'string contract' in that case was in the contemplation of the parties and therefore the sub-sale was to govern the recovery, for better or worse.[41] As Devlin J observed in another late delivery case,

> the merchant is not buying merely for re-sale generally, but upon a string contract where he will re-sell those specific goods and where he could only honour his contract by delivering those goods and no others, the measure of loss of profit on re-sale is the right measure.[42]

Similarly, in other cases the sub-sale has been found to be within the parties' contemplation and so to be taken into account as being the measure of the claimant's recovery whether or not the losses on the sub-sale are higher or lower than the difference between the market prices.[43] Thus in *Contigroup Companies Inc v Glencore AG*[44] the (compromised) liability on a butane sub-sale was not too remote and the court refused to measure loss by the difference in market value as that 'would be entirely artificial'.[45]

In contrast in *Portman v Middleton*, even if the delay caused by delivery of a useless fire-box, necessitating purchase of a replacement, led to liability of the buyer to a third party on a contract to repair a steam threshing-machine (for which the fire-box was wanted), such loss was too remote, as the seller had not known about the third party contract.[46]

In the residential property case of *Raineri v Miles*,[47] the delay in completing the sale of a home to the claimant (in third party proceedings) led to the claimant's

---

[39] *Wertheim v Chicoutimi Pulp Company* [1911] 1 AC 301 (PC).

[40] In fact the buyer in *Wertheim* was awarded 5s per ton, the difference between the market price at the due date (70s) and the sub-sale price (65s), which is not a measure of any loss suffered. However, this was not in issue in the Privy Council as there was no cross-appeal (and see argument [1911] 1 AC 301 at 303 and the comment at 307).

[41] Bankes LJ in *Slater v Hoyle & Smith Ltd* [1920] 2 KB 11 (CA) at 17 emphasised the fact that the sub-sale in *Wertheim* was of identical goods to the sale.

[42] *Kwei Tek Chao v British Traders and Shippers* [1954] 2 QB 459 (Devlin J) at 489.

[43] *Dreyfus Trading Ltd v Reliance Trading Ltd* [2004] 2 Lloyd's Rep 243 (Andrew Smith J).

[44] *Contigroup Companies Inc v Glencore AG* [2005] 1 Lloyd's Rep 241 (Glick QC).

[45] Ibid at para 80.

[46] *Portman v Middleton* (1858) 4 CB (NS) 322 (Court of Common Pleas). In any event, it appears from the headnote and argument that any such loss was caused by failure to mitigate, as if the claimant had bought a replacement promptly there would have been no liability on the third party contract.

[47] *Raineri v Miles* [1981] AC 1050 (HL).

liability to indemnify the buyer of its existing home (ie a different property to that promised by the defendant) to a third party. The defendant vendor was held liable to indemnify the claimant for its liability to its own buyer.

(iii) Carriage

In carriage cases (where the carrier rarely knows the detail of the customer's business) specific losses on specific pre-arranged sub-sales will usually be too remote and therefore the claimant can recover no more than any lost profit that would have been suffered on sale to the market.[48] In *The Pegase* it was confirmed that in some carriage cases they would not be too remote (although in that case the fact that the resale loss in part turned on the claimant's low stores of chromite sand meant that part of the resale profits were unrecoverable),[49] and in *The Baleares* Neill LJ empha-sised that in a specialised trade a carrier may have considerable knowledge.[50]

6.4 Lost Profits from Employment of the Property

A. Direct Proof and Estimation

As was observed in one tort collision case:

> The party injured is entitled to be put, as far as practicable, in the same condition as if the injury had not been suffered. It does not follow as a matter of necessity that anything is due for detention of a vessel whilst under repair. In order to entitle a party to be indemnified for what is termed in the Admiralty Court a consequential loss resulting from the deten-tion of his vessel, two things are absolutely necessary—actual loss and reasonable proof of the amount.[51]

It is possible to prove the loss of profits due to the temporary loss of use of property, as with proof of lost profits in other cases,[52] either by proving and quantifying what specific losses were suffered, or by estimating. Thus, as was explained in a ship col-lision tort case (in which the importance of not double-counting by awarding on both bases was also rightly emphasised):

> One appropriate method of calculating the damage is to prove the loss occasioned by the non-performance of the current charterparty (see *per* Bowen L.J. and Lindley L.J. in *The Argentino*). Another method, usual and admittedly convenient, is to multiply the average figure for what might have been expected to be her daily earnings by the number of days for

---

[48] *Great Western Railway Co v Redmayne* (1866) 1 LR CP 329; *Horne v Midland Railway Co* (1873) LR 8 CP 131, applying the cap principle discussed below in chapter fourteen, section 14.4. Sub-sales being held too remote is even more likely in cases of carriage by land rather than by sea, as fewer land carriages than sea carriages are for taking goods to market, Devlin J in *Heskell v Continental Express Ltd* [1950] 1 All ER 1033 at 1048.

[49] *Satef-Huttenes Albertus SpA v Paloma Tercera Shipping Co SA (The Pegase)* [1981] 1 Lloyd's Rep 175 (Goff J).

[50] *Geogas SA v Trammo Gas Ltd (The Baleares)* [1993] 1 Lloyd's Rep 215 (CA) Neill LJ at 227.

[51] *The Steamship SS City of Peking v The Compagnie des Messageries Maritimes (Hong Kong)* (1889) 15 App Cas 438 (PC) Sir Barnes Peacock at 442.

[52] See below in chapter eighteen.

which the collision caused the vessel to be unemployed, and to arrive at the figure for the daily earnings by taking three typical voyages, two before and one after the period in question. This method excludes the actual figures of loss caused by the non-performance of the interrupted charterparty, but substitutes a notional figure arrived at in the way described. But the notional figure purports, and is intended, to represent the loss of earnings by the period of detention, and to represent the whole loss resulting from the enforced deprivation of the vessel as a profit-earning instrument.[53]

Thus as Bowen LJ observed in another ship damage tort case:

> Where there is an actual charterparty [between the owner and a third party] such difficulty is reduced to a minimum. Where there is no charterparty but merely a reasonable certainty of employment, the matter is left more at large. Probably the most accurate mode of proof would be the opinion of persons acquainted with the trade and with the capacity and condition of the ship, who ought to be able to say what under the circumstances would be the ordinary earnings of such a vessel engaged to sail upon and about in a short time to sail upon such an adventure, as distinguished from all uncertain and all special profits which might or might not be reaped in a particular speculation.[54]

B. Losses from Hiring Out the Property

(i) Breach by Late Redelivery by the Hirer

The standard recovery in cases of late redelivery of hired property is the lost hire at market rates during the period of loss of use, less the hire actually paid by the breaching charterer or tenant for the period of the delay.[55] Unsurprisingly, such lost hire is rarely held to be too remote.[56] In relation to time charters in particular, the whole purpose of such charters is to convey to the defendant the earning capacity of the vessel so that it may be traded.[57]

The question of whether lost profits on a particular hire contract can be recovered was the subject of the House of Lords' decision in the leading remoteness case of *The Achilleas*.[58] On 20 April 2004, the charterer gave notice to redeliver by 2 May 2004 and, the rates being high, the owner immediately (on 21 April 2004) entered into a 4–6 month follow-on charter which the third party charterer could cancel if

---

[53] *Pacific Concord, Georgidore (Owners) v Pacific Concord (Owners) (The Pacific Concord)* [1961] 1 WLR 873 (Lord Merriman P) at 79–80.

[54] *The Argentino* (1888) 13 PD 191 (CA) Bowen LJ at 203.

[55] See the leading case on late redelivery by a charterer, *Transfield Shipping Inc v Mercator Shipping Inc (The Achilleas)* [2009] AC 61 (HL). Also *Lansat Shipping Co Ltd v Glencore Grain BV* [2009] EWCA Civ 855. Where the late delivery is under a sub-charter, the head charterer may recover an indemnity for its liability to the owner if not too remote: *Glencore Grain Ltd v Goldbeam Shipping Inc* [2002] EWHC 27 (Comm) (Moore-Bick J). As regards real property, see *Royal Bristol Permanent Building Society v Bomash* (1887) 35 Ch D 390 (Kekewich J); *Raja's Commercial College v Singh & Co Ltd* [1977] AC 312 (PC).

[56] But compare conversion case *Saleslease Ltd v Davis* [1999] 1 WLR 1664 (CA), where the loss was not too remote but the fact that it could not be mitigated by lease to another customer was, and so the loss was irrecoverable.

[57] See Hamblen J in *Sylvia Shipping Ltd v Progress Bulk Carriers Ltd* [2010] EWHC 542 (Comm) at para 62 and the quotations set out therein.

[58] *Transfield Shipping Inc v Mercator Shipping Inc (The Achilleas)* [2009] AC 61 (HL). The principle is discussed below in chapter fourteen, especially section 14.2.

the vessel was not delivered on 8 May 2004. As a result of the delayed redelivery by the defendant charterer, the owner would have missed the 8 May 2004 date and so on 5 May 2004 had to renegotiate the follow-on charter down by US$8,000 per day, the rates having fallen since 20 April 2004 on a very volatile market.

It is, of course, not unusual to fix follow-on charters before the vessel has actually been redelivered, especially where rates are high. It was accordingly perfectly predictable that a delay in redelivery would, if long enough, not only lead to a loss of hire profits for the period of the delay, but also lead to a loss or renegotiation of the follow-on charter. Charters would usually be of a specific vessel, and so the loss could not be avoided by the owner chartering a replacement vessel (and the situation is analogous to the 'string contract' situation in sale of goods cases).

However, the unpredictability of the loss from the point of the view of the parties at the date of entering into the initial contract convinced the House of Lords that such loss impliedly fell outside the charterer's scope of responsibility. The uncertainty in this case arose not only from the volatility of the market (which is a feature of many cases, including sale of goods cases) but also from the unpredictability of the length of the follow-on charter. In sale of goods cases the lost sub-sale is always a sale and therefore its size can be predicted, and its subject-matter will be of a piece with the breached head contract, whereas in charter cases the follow-on charter may be for a month or for several years. This adds an extra dimension to the unpredictability, the loss being affected not only by the date of the follow-on charter (and the rate applicable at that date) but also its length.

Thus it was held that the owner could recover for loss at the market rate only for the period of the delay (and less the rate paid in any event by the charterer during the unauthorised extension of the charter). However, the loss on the follow-on charter that was to run beyond the period of delay was outside the scope of the time charterer's duty to redeliver on time. The result in *The Achilleas* was applied in a case of late redelivery of a Boeing 737 aircraft after a five-year lease where the loss was not sustained on a follow-on lease but rather on a follow-on sale of the aircraft.[59]

(ii) Breach by the Owner/Lessor

Where un-seaworthiness interrupts charter service, the charterer can recover the ordinary lost profits during that period.[60]

(iii) Property Damage/Disrepair or Destruction

Numerous tort cases of ship collisions causing damage or destruction lay down the law in relation to temporary loss of use of property that was hired out. As in the cases discussed above of late redelivery by the charterer or interruption to charter service as a result of owner breach, the measure of loss is usually the net loss on chartering out the vessel.[61] Where there are particular engagements already made, the damages will

---

[59] *A Pindel Ltdl v AirAsia Berhad* [2010] EWHC 2516 (Comm) (Tomlinson J).
[60] *'SNIA' Societa di Navigazione Industria e Commercio v Suzuki & Co* (1924) 18 Ll L Rep 333 (CA).
[61] *The Argentino* (1889) 14 App Cas 519 (HL) Lord Herschell at 523 discussing the tort test; also the tort cases of *Ehmler v Hall* [1993] 1 EGLR 137 (CA); *Carisbrooke Shipping CV5 v Bird Port Ltd*

usually be measured by those engagements.[62] This includes charters that are already afoot when the damage or destruction occurs, and may well include losses for the entire profits on such charters where the collision led to the lawful cancellation by the charterer and this was not too remote.[63] The damages will also compensate for the loss of follow-on charters that are due to start some time after the collision, as was confirmed in the House of Lords' decision in *The Argentino*.[64]

A similar award is made where a tenant of real property returns the property in disrepair and the landlord then loses rental income while carrying out repairs that the tenant should have performed.[65] Likewise, in the sale of goods case of *Bacon v Cooper (Metals) Ltd*, the claimant recovered for lost profits resulting from the temporary outage of its scrap metal processing plant while it was being repaired as a result of damage caused by the defendant seller's non-conforming scrap.[66]

Some confusion has arisen in cases where the damage and repairs delayed completion of an existing charter. Logically the shipowner should be able to recover damages for the period of delay at the market rate from the date when the charter would have ended had the vessel not been taken out of action for a period, to compensate for being unable to charter to the market for that period. However, in *The Soya* the Court of Appeal, for mixed reasons that should be treated as unique to the case, awarded damages for lost profits during the delay period at the pre-existing charter rate.[67] The judge in *The Naxos* correctly refused to apply the result in *The Soya*.[68]

Where the claimant has a spare vessel or other property to temporarily replace the damaged or destroyed item, this may reduce the loss of profits suffered.[69]

C. Lost Profits from Other Use of the Property

Where the goods, vessel or building would have been used and not traded, damages for lost profits through unavailability for use will be recoverable on ordinary prin-

---

(*The Charlotte C*) [2005] 2 Lloyd's Rep 626 (Teare QC); '*Front Ace*' (Owners) v '*Vicky 1*' (Owners) (*The Vicky 1*) [2008] 2 Lloyd's Rep 45 (CA). See also *Lee Ting Yeung v Yeung Chung On* [2008] HKDC 254 (Hong Kong District Court) (destruction of a water-taxi).

[62] Cf the quotations in the text to nn 53 and 54 above.

[63] *The Star of India* (1876) 1 PD 466 (Sir Robert Phillimore). See also *The Consett* (1880) 5 PD 229 (Sir Robert Phillimore).

[64] *The Argentino* (1889) 14 App Cas 519 (HL). Compare the contract claim for late redelivery in *Transfield Shipping Inc v Mercator Shipping Inc (The Achilleas)* [2009] AC 61 (HL), discussed above.

[65] *Stellarbridge Management Inc v Magna International (Canada) Inc* (2004) 71 OR (3d) 263 (Ontario CA); *PGF II SA v Royal and Sun Alliance Insurance plc* [2010] EWHC 1459 (TCC) (HHJ Toulmin QC).

[66] *Bacon v Cooper (Metals) Ltd* [1982] 1 All ER 397 (Cantley J).

[67] *The Dirohys (Owners) v The Soya (Owners) (The Soya)* [1956] 1 Lloyd's Rep 557 (CA), where Jenkins LJ decided the case on (tort) remoteness but Evershed MR found that it had not been proven that in fact the vessel would have been able to avail itself of the lucrative Far Eastern market any earlier than it did, and it is not clear which approach Hodson LJ preferred.

[68] *The Naxos* [1972] 1 Lloyd's Rep 149 (Brandon J). Instead an average market rate was applied. In this case the repairs were not effected until some time after the existing charter.

[69] *The SS City of Peking* (1890) 15 App Cas 438 (PC). But as to the impact of spares on the measure of damages, see below in chapter sixteen, section 16.7A(ii), and also as to loss of use of spares, section 6.5B(i).

ciples, if not too remote. In general terms the loss of profits will rarely be too remote in commercial cases. For example it has been said (obiter) that 'in a contract to build a mill the builder knows that a delay on his part will result in the loss of business'[70] and the same will apply to many types of goods with an obvious use.

Where the loss was on specific contracts with third parties, including those already entered into by the claimant at the time of breach, these may be taken into account (i) if not too remote (although they will more frequently be too remote in contract than tort cases given the more restrictive remoteness test) and/or (ii) as evidence of the ordinary profits that would have been lost if special contracts the claimant had made are ignored. Of course, the profit must be the net profit, not gross revenue.[71]

(i) Contracts of Sale or Construction

Lost freight profits have been awarded after late delivery by a builder/seller of a ship.[72] Similarly lost profits are recoverable on late delivery by a seller of land,[73] such as damages for two crop years following non-delivery of farm land;[74] or non-delivery of land, to cover the period before replacement was possible.[75] The same principle applies where the breach causing loss of use of land was breach by a construction professional who was late in completing work.[76]

The same principle applies to goods and similar cases, thus late delivery of shares may lead to an award of lost dividends.[77] Likewise in *Cory v Thames Ironworks and Shipbuilding Company*,[78] a seller of the hull of a floating boom derrick was liable for the loss of profits during the six months of delay. Similarly, in *Victoria Laundry (Windsor) Ltd v Newman Industries Ltd*[79] an engineering company was five months late in delivering a boiler to some Windsor launderers and dyers, knowing it was wanted for immediate use (unlike in *Hadley v Baxendale*, below). As Asquith LJ put it:

> The obvious use of a boiler, in such a business, is surely to boil water for the purpose of washing or dyeing. A laundry might conceivably buy a boiler for some other purpose; for instance, to work radiators or warm bath water for the comfort of its employees or directors, or to use for research, or to exhibit in a museum. All these purposes are possible, but the first is the obvious purpose which, in the case of a laundry, leaps to the average eye.[80]

Accordingly, lost profits were recoverable.

---

[70] *Hadley v Baxendale* (1854) 23 LJ Ex 179 (Parke B) at 181.
[71] See eg *The Fortunity* [1961] 1 WLR 351 (Hewson J).
[72] *Fletcher v Tayleur* (1855) 17 CB 21.
[73] *Jaques v Millar* (1877) 6 Ch D 153 (Fry J); *Jones v Gardiner* [1902] 1 Ch 191 (Byrne J); *R v Poggioli* (1923) 32 CLR 222 (HC of Australia).
[74] *Kopec v Pyret* (1983) 146 DLR (3d) 242 (Saskatchewan QB), affirmed (1987) 36 DLR (4th) 1 (Saskatchewan CA).
[75] *Malhotra v Choudhury* [1980] Ch 52 (CA) (doctor's surgery).
[76] *Bevan Investments Ltd v Blackhall and Struthers (No 2)* [1978] 2 NZLR 97 (NZCA) (lost profits from use of a sports centre).
[77] *Sri Lanka Omnibus Co Ltd v Perera* [1952] AC 76 (PC) (the shares were only finally obtained upon specific performance).
[78] *Cory v Thames Ironworks and Shipbuilding Company* (1868) LR 3 QB 181 (QBD).
[79] *Victoria Laundry (Windsor) Ltd v Newman Industries Ltd* [1949] 2 KB 528 (CA).
[80] Ibid at 540–41.

As is discussed below,[81] in both of these cases the claimant did not recover its actual loss of profits because although lost profits in general were not too remote to be recoverable, the particularly lucrative use to which the claimant would have put the property was. In *Cory v Thames Ironworks* the damages were capped at the amount that would have been earned if but for the breach the claimant would have used the hull to store coal (the ordinary use) rather than to tranship coal (a novel use), and in *Victoria Laundry* they were capped at the amount of ordinary dyeing and laundering profits rather than those that would have been earned under the claimant's particularly lucrative dyeing contracts with the Ministry of Supply.

In *Hydraulic Engineering Ltd v McHaffie, Goslett & Co*,[82] part of a machine called a 'gun' was delivered late, meaning that the machine the claimant was producing for a third party was late and thus rejected by the third party. There was no market upon which a substitute buyer of the machine could be found, and it had only scrap value (although the parties agreed that, instead of deducting for the scrap value, the machine should be given to the defendant). The lost profit on the sub-sale, and the expenditure wasted in making the machine and which would have been recovered if it had been sold to the third party, were recoverable as not too remote because the defendant knew about the contract with the third party and the risk that it might be lost.

In a case for late delivery of a threshing machine, the rain damage to the wheat and costs of additional processes required were recoverable, although not the lost profit due to a deterioration in the market value.[83]

An important point was made by Parker J in *Croudace Construction Ltd v Cawoods Concrete Products Ltd*, who observed, in relation to the contemplated use of building materials:

> When selling building materials to a contractor for delivery on a building site, the difference in the value of the materials is, as a matter of common sense, wholly irrelevant. If between the date when the goods should have been delivered and the date when they were in fact delivered, there is a fall in the value, this is as a matter of commercial reality, of supreme indifference to the contractor and in no real sense does he suffer any loss or damage as a result of the fall. If he does, however, it appears to me to be more remote and less direct than that which begins to clock up at once, namely the cost of idle men and plant, etc.

> To take an example, suppose that a load of steel work is due on May 1, and the contractor has on site ready to install it a work force, scaffolding and lifting plant. The steel is however 14 days late. The most direct, immediate and natural damage caused by the delay is the expense of the work force scaffolding and plant. If when the steel arrives 14 days later it is worth the same as, less than, or more than it was worth on May 1 makes not the slightest difference to the contractor.[84]

---

[81] Chapter fourteen, section 14.4.

[82] *Hydraulic Engineering Ltd v McHaffie, Goslett & Co* (1878) 4 QBD 670 (CA).

[83] *Smeed v Foord* (1859) 1 E & E 602.

[84] *Croudace Construction Ltd v Cawoods Concrete Products Ltd* [1978] 2 Lloyd's Rep 55 (Parker J) at 58 (a late delivery case), affirmed [1978] 2 Lloyd's Rep 55 (CA). Discussed and approved but distinguished in *Addax Ltd v Arcadia Ltd* [2000] 1 Lloyd's Rep 493 (Morison J) at 495–96.

The point here is clear and correct. Where materials are used for construction, and that use is not too remote, the measure of loss is the actual loss on the construction project. The difference in value in the materials is irrelevant whether larger or smaller than the actual loss: the claimant would not have sold the materials on delivery and so the difference in value is not the actual loss, and the claimant cannot reasonably be expected to purchase replacements and so the difference in value is not the loss dictated by the mitigation principle.[85]

The point was also made by Lord Pearce in *The Heron II* (a late delivery case):

> Additional or 'special' knowledge … may extend the horizon to include losses that are outside the natural course of events. And of course the extension of the horizon need not always increase the damages; it might introduce a knowledge of particular circumstances, eg a subcontract, which show that the plaintiff would in fact suffer less damage than a more limited view of the circumstances might lead one to expect.[86]

Andrew Smith J has observed in *Louis Dreyfus Trading Ltd v Reliance Trading Ltd* (in effect, a late delivery case):[87]

> However, if the parties to a sale contract had within their contemplation when making their contract a particular sub-sale, different considerations can arise. In these circumstances, the buyer might be entitled to have the sub-sale brought into account to increase his damages. Equally, the seller might be entitled to have it brought into account in order to reduce the award against him.

> I consider that in a case such as the present, where the parties had in their contemplation when making their contract that the buyer was committed to deliver the same goods to a sub-buyer under a specific contract, principles of remoteness do not require that the sub-sale be disregarded in assessing the buyer's damages. It is to be taken to have been within the parties' reasonable contemplation, as a serious possibility or a consequence not unlikely to result from LD being in breach of their obligations, that the loss suffered by Reliance might depend upon the impact of the sub-sale to Boule. This being so, I reject Reliance's argument that principles of remoteness require that the sub-sale be disregarded in assessing their damages or that the sub-sale is to be treated as res inter alios acta.

This approach was adopted in the *Louis Dreyfus Trading Ltd* case of a sale of white crystal sugar at US$257.43/metric tonne for delivery to Banjul in The Gambia.[88] In that case the sub-sale pre-dated the main contract, and the main seller knew that the buyer was buying the sugar specifically to fulfil the pre-existing sub-sale (which was priced at US$290/mt for most of the sugar and US$253 for the rest). The seller breached the warranty of quiet possession that is implied by section 12(2)(b) of the Sale of Goods Act 1979 because unloading was delayed for a month by a third party's injunction. Andrew Smith J held that the measure of loss was prima facie the difference between the value had quiet possession been observed and the value at the date of delivery (ie, in effect, the late delivery measure), but that where the

---

[85] This is the same point made in relation to latent defects in *Biggin v Permanite* and *Bence Graphics*: chapter 4, sections 4.2(v)(b)–(c).
[86] *Czarnikow Ltd v Koufos (The Heron II)* [1969] 1 AC 350 (HL) at 416.
[87] *Louis Dreyfus Trading Ltd v Reliance Trading Ltd* [2004] 2 Lloyd's Rep 243 (Andrew Smith J) at paras 18 and 23.
[88] Ibid.

sub-sale was not too remote it must be taken into account. The sub-sale here was not too remote, and the appeal was allowed to remit the matter to the arbitrator to consider the proper measure of damages.

Finally, although the typical sale of goods breach leading to damages for temporary loss of use is that of late delivery, the same measure of damages may be awarded in cases of non-delivery where a replacement is available but not for some time.[89]

(ii) Contracts of Carriage

In carrier cases the consequential loss will more often be too remote than in sale cases. As Asquith LJ has observed: 'A carrier commonly knows less than a seller about the purposes for which the buyer or consignee needs the goods or about other "special circumstances" which may cause exceptional loss if due delivery is withheld'.[90] Thus, as Lord Walker observed in *The Achilleas* of the delayed delivery cases:

> The different outcomes of *Hadley v Baxendale* and the *Victoria Laundry (Windsor)* case depended in part (though only in part) on the fact that the defendant in the latter case was an engineering company supplying a specialised boiler, and not merely a carrier of goods with which it had no particular familiarity.[91]

This has been said to be 'a natural result of the fact that a carrier is supposed to know less about the commodity he carries and to undertake less responsibility in connexion with it than a seller of the same commodity would be supposed to do'.[92]

In the carriage cases of *Hadley v Baxendale*[93] and *British Columbia Saw Mill Co v Nettleship*,[94] the consequential loss of the mills being at a standstill (in the former there was delayed delivery, in the latter non-delivery leading to a delay while a replacement was sourced) were irrecoverable, although, as was said in both cases, things might have been different had the consequences of late delivery and the fact of the mills being at a standstill been brought home to the carrier before the contract was entered into.[95]

Similarly, in a Canadian case, during a train derailment a carrier damaged equipment being imported by the claimant from Belgium to Vancouver to be used in a new operation there of a plant for manufacturing wood particle boards.[96] The breach

---

[89] *Saint Line Ltd v Richardsons, Westgarth & Co Ltd* [1940] 2 KB 99 (Atkinson J); *Vanda Compania Ltda of Costa Rica v Société Maritime Nationale of Paris (The Ile Aux Moines)* [1974] 2 Lloyd's Rep 502 (Mocatta J) obiter at 505 (non-delivery); *Société des Industries Métallurgiques SA v The Bronx Engineering Co Ltd* [1975] 1 Lloyd's Rep 465 (CA) obiter at 468.

[90] *Victoria Laundry (Windsor) Ltd v Newman Industries Ltd* [1949] 2 KB 528 (CA) at 537.

[91] *Transfield Shipping Inc v Mercator Shipping Inc (The Achilleas)* [2009] AC 61 (HL) at para 67.

[92] *Montevideo Gas and Drydock Co Ltd v Clan Line Steamers Ltd* [1921] 6 Ll L Rep 539 (Roche J) at 541, decision affirmed [1921] 8 Ll L Rep 192 (CA). See also Lord Hoffmann, 'The Achilleas: custom and practice or foreseeability?' (2010) *Edinburgh Law Review* 47 at 57.

[93] *Hadley v Baxendale* (1854) 9 Exch 341.

[94] *British Columbia and Vancouver Island Spar, Lumber and Saw Mill Co v Nettleship* (1868) LR 3 CP 499.

[95] Contrast the sale of defective goods case of *Bacon v Cooper (Metals) Ltd* [1982] 1 All ER 397 (Cantley J), where damages for a scrap metal processing plant's standstill, caused by damage resulting from the defendant's non-conforming scrap, were recoverable.

[96] *Parta Industries Ltd v Canadian Pacific Ltd* (1974) 48 DLR (3d) 463 (British Columbia SC).

caused 105 days of delay in starting production. The carrier did not know the nature of the material being carried, other than that it was construction material, nor its use, but did know that speed was important (the bill of lading was marked 'RUSH'). Moreover, it could have foreseen that there would be a 45-day delay in whatever construction the material was needed for (since a replacement may obviously have to be obtained overseas) and part of the losses claimed were therefore recoverable, including the cost of labour repairing the goods, lost employee time and depreciation.

(iii) Damage or Destruction

In *The Liesbosch* the claimants had a contract with the Patras port authority and recovered

> for disturbance and loss in carrying out their contract over the period of delay between the loss of the Liesbosch and the time at which the substituted dredger could reasonably have been available for use in Patras, including in that loss such items as overhead charges, expenses of staff and equipment, and so forth thrown away.[97]

The same applied in a contract case of destruction of goods by the carrier,[98] and a tort case of destruction of a lorry.[99]

In one case a commercial vessel was, when damaged, being operated at a loss to establish a particular trading route with a view to future profit. No damages for loss of use were allowable.[100]

D. Estimation of Lost Profits from Use of the Property

(i) Estimation by Return on Capital

It has been said in the tort damage cases that 'In the ordinary case there may be no better way of estimating the value of such use than by allowing interest on the capital value of the lost vessel'.[101] This approach, as a default where better evidence is not available, has been endorsed by the House of Lords[102] and is well-established in cases of loss of use of non-commercial property.[103]

---

[97] Ibid at 468–69. Also *The Fortunity* [1961] 1 WLR 351 (Hewson J). And cf the unlawful detention detention case of *Brandeis Goldschmidt & Co v Western Transport Ltd* [1981] QB 864 (CA), where damages for the loss of use of anodes, used by the claimant as a raw material, were not proven due to the lack of evidence; and the trespass case of *Ramzan v Brookwide Ltd* [2012] 1 All ER 903 (CA), where profits were lost due to misappropriation of a function room above a restaurant.

[98] *Parta Industries Ltd v Canadian Pacific Ltd* (1974) 48 DLR (3d) 463 (British Columbia SC) discussed above at text to n 98.

[99] *Jones v Port of London Authority* [1954] 1 Lloyd's Rep 489 (Devlin J) at 490.

[100] *The Bodlewell* [1907] P 286 (Bargrave Deane J).

[101] Lord Hunter in *Clyde Navigation Trustees v Bowring Steamship Co* (1929) 34 Ll L Rep 319 (Court of Session) at 320.

[102] *The Ikala* [1929] 1 AC 196 (HL) Lord Warrington at 212.

[103] See below in section 6.5A(ii). As regards the presumption of a fair return on *cash* capital, the use of which the claimant has been deprived, see *East v Maurer* [1991] 1 WLR 461 (CA) (deceit) per Denning MR in favour of such a presumption and *Davis v Churchward Brook Haye & Co* ((CA), 6 May 1993) (deceit) Nourse LJ warning against one.

Thus in the contractual case of *British Columbia and Vancouver Island Spar, Lumber and Saw Mill Company Ltd v Nettleship*,[104] the lost profits that resulted from delayed delivery of replacement machinery to a saw-mill could not be proven and the court awarded interest at five per cent of the price of the machinery to compensate for the delay. In effect, the court assumed that the claimant would have used the machinery to make profit of five per cent on the machinery's price, since if this were not the case the claimant could have been expected to just keep the money rather than buying the machinery.

Here the court is essentially applying a presumption of a fair return on capital in the absence of better evidence,[105] and it should be rebuttable where it can be proven that the claimant would have made more or less than a fair return.[106]

(ii) Estimation by Cost of Renting a Replacement

As applied in cases of loss of use of non-profitable goods,[107] it may be appropriate to presume in profitable goods cases that the goods would have earned as much as it would cost to hire a replacement.[108]

(iii) The Presumption that Loss Equals the Cost of Running the Property

As with non-commercial property,[109] it may be appropriate to presume that a vessel would have made at least as much revenue as it cost to run. This is the best explanation for cases in which damages are measured by the cost of crew wages and other expenses incurred in relation to the vessel during the period when it was out of use.[110]

6.5 Loss of Use of Non-Profit-Earning Goods

The primary award in cases of loss of use of non-profit-earning goods is the cost of hiring a replacement, but where such a replacement is unavailable or the cost is otherwise not incurred and not deemed to have been incurred, the only award

[104] *British Columbia & Vancouver Island Spar, Lumber and Saw Mill Company Ltd v Nettleship* (1868) LR 3 CP 499.
[105] As permitted in the US by the Restatement (Second) of Contracts §348(1) where the loss is not proved with reasonable certainty.
[106] As can be seen from *The Bodlewell* [1907] P 285 (Bargrave Deane J) and *The Glenfinlas* [1918] 1 P 363 (Roscoe R), actual loss is recoverable (subject to remoteness and mitigation) in preference to estimated loss. Cf the presumption of breaking even in relation to lost profits awards, discussed below in chapter eighteen, section 18.3.
[107] See below in section 6.5A(iii).
[108] The US Restatement (Second) of Contracts §348(1) allows an award of the 'rental value of the property' the loss is not proved with reasonable certainty, in the alternative to the measure referred to at n 107 above. Cf *R v Poggioli* (1932) 32 CLR 222 (HC of Australia).
[109] See below in section 6.5A(i).
[110] Eg *Edmund Handcock (1929) Ltd v Ernesto* [1952] 1 Lloyd's Rep 467 (CA) (contract case of damage to a tug). Also *The SS City of Peking (Owners) v The Compagnie des Messageries Maritimes* (1889) 15 App Cas 438 (PC).

can be of actual loss resulting from the loss of use. Although contract damages are generally focused on harm that has financial implications, as Lord Hobhouse has explained, 'even where the chattel is non profit earning ... there may still be scope for awarding general damages for loss of use' and claimants 'do not have to survive in an environment where the law does not recognise the losses which they may have suffered and that the law is not without principles covering the provision of compensation and its assessment'.[111] The case in which Lord Hobhouse was giving judgment, like most of the others in this section, was a tort case concerning loss of use of a private car.

A. Measures of Loss

The cases show that there are two principal measures of damages in these cases where there is no cost of replacement: 'The first method is to take the cost of maintaining and operating the vehicle ... The second method is based on interest on capital and depreciation'.[112] Notably, both forms of loss would be incurred even if the claimant had not lost use of the property, and so neither describes actual sums lost as a result of the damage. Rather they are both proxies for the value of the use of the property to the claimant. The Court of Appeal has confirmed that in choosing between different measures 'there is no all-embracing principle ... other than that an award must be of such amount as will fairly compensate the claimant for his loss. Circumstances may differ and each case has to be approached on its own facts'.[113]

(i) The Presumption that Loss Equals the Cost of Running the Property: the 'Standing Charge' Method

This method takes the costs of running and maintaining the property, including a proportion of the overheads of the business, often labelled the 'standing charge'.

This method has been justified 'on the assumption [or presumption] that this figure must represent approximately the value [to] the operators'.[114] As it was put in *The Marpessa*, anything can be presumed to be worth to the owner 'at least what we are habitually paying' for it.[115] Here recovery is not of actually incurred expenditure—the asset did not need maintaining as it was out of use—but rather of the amount of expenditure that would have needed to be incurred had the asset

---

[111] *Dimond v Lovell* [2002] 1 AC 384 (HL) at 406.
[112] *Birmingham Corp v Sowsbery* [1970] RTR 84 (Geoffrey Lane J), approved in *Beechwood Birmingham Ltd v Hoyer Group UK Ltd* [2010] EWCA Civ 647. These two decisions contain useful summaries of the prior authorities.
[113] *West Midlands Travel Ltd v Aviva Insurance UK Ltd* [2013] EWCA Civ 887 (Moore-Bick LJ) at para 23.
[114] *Birmingham Corp v Sowsbery* [1970] RTR 84 (Geoffrey Lane J), approved in *Beechwood Birmingham Ltd v Hoyer Group UK Ltd* [2010] EWCA Civ 647, but see the discussion in *West Midlands Travel Ltd v Aviva Insurance UK Ltd* [2013] EWCA Civ 887 at para 27.
[115] *Mersey Docks and Harbour Board v SS Marpessa (Owners) (The Marpessa)* [1907] AC 241 (HL) at 244–45. Quoted with approval by Lord Sumner in *The Admiralty Commissioners v Owners of The Chekiang* [1926] AC 637 (HL) at 647. As to the presumption of breaking even more generally, see chapter eighteen, section 18.3, below.

been in use. This expenditure is a good proxy (on the presumption above) as to the benefit, whether non-pecuniary or pecuniary, that would have been earned by that use. Such an award has been made for periods of loss of use of residential property,[116] and of a bus.[117]

This method is particularly apt where the claimant has used its own stand-by to cover the loss of use of the damaged property,[118] and has been disapproved in other cases, where the claimant does not have a dedicated stand-by but merely makes do with capacity it has in its rotating fleet, as overcompensating the claimant.[119]

(ii) *The Presumption that Loss Equals an Interest Return on the Capital Value of the Property*

Damages on the basis of an interest return on the capital value, plus depreciation, have been awarded in a number of ship collision cases starting with *The Greta Holme*.[120] Similarly, in *Beechwood Birmingham Ltd v Hoyer Group UK Ltd*,[121] the Court of Appeal awarded interest plus depreciation following damage to a company's non-profit-earning car, in *Piper v Hales* an interest return was ordered on a classic car put out of use by the defendant's damage,[122] and in *The Hebridean Coast* the House of Lords awarded the claimant public electric company interest on the value of the damaged collier ship.[123] Similarly in cases of late delivery of goods, damages measured by depreciation may be awarded.[124] As regards damage cases, it has been suggested (probably wrongly) that this award may only be made in cases of a depreciating asset.[125]

This method was approved by the Court of Appeal in *West Midlands Travel Ltd v Aviva Insurance UK Ltd*, in which a passenger bus service provider made do from its rotating fleet, neither having a dedicated stand-by nor having to go outside its fleet to replace the out-of-use bus, and is probably the current method of choice for the courts where there is not a specific stand-by that has been brought into use (and

---

[116] *Hunt v Optima (Cambridge) Ltd* [2013] EWHC 681 (TCC) (Akenhead J) at para 263.

[117] *Birmingham Corp v Sowsbery* [1970] RTR 84 (Geoffrey Lane J), approved in *Beechwood Birmingham Ltd v Hoyer Group UK Ltd* [2010] EWCA Civ 647.

[118] *West Midlands Travel Ltd v Aviva Insurance UK Ltd* [2013] EWCA Civ 887 Moore-Bick LJ at para 23.

[119] Ibid at paras 23, 27 and 32.

[120] *No 7 Steam Sand Pump Dredger (Owners) v SS Greta Holme (Owners) (The Greta Holme)* [1897] AC 596 (HL); *SS Mediana (Owners) v Lightship Comet (Owners, Masters and Crew) (The Mediana)* [1900] AC 113 (HL); *Mersey Docks and Harbour Board v SS Marpessa (Owners) (The Marpessa)* [1907] AC 241 (HL); *Admiralty Commissioners v SS Chekiang (Owners) (The Chekiang)* [1926] AC 637 (HL); *Admiralty Commissioners v SS Susquehanna (Owners) (The Susquehanna)* [1926] AC 655 (HL).

[121] *Beechwood Birmingham Ltd v Hoyer Group UK Ltd* [2010] EWCA Civ 647 (CA).

[122] *Piper v Hales* (18.1.93) (Simon Brown QC) at para 50.

[123] *Lord Citrine (Owners) v Hebridean Coast (Owners) (The Hebridean Coast)* [1961] 1 AC 545 (HL). See also *The West Wales* [1932] P 165 (Bateson J). Cf the cases of residential leases where the non-pecuniary loss suffered due to landlord failure to repair is sometimes presumed to be equal to the notional reduction in rent that the disrepair would lead to if the property were being rented out on the market: see chapter 19, section 19.1C(iii)(b).

[124] *Sunley & Co Ltd v Cunard White Star Line Ltd* [1940] 1 KB 740 (CA): £20 awarded for one week's depreciation of a tractor and scraper machine that cost £4,500. (£16 had to be deducted to allow for profits made by the claimant with the machine while it was held at port.)

[125] *Bella Casa Ltd v Vinestone Ltd* [2005] EWHC 2807 (TCC) (Coulson QC) at para 60.

no direct financial loss proven).[126] The law was summarised by Moore-Bick LJ in the following terms:

> I think that the proper basis on which to assess general damages for the loss of use of a public service vehicle is normally interest on capital value (if it is owned) or the daily hire rate (if it is leased) together with depreciation and expenses thrown away.[127]

The Court of Appeal confirmed that the award would include not only an interest return on capital and compensation for depreciation, but also wasted expenditure, bringing in aspects of the 'standing charge' approach mentioned above; in the *West Midlands Travel* case itself such recoverable expenditure included a relevant proportion of the cost of mandatory testing, the vehicle excise licence, insurance, maintenance for degeneration over time (but not wear and tear), and possibly the cost of storage (the parking space).[128] In that case the vehicle was leased rather than owned, so the interest on capital element was replaced by the leasing cost.[129]

(iii) The Presumption that Loss Equals the Market Price of Hiring a Replacement

The market cost of hiring a replacement may also be a useful starting point for measuring damages for loss of use, even in cases where no temporary replacement is in fact hired or deemed to have been hired by the mitigation principle.[130] As one Canadian judge pointed out, the market rate may be at the high end of the range of possible awards, given that it will often cost far more (not least because of commissions etc) for a short-term rental of property than the claimant ever paid for the property as part of its purchase price.[131]

(iv) Hire Purchase

In cases of non-delivery or rejection of a car on hire purchase, the loss of use is measured as the cost of obtaining a replacement vehicle on similar hire purchase terms (not merely hiring a replacement), and the court will presume that the contract price is the same as the market price and so award the claimant damages in the amount of the hire purchase payments already made.[132] It is said that the claimant

---

[126] *West Midlands Travel Ltd v Aviva Insurance UK Ltd* [2013] EWCA Civ 887 (CA).

[127] Ibid at para 33 (Moore-Bick LJ).

[128] Ibid at para 29.

[129] Ibid at para 32.

[130] *Bee v Jenson* [2007] 4 All ER 791 (CA), where the actual replacement hire had to be ignored as it was paid for by the insurer (see below in chapter sixteen, section 16.10B(i)) and yet it was confirmed that substantial damages for loss of use were available measured by the spot rate of hire of a replacement, probably on the basis that the claimant could recover the reasonable costs the claimant should have expended but (adopting the necessary fiction that there had been no hire paid by the insurers) did not. Alternatively, it may have been presumed that the car had the same value to the claimant as a hire car would have to the market. See also *West Midlands Travel Ltd v Aviva Insurance UK Ltd* [2013] EWCA Civ 887 (CA) at para 30.

[131] *Hall v Ritchie* [2008] BCSC 1452 (British Columbia SC) at para 24 (refusal of vendor to allow purchaser to exercise rights to test drive his super-yacht before delivery).

[132] *Charterhouse Credit Co v Tolly* [1963] 2 QB 683 (CA) at 706–7 (overruled in *Photo Production Ltd v Securicor Transport Ltd* [1980] AC 827 (HL) but on a different point relating to fundamental breach).

will also have to deduct from the claim an allowance for the use made of the vehicle before rejection,[133] although this is difficult to justify since if there had been no breach the claimant would have had such use and so it was not a benefit caused by the breach.[134] The claimant may also claim for the inconvenience caused by the non-delivery or rejection and the period without use (and this will often offset the deduction for use made of the vehicle).[135]

(v) Other Measures

Although most awards will be on one of the above measures, it is open to the court to fix damages on a different basis, particularly where the loss is non-pecuniary.[136] Similarly in cases of failure to repair or develop residential property which led to loss of use of the repaired/completed property, damages for distress and physical inconvenience resulting from the delay can be recovered.[137]

B. When Will Presumptions be Rebutted and No Award Made?

Given that this is a claim for loss of use for a time (rather than loss of value), the question arises as to whether it matters that the claimant was not in fact going to get much use out of the property. Lord Halsbury posed the question in *The Mediana*:

> Supposing a person took away a chair out of my room and kept it for twelve months, could anybody say you had a right to diminish the damages by shewing that I did not usually sit in that chair, or that there were plenty of other chairs in the room?[138]

The rhetorical answer expected was no, that the claimant could still recover, and that is probably right in the particular examples given, such as consumer property.[139]

---

[133] *Charterhouse Credit Co v Tolly* [1963] 2 QB 683 (CA); *Garside v Black Horse* [2010] EWHC 190 (QB) (King J).

[134] This is probably a mistaken importation from the claim for restitution of payments made upon total failure of consideration, in which case the unjust enrichment claimant would have to make counter-restitution for the use made of the vehicle.

[135] *Farnworth Finance Facilities Ltd v Attryde* [1970] 1 WLR 1053 (CA); *Garside v Black Horse* [2010] EWHC 190 (QB) (King J).

[136] *Bernstein v Pamson Motors (Golders Green) Ltd* [1987] 2 All ER 220 (Rougier J) at 231, where £50 was awarded as contract damages for five days of being without a car (rejected as defective).

[137] Eg *Cross v Martin & Mortimer* [1989] 1 EGLR 154 (Phillips J); *Bigg v Howard Son & Gooch* [1990] 1 EGLR 173 (Hicks QC) at 175; *Wallace v Manchester City Council* [1998] 3 EGLR 38 (CA) (landlord's covenant to repair). See further below, chapter eight, section 8.3C.

[138] *The Mediana* [1900] AC 113 (HL) at 117.

[139] Cf *Piper v Hales*, 18 January 1993 (Simon Brown QC). Lord Hobhouse, dissenting in *Attorney General v Blake* [2001] 1 AC 268 (HL) at 299, answered the rhetorical question as follows: 'He would have lost the use of the chair and it, like other such amenity-value assets, can be assessed by reference to the sum which has been expended on its acquisition and/or maintenance or interest upon its capital value during the period of deprivation'. Lord Hobhouse is right for the large part, but wrong if he intended to suggest that the usefulness or uselessness of the property to the claimant can never be relevant, as the discussion of the cases in this section shows. See also *Rolls Royce Power Engineering Plc v Ricardo Consulting Engineers Ltd* [2003] EWHC 2871 (HHJ Seymour QC) at para 128.

Lord Sumner discussed the point in the House of Lords in *The Chekiang*,[140] a case of damage to a warship. He observed that the assumption that use of a vessel is worth what is paid for it may be appropriate in some non-profit cases, such as

> For a dredger, working at a limited task under settled local conditions, or a lightship always discharging the same duty in the same place [and] For some Admiralty craft ... tugs for example, and oilers, or harbour launches and ferry boats, or floating docks, or even it may be for the old Indian troopships

because

> There is a regularity of duty and a close analogy to commercial undertakings in these cases, that justify the assumption.

However, he doubted that the assumption was necessarily appropriate in the case of ships of war, where a submarine or mine-layer may have almost no value in a time of peace, and may have vast and inestimable value in a time of war.[141] In *The Chekiang* itself the registrar's award based on a rate of five per cent of the ship's value per annum was upheld, the vessel being a patrolling light cruiser that gave moral rather than material support to British interests and therefore was 'doing work for which the outlay upon her was economically well designed'.[142] And in another case the Danish government recovered substantial damages when it was deprived of use of its warship *'Heimdal'* for 22 days during peacetime, as the claimant might have wanted it for royal or fighting purposes or other purposes; it had been cruising with new conscripts when it was damaged.[143]

It has elsewhere been held that no damages are recoverable where the property was of no use at all and the owner was 'saddled' with it and would get 'no ... pleasure or other form of service' from it.[144]

(i) Loss of Use of a Spare

A private car owner has been refused damages where he had two other cars and had not been at all inconvenienced,[145] and it has been said that perhaps there would be no recovery if a private car owner was out of the country at the relevant time and already had a spare.[146]

However, a claimant Harbour Board was rightly awarded damages for loss of use of a lightship where it kept a spare in its dock for just such emergencies.[147] The Harbour Board clearly valued the availability of a spare, and in such circumstances

---

[140] *Admiralty Commissioners v Owners of SS Chekiang (The Chekiang)* [1926] AC 637 (HL) at 647–48.

[141] Ibid.

[142] Ibid at 649.

[143] *The Astrakhan* [1910] P 172 (Bargrave Deane J) at 181.

[144] Devlin LJ in *Lord Citrine (Owners) v Hebridean Coast (Owners) (The Hebridean Coast)* [1961] 1 AC 545 (CA) at 564 (affirmed by the HL, reported in the same report), following Bowen LJ in *The Argentino* (1888) 13 PD 191 (CA) at 201.

[145] *Alexander v Rolls Royce Motor Cars Ltd* [1996] RTR 95 (CA).

[146] *Bee v Jenson* [2007] 4 All ER 791 (CA) Longmore LJ at para 21.

[147] *SS Mediana (Owners) v Lightship Comet (Owners, Masters and Crew) (The Mediana)* [1900] AC 113 (HL).

the loss of use of the spare (rather than the damaged ship) was an (essentially non-pecuniary) harm to the Harbour Board, and the cost of maintaining the spare was awarded as a measure of its value.[148]

Similarly a public body was awarded substantial damages even though it had a spare pool of buses that could be used in place of the damaged item or had capacity within its rotating fleet to cover the temporary loss of a bus,[149] as was a company that had a pool of cars out of which it could replace the damaged company car used by one of its employees.[150] However, if the spare is available by fortune rather than the claimant's good planning, there may be less or no claimable loss.[151] Likewise if maintaining the spare is an unwanted burden required by legislation, the claimant does not suffer by taking the idle spare out of mothballs for temporary use as a replacement while the damaged vessel is out of action.[152]

(ii) Loss of Use of Repair Equipment

Similarly, in some cases the claimant may suffer a loss by reason of the loss of use of its undamaged property or equipment in docking or repairing the damaged property, and this loss of use is recoverable.[153]

---

[148] An alternative analysis for such cases might be that the existence of the spare was a collateral matter to be ignored, it being a form of self-insurance equivalent to insurance which is properly *res inter alios acta*: see below in chapter sixteen, section 16.7A(ii). In that case the loss would be awarded for the loss of use of the damaged item rather than, as is probably the case in *The Mediana* and similar cases, for loss of use of the spare as a spare.

[149] *Birmingham Corp v Sowsbery* [1970] RTR 84 (Geoffrey Lane J); *West Midlands Travel Ltd v Aviva Insurance UK Ltd* [2013] EWCA Civ 887 (CA). Contrast *Sealace Shipping Co Ltd v Oceanvoice Ltd (The Alecos M)* [1991] 1 Lloyd's Rep 120 (CA), a non-delivery case where it was held that there was no substantial loss from non-delivery to the buyer of a spare propeller.

[150] *Beechwood Birmingham Ltd v Hoyer Group UK Ltd* [2010] EWCA Civ 647. And see *West Midlands Travel Ltd v Aviva Insurance UK Ltd* [2013] EWCA Civ 887.

[151] See the profit case of *The SS City of Peking* (1890) 15 App Cas 438 (PC).

[152] Devlin LJ in *The Hebridean Coast* [1961] 1 AC 545 (HL) at 564.

[153] *The West Wales* [1932] P 165 (Bateson J) in relation to the use of the claimant's naval cranes and docks to repair a vessel tortiously damaged by the defendant, and *Borealis AB v Geogas Trading SA* [2011] 1 Lloyd's Rep 482 (Gross LJ) at paras 152–53 in relation to the use of claimant's equipment to repair damaged caused by the defendant in breach of contract.

7

Loss of Use of Money, Including Obligations to Pay

Damages for loss of use of money. This arises either where the defendant fails to pay the claimant, or where the defendant's breach causes the claimant to have increased costs or decreased revenue or receipts of any kind.

This chapter concerns damages for loss of use of money. These losses arise in two types of situation.

The first is where the defendant itself had a contractual obligation to pay money to the claimant. These obligations arise in many contexts. Key examples include (i) the obligation to pay the price of goods, services or hire, or an instalment of the price; (ii) the obligation to advance an agreed loan; (iii) the obligation to repay a contractual debt (eg a loan) or part of it; (iv) the obligation to pay interest on money owed; (v) the obligation to indemnify against expenses or a third party liability; (vi) the obligation (following a breach or non-performance) to pay liquidated damages as set down in an agreed damages clause. Such obligations are set down expressly or impliedly in the contract itself, and must be distinguished from legal obligations imposed by law to remedy a breach of contract, notably the court-ordered obligation to pay damages or on an action for a debt.

The second type of situation arises where although the defendant did not itself have an obligation to pay the claimant money, the defendant's breach of another obligation led to a delay in the claimant receiving money from a third party, or to the claimant not receiving the money at all. This is ubiquitous, and arises for example where the defendant seller or carrier delays the claimant's sale of its property, or where the defendant's breach causes the claimant to incur costs or pay extra for a replacement.

The actual loss of the money can be remedied by judgment at trial, leaving the claimant with the need for compensation for the temporary loss of use of the money up until that trial judgment.

7.1 The Cost of Borrowing Replacement Money

A. Cases of Breach of Promises to Pay Money

Since the House of Lords decision in *Sempra Metals Ltd v Inland Revenue Commissioners*,[1] damages for late payment of a debt (ie for the 'time value' of money) have been recoverable under ordinary damages principles.[2] (Although *Sempra* was a decision on restitution for unjust enrichment and statutory tort, there was full reconsideration of the contract authorities.[3]) Further, it is clear that loss is such an ordinary result of late payment that it will rarely be held to be too remote. As Lord Hope observed: 'The reality is that every creditor who is deprived of funds to which he is entitled and which he needs to run his business will have to incur an interest-bearing loan or employ other funds which could themselves have earned interest'.[4] Similarly, as was observed in the High Court of Australia case of *Hungerfords v Walker*, a case cited by many of the judges in *Sempra*:

> The requirement of foreseeability is no obstacle to the award of damages, calculated by reference to the appropriate interest rates, for loss of the use of money. Opportunity cost, more so than incurred expense, is a plainly foreseeable loss because, according to common understanding, it represents the market price of obtaining money. But, even in the case of incurred expense, it is at least strongly arguable that a plaintiff's loss or damage represented by this expense is not too remote on the score of foreseeability. In truth, it is an expense which represents loss or damage flowing naturally and directly from the defendant's wrongful act or omission, particularly when that act or omission results in the withholding of money from a plaintiff or causes the plaintiff to pay away money ...

> The cost of borrowing money to replace money paid away or withheld, in consequence of the defendant's breach of contract or negligence, is directly related to the wrong and is not too remote in the sense in which the common law regarded the loss attributable to late payment of damages as being too remote. We reach this conclusion more readily, knowing that legal and economic thinking about the remoteness of financial and economic loss have developed markedly in recent times. Likewise, opportunity cost should not be considered as being too remote when money is paid away or withheld.[5]

---

[1] *Sempra Metals Ltd v Inland Revenue Commissioners* [2008] 1 AC 561 (HL).

[2] Previously they had only been recoverable if they fell within the second, special communicated circumstances, limb of the *Hadley v Baxendale* remoteness rule: see *President of India v La Pintada Compania Navigacion SA* [1985] AC 104 (HL).

[3] Lord Hope at para 16, Lord Nicholls at paras 89 and 93 ff, Lord Scott at para 132, Lord Walker at para 165, Lord Mance at para 216.

[4] Ibid para 16.

[5] *Hungerfords v Walker* (1989) 171 CLR 125 (HC of Australia) Mason CJ and Wilson J at paras 26 and 30.

In *Hungerfords*, damages for the cost of borrowing replacement money were awarded against accountants whose breach led to premature payment by the claimant of its tax liabilities.

This loss by borrowing alternative funds is essentially the cost of obtaining an alternative supply, equivalent to the mitigation of loss performed by a buyer resorting to the market when the seller of goods fails to deliver. Such loss will often consist of the compound interest the claimant had to pay, as that is the usual way that both credit and debit interest are calculated.[6] This is significant, because compound interest is not available under the statutory right to interest.[7]

To claim such a loss as damages, the loss must be pleaded and proven in the usual way and the law will not simply 'assume that delay in payment of a debt will of itself cause damage'.[8] This is so even though on one view it may be unrealistic not to make that assumption,[9] although on another view it will depend upon the nature of the contract and compound interest will be too remote a loss in many everyday contracts.[10] A claimant who does not properly plead and prove such losses is left with the statutory award of interest instead.[11]

A particularly likely candidate for a successful claim for debit interest paid on an alternative loan is the claim for a breach by the defendant lender of a promise to advance a loan.[12] In such a case the need to borrow to obtain the money is unlikely to be too remote for obvious reasons. Such awards have also been made in cases of failure to return a purchaser's ship deposit that had been borrowed from a bank and should have been returned by the defendant.[13]

Another frequent situation in which a claim for loss of use of money arises is a promise to pay under a letter of credit. Where alternative funds are available, the claimant can recover the commission or other cost of obtaining the alternative funds and any other consequential costs (such as notarial and telegraphic expenses).[14]

In *Wadsworth v Lydall*, damages were awarded for borrowing costs where the defendant failed to pay the claimant the price to buy out the claimant's share of their co-owned farm, paying some of the price late and some of the price remaining unpaid at the date of trial. The claimant had bought another farm in anticipation of receipt of the money and had to take out a bridging loan when the defendant

---

[6] Lord Nicholls in *Sempra* at para 52. See also *Bank of America Canada v Mutual Trust Co* [2002] 2 SCR 601 (SC of Canada) Major J at para 24.

[7] See below in section 7.7A.

[8] Lord Nicholls in *Sempra* at para 96, also Lord Hope at para 17 and Lord Nicholls at paras 94–95.

[9] Lord Nicholls in *Sempra* at para 97.

[10] Lord Mance in *Sempra* at para 216. And see *JSC BTA Bank v Ablyazov* [2013] EWHC 867 (Comm) (Teare J) (fraud).

[11] Ibid. But see *Equitas Ltd v Walsham Bros & Co Ltd* [2013] EWHC 3264 (Comm) (Males J) and the discussion below in section 7.2C.

[12] *Astor Properties Ltd v Tunbridge Wells Equitable Friendly Society* [1936] 1 All ER 531 (Hawke J); *Bahamas (Inagua) Sisal Plantation Ltd v Griffin* (1897) 14 TLR 139 (Bigham J) obiter. Loss was not proven in *South African Territories v Wallington* [1898] AC 309 (HL). See also the comments of Lord Mance in *Sempra Metals Ltd v Inland Revenue Commissioners* [2008] 1 AC 561 (HL) at para 216.

[13] *Fast Ferries One SA v Ferries Australia Pty Ltd* [2000] 1 Lloyd's Rep 534 (Steel J) at para 38. Compare the difficulties of remoteness discussed in *Malvenna v Royal Bank of Scotland plc* [2003] EWCA Civ 1112 (CA) Waller LJ at paras 23–26 in relation to a failure to refund money to the claimant.

[14] *Prehn v Royal Bank of Liverpool* (1870) LR 5 Ex 92.

was late in paying.[15] The defendant knew the claimant's position and the loss was therefore not too remote.

The amount of the damages will, in the absence of a pleading of particular losses, usually be assumed to be the unsecured short-term rate that someone with the claimant's credit-worthiness would pay to borrow the relevant sum.[16]

B. Other Cases

The need to borrow alternative funds can arise in other cases where the defendant has caused the claimant to be without money, even where this is not by the defendant's failure to pay that money to the claimant.

(i) Lenders Induced by the Defendant to Lend

The typical examples of such losses and awards are cases of lenders induced by the negligence of surveyors or solicitors to enter into contracts of loan.[17] Sometimes the lender will prove and recover the particular costs of borrowing it incurred by specific loans or by its general wholesale or retail borrowing.[18] More usually, the court will not be interested in the particular borrowing arrangements of the bank (typically a 'basket of funds' partly on the wholesale markets and partly from different types of capital,[19] such borrowing depending upon the bank's particular capital adequacy requirements, policies, credit rating etc), such factors being *res inter alios acta*. The court will instead apply a general reasonable rate of borrowing at inter-bank rates.[20]

It has not yet been determined by the courts whether a bank can recover and/or must give credit against a negligent professional for the costs or profits of hedging arrangements it entered into alongside a loan, most typically fixed for floating swaps or equivalent arrangements entered into alongside fixed-rate loans induced by the

---

[15] *Wadsworth v Lydall* [1981] 1 WLR 598 (CA). See also *McCandless Aircraft LC v Payne* [2010] EWHC 1835 (QB) (Tugenhat J) where the seller recovered the costs of the borrowing incurred to purchase for sale to the defendant when the repayment of the borrowing was delayed, by the defendant's non-acceptance, until a replacement buyer was found.

[16] *VIS Trading Co Ltd v Nazarov* [2013] EWHC 491 (QB) (Leggatt J).

[17] Awards of lost profits the bank would have made from the money if not lent, as opposed to the cost of borrowing the money lent, are discussed below in section 7.2C(i).

[18] In *Legal & General Mortgage Services Ltd v HPC Professional Services* [1997] PNLR 567 (Langan QC) the lender was induced to enter into a loan and had itself taken out a specific loan for the money it then advanced, and the interest payable on that loan was found (obiter) to be recoverable against the defendant who induced the sub-loan. See also *ACC Bank plc v Johnston* [2011] IEHC 376 (Irish High Court) at paras 3.7–3.8, where it was necessary to ask whether a bank's rate of borrowing from its parent was reasonable. (It was.)

[19] *Lloyd's Bank plc v Parker Bullen*, 16 July 1999 (Longmore J).

[20] See *Nyckeln Finance Co Ltd v Stumpbrook Continuation Ltd* [1994] 2 EGLR 143 (Fawcus J) and *Lloyd's Bank plc v Parker Bullen*, 16 July 1999 (Longmore J). Insufficient evidence for a claim of interest as damages was advanced in *Birmingham Midshires Mortgage Services Ltd v Phillips* [1998] PNLR 468 (HHJ Bromley QC). See also the construction case of *Hutchinson v Harris* (1978) 10 BLR 19 (CA), although the interest claim was refused as not sufficiently pleaded or proven and too remote.

defendant.[21] This should be recoverable if it is an automatic and foreseeable (by the defendant) part of the bank lending at a fixed rate (like in oil trades[22]), in which case the arrangement is a foreseeable cost of borrowing arising merely from the fact that it was not practical for the bank to fund its fixed-rate loan by itself borrowing at a fixed rate. But such costs will not be recoverable if they are a particular arrangement entered into as a result of the bank's particular appetite for risk or regulatory requirements, in which case the arrangement is *res inter alios acta* like insurance.[23]

(ii) Other Cases

Other such claims arise in cases of developers or other business entities which have financed a transaction where the defendant professional's negligence delays the repayment of the finance.[24] The possibility has also been considered in a deceit case (although it had not been argued in the relevant case) that costs of borrowing may be recoverable as a cost in mitigation of loss where a claimant needed to replenish a trading fund depleted by the defendant.[25]

Unreasonably high costs of borrowing, where caused by unforeseeable impecuniosity or the bad credit rating of the claimant, will not be recoverable.[26]

7.2 Lost Profits from Use of the Money

A. General Lost Profits

In some cases, the claimant reasonably did not borrow replacement money and is entitled, subject to remoteness, to claim the lost profits that would have been made from investing the money that the defendant should have paid the claimant,[27] even if that investment would only have been on deposit in a bank.[28]

---

[21] The point was held to be arguable by the Court of Appeal in *Mortgage Agency Services Number One Ltd v Edward Symmons LLP* (22.10.13, CA), overturning the first instance court's strike out of the claim by the lender against the negligent valuer for hedging costs. Cf *Kleinwort Benson Ltd v South Tyneside Metropolitan Borough Council* [1994] 4 All ER 972 (Hobhouse J) at 985 and *Kleinwort Benson Ltd v Birmingham City Council* [1997] QB 380 (CA) at 393, which were both claims for restitution for unjust enrichment, not compensation for loss, but which nevertheless discussed the remoteness aspect that would arise in loss claims by a lender who hedged. As regards claims by the lender against the borrower itself, fixed-rate loans will often circumvent the remoteness or causation problems by including an express clause requiring the borrower to indemnify the lender for breakage costs if the borrower repays early or defaults (cf *Bank of Scotland v Dunedin Property Investment Co Ltd* 1998 SCLR 531 (Scots Inner House)).

[22] See below in section 16.10F.

[23] See below in section 16.10B.

[24] *Hartle v Laceys* [1999] Lloyd's PN 315 (CA); *Earl Terrace Properties Ltd v Nilsson Design Ltd* [2004] EWHC 136 (TCC); *Kirkton Investments Ltd v VMH LLP* [2011] CSOH 200 (Scots Outer House).

[25] *Parabola Investments Ltd v Browallia Cal Ltd* [2011] 1 QB 477 (CA) Toulson LJ at para 58.

[26] See *Compania Financiera Soleada SA v Hamoor Tanker Corp Inc (The Borag)* [1981] 1 WLR 274 (CA).

[27] *Sempra Metals Ltd v Inland Revenue Commissioners* [2008] 1 AC 561 (HL) Lord Nicholls at para 95. See also *Equitas Ltd v Walsham Bros & Co Ltd* [2013] EWHC 3264 (Comm) (Males J) at para 123(iii).

[28] Ibid Lord Scott at para 140.

Thus where a solicitor's negligence on a property acquisition led to an encumbrance which delayed the re-sale of the property, the claimant recovered interest on the profits the receipt of which was delayed.[29] Likewise where a claimant was induced to buy a doomed nursing home property it could claim for the money that would have been made on an alternative nursing home.[30]

In another case, the profits that would have been made if the defendant brokers had arranged responding insurance and there had been an insurance pay-out which could have been invested in the claimant's business were recoverable.[31]

In one case the profit a bank would have made from converting US dollars to euros and putting them on deposit was held by the High Court of Australia not to be too remote.[32] However, as one of the judges in the court below observed in that case, there are particular problems of remoteness with profits that would have been made on money because there are so many things that can be done with it (unlike goods of a certain type, say):

> The fungible nature of money further complicates the issue. It is freely negotiable and has no unique characteristic. It can be 'invested' in innumerable ways. Except in the case of bank notes, money will usually be represented by a credit with a bank or financial institution. Money is not traced except in particular trust situations. Money can be lent at interest and the interest will vary depending upon the terms of the loan, the identity of the borrower and the state of the market. Money will always represent a currency. The value of a currency constantly fluctuates as against other currencies. Currency trading is, as of necessity, a speculative activity.[33]

B. Profits from a Specific Transaction

The most common contractual situation in which claims arise for specific profits that would have been made with money is that of professional negligence inducing an unwanted transaction where, but for the negligence, the claimant would not have entered into the transaction at all. In such cases, and in similar tortious cases for negligent misstatement or deceit, the claimant is entitled to an award of any lost profits that it can prove would have been made on an alternative transaction had the money not been tied up in the unwanted transaction. Remoteness problems are minimal (even in contractual and other non-deceit cases; in deceit cases there is no remoteness requirement) where the alternative transaction is similar to the transaction the defendant induced the claimant to enter into. Such claims are discussed above in section 3.4.

---

[29] *G + K Ladenbau (UK) Ltd v Crawley & de Reya* [1978] 1 WLR 266 (Mocatta J); *McElroy Milne v Commercial Electronics Ltd* [1993] 1 NZLR 39 (NZCA), cited with approval by Lord Hoffmann in *South Australia Asset Management Corp (SAAMCo) v York Montague Ltd* [1997] 1 AC 191 (HL) at 219 and 222; *Gregory v Shepherds* (CA), 16 June 2000; *John Grimes Partnership Ltd v Gubbins* [2013] EWCA Civ 37.

[30] Eg *Havenledge Ltd v Graeme John & Partners* [2001] PNLR 17 (CA), obiter because time-barred.

[31] *Arbory Group Ltd v West Craven Insurance Services* [2007] PNLR 23 (Grenfell J).

[32] *Evans v European Bank Ltd v Evans* (2010) 240 CLR 432 (HC of Australia) (damages for breach of an undertaking), allowing the appeal.

[33] *Evans v European Bank Ltd* [2009] NSWCA 67 (NSW CA) Gyles AJA at 125.

C. Rough Quantification by the Cost of Borrowing

The law permits a certain amount of approximation when proving lost returns on money, both in relation to the statutory award of interest (discussed below) and the award of damages for loss of use of money.[34] The law routinely presumes that a claimant would not employ money without making a reasonable return (which means recovering at least for its depreciation, ie for deflation, but also recovering some profit) because money can easily be employed to make profit at low risk in a bank. Thus, as Thornton QC explained in the case of delayed completion of a housing development refurbishment, *Earl's Terrace Properties Ltd v Nilsson Design Ltd*:[35]

> If the claimant can establish that he has lost the opportunity to use the funds for a commercial purpose but he cannot establish the precise loss that arose or cannot readily quantify it, the claimant may then quantify the loss by reference to a reasonable rate of return that could have been achieved from the funds. It will, of course, have to be established what that rate might be. Obvious guidance would be obtained by ascertaining what rate of interest could have been obtained by depositing the funds so as to earn a commercial rate of interest or by lending the money on relatively short term terms. Such an assessment is permitted because the law allows an approximation of the loss to be made where a claimant can prove that he had been prevented from using funds for a commercial purpose as a result of the defendant's breach but where he cannot reasonably or readily identify the nature or extent of that loss.[36]

Although the suggestion in *Sempra Metals*[37] was that the claimant would have to plead and prove the particular lost of income resulting from loss of use of money, subsequent decisions permit an award of compound interest at a 'conventional' (ie not actually proven) rate. In particular, Males J in the *Equitas Ltd v Walsham Bros & Co Ltd* case confirmed such an approach:[38]

> unless there is some positive reason to do otherwise, the law will proceed on the basis, at any rate in the commercial context, that a claimant kept out of its money has suffered loss as a result. That represents commercial reality and everyday experience. Specific evidence to that effect is not required and, even if adduced, may well be somewhat hypothetical and thus of little assistance. For example, a business man may well be unable to say precisely what he would have done differently if a particular payment had been made to him when it ought to have been, especially if (as apparently in this case) he was unaware that the money was being withheld. Extensive disclosure, which would no doubt be demanded by the defendant, is unlikely to assist. But that does not mean that no loss has been suffered.

Males J went on to observe that usually the cost of available borrowing would cap the lost profits (since it would be unreasonable to suffer lost profits of greater than

---

[34] The same is true in cases of temporary loss of use of property. See above in chapter six.

[35] *Earl's Terrace Properties Ltd v Nilsson Design Ltd* [2004] EWHC 136 (TCC) (Thornton QC) at para 90.

[36] But see *Brandeis Goldschmidt v Western Transport Ltd* [1981] 1 QB 64 (CA), where the court refused an award where the claimant could not show when it would have released the money from its business and what it would have done with it.

[37] *Sempra Metals Ltd v Inland Revenue Commissioners* [2008] 1 AC 561 (HL). See above in section 7.1A.

[38] *Equitas Ltd v Walsham Bros & Co Ltd* [2013] EWHC 3264 (Comm) (Males J) at para 123.

that cost rather than incur the cost to mitigate such losses), and moreover that the court would presume in the ordinary case that the lost profits were equal to the cost of borrowing, whether or not the claimant did in fact borrow.[39]

(i) Profits Lenders Would have Made if they Hadn't Lent to the Specific Borrower

The issue also frequently arises in cases of lenders induced by the negligence of surveyors or solicitors to enter into contracts of loan. The courts will usually order a reasonable rate of return or else the cost of borrowing.[40] In most cases the latter will be more appropriate, unless it can be shown that the lender had limited resources and so the particular loan prevented it from lending to another good opportunity (ie that there was an 'unsatisfied demand for loans').[41]

7.3 Devaluation and Exchange Rate Losses

Where it is not too remote that a payee would have converted money into another currency after receiving or not spending it, the claimant can recover damages for loss due to devaluation (during the period of delay) of the currency the payment would have been made in against the currency it would have then been converted into.[42] As it was put in one case: 'the Belgian francs they obtain judgment for are worth less in U.S. dollar terms than the Belgian francs which they ought to have been paid on Dec. 23 1981'.[43] As to when such losses will not be too remote:

> [I]n international business, the day-to-day fluctuations of the value of currencies against each other are within the routine contemplation of international businessmen and international commerce is structured so as to take them into account. Cases where the rules of remoteness would be satisfied were previously very rare; now it must be recognized that they will be relatively common. But it will be a question of fact in every case.[44]

---

[39] Ibid.

[40] *Corisand Investments Ltd v Druce & Co* [1978] EGLR 86 (Gibson J); *Swingcastle Ltd v Alastair Gibson* [1991] 2 AC 223 (HL); *HIT Finance Ltd v Lewis & Tucker Ltd* [1993] 2 EGLR 231 (Wright J); *Arab Bank plc v John D Wood Commercial Ltd* (CA), 11 November 1999; *ACC Bank plc v Johnston* [2011] IEHC 376 (Irish High Court) at paras 3.7–3.8.

[41] *Swingcastle Ltd v Gibson* [1990] 1 WLR 1223 (CA) Neill LJ at 1231 (appeal allowed at [1991] 2 AC 223 (HL)); *ACC Bank plc v Johnston* [2011] IEHC 376 (Irish High Court) at paras 3.7–3.8.

[42] *Ozalid (Group) Export Ltd v African Continental Bank Ltd* [1979] 2 Lloyd's Rep 231 (Donaldson J), a case of non-payment under a letter of credit. See also *Isaac Naylor & Sons Ltd v New Zealand Co-operative Wool Marketing Association Ltd* [1981] 1 NZLR 361 (NZ CA), a case of late payment under a contract for sale of wool; *Volk v Hirstlens (NZ) Ltd* [1987] 1 NZLR 385 (NZ HC), a case of short payment of royalties; and *Travelers Casualty and Surety Co of Canada v Sun Life Assurance Co of Canada (UK) Ltd* [2006] EWHC 2716 (Comm) (Clarke J), a case of late payment under an indemnity policy, discussed at chapter nine n 75. Cf *Evans & Associates v Citibank Ltd* [2007] NSWSC 1004 (NSW SC), a case of refusal by a receiver to convert funds held pursuant to an undertaking.

[43] *International Minerals and Chemical Corp v Karl O Helm AG* [1986] 1 Lloyd's Rep 81 (Hobhouse J) at 101, a case of non-payment of the purchase price.

[44] *International Minerals and Chemical Corp v Karl O Helm AG* [1986] 1 Lloyd's Rep 81 (Hobhouse J) at 105. The exchange rate loss was too remote in *Mehmet Dogan Bey v GG Abdeni & Co Ltd* [1951] 2 KB 405 (McNair J).

7.4 Causing Insolvency

In one case a company claimed that the defendant's failure to pay £150,000 under invoices led to insolvency and the company sought the costs of the creditors' voluntary agreement entered into. Although the defendant had known the claimant was in financial trouble, that did not mean that insolvency was sufficiently foreseeable or within the defendant's assumption of responsibility, still less were the costs of the CVA process (which were more than the costs of winding the company up) recoverable, and further the CVA was induced by the creditors being misled, which broke the chain of causation.[45] In another case where the defendant landlord's breach impaired the claimant's profitability, damages for the loss of a 30 per cent chance of avoiding insolvency were recoverable.[46] In an Arkansas case, a bank's withdrawal of its invoice financing service caused the plaintiff's car sales business to go under, and it recovered substantial damages for the same.[47]

7.5 Other Losses

A payee will sometimes be unable to pay a third party where the payor has breached its obligation to pay. In a string contract, a seller may well depend upon the buyer's payment to itself to make payment to his own supplier.[48] The question of recovery will come down to whether or not the liability to the supplier or other third party was too remote.

Similarly, non-payment may lead to the loss of a sub-contract, or increased costs in relation thereto. This is particularly likely in cases of non-payment under a letter of credit, which can lead to a hold up of the buyer accepting the goods,[49] or cases of non-advance of an agreed loan for a specific purpose, as the purpose will therefore not be too remote.[50] Usually there will be no substantial loss on refusal to advance an agreed loan because 'if a man cannot get money in one quarter he can in another'.[51]

And where a claimant does not receive money that would cover a replacement vehicle (for example) it may have to hire replacement property until it gets the main sum. This can arise where an insurance broker is responsible for the claimant's vehicle not being covered by an insurance policy.[52]

---

[45] *Paros plc v Worldlink Group plc* [2012] EWHC 394 (Comm) (Hirst QC) at paras 87–89. In relation to remoteness and impecuniosity in general, see section 16.7 below.

[46] *Stewart v Scottish Widows & Life Assurance Society plc* [2005] EWHC 1831 (QB) (Eccles QC), appeal allowed in part on a different point [2006] EWCA Civ 999 (CA). See also *Saigol v Cranley Mansion Ltd* (2000) 72 Con LR 54 (CA).

[47] *Bank of America NA v Smith Motor Co* (2003) 106 SW 3d 425 (SC of Arkansas).

[48] *Trans Trust SPRL v Danubian Trading Co Ltd* [1952] 2 QB 297 (CA) (too remote).

[49] See *Fortis Bank SA/NV v Indian Overseas Bank* [2011] EWHC 538 (Comm) (Hirst QC), although the additional storage and other costs were not awarded on grounds of lack of factual and legal causation.

[50] *The Manchester and Oldham Bank Ltd v WA Cook & Co* (1884) 49 LT 674 Day J at 678: refusal to advance promised loan to purchase a colliery company.

[51] Ibid Day J at 678.

[52] *Ramwade Ltd v WJ Emson & Co Ltd* [1987] RTR 72 (CA), although recovery for the hire charges was barred by the then prevailing rule against losses arising from claimant impecuniosity (which rule has since been reversed: see below in section 16.7).

Where the money would have been used for non-pecuniary purposes (eg leisure, food etc), in principle such losses may be recoverable, although they will usually be regarded as too remote from the deprivation of the money.[53]

7.6 Specific Points Relating to Breach of Obligations to Pay Money

A. Getting the Money

The primary remedy for non-payment of money is an action for the sum of money itself, whether by an action for a debt[54] or by an action for damages.[55] Obligations to pay money are therefore unique in never requiring a permanent cure by obtaining an alternative; the judgment itself (of a sum of money) will always provide what was promised, and it is not possible to obtain that from a third party as a cure because to buy money costs the same amount of money. Accordingly, all claims for non-payment of money are essentially cases of *delayed* payment of money (the delay being until judgment), and the damages recovered are for losses resulting from that delay and/or the temporary cost of cure by borrowing money.

B. Mitigation

In one case of a sponsor repudiating a contract of sponsorship, the claimant had to give credit for the sponsorship money it obtained from another source that would not have been received if the original sponsorship had been received (because the original sponsor would have vetoed it).[56]

C. Loss for Non-Payment to a Third Party

Where the obligation was to pay money not to the claimant but to a third party, difficult issues arise as to whether the claimant can recover damages. The answer depends upon whether the claimant has covered, must cover or intends to cover the

---

[53] See text to chapter nineteen n 111 below.

[54] The action for debt, also known as the action for an agreed sum, is a form of specific relief, like specific performance but only for monetary obligations, and is outside the scope of this work.

[55] Usually the action is one for debt, but at least one judge has observed that on the date after payment has become due, the claim should be put in terms of an action for damages for non-payment of money rather than an action for an agreed sum, although 'in ninety-nine cases out of a hundred the amount of damages will be the sum which there has been an undertaking to pay': *Dexters Ltd v Schenker & Co* (1923) 14 Ll L Rep 586 (Greer J) at 588. Plus see the allowance of a damages claim for non-payment of a deposit, in the amount of the deposit, in *Damon Compania Naviera SA v Hapag-Lloyd International SA* [1985] 1 WLR 435 (CA) and *Griffon Shipping LLC v Firodi Shipping Ltd* [2013] 2 Lloyd's Rep 50 (Teare J) at para 28.

[56] *Force India Formula One Team Ltd v Etihad Airways PJSC* [2009] EWHC 2768 (QB) (Sir Charles Gray) at paras 90 and 105.

missing payment itself, and on the developing law as to whether substantial loss can otherwise be said to have been suffered by the claimant.[57]

D. Mental Distress

Damages for distress or other non-pecuniary loss are available for late payment of a sum, like any other breach, where not too remote.[58] In Canada such a principle has been applied to make awards of distress damages against insurers who were late in paying out under insurance policies,[59] although the same result cannot apply to indemnity insurance in England so long as an indemnity is treated by English law as the payment of damages for failure to hold harmless against the primary event.[60]

E. Damage to Reputation

Damages for damage to reputation are often available in cases of wrongful dishonour of cheques.[61] However, this loss arises from the failure to pay, not from the loss of use of money that results from the failure to pay.

F. No Damages for Failure to Pay Damages

The law will not award damages for failure to pay damages prior to judgment,[62] although interest for late payment of damages is payable under the statutory provisions[63] and, of course, interest is automatically payable after judgment on the judgment sum at the judgment rate.[64]

This is particularly important in contracts which it might sensibly be thought consisted of obligations to pay money but where the law provides that in fact they are contracts to prevent a state of affairs and therefore the obligation to pay money is actually a damages obligation (liquidated or otherwise) arising upon breach of the primary obligation. Consequently, no damages are payable for delay in paying the sums due under these contracts. Key examples are the contract of indemnity, the obligation to pay demurrage and the obligation to pay under a bill of exchange, and are discussed below in chapter nine, section 9.5B.

---

[57] Substantial damages were unavailable in *Beswick v Beswick* [1968] AC 58 (HL) (and so specific performance was awarded), and the point was further discussed in *Woodar Investment Development Ltd v Wimpey Construction Co Ltd* [1980] 1 WLR 277 (HL) where part of a purchase price was payable directly to a third party. See further below in chapter twenty-one.

[58] See the discussion in section 7.5.

[59] See below in chapter nineteen, section 19.1B(iii).

[60] See below in chapter nine, section 9.5B(i).

[61] See below in chapter eighteen, section 18.2C(iv)(a).

[62] *President of India v Lips Maritime Corp* [1988] 1 AC 395 (HL).

[63] Section 35A of the Senior Courts Act 1981 (see n 64 below) and section 69 of the County Courts Act 1984 both expressly allow awards of interest on either debts or damages.

[64] 8% since the Judgment Debts (Rate of Interest) Order 1993 (SI 1993/564).

7.7 Awards of Interest Outside the Claim for Damages

There are a number of statutory awards of interest available for late payment of a debt and for late payment of damages that do not require satisfaction of the ordinary rules of proof of loss, causation and remoteness,[65] likewise awards of interest pursuant to rights in the contract itself. These are not awards of damages, but since they often fulfil a similar role it is convenient to deal with them briefly in this book.

A. Statutory Awards of Interest

In the majority of such cases, interest is awarded pursuant to discretionary statutory powers to award interest under section 35A of the Senior Courts Act 1981[66] (in High Court actions), section 69 of the County Courts Act 1984 (in county court actions), and section 49 of the Arbitration Act 1996 (in arbitrations). Save where special rules apply,[67] these statutory powers apply to and are employed in contract claims.

All these powers provide the court with a discretion to award interest, although the claim for interest must be specifically pleaded.[68] The 1981 Act and 1984 Acts empowering interest awards in litigation expressly permit only simple interest (hence the importance of the right to award compound interest at common law as damages)[69], whereas the Arbitration Act expressly permits compound interest.[70] The power to award interest survives even if the sum due in damages has been paid before the date of judgment.[71]

The discretion is a broad one as to the rate of interest, the part (or whole) of the debt or damages on which interest may be awarded, and the period during which the interest is measured.[72] It is usually driven by the same compensatory aim as damages, and exercised with that in mind:

> The purpose of an award of interest is to achieve *restitutio in integrum*. The enquiry does
> not focus, in a case such as the present, on the profit to the defendant of the use of the

---

[65] As explained in *Sempra Metals Ltd v Inland Revenue Commissioners* [2008] 1 AC 561 (HL) Lord Scott at para 152.

[66] Formerly known as the Supreme Court Act 1981.

[67] Section 57 of the Bills of Exchange Act 1882 in relation to claims upon dishonour of bills of exchange.

[68] CPR r 16.4(2).

[69] Compound interest may therefore now be awarded as damages. The equitable power to award interest on damages, however, cannot assist in a contract claim as it only applies to limited equitable claims: *Westdeutsche Landesbank Girozentrale v Islington London Borough Council* [1996] AC 699 (HL).

[70] Section 49(3) of the Arbitration Act 1996.

[71] Section 35A(1) and (3) of the Senior Courts Act 1981, section 69(1) and (3) of the County Courts Act 1984, section 49(3)(b) of the Arbitration Act 1996. See also *Edmunds v Lloyds Italico & l'Ancora Compagnia di Assicurazione e Riassicurazione SpA* [1986] 1 WLR 492 (CA) Donaldson MR at 495–96; *Fast Ferries One SA v Ferries Australia Pty Ltd* [2000] 1 Lloyd's Rep 534 (Steel J) obiter at para 41.

[72] Although where a debt is concerned, a rate of interest set down in the contract will displace the statutory right to interest: see section 35A(4) of the Senior Courts Act 1981 and section 69(4) of the County Courts Act 1984.

money. It is directed to an estimation of the cost to the plaintiff of being deprived of the money which he should have had.[73]

Where the award is compensation for a financial loss (including either an expense or foregone receipt), or non-payment of a debt, it will compensate for the loss of use of the sum of money during the relevant period when the claimant was without that sum.[74] Where the award is compensation for a non-financial loss the award will similarly compensate for the loss of use of the damages to which the claimant became entitled at the time the loss was suffered until the time of judgment. However, where damages compensate for the loss of property and other damages compensate for the subsequent loss of use of that property (such as by lost profits) the court will not award statutory interest on the sum compensating for loss of the property during the period of loss of use, so as not to give double recovery.

The rate of interest is at the court's discretion. In commercial cases it has become normal practice to award a standard commercial rate. This will normally be one per cent above base rate or minimum lending rate[75] or its equivalent US prime rate,[76] but may also, where appropriate, be one per cent above LIBOR, or one per cent above Eurobor,[77] or any other rate (eg individuals in one case were awarded as high as base rate plus five per cent[78]). The aim is to apply a 'rate which broadly represents the rate at which [the claimants] would have had to borrow the amount recovered over the period for which interest is awarded'.[79]

The way this is applied was explained in more detail in an oft-quoted and applied[80] approach of Forbes J in *Tate & Lyle Food and Distribution Ltd v Greater London Council*:[81]

> I feel satisfied that in commercial cases the interest is intended to reflect the rate at which the plaintiff would have had to borrow money to supply the place of that which was withheld. I am also satisfied that one should not look at any special position in which the plaintiff may have been; one should disregard, for instance, the fact that a particular plaintiff, because of his personal situation, could only borrow money at a very high rate or, on the other hand, was able to borrow at specially favourable rates. The correct thing to do is to take the rate at which plaintiffs in general could borrow money. This does not, however, to my mind, mean that you exclude entirely all attributes of the plaintiff other than that he

---

[73] Steyn J in *Banque Keyser Ullman SA v Skandia (UK) Insurance Co Ltd*, 11 December 1987.

[74] Eg *AB Kemp Ltd v Tolland (t/a James Tolland & Co)* [1956] 2 Lloyd's Rep 681 (Devlin J) at 691.

[75] *FMC (Meat) Ltd v Fairfield Cold Stores Ltd* [1971] 2 Lloyd's Rep 221 (Donaldson J); *Cremer v General Carriers SA* [1974] 1 WLR 175 (Kerr J); *Shearson Lehmann Hutton v Maclaine Watson & Co (No 2)* [1990] 3 All ER 723 (Webster J); *Miskin v St John Vaughan* (CA), 19 November 1999.

[76] *Baker v Black Sea and Baltic General Insurance Co Ltd (No 2)* [1996] LRLR 353 (CA) (affirmed [1998] 1 WLR 974 (HL) on a different point); *Kuwait Airways Corp v Kuwait Insurance Co* [2000] Lloyd's Rep IR 678 (Langley J)

[77] *Benedetti v Naguib Onsi Naguib Sawiris* [2009] EWHC 1806 (Ch) (Patten LJ) at para 11, affirmed [2010] EWCA Civ 1427.

[78] *Attrill v Dresdner Kleinwort Ltd* [2012] EWHC 1468 (QB) (Owen J).

[79] *Cremer v General Carriers SA* [1974] 1 WLR 175 (Kerr J) at 182.

[80] Eg *Baker v Black Sea and Baltic General Insurance Co Ltd (No 2)* [1996] LRLR 353 (CA) (affirmed [1998] 1 WLR 974 (HL) on a different point); *Miskin v St John Vaughan* (CA), 19 November 1999; *Jaura v Ahmed* [2002] EWCA Civ 210 (CA).

[81] *Tate & Lyle Food and Distribution Ltd v Greater London Council* [1982] 1 WLR 149 (Forbes J) at 154. (Overturned [1982] 1 WLR 971 (CA) then reinstated [1983] 2 AC 509 (HL), both unrelated to the interest point.)

is a plaintiff. There is evidence here that large public companies of the size and prestige of these plaintiffs could expect to borrow at 1% over MLR [*minimum lending rate*], while for smaller and less prestigious concerns the rate might be as high as 3% over MLR. I think it would always be right to look at the rate at which plaintiffs with the general attributes of the actual plaintiff in the case (though not, of course, with any special or peculiar attribute) could borrow money as a guide to the appropriate interest rate.

Thus the parties may displace such a rate by demonstrating that an entity with the claimant's general attributes (eg global bank, prime bank,[82] small bank, Kazakh bank,[83] small business[84] or newco,[85] or individual[86]), ie following 'categorisation of the plaintiff in an objective sense',[87] could at the relevant time borrow on the markets at a particular rate. Specific features of the claimant (eg in relation to 'particular creditworthiness or his inability to "shop around"'[88]) will be disregarded in order to save time and money at trial, and so there is no need to seek to measure the 'actual loss'[89] or to investigate the actual characteristics of the claimant's borrowing.[90]

It is not uncommon for the rate of statutory interest to be argued, with evidence, after judgment has been handed down, when contesting the consequential matters that arise upon judgment.[91]

However, because the power is discretionary, the court may also take into account other issues that are irrelevant to compensation; most notably it may disallow interest for a period to penalise a claimant who without proper justification has failed to formulate or pursue its claim or otherwise delayed the recovery,[92] or reduce the interest rate awarded for a similar reason.[93]

B. Contractual Rights to Interest

(i) Generally

Although not damages in any sense, mention should be made of contractual rights to interest. Many contracts provide expressly or impliedly for a right to interest for late payment of a debt. Breach of such an obligation is a non-payment of a debt, enforceable either by the remedy of an action for a debt or by claiming damages equal to

---

[82] *Banque Keyser Ullman SA v Skandia (UK) Insurance Co Ltd*, 11 December 1987 (Steyn J).

[83] *JSC BTA Bank v Ablyazov* [2013] EWHC 867 (Comm) (Teare J) (fraud) at para 20.

[84] *Jackson v Royal Bank of Scotland* (CA), 26 June 2000; *Jaura v Ahmed* [2002] EWCA Civ 210 (CA).

[85] *Sycamore Bidco Ltd v Breslin* [2013] EWHC 174 (Ch) (Mann J).

[86] *Lindsay v O'Loughnane* [2010] EWHC 529 (QB) (Flaux J); *Attrill v Dresdner Kleinwort Ltd* [2012] EWHC 1468 (QB) (Owen J); *Challinor v Juliet Bellis & Co* [2013] EWHC 620 (Ch) (Hildyard J).

[87] *Banque Keyser Ullman SA v Skandia (UK) Insurance Co Ltd*, 11 December 1987 (Steyn J).

[88] *Jackson v Royal Bank Scotland* (CA), 28 June 2000 Potter LJ at para 41 (overturned on a different point [2005] 1 WLR 377 (HL), no appeal against the interest finding).

[89] Steyn J in *Banque Keyser Ullman SA v Skandia (UK) Insurance Co Ltd*, 11 December 1987.

[90] *Jackson v Royal Bank of Scotland* (CA) 28 June 2000.

[91] Eg *Challinor v Juliet Bellis & Co* [2013] EWHC 620 (Ch) (Hildyard J).

[92] *Fast Ferries One SA v Ferries Australia Pty Ltd* [2000] 1 Lloyd's Rep 534 (Steel J) obiter at para 39; *Socimer International Bank Ltd v Standard Bank London Ltd* [2006] EWHC 2896 (Comm) (Gloster J); *Tonkin v UK Insurance Ltd* (2006) 107 Con LR 107 (Coulson QC) at para 415.

[93] *Derby Resources AG v Blue Corinth Marine Co Ltd (No 2) (The Athenian Harmony)* [1998] 2 Lloyd's Rep 429 (Colman J).

the amount of the debt. Issues of damages and compensation do not, however, arise (save where damage results from the failure to pay the interest promptly).

(ii) The Late Payment of Commercial Debts (Interest) Act 1998

The most important interest term implied in law arises by operation of the Late Payment of Commercial Debts (Interest) Act 1998.[94] By this statute, businesses that do not otherwise provide in the contract for interest to accrue are entitled in contracts for the supply of goods or services to another business (but not to a consumer) to claim a small compensation fee—of up to £100; the amount depends upon the size of the debt—and a large rate of simple interest—currently eight per cent above base rate[95]—for all unpaid debts. The court has a discretion to vary the rate of interest in the interests of justice.[96] The reader is referred to the terms of the short Act itself in relation to the provisions as to the starting and finishing dates of the interest calculation, and the way the applicable rate for a particular period is calculated.

---

[94] The term is implied in law but may be varied by the parties: 1998 Act ss 7–10.

[95] Late Payment of Commercial Debts (Rate of Interest) (No 3) Order 2002 (SI 2002/1675).

[96] 1998 Act, s 5. See further the approach to such a discretion under the statutory right to award interest, discussed above in section 7.7A.

8

Claims by a Tenant or Hirer

Damages for non-delivery, late delivery or defective delivery by the landlord, lessor or hirer.

8.1. Non-Delivery
8.2. Late Delivery
8.3. Hire of Defective Property and Damage to Hired Property

T HE GENERAL PRINCIPLES discussed in chapters two to four in relation to services and property also apply (with minor adjustments) to cases of non-delivery or defective delivery under a contract for hire or charter. Indeed *Robinson v Harman*,[1] cited in this book and elsewhere for the key formulation of the basic compensatory principle of contract damages, was itself a case of non-delivery by a landlord. This chapter covers claims by a tenant against a lessor or third party, which are claims for loss of use (or incomplete use) of property belonging to someone else (the lessor). This contrasts with claims by a lessor for breach by the tenant, especially at the time of redelivery, which are covered in chapters four and six and are cases of deprivation of or damage to the claimant's property, and chapter five in relation to non-acceptance by the tenant.

8.1 Non-Delivery

If an owner fails to deliver the chartered vessel or the lessor fails to deliver the leased property, the damages will usually be assessed by reference to the difference between the contract rate and the market substitute rate, where the charterer or lessee reasonably did engage such a substitute or should have done so.[2]

Where a substitute vessel or property was unavailable and/or not prescribed by the mitigation rule, the claimant can (subject to remoteness) claim the lost profit it would have made using the vessel or land (for example through sale of the goods it would have carried on the vessel).[3] The same applies where there *is* a replacement

---

[1] *Robinson v Harman* (1848) 1 Ex 850.
[2] *Monarch Steamship Co Ltd v Karlshamns Oljefabriker (A/B)* [1949] AC 196 (HL); *Blackgold Trading Ltd of Monrovia v Amare SpA di Navigazione of Genoa (The Almare Seconda)* [1981] 2 Lloyd's Rep 433 (Goff J).
[3] *Watts, Watts and Co Ltd v Mitsui* [1917] AC 227 (HL).

but in relation to the period before the substitute could be acquired. Other losses may also be recoverable (such as the value of goods that perished for want of a vessel to carry them).[4]

8.2 Late Delivery

Lost profits have been awarded in cases of late delivery of business premises by a landlord where the landlord knew the tenant wanted the property for its business (and so the losses were not too remote).[5]

In voyage charter cases, late delivery of the vessel by the owner will often lead to the charterer losing or breaching a sale contract, and the charterer's liability under such a sale contract (or chain of such contracts) will often not be held too remote.[6] In *The Baleares*, late delivery of a chartered vessel led to the claimant losing a forward sale at a fixed price and having to pay the increased market price (which had increased in part because of the 'hype' arising out of the delay of the vessel, which hype and consequent increase were not held too remote) or compensate its sub-buyer.[7] The resulting loss was recoverable. And in *The Rio Claro*, late delivery of a chartered vessel led the claimant have to pay more for its oil (from the Egyptian Government), although the loss in that case was too remote.[8]

8.3 Hire of Defective Property and Damage to Hired Property

As in the case of sale, similarly in the case of lease/hire/charterparty, the lessor may have an obligation that the leased property should conform to a particular description. However, as the contract will be a lease/hire/charterparty of specific property, and the property will have to be returned at the end of the contract, it will not usually be practicable or legal for the lessee to sell the defective property and purchase a replacement, which would be the usual method of mitigation in defective *sale* cases.[9] Further, the lessee, not being owner of the property, has not suffered the diminution in value of the property (although it may sometimes suffer a diminution to the value of its leasehold interest). Accordingly the measure of damages will be

---

[4] *Heindal A/S v Questier* (1949) 82 Ll L Rep 452 (Morris J).

[5] *Ward v Smith* (1822) 11 Price 19.

[6] *ASM Shipping Ltd of India v TTMI Ltd of England (The Amer Energy)* [2009] 1 Lloyd's Rep 293 (Flaux J).

[7] *Geogas SA v Trammo Gas Ltd (The Baleares)* [1993] 1 Lloyd's Rep 215 (CA), following *Featherston v Wilkinson* (1873) LR 8 Ex 122. And as to interruption of the hire and the recoverability of lost profit, see *Sylvia Shipping Ltd v Progress Bulk Carriers Ltd* [2010] EWHC 542 (Comm) (Hamblen J) discussed below at text to n 14.

[8] *Transworld Oil Ltd v North Bay Shipping Corporation (The Rio Claro)* [1987] 2 Lloyd's Rep 173 (Staughton J).

[9] Such a sale by a lessee may be possible and reasonable in the case of a long lease of land, where it can be assigned and then replaced.

the cost of cure (where reasonable[10]) and/or any consequential losses of profit or other benefit suffered.[11]

A. Charterparties and Hire

Defects in a chartered vessel may lead to damage to the claimant charterer's goods.[12] In one charterparty case the owner refused fully to fill the hold with cargo, thus in effect forcing the charterer to accept a vessel capable of carrying 51 tonnes less than that it had contracted for.[13] Alternative capacity to carry the relevant cargo (okoume logs) on another vessel was unavailable and so the charterer recovered the lost profit that would have been made on the 51 tonnes of logs at the Cape Town destination, with no credit given for the value of the logs not shipped and so retained by the claimant, because they perished.

In *Sylvia Shipping Ltd v Progress Bulk Carriers Ltd*,[14] the owner's breach of its obligation to maintain the vessel led to an interruption in the time charter service which led the claimant charterer to lose a voyage sub-charter (although it did manage to secure a less profitable substitute time charter). The House of Lords' decision in *The Achilleas*[15] (which concerned late redelivery by a charterer to a shipowner, and where the lost profit on a follow-on charter was held to be too remote) was distinguished because in the circumstances of the interruption in the charter service in *Sylvia Shipping*, the lost sub-charter fixture was not as unpredictable as the lost follow-on charter after late redelivery to the shipowner at the end of the charter in *The Achilleas*. In the *Sylvia Shipping* situation the sub-charter was limited by the remaining period of the head charter, whereas in *The Achilleas* the loss being claimed was potentially open-ended, being the owner's loss of a follow-on fixture of unbounded duration.[16] Further there was no market understanding in this situation as there was found to be in *The Achilleas* in relation to redelivery by a charterer at the end of the charter.[17] Unless the sub-fixture was particularly lucrative, in which case it might fall outside the defendant's responsibility,[18] the loss was recoverable.[19]

---

[10] The reasonableness test is discussed above in chapter four, section 4.3B.

[11] See the hire purchase case of *Charterhouse Credit Co Ltd v Tolly* [1963] 2 QB 683 (CA), Upjohn LJ obiter at 711–12.

[12] Eg *The Folias* [1979] AC 685 (HL).

[13] *A/S D/S Heimdal v Questier & Co Ltd* (1948–49) 82 Ll L Rep 452 (Morris J).

[14] *Sylvia Shipping Ltd v Progress Bulk Carriers Ltd* [2010] EWHC 542 (Comm) (Hamblen J).

[15] *Transfield Shipping Inc v Mercator Shipping Inc (The Achilleas)* [2009] AC 61 (HL).

[16] *Sylvia Shipping* [2010] EWHC 542 (Comm) at para 73.

[17] Ibid at paras 72 and 81. And cf the late delivery to a charterer case of *Geogas SA v Trammo Gas Ltd (The Baleares)* [1993] 1 Lloyd's Rep 215 (CA).

[18] *Sylvia Shipping* [2010] EWHC 542 (Comm) at para 81. Also *'SNIA' Societa di Navigazione Industria e Commercio v Suzuki & Co* (1924) 18 Ll L Rep 333 (CA) at 337, where it was found that lost profits from the particular sub-charters were irrecoverable but were evidence of ordinary profits, which were recoverable.

[19] Cf the tort damage case of *Pacific Concord, Georgidore (Owners) v Pacific Concord (Owners) (The Pacific Concord)* [1961] 1 WLR 873 (Lord Merriman P), where (tort) remoteness was not discussed but the specific losses on the on-charter were not recoverable as they had been claimed in addition to general losses of profit and there would be duplication.

In one case an aircraft consultant's delays in doing work meant that the aircraft leased by the claimant freight carrier become unusable and uneconomic to repair for the remainder of its life.[20] But in another case, a claimant failed in a claim for lost profits following the hire of a defective second-hand tractor for the winter to keep open roads in Manitoba to enable timber haulage.[21] The owner knew the purpose for which the tractor was to be used but not the scale of the defendant's business ('whether the defendant company intended to remove 100 cords or 100,000 cords of wood'), or that all the wood had to be moved that season for particular reasons. And in a case of hire of a defective printing press, although damages for lost profits were recoverable in principle, they failed for lack of proof; however, the costs of rectifying defective printing were recovered.[22]

B. Commercial Leases

(i) Cost of Repairs

In accordance with usual principles, where reasonable, the cost of repairs that were incurred or should have been incurred will be recoverable.[23]

(ii) Lost Profits from Sub-Letting or Assignment

Where a landlord fails to provide services or keep the leased premises in repair, and the building is rented by the claimant tenant to be sub-let and not occupied by it, the tenant's recoverable loss is the lost rent from the sub-tenant, liability to the sub-tenants, or any reduction in the value of the leasehold, as applicable, if this is within the contemplation of the landlord.[24] If the claimant could nevertheless have sub-let the flats (the disrepair not being sufficient to justify not doing so) but did not do so, the claimant could still claim the difference in the rates at which it should have sub-let despite the breach, and the higher rate at which it could have sub-let but for the breach (the law deeming the claimant to have taken the steps it should have taken).[25] Where lost rental income cannot be proven and the property is out of use, the claimant may possibly recover the interest on the capital sum expended in purchasing the lease as an estimate of the value that would have been received

---

[20] *Transafrik International Ltd v Venus Corporation Ltd* (2008) 121 Con LR 78 (Akenhead J).

[21] *Munroe Equipment Sales Ltd v Canadian Forest Products Ltd* (1961) 29 DLR (2d) 730 (Manitoba CA) at 739.

[22] *Lobster Group Ltd v Heidelberg Graphic Equipment Ltd* [2009] EWHC 1919 TCC (Ramsey J).

[23] *Hawkins v Woodhall* [2008] EWHCA Civ 932 (CA) Arden LJ at para 45. For the reasonableness test, see above in chapter four, section 4.3B.

[24] *Electricity Supply Nominees Ltd v National Magazine Co Ltd* [1999] 1 EGLR 130 (Hicks QC) at 132. Such sub-letting profits will also usually be in the contemplation of the parties in cases of residential long leases, where tenants will often want to sub-let for some periods: *Mira v Aylmer Square Investments Ltd* [1990] 1 EGLR 45 (CA) Stuart-Smith LJ at 48. Cf *Hutchinson v Harris* (1978) 10 BLR 19 (CA), a construction case where the loss was avoidable so not awarded.

[25] *Marionette Ltd v Visible Information Packaged Systems Ltd*, 25 July 2002 (Warren QC).

from the property.[26] Assignment of the lease by the claimant may also be contemplated by the parties at the time of contracting, in which case the lost premium that would have been made on assignment is recoverable, plus any rent, insurance and service charges that would have been saved by having assigned the lease,[27] less the costs of procuring the assignment (which may include a licence fee payable to the landlord).

(iii) Other Lost Profits or Diminution in Value

In other cases the breach by the landlord may lead to quantifiable loss of profits to the claimant's business, in which case such loss will be recoverable.[28] The Court of Appeal confirmed in *Savva v Hussein* that proof of lost profits may be assisted by the presumption that, had the business not been shut down due to the damp caused by disrepair, the claimant would at least have earned enough revenue to pay the rent (ie to break even).[29]

Where no lost profits can be proven, and the tenant is in occupation, an award can still be made for diminution in value or general inconvenience, even though the claimant is a company or individual acting in the course of business. This was held by the Court of Appeal in *Larksworth Investments Ltd v Temple House Ltd*, where damp in a solicitor's firm's premises led to some parts being unusable and others being less pleasant, leading to a reduction in morale and a poor impression made on clients, although no particular lost profits were proven.[30] The award in that case, as interpreted and applied in subsequent cases,[31] is of damages (in addition to the costs of repair) reflecting the diminution in the value of the property to the claimant tenant, with this award (absent proof of particular lost profits) being also describable as general inconvenience and distress just as in residential cases, these being 'alternative ways of expressing the same concept'. An award for specific losses of profit would be an alternative measure to a commercial tenant's general award for diminution in value of the tenancy to the tenant.[32]

---

[26] *Bella Casa Ltd v Vinestone Ltd* [2005] EWHC 2807 (TCC) (Coulson QC). See further the discussion of this measure above in chapter six, section 6.5A(ii).

[27] *Crédit Suisse v Beegas Nominees Ltd* [1994] All ER 803 (Lindsay J), where the premium awarded was £85,000 and the rent, insurance and service charges that would have been paid were over £1.5m. See also the discussion in residential lease case *City & Metropolitan Properties Ltd v Greycroft Ltd* [1987] 1 WLR 1085 (Mowbray QC) at 1089.

[28] Eg *Stewart v Scottish Widows and Life Assurance Society plc* [2005] EWHC 1831 (QB) (Eccles QC), appeal allowed in part on a different point [2006] EWCA Civ 999 (CA); *Vasiliou v Hajigeorgiou* [2010] EWCA Civ 1475 (CA). Not proven in *Hawkins v Woodhall* [2008] EWHCA Civ 932 (CA) Arden LJ at para 53.

[29] *Savva v Hussein* [1996] 2 EGLR 65 (CA) Staughton LJ at 67. On the presumption that the claimant would have broken even more generally, see chapter eighteen, section 18.3.

[30] *Larksworth Investments Ltd v Temple House Ltd* (CA) 18 January 1999.

[31] *Clarke v Lloyds TSB Bank plc* [2002] EWHC 1025 (TCC) (Black QC) at paras 116–18. Also *Electricity Supply Nominees Ltd v National Magazine Co Ltd* [1999] 1 EGLR 130 (Hicks QC) (which predated *Larksworth*) and *Regus (UK) Ltd v Epcot Solutions Ltd* [2008] EWCA Civ 361 (CA) at paras 31 and 32.

[32] *Electricity Supply Nominees Ltd v National Magazine Co Ltd* [1999] 1 EGLR 130 (Hicks QC) at 137. For cases in which lost profits have been quantified, see above at text to n 28.

The award of damages for inconvenience may be made in the ordinary way by taking a general figure for the non-pecuniary loss, as in a case of the leaky premises of an investment bank where staff and customers suffered.[33] However, the 'notional' reduction in rent that would be attributable to the breach by the market is admissible and often useful evidence of the diminution in value. This is because 'the defendant may well not find it difficult to establish that the benefit to it ... would have been worth at least the amount of rent payable'.[34] Such notional rent reduction is not conclusive evidence of the diminution in value since 'if the parties are on an equal footing and both are satisfied with the bargain, each values what he receives rather more highly than what he gives', ie the value to the claimant may be higher than the difference in market rent.[35]

An award may be made even where a corporate tenant has engaged the property for one of its directors to occupy, the award reflecting the amenity not provided to the tenant claimant which it therefore could not pass on to its licensee.[36]

An alternative measure is the hypothetical bargain (*Wrotham Park*) measure, discussed below in chapter twenty-two. In one case of failure to provide quiet enjoyment committed by the landlord blocking a fire-door to the shopping centre unit let to the claimant, where the tenant (despite seeking and being refused an injunction) would in fact have acquiesced in exchange for a financial incentive, the hypothetical bargain measure was used and upheld by the Court of Appeal.[37]

C. Residential Leases

The ordinary principles of damages apply to residential leases and breach of the covenant to repair or provide promised amenities: '[W]hat sum will, so far as money can, place the tenant in the position he would have been in if the obligation to repair had been duly performed by the landlord?'[38] Recovery will be of financial loss if the claimant has incurred a cost of alternative accommodation,[39] or reasonably assigns the lease and buys a replacement.[40] Likewise where the claimant has to pay for repairs or should do so, which is subject to the usual test of whether a cost of cure

---

[33] *Crédit Suisse v Beegas Nominees Ltd* [1994] All ER 803 (Lindsay J) at 828.

[34] *Electricity Supply Nominees Ltd v National Magazine Co Ltd* [1999] 1 EGLR 130 (Hicks QC) at 136. Also *Larksworth Investments Ltd v Temple House Ltd*, 18 January 1999 (CA); *Clarke v Lloyds TSB Bank plc* [2002] EWHC 1025 (TCC) (Black QC).

[35] *Electricity Supply Nominees Ltd v National Magazine Co Ltd* [1999] 1 EGLR 130 (Hicks QC) at 136.

[36] *Langham Estate Management Ltd v Hardy* [2008] 3 EGLR 125 (Central London County Court, Marshall QC) at para 172.

[37] *Lunn Poly Ltd v Liverpool & Lancashire Properties Ltd* [2006] EWCA Civ 430. Note however that there was no appeal against the use of the measure, only the way it was to be applied: see Neuberger LJ at para 14.

[38] *Wallace v Manchester City Council* [1998] 3 EGLR 38 (CA) Morritt LJ at 42.

[39] Eg *Calabar Properties Ltd v Stitcher* [1984] 1 WLR 287 (CA). See also *Charsley v Jones* (1889) 53 JP 280.

[40] *Calabar Properties Ltd v Stitcher* [1984] 1 WLR 287 (CA) Griffiths LJ at 299; *City and Metropolitan Properties v Greycroft* [1987] 1 WLR 1085 (Mowbray QC) at 1088. Cf *Grosvenor Hotel Co v Hamilton* [1894] 2 QB 836 (CA).

is reasonable.[41] In *Newman v Framewood Manor Management Co Ltd*,[42] a tenant was promised use of a jacuzzi but it had been removed and replaced with a sauna. The £20,000 cost of installing a jacuzzi was out of proportion to the loss of amenity, for which £3,500 was awarded by the Court of Appeal.

Financial lost profits will be recoverable even in residential lease cases where sub-letting is, as will usually be the case at least in long leases, in the contemplation of the parties.[43] Likewise where assignment for a profit (ie purchase of a lease as a speculation) is within the parties' contemplation.[44]

Where the claimant is, or would but for the breach have been, in occupation, the primary recovery is likely to be not of financial loss but of non-pecuniary loss, which is discussed below in chapter nineteen.

Of course, damages will also be recoverable where the breach has led to personal injury[45] or property damage.[46]

---

[41] Eg *Calabar Properties Ltd v Stitcher* [1984] 1 WLR 287 (CA); *Loria v Hammer* [1989] 2 EGLR 249 (Lindsay QC). No failure to mitigate found in eg *Sturolson & Co v Mauroux* [1988] 1 EGLR 66 (CA) at 68. As to the reasonableness test applied to the cost of cure, see above in chapter four, section 4.3B.

[42] *Newman v Framewood Manor Management Co Ltd* [2012] EWCA Civ 159.

[43] *Mira v Aylmer Square Investments Ltd* [1990] 1 EGLR 45 (CA) Stuart-Smith LJ at 48; *Wallace v Manchester City Council* [1998] 3 EGLR 38 (CA) Morritt LJ at 42. See above in section 8.3B. Alternatively the claimant may recover loss of the amenity, as discussed in the following passages, that it was not able to pass on to its sub-tenant or licensee: *Calabar Properties Ltd v Stitcher* [1984] 1 WLR 287 (CA) at 290; *Langham Estate Management Ltd v Hardy* [2008] 3 EGLR 125 (Central London County Court, Marshall QC) at para 172.

[44] See the discussion, including of the relevance to remoteness of the lease clauses dealing with assignment, in *City and Metropolitan Properties v Greycroft* [1987] 1 WLR 1085 (Mowbray QC) at 1089, where the point was not decided although it was recognised that the claimant would have difficulties demonstrating that such losses were not too remote in a residential lease case.

[45] See chapter nineteen, section 19.4, below.

[46] *Hewitt v Rowlands* [1924] 93 LJKB 1080 (CA); *Marshall v Rubypoint Ltd* [1997] 1 EGLR 69 (CA) (loss of property when stolen by burglars).

9

Warranties and Indemnities

Damages for breaches of warranties or indemnities.

9.1 Introduction to Warranties

A WARRANTY IS a promise that a state of affairs exists.[1] Breach therefore arises when the state of affairs does not exist, and the measure of damages is the difference between the position the claimant is in and the position it would have been in had the state of affairs existed. The archetypal contract that includes warranties is the contract of sale. Sales and other contractual transfers of goods include a number of warranties implied by statute,[2] including that the goods conform to their description and are of satisfactory quality.

'In the case of a warranty, one compares the plaintiff's position as a result of entering into the transaction with what it would have been if the information had been accurate',[3] as Lord Hoffmann put it in *SAAMCo* (the 'information' being the warranted state of affairs). However, as with any contract term, when considering the damages measure it is very important carefully to consider the content of the particular warranty that has been breached.

9.2 Warranties of Authority

A warranty of authority is a warranty that the defendant has authority as agent on behalf of a principal. Where that warranty is breached, damages must put the claimant in the position as if it had a binding contract with that third party principal.

---

[1] This must be distinguished from the separate usage of the word 'warranty' as a term the breach of which of will never give rise to a right to repudiation, in contradistinction to 'condition' (or 'intermediate term').

[2] The Sale of Goods Act 1979 and Part I of the Supply of Goods and Services Act 1982.

[3] *South Australia Asset Management Corporation v York Montague Ltd* [1997] AC 191 (HL) at 216.

In a sale case, this means damages as if there were a binding contract of sale.[4] Similar claims arise in contracts (without authority) for settlement.[5] In litigation, it means that a solicitor may be liable to pay the other side's costs when it conducted litigation without authority from its client.[6] If there would still have been no recovery against the principal even if the agent had had authority, then no loss has been suffered.

9.3 Warranties of Quality

If the warranty is of quality, the defendant has promised that the goods are in this state. It then becomes necessary to work out what defects in the goods would not have been present if the goods had been in that state, and then calculate damages accordingly. The difference in value is the prima facie measure in such cases, as Lord Hoffmann explained in *Lion Nathan Ltd v C-C Bottlers Ltd*: 'In the case of a warranty as to the quality of the goods, the purchaser is prima facie entitled to the difference between what the goods as warranted would have been worth and what they were actually worth'.[7]

The warranties in the Sale of Goods Act (satisfactory quality, fitness for purpose, good title) are such warranties of quality, and the same prima facie measure is set down in that Act, which records in section 50 that

> (2) The measure of damages for breach of warranty is the estimated loss directly and naturally resulting, in the ordinary course of events, from the breach of warranty.
> (3) In the case of breach of warranty of quality such loss is prima facie the difference between the value of the goods at the time of delivery to the buyer and the value they would have had if they had fulfilled the warranty.[8]

Moving away from the straightforward sale of goods context, a warranty that a company's income was a particular sum (or that it owned certain assets or had certain liabilities) would be a warranty of quality in this sense, as that fact about the company affects the value and profitability of the company, and is an attribute of the company. If such a warranty is breached then, again, the question is what the shares would have been worth if the company had had income as promised. Lord Hoffmann in *Lion Nathan* again:

> If the vendor [of shares] had warranted that the earnings in the last two months would be $2,223,000, there would have been an analogy with a warranty of quality and the damages would prima facie have been the difference between what the shares would have

---

[4] *Godwin v Francis* (1870) LR 5 CP 295; *Habton Farms v Nimmo* [2003] EWCA Civ 68; *Greenglade Estates Ltd v Chana* [2012] EWHC 1913 (Ch) (Donaldson QC); and text to chapter five n 4 above.
[5] *Meek v Wendt* (1888) 21 QBD 126; *British-Russian Gazette and Trade Outlook Ltd v Associated Newspapers Ltd* [1933] 2 KB 616 (CA).
[6] *Yonge v Toynbee* [1910] 1 KB 215 (CA); *Bank of Scotland v Qutb* [2012] EWCA Civ 1661.
[7] *Lion Nathan Ltd v C-C Bottlers Ltd* [1996] 1 WLR 1438 (PC) at 1441.
[8] Section 50 Sale of Goods Act 1979.

been worth if the earnings had been in accordance with the warranty and what they were actually worth.[9]

A different measure of damages applies to warranties that reasonable care has been taken in a forecast or valuation, and this is discussed in a separate section below.[10]

A. Sale of Goods

The damages for breach of warranties of quality in sale of goods cases, ie for defective goods, are discussed above in chapter four.

B. Share Sales: The Difference in Value

Generally speaking, the ordinary rules apply to share sales as to sales of any other property.[11] As with sale of goods, and for the same reason, the prima facie measure of damages in breach of warranty of quality share sale cases is the difference in value between the shares as they were and as they would have been if the warranty had been true.

(i) The Value as Warranted

The value as warranted will be determined by valuing the shares as if the warranty had been true. The actual price will be rebuttably presumed to be the amount the shares were worth[12] (although it may be difficult to work out what was paid, given that consideration is not always a matter of a cash sum[13]), but it is open to the defendant to prove that the buyer made a bad bargain and the company even as warranted was worth less than the price.[14]

---

[9] *Lion Nathan Ltd v C-C Bottlers Ltd* [1996] 1 WLR 1438 (PC) at 1441. Also *Curtis v Lockheed Martin UK Holdings Ltd* [2008] EWHC 2691 (Comm) (Simon J) at para 112 obiter (claim failed for lack of compliant notification).

[10] See section 9.4.

[11] *AKAS Jamal v Moolla Dawood Sons & Co* [1916] 1 AC 175 (PC) (claim by seller for non-acceptance); *Sri Lanka Omnibus Co Ltd v Perera* [1952] AC 76 (PC) (late delivery, lost dividends recovered); *Asamera Oil Corporation Ltd v Sea Oil & General Corporation* [1979] 1 SCR 633 (SC of Canada), *Oxus Gold plc v Oxus Resources Corporation* [2007] EWHC 770 (Comm) (Langley J), *Bear Stearns Bank plc v Forum Global Equity* [2007] EWHC 1576 (Comm) (Andrew Smith J) and *Plumbly v BeatthatQuote.com Ltd* [2009] EWHC 321 (QB) (all non-delivery of shares by seller). Likewise the ordinary principles of damages for deceit and misrepresentation apply to share cases, such that the date of valuation of the shares for which credit must be given depends upon when it was reasonable for the claimant to sell: *Smith New Court Securities Ltd v Scrimgeour Vickers (Asset Management) Ltd* [1997] AC 254 (HL).

[12] *Senate Electrical Wholesalers Ltd v STC Submarine Systems Ltd*, 20 December 1996 (May J) (agreed by the parties); *Eastgate Group Ltd v Lindsey Morden Group Inc* [2001] Lloyd's Rep PN 51 (Andrew Smith J) Longmore LJ at para 18; *Sycamore Bidco Limited v Breslin* [2012] EWHC 3443 (Ch) (Mann J) at para 391. Also *Infiniteland Ltd v Artisan Contracting Ltd* [2004] EWHC 955 (Ch) (Park J) at para 126, appeal dismissed on a different point [2006] 1 BCLC 632 (CA).

[13] Exactly this problem arose in the short separate judgment on the point in *Sycamore Bidco Limited v Breslin* [2013] EWHC 38 (Ch) (Mann J).

[14] *Eastgate Group Ltd v Lindsey Morden Group Inc* [2002] 1 WLR 642 (CA) Longmore LJ at para 18.

(ii) The Value as Is

Where the warranty is as to a company's accounts having been true and fair, and the breach consisted in wrongly including certain elements in the turnover thus inflating it, the valuation exercise requires that the shares are valued 'on the basis of restated accounts (that is to say, accounts with all the claimed moneys omitted from turnover)'.[15] The measure is thus 'what the shares were really worth (ie with the right figures in the accounts)'.[16]

In some cases, a company may actually have no value at all.[17] In others, the breach of warranty may not have affected the value.[18] Subsequent events may shed light on the value of the company at the date of the putative sale,[19] but it is generally impermissible to take account of subsequent events as those facts would not have been available to anyone valuing the company at the relevant date.[20]

Where the claimant in fact knew of the breach of warranty, although that may or may not prevent there being a breach,[21] it may mean that the actual purchase price (which was influenced by the knowledge) is good evidence of the value as is.[22]

(a) The Market Price

The typical mechanism for identifying the value will be the market price. This is routine in sale of goods cases. In complex cases such as purchases of companies, although it is still necessary to work out what a willing buyer would have paid a willing seller[23] (essentially the definition of market price), it may be necessary to perform the modelling and calculations that a prospective purchaser would have performed. When assessing the value of companies or shares in companies, it is common to have expert evidence and to base calculations on a discounted cash flow or price/earnings ratio,[24] or a net asset value,[25] which is what company purchasers do.

---

[15] *Sycamore Bidco Limited v Breslin* [2012] EWHC 3443 (Ch) (Mann J) at para 398.

[16] Ibid at para 397.

[17] Eg *Bottin v Venson* [2006] EWHC 3112 (Ch) (Blackburne J) obiter at para 415 (deceit).

[18] *Sycamore Bidco Limited v Breslin* [2012] EWHC 3443 (Ch) (Mann J) at para 405.

[19] *Infiniteland Ltd v Artisan Contracting Ltd* [2004] EWHC 955 (Ch) (Park J) at paras 132–34, appeal dismissed on a different point [2006] 1 BCLC 632 (CA); *Bottin v Venson* [2006] EWHC 3112 (Ch) (Blackburne J) obiter at para 415 (deceit).

[20] *Buckingham v Francis* [1986] 2 All ER 738 (Staughton J) at 740; *Joiner v George* [2002] EWCA Civ 1160 (CA) at paras 68–75; *Ng v Crabtree* [2011] EWHC 1834 (Ch) (Arnold J) at para 17.

[21] In many share purchase agreements there is a clause stating that knowledge is irrelevant if the matter is not disclosed through the disclosure letter or proper channels, although that may possibly be circumvented by an agreement that a matter is not to be treated as material or by construction of the relevant clause: *Eurocopy plc v Teesdale* [1992] BCLC 1067 (CA) at 1071. In others there is a clause providing that anything known by the claimant cannot be treated as undisclosed, in which case knowledge goes to whether there was a breach of warranty and not merely to damages. See the clause in *Infiniteland Ltd v Artisan Contracting Ltd* [2004] EWHC 955 (Ch) (Park J) at paras 116 ff.

[22] See *Eurocopy plc v Teesdale* [1992] BCLC 1067 (CA), especially Nourse LJ and Lloyd LJ at 1073.

[23] *Sycamore Bidco Limited v Breslin* [2012] EWHC 3443 (Ch) (Mann J) at paras 405, 454, 464.

[24] *ADO Ltd v BDO Binder Hamlyn*, 6 December 1995 (May J) (misrep); *Lion Nathan Ltd v C-C Bottlers Ltd* [1996] 1 WLR 1438 (PC); *Senate Electrical Wholesalers Ltd v Alcatel Submarine Networks Ltd* [1999] 2 Lloyds Rep 423 (CA) Stuart-Smith LJ at para 33.

[25] See the discussion in *ADO Ltd v BDO Binder Hamlyn*, 6 December 1995 (May J).

Further, where information that would have affected the value of the property is unknown by the market, the market value of publicly traded shares is not a fair test of the true value as is, because the market price is artificial.[26] In such cases the market price after the information becomes public may be better evidence of the real market value of the shares.[27]

(b) The Relevance of How the Claimant Actually Valued the Company

In working out the actual value the court will often look at the way the claimant itself valued the company, as that is evidence of the way the market would value the property or business.[28] However, the court is not bound to adopt the method of valuation that the buyer actually adopted, especially where the experts agreed on a different method.[29]

(c) The Relevance of What the Claimant Would Have Done

The price the claimant itself would have paid if the proper accounts had been presented is good (but not conclusive) evidence of what the market would have paid, and factors such as competition for the business and how parties in fact pragmatically conduct bidding (which is not merely a mathematic application of models as to value) are to be taken into account. In *Senate v Alcatel*, the first instance judge adopted the buyer's actual method and motivations and relied upon the price the buyer actually would have paid because it was the 'only valuation evidence ... which is other than entirely theoretical' and the only evidence of 'the way in which people in real life valued this Business'.[30] In *Sycamore Bidco* the judge confirmed that the difference in price measure adopted by the first instance judge in *Senate v Alcatel* was only an attempt to get at 'what the shares were really worth (ie with the right figures in the accounts)' and that what the claimant would have paid is just a way of measuring the 'actual value' and so what the claimant would in fact have done is not determinative.[31]

---

[26] See deceit case *Derry v Peek* (1887) 37 Ch D 541 (CA) at 591.

[27] *Kerr v Danier Leather Inc* (2004) CanLII 8186 (Ontario Superior Court of Justice) at paras 338–39 (appeal allowed on liability (2005) 77 OR (3d) 321 (Ontario Court of Appeal), further appeal dismissed [2007] 3 SCR 331 (Supreme Court of Canada), both appellate courts declining to consider the damages issues).

[28] *Senate Electrical Wholesalers Ltd v Alcatel Submarine Networks Ltd* [1999] 2 Lloyds Rep 423 (CA) Stuart-Smith LJ at paras 33 and 37; *Sycamore Bidco Limited v Breslin* [2012] EWHC 3443 (Ch) (Mann J).

[29] *Senate Electrical Wholesalers Ltd v Alcatel Submarine Networks Ltd* [1999] 2 Lloyds Rep 423 (CA) Stuart-Smith LJ at para 34; *Sycamore Bidco Limited v Breslin* [2012] EWHC 3443 (Ch) (Mann J) (claimant's method not adopted).

[30] *Senate Electrical Wholesalers Ltd v STC Submarine Systems Ltd*, 20 December 1996 (May J). The Court of Appeal allowed the appeal on notification grounds but obiter disapproved the award as the claimant had not pursued a claim for the difference between the price paid and that which would have been paid but had instead pursued a different measure for 'jackpot damages', and so it was not open to the judge to make the £5m award he did: *Senate Electrical Wholesalers Ltd v Alcatel Submarine Networks Ltd* [1999] 2 Lloyds Rep 423 (CA) Stuart-Smith LJ at paras 47–49, 51 and 54, a point discussed below in chapter eighteen, section 18.2B.

[31] *Sycamore Bidco Limited v Breslin* [2012] EWHC 3443 (Ch) (Mann J) at paras 393–97 and 403–5.

In this context, it will be relevant not only what figure a pricing model produces, but also what demand and competition there was in the market, such that there were other bids that a successful purchaser would have to beat.[32] In some cases the realities of commercial bargaining and particular keenness to acquire a business (eg for strategic, synergistic or sentimental reasons), or the competitive reality, mean that the parties would have departed from the price the model produced. In one case this competitive reality was referred to as the 'haggle factor'.[33]

(iii) The Date of Assessment

As with sales of goods, with share sales prima facie the difference in value is taken at the date of purchase.[34] However, as with goods cases, this presumption is rebuttable according to the proper application of the mitigation and causation rules.[35]

In *Intrum Justitia BV v Legal and Trade Financial Services Ltd*[36] (a breach of warranty case), the effect of the warranty was to promise that a company had not suffered an undisclosed embezzlement in its recent past, when it in fact had. The shares had negligible value at the date of acquisition given the embezzlement, and the reasonable thing to do (especially where the shares were bought to be held) was to hold on to the shares, put the embezzled money back in, pay for a proper forensic investigation and wait until the embezzlement had been forgotten by the market. Such losses, plus a figure for the chance of lost profits, were therefore awarded by the Irish High Court.

In *Great Future International Ltd v Sealand Housing Corp* (a breach of warranty and misrepresentation case), the court confirmed that a later date than the date of acquisition could be taken for the valuation of the shares where justice required but refused to defer the date in the instant case (where to do so would have reduced the award), despite the purchase being a long-term acquisition.[37]

And in the deceit case of *Smith New Court Securities* (where slightly different considerations applied) the claimant was 'locked in' to the purchase and so the House of Lords awarded damages based on the value of the shares at the later date when it did sell the shares after the defect had become patent (this was a larger award than if losses had been awarded at the date of acquisition).[38]

---

[32] *Senate Electrical Wholesalers Ltd v Alcatel Submarine Networks Ltd* [1999] 2 Lloyds Rep 423 (CA) obiter Stuart-Smith LJ at para 66; *Sycamore Bidco Limited v Breslin* [2012] EWHC 3443 (Ch) (Mann J) at para 405.

[33] *Sycamore Bidco Limited v Breslin* [2012] EWHC 3443 (Ch) (Mann J) at para 464, and generally paras 403–43.

[34] Ibid at para 391.

[35] The breach of warranty shares are referred to in the body of the text, but for share non-delivery cases confirming that the date of assessment is the date when the buyer should have gone to the market see *Asamera Oil Corporation Ltd v Sea Oil & General Corporation* [1979] 1 SCR 633 (SC of Canada); *Bear Stearns Bank plc v Forum Global Equity* [2007] EWHC 1576 (Comm) (Andrew Smith J).

[36] *Intrum Justitia BV v Legal and Trade Financial Services Ltd* [2009] 4 IR 417 (Irish High Court).

[37] *Great Future International v Sealand Housing Corp* [2002] EWHC 2454 (Ch) (Lightman J), appeal allowed on an evidential point [2002] EWCA Civ 1183 (CA). The point was res judicata so the point is obiter, but the judge's approach is nevertheless problematic, as described above in chapter four, section 4.2B(v)(d).

[38] *Smith New Court Securities Ltd v Scrimgeour Vickers (Asset Management) Ltd* [1997] AC 254 (HL).

Sometimes courts seek to achieve the result of deferring the date of assessment by instead purporting to take the value of shares at the date of breach but taking into account post-purchase events.[39]

C. Share Sales: Other Measures of Damages

Shares provide an additional complication not present in cases of sale of property or a business itself, because the shareholder is at one remove from the business's profits and losses. If one buys a business (ie the assets and goodwill), and not merely the company vehicle that operates a business, then a breach of warranty of quality means that the claimant's loss will often be the costs and lost profits that the business has suffered as a result of the business not being as described, just as in a sale of goods case.

However, shareholders do not so easily feel a change in the costs or profits of the business directly in their pocket. Most usually and most obviously, a shareholder will feel any breach in a change in the value of its shareholding or (more rarely) the amount of dividends received.[40] The case law almost all concerns a claim for the decreased value of the shareholding.

A shareholder will rarely be able to claim the cost of curing a defect in the business, or lost profits to the business, because usually the business will be left to its own devices and not draw on shareholders for further sums. In one case, however, the claimant recovered the cost of injecting money into a company to solve the problem (of embezzlement) revealed by the breach of warranty and to repair the company.[41]

9.4 Warranties of Reasonable Care

A. The Measure of Damages

In *Esso Petroleum Co Ltd v Mardon*,[42] a seller's business forecast was found to have been not a warranty as to the forecast being true, but rather a warranty that the seller had taken reasonable care in preparing the forecast. The measure of damages was confirmed as being the misstatement/negligent advice measure, involving asking not what the claimant would have earned if the forecast had been true, but what the

---

[39] Hence courts' willingness to look at post-purchase events when working out the actual value of the company: *Infiniteland Ltd v Artisan Contracting Ltd* [2004] EWHC 955 (Ch) (Park J) at paras 132–34, appeal dismissed on a different point [2006] 1 BCLC 632 (CA); *Bottin v Venson* [2006] EWHC 3112 (Ch) (Blackburne J) obiter at para 415 (deceit). This is just a way of adapting the capital value to better measure the actual lost profits or lost future value.

[40] For an example of an award of lost dividends in a late delivery of shares case, see *Sri Lanka Omnibus Co Ltd v Perera* [1952] AC 76 (PC). Such an award was also approved in *George Fischer (Great Britain) Ltd v Multi Construction Ltd and Dexion Ltd* [1995] 1 BCLC 260 (CA), although no such claim was made.

[41] *Intrum Justitia BV v Legal and Trade Financial Services Ltd* [2009] 4 IR 417 (Irish High Court).

[42] *Esso Petroleum Co Ltd v Mardon* [1976] QB 801 (CA).

claimant would have done if a different, more careful forecast had been provided. In that case the claimant would not have taken the tenancy of the business, and damages were assessed on that basis.

The same approach was taken by the Privy Council in share sale case of *Lion Nathan Ltd v C-C Bottlers Ltd* to a warranty that the seller's forecast that a company's profits would be US$2,223,000 before interest and tax for the two months after completion had been calculated 'on a proper basis' and was 'achievable based on current trends and performance'.[43] The actual profits during those two months were around US$1m lower at US$1,233,000. The Privy Council, the court's judgment being given by Lord Hoffmann, found that this was not a warranty that the profits would be US$2,223,000, but only that reasonable care had been taken in preparing the forecast, the difference being that 'The forecast, though prepared with reasonable care, may on account of unknown or unforeseeable factors turn out to be substantially inaccurate. It therefore does not warrant that the company has any particular quality'.[44] Alternatively, there may be post-purchase events which are not too remote but are not captured by (because not foreseen by) a difference in value measure. Again, in such a case the measure must be adjusted to take account of these losses.[45]

That being the case, and consistently with *Esso v Mardon* (not mentioned in *Lion Nathan*), the court asks what the claimant would have done if a careful forecast had been provided. As Lord Hoffmann explained in *Lion Nathan*:

> In this case the vendor represented to the purchaser that $2,223,000 was a figure upon which he could rely in calculating the price. The figure was in fact used in the calculation of the price. If the vendor had made a forecast in accordance with the terms of the warranty, he would have produced a lower figure and the price would have been correspondingly lower. The damages are therefore the difference between the price agreed on the assumption of $2,223,000 earnings and what the price would have been, using the same method of calculation, if the forecast had been properly made.[46]

The measure of damage therefore depends upon what would have happened but for the breach, as in misstatement or negligent advice cases[47] (and in share sale cases it is noteworthy that breach of warranty claims often sit alongside negligent misstatement or deceit claims).

---

[43] *Lion Nathan Ltd v C-C Bottlers Ltd* [1996] 1 WLR 1438 (PC).

[44] Ibid Lord Hoffmann at 1442. In fact there was an absolute warranty that the forecast up to the date of completion would be met, but only a warranty that care had been taken as regards the forecast for the two months following completion. The dispute in *Lion Nathan* only related to the two post-completion months. The pre-completion shortfall in profits below the forecast was dealt with by a price adjustment clause.

[45] Hence courts' willingness to look at post-purchase events when working out the actual value of the company: *Infiniteland Ltd v Artisan Contracting Ltd* [2004] EWHC 955 (Ch) (Park J) at paras 132–34, appeal dismissed on a different point [2006] 1 BCLC 632 (CA); *Bottin v Venson* [2006] EWHC 3112 (Ch) (Blackburne J) obiter at para 415 (deceit). This is just a way of adapting the capital value to better measure the actual lost profits or lost future value.

[46] *Lion Nathan Ltd v C-C Bottlers Ltd* [1996] 1 WLR 1438 (PC) Lord Hoffmann at 1442.

[47] The measure for contractual misstatement, or misadvice, cases is discussed above in chapter three.

(i) The Claimant Would Have Paid Loss: Recover the Extra Price Paid

It may be that had the relevant care been taken the claimant would have paid less, in which case this difference in price is recoverable;[48] and it will be even easier to prove the claimant would have paid less where the price paid was derived by a formula from the erroneous figures in the accounts.[49] It may be that, for example because of the claimant's keenness to buy the property and/or the presence of rival buyers, the claimant would have paid exactly the same;[50] likewise because an undisclosed claim against the acquired company was so weak.[51]

(ii) The Claimant Would Not Have Entered the Transaction at All: Recover the Net Losses

It may be that the claimant would not have entered into the transaction at all, in which case the net losses from the purchase are recoverable, as in *Esso v Mardon*.[52] This involves comparing the price paid (plus any subsequent costs) with the value of the property received.

(iii) Other Types of Loss

There could be other consequences: in one case it was argued that the claimant would have provided for the missed charge if it had been identified in the accounts, with various consequences, although the point was not decided.[53] In another, it was argued that the buyer would have obtained indemnities in relation to a third party claim, although this was rejected on the facts.[54] In some cases it may be that if the accounts or other information had been properly prepared there would have been a full accountants' investigation, in which case it must be assumed (in working out what would have happened) that this would have taken place and disclosed whatever matters it would have revealed, and then asked what would the claimant have done.[55]

---

[48] *Lion Nathan Ltd v C-C Bottlers Ltd* [1996] 1 WLR 1438 (PC) Lord Hoffmann at 1442; *Macquarie Internationale Investments Ltd v Glencore UK Ltd (No 2)* [2010] 1 BCLC 238 (Andrew Smith J) obiter.

[49] As in *Macquarie Internationale Investments Ltd v Glencore UK Ltd (No 2)* [2010] 1 BCLC 238 (Andrew Smith J) obiter at para 238, affirmed without considering damages at [2011] 1 BCLC 561 (CA).

[50] Cf *Sycamore Bidco Limited v Breslin* [2012] EWHC 3443 (Ch) (Mann J) at para 405; *Welven Ltd v Soar Group Ltd* [2011] EWHC 3240 (Comm) (Eder J) (misrepresentation).

[51] *Curtis v Lockheed Martin UK Holdings Ltd* [2008] EWHC 2691 (Comm) (Simon J) at para 114 obiter.

[52] *Esso Petroleum Co Ltd v Mardon* [1976] QB 801 (CA). In the usual way, the claimant will usually have to give credit for the value of the shares at the date on which it could reasonably have been expected to sell them (or any decision not to do so is a matter of the claimant's own speculation): *Smith New Court Securities Ltd v Scrimgeour Vickers (Asset Management) Ltd* [1997] AC 254 (HL) (deceit).

[53] *Macquarie Internationale Investments Ltd v Glencore UK Ltd (No 2)* [2010] 1 BCLC 238 (Andrew Smith J) obiter at para 244, affirmed without considering damages at [2011] 1 BCLC 561 (CA).

[54] *Curtis v Lockheed Martin UK Holdings Ltd* [2008] EWHC 2691 (Comm) (Simon J) at para 115.

[55] Eg *ADO Ltd v BDO Binder Hamlyn*, 6 December 1995 (May J) (misrep by accountant).

B. Identifying Reasonable Care-type Warranties?

The *Lion Nathan* decision and principle are rarely cited and discussed in relation to the measure of loss,[56] and in the majority of cases, whatever the nature of the warranty breached, the court adopts the 'warranty of quality' approach of awarding the difference between the value as is and the value as warranted.[57] This makes it difficult to work out what warranties (other than that a forecast is on a proper basis or prepared with reasonable care) should be governed by the *Lion Nathan* approach, and indicates that the *Lion Nathan* approach is applied fairly restrictively (although often without express consideration).

(i) True and Fair View in Accounts?

A key warranty in a share or company sale is that certain accounts were prepared on a true and fair basis and in accordance with relevant accounting standards. These accounts will often form the basis of the buyer's valuation, and the buyer needs to be able to rely on them. On a proper legal analysis of the 'true and fair' basis, it is clear that it is not a warranty that the accounts are true but rather that a certain amount of care has been taken in preparing them.[58] Indeed, the warranty may not be breached even if the accounts do not record the true position as to the company: the preparer of accounts cannot be criticised if they did not know about the relevant matter and should not have discovered it at the date of preparation of the accounts, and indeed it would be improper to include such a matter unless there is sufficient evidence of it at the date of preparation of the accounts.[59]

A warranty of this sort is therefore apparently similar to a duty to take reasonable care (albeit that the care or other process required will depend upon the wording of the warranty), and one would have thought that the *Lion Nathan* measure rather than the difference in value/warranty of quality measure should apply. The comments of Lord Hoffmann in relation to the forecast warranty that he found to be this type of warranty in *Lion Nathan* also apply to the true and fair warranty: 'The forecast, though prepared with reasonable care, may on account of unknown or unforeseeable factors turn out to be substantially inaccurate. It therefore does not warrant that the company has any particular quality'.[60]

The prevailing approach, however, is nevertheless to apply the difference in value/warranty of quality measure to the true and fair warranty, occasionally with express consideration of the *Lion Nathan* point,[61] but more often by agreement between

---

[56] Although the decision is often cited for the different principle as to how one measures what a valuation would have been if reasonable care had been taken. See below in chapter thirteen, section 13.3B(ix).

[57] See above in section 9.3B.

[58] *Thomas Witter Ltd v TBP Industries Ltd* [1996] 2 All ER 573 (Jacob J); *Macquarie Internationale Investments Ltd v Glencore UK Ltd (No 2)* [2011] 1 BCLC 561 (CA).

[59] *Macquarie Internationale Investments Ltd v Glencore UK Ltd (No 2)* [2010] 1 BCLC 238 (Andrew Smith J), affirmed [2011] 1 BCLC 561 (CA).

[60] *Lion Nathan Ltd v C-C Bottlers Ltd* [1996] 1 WLR 1438 (PC) at 1442.

[61] *Intrum Justitia BV v Legal and Trade Financial Services Ltd* [2009] 4 IR 417 (Irish High Court).

the parties and with little or no express consideration by the judge.[62] However, in one case Andrew Smith J accepted that the difference in the price that would have been made was the correct measure, although again without argument or express consideration of *Lion Nathan*.[63]

(ii) Other Warranties

As regards other warranties, in one case the court expressly considered whether the difference in price measure should apply and held that the proper measure for warranty claims was the difference in value, citing *Lion Nathan* but not considering the warranty of quality/warranty of reasonable care distinction set out there.[64] The warranties in that case include that full details of a pension scheme had been disclosed, and that a report on a certain contract was inaccurate and did not comply with proper accounting practices.

In another case the *Lion Nathan* distinction was expressly considered, and it was held obiter that the difference in value/warranty of quality measure did not apply to warranties that the information given by the vendor is 'true, accurate and complete in all respects', or that there is no material agreement that has not been disclosed and is likely to give rise to liability, and no litigation pending.[65] However, in an Irish decision the *Lion Nathan* point was also expressly considered and it was concluded that a warranty that information was true and accurate was a warranty of quality.[66]

C. Identifying the Careful Forecast or Other Information

Damages for breach of these type of warranties require identification of what the forecast or accounts would have looked like at the time of their preparation if they had been prepared on the proper basis: 'the crucial question ... is the ascertainment of what a properly prepared forecast would have been'.[67] In working out

---

[62] *Senate Electrical Wholesalers Ltd v STC Submarine Systems Ltd*, 20 December 1996 (May J) and *Senate Electrical Wholesalers Ltd v Alcatel Submarine Networks Ltd* [1999] 2 Lloyds Rep 423 (CA) Stuart-Smith LJ at para 24 (*Lion Nathan* was cited but this point not considered), although the court did not seem to disapprove of the difference in price measure, had it been properly pleaded: Stuart-Smith LJ at paras 47–49 and 55; *Eastgate Group Ltd v Linsey Morden Group Inc* [2001] Lloyd's Rep PN 51 (Andrew Smith J) at paras 4 and 13, appeal allowed on a different point but this point affirmed at [2002] 1 WLR 642 (CA) Longmore LJ at para 18; *Infiniteland Ltd v Artisan Contracting Ltd* [2004] EWHC 955 (Ch) (Park J) at para 100, appeal dismissed on a different point [2006] 1 BCLC 632 (CA); *Sycamore Bidco Limited v Breslin* [2012] EWHC 3443 (Ch) (Mann J) at paras 391–92 and 467 (point not disputed, although the defendant unsuccessfully tried to argue that what the defendant would have done was nevertheless relevant to causation).

[63] *Macquarie Internationale Investments Ltd v Glencore UK Ltd (No 2)* [2010] 1 BCLC 238 (Andrew Smith J) at para 239, affirmed [2011] 1 BCLC 561 (CA).

[64] *RWE Nukem Ltd v AEA Technology plc* [2005] EWHC 78 (Comm) (Gloster J) at para 5, appeal allowed on a different discrete point: [2005] EWCA Civ 1192.

[65] *Curtis v Lockheed Martin UK Holdings Ltd* [2008] EWHC 2691 (Comm) (Simon J) obiter at para 113. It is not clear that the point was properly understood, as the discussion at para 114 seems to consider that the relevant calculation is nevertheless the difference in value.

[66] *Intrum Justitia BV v Legal and Trade Financial Services Ltd* [2009] 4 IR 417 (Irish High Court).

[67] *Lion Nathan Ltd v C-C Bottlers Ltd* [1996] 1 WLR 1438 (PC) Lord Hoffmann at 1442, also 1446.

what the forecast or accounts would have looked like if properly prepared, subsequent events that would not have been available to the accountants or forecaster must be ignored,[68] save that the actual outcome can be rebuttably presumed to be what the accountants would have foreseen. To the extent that subsequent events are unforeseeable by the accountants, they must be ignored for the purposes of working out what the accounts of the forecaster would have stated if properly prepared.[69]

9.5 Indemnities

A. Quantum

The quantum of an indemnity depends upon the terms of the indemnity. Some indemnities require payment of expenses regardless of whether or not they were foreseeable or a direct consequence.[70] The amount of the indemnity is not subject to a duty to mitigate.[71]

B. Obligations to Pay Damages, Not Merely a Debt

As a matter of law, under a contract of indemnity the indemnifier is in breach when the claimant pays out something for which the indemnifier is required to indemnify, and the indemnifier is then required to compensate for the loss suffered by the claimant in making the latter's payment.[72] As a consequence, any failure to pay under an indemnity is a failure to pay damages not a failure to pay a debt, and such failure cannot itself give rise to compensation because of the rule that there can be no damages for failure to pay damages.[73]

(i) Indemnity Insurance

This applies to indemnity insurance, under which the obligation to make the insurance payout (eg for reinstatement costs) is treated as an obligation to pay unliquidated damages,[74] under the fiction that the insurer's obligation was a

---

[68] *Macquarie Internationale Investments Ltd v Glencore UK Ltd (No 2)* [2010] 1 BCLC 238 (Andrew Smith J) obiter at para 239, appeal dismissed [2011] 1 BCLC 561 (CA).

[69] *Lion Nathan Ltd v C-C Bottlers Ltd* [1996] 1 WLR 1438 (PC) Lord Hoffmann at 1447–48. In that case Lord Hoffmann did not identify any factors which would displace that presumption.

[70] See the discussion in *Parbulk AS v Kristen Marine SA* [2011] 1 Lloyd's Rep 220 (Burton J) at para 25 and the cases cited therein.

[71] Eg *Royscot Commercial Leasing Ltd v Ismail* (CA), 29 April 1993.

[72] *Chandris v Argo Insurance Co Ltd* [1963] 2 Lloyd's Rep 65 (Megaw J) at 73–74.

[73] See above in chapter seven, section 7.6F.

[74] *Chandris v Argo Insurance Co Ltd* [1963] 2 Lloyd's Rep 65 (Megaw J) at 73–74 and the authorities in n 75 below. The position is different in Scotland: *Strachan v Scottish Boatowners' Mutual Insurance Association* [2001] Scot CS 138, [2010] SC 367 (Outer House, Court of Session). See further the Law Comm and Scots Law Comm Consultation Paper, *Insurance Contract Law: Issues Paper 6: Damages for Late Payment and the Insurer's Duty of Good Faith* (2010), which recommend reversal of the rule.

primary duty to hold the insured harmless, which is then breached whenever an insured event occurs, and for which the indemnity is itself a damages payment.[75] Under English law there can therefore be no damages awarded (for consequential costs of borrowing, distress or anything else) in a case of an insurer's failure to pay or delay in paying out under such a policy.[76] However, if some separate obligation in the insurance policy is breached in failing to approve a loss or promptly to inspect the damaged property or accept liability then the rule would not apply, as breach of that obligation would give rise to liability for compensation for loss in the usual way.[77]

(ii) Demurrage

The same applies to a shipowner's claim under a charter for demurrage (the claim for payment where the charterer exceeds the agreed lay-time for loading and unloading), which is a claim for liquidated damages for detaining the vessel in breach of contract, and so there can be no claim for loss caused by failure to pay, or late payment of, demurrage.[78]

---

[75] *Firma C-Trade SA v Newcastle Protection and Indemnity Association (London) Ltd (The Fanti)* [1991] 2 AC 1 (HL) Lord Goff at 35–36.

[76] *Ventouris v Trevor Rex Mountain (The Italia Express (No 2))* [1992] 2 Lloyd's Rep 281 (Hirst J) at 292; *Sprung v Royal Insurance (UK) Ltd* [1999] Lloyd's Rep IR 111 (CA); *Normhurst Ltd v Dornoch Ltd* [2004] EWHC 567 (Comm) (Chambers QC); *Mandrake Holdings Ltd v Countrywide Assured Group plc* [2005] EWCA Civ 940; *Tonkin v UK Insurance Ltd* (2006) 107 Con LR 107 (Coulson QC). But see *Travelers Casualty and Surety Co of Canada v Sun Life Assurance Co of Canada (UK) Ltd* [2006] EWHC 2716 (Comm) (Clarke J), where the point appears to have been overlooked and damages were awarded to compensate for devaluation losses. And contrast the position where the insurer's breach is in not itself reinstating the property, in which cases damages for delay are available: *Axa Insurance UK plc v Cunningham Lindsey United Kingdom* [2007] EWHC 3023 (TCC). There are proposals to reverse the position in relation to indemnity insurance and allow damages for delay beyond a reasonable time: The Law Commission, Consultation Paper: *Insurance Contract Law: Post Contract Duties and Other Issues* (2011) and *Summary of Responses* (2012).

[77] *Sprung v Royal Insurance (UK) Ltd* [1999] Lloyd's Rep IR 111 (CA) Evans LJ at 116; *Tonkin v UK Insurance Ltd* (2006) 107 Con LR 107 (Coulson QC) obiter at paras 37–38. Such an implied duty to act with reasonable dispatch was rejected in *Insurance Corporation of the Channel Islands Ltd v McHugh* [1997] Lloyd's Rep IR 94 (Mance J). Pill LJ in *Sprung* also wondered whether there may be an exception 'where a policy is entered into whose whole purpose is to provide for the immediate repair of damaged plant and equipment', but although that may well explain that losses would not be too remote in such a case, the claim would still fall foul of the rule that the losses were caused by failure to pay damages not by the breach itself. See further the discussion and authorities cited in the Law Commission Consultation Paper, ibid, at paras 2.40–51. However, the Court of Appeal was wrong, in *Ramwade Ltd v WJ Emson & Co Ltd* [1987] RTR 72 (CA), to hold, obiter, that an insurance broker could not be liable for harm resulting from an insurer not paying the insured, as this was not liability for the broker's failure to pay damages, but liability for loss caused by the broker and resulting from the insurance policy not responding. Although the insurer would not be liable for harm consequent upon its own late payment of damages under the policy, the broker can be liable for harm consequent upon the insurer's non- or late payment of damages under the policy. See *Arbory Group Ltd v West Craven Insurance Services* [2007] PNLR 23 (Grenfell J).

[78] *President of India v Lips Maritime Corp (The Lips)* [1988] 1 AC 395 (HL). But as for a demurrage clause in a sale contract, see *Fal Oil Co Ltd v Petronas Trading Corp SDN BHD (The Devon)* [2004] 2 Lloyd's Rep 282 (CA).

(iii) Other Contracts of Indemnity

Likewise some contracts of suretyship that are, on their proper construction, promises to procure that the principal debt is paid or to indemnify the creditor are contracts for which the failure to pay by the surety is a failure to pay damages and not a debt (and so cannot sound in further damages).

The same applies to liability under a bill of exchange, which is deemed to be a liability in liquidated damages.[79]

---

[79] Section 57 of the Bills of Exchange Act 1882.

10

Negative Covenants

Damages for breaches of negative covenants, including property covenants, non-compete clauses and exclusive jurisdiction clauses.

10.1. Introduction
10.2. Property-Related Restrictive Covenants
10.3. Exclusive Jurisdiction and Arbitration Clauses
10.4. Non-Compete, Non-Solicitation, Exclusivity, Business Secret and Confidentiality
     Clauses

10.1 Introduction

THERE IS LITTLE that is special about negative covenants, ie promises not to do something. Certainly they more commonly give rise to specific relief, because it is easier to get a restraining injunction than it is to get an order for positive performance, but as regards contract damages no special principles apply save possibly for (i) the greater prevalence of damages on the *Wrotham Park* measure, because that type of award originated in negative covenant cases such as *Wrotham Park* itself,[1] and (ii) that in negative covenant cases the *Lavarack* principle does not apply.[2] Nevertheless, it is convenient to gather together a few categories of negative covenant cases which do not otherwise get much coverage in the other chapters of this book.

10.2 Property-Related Restrictive Covenants

Restrictive covenants are negative promises between neighbouring properties, usually originating upon separation of a larger property into two by a sale of part, and primarily concern restrictions on construction, development or use of the property (such as height or type restrictions). They are proprietary interests that run with the land and bind the owners of the land even if not the original promisees, outside the rules of ordinary contractual privity.[3]

---

[1] As to whether the *Wrotham Park* measure is restricted to negative promise cases, see chapter twenty-two, section 22.3C.
[2] See the discussion below in chapter thirteen, section 13.3B(viii).
[3] The principle from *Tulk v Moxhay* (1848) 41 ER 1143.

As discussed in chapter twenty-two, the typical award in cases of breaches of restrictive covenant (such as the *Wrotham Park* case itself) is an award of *Wrotham Park* reasonable licence fee damages.[4] This is because in most cases, by the usual measures no loss can be proven.[5]

In principle, non-pecuniary loss should be recoverable in restrictive covenant cases under the ordinary rules, eg where the defendant promised not to operate a business next door to the claimant's home and breached it by running a girls' school.[6] Indeed, as one commentator explains, in the classic restrictive covenant cases like *Wrotham Park*,

> [t]he undesired consequence was non-pecuniary: the views from the claimant's land were now views of a development rather than the undeveloped 'green belt'. The trial judge found that this was undesired by the claimant developer, Wrotham Park Estate Co, and reasonably so. There was a loss but it was not a pecuniary loss.[7]

In negative promises in relation to intellectual property, the *Wrotham Park* award is also common. Two of the leading Court of Appeal decisions on such awards, *Experience Hendrix LLC v PPX Enterprises Inc*[8] and *WWF v World Wrestling Federation Entertainment Inc*,[9] both fall into this category. Both decisions arose out of breaches of compromise agreements not to use or infringe such intellectual property, the *Experience Hendrix* decision relating to a promise not to exploit certain Jimi Hendrix recordings and the *WWF* decision, a promise by the former Worldwide Wrestling Federation to the Worldwide Fund for Nature not to trade under its then WWF name. The view of this author is that such awards of reasonable licence fee damages are, in the contractual context, a measure of award of compensatory damages for non-pecuniary loss.[10]

---

[4] *Wrotham Park Estates Ltd v Parkside Homes Ltd* [1974] 1 WLR 798 (Brightman J). See also *Jaggard v Sawyer* [1995] 1 WLR 269 (CA); *Gafford v Graham* [1999] 3 EGLR 75 (CA). And see the easement case of *Bracewell v Appleby* [1975] 1 Ch 408 (Graham J); *Lane v O'Brien Homes Ltd* [2004] EWHC 303 (QB) (Clarke J) on a collateral contract restricting use of land; and *Lunn Poly Ltd v Liverpool & Lancashire Properties Ltd* [2005] 2 EGLR 29 (CA) on breach of a commercial landlord's covenant of quiet enjoyment. And cf *Michael Green (Leasing) Ltd v Greatsunny Ltd* [2010] Ch 558 (Strauss QC), where obiter the judge would have been willing to make such an award had the defendant breached its landlord's waiver agreement and failed to give notice enabling the claimant to remove property fixed to the leased premises.

[5] An exception where financial loss can be proven is *British Motor Trade Association v Gilbert* [1951] 2 All ER 641 (Danckwerts J). There, the breach of a covenant not to resell a car within two years after purchase (the supply of which was limited by government regulation) without giving the seller the option to repurchase it at the list price. The recoverable loss was held to be the difference between the list price and the market price that could have been obtainable after two years, correct on the assumption that but for the breach the buyer would have sold the car back to the seller at the list price and the seller would then have sold the goods on the market.

[6] *Kemp v Sober* (1851) 61 ER 200 at 200 (actually an injunction not damages case, but anxiety damage was acknowledged).

[7] J Edelman, 'The Meaning of Loss and Enrichment' in R Chambers, C Mitchell and J Penner, *Philosophical Foundations of the Law of Unjust Enrichment* (Oxford, OUP, 2009) at 214 and 217.

[8] *Experience Hendrix LLC v PPX Enterprises Inc* [2003] EWCA Civ 323 (CA).

[9] *WWF v World Wrestling Federation Entertainment Inc* [2008] 1 WLR 445 (CA).

[10] See below text to chapter nineteen, section 19.2C(ii)(c).

10.3 Exclusive Jurisdiction and Arbitration Clauses

The primary means of enforcement of an exclusive jurisdiction clause is an injunction, but damages are available to compensate for the costs of responding to foreign litigation embarked upon in breach of a contractual clause granting exclusive jurisdiction to a jurisdiction other than that in which the litigation took place (indeed, the local costs regime may be one reason the claimant preferred the jurisdiction that was granted exclusivity),[11] or for the amount by which the result in the foreign court was worse than that in the English court.[12] Likewise damages for additional costs or the amount by which court proceedings were worse for the claimant are recoverable where the defendant litigated in breach of an arbitration clause.[13] Such damages may have to take the form of a 'loss of a chance' award, as they do in lost litigation cases.[14]

10.4 Non-Compete, Non-Solicitation, Exclusivity, Business Secret and Confidentiality Clauses

Where a defendant has breached a promise not to solicit the claimant's clients or similar, it is for the claimant to prove its lost business, which will usually but not always[15] be on a loss of a chance basis: namely the lost chance that the third party client would have sent more profitable business the claimant's way. If the clients would have gone to the defendant or another supplier than the claimant in any event, then no loss has been suffered:[16] in *Sanders v Parry* it was found that the relevant client would have changed his solicitor from the claimant after a year in any event.[17] Natural occurrences and competition mean that all business relationships eventually end.[18]

---

[11] *Union Discount Co Ltd v Zoller* [2002] 1 WLR 1517 (CA); *Donohue v Armco Inc* [2002] 1 All ER 749 (HL) Lord Bingham at para 48; *Starlight Shipping Co v Allied Marine & Aviation Versicherungs AG* [2011] EWHC 3381 (Comm) (Burton J) at para 35; *Morgan Stanley & Co International plc v China Haisheng Juice Holdings Ltd* [2011] 2 BCLC 287 (Teare J) at para 35. Loss not proven in *Elafonissos Fishing and Shipping Co v Aigaion Insurance Co SA* [2012] EWHC 1512 (Comm) (Blair J). And see *National Westminster Bank plc v Rabobank Nederland (No 3)* [2007] EWHC 1742 (Comm) (Colman J) (anti-suit clause).

[12] For further discussion of damages claims for breaches of exclusive jurisdiction clauses, which raise comity and other issues, see N Yeo and D Tan, 'Damages for Breach of Exclusive Jurisdiction Clauses' in S Worthingon (ed), *Commercial Law & Commercial Practice* (Oxford, Hart Publishing, 2003).

[13] *Mantovani v Carapelli SpA* [1989] 1 Lloyd's Rep 374 (CA) Browne LJ at 383; *A v B (No 2)* [2007] EWHC 54 (Comm) (Colman J); *CMA CGM SA v Hyundai Mipo Dockyard Co Ltd* [2009] 1 Lloyd's Rep 213 (Burton J).

[14] See below in chapter thirteen, section 13.5.

[15] *Safetynet Security Ltd v Coppage* [2013] IRLR 970 (CA).

[16] Cf *Universal Thermosensors Ltd v Hibben* [1992] 1 WLR 840 (Nicholls V-C). No loss was proven in *Lighthouse Carwood Ltd v Luckett* [2007] EWHC 2866 (QB) (MacDuff QC).

[17] *Sanders v Parry* [1967] 1 WLR 753 (Havers J). See also the obiter discussion in *Dunedin Independent plc v Welsh* [2006] CSOH 174 (Court of Session, Outer House).

[18] See the approach taken in *Jackson v Royal Bank of Scotland* [2005] 1 WLR 377 (HL), which was not a non-solicitation clause case.

In business secrets and breach of confidence cases the measure will depend upon what the claimant would have done. As has been correctly summarised by Arnold J:[19]

> Where the Claimant exploits the confidential information by manufacturing and selling products for profit, and his profits have been diminished as a result of the breach, then he can recover his loss of profit.[20] Where the Claimant exploits the confidential information by granting licences to others, and his licence revenue has been diminished as a result of the breach, he can recover the lost revenue.[21] Where the Claimant would have 'sold' the confidential information but for the breach, he can recover the market value of the information as between a willing seller and a willing buyer. Where the Claimant cannot prove he has suffered financial loss in any of these ways, he can recover such sum as would be negotiated between a willing licensor and a willing licensee acting reasonably as at the date of the breach for permission to use the confidential information which has been misused in the manner in which the Defendant has used it [*ie Wrotham Park damages*].[22]

In cases of promises to pursue a business opportunity together, which can be exclusivity or joint venture agreements and often include confidentiality elements, the claimant may be able to show that but for the breach the parties would have won a particular bid and/or made various profits together.[23] Alternatively, the appropriate award may be *Wrotham Park* damages for the amount for which the defendant would have bought out its obligations in a hypothetical bargain.[24]

In *Walford v Miles*,[25] Bingham LJ, dissenting, found that there was a binding agreement locking the defendant out of selling to anyone but the claimant while negotiations continued, and held that damages would depend upon whether the claimant and defendant would have come to terms.

---

[19] *Force India Formula One Team Ltd v Malaysia Racing Team SDN BHD* [2012] EWHC 616 (Ch) (Arnold J) at para 424. See also *Dowson and Mason Ltd v Potter* [1986] 1 WLR 1419 (CA); *JN Dairies Ltd v Johal Dairies Ltd* [2010] EWHC 1689 (Ch) (HHJ Cooke).

[20] *Dowson and Mason Ltd v Potter* [1986] 1 WLR 1419 (CA); *Cadbury Schweppes Inc v FBI Foods Ltd* [1999] 3 LRC 457 (SC of Canada). And see the loss of chance award in *Indata Equipment Supplies Ltd (t/a Autofleet) v ACL Ltd* [1998] 1 BCLC 412 (CA) and *Jackson v Royal Bank of Scotland* [2005] 1 WLR 377 (HL), both of which involved the revealing to a customer, in breach of contract, of the amount of the claimant's commission.

[21] *Seager v Copydex Ltd (No 2)* [1969] 1 WLR 809 (CA) as explained in *Dowson and Mason Ltd v Potter* [1986] 1 WLR 1419 (CA).

[22] *Gorne v Scales* [2006] EWCA Civ 311; *Vercoe v Rutland Fund Management Ltd* [2010] EWHC 424 (Ch) (Sales J); *Pell Frischmann Engineering Ltd v Bow Valley Iran Ltd* [2011] 1 WLR 2370 (PC); *Force India Formula One Team Ltd v Malaysia Racing Team SDN BHD* [2012] EWHC 616 (Ch) (Arnold J).

[23] *Jones v IOS (RUK) Ltd* [2012] EWHC 348 (Ch) (Hodge QC), obiter.

[24] *Pell Frischmann Engineering Ltd v Bow Valley Iran Ltd* [2011] 1 WLR 2370 (PC); *Jones v IOS (RUK) Ltd* [2012] EWHC 348 (Ch) (Hodge QC), obiter at paras 96 ff. The appropriate award may even be restitutionary damages, as in *Jostens Canada Ltd v Gibsons Studios Ltd* 1998 CanLII 3952 (British Columbia SC) and *Denaro Ltd v Onyx Bar & Café (Cambridge) Ltd* [2011] NZHC 52 (NZ High Court), although in Canada and New Zealand such awards are more readily made than in England. As to restitutionary damages awards and their rarity, see chapter twenty-three, section 23.2, below.

[25] *Walford v Miles* [1991] 2 EGLR 185 (CA) Bingham LJ dissenting at 189, refusing to apply the minimum obligation rule from *Lavarack v Woods of Colchester Ltd* [1967] 1 QB 278 (CA) (discussed below in chapter thirteen, section 13.3), the majority's decision upheld by the HL [1992] 2 AC 128.

Part 3

Factual Causation and Actual Loss

11

Introduction to Factual Causation

An introduction to factual causation, as dealt with by chapters twelve and thirteen.

11.1. Factual 'But For' Causation
11.2. Harm That Would Have Happened Anyway

11.1 Factual 'But For' Causation

AS INTRODUCED ABOVE,[1] the basic compensatory calculation is a simple factual comparison between what actually happened (the breach position) and what would but for the breach have happened (the non-breach position). As Hicks QC clearly put it in one High Court decision:

> I take the governing principle to be that damages should be such as will restore the plaintiff, so far as a monetary award can do so, to the position which it would have occupied had the breaches found to have been committed by the defendant not occurred. On that basis an inquiry into damages should therefore normally take the form of a comparison, in financial terms, between the events which have actually happened, and those which would have happen[ed] had the relevant breach not occurred, the former being susceptible of direct evidence, the latter being necessarily hypothetical.[2]

Teare J put the same point in this way: 'Damages are assessed by comparing the position that the innocent party would have been in had the contract been performed (necessarily, as just explained, a hypothetical exercise because the contract had not been performed) with the position that the innocent party was in fact in as a result of the breach'.[3]

The rules of legal causation and remoteness can be put aside for the time being. They are covered below in chapters fourteen to sixteen. This part (chapters eleven to thirteen) deals with the largely factual questions of the breach position and the non-breach position, and the legal rules (such as the loss of chance principle) that apply to the process of answering these factual questions.

---

[1] See above in chapter one, sections 1.3A–B.
[2] *Stephenson Blake (Holdings) Ltd v Streets Heaver Ltd* [2001] Lloyd's Rep PN 44 (Hicks QC) at para 158.
[3] *Flame SA v Glory Wealth Shipping PTE Ltd* [2013] EWHC 3153 (Comm) (Teare J) at para 18.

11.2 Harm That Would Have Happened Anyway

A simple consequence of the basic test of factual causation—that the defendant's breach must have caused the loss—is that a harm that would have occurred even but for the breach, or gain that would not have been received even if the breach had not taken place, are not recoverable as they are not losses caused by the defendant. A few examples of this may assist:

A. The Claimant Would Have Ignored the Advice or Help

A defendant's breach may not lead to loss where the claimant would have acted the same way even but for the breach.[4]

B. Expenses That Would Have Been Incurred Anyway

A claimant cannot recover expenses that would have been incurred even but for the breach, whether on the same or an alternative transaction.[5]

In *Calvert v William Hill Credit Ltd*,[6] a bookmaker who broke a (non-contractual) agreement made with an addicted gambler not to let him gamble was not liable for the £2m losses he sustained because the gambler would have suffered them anyway, gambling with another bookmaker who had not made such an agreement.[7]

C. Already Necessary Repairs

The tort case of *Performance Cars Ltd v Abraham*[8] illustrates this point. A claimant could not recover from a defendant, who caused damage to his Rolls Royce car, for a re-spray because the car already needed a re-spray as a result of an earlier accident that had led to judgment against a third party for the cost of the re-spray. The re-spray cost would therefore have been spent anyway.[9]

---

[4] See above section thirteen, section 13.2B. Also *Simply Irresistible Pty Ltd v Couper* [2010] VSC 601 (SC of Victoria).

[5] See above in chapter three, section 3.4C.

[6] *Calvert v William Hill Credit Ltd* [2009] 1 Ch 330 (CA).

[7] The Court of Appeal relied upon the scope of the claimant's duty, but properly the matter is one of causation: the breach was not even a 'but-for' cause of the loss.

[8] *Performance Cars Ltd v Abraham* [1962] 1 QB 33 (CA).

[9] However, where the other cause of the need for the expense post-dates the defendant's breach, it will often break the chain of causation and so be irrelevant to the claim against the defendant. See the discussion of *Performance Cars* below at chapter sixteen n 408 and the discussion at section 16.13D.

D. But Reject the General Argument That the Claimant Would Have Spent the Money Anyway

Of course, it is no answer for a defendant to say that the claimant would have spent the money *on something else entirely* anyway (on a holiday, etc), because such a claimant would have been able to choose to do so and had value for it.[10] If the defendant can prove that the money it cost the claimant would have been given to charity, that nevertheless does not reduce the claimant's claim,[11] nor if the claimant would have spent the money on 'extravagant living'[12] or even on drink.[13] Likewise, the fact that a company would, upon receipt of money, have passed it over to its lender,[14] ultimate beneficial owner,[15] or shareholders, is entirely irrelevant.

All money is spent, but that does not mean that the claimant has not suffered a loss by an expense necessitated by the claimant. Tort provides further examples, eg by which a claimant's nursing home expenses are recoverable even though the claimant saves the cost of hotel bills.[16] (Similarly, the House of Lords rightly rejected the argument that a warship was of no value because it would probably be lost in battle at some point anyway.[17] That loss would be in use, and is very different to loss depriving the claimant of use of the property.)

The converse is also true: if the claimant obtained money on loan and then spent it, it can rarely complain that the defendant who caused the loan has caused the claimant a loss.[18] And the loss of enjoyment resulting from being deprived of a sum of money will usually be too remote because the achievement of the money will be the object of the contract but not the further step of what might be done with it.[19]

E. The Delay Would Have Occurred Anyway

Where a defendant causes delay but the claimant concurrently caused the delay, the claimant cannot recover damages for it.[20]

---

[10] As to an attempt to begin to grapple with this issue (when is a loss that would have been suffered similar enough to the loss actually suffered to prevent recovery, and when is it something completely different, that is *res inter alios acta*?), see Mark Stiggelbout, 'The case of "loss in any event": a question of duty, cause or damages?' (2010) 30 *Legal Studies* 558.

[11] *Parabola Investments Ltd v Browallia Cal Ltd* [2011] 1 QB 477 (CA) Toulson LJ at para 55. But the judge goes too far in that dictum, see the discussion above in chapter three text to n 178.

[12] *Woods v Martins Bank* [1959] 1 QB 255 (Salmon J) at 73.

[13] Obiter in *Calvert v William Hill Credit Ltd* [2009] 1 Ch 330 (CA) at para 35.

[14] *Slocom Trading Ltd v Tatik Inc* [2013] EWHC 1201 (Ch) (Roth J) obiter at para 33.

[15] Ibid at para 34.

[16] *Shearman v Folland* [1950] 2 KB 43 (CA).

[17] *Clydebank Engineering Co v Don Jose Ramos Ysquierdo y Castaneda* [1905] AC 6 (HL) Halsbury LC at 13.

[18] See below text to chapter sixteen, section 16.6A(i).

[19] See text to chapter nineteen n 112 below.

[20] *De Beers UK Ltd v Atos Origin IT Services UK Ltd* [2010] 134 Con LR 151 (Edwards-Stuart J) at paras 177–78.

F. Personal Injury or Property Damage or Loss Would Have Occurred Anyway

The rules concerning concurrent personal injury and property damage are discussed below.[21] In summary, where an event breaks the chain of causation it is disregarded. Accordingly, even though as a matter of fact damage or destruction would have occurred subsequent to the breach in any event, that will be ignored if the subsequent damaging event breaks the chain of causation.

If a disease or condition would have come about anyway, but was accelerated by the defendant, damages are assessed only for the period of the acceleration.[22]

---

[21] See chapter sixteen, section 16.13D.

[22] Eg dictum of *McLelland v Greater Glasgow Health Board* 1999 SLT 543, 1999 SC 305 (Court of Session, Outer House) Lord Macfayden at 552. There was a similar finding at first instance in relation to nervous breakdown but that was then overturned on appeal in *Brown v Richmond Upon Thames London Borough Council* [2012] EWCA Civ 1384 (CA).

12

The Breach Position: Proving What Actually Happened

The first half of the factual causation equation: proving what actually happened and will happen, following the breach.

12.1. What Happened from Breach to Trial?
12.2. What Will Happen Post-Trial (The Chance of a Loss Principle)?

12.1 What Happened from Breach to Trial?

PROVING WHAT ACTUALLY happened, whether prior to the breach or after the breach but prior to trial, must be done on the balance of probabilities. There is no question of loss of a chance (which sometimes applies to what would have happened[1]), because neither hypothetical nor future events are involved, and the only uncertainty is that of evidence.[2] In truth, the question being answered on the balance of probabilities when proving what happened is not as to the probability of the event (which either did or did not happen) but the probability that the proffered account (that the event did happen or did not happen) is correct.[3] The burden falls on the claimant to satisfy the court 'on rational and objective grounds that the case for believing that the suggested means of causation occurred is stronger than the case for not so believing'.[4]

The events up to the date of trial will, of course, be taken into account.[5] Thus if the trial in *Giedo van der Garde BV v Force India Formula One Team Ltd*,[6] in which Mr van der Garde fought the Spyker formula one team for damages to compensate him for his lost career when they failed to provide access to the track practice laps he'd paid for, had taken place in 2013 rather than 2008–10 (judgment September 2010), the assessment might have been very different: in 2010 it was

---

[1] See below in chapter thirteen, section 13.5.
[2] See the following dicta in key tort cases: *Mallett v McMonagle* [1970] AC 166 Lord Diplock at 176; *Davies v Taylor* [1974] AC 207 (HL) Lord Reid at 213; *Gregg v Scott* [2005] 2 AC 176 Lord Nicholls at paras 9 and 15; *Nulty v Milton Keynes Borough Council* [2013] EWCA Civ 15 Toulson LJ at para 35.
[3] *Nulty v Milton Keynes Borough Council* [2013] EWCA Civ 15 Toulson LJ at para 35.
[4] Ibid.
[5] See further chapter seventeen, section 17.1A(iii).
[6] *Giedo van der Garde BV v Force India Formula One Team Ltd* [2010] EWHC 2373 (QB) (Stadlen J) at 496.

thought that his career had been severely damaged, whereas in 2013 he in fact joined a formula one team.

12.2 What Will Happen Post-Trial (The Chance of a Loss Principle)?

Damages awards are made at trial, once and for all, and must therefore measure future losses (gains that would have been made post-trial, or losses that will be incurred or will continue to be incurred post-trial) as well as past losses.[7]

However, whereas what has happened pre-trial is a matter of fact to be proven on the balance of probabilities, what will in fact happen (will the claimant find another job? will the disease get worse?) is proven on a contingency basis. In other words, the damages are discounted according to the chances that something will or won't happen. As Lord Nicholls observed in *Gregg v Scott*: 'Whether an event will happen in the future calls for an assessment of the likelihood of that event happening, because no one knows for certain what will happen in the future'.[8]

The loss of chance doctrine is discussed below, in relation to proof of what would have happened but for the breach.[9] Where what is being considered is what will happen not what would have happened, this is not really recovery of the *loss of a chance*, rather it is about measuring the *chance of a (future) loss*: had the trial been much later the loss would have been proven as (on the balance of probabilities) having in fact occurred or not having in fact occurred, but because it is too early to say there must be a discount for the chance the loss will not be suffered.[10] The approach and arithmetic are similar to that of loss of a chance, however.

Thus a claimant exposed to tax liabilities that had still not crystallised into a final figure could recover 'the value of the contingency of the potential tax liabilities in the circumstances as they appear at the trial'.[11]

The chances of earning profits from charterparties decrease over time, and allowance must be made for this.[12] Similarly, in personal injury awards for loss of future income or loss of amenity, the court must make a reduction for the natural vicissitudes of life that may reduce that loss or cut it short, or an increase for the chance that a condition will develop.[13] And in discriminatory dismissal cases the court must assess the income that the claimant may in fact earn in the future, while giving credit for that against the income the claimant would have earned but for the breach.[14]

---

[7] See above chapter one, section 1.2C(ii).

[8] *Gregg v Scott* [2005] 2 AC 176 (HL) at para 9.

[9] See below in chapter thirteen, section 13.5.

[10] In contrast, what would have happened but for the breach will always be hypothetical, even when assessed after the date of the relevant event.

[11] *Pegasus v Ernst & Young* [2012] EWHC 738 (Ch) (Mann J) at para 5.

[12] *The Racine* [1906] P 273 (CA) at 278.

[13] Eg *Johnston v Great Western Railway Co* [1904] 2 KB 250 (CA). See *Golden Strait Corp v Nippon Yusen Kubishika Kaisha (The Golden Victory)* [2007] 2 AC 353 (HL) Lord Carswell at para 64.

[14] Eg *Wardle v Crédit Agricole Corporate and Investment Bank* [2011] IRLR 604 (CA).

When considering what jobs the claimant might get in the future, this contingency approach applies.[15]

Sometimes there is no need to adjust the chance up or down, because where there are a range of things that could occur and the court estimates the mean outcome, that naturally allows for any reduction in the award for the chance that the harm will be greater than the median to be outweighed by an increase for the chance that the harm will be less. Thus:

> In the normal case if a tribunal assesses that the employee is likely to get an equivalent job by a specific date, that will encompass the possibility that he might be lucky and secure the job earlier, in which case he will receive more in compensation than his actual loss, or he might be unlucky and find the job later than predicted, in which case he will receive less than his actual loss. The tribunal's best estimate ought in principle to provide the appropriate compensation. The various outcomes are factored into the conclusion. In practice the speculative nature of the exercise means that the tribunal's prediction will rarely be accurate. But it is the best solution which the law, seeking finality at the point where the court awards compensation, can provide.[16]

Where there is really no evidence as to what will happen after trial the court will presume that the current state of affairs will continue without change (eg that a particular market has plateaued and will continue as it is).[17]

---

[15] *Bank of Credit & Commerce International SA v Ali (No 2)* [1999] 4 All ER 83 (Lightman J) at para 67.
[16] *Wardle v Crédit Agricole Corporate and Investment Bank* [2011] IRLR 604 (CA) per Elias LJ at para 52.
[17] *Evans Marshall & Co Ltd v Bertola SA* [1976] 2 Lloyd's Rep 17 (HL).

13

The Non-Breach Position: Proving What Would Have Happened but for the Breach

The second half of the factual causation equation: proving what would have happened but for the breach. Split into sections on what the claimant would have done, what the defendant would have done, what natural events would have occurred, and what third parties would have done. Includes such legal principles as the minimum performance rule (in relation to defendants) and the loss of chance principle (in relation to third parties).

13.1 Summary

THE NON-BREACH POSITION—what would have happened but for the breach—is necessarily more difficult to prove than the breach position—what in fact happened. It is nevertheless no less important in calculating damages, which are always relative to the non-breach position. Without knowing the non-breach position, the claimant cannot be placed in 'the same situation … as if the contract had been performed';[1] a harm that actually happens is only a recoverable loss if it would not have happened but for the breach, and a gain that is not received is only a recoverable loss if it would have been received but for the breach. The breach position of what actually happened must therefore be distinguished

---

[1] See further above in chapter one, section 1.3B.

from the non-breach position which concerns what might be called 'hypothetical causation'.[2]

A. Proof Depends upon the Type of Event

In general terms, and as explained further in the following sections, (i) the claimant must prove on the balance of probabilities what the claimant would have done, and what physical (non-human) events would have occurred; (ii) the claimant must prove on the balance of probabilities what the defendant would have done, although as an exception, the defendant may sometimes reduce liability by showing what it *could* have done even if that is not what it *would* have done (the *Lavarack*[3] minimum obligation rule); (iii) the claimant must prove a significant chance that a third party would have acted as the claimant alleges, and damages are then awarded on a 'loss of a chance' basis;[4] (iv) where the question is as to whether the claimant would have suffered an injury, in medical negligence failure to warn cases a special rule applies from *Chester v Afshar*.[5]

B. The 'Fair Wind' Principle

Generally speaking, as it is the defendant's fault that the court does not know what would have happened but for its breach, evidential uncertainties in establishing what would have happened should be resolved in favour of the claimant,[6] ie the burden is to an extent reversed so that it falls on the defendant to prove that the loss would not have occurred but for the breach.[7] This is sometimes described by the maxim '*omnia praesumuntur contra spoliatorem*'—everything is presumed against the wrongdoer—but that probably goes too far, and the maxim should only apply

> where the wrongdoer's acts make it difficult or impossible for the innocent party to prove its loss or where the facts needed to prove the loss are known solely by the wrongdoer and the wrongdoer does not disclose these facts to the innocent party.[8]

---

[2] *Första AP-Fonden v Bank of New York Mellon SA/NV* [2013] EWHC 3127 (Comm) (Blair J) at para 472.

[3] *Lavarack v Woods* [1967] 1 QB 278 (CA).

[4] For an example of care being taken to apply the different approaches to the claimant and to third parties, see *Ball v Druces & Attlee (No 2)* [2004] EWHC 1402 (QB) (Nelson J).

[5] *Chester v Afshar* [2005] 1 AC 134 (HL).

[6] *Double G Communications Ltd v New Group International Ltd* [2011] EWHC 961 (QB) (Eady J) at para 5 and the cases cited therein. But see further section 13.5B(iv) and chapter eighteen, section 18.2A(iii) below.

[7] *Phethean-Hubble v Coles* [2012] EWCA Civ 349 (tort, road traffic) Longmore LJ at para 90; *West v Ian Finlay & Associates* [2013] EWHC 868 (TCC) (Edwards-Stuart J) (construction) at para 181.

[8] *Ticketnet Corp v Air Canada* (1997) 154 DLR (4th) 271 (Ontario CA) Laskin JA at para 85.

13.2 What Would the Claimant Have Done?

A. The Test

(i) The Test is the Balance of Probabilities

The burden is on the claimant to show on the balance of probabilities what it would have done had the breach not occurred, and the doctrine of loss of a chance can have no application to such a question.[9]

Thus in a sale of goods case where the claimant seller had an option to supply up to 10 per cent above or below a specified amount, it was found on the balance of probabilities that the seller would have supplied the maximum permitted and damages were quantified on that basis.[10] Likewise the question of how many aircraft a claimant would have asked the defendant to maintain during the life of a contract was answered on the balance of probabilities.[11]

(The exception is the statutory unfair dismissal action, to which loss of chance operates on the question of what the claimant would have done by the *Polkey* principle, discussed below at section 13.3B(iv)(b).)

(ii) No Minimum or Maximum Obligation Test

The minimum obligation test, which assumes in certain circumstances that *defendants* would have done that which was most beneficial to them, does not apply to proof of what the *claimant* would have done. Thus where the question is what the claimant sellers would have supplied and there is a contractual tolerance, the court merely asks what the sellers would in fact have supplied, not assuming that they would have supplied the maximum (or minimum) allowable.[12]

(iii) Third Parties Linked to the Claimant

There is Court of Appeal authority that the actions of those third parties closely linked to the claimant are also to be proven on the balance of probabilities and not on a loss of chance basis, which is the rule applicable to third parties. In *Veitch v Avery* the question of whether the claimant's father would have lent the claimant

---

[9] *Sykes v Midland Bank Executor Co* [1971] 1 QB 113 (CA); *Allied Maples Group Ltd v Simmons and Simmons (a firm)* [1995] 1 WLR 1602 (CA); *Hartle v Laceys (a firm)* [1999] Lloyd's PN 315 (CA); *North Sea Energy Holdings NV v Petroleum Authority of Thailand* [1999] 1 Lloyd's Rep 483 (CA) Waller LJ at 494. But for discussion of the position where the personal representative is suing and proving what the deceased would have done, see *Feltham v Bouskell* [2013] EWHC 1952 (Ch) (Hollander QC) at para 111.

[10] *Toprak Mahsulleri Ofisi v Finagrain Compagnie Commerciale Agricole et Financière* [1979] 2 Lloyd's Rep 98 (CA) Denning LJ at 115.

[11] *Jet2.com Ltd v SC Compania Nationala de Transporturi Aeriene Romane Tarom SA* [2012] EWHC 2752 (QB) (Mackie QC) affirmed [2014] EWCA Civ 87.

[12] *Sudan Import & Export Co (Khartoum) v Société Générale de Compensation* [1958] 1 Lloyd's Rep 310 (CA) at 317 (where the court found that the sellers would have supplied 2000 tons and not made use of the tolerance either way); *Toprak Mahsulleri Ofisi v Finagrain Compagnie Commerciale Agricole et Financière* [1979] 2 Lloyd's Rep 98 (CA).

money was said to be governed by the balance of probabilities 'since the son and father were for practical purposes a unity' and so the question was essentially one of 'what would the plaintiff have done'.[13] The same principle has been applied to the administratrix of the claimant's estate.[14]

(iv) Take into Account What Actually Happened

The court will take account what the claimant actually did up to the date of trial in determining what would have happened during that period, for example it will take into account the fact that the claimant committed suicide[15] (although it will have to satisfy itself that this would have happened but for the breach).

(v) Assume the Claimant Would Have Acted Legally

Broadly speaking, it must be assumed (partly as a result of the doctrine of illegality) that the claimant would have acted lawfully and not, for example, earned greater profits by committing falsehoods against third parties.[16]

B. Negligent Professionals Cases

The question of what the claimant would have done is particularly important in professional negligence cases involving advice, where the damages claim depends upon showing that things would have been different if the claimant had been properly advised, eg it would not have entered into the transaction at all (that it is a 'no-transaction' case), or would have paid less (in a 'successful transaction' case).[17]

(i) Did the Claimant Rely?

If the claimant cannot show that it would have done anything different (eg would have ignored the proper advice or was already committed to the transaction[18]) it has suffered no loss. There are examples of such a finding in cases of a failure by a solicitor to advise of the unusual clauses in the lease[19] or the risks of litigation,[20] or where the solicitor did not hold all of the purchase monies in a transaction;[21] failure by a financial advisor to advise of the possibility of moving the claimant's

---

[13] *Veitch v Avery* (2007) 115 Con LR 70 (CA) at para 26.

[14] Salmon LJ in *Sykes v Midland Bank Executor Co* [1971] 1 QB 113 (CA) at 130 and Stuart-Smith LJ in *Allied Maples Group Ltd v Simmons and Simmons* [1995] 1 WLR 1602 (CA) at 1612B–C, discussing *Otter v Church, Adams, Tatham & Co* [1953] Ch 280 (Upjohn J).

[15] *Whitehead v Hibbert Pownall & Newton (a firm)* [2009] 1 WLR 549 (CA).

[16] *ParkingEye Ltd v Somerfield Stores Ltd* [2013] 2 WLR 939 (CA).

[17] The terms 'no-transaction' and 'successful transaction' are discussed above in chapter three, section 3.1B(i).

[18] *AW Group Ltd v Taylor Walton* [2013] EWHC 2610 (Ch) (Hodge QC).

[19] *Sykes v Midland Bank Executor & Trustee Co Ltd* [1971] 1 QB 113 (CA) (solicitor negligence).

[20] *Benedict White v Paul Davidson & Taylor (a firm)* [2004] EWCA Civ 1511.

[21] *Godiva Mortgages Ltd v Khan* [2012] EWHC 1757 (Ch) (Cooke).

pension into an immediate annuity rather than a broker-managed fund;[22] failure by a doctor to advise of the risk of failure of an operation;[23] and failure by a surveyor to advise of contamination.[24] In some cases the defendant will have an uphill battle trying to disprove reliance, for example where the defendant advised the claimant to commence proceedings and proceedings were then commenced.[25]

Of course, a claimant failing to show it would not have entered into the transaction does not mean it cannot show that it would not have done *anything* different. A claimant may be able to show that it would have ended up paying less to enter the transaction or in consequential costs, as a result of which that will be the measure of loss.[26] Proving this may be a mixed question as to what the claimant would have done and what the third party would have done, since it might be said that the third party would have (eg) refused to drop the price or alter the relevant clause. The claimant must prove on the balance of probabilities that it would have sought a lower price, but proof that the third party (eg vendor) would have accepted it is on the loss of chance measure, as discussed below.[27] *Allied Maples Group Ltd v Simmons & Simmons* is an example of this.[28]

(ii) The Test of Reliance and Inducement

In misadvice or misstatement cases, certain complexities emerge when considering whether the claimant would have acted differently. It has been held that:

> as long as a misrepresentation plays a real and substantial part, though not by itself a decisive part, in inducing a Plaintiff to act, it is a cause of his loss and he relies on it, no matter how strong or how many are the other matters which play their part in inducing him to act.[29]

The meaning of this was unpacked, and the case law set out, in considerable detail by Clarke J in the misrepresentation case of *RZO AG v RBS plc*.[30] The judge confirmed that it is necessary that the claimant show that but for the representation it would not have acted differently, meaning that if the representation had not been made *at all* the claimant would have acted differently. However, it was held that it is

---

[22] *Beary v Pall Mall Investments* [2005] EWCA Civ 415.

[23] *Smith v Barking, Havering and Brentwood Health Authority* [1994] 5 Med LR 285 (Hutchison J). However, compare *Chester v Afshar* [2005] 1 AC 134 (HL), which laid down a special rule for failure to warn cases where the medical procedure would have gone ahead anyway, but at a different time: see the discussion in chapter fourteen, section 14.5B(ii)(e) below.

[24] *Dancorp Developers v Auckland City Council* [1991] 3 NZLR 337 (HC of New Zealand). Or in the non-professional negligence context see *McWilliams v Sir William Arrol & Co* [1962] 1 WLR 295 (HL) (the deceased would not have worn a seatbelt even if there had been one).

[25] *Levicom International Holdings BV v Linklaters (a firm)* [2010] EWCA Civ 494 at paras 261, 282 and 284.

[26] See above in chapter three, section 3.4.

[27] See section 13.5, below.

[28] *Allied Maples Group Ltd v Simmons & Simmons* [1995] 1 WLR 1602 (CA).

[29] *JEB Fasteners Ltd v Marks Bloom & Co* [1983] 1 All ER 582 (CA) Stephenson LJ at 589. Approved and applied in eg *Housing Loan Corp plc v William H Brown Ltd* (CA), 18 December 1998; *Capita Alternative Fund Services (Guernsey) Ltd v Drivers Jonas (a firm)* [2011] EWHC 2336 (Comm) (Eder J).

[30] *Raiffeisen Zentralbank Osterreich AG v Royal Bank of Scotland plc* [2011] 1 Lloyd's Rep 123 (Clarke J) at paras 153–99.

not necessary that the claimant show it would have acted differently if it had known the truth (ie enough information to correct the falsehood), and that is not relevant save as evidence of what was important and so what the claimant would have done if the representation had not been made.

This is somewhat counterintuitive and it is not the way the law is applied generally. If it were, a lender could blame a valuer for a slight overvaluation merely because it would not have lent if it had had no valuation at all, even though it would have lent even if reasonable care had been taken and the true value had been given (eg because the true value was, like the advised value, within the lender's loan-to-value ratio policy limits). Clearly lenders and other claimants do not have such an easy ride, and the courts ask what would have happened if the defendant had taken reasonable care, which will often involve asking what would have happened if the defendant had given different advice or a different statement, and only fairly rarely asking what would have happened if the defendant had given no advice or made no statement.

A minor wrinkle discussed in *RZO v RBS* is the situation where the representation or advice makes important to the claimant a particular point that was not previously important; but for the representation or advice the claimant would have done the same, but once the representation had been given the matter was important and such a falsehood still counts as inducing the action of the claimant.[31] The test proposed in an earlier case and supported in *RZO* was that the defendant would have to show 'at least, the [relevant factor] having been brought to his attention, that [the claimant] would not have made enquiries to establish the true position but would have gone ahead anyway'.[32]

(iii) Indirect Reliance

In many cases of transactions that depend upon a valuation or other professional service, investors or others that have a cause of action against the professional (for example because the professional expressly undertook responsibility towards the investors) may want to complain of the professional's negligent valuation or information on the basis not that the claimant itself noticed and relied upon it being true and was thereby induced to invest, but that had the professional taken reasonable care the project or fund-raising would not have been carried out at all because someone other than the claimant would have pulled the plug. Furthermore, the claimant may have known that the valuation or information would have to satisfy that third party and taken comfort from that fact without looking at the valuation or information itself.

This sort of argument was approved by the House of Lords in *Harris v Wyre Forest DC*,[33] where the claimant property purchaser's claim against the defendant

---

[31] Ibid at para 191.

[32] *Dadourian Group International Inc v Simms* [2006] EWHC 2973 (Ch) (Warren J) at paras 548 and 552 (affirmed without discussing this point: [2009] EWCA Civ 169, esp at paras 100–105), cited with approval in *Raiffeisen Zentralbank Osterreich AG v Royal Bank of Scotland plc* [2011] 1 Lloyd's Rep 123 (Clarke J) at para 191.

[33] *Harris v Wyre Forest District Council*; heard with *Smith v Eric S Bush* [1990] 1 AC 831 (HL). Also *Yianni v Edwin Evans & Sons* [1982] QB 438 (Park J), approved in *Smith v Eric S Bush*.

valuer was not defeated by the fact that the claimant had not seen the valuation report; it simply relied on its knowledge that the mortgage lender had procured the report and was satisfied with it. Such an argument was also raised in *Banque Bruxelles Lambert SA v Eagle Star Insurance Co Ltd* at first instance.[34] Phillips J, obiter, agreed that if the negligent valuation induced the insurer to approve the loan (which he found it did not), and if the claimant bank relied on the insurer's approval in determining whether itself to advance the money, the bank could claim against the valuer. In American securities litigation, the 'fraud on the market' theory similarly allows a claimant in a case of a misleading statement (for example, in a prospectus) to satisfy the reliance requirement by showing that although the claimant did not read or hear the particular statements, the claimant relied on the market to value the shares and the market (being efficient) read or heard and relied on the statements.[35]

If a duty to take care and breach are found then, subject to points on the scope of duty, recovery should only require that the breach in fact caused the loss. It is not essential that the claimant read the information supplied by the defendant, or even knew about it. Where tort law is concerned, however, the difficulty will be the duty of care: usually it is only where the claimant at least relies on the defendant taking reasonable care that a duty will be found, although that will not always be the case.[36] Even in contract law, the scope of duty may provide a problem. It may be found that the duty of the defendant did not extend to advising a third party and thus it is not liable for the indirect consequences of such misadvice for the claimant. In one solicitor's negligence case, the lender failed because the only causal link from the solicitor's breach in failing to spot a restrictive covenant and the transaction was that if the solicitor had taken reasonable care the borrower (not the lender) would not have wanted to proceed, and this was held to be outside the scope of the solicitor's duty to the lender.[37]

C. Would the Claimant Have Repudiated?

In cases of termination for repudiatory breach, the claimant is sometimes said to be entitled to a general presumption that it would, but for the termination, have performed the contract, because the calculation of damages is on the premise that by

---

[34] *Banque Bruxelles Lambert SA v Eagle Star Insurance Co Ltd* [1995] 2 All ER 769 (Phillips J) at 794–95.

[35] *Basic Inc v Levinson* (1988) 485 US 224 (Supreme Court). But see *Amgen Inc v Connecticut Retirement Plans and Trust Funds* (27.2.2013, Supreme Court). In these cases the cause of action is a claim under the tort-like common law cause of action implied from the offence under rule 10b-5 of the Securities and Exchange Commission. The same lack of a requirement of individual reliance appears to be applicable to the English claim for misleading prospectus statements under section 90A of the Financial Services and Markets Act 2000.

[36] *White v Jones* [1995] 2 AC 207 (HL) (solicitors owed a duty to the intended beneficiaries of a will); *Spring v Guardian Assurance plc* [1995] 2 AC 296 (HL) (provider of a negligent reference owes a duty to the former employee who does not see the reference, as well as to the recipient).

[37] *Crosse and Crosse v Lloyd's Bank plc* [2001] EWCA Civ 366.

repudiating the defendant has waived its right to performance.[38] This is something of a non sequitur. At the very least, it is clear that this approach does not apply where repudiation by the claimant was 'predestined':

> [I]f the repudiating party can show that certain events were, at the date of acceptance of the repudiation, predestined to happen, which would have meant that the contract could not or would not have been performed, then the innocent party cannot recover damages on the normal assumption that he would have performed the contract according to its terms.[39]

It therefore seems that where the claimant in fact subsequently commits a repudiatory breach and this can be shown to have been predestined, that will be taken into account as something that would have happened even but for the defendant's earlier breach (unless the claimant's breach was somehow caused by the defendant's earlier breach).[40]

Indeed, the better approach must be that ordinary principles apply and even if a repudiatory breach was not predestined, if it is proven on the balance of probabilities that it would have occurred (and the defendant would have accepted the repudiation[41]) it must be taken into account.[42] This may be because 'predestined' merely means 'would have happened'[43] and so there is no separate 'predestiny' rule merely the balance of probabilities rule. Or it may be because the predestiny principle is simply wrong.[44] Indeed, the modern position appears to be that the burden falls on the claimant to prove that it would have performed.[45]

D. Would the Claimant Have Terminated Later for the Defendant's Further Breach?

If it can be shown that, but for the defendant's breach (A), the claimant would have terminated the contract at a later date for another breach (B) by the defendant, that

---

[38] *Chiemgauer Membran und Zeltbau GmbH v The New Millenium Experience Co Ltd*, 15 December 2000 (Vos J) at paras 43–44 and 47–51.

[39] Ibid at para 53, following the 'predestiny' principle from *Maredelanto Compania Naviera SA v Bergbau-Handel GmbH (The Mihalis Angelos)* [1971] 1 QB 164 (CA) Megaw LJ at 209–10 (without majority support) and *North Sea Energy Holdings NV v Petroleum Authority of Thailand* [1999] 1 Lloyd's Rep 483 (CA) (discussed at text to chapter five n 79) obiter Waller LJ at 496 (in that case predestiny was found).

[40] *Maredelanto Compania Naviera SA v Bergbau-Handel GmbH (The Mihalis Angelos)* [1971] 1 QB 164 (CA).

[41] Although as to whether the defendant would have exercised its right, see section 13.3B(iv) below.

[42] *BS & N Ltd (BVI) v Micado Shipping Ltd (Malta) (The Seaflower)*, 19 April 2000 (Walker J) at paras 43–45. There is therefore something of a clash at first instance given the decision in *Chiemgauer Membran und Zeltbau GmbH v The New Millenium Experience Co Ltd*, 15 December 2000 (Vos J) which supports the 'predestiny' principle. But see n 45 below.

[43] Cf *Commonwealth v Amann Aviation Pty Ltd* (1992) 174 CLR 64 (HC of Australia) obiter at paras 31–33, where a loss of chance test seemed to be applied as predestiny was not shown: there was a 20% chance of lawful termination by the services employer had it not unlawfully repudiated, but this did not ultimately affect the damages because they were calculated by reference to an unrebutted presumption that the claimant would have broken even: see text to chapter 18 nn 103 and 113 below.

[44] See the discussion in *Golden Strait Corp v Nippon Yusen Kubishika Kaisha (The Golden Victory)* [2007] 2 AC 353 (HL) Lord Carswell at para 61.

[45] *Flame SA v Glory Wealth Shipping PTE Ltd* [2013] EWHC 3153 (Comm) (Teare J), especially at para 85. That was a case of a shipowner who had to prove that had the charterer declared laycans for its shipments (which in breach it did not do), the owner would have been able to provide the necessary vessels.

later date provides an end limit on the lost profits that can be claimed for breach A because but for breach A, profits after that date would not have been earned.[46] However, the claimant should be able to claim under breach A for lost damages that would have been recoverable upon a claim for breach B, which claim the claimant now will not have because the contract was brought to an end early, and so the end result should be similar.

In some cases, it may be proven that the claimant would have terminated for its own reasons, eg where an employee would have resigned even if not constructively dismissed.[47]

13.3 What Would the Defendant Have Done?

A. Introduction

(i) Assume that the Defendant Would Have Performed the Contract

The premise of the hypothetical question as to what would have happened but for the breach (the non-breach position) is, tautologically, that the defendant would have performed the contractual obligation that it in fact breached.[48] As Diplock LJ has observed:

> It involves assessing that what has not occurred and never will occur has occurred or will occur, ie that the Defendant has since the breach performed his legal obligations under the contract, and if the estimate is made before the contract would otherwise have come to an end, that he will continue to perform his legal obligations thereunder until the due date of its termination. But the assumption to be made is that the Defendant has performed or will perform his legal obligations and nothing more.[49]

(ii) Thus Focus on the Defendant's Obligation

It becomes important properly to identify what the defendant was obliged to do. Sometimes it will have had a free discretion within limits, but sometimes the obligation will have been expressly or impliedly subject to fetters.[50] Where a defendant promised five years of remuneration and its factory burned down after two, that was irrelevant: the promise was of five years' work and the damages were assessed on that basis.[51] (Of course, things would have been different if the contract had been or would, if still in force, have been frustrated by the fire or terminated on some option of the defendant.)

---

[46] *Leofelis SA v Lonsdale Sports Ltd* [2012] EWHC 485 (Ch) (Roth J), obiter, affirmed [2012] EWCA Civ 1366.

[47] *Ahsan v Labour Party* (29.7.11, EAT); *Osei-Adjei v RM Education Ltd* (24.9.13, EAT).

[48] It need not be assumed that the defendant would have performed all other contractual obligations as well. See further text to n 46 above.

[49] *Lavarack v Woods of Colchester Ltd* [1967] 1 QB 278 (CA) at 294. And see *SC Compania Nationala de Transporturi Aeriene Romane Tarom SA v Jet2.com Ltd* [2014] EWCA Civ 87.

[50] See below in section 13.3B(v).

[51] *Turner v Goldsmith* [1891] 1 QB 544 (CA).

Difficulties arise when faced with the common situation in which there is more than one way in which the defendant could have performed the contract, as explained in the following sections.

(iii) Third Parties Linked to the Defendant

It has been held that the loss of chance doctrine (which applies to third parties) and not the balance of probabilities test (the ordinary test for what defendants would have done) applies to the hypothetical actions of a company distinct from but in the same group as the defendant.[52] In other words, authority does not support the application of the *Veitch v Avery* principle—by which those linked to the claimant are in some cases treated like the claimant for causation purposes—to the defendant.[53]

(iv) Minimum Obligation or Balance of Probabilities Not Loss of Chance

As explained in the following sections, the loss of chance doctrine is inapplicable to determining what the defendant would have done, which is instead a mixture of the balance of probabilities test and the minimum obligation rule. (The exception is the statutory unfair dismissal action, to which loss of chance operates by the *Polkey* principle, discussed below at section 13.3 B(iv)(b).)

B. Assume that the Defendant Would Have Done What was Least Burdensome to it

(i) Introduction to the Minimum Obligation Rule

In general terms, in determining the benefits that the claimant would have received had the contract been performed the court assumes that, where the defendant had an option about how to perform the contract, the defendant would perform in the way that benefited it and not the claimant (which usually means the defendant performs in the way cheapest for it). It need not be shown that the defendant would in fact probably have exercised that choice, only that it could have done, and the court will even ignore evidence that the defendant would not have done so, because the claimant's loss is only that to which it was entitled from the defendant, not that which it would have actually received. Diplock LJ explained in the leading case of *Lavarack v Woods* that 'the assumption to be made is that the defendant has performed or will perform his legal obligations under his contract with the plaintiff and nothing more',[54] and confirmed that it must be assumed that the defendant would have exercised any options so as to perform 'in the manner least burthensome to themselves'.[55] Or as Davies LJ put it in *The Mihalis Angelos*, it must be assumed

---

[52] *Jones v IOS (RUK) Ltd* [2012] EWHC 348 (Ch) (Hodge QC) at para 86.
[53] *Veitch v Avery* (2007) 115 Con LR 70 (CA). See above in section 13.2A(iii).
[54] *Lavarack v Woods of Colchester Ltd* [1967] 1 QB 278 (CA) at 294.
[55] Maule J in *Cockburn v Alexander* (1848) 6 CB 791 at 814, approved in *Lavarack v Woods of Colchester Ltd* [1967] 1 QB 278 (CA) Diplock LJ at 293, 296 and 297, and Denning LJ dissenting at

that the defendant would 'have performed his legal obligation and no more'.[56] This is sometimes called the 'minimum obligation' rule.

The reader should not stop reading here, however, because over time there has been a move to limit and confine (although not eliminate) the rule, returning in many situations to the ordinary compensatory principle that the claimant can recover for losses it can prove on the balance of probabilities that it would not have suffered but for the wrong.

(ii) Would the Defendant Have Conferred a Discretionary Benefit or Extended the Contract?

The cleanest application of the rule remains in the context in which *Lavarack* was itself decided. Thus a dismissed employee can claim damages for lost earnings to which he or she was contractually entitled (including salary, but also a discretionary bonus that had become mandatory for the particular year by the employer exercising the discretion prior to the dismissal[57]), but not for a retirement contribution the employer could have discontinued for any employee at any time,[58] nor for the loss of the chance of a raise that the employee could have expected to have followed the discontinuance of the pension scheme shortly after the dismissal (and which raise did follow for many, although not all of those still employed at that time).[59] In such situations it will be assumed against the claimant that the defendant would not have 'voluntarily subjected himself to an additional contractual obligation in favour of the Plaintiff'.[60]

Similarly, a claimant cannot usually claim for the chance that the defendant would have chosen to extend the employment, or other contract profitable to the claimant, beyond the contractual period.[61]

However, in one High Court of Australia decision, the claimant wife recovered damages for breach of an agreement with her husband for both the benefit she would have received during the six months of promised consortium, had he honoured the agreement and not repudiated it early, and damages on a loss of chance basis for the benefits she would have received had a reconciliation with her husband been effected.[62] The modern English approach, at least, is to apply a balance

288. Where there is a difference between the two, the focus must be on what was best for the defendant not what was worst for the claimant: see *Pacific Maritime (Asia) Ltd v Holystone Overseas Ltd* [2008] 1 Lloyd's Rep 371 (Clarke J) at para 39.

[56] *Maredelanto Compania Naviera SA v Bergbau-Handel GmbH (The Mihalis Angelos)* [1971] 1 QB 164 (CA) at 203. See also the approval of the general rule, obiter, in *Lion Nathan Ltd v C-C Bottlers Ltd* [1996] 1 WLR 1438 (PC) Lord Hoffmann at 1446.
[57] *Lavarack v Woods of Colchester Ltd* [1967] 1 QB 278 (CA).
[58] *Beach v Reed Corrugated Cases Ltd* [1956] WLR 807 (Pilcher J) at 817.
[59] The majority in *Lavarack v Woods of Colchester Ltd* [1967] 1 QB 278 (CA).
[60] *Lavarack v Woods of Colchester Ltd* [1967] 1 QB 278 (CA) Russell LJ at 298.
[61] Diplock LJ in *Lavarack v Woods of Colchester Ltd* [1967] 1 QB 278 (CA) at 298. See also *Days Medical Aids v Pihsiang Machinery Manufacturing Co Ltd* [2004] EWHC 44 (Comm) (Langley J) at 267(5), although the judge did not put it in exactly these terms. But see *Commonwealth v Amann Aviation Pty Ltd* (1992) 174 CLR 64 (HC of Australia), discussed below in section 13.3B(vi).
[62] *Fink v Fink* (1946) 74 CLR 127 (HC of Australia).

of probabilities approach to ask what would have happened between the claimant and defendant.

(iii) Alternative Modes of Performance

Where there are contractually specified alternative modes of performance or a contractually specified range or tolerance within which performance must fall, the court will assume that the defendant would have chosen the mode least onerous to it. Where the defendant can deliver to two ports but delivers to neither, damages will be measured as if it had delivered to the nearer one.[63] Where the defendant seller should have delivered goods and had a contractual tolerance for the shipment, it is assumed that the defendant would have delivered the lowest amount contractually permitted.[64] Likewise where the defendant buyer should have accepted goods and had a contractual tolerance, it is assumed that the defendant would have bought the least amount permitted.[65] Where the defendant seller's failure to have all the documents in order delayed the vessel's berthing, but the seller loaded at a faster rate than that expressly permitted in the contract (ie chose the fastest mode of performance) and so would have finished within the period of lay-time permitted even had it started at the proper date, no loss had been caused.[66] Where a charterer repudiated, it was assumed that on the final voyage the vessel would have been underladen and gone to the nearest port so as to give the minimum hire payable to the claimant owner.[67] And where a charterer would have had an option as to the way in which it would have required the claimant shipowner to perform its contract, it must be assumed that it would have operated it in the way most favourable to it.[68]

(iv) Would the Defendant Have Lawfully Terminated the Contract Anyway?

The minimum obligation rule also seems broadly to apply to the situation where a defendant repudiates but would have had an option lawfully to terminate at that date or at a later date. In such a situation it must be assumed that it would have exercised that option. This applies where the defendant would have had a common

---

[63] *Abrahams v Herbert Reiach* [1922] 1 KB 477 (CA) Atkin LJ obiter at 483.

[64] *Re Thornett & Fehr* [1921] 1 KB 219 (contract to deliver '200 tons, 5 per cent. more or less', the court assuming the defendant would have delivered 190 tons); *Johnson Matthey Bankers Ltd v The State Trading Corp of India Ltd* [1984] 1 Lloyd's Rep 427 (Staughton J).

[65] *Phoebus D Kyprianou Coy v Pim & Co* [1977] 2 Lloyd's Rep 570 (Kerr J); *Bunge Corp v Tradax Export SA* [1981] 1 WLR 711 (HL) Lord Roskill at 731.

[66] *Kurt A Becher GmbH & Co KG v Roplak Enterprises SA (The World Navigator)* [1991] 2 Lloyd's Rep 23 (CA). This decision is difficult to explain, as Toulson LJ found in *Durham Tees Valley Airport* at paras 137–43. Patten LJ's explanation at paras 74–78 appears correct: in *The World Navigator* there was a minimum loading rate specified and the defendant was entitled to take advantage of it when damages were being calculated. See also *Spiliada Maritime Corp v Louis Dreyfus Corp* [1983] Com LR 268 (Parker J) where it was assumed that the defendant would have used all lay-days.

[67] *Santa Martha Baay Scheepvaart and Handelsmaatschappij NV v Scanbulk A/S (The Rijn)* [1981] 2 Lloyd's Rep 267 (Mustill J) at 272.

[68] *Kaye Steam Navigation Co Ltd v W & R Barnett Ltd* (1932) 48 TLR 440; *SIB International SRL v Metallgesellschaft Corp (The Noel Bay)* [1989] 1 Lloyd's Rep 361 (CA), especially Staughton LJ at 363.

law right to terminate for repudiatory breach[69] (assuming it has already been proven that the claimant would have repudiatorily breached, an issue discussed above in section 13.2C), and where the defendant would have a right to terminate for material breach under an express clause.[70]

It also applies where the defendant would have terminated under an express clause for some reason other than breach, as arose in *The Golden Victory*.[71] It was found by the arbitrator as a fact that the charterer would have lawfully terminated the charter under the war clause in 2003, rather than kept it up until it expired in 2005,[72] and this was common ground by the time the matter reached the House of Lords,[73] although the correctness of the finding may be doubtful (given that charterers rarely terminate on a rising market and the Second Gulf War led the market to rise) and it may be that the point can be explained on the alternative basis that it has to be presumed in the charterer's favour under the rule from *Lavarack*, as the arbitrator also apparently found.[74]

The approach in *The Golden Victory* reflects that of the Supreme Court of Canada a few years earlier in *Hamilton v Open Window Bakery Ltd*, where the court assumed that but for its wrongful repudiation of the marketing agency and distribution agreement after 16 months, the defendant would have exercised its right to terminate at the earliest possible opportunity, giving three months' notice after 18 of the 36 months of the contract had run, and so damages were limited to the profits the claimant would have made had the contract run for 21 months.[75] The principle was subsequently applied in the oil sale case of *Novasen SA v Alimenta SA*.[76]

In hire-purchase cases the usual assumption is that the debtor would have paid off all the instalments and not terminated earlier,[77] although in practice this does not matter because hire-purchase agreements include a minimum payment clause which means that a hire-purchaser will pay no less by terminating earlier than by upholding the agreement to term.

---

[69] *Maredelanto Compania Naviera SA v Bergbau-Handel GmbH (The Mihalis Angelos)* [1971] 1 QB 164 (CA) (charterparty): 'if the Defendant has under the contract an option which would reduce or extinguish the loss, it will be assumed that he would exercise it' Lord Denning MR at 196; *Kurt A Becher GmbH & Co KG v Roplak Enterprises SA (The World Navigator)* [1991] 2 Lloyd's Rep 23 (CA) Staughton LJ at 32.

[70] *Total Spares and Supplies Ltd v Antares SRL* [2004] EWHC 2626 (Ch) (David Richards J) esp at para 210. See also *Leofelis SA v Lonsdale Sports Ltd* [2012] EWHC 485 (Ch) (Roth J) (trademark licence), affirmed [2012] EWCA Civ 1366.

[71] *Golden Strait Corp v Nippon Yusen Kubishika Kaisha (The Golden Victory)* [2007] 2 AC 353 (HL). See above in section1 3.2D. See also *Automotive Latch Systems Ltd v Honeywell International Inc* [2008] EWHC 2171 (Comm) (Flaux J) at paras 705 ff.

[72] *The Golden Victory* [2006] 1 WLR 533 (CA) at para 6 (Lord Mance).

[73] Ibid [2007] 2 AC 353 (HL) at para 28 (Lord Scott).

[74] Lord Mance in the Court of Appeal: [2006] 1 WLR 533 (CA) at para 6.

[75] *Hamilton v Open Window Bakery Ltd* [2004] 1 SCR 303 (SC of Canada).

[76] *Novasen SA v Alimenta SA* [2013] EWHC 345 (Comm) (Popplewell J) at para 23, although the point was sensibly not disputed (see paras 12–14) despite Hamblen J's obiter comments in *Bunge SA v Nidera BV (The Union Power)* [2013] EWHC 84 (Comm) at paras 54–55.

[77] *Yeoman Credit Ltd v Waragowski* [1961] 1 WLR 1124 (CA); *Overstone Ltd v Shipway* [1962] 1 WLR 117 (CA). See further the developments in *Financings Ltd v Baldock* [1963] 2 QB 104 (CA).

(a) Wrongful Dismissal from Employment (the Common Law Claim)

The *Lavarack* minimum obligation principle is the major limiting factor in the common law claim for wrongful dismissal (ie dismissal in breach of the contract of employment), which is where the principle originated. The recovery in a wrongful dismissal case is therefore the additional amount the claimant would have earned if the defendant had lawfully terminated the employment, which usually confines damages to the period of extra employment during any contractual dismissal process or, more usually, contractual or statutory minimum notice period.[78]

(b) Unfair Dismissal from Employment (the Statutory Action)

The position is different in relation to the statutory action for unfair dismissal which, in summary, applies a loss of chance approach to what the defendant employer would have done (in contrast with the general rule in contract law).

By way of introduction to the action: unfair dismissal awards are statutory and include a 'basic award' which is non-compensatory and depends upon the length of time the claimant has been employed and various other factors.[79] The award also includes a statutory 'compensatory award'[80] which applies largely the same principles as common law contract damages.[81] The similarities with the common law principles should not be overstated. First, the statutory award is subject to a statutory cap.[82] Secondly, the 'loss' recoverable under the statutory award is only economic loss.[83] Thirdly, the judge making a statutory award has an overriding discretion to do what is just and equitable,[84] and it has therefore been held that the ordinary principles of remoteness do not strictly apply.[85] However, the general principles of factual causation

---

[78] *British Guiana Credit Corp v Da Silva* [1965] 1 WLR 248 (PC); *Gunton v London Borough of Richmond-upon-Thames* [1981] Ch 448 (CA); *Mining Supplies (Longwall) Ltd v Baker* [1988] ICR 676 (EAT); *Ministry of Defence v Cannock* [1995] 2 All ER 449 (EAT); *Boyo v London Borough of Lambeth* [1994] ICR 727 (CA); *Fosca Services (UK) Ltd v Birkett* [1996] IRLR 325 (EAT); *Janciuk v Winerite Ltd* [1998] IRLR 63 (EAT); *Silvy v Pendragon plc* [2001] IRLR 685 (CA); *Wise Group v Mitchell* [2005] ICR 896 (EAT). If the contract is fixed term without a right to terminate on notice, then the damages will ordinarily be for the full period of the term. Statutory minimum notice periods are found in the Employment Rights Act 1996 s 86.

[79] Employment Rights Act 1996 ss 119–22.

[80] Employment Rights Act 1996 s 123.

[81] See the definition of loss (including a factual causation test) in s 123(1) and the express incorporation of the common law mitigation rule by s 123(6).

[82] Employment Rights Act 1996 s 124. The cap at the time of writing was whichever is lower of £74,200 and 52 weeks' pay, with 'pay' as defined in Chapter II Employment Rights Act 1996.

[83] *Norton Tool Co Ltd v Tewson* [1973] 1 WLR 45 (National Industrial Relations Court); *Dunnachie v Kingston upon Hull City Council* [2005] 1 AC 226 (HL). And see further the discussion above in chapter five, section 5.4A.

[84] Employment Rights Act 1996 s 123(1). And see the discussion of Viscount Dilhorne in *W Devis & Sons Ltd v Atkins* [1977] AC 931 (HL) at 955. This includes making adjustments for failure to comply with statutory codes of practice: see Employment Rights Act 1996 s124A.

[85] *Leonard v Strathclyde Buses Ltd* [1998] IRLR 693 (Court of Session), approved in *Jones v Lingfield Leisure plc* (CA), 20 May 1999 and applied in *Balmoral Group Ltd v Rae* (EAT), 25 January 2000, although it is far from clear that the same results would not have been reached on correct application of conventional common law principles of causation and remoteness, rather than by rejecting them (ie the decision on this point may be obiter).

and mitigation are the same.[86] Fourthly, as part of this just and equitable principle, judges can reduce the award for contributory fault.[87]

A further striking difference is the approach to proving what would have happened but for the unfair dismissal. Even when considering what the defendant would have done, the *Lavarack* principle does not apply and there is no assumption that the defendant would have dismissed the employee lawfully as soon as possible. Instead, a loss of chance approach applies, whether the issue is what the defendant employer would have done (and in particular whether the employer would have lawfully dismissed the employee had the proper consultation or other procedure or decision-making process taken place); what the claimant would have done (and in particular whether he or she would have left of their own accord); or what external events such as illness or collapse of the business would have occurred.

This loss of chance principle in unfair dismissal cases comes from *Polkey v AE Dayton Services Ltd*[88] and a reduction for such a chance is known as a '*Polkey* reduction' (and, alongside the reduction for contributory fault and the reduction for the likely replacement job that the claimant will find in mitigation of loss, forms a routine reduction in unfair dismissal cases). Such a reduction is made as part of the determination of what award is just and equitable.[89] The court must consider not a hypothetical employer but 'the employer who is before the Tribunal, on the assumption that the employer would this time have acted fairly',[90] ie what the actual employer would or might have done.

Accordingly, an employee will have his or her award reduced to reflect the chance that, even if the employee had not been unfairly dismissed, it would or might have been fairly dismissed at some later point. This may be because the business would or might have closed down;[91] the employer would or might have fairly dismissed the employee for misconduct or another reason;[92] the claimant would or might have left the job voluntarily (but not where, as is more likely, the claimant would have only left for a better job than that with the defendant or than the claimant has in fact secured after the dismissal),[93] or on expiry of a work permit,[94] or due to illness;[95] or, for example, a long army career would or might have ended

---

[86] Employment Rights Act 1996, s 123(4). And therefore the same as in non-statutory claims where the claimant is deprived of employment, for example through breach of the mutual obligation of trust and confidence: obiter in *Malik v Bank of Credit & Commerce International SA* [1998] 1 AC 20 (HL).

[87] Employment Rights Act 1996 sub-ss 122(2) and 123(6); *Nelson v British Broadcasting Corp* [1979] ICR 110 (CA).

[88] *Polkey v AE Dayton Services Ltd* [1988] ICR 442 (HL). See also *Fisher v California Cake & Cookie Ltd* [1997] IRLR 212 (EAT); *Software 2000 Ltd v Andrews* [2007] ICR 825 (EAT), especially at para 54; *Scope v Thornett* [2007] ICR 236 (CA) (where the general principle and previous authorities were discussed); *Chagger v Abbey National plc* [2010] ICR 397 (CA), especially at paras 57 and 76.

[89] *Gover v Propertycare Ltd* [2006] 4 All ER 69 (CA).

[90] *Hill v Governing Body of Great Tey Primary School* [2013] ICR 691 (EAT) at para 24.

[91] *James W Cook & Co (Wivenhoe) Ltd v Tipper* [1990] IRLR 386 (CA).

[92] *Polkey v AE Dayton Services Ltd* [1988] ICR 442 (HL); *O'Donughue v Redcar & Cleveland Borough Council* [2001] IRLR 615 (CA) (discriminatorily dismissed barrister would have been lawfully dismissed within six months due to antagonistic attitude).

[93] *Chagger v Abbey National plc* [2010] ICR 397 (CA) Elias LJ at para 71; *Wardle v Crédit Agricole Corporate and Investment Bank* [2011] IRLR 604 (CA) Elias LJ at para 65.

[94] *Kings Castle Church v Okukusie* (EAT) 13 June 2012.

[95] *Seafield Holdings Ltd v Drewett* [2006] ICR 1413 (EAT).

for some other reason.[96] Because the minimum obligation principle does not apply here, if an employer in fact had a fair ground upon which it could have dismissed the employee but would not or might not have done so, the compensatory award for unfair dismissal will not be reduced on account of the fair ground for dismissal.[97]

If upon the correct observance of a redundancy procedure another job would have been offered, the court had to assess the profits that would have been earned under that job.[98]

Given the many contingencies that can arise and the fluidity of employment, it will rarely be appropriate to find that the claimant would have remained employed by the defendant for his or her full career and/or that the claimant will not (in mitigation) find a replacement job at any time in their remaining career.[99]

(v) Limits on the Defendant's Discretion

One set of situations in which the operation of the minimum obligation principle is confined is where there is a contractual limit on the defendant's discretion under its obligation. To put it another way the defendant's minimum obligation is not unfettered. Sometimes, the fetter will be express;[100] more often it will only be implied.

The minority explanation of *Abrahams v Reiach (Herbert) Ltd*[101] was that a publisher which was obliged to publish a book could not limit its damages payable to the author on the grounds that they would have published the absolute minimum number of copies that could amount to a publication, as the publisher was impliedly obliged to act reasonably.[102] The same was true of a purchaser of a large amount of clothing in *Paula Lee Ltd v Robert Zehil & Co Ltd*, which was impliedly required to make a reasonable selection of clothing when purchasing.[103] Where, in *Chaplin v Hicks*, the claimant had lost the chance that the defendant would award her a prize in the competition, the claimant was still able to recover for the lost chance because the defendant was obliged to pick a winner (rather than giving no one the prize) and indeed had an implied obligation to do so in good faith.[104] And in the case of *Lion Nathan Ltd v C-C Bottlers Ltd*, which concerned a share sale contract in which the vendor had warranted that forecasts had been prepared on a proper (careful) basis, the court would not assume that but for the breach the vendor would have produced

---

[96] *Ministry of Defence v Wheeler* [1998] 1 WLR 637 (CA).

[97] *Trico-Folberth Ltd v Devonshire* [1989] ICR 747 (CA).

[98] *Polkey v AE Dayton Services Ltd* [1988] ICR 442 (HL); *Red Bank Manufacturing Co Ltd v Meadows* [1992] ICR 204 (EAT).

[99] *Wardle v Crédit Agricole Corporate and Investment Bank* [2011] IRLR 604 (CA) Elias LJ at para 50; but such a finding was made in *Chagger v Abbey National plc* [2010] ICR 397 (CA).

[100] Eg *Commonwealth v Amann Aviation Pty Ltd* (1992) 174 CLR 64 (HC of Australia), especially Mason CJ and Dawson J at para 62.

[101] *Abrahams v Reiach (Herbert) Ltd* [1922] 1 KB 477 (CA).

[102] Ibid Scrutton LJ. This case is discussed further below at text to n 118.

[103] *Paula Lee Ltd v Robert Zehil & Co Ltd* [1983] 2 All ER 390 (Mustill J).

[104] *Chaplin v Hicks* [1911] 2 KB 786 (CA), discussed by Diplock LJ in *Lavarack v Woods of Colchester Ltd* [1967] 1 QB 278 (CA) at 295. See similarly *MJB Enterprises Ltd v Defence Construction (1951) Ltd* [1999] 1 SCR 619 (SC of Canada): defendant failed to follow tender rules and picked a third party; court ignored defendant's technical right under a 'privilege clause' to reject all of the tenders, presumably because it was contrary to business sense and the defendant's interests, and found had it followed the tender rules the claimant would have won the contract and so lost the profits of that contract.

the *highest* careful forecast figure but instead assumed it would have produced the *most likely* careful figure, as the forecast is a good faith prediction of the most probable outcome (and therefore usually somewhere in the middle of the range).[105]

Thus in *Cantor Fitzgerald International v Horkulak*,[106] a manager at a swaps brokership was entitled to damages for loss of his discretionary bonus (which was very much a central part of the remuneration structure in that industry) because the employer had been obliged to exercise its discretion as regards the bonus in good faith and rationally. In such a case the claimant can recover the minimum reasonable sum that could have been awarded. Similarly in *Clark v BET plc*[107] the claimant was obliged to pay a bonus but had a discretion as to the amount, although could not exercise that discretion irrationally or capriciously, and therefore the defendant was obliged to compensate for loss of a bonus properly determined. A similar requirement that the claimant not act irrationally has also been implied into a clause giving an express right to terminate if in the claimant's sole discretion it determines that continued performance is not commercially viable.[108] Such a fetter on discretion will not always be implied, however, and will depend upon the particular contract.[109]

(vi) *The Court Will Not Make Unrealistic Assumptions as to the Defendant's Business Decisions*

> [O]ne must not assume that [the defendant] will cut off his nose to spite his face and so control these events as to reduce his legal obligations to the plaintiff by incurring greater loss in other respects.[110]

By this principle, although a defendant might have only been obliged to pay the claimant for as long the defendant continued in business, it cannot be assumed that the defendant would have ceased its business. Indeed this would not be the least burdensome mode of performance for the defendant. If a defendant might only have been obliged to pay the claimant a pension for so long as the employee pension scheme continued, it cannot be assumed that the defendant would have stopped the pension scheme[111] (although it might be proven that the scheme would in fact have been discontinued, for example by evidence that it had been discontinued by the date of trial).

In the important Australian case of *Commonwealth v Amann Aviation Pty Ltd*,[112] Amann sought damages for loss of development of its business upon repudiation of a contract for them to provide coastline aerial surveillance services. In a renewal tender, Amann (having already sunk the front-end costs) would have been much cheaper than its competitors (indeed the profitability of the venture for Amann was

---

[105] *Lion Nathan Ltd v C-C Bottlers Ltd* [1996] 1 WLR 1438 (PC). See further below in section 13.3B(ix).

[106] *Cantor Fitzgerald International v Horkulak* [2008] EWCA Civ 1287.

[107] *Clark v BET plc* [1997] IRLR 348 (Timothy Walker J).

[108] *Automotive Latch Systems Ltd v Honeywell International Inc* [2008] EWHC 2171 (Comm) (Flaux J) at para 711.

[109] Compare *Rutherford v Seymour Pierce Ltd* [2010] EWHC 375 (QB) (Coulson J).

[110] *Lavarack v Woods of Colchester Ltd* [1967] 1 QB 278 (CA) Diplock LJ at 294–96.

[111] *Bold v Brough, Nicholson & Hall Ltd* [1964] 1 WLR 201 (Phillimore J).

[112] *Commonwealth of Australia v Amann Aviation Pty Ltd* (1992) 174 CLR 64 (HC of Australia).

dependent upon getting renewal), and so as the court assumed that the employer would have acted in its own interests it had to assume that the employer probably would have renewed the contract.[113]

Other decisions may be partly explicable on this basis, such as the clothing supply case of *Paula Lee Ltd*.[114] The damages payable by a repudiating clothing distributor who had undertaken to buy 16,000 garments from the claimant for each of two seasons would not be assessed on the basis that the defendant would have bought 16,000 of the cheapest garments, as it never would have done this, such a collection being entirely unsellable and alienating the defendant's wholesalers (although the decision was explained by Mustill J as based on an implied obligation to make a reasonable selection).[115]

(vii) The Rule Does Not Apply to Resolve Vagueness of a Single Obligation

The biggest cut-back of the minimum obligation principle is that it only applies to optional extras (such as in *Lavarack*) or alternative modes of performance identified in a contract (such as alternative ports or a contractual tolerance) and not a single but vague obligation which admits of different levels of performance but where the range is not specified within the contract. In these latter cases the minimum obligation rule does not apply and a more practical approach is taken. The approach is found in a passage in Patten LJ's judgment in *Durham Tees Valley Airport Ltd v bmibaby Ltd*, approved by the rest of the Court of Appeal:

> The court, in my view, has to conduct a factual inquiry as to how the contract would have been performed had it not been repudiated. Its performance is the only counter-factual assumption in the exercise. On the basis of that premise, the court has to look at the relevant economic and other surrounding circumstances to decide on the level of performance which the Defendant would have adopted. The judge conducting the assessment must assume that the Defendant would not have acted outside the terms of the contract and would have performed it in his own interests having regard to the relevant factors prevailing at the time. But the court is not required to make assumptions that the defaulting party would have acted uncommercially merely in order to spite the Claimant. To that extent, the parties are to be assumed to have acted in good faith although with their own commercial interests very much in mind.[116]

The Court therefore directed that there be an assessment of the loss of profits suffered by reason of the defendant failing to operate a two-aircraft-based operation at the claimant's airport for the relevant period on that basis, and not on the assumption that the defendant would have operated the minimum number of flights

---

[113] See also the discussion of in *Mulvenna v Royal Bank of Scotland plc* [2003] EWCA Civ 1112 Sir Anthony Evans at para 35.

[114] *Paula Lee Ltd v Robert Zehil & Co Ltd* [1983] 2 All ER 390 (Mustill J).

[115] Note also that, according to *Page v Combined Shipping and Trading Co Ltd* [1997] 3 All ER 656 (CA), damages under the Commercial Agents (Council Directive) Regulations 1993 are based not on the minimum obligation principle but on the normal commission that would have been earned.

[116] *Durham Tees Valley Airport Ltd v bmibaby Ltd* [2011] 1 Lloyd's Rep 68 (CA) Patten LJ at para 79, with which paragraph Toulson LJ expressly agreed at para 147 after a reasoned judgment, Mummery LJ agreeing with both judgments at para 150.

possible under the contract whilst allowing in the defendant's favour for the maximum number of groundings for maintenance, etc.

This distinction between alternative modes of performance and a single obligation was taken from the majority decision of the Court of Appeal in *Abrahams v Reiach (Herbert) Ltd*,[117] where the obligation to publish the claimant's book could not be assumed to have been satisfied by printing the minimum number of copies but rather it was held that the court must enquire as to a normal amount that would have been published in such a print run.[118] As Toulson LJ explained in *Durham Tees Valley Airport*,

> the question [*in Abrahams*] was not how the Defendants might have carried on their business in a way that would involve the least obligation towards the Plaintiff. The proper method of assessment was quite different, namely to make a reasonable computation of the amount which the Plaintiffs would have received, taking into account everything that was likely to have affected the size of the publication.

This distinction, which will not always be easy to apply, was justified and explained by Toulson LJ in *Durham Tees Valley Airport* on the basis of practicality:

> There is good practical reason for this. Where a contract imposes alternative obligations the contract itself will identify them. But where there is a single obligation expressed in broad terms, it may be conceptually very difficult to identify as a theoretical exercise what would have been a minimum performance level, as *Abrahams v Reiach* demonstrated. In that case the damages of £100 which the Court of Appeal considered appropriate would have been equivalent to the royalties on 6,000 copies. Would the printing of 6,000 copies have been a minimum contractual performance? If so, why? Why not 5,500 or 5,000? The questions are impossible to answer and it is notable, as I have said, that although Scrutton LJ stated that he considered what was the minimum number which would constitute a contractual performance, he did not state his conclusion or reasoning. It would be more possible, as the majority did, to make a broad brush assessment of the number of copies which the publishers would have been likely to print having regard to the potential saleability of the book. For that reason, the approach of Atkin and Bankes LJ affords a more practical and realistic way of assessing the true loss suffered by the breach. Indeed, the logic of the publishers' argument, as their counsel submitted, was that the authors should have recovered only nominal damages. This would not have done justice.[119]

This gives some assistance in application of the distinction. Where the contract provides a minimum level of obligatory performance or different alternatives, the defendant is entitled to the assumption that it would have done the least burdensome thing, but where there is no such express or implied specification of the minimum or of alternatives, the court must take a more realistic view rather than seeking itself

---

[117] *Abrahams v Reiach (Herbert) Ltd* [1922] 1 KB 477 (CA). See also *TCN Channel 9 Ltd v Hayden Enterprises Ltd* (1989) 16 NSWLR 130 (New South Wales CA) at 153.

[118] Bankes and Atkin LJJ in *Abrahams*. Scrutton LJ implied a term that the print run had to be reasonable, and so avoided the point. See the discussion in *Durham Tees Valley Airport Ltd v bmibaby Ltd* [2011] 1 Lloyd's Rep 68 (CA) Patten LJ at paras 65–69 and 79 and Toulson LJ at paras 121–32, Toulson LJ at 135 and 144 doubting Mustill LJ's analysis of *Abrahams* in *Paula Lee Ltd v Robert Zehil & Co Ltd* [1983] 2 All ER 390 at 394. See also Lord Denning MR's dissent in *Abrahams* in his dissent in *Lavarack v Woods of Colchester Ltd* [1967] 1 QB 278 (CA), approved by Toulson LJ in *Durham Tees Valley Airport* [2011] 1 Lloyd's Rep 68 at para 131.

[119] *Durham Tees Valley Airport* [2011] 1 Lloyd's Rep 68 at para 132. See also para 144.

to work out what would have been the minimum the defendant could have done. Viewed in this way, the *Lavarack* principle is relatively confined.

(viii) The Rule Does Not Apply to Negative Obligations

In *Jones v IOS (RUK) Ltd*,[120] it was alleged that the defendant had breached a confidentiality agreement and, had it not done so, would have entered a joint bid with the claimant and won the tender. At the summary judgment stage, Roth J considered the *Durham Tees Valley Airport* decision[121] and held that the minimum obligation principle had no application to negative promises because there the question is not what benefits would have been provided.[122] Thus, in asking what the defendant would have done if it had not used the claimant's confidential information, the court must apply the simple balance of probabilities test.[123] Roth J had relied upon Bingham LJ's dissent in *Walford v Miles*[124] that if there were a binding lock-out agreement in that case the court would have to just determine on ordinary principles whether or not the negotiations of the claimant and defendant would have ended in an agreement.

At trial, Hodge QC supported Roth J's finding, although not expressing a view as to the positive/negative obligation distinction, and instead correctly pointing out that the case was one where the loss did not in fact turn upon the decision or action of the defendant but rather that of RIA, a separate company in the same group as the defendant but not a party to the contract, and so was a loss of chance case and did not give rise to the minimum obligation principle.[125]

It remains to consider whether the positive/negative obligation distinction has merit as regards the minimum obligation rule. At heart the problem may be, as Hodge QC observed, that the overall *Lavarack* rule is questionable and a basic balance of probabilities rule fairer: 'One may question whether such an attitude merits the application of a blanket rule of law, operating by way of an irrebuttable presumption, governing the hypothetical future actions of the contract-breaker'.[126] However, if the *Durham Tees Valley Airport* principle—which does have the authority of the Court of Appeal—is the correct basis for circumscribing the scope of the *Lavarack* rule, then Roth J is correct that it is difficult to see how the rule could be applied in negative covenant cases. In such cases the contract does not provide for alternative methods of performance or a fixed tolerance for performance (of which it might be assumed that the defendant would have chosen the least burdensome), instead merely providing for what the defendant must not do. Accordingly, on the authority of *Durham Tees Valley Airport*, in a negative covenant case the inquiry

---

[120] *Jones v IOS (RUK) Ltd* [2010] EWHC 1743 (Ch) (Roth J).

[121] *Durham Tees Valley Airport Ltd v bmibaby Ltd* [2011] 1 Lloyd's Rep 68 (CA), discussed in the previous section.

[122] *Jones v IOS (RUK) Ltd* [2010] EWHC 1743 at para 74.

[123] Ibid at para 75.

[124] *Walford v Miles* [1991] 2 EGLR 185 (CA) Bingham LJ at 189 refusing to apply the minimum obligation rule from *Lavarack*. See Roth J at paras 77–78 in *Jones v IOS (RUK) Ltd*.

[125] *Jones v IOS (RUK) Ltd* [2012] EWHC 348 (Ch) (Hodge QC) at paras 83 ff.

[126] Ibid at para 86.

into what the defendant would have done is a question of fact and not a question of the minimum obligation principle.

(ix) Duty of Care Cases

Dealing first with a slightly different point: when determining whether a professional or other has *breached* its duty of care, it must be shown that no reasonable professional would have acted in the way the defendant acted. This is because there is more than one way of giving reasonable advice and reasonable professionals may disagree (without being negligent).[127] In valuation cases, where the advice is essentially as to a figure (the value of the property), this margin of discretion is particularly stark: the court will work out what the central reasonable value is and then put a 'bracket' or 'band' around that of usually 5/10/15 per cent, and only if the valuation fell outside this range within which a reasonably competent valuer could have valued the property may the valuation be found to be negligent.[128]

If the conduct does fall outside the bracket and is negligent, the question then arises at the causation and loss stage as to what value it is assumed that the valuer would have chosen if non-negligent, or, more generally, what a negligent defendant would have done if it had acted carefully. Is the defendant assumed but for the breach to have performed at the centre of the band of reasonable conduct, or is it (by the minimum obligation rule) the highest non-negligent valuation or the other non-careless performance most favourable to the defendant (ie the upper end of the band)? The answer provided by Lord Hoffmann in the *SAAMCo* case is the former, as the court must form a view as to

> the figure which it considers most likely that a reasonable valuer, using the information available at the relevant date, would have put forward as the amount which the property was most likely to fetch if sold upon the open market. While it is true that there would have been a range of figures which the reasonable valuer might have put forward, the figure *most* likely to have been put forward would have been the mean figure of that range. There is no basis for calculating damages upon the basis that it would have been a figure at one or other extreme of the range. Either of these would have been less likely than the mean.[129]

Lord Hoffmann elaborated upon this, and the nature of giving reasonable valuations, in *Lion Nathan Ltd v C-C Bottlers Ltd*, in relation to financial forecasts of

---

[127] *Bolam v Friern Hospital Management Committee* [1957] 1 WLR 582 (McNair J).

[128] *Merivale Moore plc v Strutt & Parker* [1999] 2 EGLR 171 (CA); *Capita Alternative Fund Services (Guernsey) Ltd v Drivers Jonas (a firm)* [2011] EWHC 2336 (Comm) Eder J at para 145 (appeal partially allowed as to other points at [2012] EWCA Civ 1407).

[129] *South Australia Asset Management Corp v York Montague Ltd* [1997] 1 AC 191 (HL) at 221–22. See also *Goldstein v Levy Gee (a firm)* [2003] EWHC 1575 (Ch) Lewison J at para 46 and *Capita Alternative Fund Services (Guernsey) Ltd v Drivers Jonas* [2011] EWHC 2336 (Comm) Eder J at para 146 (appeal partially allowed as to other points at [2012] EWCA Civ 1407 (CA)), and the discussion of Lord Hoffmann in *Lion Nathan Ltd v C-C Bottlers Ltd* [1996] 1 WLR 1438 (PC) at 1445–47 of choosing the figure that is the middle of a bell curve of possible figures.

a business.[130] Thus the bracket becomes irrelevant once the question of causation arises.[131] Similarly, in a case of mis-investment by a trustee, the right approach in assessing the non-breach position was to take what a prudent trustee would have done, not the least that might have been achieved in the range of outcomes the prudent trustee might have taken.[132]

Of course, the above only applies where the result of the conduct would have differed. In one case a defendant valuer was careless in *preparing* a report but had it taken care the report would nevertheless have been the same.[133]

C. Take into Account Actual Post-Breach Pre-Trial Events

In determining what the defendant would have done after the breach, the court will take into account pre-trial events it knows about. There could be no claim for a loss of a bonus where an employer did terminate an employee-wide bonus scheme shortly after dismissal for reasons unrelated to the claimant's dismissal[134] (and so would have done so even but for the breach). In another case, the defendant's actually having terminated for the claimant's repudiatory breach was also taken into account when determining what would have happened but for the defendant's breach.[135]

13.4 What Natural Events Would Have Occurred?

Pre-trial natural events (eg the development of disease, the occurrence of weather, the spread of fire) are governed by the ordinary burden of proof on the balance of probabilities.[136] Thus if at the time of trial the court does not know whether the property would have been out of use but for the breach, it may be necessary

---

[130] *Lion Nathan Ltd v C-C Bottlers Ltd* [1996] 1 WLR 1438 (PC). Lord Hoffmann explained the usual process of an expert establishing such a figure at 1444: 'He is saying that $2,223,000 is in his opinion the most probable outcome, but that figures slightly higher or lower are almost equally probable and that on either side of them there is a range of possible figures which become increasingly less probable as they deviate from the mean'. (This describes selecting the high point of a bell curve).

[131] See also *Scotlife Homeloans (No 2) Ltd v Kenneth James & Co* [1995] EGCS 70 (Crawford QC).

[132] *Nestle v National Westminster Bank plc* [1993] 1 WLR 1260 (CA) Dillon LJ at 1268–69. Cf the competition case of *Albion Water Ltd v Dwr Cymru Cyfyngedig* [2013] CAT 6 at para 71.

[133] *Platform Funding Ltd v Anderson & Associates Ltd* [2012] EWHC 1853 (QB) (Thornton QC) at para 108.

[134] *Lavarack v Woods of Colchester Ltd* [1967] 1 QB 278 (CA).

[135] *Leofelis SA v Lonsdale Sports Ltd* [2012] EWHC 485 (Ch) (Roth J), obiter, affirmed [2012] EWCA Civ 1366.

[136] As confirmed in *Hotson v East Berkshire Area Health Authority* [1987] AC 750 (HL) and *Gregg v Scott* [2005] 2 AC 176 (HL). But see *Janiak v Ippolito* [1985] 1 SCR 146 (SC of Canada). Lord Brown in *Golden Strait Corp v Nippon Yusen Kubishika Kaisha (The Golden Victory)* [2007] 2 AC 353 (HL) at para 76 was therefore wrong to say that where a shipowner is claiming for wrongful repudiation of a charterparty, and at the date of trial there is a chance that war will break out and give the charterparty a right lawfully to terminate, the shipowner's damages should be measured as the loss of a chance of profits beyond that date. The profits beyond that date depend upon whether war would later have broken out, which should be proven on the balance of probabilities

to reduce the award to allow for the chance that the loss of earnings would not have been suffered, for example due to the property being damaged or destroyed anyway.[137]

Many claims for future loss of amenity or lost profits will be reduced to allow for any chance that the amenity or profits would not have been enjoyed even but for the wrong, due to some independent reason such as an injury by a future wrongdoer or illness (whether the same as caused by the defendant or a different one) that might in the future occur or have occurred (through the general vicissitudes of the claimant's life or for a specific reason),[138] or unforeseen catastrophes in the market or other business contingencies.[139]

However, where particular third party human events are involved, the question again becomes one of loss of a chance as discussed below in this chapter: thus where loss depended upon whether, but for the defendant's carelessness, a fire would have spread past a certain point, the involvement of the fire brigade in the hypothetical made the case a loss of chance case.[140]

A. Take into Account Actual Post-Breach Pre-Trial Events

Where we know what would have happened because it has happened, then, if it would have happened even but for the breach, it must be taken into account.

The outbreak of war was the event in question in *The Golden Victory*, and the court took into account that by the date of trial it was known that war would have broken out.[141] Lord Scott confirmed that had an external event which would have frustrated the contract even but for the breach, such as legislation, taken place after the breach but before trial, this too must be taken into account when assessing damages.[142] (Of course, if the contract was marketable and would have been sold before the frustrating or similar event, then the claimant may prove that it lost the sale value of the contract, as it would not have been left holding the contract when the metaphorical music stopped, but that was not the case in *The Golden Victory*.[143])

Similarly, when considering whether an award of lost earnings should be reduced for the chance that property would have been damaged anyway, where at the time of trial the court knows the property would *not* have been damaged then it must not make such a reduction.[144] And likewise in the personal injury context, eg where

---

[137] *The Kingsway* [1918] P 344 (CA) Hill J at first instance at 354; Lord Normand in *Carslogie Steamship Co Ltd v Royal Norwegian Government* [1952] AC 292 (HL) at 307.

[138] *Heil v Rankin* [2000] PIQR Q16 (CA)—police dog handler with post-traumatic stress disorder had a 75% chance that the condition would have become serious as a result of another incident even but for the defendant's wrong.

[139] *Leche Pascual SA v Collin & Hobson plc* [2004] EWCA Civ 700; *Zodiac Maritime Agencies Ltd v Fortescue Metals Group Ltd (The Kildare)* [2011] 2 Lloyd's Rep 360 (Steel J) at para 73.

[140] *J Sainsbury Plc v Broadway Malyan* (1998) 61 Con LR 31 (HHJ Humphrey Lloyd QC) at 38.

[141] *Golden Strait Corp v Nippon Yusen Kubishika Kaisha (The Golden Victory)* [2007] 2 AC 353 (HL).

[142] Ibid at para 35.

[143] Ibid Lord Scott at para 37.

[144] Lord Normand in *Carslogie Steamship Co Ltd v Royal Norwegian Government* [1952] AC 292 (HL) at 307: tortious damage to ship.

but for the breach the claimant would have died anyway,[145] or been disabled.[146] An extreme example can be found in the US case of *Dillon v Twin State Gas & Electric Co*, where a defendant would not be responsible for the claimant's death by electrocution on grabbing an uninsulated wire to arrest his fall from a girder where, had the wire not been there, the claimant would have fallen to his death anyway.[147]

13.5 What Would Third Parties Have Done? (The Principle of Loss of a Chance)

A. Introduction

(i) The Loss of Chance Rule

In contrast with past facts and the hypothetical behaviour of the claimant and defendant, the hypothetical behaviour of third parties is to be determined on a loss of a chance basis (unless the parties concede otherwise[148]).[149] This means that the claimant does not have to show that on the balance of probabilities (ie to a more than 50 per cent likelihood) the third party would have behaved so as to confer a benefit or prevent a loss, it is enough if the claimant can prove that there is a 'substantial' chance, which may well be less than 50 per cent, that the third party would have behaved in this way. The claimant can then recover the fraction of the hypothetical loss that corresponds with the chance that the third party would have acted in such a way as to make it come about.

One of the leading contract cases setting down this rule is the Court of Appeal decision in the beauty contest case of *Chaplin v Hicks*.[150] The claimant was one of 50 finalists out of around 6,000 entries who submitted their photograph and details, competing in a contest for one of 12 prizes of a job for three years as an actress at an average wage of £4 per week (some of the jobs paid more, some less). The defendant breached in failing to give the claimant an alternative appointment so that she could attend before the defendant and committee who selected the final 24 competitors, whose pictures would then be published in a newspaper from which the readers would select the 12 winners. The Court of Appeal upheld the jury's award of £100

---

[145] *The Kingsway* [1918] 1 P 344 (CA) Scrutton LJ at 362.
[146] *Jobling v Associated Dairies Ltd* [1982] AC 794 (HL).
[147] *Dillon v Twin State Gas & Electric Co* 85 NH 449, 163 A 111 (1932) (SC of New Hampshire), although query whether the proper counterfactual is what would have happened if the wire had been insulated, not if the wire had not been there at all.
[148] Such a concession was conclusive in *Multi Veste 226 BV v NI Summer Row Unitholder BV* [2011] EWHC 2026, (2011) 139 Con LR 23 (Lewison J), paras 12–13 and 213.
[149] This rule does not only apply to contract cases. See the obiter discussion in the tort case of *Feltham v Freer Bouskell* [2013] EWHC 1952 (Ch) (Hollander QC), based on the duty of care owed by solicitors to beneficiaries in *White v Jones* [1995] 2 AC 207 (HL).
[150] *Chaplin v Hicks* [1911] 2 KB 786 (CA).

at trial (equivalent to approximately a one in six chance, as against the ratio of finalists to jobs of around 4:1).[151]

The leading case confirming and delimiting this rule and explaining how it operates is the solicitor's negligence decision of the Court of Appeal in *Allied Maples v Simmons and Simmons*.[152] The claimant was seeking to buy some department stores through an asset takeover agreement. Had the defendant solicitors noticed and advised the claimant that the vendor had, in the course of drafting and negotiations, narrowed a particular draft warranty in an asset takeover agreement, the question then arose whether the claimant would have sought to put back the wider warranty, and whether the vendor and its solicitors would have agreed. The former question was a matter for proof on the balance of probabilities,[153] but the latter was a question of loss of a chance, as Stuart-Smith LJ explained:[154]

> In many cases the plaintiff's loss depends on the hypothetical action of a third party, either in addition to action by the plaintiff, as in this case, or independently of it. In such a case, does the plaintiff have to prove on balance of probability, as Mr. Jackson submits, that the third party would have acted so as to confer the benefit or avoid the risk to the plaintiff, or can the plaintiff succeed provided he shows that he had a substantial chance rather than a speculative one, the evaluation of the substantial chance being a question of quantification of damages?

> … in my judgment, the plaintiff must prove as a matter of causation that he has a real or substantial chance as opposed to a speculative one. If he succeeds in doing so, the evaluation of the chance is part of the assessment of the quantum of damage, the range lying somewhere between something that just qualifies as real or substantial on the one hand and near certainty on the other. I do not think that it is helpful to seek to lay down in percentage terms what the lower and upper ends of the bracket should be.

The Court of Appeal was addressing, as a preliminary issue, whether there was a 'real and substantial chance' of the vendor having agreed to a broader warranty. They found by a majority (Millett LJ dissenting) that there was. The chance, when quantified (at a later hearing), would then be multiplied by the lost benefit to calculate the damages.

(a) Are All Cases Involving Third Parties Loss of Chance Cases?

Not every case involving a third party is a loss of chance case.[155] If the third party would have to apply objective criteria and value something then a loss of chance approach is inappropriate and the court must instead make a finding as to the valuation that would have been reached.[156]

---

[151] If it was the defendant who made the decision then this should not be a loss of chance case by the rule from *Allied Maples Group Ltd v Simmons and Simmons* [1995] 1 WLR 1602 (CA), as Walker LJ observed in *Bank of Credit and Commerce International v Ali (No 3)* [2002] All ER 750 (CA) at para 60. However, it does appear that it was not just the defendant but also a committee and then the public who made the relevant decision: see the facts in *Chaplin v Hicks* [1911] 2 KB 786 (CA) at 786–87.

[152] *Allied Maples Group Ltd v Simmons and Simmons* [1995] 1 WLR 1602 (CA).

[153] See also *Maden v Clifford Coppock & Carter* [2005] 2 All ER 43 (CA) Neuberger LJ at para 50.

[154] *Allied Maples Group Ltd v Simmons and Simmons* [1995] 1 WLR 1602 (CA) at 1609 ff and 1614. See also Millett LJ at 1623.

[155] *Law Debenture Trust Corp plc v Elektrim SA* [2010] EWCA Civ 1142 Arden LJ at para 45.

[156] Ibid.

(b) Why are Third Parties Treated Differently?

Although largely academic, because the rule is well settled, it is worth asking why hypothetical third party actions are governed by the loss of a chance rule, whereas hypothetical natural events or claimant or defendant actions are governed by the ordinary balance of probabilities rule.

The difference between natural events and human events may rest on certain physical and metaphysical assumptions: causal determinism means that all natural events are entirely predictable, if only there was enough evidence, whereas events based on human choice are, because of free will, profoundly indeterminate.[157] The loss of a chance doctrine is a way of accepting this indeterminacy.

The difference between third parties and the claimant or defendant is more difficult still. All are (or act through) human actors with free will. Claimants and defendants have no better access to knowledge about what they would have done than third parties do. However, there is an intuitive appeal to the distinction between claimants and third parties that is captured in Lord Nicholls' observation that the loss of a chance doctrine applies to the loss of an opportunity to achieve a result 'whose achievement was outside [the claimant's] control'.[158]

B. Proving Loss of a Chance

(i) The Burden of Proof

The claimant has the burden of proving (on the balance of probabilities[159]) that it lost a substantial chance, but does not have the burden of proving the precise amount of that chance, which is at large for the court's reasonable assessment and 'making the best attempt it can to evaluate the chances, great or small (unless those chances amount to no more than remote speculation), taking all significant factors into account'.[160]

(ii) A Real and Substantial Chance

If there is no real and substantial chance that the claimant would, but for the wrong, have received the benefit or avoided the harm, then no damages are awarded. There is no minimum percentage for 'real and substantial', but courts will not usually be convinced to make awards for, say, a two or three per cent chance.[161]

The same applies at the other end of the range. If the claimant would almost certainly, but for the wrong, have received the benefit or avoided the harm, then the

---

[157] *Gregg v Scott* [2005] 2 AC 176 (HL), Lord Hoffmann at para 79 and Lady Hale at 220, both approving Helen Reece, 'Losses of Chances in the Law' (1996) 59 *MLR* 188.

[158] *Gregg v Scott* [2005] 2 AC 176 (HL) at para 15. See further the discussion in *Feltham v Bouskell* [2013] EWHC 1952 (Ch) (Hollander QC) at paras 110–11.

[159] *North Sea Energy Holdings v Petroleum Authority of Thailand* [1999] 1 Lloyd's Rep 483 (CA) Waller LJ at 494.

[160] *Parabola Investments Ltd v Browallia Cal Ltd* [2011] 1 QB 477 (CA) Toulson LJ at paras 22–23 (deceit).

[161] See *BCCI v Ali (No 3)* [2002] All ER 750 (CA) at para 25.

court will award 100 per cent of the loss. In other words, if there is not a real and substantial chance that the harm would *not* have been suffered, the damages will not be reduced for unreal or insubstantial (eg two per cent) chance.[162] However, unless a judge is 'certain, or very close to certain' that the harm would not have been suffered or the gain would have been received he or she should discount the award of damages 'to take into account the uncertainty'.[163]

The effect is that the loss of chance approach is applied consistently (eg if the chance is 0 per cent or 100 per cent then that is applied too, although in those cases the result is the same as if the balance of probabilities approach were being applied) but the court has a de minimis threshold, which is probably partly to discourage, for example, the attack by defendants on even clear causational steps involving third parties merely to try to reduce damages by a couple of percentage points.[164]

(iii) No Minimum Obligation Rule

As explained above, when determining what a defendant would have done but for the breach, it is to an extent necessary to assume or presume that the defendant would have acted in its own interests under the minimum obligation rule.[165] For the avoidance of doubt, this does not apply when determining what a third party would have done.[166] (Thus, for example, the fact that an insurer could legally have refused the insured claimant's claim even but for the defendant broker's breach does not prevent full recovery if the insurer would have paid out or partial recovery if there was a substantial chance the insurer would have paid out.[167])

(iv) The 'Fair Wind' Principle: An Evidential Presumption in Favour of the Claimant?

There is in practice something of an exception developed in lost litigation cases against negligent solicitors (but broadly applicable to other cases turning on third party actions). Because it was the defendants' fault that the claimant never got to fight the litigation, the law imposes an evidential burden on the defendants to show that 'despite their having acted for the plaintiff in the litigation and charged for their services, that litigation was of no value to their client, so that he lost nothing by their negligence in causing it to be struck out'.[168] As Parker LJ has observed, reviewing and approving this principle, 'The practical effect of that is to give the claimant a fair wind in establishing the value of what he has lost'.[169] Once the evidential burden has been raised by the defendant putting forward a credible case that the

---

[162] Eg *Dickinson v Jones Alexander & Co* [1993] 2 FLR 321.
[163] *Maden v Clifford Coppock & Carter* [2004] EWCA Civ 1037.
[164] See eg *Nicholson v Knox Ukiwa & Co (a firm)* [2008] PNLR 33 (Saunders J).
[165] See above in section 13.3(B)(i).
[166] *Jones v IOS (RUK) Ltd* [2012] EWHC 348 (Ch) (Hodge QC) at para 86, obiter.
[167] See below in section 13.5B(viii).
[168] *Mount v Barker Austin (a firm)* [1998] PNLR 493 (CA) Simon Brown LJ at 510. See further *Phillips & Co v Whatley (Gibraltar)* [2007] UKPC 28 Lord Mance at para 45, relying on the principle from *Armory v Delamirie* (1722) 1 Strange 505.
[169] *Browning v Bracher* [2005] EWCA Civ 753 at para 210.

claimant would have lost, the usual burden of proving the chance of success falls back to the claimant. Of course, where the defendants had the opportunity to advise on the litigation and themselves did not advise that it was hopeless, their burden will be all the greater simply because that itself provides evidence weighing against them.[170] This reversal of the evidential burden is not a rule of law but merely arises because the fact that the defendant acted for the claimant is some evidence, without more, that the litigation was worth something and might have succeeded. The same approach has been said to apply to questions of what an insurer would have paid out had the policy been valid.[171]

(v) Evidence from the Third Party

A natural source of evidence as to what the third party would have done will be the third party himself. There have been judicial suggestions that where the third party is giving evidence there is no need for a loss of chance analysis at all,[172] but the better view is to the contrary.[173] Indeed in the leading loss of chance decision, *Allied Maples*, Stuart-Smith LJ contemplated that the third party might give evidence, although doubted its usefulness.[174]

The court is not bound to accept that a witness would have done what it at trial says it would have done,[175] as witnesses, even if telling the truth, will, with hindsight, not always be the most reliable judge of what they would have done.[176] In some cases, however, clear evidence from an impartial and reliable witness will convince a judge. In these cases the court will often find that there was no substantial chance that the third party would have taken anything but a particular course, and so the claimant will recover all or none of the loss (but not a percentage part of it).[177]

(vi) Net Loss

The chance percentage multiplier must be applied to the net gain/net decrease in loss of which it is the chance. Thus in *Hartle v Laceys*, the claimant actually sold property for £150,000 but lost a 60 per cent chance of selling earlier for net proceeds

---

[170] *Mount v Barker Austin* [1998] PNLR 493 (CA) Simon Brown LJ at 510.

[171] *Ramco Ltd v Weller Russell & Laws Insurance Brokers Ltd* [2009] Lloyd's Rep IR 27 (David Donaldson QC) at para 41. As to the principle in other cases, see above in section 13.1B.

[172] *Stone Heritage Developments Ltd v Davis Blank*, 31 May 2006 at paras 333–34; *Aercap Partners 1 Ltd v Avia Asset Management AB* [2010] EWHC 2431 (Comm) (Gross LJ) at para 76(v).

[173] *4 Eng Ltd v Harper* [2008] 3 WLR 892 (David Richards J) at para 57; *Tom Hoskins plc v EMW Law (a firm)* [2010] EWHC 479 (Ch) (Floyd J) at paras 126 to 128. Both of these cases partly relied on the fact that not all the possible evidence as to what the third party would have done was before the court, and therefore there remains a dispute at first instance as to whether the loss of chance approach applies where all such evidence *is* before the court, although the better view is that it does apply.

[174] *Allied Maples Group Ltd v Simmons and Simmons* [1995] 1 WLR 1602 (CA) at 1614.

[175] *Alliance & Leicester Building Society v Robinson* (CA), 4 May 2000, Chadwick LJ at paras 32–33.

[176] See eg *Talisman Property Co (UK) Limited v Norton Rose* [2006] EWCA Civ 1104 Moses LJ at para 41.

[177] See for example *Hicks v Russell Jones & Walker* [2007] EWHC 940 (Ch) (Henderson J), affirmed [2008] EWCA Civ 340, where counsel's evidence as to what he would have advised was accepted by the court.

of £360,000, and so the correct measure of loss was to multiply the net loss of £210,000 by 60 per cent to give £126,000.[178] Had the earlier sale gone ahead the claimant would have received £360,000 it did not receive but not received £150,000 it did receive (and would also have avoided paying debit interest on the £126,000 which it had to continue to borrow but would have been able to pay off, which loss was also recovered in this case).

(vii) Mathematics and Cumulative Chances

Often there will be more than one third party decision or action, all of which would have had to occur for the claimant to have received the benefit/avoided the loss. In such cases, and providing the events are independent, it is (at least in principle) necessary to multiply the chance of each event to find the chance of the result that depended upon them.

In one case it was necessary to multiply the 50 per cent chance of a third party not going to counsel for advice (and thus not discovering its true entitlement) by the 70 per cent chance of the third party, if it had not gone to counsel, reaching agreement with the claimant, giving a 35 per cent chance of the deal being done.[179] Similarly where there would have been a 70 per cent chance of getting judgment against the insolvent defendants in the lost litigation, and a 40 per cent chance of recovering from the defendant's insurers if judgment were obtained (no more than 40 per cent because the insurers had been late notified by their insured, the defendant), the claimant lost a 28 per cent chance of recovery.[180]

The situation is different where the multiple events are not independent. For example, in one lost insurance claim case Roch LJ in the Court of Appeal pointed out that the various arguments raised by the insurer were not independent, because 'Although the issues are discrete, success for the respondent on the major issue would have been bound to have improved his chances of success against his insurers on the other two issues'.[181] The same conclusion was reached in a solicitor negligence case where the chances of a third party agreeing to provide a guarantee and the chances of completion of a sale by a certain date were not independent, so it was better to assess the 'overall chances' of the sale completing by that date with guarantee provided.[182]

(viii) Approaches to Quantifying the Chance Where there are Several Possible Outcomes

In many cases there will be many possible outcomes dependent upon the hypothetical action of the third party. In a civil case a judge will often have a choice not just between finding for the claimant or not, but between several or even thousands

---

[178] *Hartle v Laceys* [1999] Lloyd's PN 315 (CA).
[179] *Talisman Property Co (UK) Limited v Norton Rose (a firm)* [2006] EWCA Civ 1104.
[180] *Phillips & Co v Whatley (Gibraltar)* [2007] UKPC 28 (PC). See also *Joyce v Bowman Law Ltd* [2010] EWHC 251 (Ch) (Vos J) at paras 108–15.
[181] *Hanif v Middleweeks (a firm)* [2000] Lloyd's Rep PN 920 (CA) at para 71.
[182] *Tom Hoskins plc v EMW Law (a firm)* [2010] EWHC 479 (Ch) (Floyd J) at paras 133–34. See further Hugh Evans, 'Lies, damn lies, and loss of a chance' (2006) 22 *Professional Negligence* 99.

of possible awards. Likewise, in a negotiation there are many different outcomes. (Rather than agreeing or disagreeing, the vendor in *Allied Maples* might have exacted a price of some kind in exchange for reverting to the broader warranty, and then one has to identify which of the possible prices.) As Hobhouse LJ observed in *Allied Maples*:

> The judge will have to assess the plaintiffs' loss on the basis of the value of the chance they have lost to negotiate better terms. This involves two elements: what better terms might have been obtained—there may be more than one possibility—and what were the chances of obtaining them. Their chance of obtaining some greater improvement, although significant, may be less good than the chances of obtaining some other lesser improvement.[183]

In weighing up the lost chance, the court has to weigh up the small chance of a huge reward, the large chance of a medium reward, the small chance of a small reward, and the small chance of no reward (for example).

Some judges will explicitly break the chances down into separate chances and add them together or average them off. In *Jackson v RBS*[184] the bank of a dog-chew seller carelessly delivered to the purchaser documents revealing how much the seller was taking as middle man in the supply chain, leading the purchaser to break off the relationship with the seller. The question arose as to how long the profitable supply relationship would have continued but for this slip. The first instance judge's approach was to say that there was a 57 per cent chance it would have continued for a year, a 46 per cent chance it would have continued for two years, 29 per cent for three years and 16 per cent for four years, with no real chance it would have continued for more than four years.[185] Each percentage was multiplied by the amount that the seller proved would have been earned in that year had the relationship continued, and the total was awarded as the lost chance of profit.

Other judges will do the weighing in their head, merely identifying the most likely reward (eg the amount of damages that would probably have been recovered in lost litigation) and the chance of winning a reward, and multiplying them to find the loss.[186] This is not wrong where the most likely reward sits in the middle of a bell or similar curve, because the chance of a higher reward is balanced by the chance of a lower reward. As to the equivalence of the two approaches, note Jack J's comments in *Earl of Malmesbury v Strutt & Parker*, expressing a preference for the simpler approach:[187]

> If there was no significant chance that terms could have been negotiated including provision for a turnover rent, the claimants fail. If there would have been a, say, 60 per cent chance, the claimants are entitled to 60 per cent of the value of the chance lost. If the figure for

---

[183] *Allied Maples Group Ltd v Simmons and Simmons* [1995] 1 WLR 1602 (CA) at 1621.

[184] *Jackson v Royal Bank of Scotland plc* [2005] 1 WLR 377 (HL). Another vivid example of this approach is the tort case of *Langford v Hebron* [2001] EWCA Civ 361, concerning an injured amateur kickboxing champion. The court separately analysed and spelled out the chances of the claimant having won a national or European title, gone to the US and won State titles, become a world champion, maintained his world title and become a professional instructor.

[185] See the discussion in the Court of Appeal at [2000] EWCA Civ 203 at para 16.

[186] The Court of Appeal approved this approach in *Browning v Messrs Brachers* [2005] EWCA Civ 753 at para 212.

[187] *Seventh Earl of Malmesbury v Strutt & Parker* [2007] EWHC 999 (QB) (Jack J) at para 149.

turnover split most likely to have been agreed in a negotiation in which the principle of a turnover rent was accepted was 20 per cent in favour of the claimants the hypothetical lease is to be valued on that basis. The claimants would have lost 60 per cent of the resulting figure, because they had a 60 per cent chance of obtaining it if Mr Ashworth had carried out his duty. There are other ways of looking at the problem, but they achieve the same result. Thus one could say, for example, that there was, on the basis that the principle of a turnover element was accepted by BIA, then a fifty per cent chance of achieving a turnover split of 10 per cent and a similar chance of achieving 30 per cent, so one would take 20 per cent. In my judgment, it is most helpful and realistic to decide what the most likely figure is rather than looking at the chances of a range of figures. That accords with *Browning v Bracher* [2005] EWCA Civ 753, paragraphs 122 and 212.

And there are dangers in extending the break-down approach to 'to commercial cases, especially valuation cases where permutations may be almost infinite'[188] and where a valuation is essentially the middle (and so most likely) of a curve of possible prices that a third party would have paid.[189] Once a substantial chance has been identified the court is bound to come up with a figure however rough its assessment.[190]

(ix) The Chance of Making a Loss

When damages are ordinarily calculated, any saving made by the claimant must be deducted from any lost profit to find how much better or worse off the claimant would have been but for the wrong.

The question arises as to whether the chance of suffering a loss must be set off against the chance of making a profit when calculating a loss of a chance. Logic and authority say yes. Assuming the chances of making a large loss (including, for example, the amount of legal costs a claimant may have been liable for if the litigation had gone ahead and the claimant had lost) were the same as those of making a large profit (say, if the claimant had won the lost litigation), it would clearly be unfair to allow recovery of the lost chance to profit. Thus in one case where a claimant could not prove that the chance of profiting from commodity trading was greater than the risk of making a loss, no recovery was allowed.[191]

(x) No Need to Try the Lost Litigation in the Professional Negligence Action by a Mini-trial

In trying to assess the chances of succeeding in lost litigation, a judge in the professional negligence action should not seek to go through the all the steps of the lost trial,[192] but should weigh up all the evidence now available and do the best he

---

[188] *Law Debenture Trust Corp plc v Elektrim SA* [2010] EWCA Civ 1142 Arden LJ at para 48.
[189] *Lion Nathan Ltd v C-C Bottlers Ltd* [1996] 1 WLR 1438 (PC).
[190] *Giedo van der Garde BV v Force India Formula One Team Ltd* [2010] EWHC 2373 (QB) (Stadlen J) at 386–88 and 410–12.
[191] *E Bailey & Co Ltd v Balholm Securities Ltd* [1973] 2 Lloyd's Rep 404 (Kerr J), obiter; *ATA v American Express Bank Ltd* (CA), 17 June 1998.
[192] *Sharif v Garrett & Co (a firm)* [2002] 1 WLR 3118 (CA).

or she can.[193] It is important in doing so to take into account the chances of settlement.[194] As always, the court should evaluate what the net gain from the litigation would have been, which requires consideration of whether costs would have been recoverable.[195]

C. Examples of Application of the Loss of a Chance Rule

(i) Lost Profits on a Sale or Otherwise

See chapter eighteen, section 18.2D, below.

(ii) The Chance of Earning Commission

A broker who was deprived of the chance of seeking to sell all of a company's shares with subscribers for a reward of £400 was awarded £250.[196] A similar result obtained in a residential property sale case, where a vendor breached a sole agency agreement.[197]

(iii) The Chance of Successfully Completing Negotiations/Winning a Tender/Auction

The chance of negotiations with a third party leading to better contract terms than were entered into was the subject of the *Allied Maples* case discussed above.[198] Another good example is *Jones v IOS (RUK) Ltd*,[199] where it was concluded obiter that but for a breach of a confidentiality agreement (which breach was not found), the defendant's sister company would have entered a joint bid with the claimant and they would have won.[200] And in *4 Eng v Harper* it was concluded that there was an 80 per cent chance that, but for the defendant's deceit, the claimant would have bought a particular alternative business.[201]

---

[193] *Hatswell v Goldbergs (a firm)* [2001] EWCA Civ 2084 at para 50.

[194] See the discussion in *Harrison v Bloom Camillin (a firm) (No 2)* [2000] Lloyd's Rep PN 89 (Neuberger J).

[195] Eg in *Corfield v DS Bosher & Co* [1992] 1 EGLR 163 (Peter Crawford QC) where a successful outcome would have included the claimant bearing his own costs and half the arbitrator's fee.

[196] *Inchbald v Western Neilgherry Coffee, Tea & Cinchona Plantation Co Ltd* (1864) 17 CB (NS) 733.

[197] *Nicholas Prestige Homes v Sally Neal* [2010] EWCA Civ 1552. See also *Richardson v Mellish* (1824) 2 Bing 229.

[198] Above n 26. See also *Football League Ltd v Edge Ellison (a firm)* [2006] EWHC 1462 (Ch) (Rimer J); *Earl of Malmesbury v Strutt & Parker* [2007] EWHC 999 (QB) (Jack J); *Perkin v Lupton Fawcett (a firm)* [2008] EWCA Civ 418.

[199] *Jones v IOS (RUK) Ltd* [2012] EWHC 348 (Ch) (Hodge QC) at para 87.

[200] The conclusion was academic as not only was there no breach, but the claimant won the tender in any event, jointly with another company.

[201] *4 Eng Ltd v Harper* [2009] Ch 91 (Richards J). See also *Thomas Eggar Verrall Bowles v Rice*, 21 December 1999 (Rimer J) as to the chances of winning an auction.

(iv) The Chance of Earning Tips

A claimant is entitled to claim the loss of a chance of receiving a voluntary donation from a third party as with any other type of benefit. Thus damages for a hairdresser's dismissal must include an allowance for the tips that might or would have been made during the proper period of notice.[202]

(v) The Chance of Winning a Job

A claimant may be able to prove that the defendant's breach cost it the chance of a job.[203] Indeed beauty contest case *Chaplin v Hicks* was such a case.[204]

(vi) The Chance of Being Named in a Will

The lost chance of receiving property in a will is recoverable where the solicitor preparing a will owes the would-be beneficiary a duty of care, usually in tort.[205] It may also arise in claims against solicitors who misadvise as to steps that affect whether the claimant will receive a bequest under a will.[206]

(vii) The Chances of Succeeding in a Property Development

The chance of obtaining planning permission and getting funding for a development must be assessed on a loss of a chance basis.[207]

(viii) The Chance of Being Covered by Insurance

Insurance broker negligence cases often involve claims for the lost chance that a third party insurer would have paid out on a particular insurance claim if the broker had arranged suitable insurance, properly disclosed all material issues to the insurer at the time of placement, or kept the insured informed (therefore depriving the insurer of the right to avoid for non-disclosure or breach). The likelihood that an insurer would have taken a different point available to it to refuse cover is a question

---

[202] *Manubens v Leon* [1919] 1 KB 208.

[203] See also *Spring v Guardian Assurance plc* [1995] 2 AC 296 (HL) Lord Lowry at 327 (tortious and contractual negligent misstatement in preparation of a job reference). And see the discussion of this point in *Bank of Credit and Commerce International v Ali (No 2)* [1999] 4 All ER 83 (Lightman J) at paras 74–81.

[204] *Chaplin v Hicks* [1911] 2 KB 786 (CA).

[205] Applying the principle from *White v Jones* [1995] 2 AC 207 (HL). A loss of chance approach was apparently applied, obiter, in *Bacon v Howard Kennedy (a firm)* [1999] PNLR 1 (Bromley QC) although there was only a speculative chance that a bequest would not have been made so the award was equivalent to a 100% chance, and see similarly *Cancer Research Campaign v Ernest Brown & Co* [1998] PNLR 592 (Harman J).

[206] *Hall v Meyrick* [1957] 2 QB 455 (CA).

[207] *Joyce v Bowman Law Ltd* [2010] EWHC 251 (Ch) (Vos J).

of fact and loss of chance.[208] Uncertainty as to the sum the insurer would have paid out should be resolved in the favour of the claimant.[209]

(ix) Lost Litigation

A common category of loss of chance professional negligence cases is that of lost litigation. Since *Kitchen v RAF*[210] it has been established that lost litigation cases are evaluated on a loss of a chance basis. Thus the loss of chance approach applies where a solicitor's carelessness (failing to spot a limitation period, missing the deadline for filing and serving a defence, etc) led to a claimant losing the opportunity to present its case at trial or best present its case at trial, and therefore to earn an award by judgment[211] or settlement[212] or a higher award than was achieved,[213] or to enforce that award before the defendant went into insolvency.[214] Similarly where such carelessness led to loss of a chance to avoid a judgment or a conviction against the claimant (where it was defendant in the litigation).[215]

D. Take into Account Actual Post-Breach Pre-Trial Events

In determining what would have happened, the court will take into account pre-trial events it knows about. Thus in one case a claimant was entitled to damages for the loss of a bonus that would have been payable post-breach but pre-trial, given how well the claimant Formula One team actually did during that period.[216] In *The Golden Victory* the profits the owner would have made (before war broke out) under the existing charter with the defendant depended in part on market movements, as the charter included a profit-share provision, and the actual post-breach pre-trial market movements had to be taken into account in quantifying such lost profits.[217]

---

[208] *Fraser v BN Furman (Productions) Ltd* [1967] 1 WLR 898 (CA); *Everett v Hogg Robinson* [1973] 2 Lloyd's Rep 217 (CA); *Dunbar v A & B Painters* [1986] 2 Lloyd's Rep 38 (CA); *O & R Jewellers Ltd v Terry* [1999] Lloyd's Rep IR 436 (Le Quesne QC).

[209] *Ramco Ltd v Weller Russell & Laws Insurance Brokers Ltd* [2009] Lloyd's Rep IR 27 (David Donaldson QC) at para 41.

[210] *Kitchen v Royal Air Force Association* [1958] 1 WLR 563 (CA).

[211] *Kitchen v RAF Association* [1958] 1 WLR 563 (CA); *Gascoine v Ian Sheridan & Co* (1994) 5 Med LR 437 (Mitchell J); *Hanif v Middleweeks (a firm)* [2000] Lloyd's Rep PN 920 (CA); *Phillips & Co v Whatley (Gibraltar)* [2007] UKPC 28 (PC); *Nicholson v Knox Ukiwa & Co* [2008] PNLR 33 (Reddihough J).

[212] For an example of loss of the chance of reaching a particular out of court settlement see *Maden v Clifford Coppock & Carter* [2005] 2 All ER 43 (CA).

[213] *Hickman v Blake Lapthorn* [2006] PNLR 20 (Jack J).

[214] *Pearson v Sanders Witherspoon* [2000] PNLR 110 (CA).

[215] *Acton v Graham Pearce & Co (a firm)* [1997] 3 All ER 909 (CA); *Feakins v Burstow* [2005] EWHC 1931 (QB) (Jack J).

[216] *Force India Formula One Team Ltd v Etihad Airways PJSC* [2009] EWHC 2768 (QB) (Sir Charles Gray) at paras 107–9.

[217] *Golden Strait Corp v Nippon Yusen Kubishika Kaisha (The Golden Victory)* [2007] 2 AC 353 (HL) Lord Brown at para 81, and see also the Court of Appeal decision [2006] 1 WLR 533 Lord Mance at paras 13 and 25.

13.6 The Future: What Would Have Happened after Trial

Damages awards are made at trial, once and for all, and must therefore, as well as measuring past losses, also measure future losses: gains that would have been made post-trial but will not be made because of the breach, and harms that will be incurred post-trial but would not have been but for the breach.[218]

A. Lost Post-Trial Profits

Thus a claimant who was induced to give up a favourable pub tenancy agreement was entitled to damages for the lost income for the nine years after trial.[219] A claimant whose telephone equipment supply contract was repudiated was entitled to lost profits for the one year up to trial and the five remaining years of the contract after trial.[220] A different telephone answering machine supplier was entitled to lost rental profits, including for the six years after trial.[221] A wrongfully dismissed employee can recover for the net loss of future earnings.[222]

B. Future Post-Trial Liability to a Third Party

Similarly, in some cases a court will seek to quantify the liability that a claimant will suffer to a third party in the future, and make the defendant liable for that sum.[223]

C. Future Post-Trial Costs

Where the cost is of repair that has not yet been carried out, proof will involve showing (as part of the reasonableness requirement) an intention to do the work.[224] The cost of the works can be estimated and discounted to the date of award.[225]

D. Discount for Chance

It has been noted above that when proving what will happen post-trial, the court discounts for the contingency of the future event.[226] The same seems to apply when proving what would have happened post-trial. A good example is provided

---

[218] See above in chapter one, section 1.2C(ii).
[219] *Plummer v Tibsco Ltd*, 9 March 2001 (Neuberger J).
[220] *Interoffice Telephones Ltd v Robert Freeman Co Ltd* [1958] 1 QB 190 (CA).
[221] *Robophone Facilities Ltd v Blank* [1966] 1 WLR 1428 (CA).
[222] *Lavarack v Woods of Colchester Ltd* [1967] 1 QB 278 (CA).
[223] See above in chapter one, section 1.2C(ii).
[224] See above in chapter four, section 4.3B(iv).
[225] *Tabcorp Holdings Ltd v Bowen Investments Pty Ltd* (2009) 236 CLR 72 (HC of Australia) at para 26.
[226] See above in chapter twelve, section 12.2.

by *The Golden Victory*, albeit obiter. War had already broken out by the date of trial, but had it not done so the majority confirmed that it would have been necessary to evaluate the future income under the charterparty as subject to reduction for the chance that war would have broken out and the claimant would then have terminated early.[227]

E. Accelerated Receipt

In all of these cases, the award of damages for future losses is subject to a deduction for accelerated receipt.[228]

13.7 Tax

Since the House of Lords' decision on the effect of income tax in the personal injury case of *British Transport Commission v Gourley* in 1955,[229] the general approach of English law has been to take into account in calculating damages the amount of tax the claimant would have had to pay but for the breach, but will not have to pay on the damages award,[230] whether under English or foreign tax laws.[231] This applies equally to contract cases. Thus in *Shove v Downs Surgical plc*[232] the damages on a wrongful dismissal claim took account both of the income tax the claimant would have paid on the income he would have earned but for the breach, and the income tax he was in fact liable to pay on the damages award.[233]

This is the correct approach in principle, although in practice to avoid the costs of evidence and argument on tax, unless either of the parties presses the point because the tax treatment of the damages is significantly different to the tax treatment that would have been applied to the benefit lost by the breach, the court will merely assume by way of rough justice that the tax (income tax or corporation tax or capital gains tax) payable on the sum that would have been received but for the breach is the same as the tax that will have to be paid on the damages, and therefore make no adjustment for tax and awards the gross loss.[234]

---

[227] *Golden Strait Corp v Nippon Yusen Kubishika Kaisha (The Golden Victory)* [2007] 2 AC 353 (HL) Lord Carswell at para 66 and Lord Brown at para 76.

[228] See above in chapter one, section 1.1C(v).

[229] *British Transport Commission v Gourley* [1956] AC 185 (HL).

[230] This diverges from the approach taken in Canada and the US.

[231] See *Julien Praet et Compagnie SA v HG Poland Ltd* [1962] 1 Lloyd's Rep 566 (Mocatta J).

[232] *Shove v Downs Surgical plc* [1984] 1 All ER 7 (Sheen J).

[233] Damages on a claim for loss of office are tax free up to £30,000: Income Tax (Earnings and Pensions) Act 2003 ss 401 ff. See also the application of these principles to the professional negligence claim in *Capita Alternative Fund Services (Guernsey) Ltd v Drivers Jonas (a firm)* [2012] EWCA Civ 1407 in relation to tax credits achieved as part of the wrongfully induced transaction. See also an Australian case in which tax on the damages award had to be taken into account: *Airloom Holdings Pty Ltd v Thales Australia Ltd* [2011] NSWSC 1513 (S C of New South Wales).

[234] See eg *Diamond v Campbell-Jones* [1961] Ch 22 (Buckley J); *Julient Praet et Compagnie SA v HG Poland Ltd* [1962] 1 Lloyd's Rep 566 (CA); *Parsons v BNM Laboratories Ltd* [1964] 1 QB 95 (CA); *Deeny v Gooda Walker Ltd (No 2)* [1995] STC 439 (CA), affirmed on different points [1996] 1 WLR 426 (HL).

In practice, therefore, there is a presumption that no adjustments for tax will be made, and the burden falls on the party seeking to displace that rule to demonstrate why.[235] In some cases the presumption will remain unrebutted.[236] But where enough is at stake, the courts will tend to allow evidence to displace the rule.[237] This will arise, for example, where the claimant is insolvent and so it (or its liquidator) will not pay tax on the damages received.[238] Further, where part of an income is lost, the courts have shown a willingness to calculate the difference between the position as it was and the position as it would have been if the income had been earned, thereby assuming that the part lost would have been notionally lost during the tax year, and so would have attracted tax at the claimant's highest rate.[239]

Furthermore, the calculation of interest on damages should allow for the taxation position: even if the claimant will end up paying the same tax on the damages as would have been paid on a sum that would but for the breach have been received earlier, the interest calculation must allow for the fact that the claimant would have paid the tax earlier and so has from that date been kept out of the net and not gross sum.[240]

13.8 Inflation[241]

Inflation in prices (often measured by the consumer price index) has the effect that £1 today will not buy as much as £1 in a year's time. The effect this should have on damages varies depending upon the damages being awarded.

A. The Cost of Buying Something Has Gone Up

If what is being awarded at trial is the cost of a cure or some other step the claimant has to take (which the claimant cannot be blamed for not having taken yet), the only fair way of assessing that cost is to measure the cost of cure at the date of trial rather than at an earlier date (since the award of the earlier cost of cure will not pay for the

---

[235] *Finley v Connell Associates (a firm)*, 27 July 2001 (Ouseley J).

[236] Eg *Raja's Commercial College v Singh & Co Ltd* [1977] AC 312 (PC).

[237] Eg *Amstrad plc v Seagate Technology Inc* (1998) 86 BLR 34 (Lloyd QC); *BSkyB Ltd v HP Enterprise Services UK Ltd (No 2)* (2010) 131 Con LR 42 (Ramsey J). On one view the *Amstrad* case goes too far as *Gourley's* case only allows adjustment where the lost income would have been taxed and the damages award is not, but there is no principled reason to refuse to make the opposite adjustment.

[238] On the correct approach in such cases see *Finley v Connell* [2002] Lloyd's Rep 62 (Ouseley J); *Stewart v Scottish Widows and Life Assurance Society plc* [2005] EWHC 1831 (QB) (Eccles QC), appeal allowed in part on a different point [2006] EWCA Civ 999 (CA).

[239] *Lyndale Fashion Manufacturers v Rich* [1973] 1 WLR 73 (CA).

[240] See the discussion in *BSkyB Ltd v HP Enterprise Services UK Ltd (No 2)* (2010) 131 Con LR 42 (Ramsey J) at paras 78–82, in relation to the usual award of interest under s 35A of the Senior Courts Act 1981 (formerly called the Supreme Court Act 1981).

[241] See further A Burgess, 'Avoiding Inflation Loss in Contract Damages Awards: The Equitable Damages Solution' (1985) 34 *ICLQ* 317; C Proctor, 'Changes in Monetary Values and the Assessment of Damages' in D Saidov and R Cunnington (eds), *Contract Damages: Domestic and International Perspectives* (Oxford, Hart Publishing, 2008).

cure at the date of trial).[242] As Nourse J held in *Jarvis v Richards & Co*, 'it would be quite wrong for Mrs. Jarvis ... to be left with damages which made no allowance for the inflation of a period during which she could do nothing effective to help herself'.[243] It has been said that the claimant's duty to mitigate does not extend to protecting the defendant from the effects of inflation and that the claimant does not fail to mitigate by waiting until trial before performing the works.[244]

B. General Devaluation of Money

If what is being awarded is an indemnity for a cost already incurred by the claimant, then awarding the same sum at trial will not be fair compensation. The claimant could have bought more with it at the relevant date than at the date of trial; the money has devalued in the meantime. In practice, no allowance is made for this inflation, and what the claimant would have done with the money will usually be too remote or *res inter alios acta*. A slightly more generous interest rate might be calculated for the interim period to allow for inflation, but the primary purpose of the interest award is to compensate for loss of use of the money and not inflation.

If what is being awarded at trial is compensation for loss of future income or for future costs, then inflation is relevant because the claimant will have more buying power with the money awarded at trial than it would at the later date, although this can be disregarded as the money is going to have to be invested to provide the future income by alternative means. The main adjustment necessary is therefore not for inflation, but to allow for the claimant's advantage in having the money earlier and so being able to earn interest on it, and a reduction is therefore needed for accelerated receipt.[245] The general approach to awards of economic loss in personal injury cases is to ignore inflation save in extreme cases, on the basis that it is difficult to predict and will be balanced by the investment policy of the lump sum received by the damages award.[246]

---

[242] See eg *Anchorage Asphalt Paving Company v Lewis* 629 P 2d 65 (1981) (SC of Alaska), where this point was explicitly made by Matthews J at para 6; *Johnson v Perez* (1988) 166 CLR 351 (HC of Australia) Mason CJ at paras 4, 8 and 15; *The Board of Trustees of National Museums and Galleries on Merseyside v AEW Architects and Designers Ltd* [2013] EWHC 2403 (TCC) (Akenhead J) at para 108. See also *Dodd Properties (Kent) Ltd v Canterbury City Council* [1980] 1 WLR 433 (CA).

[243] *Jarvis v Richards & Co*, 30 July 1980 (Nourse J).

[244] Ibid. See also D Feldman and DF Libling, 'Inflation and the Duty to Mitigate' (1979) 95 *LQR* 270.

[245] See above in section 13.6E.

[246] *Taylor v O'Connor* [1971] AC 115 (HL); *Cookson v Knowles* [1979] AC 556 (HL); *Lim Poh Choo v Camden Islington Area Health Authority* [1980] AC 174 (HL); *Hodgson v Trapp* [1989] AC 807 (HL).

Part 4

Legal Principles of Remoteness, Mitigation and Legal Causation

14

Remoteness and Scope of Duty

The remoteness principle applies to determine which losses are recoverable. It is one of the major contractual principles that prevents recovery of losses despite their having in fact been caused by the breach, ie even though but for the breach those losses would not have occurred. Remoteness (and its minor cousin, 'scope of duty') does this by focusing on whether the losses were foreseeable at the time of contracting, and whether they were within the implied assumption of responsibility or scope of duty of the defendant.

14.1. Start with Foreseeability
14.2. The Assumption of Responsibility Basis
14.3. The Reasonable Contemplation Test of Remoteness
14.4. The Cap Rule from *Cory v Thames Ironworks*
14.5. Displacing the Reasonable Contemplation Test by the Remoteness and Scope of Duty Principles
14.6. Factors Relevant to Scope of Duty and Assumption of Responsibility
14.7. The Interaction of Scope of Duty with Contribution and Contributory Negligence

14.1 Start with Foreseeability

AT THE HEART of the test of remoteness is a foreseeability test, and this remains the case despite the developments described below. By this test, losses which are not reasonably foreseeable at the time of contracting are too remote and so unrecoverable. Losses which are reasonably foreseeable are recoverable. However, in part to distinguish it from the slightly different tortious remoteness test of reasonable foreseeability,[1] the contractual test has always been phrased not in terms of 'foreseeability' but in terms of whether the loss was in the 'reasonable contemplation' of the parties, this phrase and the test itself deriving from the still leading nineteenth century decision of Baron Alderson, *Hadley v Baxendale*.[2]

---

[1] *Overseas Tankship (UK) Ltd v Morts Dock & Engineering Co Ltd (The Wagon Mound)* [1961] AC 388 (PC).

[2] *Hadley v Baxendale* (1854) 9 Exch 341.

14.2 The Assumption of Responsibility Basis

A. Introduction

In *The Achilleas*,[3] the House of Lords explained contract remoteness (including the reasonable contemplation test) as being based upon an 'assumption of responsibility' rather than an external rule applying a test of foreseeability for its own sake. The reasonable contemplation test must therefore be understood as a general application of, or rule of thumb for, the assumption of responsibility test. As Toulson LJ summarised in the important post-*Achilleas* Court of Appeal decision of *Siemens Building Technologies FE Ltd v Supershield Ltd*:

> *Hadley v Baxendale* remains a standard rule but it has been rationalised on the basis that it reflects the expectation to be imputed to the parties in the ordinary case, ie that a contract breaker should ordinarily be liable to the other party for damage resulting from his breach if, but only if, at the time of making the contract a reasonable person in his shoes would have had damage of that kind in mind as not unlikely to result from a breach.[4]

B. The Assumption of Responsibility

In *The Achilleas* a majority of the House of Lords explained that remoteness was based upon the parties' 'presumed intentions' (Lord Hoffmann); 'assum[ed] responsibility', 'presumed intention' (Lord Hope); 'common basis', 'shared understanding', 'common intention' and 'common expectation, objectively assessed' (Lord Walker).[5] Despite the majority support for this common principle, there is a fairly arid debate as to whether the assumption of responsibility basis had majority support of the House. Lord Rodger and Baroness Hale maintained that the decision could be justified by the traditional reasonable contemplation test, and Lord Walker (by agreeing with Lords Hoffmann and Hope but also Rodger) appears to support that as an alternative ratio of the court.

The reasons the debate is arid, however, are these:

First, the explicit reasoning of Lords Hoffmann, Hope and Walker cannot be, was not likely to be, and has not been ignored.

Secondly, the new approach has in fact been adopted by the Court of Appeal in several post-*Achilleas* decisions, and is now clearly part of the law.[6]

Thirdly, Lords Hoffmann, Hope and Walker were correctly describing the existing law. There is the established principle of scope of duty from *SAAMCo*.[7] There are

---

[3] *Transfield Shipping Inc v Mercator Shipping Inc (The Achilleas)* [2009] AC 61 (HL). The facts are discussed above at text to chapter six n 58.

[4] *Siemens Building Technologies FE Ltd v Supershield Ltd* [2010] EWCA Civ 7 at para 43.

[5] [2009] AC 61 at paras 12, 24, 36, 69, 78 and 84.

[6] *Ryan v London Borough of Islington* [2009] EWCA Civ 578; *Siemens Building Technologies FE Ltd v Supershield Ltd* [2010] EWCA Civ 7; *Rubenstein v HSBC Bank plc* [2012] EWCA Civ 1184; *John Grimes Partnership Ltd v Gubbins* [2013] EWCA Civ 37.

[7] *South Australia Asset Management Corp (SAAMCo) v York Montague Ltd* [1997] 1 AC 191 (HL), discussed below in section 14.5B.

the clear dicta of Goff J in *The Pegase* and the Court of Appeal in *Mulvenna v Royal Bank of Scotland plc*.[8] There is the evolving principle governing recovery of damages for mental distress.[9] And there is the unworkability of the existing test at its borders (ie in determining what is a type of loss, what is foreseeable as being not unlikely, and in the apparent conclusion that merely communicating information at the time of contracting about a potential loss can render the other party liable for it).

The assumption of responsibility principle is therefore here to stay, although it does not entail the radical rewriting of the remoteness test, at least in practice, that some feared.

C. Identifying the Implied Assumption of Responsibility by Construction

The assumption of responsibility approach involves 'the interpretation of the contract as a whole against its commercial background'.[10] It therefore involves addressing the usual construction questions of the words used, the contractual context, the broader matrix of fact, and the purpose of the contract. As to this process, the following comments of Professor Leon Green in *The Rationale of Proximate Cause* (published in 1927) are difficult to improve upon:

> Parties, in making contracts, rarely contemplate *the losses* which would result from its breach. But they do count the advantages they will gain from its performance. *What interests does the contract promote or serve?* These are actually considered in the most part, and those which are shown to have been considered or reasonably falling within the terms in view of the language used and background of the transaction, mark its boundaries—the limits of protection under it. Did the parties intend (using intention in the sense indicated above) that the injured interest was to be protected? Did this agreement fairly comprehend the advantage now claimed to have been lost?[11]

Some of the key factors in the construction task are discussed below (section 14.6), but *The Achilleas* itself throws up a few examples of factors that could not have been taken into account under the traditional view of the remoteness test, but which can now that remoteness is understood as being a construction task based on discerning the implied assumption of responsibility. One is the contractual power of the shipowner to refuse to obey an illegitimate last voyage order by the charterer. This arguably shows that the shipowner is not at the mercy of the charterer and has at least a limited ability to minimise the risk of overrun where the consequences for the shipowner will be great, therefore supporting the view that (as found by the House of Lords) the shipowner takes the responsibility of losses on follow-on charters.[12] Another factor is the absence of an express term (especially an exclusion

---

[8] *Satef-Huttenes Albertus SpA v Paloma Tercera Shipping Co SA (The Pegase)* [1981] 1 Lloyd's Rep 175 (Goff J) at 183; *Mulvenna v Royal Bank of Scotland plc* [2003] EWCA Civ 1112. Both were cited by Lord Hoffmann in *The Achilleas*.

[9] See below in chapter nineteen, section 19.1E.

[10] Lord Hoffmann in *The Achilleas* [2009] AC 61 at paras 25–26.

[11] L Green, *The Rationale of Proximate Cause* (Kansas City, MO, Vernon Law Book Co, 1927).

[12] See Lord Hoffmann in *The Achilleas* [2009] AC 61 at para 23.

clause) governing the risk.[13] A third factor is the general market understanding as to how the responsibilities were allocated.[14]

As with all construction questions, the one concerning the assumption of responsibility is complicated. It is important that the loss is sufficiently salient (either by being likely and so foreseeable, or being closely linked to the apparent purpose of the duty) that the defendant could have been expected, had it so wished, to disclaim or limit responsibility by an exclusion or limitation clause, to insure against liability for the loss, or to price the possible liability into the price it was charging or paying under the contract. It is also relevant to this construction task whether the loss is sufficiently quantifiable that these things are possible; which party could more easily and cheaply have insured against the loss; and how generally the defendant prices, ie whether it could realistically have factored the risk into its price.[15]

D. The History of the Assumption of Responsibility Rationale

The assumption of responsibility test is a reworking of a version of the remoteness test that reached its zenith in the latter half of the nineteenth century with English decisions such as *British Columbia and Vancouver's Island Spar, Lumber, and Saw-Mill Co v Nettleship*.[16] It was championed in the US by Oliver Wendell Holmes Jr both on and off the bench, who said in his judgment in *Globe Refining Co v Landa Cotton Co* that remoteness was a matter of determining 'terms which it fairly may be presumed [the defendant] would have assented if they had been presented to his mind'.[17]

Originally it dates back to the continental sixteenth-century jurist Molinaeus and eighteenth-century jurist Pothier, who imposed a foreseeability test because it could be presumed that the defendant submitted to responsibility for foreseeable losses only.[18] That nineteenth-century version of the test, at least on some readings, required identification of an implied promise to pay damages for a particular harm. This was rejected in England and the United States.[19]

---

[13] Lord Hoffmann (ibid at para 26) thought this was of no significance to the construction question at hand. Baroness Hale at para 90 thought that it pointed towards the assumption of responsibility by the defendant (ie against the finding of the House of Lords), although it is worth noting that under her preferred approach—the traditional approach based solely on reasonable contemplation with no reference to assumption of responsibility—the lack of an express term (as noted by her) cannot feature in the remoteness reasoning at all.

[14] Lord Hoffmann (ibid) at paras 6–7 and 9.

[15] See further below in section 14.6.

[16] *British Columbia and Vancouver's Island Spar, Lumber, and Saw-Mill Co v Nettleship* (1868) LR 3 CP 499.

[17] *Globe Refining Co v Landa Cotton Oil Co* 190 US 540 at 543 (1903). See also OW Holmes Jr, *The Common Law* (Boston, MA, Little, Brown & Co, 1881) at 302–3.

[18] For more discussion of the nineteenth-century test see A Kramer, 'An Agreement-Centred Approach to Remoteness and Contract Damage' in Cohen and McKendrick (eds), *Comparative Remedies for Breach of Contract* (Oxford, Hart Publishing, 2005). This test still applies in Arkansas: see eg *Morrow v First National Bank of Hot Springs* 550 SW 2d 429 (1977) (SC of Arkansas) and *Bank of America NA v Smith Motor Co* 106 SW 3d 425 (2003) (SC of Arkansas).

[19] *Czarnikow Ltd v Koufos (The Heron II)* [1969] 1 AC 350 (HL) obiter Lord Upjohn at 421–22; US Restatement (Second) of Contracts §351 cmt a; Uniform Commercial Code s 2-715 cmt 2. But see in South Africa: *Shatz Investments (Pty) Ltd v Kalovyrnas* 1976 (2) AD 545 (SC of South Africa) at 551

The modern test does not go so far: what is implied is the allocation of responsibility, as with the scope of duty principle. The obligation to pay damages itself (which gives effect to the implied allocation of responsibility) is imposed by law.

The nineteenth-century version did not achieve the permanence of the twenty-first-century version. This may be because the nineteenth-century version followed too hard on the heels of *Hadley v Baxendale* itself, and more time was needed to discover that the reasonable contemplation test applied across the range of contract law, but gave an incomplete answer in particular situations. More simply, of course, the nineteenth-century version did not have the House of Lords' authority that the twenty-first-century version has.

E. The Consequences of *The Achilleas* for the Reasonable Contemplation Test

The discovery of this new rationale for the contract remoteness test has three consequences.

The first is the absence of a consequence. The reasonable contemplation test will usually still give the right answer and should be treated as the default test. This is entirely consistent with the assumption of responsibility test. As Bridge LJ has observed (prior to *The Achilleas*)

> If a party entering into a contract would as a reasonable man foresee that his breach would be likely to cause loss of a certain kind to the other contracting party, then it must be, I would say, from that and nothing else that the implication would arise of his contractual willingness to accept liability for that loss.[20]

The main change made by *The Achilleas* to this approach is that a loss being sufficiently foreseeable is no longer a conclusive indication that the defendant assumed responsibility; rather it is good evidence or raises a rebuttable presumption.[21] Accordingly it is still convenient to explain remoteness in terms of the foreseeability-based reasonable contemplation test, as it is in this chapter in section 14.3. As Lord Hoffmann summarised extra-judicially, 'Foreseeability will play a part, usually a very big part' in answering the remoteness question,[22] but:

> The question is: what obligation to make compensation for breach of contract would a reasonable observer understand the contracting party to have undertaken? In the ordinary way, that will be compensation for any loss which the parties would reasonably have regarded as likely to flow from the breach. But there may be cases in which a reasonable man would consider that a greater or lesser obligation was being accepted.[23]

---

and *Thoroughbred Breeders' Association of South Africa v Price Waterhouse* (2001) (4) SA 551 (SC of South Africa) at 582 and 597. And in the US: *Wells Fargo Bank, NA v United States* 33 Fed Cl 233 (1995) at 242–44 fn 8.

[20] *GKN Centrax Gears Ltd v Matbro Ltd* [1976] 2 Lloyd's Rep 555 (CA) at 580. Also *Czarnikow Ltd v Koufos (The Heron II)* [1966] 2 QB (CA) Diplock LJ at 728 and 731 and Salmon LJ at 739; *Jackson v Royal Bank of Scotland plc* [2005] 1 WLR 377 (HL) Lord Hope at para 26.

[21] Eg *John Grimes Partnership Ltd v Gubbins* [2013] EWCA Civ 37 at para 20.

[22] Lord Hoffmann, '*The Achilleas*: custom and practice or foreseeability?' (2010) *Edinburgh L Rev* 47 at 58.

[23] Ibid at 55.

The second consequence (evident from *The Achilleas* itself, and summarised in that quotation from Lord Hoffmann) is that the reasonable contemplation test will sometimes give the wrong answer, and the question of remoteness will ultimately be determined by other factors than reasonable contemplation, which will displace the reasonable contemplation test. This is discussed below in sections 14.5 and 14.6, after consideration of the foreseeability-based reasonable contemplation test.

The third consequence is that the foreseeability-based reasonable contemplation test must itself be applied with the assumption of responsibility rationale in mind. Thus in determining whether a loss is sufficiently foreseeable, or how broadly to categorise a type of loss before determining foreseeability, the court must have in mind the reason for asking the questions, namely the search for the implied allocation of responsibility of the parties. This point is elaborated upon in the following sections.

14.3 The Reasonable Contemplation Test of Remoteness

The basis of the reasonable contemplation test is the question of whether the type of loss, of which the actual loss suffered is an example, was foreseeable at the date at which the contract was entered into as being sufficiently likely. If it was, the actual loss will (subject to other rules such as mitigation and causation) be recoverable as not being too remote.

A. *Hadley v Baxendale*

Hadley v Baxendale[24] is probably the most cited contract law decision of all. The claimant had a corn mill in Gloucester operating by steam engine. The engine's crank shaft broke, and the claimant ordered a new one from a Greenwich manufacturer who needed the broken shaft so as to ensure that the new shaft would fit into the existing engine and mill. The claimant engaged the defendant common carrier to carry the broken shaft to Greenwich, but the defendant delayed in breach of contract, causing the mill to be at a standstill for an additional five days. Profits were lost, and the claimant had to buy in flour, sharps and bran to supply its customers, and it claimed damages for these losses.

Baron Alderson, giving the judgment of the four-judge Court of Exchequer, laid down the rule of remoteness in the following terms:

> Where two parties have made a contract which one of them has broken the damages which the other party ought to receive in respect of such breach of contract should be such as may fairly and reasonably be considered as either arising naturally, ie, according to the usual course of things, from such breach of contract itself, or such as may reasonably be supposed to have been in the contemplation of both parties at the time they made the contract as the probable result of the breach of it. If special circumstances under which the contract was actually made were communicated by the plaintiffs to the defendants, and thus known

[24] *Hadley v Baxendale* (1854) 9 Exch 341.

to both parties, the damages resulting from the breach of such a contract which they would reasonably contemplate would be the amount of injury which would ordinarily follow from a breach of contract under the special circumstances so known and communicated. But, on the other hand, if these special circumstances were wholly unknown to the party breaking the contract, he, at the most, could only be supposed to have had in his contemplation the amount of injury which would arise generally, and in the real multitude of cases not affected by any special circumstances, from such a breach of contract. For, had the special circumstances been known, the parties might have specially provided for the breach of contract by special terms as to the damages in that case; and of this advantage it would be very unjust to deprive them.

Although at the time of contracting the defendant carrier knew that the article being carried was a broken shaft from the claimant's mill, in most cases this would not be enough to make clear to the carrier that the mill was at a standstill and profits being lost, as, for example, for all the defendant knew the claimant had a spare shaft or the mill was at a standstill due to other defects in addition to a broken shaft.[25] Thus:

> It follows, therefore, that the loss of profits here cannot reasonably be considered such a consequence of the breach of contract as could have been fairly and reasonably contemplated by both the parties when they made this contract. For such loss would neither have flowed naturally from the breach of this contract in the great multitude of such cases occurring under ordinary circumstances, nor were the special circumstances, which, perhaps, would have made it a reasonable and natural consequence of such breach of contract, communicated to or known by the defendants.

The jury, who had awarded lost profits, had been misdirected, and a retrial was ordered.

B. Foreseeability Not Foreseen

It is worth making the basic point that for a loss to be in the parties' reasonable contemplation it must be something on their 'horizon'[26] that they could have foreseen as sufficiently likely, but it is certainly not necessary (or relevant) that the claimant in fact considered or foresaw the particular loss.[27] This is entirely consistent with the basis of contractual responsibility (and the interpretation of contract terms to discover the parties' obligations) being objective not subjective.

---

[25] The headnote of *Hadley v Baxendale* states that the claimant told the defendant's clerk at the time of contracting that the mill was in fact stopped. This runs counter to the tenor of Baron Alderson's judgment in *Hadley*, and appears to be wrong, as is observed by Asquith LJ in *Victoria Laundry (Windsor) Ltd v Newman Industries Ltd* [1949] 2 KB 528 (CA) at 537–38. Of course, it may be that merely telling the defendant of a fact does not mean that the defendant takes responsibility for it, as discussed below in section 14.3E, but Baron Alderson appeared to understand that the defendant did not even know that the mill was at a standstill.

[26] *C Czarnikow Ltd v Koufos (The Heron II)* [1969] 1 AC 350 (HL) Lord Pearce at 416; *Transfield Shipping Inc v Mercator Shipping Inc (The Achilleas)* [2009] AC 61 (HL) Lord Walker at para 78.

[27] *Hammond & Co v Bussey* (1887) 20 QBD 79 (CA) Lord Goddard CJ at 88; *Victoria Laundry (Windsor) Ltd v Newman Industries Ltd* [1949] 2 KB 528 (CA) Asquith LJ at 550 pt 5.

C. Contemplation is Usually Tested at the Date of Contracting

The first point to note is that the question of contract remoteness is to be applied at the date of contracting,[28] whereas tort remoteness is tested at the date of breach. This follows from the 'assumption of responsibility' basis of the rule of contract remoteness: it is only at the date of contracting that the parties

> have the opportunity to limit their liability in damages when they are making their contract. They have the opportunity ... to draw attention to any special circumstances outside the ordinary course of things which they ought to have in contemplation when entering the contract[29]

and, crucially, only at the date of contracting that they can fix their price or exclusion/limitation clauses accordingly. (As Baron Alderson observed in *Hadley v Baxendale*, had the carrier been aware that delay might lead to a prolonged standstill of the mill 'the parties might have specially provided for the breach of contract by special terms as to the damages'.) As Hobson CJ explained in the Kentucky Court of Appeal:

> If one party could by a subsequent notice make the other party liable for such special damages, then the rights of the parties would not be determined by the contract between them or by their situation at that time, but by the act of one or the parties alone. The rule that notice should be given at the time the contract is entered into rests upon the ground that the person to whom the notice is given may have an opportunity to protect himself by the contract which he makes or by special precautions to avoid loss. A notice given afterwards by one party would afford no such opportunity for self-protection.[30]

Thus the parties are presumed to have assumed responsibility (and provided in the contract to the extent they wish to) for all losses that were sufficiently foreseeable at the date of contracting, but not those which only became sufficiently foreseeable at a later date.

(i) But a Later Date Where the Contract is Varied or is a Long-Term Contract?

As a limited exception to this, logic and some authority supports the view that where a contract is amended, the remoteness test may be reset, at least in relation to the obligations that were amended, since (and to the extent that) at the time of variation the parties have the opportunity again to adjust the price or add exclusion or limitation clauses, adjust their insurance or redouble their efforts to perform.[31]

Likewise, in long-term relationship contracts such as a solicitor's retainer, arguably it makes no sense to fix the assumption of responsibility at 'the moment when the plaintiff, as it were, walked into the defendants' office'.[32] A more flexible approach,

---

[28] Eg Lord Hope in *Jackson v Royal Bank of Scotland plc* [2005] 1 WLR 377 (HL) at para 36.

[29] Lord Hope in *Jackson v Royal Bank of Scotland plc* [2005] 1 WLR 377 (HL) at para 36.

[30] *Patterson v Illinois Central Railroad Corp Inc* 97 SW 423 (1906).

[31] A Kramer, 'Remoteness: New Problems with the Old Test' in D Saidov and R Cunnington, *Contract Damages: Domestic and International Perspectives* (Oxford, Hart Publishing, 2008) at 297–98.

[32] *Malyon v Lawrence, Messer & Co* [1968] 2 Lloyd's Rep 539 (QB) (Brabin J) at 550; A Kramer, ibid at 296–302.

fixing the scope of responsibility later, was applied in the solicitor's negligence case of *Pearson v Sanders Witherspoon*.[33] The same approach has been taken in cases of long-term banker/customer contracts that are terminable at will,[34] and in the context of the cross-undertaking in damages given upon the grant of an interim injunction, given that such injunctions are susceptible to variation or discharge by the court at any time.[35]

D. Knowledge: Two Limbs, One Rule

Baron Alderson's formulation in *Hadley v Baxendale*, quoted above,[36] appears to divide the remoteness rule into two parts. The first is losses arising 'naturally, ie, according to the usual course of things' or which 'flowed naturally from the breach of this contract in the great multitude of such cases occurring under ordinary circumstances', and the second 'such as may reasonably be supposed to have been in the contemplation of both parties, at the time they made the contract, as the probable result of the breach of it'.

Asquith LJ in *Victoria Laundry* explained that (as Baron Alderson himself indicates) there is really only one rule that the claimant can only recover loss 'as was at the time of the contract reasonably foreseeable as liable to result from the breach' but 'What was at that time reasonably so foreseeable depends on the knowledge then possessed by the parties'. The dichotomy applies to that knowledge, as there are two kinds:

> [O]ne imputed, the other actual. Everyone, as a reasonable person, is taken to know the 'ordinary course of things' and consequently what loss is liable to result from a breach of contract in that ordinary course. This is the subject matter of the 'first rule' in Hadley v. Baxendale. But to this knowledge, which a contract-breaker is assumed to possess whether he actually possesses it or not, there may have to be added in a particular case knowledge which he actually possesses, of special circumstances outside the 'ordinary course of things,' of such a kind that a breach in those special circumstances would be liable to cause

---

[33] *Pearson v Sanders Witherspoon* [2000] Lloyd's Rep PN 151 (CA), discussed below at text to n 176. But compare *Cadoks Pty Ltd v Wallace Westley & Vigar Pty Ltd* [2000] VSC 167 (SC of Victoria), obiter.

[34] *National Australia Bank Ltd v Nemur Varity P/L* [2002] 4 VR 252 (Victoria CA) Batt JA at para 49, concerning a current account. See also the dicta in *Murano v Bank of Montreal* (1995) 20 BLR (2d) 61 (Ontario Court of Justice) at paras 160 and 193 (appeal dismissed (1998) 163 DLR (4th) 21 (Ontario CA): 'Where a party can demand full payment of a loan at will, that party can assess daily whether to break off its contractual relationship. In the case of a demand loan, it can do so without breaching its contract provided it gives reasonable notice. In that particular context, it seems strange to be thrown back to the original date of contract for the purposes of foreseeability. In fact, confining loss assessment to the formation of a long standing "at will" banking relationship seems artificial and may be inconsistent with the general trend of authority harmonizing rules in tort and contract. Indeed, in this case, judging the foreseeability of loss in light of the Bank's knowledge closer to the date of breach is not likely to upset contractual intentions given the expectations of the parties at the date of contract formation that the plaintiffs' changing conditions would be closely monitored'.

[35] *Abbey Forwarding Ltd v Hone* [2012] EWHC 3525 (Ch) (Pelling QC) at paras 28–29.

[36] See section 14.3A.

more loss. Such a case attracts the operation of the 'second rule' so as to make additional loss also recoverable.[37]

As has later been confirmed, there is only, therefore a single rule.[38] The defendant is only liable for what is within its reasonable contemplation, but what is within its reasonable contemplation depends both on what the claimant could have foreseen because of its general knowledge of what ordinarily happens, and also because of the knowledge the defendant has been specifically given by the claimant prior to contracting. Thus:

> A party for this purpose is on notice of facts (i) which were actually known by him, (ii) which were known by his agent and which it was his agent's duty to communicate to him, and (iii) which he should reasonably have deduced from (i) and (ii).[39]

All that matters is 'the shared knowledge of both parties when the contract was made'.[40] The source of that knowledge is rarely important.

(i) The First Limb: Ordinary Knowledge Imputed to the Defendant

A useful illustration of the importance of the knowledge imputed to the defendant arises in the House of Lords' decision in *Balfour Beatty Construction (Scotland) Ltd v Scottish Power plc*.[41] There the electricity supplier would have known that interrupting supply would interrupt the claimant's aqueduct and road-building, but was not in that industry so did not know that concrete pouring was involved or in any event that if a concrete pour were interrupted that would irreversibly damage that concrete. As Lord Jauncey observed:

> It must always be a question of circumstances what one contracting party is presumed to know about the business activities of the other. No doubt the simpler the activity of the one, the more readily can it be inferred that the other would have reasonable knowledge thereof. However, when the activity of A involves complicated construction or manufacturing techniques, I see no reason why who supplies a commodity that A intends to use in the course of those techniques should be assumed, merely because of the order for the commodity, to be aware of the details of all the techniques undertaken by A and the effect thereupon of any failure of or deficiency in that commodity. Even if the Lord Ordinary had made a positive finding that continuous pour was a regular part of industrial practice it would not follow that in the absence of any other evidence suppliers of electricity such

---

[37] *Victoria Laundry (Windsor) Ltd v Newman Industries Ltd* [1949] 2 KB 528 (CA) at 539.
[38] See further Lord Reid in *C Czarnikow Ltd v Koufos (The Heron II)* [1969] 1 AC 350 (HL) at 385; Goff J in *Satef-Huttenes Albertus SpA v Paloma Tercera Shipping Co SA (The Pegase)* [1981] 1 Lloyd's Rep 175 at 182; *Transfield Shipping Inc v Mercator Shipping Inc (The Achilleas)* [2007] 2 Lloyd's Rep 555 (CA) Rix LJ at para 88 (appeal allowed [2009] AC 61 (HL)). The distinction between the two rules may still matter when construing exclusion clauses, which are often (depending upon their wording) taken to only exclude liability for loss of the special type (under the so-called second rule), which does not arise in the ordinary course of things (first rule loss).
[39] *Seven Seas Properties Ltd v Al-Essa (No 2)* [1993] 1 WLR 1083 (Lightman QC) at 1088.
[40] *Robophone Facilities Ltd v Blank* [1966] 1 WLR 1428 (CA) at 1448; *Kpohraror v Woolwich Building Society* [1996] 4 All ER 119 (CA) at 127–28; *Jackson v Royal Bank of Scotland plc* [2005] 1 WLR 377 (HL) Lord Hope at para 29 and Lord Walker at para 49.
[41] *Balfour Beatty Construction (Scotland) Ltd v Scottish Power plc* (1994) 71 BLR 20 (HL), [1994] SC(HL) 20.

as the Board should have been aware of that practice. I consider that the Lord Ordinary correctly interpreted Lord Wright's statements in the *A/B Karlshmans* [sic][42] case.

This rightly stresses the importance of asking how involved the defendant is in the claimant's industry, as this informs what the defendant can be expected to know and anticipate in relation to the consequences for the claimant of its breach.[43]

In the New York telegraph case of *Kerr Steamship v Radio Corporation of America*, an international message was sent in code at a cost of US$26.78 to instruct an agent to load cargo onto a vessel.[44] This was not done and freight worth US$6,675.29 was lost. Cardozo J explained that

> The defendant upon receiving from a steamship company a long telegram in cipher to be transmitted to Manila would naturally infer that the message had relation to business of some sort. Beyond that, it could infer nothing.

Telegraphers, like carriers and electricity suppliers, can by their breach cause damage to their business customers but have such a range of customers that the knowledge imputed to them as to the damage they might cause is very limited. Moreover, their pricing is general (not bespoke) and relatively low and it is not reasonable to understand such suppliers to undertake responsibility for the specific huge losses that a particular customer can incur:

> The sender can protect himself by insurance in one form or another if the risk of nondelivery or error appears to be too great. The total burden is not heavy since it is distributed among many, and can be proportioned in any instance to the loss likely to ensue. The company, if it takes out insurance for itself, can do no more than guess at the loss to be avoided. To pay for this unknown risk, it will be driven to increase the rates payable by all, though the increase is likely to result in the protection of a few.[45]

Accordingly, the loss was too remote and the damages were limited to the return of the price paid (presumably on the basis of restitution following termination).

E. Specially Communicated Information: Is Mere Notice Enough?

(i) Specially Communicated Information Increasing Liability

One of the key problem situations for the law of contract remoteness is that in which the claimant, at or before the time of contracting, conveys to the defendant information which renders foreseeable and quantifiable a loss that would otherwise (ie taking into account only the ordinary matters that would be imputed to the defendant) be unforeseeable or unquantifiable. If the remoteness test were simply about foreseeability, then the communication of such information to the defendant or its agent would be sufficient to render the loss foreseeable. Given, however, that

---

[42] This is a reference to *Monarch Steamship Co Ltd v Karlshamns Oljefabriker (A/B)* [1949] AC 196 (HL), in which Lord Wright at 224–25 discusses the extent to which 'As reasonable business men each must be taken to understand the ordinary practices and exigencies of the other's trade or business'.

[43] See further on this point below in section 14.6A(iii).

[44] *Kerr Steamship Co Inc v Radio Corporation of America* 245 NY 284 (1927) (NYCA).

[45] Ibid.

the test is and always has been about an assumption of responsibility, the law has always rightly resisted a finding of liability where the information was conveyed in casual terms, to a junior employee, or at the last minute, or otherwise in circumstances in which the parties would well have understood that the defendant did not re-evaluate the contract, including its terms, price and risks, and therefore nothing has changed as regards the implied assumption of responsibility.

The problem principally arises where the defendant is not in the same industry as the claimant and provides its service to all sorts of claimants for all sorts of purposes, as a carrier often does. Typically it will price its service accordingly and in general terms. This generic pricing could take into account extreme losses that could arise to particular customers, but usually will not, as it would be uncompetitive for most customers to have to pay a price that spreads extreme losses that cannot arise in their own cases among them. Nowadays financial losses will usually be expressly excluded in such carriage contracts, but even if not, it will rarely be reasonable to understand the carrier to have taken responsibility for such idiosyncratic losses:[46]

> For example, an innkeeper furnishes a chaise to a son to drive to see his dying father; the chaise breaks down; the son arrives too late to see his father, who has cut him out of his will in his disappointment at his not coming to see him; in such a case it is obvious that the actual damage to the plaintiff has nothing to do with the contract to supply the chaise.[47]

The innkeeper is not liable. Crucially, the point should usually not be resolved any differently even if the son communicated to the innkeeper, at the time of contracting, the reason he needed the chaise. Or:

> Take the case of a barrister on his way to practise at the Calcutta bar, where he may have a large number of briefs awaiting him: through the default of the Peninsular & Oriental Company he is detained in Egypt or in the Suez boat, and consequently sustains great loss; is the company to be responsible for that, because they happened to know the purpose for which the traveller was going?[48]

The answer is no.[49] The updated version of this example is that of the taxi-driver:

> If I tell my taxi driver that I will miss the opportunity of making a profit of £1m if I fail to reach an appointment on time, his acceptance of me as a passenger should not lead to the inference that he accepts the risk.[50]

---

[46] See further the cases above in chapter four, section 4.2B(vi)(a).

[47] *Chaplin v Hicks* [1911] 2 KB 786 (CA) Fletcher Moulton LJ at 794, obiter. See also the example of the taxi driver who injures the passenger on his way to buy a winning lottery ticket: *Aldgate Construction Co Ltd v Unibar Plumbing and Heating Ltd* (2010) 130 Con LR 190 (Akenhead J).

[48] *British Columbia and Vancouver's Island Spar, Lumber and Saw-Mill Co Ltd v Nettleship* (1868) LR 3 CP 499 Willes J at 510.

[49] The problem is even starker in the days of common carriers, who were obliged to carry everyone and therefore their continuing to contract even after learning the information could not indicate any assumption of risk, although arguably this rule of common carriage did not apply in cases of extraordinary risk. See further *Horne v Midland Railway Co* (1873) LR 8 CP 131 at 145; *Rivers v George White and Sons Co Ltd* (1919) 46 DLR 145 (Saskatchewan CA) at 147; *C Czarnikow Ltd v Koufos (The Heron II)* [1966] 2 QB 695 (CA) Diplock LJ at 728.

[50] D Harris, D Campbell and R Halson (eds), *Remedies in Contract and Tort*, 2nd edn (London, Butterworths, 2002) at 97, discussed in A Kramer, 'An Agreement-Centred Approach to Remoteness and Contract Damage' in Cohen and McKendrick (eds), *Comparative Remedies for Breach of Contract* (Oxford, Hart Publishing, 2005) at 269–70 and Lord Hoffmann, 'The Achilleas: custom and practice or

However, if the taxi-driver ups his fare to £100,000 then it is clear that he should then be liable.[51] The question is why? The answer (although these points and this result can have no purchase under the traditional pre-*Achilleas* view of remoteness) is that before changing the fare, the driver has clearly not priced the service to take account of such risks as the £1m lost profit, and it would be commercially absurd to expect the driver to have taken that risk in return for the ordinary modest fare.[52] Knowledge of the risk of loss is nothing to the point; the information has not been factored into the contract terms or economics. However, if the driver ups his fare to £100,000, that signals a clear adjustment of the economics of the taxi service, the price rise being clearly a response to the increased risk of loss and importance to the customer, in which circumstances it is reasonable to understand the driver to be taking the risk of being late and causing the £1m loss.

Even before the *Achilleas*, the law had recognised this reality and developed the tools to deal with it. Thus the nineteenth-century cases, including *British Columbia and Vancouver's Island Spar, Lumber and Saw-Mill Co Ltd v Nettleship*, from which the barrister travelling to Calcutta example comes, made clear that merely being told something was not enough, and it was necessary that the loss be 'brought home' to the defendant at or before the time of contracting:

> [I]t could not be contended that the mere fact of knowledge, without more, would be a reason for imposing upon him a greater degree of liability than would otherwise have been cast upon him. To my mind, that leads to the inevitable conclusion that the mere fact of knowledge cannot increase the liability. The knowledge must be brought home to the party sought to be charged, under such circumstances that he must know that the person he contracts with reasonably believes that he accepts the contract with the special condition attached to it.[53]

This approach was subsequently disapproved,[54] but then nevertheless revived, for example in Lightman QC's comments in *Seven Seas Properties Ltd v Al-Essa (No 2)* that it is necessary that the claimant 'signalised' to the defendant his purpose and the consequences of breach,[55] or requirements that they were 'brought home' to him,[56]

---

foreseeability?' (2010) *Edinburgh L Rev* 47 at 56. The example is discussed by Phang Boon Leong JA in *MFM Restaurants Pte Ltd v Fish & Co Restaurants Pte Ltd* [2011] 4 LRC 1 (Singapore CA) at paras 118–20, and Menon CJ in *Out of the Box Pte Ltd v Wanin Industries Pte Ltd* [2013] SGCA (Singapore CA) at paras 30–34, although that court in both cases rejected the implied assumption of responsibility test and preferred to allow the court to reject liability for the taxi driver on grounds of reasonableness, policy or justice.

[51] See Harris, Campbell and Halson ibid; Kramer ibid; and Hoffmann ibid.

[52] Disproportion between price and risk is discussed further below in section 14.6D.

[53] *British Columbia and Vancouver's Island Spar Lumber and Saw-Mill Co Ltd v Nettleship* (1868) LR 3 CP 499 Willes J at 509 also at 505 (and note that Willes J had been counsel for Mr Baxendale in *Hadley v Baxendale*). See also *Horne v Midland Railway Co* (1873) LR 8 CP 131; and JD Mayne, *A Treatise on the Law of Damages* (London, Sweet, 1856) at 8, the first edition of the book that later became *McGregor on Damages*.

[54] *Czarnikow Ltd v Koufos (The Heron II)* [1969] 1 AC 350 (HL) obiter per Lord Upjohn at 421–22; US Restatement (Second) of Contracts §351 cmt a; Uniform Commercial Code s 2-715 cmt 2.

[55] *Seven Seas Properties Ltd v Al-Essa (No 2)* [1993] 1 WLR 1083 (Lightman QC) at 1088. Cf *Satef-Huttenes Albertus SpA v Paloma Tercera Shipping Co SA (The Pegase)* [1981] 1 Lloyd's Rep 175 (Goff J) at 184.

[56] *Out of the Box Pte Ltd v Wanin Industries Pte Ltd* [2013] SGCA 15 (Singapore CA) at para 47 (although expressly applying a policy, not assumption of responsibility, approach to remoteness).

and did not come to him 'casually'.[57] Following *The Achilleas*, we can now accept this as part of the principle of assumption of responsibility.

The law is therefore as Mayne described in 1877 in the third edition of what became *McGregor on Damages*:

> Where a person who has knowledge or notice of such special circumstances might refuse to enter into the contract at all, or might demand a higher remuneration for entering into it, the fact that he accepts the contract without requiring any higher rate will be evidence, although not conclusive evidence, from which it may be inferred that he has accepted the additional risk in case of breaches.[58]

In *Hadley v Baxendale* itself, it does not necessarily follow that even if the carrier knew the mill was at a standstill it would be liable for the consequences. A similar example was given in an Arkansas case of a large manufacturing establishment brought to a stop by a single machine. In this example, the defendant is a machinist or blacksmith called out to repair it. Nevertheless, the machinist or blacksmith would not normally be liable for losses of the entire business even if he or she breached the contract and knew that the business was dependent upon his or her work,

> in the absence of a contract on his part to be thus liable, unless the notice and the circumstances under which he made the contract were such that he ought reasonably to have known that in the event of his failure to perform his contract the other party would look to him to make good the loss.[59]

(ii) Specially Communicated Information that Reduces Liability

The defendant's knowledge is relevant to the scope of its assumption of responsibility. This (like the assumption of responsibility rule generally) can cut both ways. It is possible for knowledge and circumstances to reduce the scope of the defendant's responsibility. In one solicitor negligence case where the solicitor failed to tell the claimant of the date of an auction, it was accepted that if the claimant had only told the solicitor that the claimant wanted to know about the auction to satisfy its curiosity, losses resulting from the claimant's missing the opportunity to buy at the auction would have been outside the scope of the defendant's responsibility.[60] The result is questionable—mere knowledge (unless there is an estoppel) should not be enough to reduce the defendant's responsibility, just as it is not enough to increase it—but the example is a useful illustration of the point that liability can be adjusted so as either to include or exclude the loss that actually occurs.[61]

---

[57] *Transfield Shipping Inc v Mercator Shipping Inc (The Achilleas)* [2007] 2 Lloyd's Rep 555 (CA) Rix LJ at para 115.

[58] JD Mayne and L Smith, *Mayne's Treatise on Damages*, 3rd edn (London, Stevens and Hayes, 1877) at 33.

[59] *Hooks Smelting Co v Planters' Compress Co* 79 SW 1052 (1904) (SC of Arkansas).

[60] *Thomas Eggar Verrall Bowles v Rice*, 21 December 1999 (Rimer J).

[61] See more generally on this point section 14.5A below.

F. Likelihood

A rather unnecessary semantic discussion in the House of Lords during its decision in *The Heron II*[62] canvassed several possibilities as to how likely the loss must be foreseen as being for it not to be found too remote, but the most that was concluded in that case was that (a) for a loss to be recoverable it will usually have to be foreseeable as 'not unlikely' or as having a 'substantial degree of probability',[63] and (b) this level of likelihood is higher than that at which a loss must be foreseeable to be recoverable in the tort of negligence.

These two points will be dealt with separately.

(i) How Likely

Although Lord Reid's formulation in *The Heron II* that a loss must be foreseeable as a 'not unlikely' consequence of breach is the most commonly adopted test,[64] Lord Walker correctly explains in *The Achilleas*:

> [I]t is not simply a question of probability. It is also a question of what the contracting parties must be taken to have had in mind, having regard to the nature and object of their business transaction. If a manufacturer of lightning conductors sells a defective conductor and the customer's house burns down as a result, the manufacturer will not escape liability by proving that only one in a hundred of his customers' buildings had actually been struck by lightning.[65]

Similarly, Lord Pearce in *The Heron II* said:

> Suppose a contractor was employed to repair the ceiling of one of the Law Courts and did it so negligently that it collapsed on the heads of those in court. I should be inclined to think that any tribunal (including the learned baron himself) would have found as a fact that the damage arose 'naturally, ie, according to the usual course of things.' Yet if one takes into account the nights, weekends, and vacations, when the ceiling might have collapsed, the odds against it collapsing on top of anybody's head are nearly ten to one.[66]

It is simply enough (for foreseeability purposes) that the loss is sufficiently likely to feature in the 'horizon of the parties' contemplation,[67] ie it is sufficiently salient or obvious to the promisor (and likelihood is an important aspect of this) that it would

---

[62] *Czarnikow Ltd v Koufos (The Heron II)* [1969] 1 AC 350 (HL).

[63] As later recorded in *Balfour Beatty Construction (Scotland) Ltd v Scottish Power plc* [1994] SC(HL) 20, (1994) 71 BLR 20 (HL).

[64] Eg *Transworld Oil Ltd v North Bay Shipping Corporation (The Rio Claro)* [1987] 2 Lloyd's Rep 173 (Staughton J) at 175; *Brown v KMR Services Ltd* [1995] 4 All ER 598 (CA) Stuart-Smith LJ at 621; *Siemens Building Technologies FE Ltd v Supershield Ltd* [2010] EWCA Civ 7 at paras 38 and 42–43; *Borealis AB v Geogas Trading SA* [2011] 1 Lloyd's Rep 482 (Gross LJ) at para 48. And see earlier *Re Hall (R and H) Ltd and WH Pim Junior & Co's Arbitration* [1928] All ER Rep 763 (HL) Lord Shaw at 769–70.

[65] *Transfield Shipping Inc v Mercator Shipping Inc (The Achilleas)* [2009] AC 61 (HL) at para 78.

[66] *C Czarnikow Ltd v Koufos (The Heron II)* [1969] 1 AC 350 (HL) Lord Pearce at 417. For a real ceiling collapse case where there was recovery for personal injury, see *Pope v St Helen's Theatre Ltd* [1947] KB 30 (Sellers J).

[67] *C Czarnikow Ltd v Koufos (The Heron II)* [1969] 1 AC 350 (HL) Lord Pearce at 416; *Transfield Shipping Inc v Mercator Shipping Inc (The Achilleas)* [2009] AC 61 (HL) Lord Walker at para 78; *Out of the Box Pte Ltd v Wanin Industries Pte Ltd* [2013] SGCA 15 (Singapore CA) at paras 13 and 17.

feature in any setting of the price, insurance and exclusion clauses and it can therefore be assumed (absent an exclusion clause, of course) that the promisor assumed responsibility for it. More important in the ceiling case is that the Lord Chancellor's Department would be able to say

> We employed you to repair the ceiling so that it should not fall down. In undertaking to repair it, you accepted liability to compensate us for any loss which might be caused by it falling down, however unlikely that particular loss might be.[68]

As explained below in section 14.6A, an important aspect of this, especially in *The Achilleas*, is not merely whether the type of loss is foreseeable by the defendant at the time of contracting, but whether it is (roughly) *quantifiable*.

(ii) More Likeliness is Required than under the Tort Test

As for the latter point, this was doubted by all of the Court of Appeal in *Parsons (Livestock) Ltd v Uttley Ingham & Co Ltd*,[69] who were of the view that the tests in contract and tort were the same (Lord Denning MR contending that they were only the same in physical damage cases).[70] However, it was confirmed by the House of Lords in *The Heron II* that the contract test is indeed different from the tort test, and that contract liability requires the loss to have been foreseeable as more likely than merely 'reasonably foreseeable' as in the tort test.[71]

As is explained by Lord Reid in *The Heron II*, in justifying the difference, in a contract situation the claimant can direct the defendant's attention to any unusual loss, whereas in a tort case 'the tortfeasor cannot reasonably complain if he has to pay for some very unusual but nevertheless foreseeable damage which results from his wrongdoing'.[72]

G. When Considering Remoteness, Assume Breach

It was made clear by the Court of Appeal in *Parsons (Livestock) Ltd v Uttley Ingham & Co Ltd*, and must be right, that the question is as to whether a loss was a sufficiently foreseeable consequence of a *breach*, ie assuming that the breach (however unlikely) has occurred.[73] The fact that a particular breach is unlikely does

---

[68] Lord Hoffmann, 'The Achilleas: custom and practice or foreseeability?' (2010) *Edinburgh L Rev* 47 at 55.

[69] *Parsons (Livestock) Ltd v Uttley Ingham & Co Ltd* [1978] QB 791 (CA).

[70] The tort test referred to in the text is that in negligence and was laid down by the Privy Council in *Overseas Tankship (UK) Ltd v Morts Dock & Engineering Co Ltd (The Wagon Mound)* [1961] AC 388 (PC).

[71] *C Czarnikow Ltd v Koufos (The Heron II)* [1969] 1 AC 350 (HL) Lord Reid at 385–87 and 389, Lord Hodson at 411, Lord Pearce at 414, Lord Upjohn at 422. Lord Denning's minority views in *Parsons v Uttley Ingham & Co Ltd* [1978] QB 791 (CA) that the contract and tort test were the same in cases of physical damage or personal injury have not been taken up and are not good law.

[72] [1969] 1 AC 350 at 386. As to whether this distinction justifies a difference in all tort cases—it is this writer's view that it cannot in *Hedley Byrne*-type assumption of responsibility cases—see below in section 14.5C.

[73] *Parsons (Livestock) Ltd v Uttley Ingham & Co Ltd* Scarman LJ at [1978] QB 791 (CA), Lord Denning MR at 802.

not affect the remoteness question, as the question is what losses the defendant can be assumed to have taken responsibility for in relation to the particular obligation, and so the court must assume the parties were considering the particular obligation when considering their responsibilities.

H. The Type or Kind of Loss

The precise extent and particular circumstances of the loss that occurs need not be foreseeable, and indeed at the time of contracting any precise occurrence of loss resulting from breach will be highly unlikely (given all the other precise occurrences that may come about). Instead it is only necessary that the 'loss or injury was of a type which the parties could reasonably be supposed to have in contemplation',[74] although the reference to 'type' of loss is sometimes replaced by a reference to the 'kind' of loss.[75] It accordingly does not matter that the 'extent'[76] or 'scale or amount'[77] was unforeseeable. It is necessary that the 'type of consequence, not necessarily the specific consequence' was foreseeable as sufficiently likely.[78]

This principle was applied by the Court of Appeal in *Victoria Laundry (Windsor) Ltd v Newman Industries Ltd*,[79] one of the leading cases on remoteness. The case concerned the contract for sale of a boiler to a laundering and dyeing company. It was held to be not too remote that if the boiler was delivered late the claimant would suffer dyeing and laundering lost profits, but the lost profits from a particularly lucrative Ministry of Supply dyeing contract (of which the defendant was unaware at the time of contracting) *were* too remote. (The recovery was therefore limited to the ordinary profits, as discussed below.[80])

In *Parsons (Livestock) Ltd v Uttley Ingham & Co Ltd*[81] it was held by the Court of Appeal that illness of pigs was a foreseeable consequence of a bulk pig food storage hopper having its ventilator improperly sealed (a breach of a sale warranty that the hopper be fit for purpose, or of the duty to erect the hopper carefully), because the inadequate ventilation might (and did) lead to mouldy pignuts stored in the hopper. Although this was only a slight possibility, and the particular illness that resulted—E coli resulting from diarrhoea and leading to the death of 254 pigs—was far more serious than was reasonably foreseeable as even a slight possibility, none of that prevented recovery. The importance of the case is in the refusal to narrowly define the type of loss that had to be foreseeable as E coli, and the emphasis instead that 'pig illness' was a foreseeable result of mouldy nuts. However, given that the

---

[74] Ibid Scarman LJ at 806, with whom Orr LJ agreed.
[75] *C Czarnikow Ltd v Koufos (The Heron II)* [1969] 1 AC 350 (HL) Lord Reid at 382 and 385.
[76] *Brown v KMR Services Ltd* [1995] 4 All ER 598 (CA) Stuart-Smith LJ at 621.
[77] Ibid.
[78] *Parsons (Livestock) Ltd v Uttley Ingham & Co Ltd* [1978] QB 791 (CA) Scarman LJ at 813. See also *Transworld Oil Ltd v North Bay Shipping Corporation (The Rio Claro)* [1987] 2 Lloyd's Rep 173 (Staughton J) at 175.
[79] *Victoria Laundry (Windsor) Ltd v Newman Industries Ltd* [1949] 2 KB 528 (CA), referred to above in chapter six, section 6.4C(i). See also *Cory v Thames Ironworks and Shipbuilding Co Ltd* (1868) LR 3 QB 181 (QBD), discussed below in section 14.4.
[80] See section 14.4.
[81] *Parsons (Livestock) Ltd v Uttley Ingham & Co Ltd* [1978] QB 791 (CA).

pig farmer did not see any real risk in nuts he knew were mouldy making pigs ill (which is why he knowingly fed mouldy nuts to the pigs),[82] and that 'as a rule, mouldy nuts do not harm pigs',[83] the decision is a surprising one: the main loss that is in the contemplation of the parties as a result of this breach is the cost of buying replacement pignuts.

In *Brown v KMR Services Ltd*[84] some Lloyd's members' agents negligently failed to warn a Lloyd's name of the risks of joining various underwriting syndicates, but claimed that the number of catastrophes that struck in the relevant years subsequently was unforeseeable and could never have been predicted. Although the agents were right about this, it was held by the Court of Appeal, which explicitly engaged with the type/extent issue, to be irrelevant. The *type* of risk was foreseeable and was what the agents should have protected the names against, and the unforeseeable extent was neither here nor there.

As Lord Hoffmann observes in *The Achilleas*, judges can only determine what losses are of the same 'type' and what are not, ie how generally a type is drawn, by applying the underlying purpose of the rule. Otherwise all financial losses could be of the same type; or all financial losses from a particular use of property;[85] or all financial losses from a particular use of property involving only ordinarily profitable onward contracts. Thus, Lord Hoffmann stated:

> What is the basis for deciding whether loss is of the same type or a different type? It is not a question of Platonist metaphysics. The distinction must rest upon some principle of the law of contract. In my opinion, the only rational basis for the distinction is that it reflects what would reasonably have been regarded by the contracting party as significant for the purposes of the risk he was undertaking.[86]

Accordingly, 'the vendor of the boilers [in the *Victoria Laundry* case] would have regarded the profits on these contracts as a different and higher form of risk than the general risk of loss of profits by the laundry'.[87] Merely seeking to apply a 'type versus extent' principle makes *Victoria Laundry* a difficult case to justify. Dyeing profits on a particular lucrative contract would, as matter of plain English, usually be viewed as different from ordinary dyeing profits only in extent and not type, and therefore they should on that basis be recoverable. But when 'type' is understood as merely allowing the court to demarcate losses that the parties would treat as significantly different, for example because they are outside the range of losses that the defendant would be expected to take into account when pricing or insuring, then the law regains coherence and sense, and the decision can be justified.

Likewise the charterer in *The Achilleas* would have regarded losses on a follow-on charter as being of a different and higher form of risk than the general risk of loss

---

[82] Ibid Lord Denning MR at 799.

[83] Ibid.

[84] *Brown v KMR Services Ltd* [1995] 4 All ER 598 (CA).

[85] For a rare example of an explicit discussion of the effect of drawing the type in different ways, see *British & Commonwealth Holdings plc v Quadrex Holdings Inc* (CA), 10 April 1995 at transcript p 63.

[86] *Transfield Shipping Inc v Mercator Shipping Inc (The Achilleas)* [2009] AC 61 (HL) at para 22.

[87] Ibid per Lord Hoffmann at para 22. See also the discussion of *Victoria Laundry* in *Brown v KMR Services Ltd* [1995] 4 All ER 598 (CA), Stuart-Smith LJ at 621.

of profits for the period of the overrun.[88] (Seeking to explain this by the traditional approach, divorcing the remoteness test from its underlying rationale, descends into absurdity. Lord Rodger attempted to apply the traditional test without any reference to implied understandings, and was forced to declare that it was the sheer 'extent' of the losses on follow-on charters that made them of a different type.[89])

In the *Rubenstein* mis-selling dispute, the bank's breach of duty was in failing to warn the claimant that the investment involved some risk, and therefore the bank was liable upon the market collapse despite the extent of the collapse being unforeseeable.[90] However, the complication was that the claimant had told the bank that he was intending to invest only in the short term, and had he stuck to that the losses due to market collapse after two years would not have been suffered. This caused the Court of Appeal concern, but this powerful argument of the bank (that the loss was too remote, the chain broken by keeping the investment, or that losses after a year were outside the scope of the bank's duty) ultimately failed on the facts, as the claimant expected to hold the investments until he had bought his new home and although he expected that to be within a year the parties knew it might not be, and further the claimant's choice to hold the investments longer was very much informed by his false understanding that he had no risk.[91]

Of course, in these cases merely identifying a different type of loss does not answer the question. The point is that although the higher forms of risk were probably also foreseeable, they were losses for which the parties would not reasonably understand the defendant to have taken responsibility.

(i) The Type Test and Physical Damage

Lord Denning MR in *Parsons* explained the finding of lack of remoteness on the basis that where physical damage is concerned, the more relaxed tort test of reasonable foreseeability applies, whether the cause of action is in contract or tort.[92] The majority (Orr and Scarman LJJ) rejected this reasoning and came to the same conclusion but on conventional grounds, applying the contract remoteness test. However, it is worth examining Lord Denning's reasoning, which was justified by two false premises. First, he drew support from latent defect cases where the defect was often highly unforeseeable. However, as explained in the *Parsons* case and above,[93] it is necessary to apply the foreseeability (contemplation) test to the consequences of a breach once it is assumed that the breach is known of; it is the

---

[88] *Transfield Shipping Inc v Mercator Shipping Inc (The Achilleas)* [2009] AC 61 (HL) Lord Hoffmann at para 22.

[89] Ibid Lord Rodger at para 53. This makes even less sense in *The Achilleas* than in *Victoria Laundry*. At least in *Victoria Laundry* the contract was at a specially high price, and further the cap rule discussed below at section 14.4 meant that the claimant recovered the ordinary lost profits that it would have suffered but for the particularly lucrative contract. In *The Achilleas* the particular follow-on charter was merely at the market rate (although the market was high) and fairly but not extremely long, and moreover there was no award of lost profits on a cheaper shorter follow-on charter, only of lost profits for the few days of the overrun.

[90] *Rubenstein v HSBC Bank plc* [2012] EWCA Civ 1184, discussed further below at text to n 208.

[91] Ibid at paras 120–22.

[92] *Parsons (Livestock) Ltd v Uttley Ingham & Co Ltd* [1978] QB 791 (CA) at 803–4.

[93] See section 14.3G.

loss, not the breach itself that must be in the parties' contemplation. Secondly, Lord Denning drew support from the argument that in concurrent liability cases the remoteness test should be the same. As is argued below,[94] this is broadly correct, but Lord Denning was wrong to say that in such cases the test should be the tort test, as it should be the contract test.

Nevertheless, Lord Denning was correct that in general terms physical damage is more rarely found too remote than economic loss such as lost profits.[95] This is explicable now that remoteness is understood as being about assumption of responsibility. Certainly, it is easier and more usual for a defendant to take out an indemnity policy for liability for physical damage or personal injury than for lost profits. In addition, a claimant is less likely to accept the risk of physical damage or personal injury in a sanguine manner as one of the costs of the business or activity, not least because whereas economic losses are merely a matter of money to be offset by profit, most claimants would not trade physical damage and personal injury for profits. Finally, many physical damage and personal injury cases are consumer cases, and in such contracts it would be normal to assume that the supplier takes the risk of the goods or service being physically unsafe.

I. Remoteness Not of the Loss but of its Non-Mitigability

Where the shared expectation was that the claimant would be able to mitigate the otherwise contemplated loss, the loss will usually not be within the scope of the defendant's assumption of responsibility. This is one reason why damages from a sub-sale are rarely recoverable in patently defective or destroyed goods cases: unless the defendant could have known that the sub-sale was a chain sale that required the exact goods the defendant was supplying, it will usually reasonably have assumed that the claimant would be able to mitigate any losses by resort to the market.[96]

An illustration can be taken from the conversion case of *Saleslease Ltd v Davis*.[97] The defendant detained the claimant's equipment, causing it to lose the benefit of a leasing arrangement that, to the defendant's knowledge, the claimant had with a third party (the defendant's tenant). However, the defendant did not know and could not have been expected to know that the claimant would not be able to lease the equipment to anyone else and that therefore a loss of hiring profits was unavoidable. The majority of the Court of Appeal therefore awarded the claimant nothing, as it had successfully sold the goods to the market upon their return.

---

[94] See section 14.5C.

[95] That the rules are not applied in quite the same way to physical damage is implied by Lord Walker in *Transfield Shipping Inc v Mercator Shipping Inc (The Achilleas)* [2009] AC 61 (HL) at para 82.

[96] See eg *Kwei Tek Chao v British Traders and Shippers Ltd* [1954] 2 QB 459 (Devlin J) at 489–90: 'no evidence to show that it could ever have been contemplated that if the goods were not delivered it would be necessary for the plaintiffs to do anything except go out into the market and buy similar goods which would have taken their place'.

[97] *Saleslease Ltd v Davis* [1999] 1 WLR 1664 (CA), esp Waller LJ at 1671.

J. The Test Applies to Both the Actual and the Hypothetical

All losses depend upon a comparison of what actually happened (the breach position) with what would have happened but for the breach (the non-breach position). Both sides of this comparison fall within the remoteness enquiry. Thus a loss may be too remote because the explosion or flood that actually occurred following the breach was too unlikely and so remote. Alternatively, a loss may be too remote because the profitable use to which the claimant *would* have put property but for the breach was too unlikely and so remote.

The first half of this enquiry, the investigation of what actually happened after the breach, is also governed by the principles of legal causation (certain events may break the chain of causation) and mitigation (it may be that the claimant acted unreasonably after the breach).

The second half of the enquiry, dealing with whether there are features of what would have happened but for the breach which render the loss irrecoverable, is almost solely a matter for the remoteness principle.[98]

14.4 The Cap Rule from *Cory v Thames Ironworks*

An important, although often overlooked, rule within remoteness is that by which if part of the actual loss suffered is too remote, the claimant can nevertheless recover damages for loss up to the 'cap' of a non-remote (albeit not suffered) loss. As Hobhouse J (as he then was) observed: 'Remoteness of damages in contract cases is not to be decided on an all or nothing basis'.[99]

A. The Cases

In *Cory v Thames Ironworks and Shipbuilding Company*,[100] a seller of a floating boom derrick hull was liable for the loss of profits during six months of delay. The ordinary use for such a hull would be to store coal, but the claimant had in mind a novel use of transhipping coals from collieries to barges (after putting a hydraulic crane on the hull), which the defendant could never have anticipated. The claimant accepted that the special use was too remote and only claimed for the smaller amount of profits it would have made had it been employing the hull for its ordinary use.[101] The court found for the claimant and awarded damages measured by the amount that would have been lost had the claimant been intending the ordinary

---

[98] Although see below as to whether legal causation applies to the non-breach position.

[99] *Islamic Republic of Iran Shipping Lines v Ierax Shipping Co of Panama (The Forum Craftsman)* [1991] 1 Lloyd's Rep 81 (Hobhouse J) at 85.

[100] *Cory v Thames Ironworks and Shipbuilding Co Ltd* (1868) LR 3 QB 181 (QBD).

[101] That the claimant only sought the smaller amount can be seen from the summary of the claimant's argument ibid at 185.

use for the hull. Blackburn J then explained why the contemplated but not suffered loss was recoverable:

> But Mr. Coleridge's argument would come to this, that the damages could never be anything but what both parties contemplated; and where the buyer intended to apply the thing to a purpose which would make the damages greater, and did not intend to apply it to the purpose which the seller supposed he intended to apply it, the consequence would be to set the defendant free altogether. That would not be just.[102]

In the same case, Cockburn J explained the result as follows:

> [I]f the two parties are not *ad idem quoad* the use to which the article is to be applied, then you can only take as the measure of damages the profit which would result from the ordinary use of the article for the purpose for which the seller supposed it was bought.[103]

The same principle was applied by the Court of Appeal in *Victoria Laundry (Windsor) Ltd v Newman Industries Ltd*,[104] discussed above.[105] The particularly lucrative Ministry of Supply dyeing contract was too remote, but the court awarded a 'general (and perhaps conjectural) sum for loss of business in respect of dyeing contracts to be reasonably expected',[106] even though the claimant had no intention of conducting such ordinary business.[107] This was expressly approved by the Lord Reid in the House of Lords in *The Heron II*, also describing them as 'conjectural'.[108]

This approach was applied by Lord Caplan sitting in the Scottish Outer House in the context of a breach of contract by sub-contractors on the British Piper Alpha off-shore oil platform, where an explosion in 1988 killed 165 people.[109] Liability on the part of the claimant head contractor in a Texas court, where large jury-awarded punitive damages were available, was held to be for a different type of loss to that of liability generally and too remote, as the reasons why the claimant was vulnerable to third party victims successfully establishing Texas jurisdiction and pursuing a Texas claim (that the claimant operated its business partly in Texas) were unknown to the defendants. The more normal amount if an award against the head contractor had been made in Scotland rather than Texas was still awarded as damages under the *Cory* rule. In this case settlement was reached with the victims on a mid-Atlantic basis, but it was unrecoverable against the defendant to the extent to which it was uplifted to allow for the possibility that the claim would be fought in Texas.[110]

---

[102] Ibid at 191.

[103] Ibid at 188.

[104] *Victoria Laundry (Windsor) Ltd v Newman Industries Ltd* [1949] 2 KB 528 (CA), referred to above at text to chapter six n 81.

[105] See text to n 79.

[106] [1949] 2 KB 528 Asquith LJ at 543. Tettenborn describes them as 'putative': Tettenborn and Wilby, *The Law of Damages*, 2nd edn (London, LexisNexis, 2010) at para 6.37.

[107] As is pointed out by JD McCamus, *The Law of Contracts* (Toronto, Irwin Law Inc, 2005) at 862.

[108] *Czarnikow Ltd v Koufos (The Heron II)* [1969] 1 AC 350 (HL) at 389.

[109] *Elf Enterprise Caledonia Ltd v London Bridge Engineering Ltd* (Court of Session, Outer House), 2 September 1997 at sections 9.3.7–9.3.8 and 13. The case actually turned on construction of indemnity clauses in the sub-contracts, but the conclusions were reached by the importation of common law remoteness rules. See [2000] Lloyd's Rep IR 249.

[110] But a different result was reached by the House of Lords on construction of the insurance policy covering the losses: *Caledonia North Sea Ltd v Norton (No 2)* [2002] SCLR 346 (HL), especially Lord Mackay at para 69.

The approach has also been applied to the recovery, against a non-delivering seller, of lost profits on a sub-sale where the sub-sale was unusually at a fixed price but the recoverable loss treated the sub-sale as if the price was pegged to the Platt's index,[111] or where the sub-sale contained a high liquidated damages clause,[112] or was otherwise 'extravagant and unusual';[113] to a claim by a seller for non-acceptance where the profit the claimant would have made was too 'extravagant or unusual';[114] and to claims against a late delivering carrier for lost profits on a sub-sale (a military shoe sub-sale to the French army was at an unusually high price,[115] and in another case the delay was unforeseeably long,[116] and in another the losses were exacerbated by the claimant's low stock levels of which the defendant was unaware.[117]) Likewise the approach has been applied to cases of a charterer's lost profits on sub-fixtures caused by interruption of hire due to the shipowner's breach,[118] and an unforeseeably long delay to a voyage caused by the defendant's breach which wet the claimant's sugar,[119] and (until *The Achilleas*) a late redelivery by the charterer.[120]

Although this rule is not explicitly discussed very often, it is applied in a much broader range of cases than these. Thus in *The Achilleas* itself,[121] the claimant recovered the difference between the market rate and the contract rate for the period of the overrun of the charter. In fact the shipowner did not suffer this loss, as had the vessel been returned it would not have chartered the vessel out on the market at the date of redelivery, it having already chartered the vessel at a much higher rate for 4–6 months to begin on redelivery by the defendant. That follow-on charter loss

---

[111] *Coastal International Trading Ltd v Maroil AG* [1988] 1 Lloyd's Rep 92 (Leggatt J) at 96. Cf *Duff & Co v The Iron and Steel Fencing and Buildings Co* (1891) 19 R 199 (Court of Session, 1st Division) at 205 where it was confirmed that only 'ordinary commercial profit' is in the parties' contemplation.

[112] *Die Elbinger Actien-gesellschaft Für Fabrication von Eisenbahn Materiel v Armstrong* (1874) LR 9 QB 473; *Grébert-Borgnis v J & W Nugent* (1885) 15 QBD 85 (CA), Brett MR at 90. See also *Re Hall (R and H) Ltd and WH Pim Junior & Co's Arbitration* [1928] All ER Rep 763 (HL) Viscount Dunedin at 767.

[113] *Re Hall (R and H) Ltd and WH Pim Junior & Co's Arbitration* [1928] All ER Rep 763 (HL) obiter Viscount Dunedin at 767.

[114] *North Sea Energy Holdings v Petroleum Authority of Thailand* [1997] 2 Lloyd's Rep 418 (Thomas J) at 438–39, affirmed [1999] 1 Lloyd's Rep 483 (CA), approved in *Transfield Shipping Inc v Mercator Shipping Inc (The Achilleas)* [2007] 2 Lloyd's Rep 555 (CA) at para 112. This was obiter, as in fact it was found that the claimant could not have supplied the oil, and further there was insufficient evidence of the 'market claim' of ordinary profits which would have provided a cap for a permissible recovery under the *Cory* rule in place of the actual losses.

[115] *Horne v Midland Railway Co* (1872) 7 LR CP 583, where only the difference between the market value at the date of delivery and that at the date of promised delivery was recoverable.

[116] *Parta Industries Ltd v Canadian Pacific Ltd* (1974) 48 DLR (3d) 463 (British Columbia SC).

[117] *Satef-Huttenes Albertus SpA v Paloma Tercera Shipping Co SA (The Pegase)* [1981] 1 Lloyd's Rep 175 (Goff J).

[118] *'SNIA' Societa di Navigazione Industria e Commercio v Suzuki & Co* (1924) 18 Ll L Rep 333 (CA) at 337; *Sylvia Shipping Ltd v Progress Bulk Carriers Ltd* [2010] EWHC 542 (Comm) (Hamblen J) obiter at para 81.

[119] *Islamic Republic of Iran Shipping Lines v Ierax Shipping Co of Panama (The Forum Craftsman)* [1991] 1 Lloyd's Rep 81 (Hobhouse J) at 85–86.

[120] Such losses on the follow-on charter were held too remote in *Transfield Shipping Inc v Mercator Shipping Inc (The Achilleas)* [2009] AC 61 (HL), but in the Court of Appeal (when they were held recoverable) Rix LJ confirmed that that losses under the follow-on charter would nevertheless not be recoverable to the extent that they were 'extravagant or unusual', and possibly even if it was longer than the fixture with the defendant: [2007] 2 Lloyd's Rep 555 (CA) at para 112.

[121] *Transfield Shipping Inc v Mercator Shipping Inc (The Achilleas)* [2009] AC 61 (HL).

being too remote, the claimant nevertheless recovered loss at the capped amount of the market loss for the few days of the overrun.

And the rule that where the costs of repair or replacement are available, only reasonable costs may be recovered (ie the reasonableness test from *Ruxley Electronics*), may itself be an application of the cap rule: recovery is capped at the reasonable cost.[122]

B. Discussion: the Cap

It therefore appears that the actual loss is recoverable even if too remote, but (as one leading textbook puts it) the contemplated loss provides a 'ceiling' or 'cap' on recovery.[123] The Vienna Convention on Contracts for the International Sale of Goods takes this approach, providing that damages should measure the loss suffered but '[s]uch damages may not exceed the loss which the party in breach foresaw or ought to have foreseen at the time of the conclusion of the contract'. As one commentator puts it, 'the amount expected from normal use simply placed a *ceiling* on his recovery',[124] and as another says, permits recovery of an 'equivalent' of the actual loss.[125] Thus although Asquith LJ in *Victoria Laundry* said that 'the aggrieved party is only entitled to recover such part of the loss actually resulting as was at the time of the contract reasonably foreseeable as liable to result',[126] the correct position is that the aggrieved party is entitled to recover such part of the loss actually resulting as is no greater than such loss (even if not actually resulting) as was reasonably foreseeable as liable to result. Blackburn J has confirmed that a claimant's actual loss forms the 'extreme limit of the damage they can recover' and that remoteness determines 'whether the defendants were liable for as much'.[127]

Accordingly, the claimant can recover the lower of the actual loss and the non-remote loss, even if the actual loss is entirely too remote in type, provided the other type of loss not suffered was not too remote.[128]

The parallel with the separately evolved scope of duty principle, discussed below in section 14.5 and presented in this text as part of the remoteness principle, is obvious: there too a 'cap' has evolved (although there has been some resistance to the term) whereby, in the central case of the lender against the valuer, the lender can recover against the valuer the lower of the actual loss and the amount of the

---

[122] *Axa Insurance UK plc v Cunningham Lindsey United Kingdom (an unlimited company)* [2007] EWHC 3023 (TCC) (Akenhead J) at para 258.

[123] *Chitty on Contracts*, 31st edn (London, Sweet & Maxwell Ltd, 2012) at para 26–114.

[124] R Halson in D Harris, D Campbell and R Halson (eds), *Remedies in Contract & Tort*, 2nd edn (London, Butterworths, 2002) at 99.

[125] A Burrows, *Remedies for Torts and Breach of Contract*, 3rd edn (Oxford, OUP, 2004) at 96.

[126] *Victoria Laundry (Windsor) Ltd v Newman Industries Ltd* [1949] 2 KB 528 (CA) at 539.

[127] *Elbinger Aktiengesellschaft v Armstrong* (1874) LR 9 QB 473 at 479.

[128] Another way of approaching the point, with much the same result in most cases, is to say that the claimant is deemed to have suffered the not too remote loss and not the actual loss. This latter formulation has the same result as the former in most cases, but leaves open the possibility of recovering *more* than the actual loss where the not too remote loss is greater. Such a true deeming, where the actual loss is replaced with the deemed loss even if greater, can occur in cases of mitigation and causation: see above in chapter fourteen, 15.2B(ii) and 15.3(iv). Realistically, however, it seems unlikely that a non-remote loss greater than the actual loss would be awarded, and therefore the simple cap approach best describes the law.

overvaluation (a rough assessment of the loss that would have been suffered if the valuation had been true).

14.5 Displacing the Reasonable Contemplation Test by the Remoteness and Scope of Duty Principles

As explained above, the reasonable contemplation test will not always give the right answer to the question of whether responsibility for a loss was impliedly assumed. In other words, the parties will sometimes assume responsibility for losses that are unlikely to occur, or not assume responsibility for losses that are likely (or not unlikely) to occur.

A. It Can Extend or Restrict Liability

It is important to understand that, as Toulson LJ explained in *Siemens v Supershield*,[129] the displacement can work either way: to restrict liability so as to exclude losses that would have been foreseeable as not unlikely (as occurred in *SAAMCo* and in *The Achilleas*) or to extend liability to include losses that were not foreseeable as not unlikely or would otherwise be barred by the rule of legal causation (as occurred in *Siemens v Supershield* itself, and *Rubenstein v HSBC Bank plc*[130]).

B. Scope of Duty

The application of the assumption of responsibility test (developed by Lord Hoffmann in *The Achilleas*) to displace the reasonable contemplation test is most developed in the field of professional negligence, specifically cases of advice or information provision, where it was developed under the title 'scope of duty', most notably in the *South Australia Asset Management v York Montague Ltd* decision, also by Lord Hoffmann but prior to *The Achilleas*. The interaction with the *Achilleas* test will be discussed below (at heart, they are the same) but it is convenient to deal with the scope of duty/professional negligence cases separately and first.

(i) SAAMCo, *Valuers and Coincidental Loss*

(a) An Introduction to *SAAMCo* and Valuers

In *South Australia Asset Management v York Montague Ltd* (also known as *Banque Bruxelles Lambert SA v Eagle Star Insurance Co Ltd* and often shortened to 'SAAMCo'),[131] the claimant mortgage lender made a secured loan during the 1980s

---

[129] *Siemens Building Technologies FE Ltd v Supershield Ltd* [2010] EWCA Civ 7 at para 43. See also *Earl's Terrace Properties Ltd v Nilsson Design Ltd* [2004] EWHC 136 (TCC) (Thornton QC) at para 106.

[130] *Rubenstein v HSBC Bank plc* [2012] EWCA Civ 1184. See also *Calvert v William Hill Credit Ltd* [2009] 1 Ch 330 (CA), discussed below in chapter sixteen, section 16.8D, especially Sir Anthony May P at para 46.

[131] *South Australia Asset Management Corp v York Montague Ltd* [1997] 1 AC 191 (HL).

property boom, induced by the defendant valuer's valuation of the property being purchased and used as security for the loan. The borrower defaulted and the lender enforced its security but still suffered a loss (ie failed to recover some of its loan and expenses from the proceeds of sale of the property). The House of Lords held that even if the lender would not have made the loan but for a defendant valuer's negligence, and so the negligence was a 'but for' cause of all the lender's loss, the claimant could still not recover damages for losses that were in part due to a market drop which took some of the value off the security property (and so reduced the lender's recovery when it came to call in the security). Lord Hoffmann (with the rest of the House agreeing) emphasised that such a 'kind of loss' did not fall within the contractual and concurrent tortious 'scope of duty' of care of the valuer. Because a valuer provided information that assisted a claimant in deciding whether to enter into a transaction, but did not actually advise on whether to enter into the transaction, he is not 'generally regarded as responsible for all the consequences of that course of action. He is responsible only for the consequences of the information being wrong'.[132]

(b) Coincidental Loss

At this juncture it is necessary to introduce the concept of 'coincidental' loss. A useful example was given in *Chester v Afshar* (which post-dates *SAAMCo*) by Lord Walker:[133]

> When a traveller was delayed through a railway company's fault and a lamp exploded in the hotel where she was compelled to spend the night (the well-known case of *Central of Georgia Railway Co v Price* (1898) 32 SE 77) that was simply an unfortunate coincidence. Similarly, if a taxi-driver drives too fast and the cab is hit by a falling tree, injuring the passenger, it is sheer coincidence. The driver might equally well have avoided the tree by driving too fast, and the passenger might have been injured if the driver was observing the speed limit.

The taxi driver example is the cleanest.[134] In such cases of coincidental loss[135] the defendant's wrong (whether a tort or breach of contract) has caused the loss in a but-for sense: had the defendant not committed the breach, the harm would not have occurred because the chances are that in those slightly different circumstances the unlikely harm would not have come about. However (using the language of legal causation), the breach is said not to be an effective cause of the wrong. This is not merely because the injury was unlikely. The key point in a situation like this which is properly described as 'coincidence' is that the wrong neither created nor increased

---

[132] Ibid at 211–14.

[133] *Chester v Afshar* [2005] 1 AC 134 (HL) at para 94.

[134] Another example is of a driver who carefully drives but is aware of or careless as to his lack of a licence, and the damage caused by him is unconnected with not having a licence: Lord Hoffmann in *South Australia Asset Management Corp v York Montague Ltd* [1997] 1 AC 191 (HL) at 212–13. Or of an injured person who is then further injured or killed by a fire that starts in the hospital he visits: Lord MacDermott in *Hogan v Bentinck Collieries* [1949] 1 All ER 588 (HL) at 601.

[135] The term 'coincidental' or 'coincidence' was used in the pure sense where the breach does not increase the risk of harm in *Chappel v Hart* (1998) 195 CLR 232 (HC of Australia) at paras 33 and 93 and adopted in *Chester v Afshar* [2005] 1 AC 134 (HL) by Lord Walker at paras 93–94. See also HLA Hart and T Honoré, *Causation in the Law*, 2nd edn (Oxford, OUP, 1985) at 164–68 and 324.

the risk in any relevant sense. As Mason CJ has observed in the High Court of Australia, cited with approval by Lord Walker in *Chester v Afshar*,

> a factor which secures the presence of the plaintiff at the place where and at the time when he or she is injured is not causally connected with the injury, unless the risk of the accident occurring at that time was greater.[136]

The delayed traveller is a less clean example and probably best not described as 'coincidental' loss because although the breach did not increase the risk of the lamp exploding, it did increase the risk of the claimant being present when the lamp exploded (unlike in the taxi example), ie it increased the risk of the accident. In the traveller example the point is that although the breach did increase the risk of the injury, the risk was not something the duty that was breached was aimed at protecting against, and/or the claimant simply cannot be held to be responsible for what happened. The injury will therefore be held to be too remote or a break in the chain of causation. (So the result might be different if eg goods are left at a dockside and then harmed in a storm and storms are an established risk of leaving goods there.[137])

(c) The Mountaineer Example

In *SAAMCo* Lord Hoffmann discussed this type of problem in the context of professional advisors, first of all by giving his famous mountaineer example:

> A mountaineer about to undertake a difficult climb is concerned about the fitness of his knee. He goes to a doctor who negligently makes a superficial examination and pronounces the knee fit. The climber goes on the expedition, which he would not have undertaken if the doctor had told him the true state of his knee. He suffers an injury which is an entirely foreseeable consequence of mountaineering but has nothing to do with his knee.

> On the Court of Appeal's principle, the doctor is responsible for the injury suffered by the mountaineer because it is damage which would not have occurred if he had been given correct information about his knee. He would not have gone on the expedition and would have suffered no injury. On what I have suggested is the more usual principle, the doctor is not liable. The injury has not been caused by the doctor's bad advice because it would have occurred even if the advice had been correct.[138]

Here but for the breach by the doctor the mountaineer would not have gone on the expedition and suffered the injury (from an avalanche, say).[139] Accordingly, the breach did increase the risk of the injury in that sense and the loss cannot be said to be (and was not said by Lord Hoffmann to be) coincidental,[140] as it was in the taxi

---

[136] Mason CJ in *March v E & MH Stramare Pty Ltd* (1991) 171 CLR 506 (HC of Australia) at 516; Lord Walker in *Chester v Afshar* [2005] 1 AC 134 (HL) at para 94.

[137] See the cases at chapter sixteen n 444 below.

[138] *South Australia Asset Management v York Montague Ltd* [1997] 1 AC 191 (HL) in 213.

[139] The case is therefore like a 'no transaction' case where the transaction would not have gone ahead but for the wrong (see the discussion of such cases above in chapter three, section 3.1B(i)). One judge therefore described it as a 'no travel' case, as the mountaineer would not have travelled: *ACC Bank plc v Johnston* [2011] IEHC 376 (Irish High Court) at paras 7.14.

[140] Counsel Mr Sumption QC (as he then was) used the term 'coincidental' in this context in argument in *SAAMCO* [1997] 1 AC 191 (HL) at 209, as was adverted to but not adopted by Lord Hoffmann at 220; this followed Sumption QC's using the term in argument in a similar context in *Smith New Court Securities Ltd v Scrimgeour Vickers (Asset Management) Ltd* [1997] 1 AC 254 (HL) at 259. Macaulay QC used it this

driver example. The loss is not truly coincidental in the pure sense of something not having increased the risk of the claimant suffering the injury.

The important thing, then, is to work out why one intuitively thinks that the doctor should not be blamed for the injury. This is not easy to put into words, but the essence of it is that the doctor did not advise the mountaineer to go on the expedition but instead merely advised the mountaineer in relation to his knee. Consequently, the doctor cannot be said to have taken the risk of the entire expedition,[141] only of knee-related accidents. The fact that the advice in relation to the knee in fact determined whether the claimant went on the expedition did not mean that the success of the entire expedition could be laid at the doctor's feet. As Rix LJ has subsequently explained:[142]

> Although the mountaineer would not have gone on the mountain unless he had been given the all clear from the doctor, we would not select the doctor's negligent advice as the cause of the mountaineer's injury *unless* the injury had been contributed to in some material way by the unfitness of the knee. This is despite the fact that an accident on the mountains— whether it is due to something entirely fortuitous such as an avalanche, or is the result of some faulty piece of equipment, or of the weather, always unpredictable but inherently so—is always, more or less but readily, foreseeable. However, the doctor is responsible for the mountaineer's knee, but not for the weather, the equipment, or sheer bad luck.

Accordingly 'advice and the loss were ... disconnected by an unforeseeable event beyond the scope of the [doctor's] duty'.[143]

An important test in such cases is what damages would have been recoverable if the information or advice had been warranted. In such cases the damages measure the difference between the actual position and the position if the advice had been correct. If the doctor's advice that the knee was safe had been correct then the claimant would still have gone on the expedition and still suffered an injury. If, however, the injury had been suffered when the knee gave way on the mountainside then clearly the incorrectness of the doctor's advice that the knee was safe did determine matters, as had it been correct, the knee would not have given way. As Lord Hoffmann explained in the final sentence in the above quotation, 'The injury has not been caused [in a legal sense] by the doctor's bad advice because it would have occurred even if the advice had been correct', and it would be strange if the doctor were liable for failing to take care in relation to information when the doctor wouldn't be liable if the information were warranted.[144]

This is because the purpose of the duty to take care as to information is to try to ensure that the information is true, and therefore breach gives rise only to liability for 'the loss attributable[145] to the inaccuracy of the information which the plaintiff

---

context in the Scottish Outer House in *Watts v Bell & Scott WS* [2007] CSOH 108 at para 93. See further eg A Burrows, *Remedies for Torts and Breach of Contract*, 3rd edn (Oxford, OUP, 2009) at 114.

[141] Lord Hoffmann [1997] 1 AC 191 at 214.
[142] *Rubenstein v HSBC Bank plc* [2012] EWCA Civ 1184 at para 102.
[143] Ibid at para 118.
[144] *SAAMCO* [1997] 1 AC 191 at 213–14.
[145] Lord Hoffmann uses this term many times in his judgment in *SAAMCo*, and also in in *Nykredit Mortgage Bank plc v Edward Erdman Group Ltd (No 2)* [1997] WLR 1627 (HL) at 1638. And as Parker LJ has observed, it is important to ask '(a) what is the particular breach of duty in respect of which damages are sought, and (b) what loss is attributable to that breach?': *Crosse and Crosse v Lloyd's Bank plc* [2001] EWCA Civ 366 at para 95.

has suffered by reason of having entered into the transaction on the assumption that the information was correct'.[146] So the court must ask what would have happened if that assumption had been satisfied and the information given (the knee is safe) had been correct, not only what would have happened if different correct information (the knee is unsafe) had been given.

(d) The General Principles from *SAAMCo*

The general principles arising out of Lord Hoffmann's conclusions in relation to the mountaineer are as follows:

First, as a general matter, the scope of liability of a professional adviser, or other person under a duty to take reasonable care[147] to provide information on which someone else will decide upon a course of action, usually dictates that the person is 'responsible only for the consequences of the information being wrong'.[148] Accordingly, damages are not recoverable for injury that would have been suffered even if the information given had been correct (as only that injury is a consequence of the information being wrong).

Secondly, it is therefore necessary to identify the information provided and so work out what would have happened had the information provided been true:

> The principle thus stated distinguishes between a duty to *provide information* for the purpose of enabling someone else to decide upon a course of action and a duty to *advise* someone as to what course of action he should take. If the duty is to advise whether or not a course of action should be taken, the adviser must take reasonable care to consider all the potential consequences of that course of action. If he is negligent, he will therefore be responsible for all the foreseeable loss which is a consequence of that course of action having been taken. If his duty is only to supply information, he must take reasonable care to ensure that the information is correct and, if he is negligent, will be responsible for all the foreseeable consequences of the information being wrong.[149]

This is not really a separate principle, it is an application of the first. If a professional has advised that the course of action be taken then anything that goes wrong during the course of action would not have occurred if the advice given had been correct. Thus if the nature, even if not the content, of the advice from the doctor had been not merely that the knee is safe but also that the expedition is a good idea and will overall be safe, then any avalanche injury is attributable to that advice because not only would the mountaineer not have proceeded if the doctor had taken reasonable care and warned the mountaineer off, which we have established is not enough for liability, but the mountaineer would not have suffered the avalanche or other

---

[146] *SAAMCO* [1997] 1 AC 191 at 216.

[147] Although not a matter of contract damages, it is worth observing in passing that this scope of duty approach limiting liability to the loss had the information been true does not apply in deceit cases, where the defendant is liable for all the direct consequences of entering into the transaction. See further *Smith New Court Securities Ltd v Scrimgeour Vickers (Asset Management) Ltd* [1997] AC 254 (HL) Lord Browne-Wilkins at 267 and Lord Steyn at 283, disapproving Hobhouse LJ in *Downs v Chappell* [1997] 1 WLR 426 (CA) at 444 on this point, and see *Twycross v Grant* (1877) 2 CPD 469 (CA) Bramwell LJ at the foot of 504 and *SAAMCo* Lord Hoffmann [1997] 1 AC 191 at 215–16.

[148] [1997] 1 AC 191 at 214, also 213.

[149] Ibid at 214.

injury if the doctor had been correct and the expedition had been safe. The factual loss therefore all falls within the scope of duty.

(e) The valuers in *SAAMCo*

As has been seen, the House of Lords in *SAAMCo* applied those general principles to valuers by determining that usually valuers merely provide information to enable a lender or buyer to make a lending or buying decision, but do not generally advise on the overall sense of that decision, which involves other factors than the value of the security property to which the valuer will ordinarily not be privy

> such as how much money he has available, how much the borrower needs to borrow, the strength of his covenant, the attraction of the rate of interest or the other personal or commercial considerations which may induce the lender to lend.[150]

The valuer is therefore an information-giver, not an adviser, in the sense discussed above, and so its liability is limited to the consequences of the information in fact given not being correct, ie the losses that would not have been suffered if the valuation in fact given had been accurate. To show recoverable loss, a lender must show that he is 'worse off as a lender than he would have been if the security had been worth what the valuer said'.[151]

This cuts out losses such as the costs of pursuing the borrower and failure to recover due to the market crashing and wiping value of the security property—as if the valuation had been accurate the lender would still have lent and suffered those losses—but still includes the amount by which the bank's recovery is less because the valuer overvalued the property. These are 'the consequences of risks the lender would have taken upon himself it the valuation advice had been sound'.[152]

This scope of duty explanation also works for the taxi driver[153] (in addition to the explanation that the risk was not increased and so the loss is coincidental): the taxi driver's duty not to drive too fast was aimed at avoiding accidents that do not happen when driving more slowly, not at avoiding unknown tree falls or lightning strikes, the risk of which is in no way affected by the driver's speed.

So the court must ask what would have happened if the valuation had been accurate (answer: the property would have been worth a bit more, so the lender would have had a bit less loss, but still suffered a market drop and shortfall against its lending), not what would have happened if the valuer had taken care (and so given a true low valuation, which would have led to the lender not lending at all).

(f) Operation of the Cap and the Two-Stage Approach

The effect *should be* to cap the recoverable damages at the warranty measure, and this is often referred to as the 'SAAMCo cap'.[154] The upshot of all of this *should be*

---

[150] Lord Hoffmann [1997] 1 AC 191 at 211 and 222.

[151] *Siemens Building Technologies FE Ltd v Supershield Ltd* [2010] EWCA Civ 7 at para 43.

[152] Lord Nicholls in *Nykredit Mortgage Bank plc v Edward Erdman Group Ltd (No 2)* [1997] 1 WLR 1627 (HL) at 1631.

[153] See above in section 14.3E(i).

[154] Eg in *Platform Home Loans Ltd v Oyston Shipways Ltd* [2000] 2 AC 190 (HL) Lord Hobhouse at 206 (although some reports refer to it as the '*Banque Bruxelles* cap', after the alternative name for the *SAAMCo* case).

that the claimant recovers *the lower of the actual loss suffered and the warranty measure*. It is important to understand that this does not mean that the duty is in fact a warranty, or that the lender can recover the overvaluation (the amount of the cap) come what may. If the lender is no worse off than it would have been if it had not entered into the transaction, it cannot complain that it would nevertheless have had more profit if the valuation had been true.[155] Unlike in pure warranty cases, where the measure of loss is simply that which would have not been suffered if the information warranted had been correct,[156] a two-stage process therefore arises: 'A plaintiff has to prove both that he has suffered loss and that the loss fell within the scope of the duty'.[157] We shall return to the amount of the cap in due course, but first it is necessary to consider the two-stage process.

Lord Hobhouse explained this clearly in the *Platform Home Loans* case:

> The first step is to establish what was the *basic loss* of the lender. The second step is to see whether that basic loss exceeds the amount of the overvaluation and, if it does, the lender's right to recovery from the valuer is limited to the extent of the overvaluation.[158]

Lord Millett also explained the point in the same case:

> Two calculations are required. The first is a calculation of the loss incurred by the lender as a result of having entered into the transaction. This is an exercise in causation. The main component in the calculation is the difference between the amount of the loan and the amount realised by enforcing the security.[159]

Pausing there, the first calculation identifies the actual loss on factual causation principles. What would have happened if the defendant had taken reasonable care?[160] This is sometimes called the 'basic loss'.[161] Then turning to the second calculation:

> The second calculation has nothing to do with questions of [factual] causation: see the Nykredit case, at p. 1638, per Lord Hoffmann. It is designed to ascertain the maximum amount of loss capable of falling within the valuer's duty of care. The resulting figure is the difference between the negligent valuation and the true value of the property at the date of valuation. The recoverable damages are limited to the lesser of the amounts produced by the two calculations.
>
> It is to be observed that neither amount is an element or component of the other. Either may be the greater, for they are the results of completely different calculations. In mathematical terms, they bear the same relationship to each other as a-b does to c-d. The figure produced by the second calculation is simply the amount of the overvaluation. It is not the loss or any part of it, and cannot be equated with the amount of the loss sustained by the lender in consequence of the overvaluation. The two are the same only in a case where the lender has advanced 100 per cent of valuation.[162]

---

[155] Lord Hoffmann in *Nykredit Mortgage Bank plc v Edward Erdman Group Ltd (No 2)* [1997] 1 WLR 1627 (HL) at 1638, also in *SAAMCo* [1997] 1 AC 191 at 216.
[156] Lord Hoffmann distinguishes the warranty measure in *SAAMCo* (ibid at 216, 3rd para).
[157] Lord Hoffmann in *SAAMCo*, ibid at 218.
[158] *Platform Home Loans Ltd v Oyston Shipways Ltd* [2000] 2 AC 190 (HL) at 201.
[159] Ibid.
[160] See also Lord Hoffmann, ibid, at 220.
[161] *Platform Home Loans Ltd v Oyston Shipways Ltd* [2000] 2 AC 190 (HL) Lord Hobhouse *passim*.
[162] Ibid Lord Millett at 214–15.

This second calculation therefore works out a cap of the amount of the overvaluation, to give effect to the scope of duty requirement.[163]

If the valuer overvalues by £50,000 then, whatever loan to value ratio the lender lends on, the lender's security is £50,000 less than it assumed (in reliance on the valuation). If the valuation had been true, the lender would have had £50,000 more security. The loss is therefore capped at £50,000.

In a no transaction case (where but for the negligence the lender would not have lent at all), if the borrower's covenant turns out to be good and/or the value of the security property goes up, the lender may in fact suffer no loss because the covenant and security rights are worth what the lender lent and/or it ultimately recovers through them its entire advance plus costs, plus any profit it can show it would have made on an alternative transaction. If, however, the lender does suffer a loss because the borrower does not pay and/or the security property drops in value (beyond any cushion the lender had allowed in its loan to value ratio) then its loss is nevertheless capped at £50,000.

In a successful-transaction case (where but for the negligence the lender would have lent a lesser amount) the lender's actual loss is the amount by which its loan would have been lower if the valuer had taken reasonable care (usually the loan to value ratio multiplied by the amount of the overvaluation) to the extent that this sum is not recovered from the borrower and security property, plus any profit the lender can show it would have made using this additional sum elsewhere. Again, this will be capped at £50,000.[164]

Logically therefore, there are two possibilities. First, the actual loss may be less than the cap and so the scope of duty does not in any way limit recovery. This is what happened in the first of the three cases considered in *SAAMCo, South Australia Asset Management v York Montague* itself, where the actual loss fell just below the £10m overvaluation sum and fell well below when contributory negligence was taken into account.[165] Secondly, the actual loss may be more than the cap, in which case the scope of duty limits the liability to the amount of the cap. This is what happened in the second and third of the three cases considered in the *SAAMCo* proceedings, *United Bank of Kuwait Plc v Prudential Property Services Ltd*, where the loss was about £1.3m but the overvaluation either £650,000 or £700,000 and recovery limited to this sum, and *Nykredit Mortgage Bank Plc v Edward Erdman Group Ltd*, where the loss was about £3m but the overvaluation £1.5m, and recovery was limited to this sum.

All of the above makes sense, save for the precise (or rather, imprecise) way the cap is calculated. The astute reader will recognise that the principle behind the cap would justify capping recoverable loss at the amount that would have been suffered if the valuation had been warranted, ie the amount by which the proceeds of sale are lower than they would have been had the valuation been correct.

---

[163] Lord Hoffmann ibid at 220.

[164] At 218 Lord Hoffmann disapproved the use of the terms 'no transaction' and 'successful-transaction' but they are useful when identifying the basic loss because they focus on what the claimant would have done. See further chapter three, section 3.1B(i), above.

[165] The particular facts of the three cases are considered in *SAAMCo* [1997] 1 AC 191 at 222–24. As to the way contributory negligence interacts with scope of duty, see below in section 14.7.

Instead, the cap is fixed at the amount of the overvaluation. This can only ever be a rough measure of the warranty loss, and will become rougher the more time passes from the date of valuation to the date of sale. If a £200,000 property is overvalued by £50,000 in 2000, and the property is sold under the lender's mortgage in 2010 following borrower default, the loss on the warranty measure would be the difference between the actual proceeds of sale in 2010 and the proceeds in 2010 if the property had been worth £250,000 and not £200,000 10 years earlier in 2000. This difference *may* be £50,000, but will not necessarily be. For example, if the property market has halved in the 10 years between valuation and sale, then the overvaluation of £50,000 may have only translated into a £25,000 reduction in the proceeds of sale. If the market has risen, the overvaluation may well result in a greater decrease in proceeds than £50,000.

The cap is therefore a practical and easy-to-apply measure that requires far less evidence than the warranty measure does,[166] only requiring the amount of the overvaluation (which is found by the judge when determining liability) and not expert evidence as to how the higher value property would have been affected by post-valuation property movements. The cap is, however, somewhat illogical given the principles justifying it.[167]

(g) The Label

Since *SAAMCo*, Lord Hoffmann has said, extra-judicially, that he should have called the 'scope of duty' principle the 'extent of liability' principle.[168] The label does not much matter, but this comment emphasises the connection between this principle and the general 'assumption of responsibility' test of remoteness.[169]

(ii) Applying the Scope of Duty Principle

(a) Valuer Cases

The *SAAMCo* approach has become the standard approach in valuation cases. It has been held that it probably applies to an overvaluation of rental income, as well as capital value.[170]

Even in commercial valuations of a development or business, it has been held (including in *Nykredit*, the third case in the *SAAMCo* proceedings themselves) that commercial advice contained in a valuation is all part of the information of the valuation and supports the valuation figure, and that the scope of the defendant's responsibility did not include the claimant relying on the commercial advice

---

[166] Cf the comments of Lord Hobhouse in *Platform Home Loans Ltd v Oyston Shipways Ltd* [2000] 2 AC 190 (HL) at 212.

[167] One justification could be to say that the warranty measure provides a cap *but* post-acquisition market movements are *res inter alios acta*, even to the extent that they would have acted on the overvalued part of the property value. This is difficult to justify, however, as valuers know that lenders will suffer any loss after such market movements and it is difficult to see why they should be too remote or outside the scope of duty. See further below in chapter sixteen, section 16.13C.

[168] Lord Hoffmann, 'Causation' (2005) 121 LQR 592 at 596.

[169] See below in section 14.5B(iii). Indeed, in *The Achilleas*, Lord Hoffmann used the phrase 'extent of liability' to refer to the subject matter of the remoteness principle [2009] AC 61 at para 23.

[170] *Scullion v Colleys* [2010] EWHC 2253 (Ch) (Snowden QC) at paras 62 ff.

separately and therefore damages were limited to the amount of the over-payment.[171] Thus the courts have resisted finding that a valuer has a broader advice-type scope of duty and is not merely providing information.

A twist on the standard valuer claim arose in *Broker House Insurance Services Ltd v OJS Law*,[172] where the solicitor obtained for the lender a second charge on property protected by agreed notice on the register, rather than protected as a registered charge, and failed to get the consent of the first chargee. The lender would not have lent if it had known the first chargee had not consented, but the court confirmed that the lender could only recover if and to the extent that (as does not appear to be the case) the lack of consent or failure to register the charge actually led to a lower recovery by the lender.

(b) Advice with Limited Scope: The Example of Default Risk

The information/advice distinction is not conclusive: the important thing to focus on where advice is given is whether the loss falls within the scope of responsibility assumed by the advisor.

In the *Haugesund Kommune* case, although the solicitors negligently advised that a loan contract with a Norwegian municipality was valid, the risk of creditworthiness of the municipality was assumed by the lender.[173] The contract was void, a right to restitution arose, and the lender's principal loss only arose because the municipality could not afford to repay the loaned monies. Had the solicitors advised that the contract would be void, then of course the lender would never have loaned the money (and thus all loss was factually caused by the negligence), however the loss nevertheless fell outside the solicitors' scope of duty, as it was caused by the municipality's impecuniosity. (The unrecovered legal costs of the lender proving its right to restitution, which arose because that right was disputable and disputed where a simple right under a loan would not have been, were recoverable.[174])

Similarly, in one case of alleged investment mis-selling it was held, obiter, that even if the relevant product was mis-sold, the failings had nothing to do with what was said or not said about the risk of issuer default in relation to the product sold, which default was highly unlikely and unforeseeable at the time of the sale (the issuer was a Lehman Brothers entity). Accordingly, since the product was otherwise profitable, the risk of issuer default fell outside the scope of the investment adviser's duty.[175]

---

[171] *SAAMCo* [1997] 1 AC 191 at 222–23; *Capita Alternative Fund Services (Guernsey) Ltd v Drivers Jonas (a firm)* [2011] EWHC 2336 (Comm) (Eder J) at paras 305–9.

[172] *Broker House Insurance Services Ltd v OJS Law* [2010] EWHC 3816 (Ch) (Lewison J).

[173] And this was common ground. See *Haugesund Kommune v DEPFA ACS Bank* [2012] QB 549 (CA), Gross LJ at para 96.

[174] And this also was common ground. See Rix LJ at para 81.

[175] *Camerata Property Inc v Credit Suisse Securities (Europe) Ltd* [2012] EWHC 7 (Comm) (Flaux J) at paras 100–103. The point is not discussed at length in the judgment but this seems to be the reasoning of the judge, who explicitly relied on *SAAMCo*. *Camerata* is discussed and distinguished by Rix LJ in *Rubenstein v HSBC Bank plc* [2012] EWCA Civ 1184 at para 112. The opposite situation arose in *Andrews v Barnett Waddingham LLP* [2006] EWCA Civ 93: the negligent advice related to the risk of unprotected issuer default, but the issuer did not default and the loss was caused otherwise.

Likewise a litigating solicitor is not automatically liable for failing to protect against the un-credit-worthiness of the opposing party. In *Pearson v Sanders Witherspoon*[176] a breach of the duty of care to progress the dispute with reasonable dispatch led to the counterclaim not being concluded until the defendant to the counterclaim had fallen insolvent. However, that risk, being of the usual order at the time the retainer incepted, did not fall within the scope of the solicitor's duty to act promptly, which was geared towards preventing the claim being struck out for want of prosecution (which would, if it had occurred, have fallen within the scope of the solicitor's responsibility). Once the solicitor learned in the press of the potential impecuniosity of the opposing party (Ferranti), and continued to act, he then assumed responsibility for the consequences of that impecuniosity if caused by his negligent delay after that date, and was liable for the loss of chance that judgment could have been obtained and enforced had he done so.[177]

In another case the particular breach of the solicitor was in failing to warn the claimant as to credit-worthiness checks that should be done, and there the default risk was clearly not outside the scope of responsibility and the solicitor was liable for the losses caused by selling the business to the particular buyer.[178] Similarly credit-worthiness will often fall within a solicitor's scope of responsibility where the solicitor is advising a lender.[179]

(c) Advice with Limited Scope: Other Cases

The purpose of the defendant's service or other obligation is clearly important.

Where, although the loss would not have happened but for the breach, the prevention of the loss is no part of the purpose of the service, the loss will often be outside the scope of the defendant's duty. Thus in *Galoo v Bright Grahame Murray*[180] (decided on the basis of legal causation, before *SAAMCo* and the formulation of the scope of duty principle[181]) negligent auditors were not liable to the companies audited for trading losses even though, had they taken reasonable care, a fraud would have been discovered and so the companies put into liquidation, preventing them from incurring trading losses. Although the judgment does not formulate the point in these terms, it is clear that the auditors' failure did not lie in giving advice

---

[176] *Pearson v Sanders Witherspoon* [2000] Lloyd's Rep PN 151 (CA).

[177] This decision appears at first sight to conflict with the basic principle by which the contract remoteness test is applied, and therefore the scope of responsibility for breach of a contractual obligation is fixed, at the date of contracting, the Court of Appeal here clearly finding that the scope of duty expanded part way through the retainer, when the solicitor learned of the particular risk of Ferranti's insolvency. To be clear: the duty to take reasonable care to proceed with dispatch was present throughout, but the risk of non-recovery due to Ferranti's insolvency was initially outside the solicitor's initial scope of responsibility for breach of that obligation, and later within it. But see further the discussion above at 14.3C(i) as to when a strict 'date of contracting' rule is inappropriate to the fixing of the scope of responsibility/remoteness, including discussion of this case.

[178] *Matlaszek v Bloom Camillin (a firm)*, 15 February 2001 (Hart J) and then the decision on quantum at [2003] EWHC 2728 (Ch) (Park J).

[179] *Omega Trust Co Ltd v Wright Son & Pepper (No 2)* [1998] PNLR 337 (Douglas Brown J).

[180] *Galoo v Bright Grahame Murray* [1994] 1 WLR 1360 (CA). Compare *Tom Hoskins plc v EMW Law* [2010] EWHC 479 (Ch) (Floyd J) at paras 143–56, where *Galoo* was discussed and distinguished.

[181] But explained as a scope of duty case by Lord Hoffmann, 'Common Sense and Causing Loss' (Lecture to the Chancery Bar Association, 15 June 1999) and by Langley J in *Equitable Life Assurance Society v Ernst & Young* [2003] EWHC 112 (Comm) at para 93.

that the business was profitable, and the benefit of ceasing to incur trading losses would have been incidental to the discovery of the fraud. (Or, to put it another way, the claimant company's trading unprofitably is the cause that is really responsible for the losses.) And where advice was given as to a particular levy not being due on a dairy business, liability was limited to the liability to pay that levy, and did not extend to the full consequences of continuing to operate the business even if the claimant would not have done so but for the advice.[182] It will often be the case that merely causing a business to continue to run does not include responsibility for all the consequences that follow (including the losses the business suffers through trading).[183]

Similarly, in a fairly clearly analogous case to Lord Hoffmann's mountaineer, *Andrews v Barnett Waddingham*, the solicitor failed to advise as to a pension not being government-guaranteed against insolvency, but as the provider did not become insolvent and the loss was otherwise caused, the loss fell outside the scope of duty.[184] In the *Colin Bishop* claim, which formed part of the *Bristol and West BS v Fancy & Jackson* litigation,[185] a solicitor's breach in failing to advise that the transaction was a back-to-back sale did not hide from the bank information that would have dissuaded the bank from lending to this borrower at all, but only information indicating that the bank would need to be sure of the valuation, and accordingly the solicitor had the limited scope of duty equivalent to a valuer.[186] In *Crosse and Crosse v Lloyd's Bank plc*[187] the solicitor's failure to disclose restrictive covenants was equivalent to an overvaluation and the solicitor's liability limited accordingly. The fact that the transaction would not have gone ahead but for the breach, because the borrower (rather than the lender)[188] would not have wished it to, was outside the defendant's scope of duty.

In *Peterson v Rivlin*[189] the defendant should have advised that a particular clause did not limit a particular liability to £10,000 but was instead open-ended. The litigation costs were outside the scope of the defendant's responsibility, as although the claimant would not have entered into the transaction and so not incurred those costs, such general consequences were outside the defendant's responsibility. Had the claimant's understanding (that there was a limit of £10,000) been true (ie the warranty measure) the costs would still have been incurred.

Likewise, where a solicitor should have obtained security for a loan and, had it done its job properly, circumstances would have come to light that would have meant the lender did not lend, the breach related solely to the security and the lender's claim was limited to the extra amount it would have recovered if the security had

---

[182] *Intervention Board for Agricultural Produce v Leidig* [2000] Lloyd's Rep 144 (CA).

[183] Ibid Robert Walker LJ at 149, quoting *Alexander v Cambridge Credit Corporation Ltd* (1987) 9 NSWLR 310.

[184] *Andrews v Barnett Waddingham LLP* [2006] EWCA Civ 93.

[185] *Bristol and West Building Society v Fancy & Jackson (a firm)* [1997] 4 All ER 582 (Chadwick J).

[186] Ibid at 623. See also *Gabriel v Little* [2013] EWCA Civ 1513. Compare the *Steggles Palmer* case discussed below.

[187] *Crosse and Crosse v Lloyd's Bank plc* [2001] EWCA Civ 366.

[188] Ibid, Parker LJ at paras 71–72.

[189] *Peterson v Rivlin* [2002] EWCA Civ 194.

been in place: it could not recover the total losses on the loan.[190] If the breach related to failure to obtain a protected search but ultimately the security obtained was not flawed and just as intended (ie no harm came from the lack of an official search certificate) there was no loss recoverable against the solicitor.[191]

In some cases an architect's duty will be limited to the consequences of information being wrong. This was so in *HOK Sport Ltd v Aintree Racecourse Co Ltd*,[192] where, despite a failure to warn the client racecourse owner that certain design changes would mean fewer standing places at the racecourse stand, and although that warning would foreseeably have led to a redesign which might have reinstated the original number of places, the architect was not liable for the loss of places. In another case, losses due to movements in the market were held to be outside the scope of duty of an architect who had negligently caused a 15-month delay in completion of properties, although £6m costs of funding during the delay were in principle recoverable.[193]

Where a defendant surveyor's negligence led to the claimant acquiring property with planning issues, it was held (obiter) that the claimant's damages would be limited to the amount of the overpayment for the property that was attributable to the lack of planning consent only.[194]

(d) Advice with a Broader Scope of Duty

In *Aneco*, a reinsurance broker was liable for its client's entire US$35m loss as a result of entering into an insurance treaty that it would not have entered into had it been told that reinsurance was unavailable, even though had the broker's advice that there was reinsurance available been correct that would only have covered US$11m of the loss (the client retaining the rest of the risk itself).[195] The brokers had a duty to advise, with all that implied, and not merely a duty to provide information. The availability of reinsurance was too deeply intertwined with the question of whether to enter into the treaty to be held to be a narrower and more limited informational duty.[196]

In the bank claim against solicitors in *Steggles Palmer*, one of the conjoined cases in the *Bristol and West BS v Fancy & Jackson* litigation,[197] the lender's entire loss on a loan it would not have entered into but for the defendant's breach was recoverable because the failure of the solicitor led not merely to a misunderstanding as to the financial viability of the transaction or to a willingness to lend more than it would otherwise have lent (as in valuer cases), but to the bank not knowing information which would have revealed to it that the borrower was one 'to whom it did not wish to lend' at all.[198] (Compare the *Colin Bishop* case in the same litigation, discussed in

---

[190] *ACC Bank plc v Johnston* [2011] IEHC 376 (Irish High Court).
[191] *Bristol and West Building Society v Fancy & Jackson (a firm)* [1997] 4 All ER 582 (Chadwick J) at 621–22.
[192] *HOK Sport Ltd v Aintree Racecourse Co Ltd* [2002] EWHC 3094 (TCC).
[193] *Earl Terrace Properties Ltd v Nilsson Design Ltd* [2004] EWHC 136 (TCC).
[194] *AW Group Ltd v Taylor Walton* [2013] EWHC 2610 (Ch) (Hodge QC) at para 241.
[195] *Aneco Reinsurance Underwriting Ltd v Johnson & Higgins Ltd* [2002] 1 Lloyd's Rep 156 (HL).
[196] Ibid Lord Steyn at para 41.
[197] *Bristol and West Building Society v Fancy & Jackson (a firm)* [1997] 4 All ER 582 (Chadwick J).
[198] At 622.

the previous section.) The particular breaches by the solicitor were in failing to advise that they could not confirm that the purchase monies came from the borrower, and that the sale was by way of sub-sale. Accordingly, all the consequences of lending (subject to any further arguments that could be made on causation) were within the defendant's scope of duty in relation to the particular obligations breached.

As Otton LJ explained in *Portman Building Society v Bevan Ashford*, where this approach was applied,

> where a negligent solicitor fails to provide information which shows that the transaction is not viable or tends to reveal an actual or potential fraud on the part of the borrowers, the lender is entitled to recover the whole of its loss. In other words, the whole of the loss suffered by the lender is within the scope of the solicitor's duty and is property recoverable.[199]

In that case the solicitors had failed to reveal that the borrowers were not providing their share of the funds from their own resources, as they had said on the application form, but instead were providing them by way of a second mortgage, and so were fraudsters to whom the bank would not have wished to lend. The entire loss was within the defendant's scope of duty. The same applied where solicitors failed to provide information revealing a borrower's previous bankruptcy.[200]

In the Australian valuation case of *Kenny & Good Pty Ltd v MGICA (1992) Ltd*,[201] a valuer was held liable for the entirety of the claimants' losses, including that part due to a market drop. Some members of the High Court of Australia appeared to reject the *SAAMCo* principle, but the particular valuation confirmed that the property was suitable security 'for investment of trust funds to the extent of our valuation for a term of 3–5 years' and it was expressly stated that it could be relied upon by the bank and MGICA, the bank's mortgage insurer. These special facts (which emphasised the investment itself and that the property value was not just accurate at the date of the valuation but would in effect be safe for 3–5 years) meant that the particular valuer didn't merely assume the usual duty to inform, but also a duty to advise on entering into the transaction, and this was certainly the approach McHugh J took.[202] Further, had the valuation been true the same loss would still have been suffered.

In a solicitor's negligence claim, the trading losses that resulted from the solicitor's negligence leading to the claimant company's sale of its entire business being delayed were recoverable.[203] Although the solicitor did not know that the claimant was actually trading at a loss, that was entirely foreseeable given that an urgent sale of the entire business was being conducted, and *Galoo v Bright Grahame Murray*[204] was distinguished. Similarly in *Esso Petroleum Co Ltd v Mardon*,[205] responsibility

---

[199] *Portman Building Society v Bevan Ashford* [2000] 1 EGLR 81 (CA) at 86.
[200] *Omega Trust Co v Wright Son & Pepper (No 2)* [1998] PNLR 337 (Douglas Brown J).
[201] *Kenny & Good Pty Ltd v MGICA (1992) Ltd* (1999) 163 ALR 611 (HC of Australia).
[202] Ibid at paras 59 to 61. See also Gummow J at paras 80 to 87, and cf Gaudron J at paras 23–24.
[203] *Tom Hoskins plc v EMW Law* [2010] EWHC 479 (Ch) (Floyd J) at paras 143–56.
[204] *Galoo v Bright Grahame Murray* [1994] 1 WLR 1360 (CA).
[205] *Esso Petroleum Co Ltd v Mardon* [1976] QB 801 (CA).

for advice as to a business's profitability encompassed all the consequences of embarking upon the business.[206]

Where an architect's job was to seek planning permission for a property, the reduction in sale price caused by the market drop during the careless delay would be recoverable.[207]

In *Rubenstein v HSBC Bank plc*, a case of investment misadvice, the collapse of the market following the Lehman Brothers insolvency was held by the Court of Appeal not to be outside the scope of the advisor's duty, the breach being recommendation of a particular bond when the client had made clear he wanted a risk-free investment:[208]

> The doctor did not advise, let alone recommend, his patient to go mountaineering: he merely told him that his knee was in good shape. Mr Marsden, however, not only advised Mr Rubenstein on the investment of his capital, he recommended a particular investment. He, so to speak, put him in it. If such an investment goes wrong, there will nearly always be other causes (bad management, bad markets, fraud, political change etc): but it will be an exercise in legal judgment to decide whether some change in markets is so extraneous to the validity of the investment advice as to absolve the adviser for failing to carry out his duty or duties on the basis that the result was not within the scope of those duties.

The particular feature of the case which gave the Court most pause was that the client had said he expected to only need the investment until he bought a house and this was expected to be within a year, but the client in fact did not find a house and held the investment for longer than a year, and indeed only suffered losses on the market collapse after three years. The bank argued that any losses after a year were too remote, but the Court disagreed, as the losses were caused by the client holding his money in an investment with some risk when the client thought (because of the misadvice) that it was risk-free.[209]

A difficult case, very much on the borderline, was *British Racing Drivers' Club Ltd v Hextall Erskine & Co*.[210] There the solicitor negligently and incorrectly advised the claimant that it did not need members' approval under section 320 of the Companies Act 1985 before purchasing shares in a transaction connected with directors. It was found that the amount by which the claimant overpaid for the shares was within the defendant's scope of duty because had a general meeting of members been held, the directors' unconscious conflicts of interest would have been ironed out and the discussion would have led to a lower purchase price, and the danger of this not happening and of a fuller than commercial price being paid were within the dangers against which the duty to advise on section 320 was supposed to protect.

---

[206] See the explanation of *Esso* in *Intervention Board for Agricultural Produce v Leidig* [2000] Lloyd's Rep 144 (CA) Simon Brown LJ at 148, where *Esso* was distinguished.
[207] Obiter in *Hancock v Tucker* [1999] Lloyd's Rep PN 814 (Toulson J).
[208] *Rubenstein v HSBC Bank plc* [2012] EWCA Civ 1184 Rix LJ at para 103. See also para 118.
[209] Ibid at paras 120–24.
[210] *British Racing Drivers' Club Ltd v Hextall Erskine & Co* [1996] 3 All ER 667 (Carnwath J).

(e) Coincidental Loss and the Special Rule in Medical Negligence Cases of Failure to Warn

Contrary to the coincidental loss principle explained above in section 14.5B(i)(b), a special rule has developed in England in medical failure to warn cases, arising out of the medical negligence case of *Chester v Afshar*,[211] which concerned private medical care and so was a contractual as well as tortious case. Three days before a recommended spinal procedure, a neurosurgeon failed to warn Miss Chester of the unavoidable 1–2 per cent risk of a particular nerve damage complication, and when the procedure was performed the complication eventuated. Had the doctor warned the patient, she would still have had the operation, but not until some time later than she did, as she would have wanted to get a second opinion. At that later date when she would have had the operation the risk would have been the same. As the risk was small, it could be said that although the risk would have been the same at the time she would have had the operation, the risk would not have eventuated (the chance was independent and in any particular case it would probably not occur) and so the loss was, in that but-for sense, caused by the failure to warn.

A 3:2 majority of the House of Lords found that Miss Chester was entitled to substantial damages, on the basis that the rules of causation should be modified to protect the patient's right to autonomy and dignity and to give informed consent, and that in medical causes the fact that the patient would have gone ahead anyway and that the risk was not increased (ie the loss was coincidental loss as referred to above[212]) was irrelevant: if the doctor fails to warn he or she is liable (as if an insurer) if the thing he or she should have warned about occurred.[213] Lord Walker distinguished a non-negligent accident of anaesthesia or the operating theatre being struck by lightning, which would be coincidental,[214] from the nerve damage risk which was what the claimant should have warned of.

The minority's view (Lords Hoffmann and Bingham) was that ordinary rules should apply, the risk was not created or increased by the failure to advise and was therefore coincidental, and so the failure to advise was not the effective cause of the loss.[215] To put it another way (and not as they put it), the scope of the duty to warn is to allow the claimant to avoid the nerve damage complication by deciding not to have the operation, not to avoid the nerve damage complication fortuitously

---

[211] *Chester v Afshar* [2005] 1 AC 134 (HL). See also *Chappel v Hart* (1998) 195 CLR 232 (HC of Australia).

[212] The mountaineer example discussed above would still have the same result even applying this approach from *Chester*: the doctor's failure to warn was of knee collapse not avalanche injury. This point was made by Sir Denis Henry giving the judgment of the Court of Appeal in *Chester v Afshar* at [2003] QB 356 (CA) para 46.

[213] Thus the fact that the claimant would have delayed her operation is not necessary to the majority's decision.

[214] [2005] 1 AC 134 at para 94.

[215] See further Lord Hoffmann, 'Common Sense and Causing Loss' (Lecture to the Chancery Bar Association, 15 June 1999), commenting on *Chappel v Hart* (1998) 195 CLR 232 (HC of Australia).

by random chance of having the operation on another day. However, that minority view is not the law in medical negligence cases, where this special rule applies.[216]

The Court of Appeal has (rightly) refused to extend the *Chester v Afshar* rule to a case of failure to warn by a solicitor[217] or by a financial advisor.[218]

(iii) The Link between 'Scope of Duty' and Remoteness ('Assumption of Responsibility')

Scope of duty and assumption of responsibility (the modern test behind remoteness) are essentially the same thing: they both describe implied scope of the responsibility assumed by the defendant.

Lord Hoffmann in *The Achilleas* in 2008 expressly linked the remoteness principle as applied in that case with the scope of duty principle from his judgment in *SAAMCo* 12 years earlier.[219] Toulson LJ in *Siemens v Supershield* described both *SAAMCo* and *The Achilleas* as cases in which 'the standard approach [*the remoteness test from Hadley v Baxendale*] would not reflect the expectation or intention reasonably to be imputed to the parties'.[220] In *Haugesund Kommune v Depfa ACS Bank*,[221] in which the duty arose only in contract, the *SAAMCo* test was applied but Rix LJ (nodding to *The Achilleas*) observed that 'It may be that in the context of contract that might have to be rephrased as a question of assumption of responsibility'.[222] Put simply, as Professor Burrows says, 'with the benefit of hindsight of the reasoning in *The Achilleas*, *SAAMCo* should now be regarded as a decision on remoteness'.[223] Because of their origins and terminology, it is likely that the label 'scope of duty' will continue to be used in cases of duty of care, and 'assumption of responsibility' in cases of strict duties,[224] but the essence is the same.

---

[216] But in Australia there is legislation focusing on the scope of duty in this context. See *Wallace v Kam* [2013] HCA 19 (HC of Australia) and s 5D of the Civil Liability Act 2002 of New South Wales. And see *M's Guardian v Lanarkshire Health Board* [2013] CSIH 3 (Inner House), which sought to limit the application of *Chester* even in the medical negligence field.

[217] *Benedict White v Paul Davidson & Taylor* [2004] EWCA Civ 1511.

[218] *Beary v Pall Mall Investments (a firm)* [2005] EWCA Civ 415, especially at para 41.

[219] *Transfield Shipping Inc v Mercator Shipping Inc (The Achilleas)* [2009] AC 61 (HL) at paras 15 to 19. See also Baroness Hale's comments at para 93, although she linked the two when arguing that the principle should not apply to non-negligence-based contractual duties. See also *Platform Home Loans Ltd v Oyston Shipways Ltd* [2000] 2 AC 190 (HL) Lord Hobhouse at 208, and *Aneco Reinsurance Underwriting Ltd v Johnson & Higgins Ltd* [2002] 1 Lloyd's Rep 156 (HL) Lord Lloyd at para 11, linking scope of duty and remoteness even before the developments in *The Achilleas*.

[220] *Siemens Building Technologies FE Ltd v Supershield Ltd* [2010] EWCA Civ 7 at para 43. See also the pre-*Achilleas* comments of Evans LJ in *Cossey v Lonnkvist* [2000] Lloyds Rep PN 885 (CA) at 888.

[221] *Haugesund Kommune v Depfa ACS Bank* [2012] QB 549 (CA).

[222] Ibid at para 73. The scope of duty test also applies to purely tortious liability: *Calvert v William Hill Credit Ltd* [2009] Ch 330 (CA).

[223] A Burrows, 'Comparing Compensatory Damages in Contract and Tort: Some Problematic Issues' in S Degeling, J Edelman and J Goudkamp (eds), *Torts in Commercial Law* (Sydney, Law Book Co, 2011).

[224] Thus, for example, Field J was resistant (prior to *The Achilleas*) to the attempt to apply 'scope of duty' language to an action under a seller's strict duty to deliver goods, but was happy to use language of remoteness and causation: *CTI Group Inc v Transclear SA (The Mary Nour) (No 2)* [2008] 1 Lloyd's Rep 250 at para 9. Similarly, Lord Walker in *Sentinel International Ltd v Cordes* [2008] UKPC 60 at para 50 said (after *The Achilleas* but without referring to it) that the *SAAMCo* principle did not apply to ordinary loss of bargain claims.

C. Remoteness in the Tort of Negligence

It might be said that the scope of duty and assumption of responsibility principles cannot be the same because the scope of duty test clearly applies not only to contract but also to tort cases of professional liability, ie liability under a duty of care arising out of an assumption of responsibility by the principle from *Hedley Byrne & Co Ltd v Heller & Partners Ltd*[225] and *Henderson v Merrett Syndicates Ltd*,[226] and that it is well-established (eg by *The Heron II*[227]) that the remoteness test in the tort of negligence is different to that in contract. The answer to this is that the remoteness test in cases where the tortious duty of care arises out of an 'assumption of responsibility' (quoting Lord Devlin in *Hedley Byrne* when explaining the basis of the duty of care)[228] is the same test as the contract test: a construction question as to the scope of the defendant's 'assumption of responsibility' (quoting Lord Hoffmann in *The Achilleas* in relation to the question of loss). However, although logic and a body of considered opinion favour this conclusion,[229] there is as yet no clear and conclusive decision determining the point.

14.6 Factors Relevant to Scope of Duty and Assumption of Responsibility

The assumption of responsibility and scope of duty principles (or, really, 'principle' singular) require construction of the contract as a whole. Accordingly, there are an infinite variety of factors that affect the question of whether responsibility has been assumed, including the broader context and the other terms of the contract. Nevertheless, the following are important features in many cases:

A. Could the Defendant Have Estimated the Loss at the Date of Contracting?

The first and probably most important aspect of the remoteness requirement is whether the possible harm to which the breach exposed the claimant was easy, difficult or impossible for the defendant to estimate, and so price into the contract or insure against if it wished to and had the negotiating power to do so. Important factors in answering this question include:

---

[225] *Hedley Byrne & Co Ltd v Heller & Partners Ltd* [1964] AC 465 (HL).
[226] *Henderson v Merrett Syndicates Ltd* [1995] 2 AC 145.
[227] *C Czarnikow Ltd v Koufos (The Heron II)* [1969] 1 AC 350 (HL).
[228] [1964] AC 465 at 528.
[229] See A Kramer, 'Remoteness: New Problems with the Old Test' in Cunnington and Saidov (eds), *Contract Damages: Domestic and International Perspectives* (Oxford, Hart Publishing, 2008) and the cases and articles cited therein, especially J Cartwright, 'Remoteness of Damage in Contract and Tort: A Reconsideration' (1996) 55 *CLJ* 488.

(i) Was the Loss Foreseeable as Not Unlikely at the Date of Contracting?

This is the default 'reasonable contemplation' test, from which an assumption of responsibility can usually be inferred.[230] If a loss is not foreseeable the defendant could not be expected to allow for it and so to have taken responsibility for it, as discussed earlier in this chapter.

(ii) Is the Defendant Conducting a Normal Business or Doing Something Special?

An important factor rendering losses too remote in some cases is that the particular losses suffered by the claimant were abnormal even for the claimant's industry or even for its own business. Key examples include the abnormal use of the derrick in *Cory v Thames Ironworks*,[231] and the particularly lucrative contracts in *Victoria Laundry*.[232] Likewise, when ordering a spare part it is not usual that the claimant's entire business is waiting on its delivery (*Hadley v Baxendale*[233]).

(iii) The Relationship between the Defendant and Claimant and Whether They Share the Same Markets

The extent of the defendant's knowledge and understanding of and engagement with the claimant's industry will be relevant to the extent of losses the defendant can be expected to have anticipated causing and so reasonably understood to have taken responsibility for. A key contrast is between claims against sellers (who are in the same industry as the claimant buyer) and claims against carriers (who could be carrying anything and may know little about the industry). *Hadley v Baxendale* is a carrier case, whereas *Bacon v Cooper (Metals) Ltd* (where the claimant's business was also brought to a standstill but the losses were not too remote),[234] *Victoria Laundry* and *The Heron II*[235] are sales cases.[236] The limited scope of duty of many professionals may be partly explained by the fact that they are not in the lending business, whereas a broader scope was found in *Aneco*[237] where the defendant broker and claimant insurer 'share the same markets',[238] and in *Brown v KMR Services Ltd* where the Lloyd's members' agents shared the industry with the Lloyd's members.[239] The remoteness of the losses in *Balfour Beatty Construction (Scotland) Ltd v Scottish Power plc*,[240] a dispute between a road builder and an electricity supplier, very much

---

[230] See section 14.2E above.

[231] *Cory v Thames Ironworks and Shipbuilding Co Ltd* (1868) LR 3 QB 181 (QBD), discussed above in section 14.4A.

[232] *Victoria Laundry (Windsor) Ltd v Newman Industries Ltd* [1949] 2 KB 528 (CA), discussed above at text to nn 79 and 104.

[233] *Hadley v Baxendale* (1854) 9 Exch 341, discussed above in section 14.3A.

[234] *Bacon v Cooper (Metals) Ltd* [1982] 1 All ER 397 (Cantley J).

[235] *C Czarnikow Ltd v Koufos (The Heron II)* [1969] 1 AC 350 (HL), discussed above at text to n 62.

[236] For explicit judicial recognition of this point, see text to chapter six nn 92 to 94.

[237] *Aneco Reinsurance Underwriting Ltd v Johnson & Higgins Ltd* [2002] 1 Lloyd's Rep 156 (HL), discussed above in section 14.5B(ii)(d).

[238] This was a point made by Rix LJ in *Haugesund Kommune v Depfa ACS Bank* [2012] QB 549 (CA) at para 76 when distinguishing the *Aneco* decision.

[239] *Brown v KMR Services Ltd* [1995] 4 All ER 598 (CA), discussed above at text to n 84.

[240] *Balfour Beatty Construction (Scotland) Ltd v Scottish Power plc* (1994) 71 BLR 20 (HL).

depended upon the latter's lack of detailed understanding of the former's business and the importance and mechanics of the continuous concrete pour.[241]

(iv) Was the Loss Quantifiable, at Least Roughly, at the Time of Contracting?

One of the important features of *The Achilleas* itself was that although the defendant could foresee the type of loss that the claimant might suffer upon late redelivery of the vessel, it could have 'no idea when that would be done or what its length [*ie that of the follow-on charter*] or other terms would be'[242] and so no way of estimating the extent of the loss. As Lord Hope put it in that case:

> [A] party cannot be expected to assume responsibility for something that he cannot control and, because he does not know anything about it, cannot quantify. It is not enough for him to know in general and on open-ended terms that there is likely to be a follow-on fixture. This was the error which lies at the heart of the decision of the majority. What he needs is some information that will enable him to assess the extent of any liability.[243]

The length of the possible follow-on charter is a key feature: the shipowner might have made a short or very long follow-on charter, and this provided an impossibly large range of possible losses.[244] It is not merely that the losses depend upon the market, but rather that they depend upon the specific arrangements made by the claimant with a third party, which arrangements can vary dramatically.[245] The same ordinarily applies as regards a buyer who tries to hold a seller responsible for losses on a particular pre-arranged sub-sale, for the same reasons.[246]

An analogy can be drawn with contracts of carriage in the age of sail. In those days the arrival time and therefore consequent market movements were so impossible of estimation that losses due to market fluctuations were held to be too remote by the rule in *The Parana*,[247] and it was partly because modern sea transportation and therefore the losses from delay are far more predictable that the rule from *The Parana* was reversed in *The Heron II*.[248]

---

[241] See above at text to n 41.

[242] *Transfield Shipping Inc v Mercator Shipping Inc (The Achilleas)* [2009] AC 61 (HL) Lord Hoffmann at para 23. See also Lord Hope at para 34, Lord Rodger at para 61 and Lord Walker at para 86. Also Lord Hoffmann, 'The Achilleas: custom and practice or foreseeability?' (2010) *Edinburgh L Rev* 47 at 59.

[243] [2009] AC 61 at para 36.

[244] In contrast, where the breach of the shipowner interrupts the charter the possible losses on the sub-charter are more confined as they cannot run beyond the period of the head charter and will usually be voyage charters. See *Sylvia Shipping Ltd v Progress Bulk Carriers Ltd* [2010] EWHC 542 (Comm) (Hamblen J) (interruption of hire) and *Geogas SA v Trammo Gas Ltd (The Baleares)* [1993] 1 Lloyd's Rep 215 (CA) (late delivery at the start of hire), in both of which the lost profits on the sub-charter were recoverable.

[245] See especially Lord Hope [2009] AC 61 at para 34.

[246] *Williams v Reynolds* (1865) 34 LJQB 221. See the quotation at text to chapter four n 122 above. See also a similar point in *Kerr Steamship Co, Inc v Radio Corporation of America* (1927) 245 NY 284 (NYCA).

[247] *The Parana* (1877) 2 PD 118 (CA).

[248] *C Czarnikow Ltd v Koufos (The Heron II)* [1969] 1 AC 350 (HL) Lord Upjohn at 428–29 and *Dunn v Bucknall Brothers* [1902] 2 KB 614 (CA) Collins MR at 623. See also Lord Hoffmann, 'The Achilleas: custom and practice or foreseeability?' (2010) *Edinburgh L Rev* 47 at 56.

The same applies where the claimant's entire business, the detail and scale of which is unknown by the defendant, rests on the good working order of the defendant's equipment, in which case the lost profits will likely be held too remote.[249] And if a defendant is manufacturing a product with modest cost and minimum quantity it has no way of knowing without being told that the purchaser is engaged in a hugely expensive advertising campaign (which will be wasted if the product is defective).[250]

In this context, it should be noted that although the volatility of a market (which was a feature in *The Achilleas*) does not rule out the defendant's having assumed responsibility for damages resulting from it (eg by delay), it can point against such an assumption.[251]

B. Was the Purpose of the Breached Duty the Protection of the Claimant against the Harm that Eventuated, or Conversely Was the Harm that Eventuated Incidental to the Purpose?

Where a duty was to protect against a particular harm or to protect a particular interest that such a harm interferes with, then no matter how unlikely that harm is, it will almost certainly fall within the defendant's responsibility.[252] This was important in the *Supershield* and *Rubenstein* cases,[253] and in various other cases of external events and claimant events discussed in more detail below in sections 16.8 and 16.13. The question of whether a professional is providing information or advice on a specific point, or is generally advising or acting as an *homme des affaires*,[254] also falls under this heading. The court must look at the role the defendant is undertaking by the relevant duty, and the purpose the reasonable person would understand the duty to have for the claimant.

C. Where the Defendant was Given Specific Information by the Claimant, What Were the Circumstances?

As explained above (section 14.2E), where information is communicated to the defendant that renders a loss foreseeable and/or quantifiable, whether that also makes the defendant impliedly responsible for that loss depends upon the circumstances in which the information was communicated, including whether it was casual or formal,

---

[249] *Munroe Equipment Sales Ltd v Canadian Forest Products Ltd* (1961) 29 DLR (2d) 730 (Manitoba CA).

[250] *Out of the Box Pte Ltd v Wanin Industries Pte Ltd* [2013] SGCA 15 (Singapore CA) at para 54 (although expressly applying a policy, not assumption of responsibility approach to remoteness).

[251] *John Grimes Partnership Ltd v Gubbins* [2013] EWCA Civ 37 Tomlinson LJ at paras 33–34, doubting his earlier comments in *A Pindell Ltd v AirAsia Berhad* [2010] EWHC 2516 (Comm) (Tomlinson J), and Sir David Keene at para 27.

[252] See text to n 11.

[253] *Siemens Building Technologies FE Ltd v Supershield Ltd* [2010] EWCA Civ 7 and *Rubenstein v HSBC Bank plc* [2012] EWCA Civ 1184.

[254] See Rix LJ in *Haugesund Kommune v Depfa ACS Bank* [2012] QB 549 (CA) at para 76, and the discussion above in section 14.5B.

whether to a junior or senior employee, and when, and whether the contract price and terms were or could realistically have been adjusted after the information was imparted.

D. Pricing

(i) Disproportionality of the Price as Compared with the Magnitude of Losses

Although it will rarely point conclusively in either direction, comparing the price paid by the promisor with the size of potential losses for which the promisor is said to have taken the risk can assist in resolving the construction question of the implied assumption of responsibility.[255] The simple point is (as an Arkansas judge put it) that

> where the damages ... are so large as to be out of proportion to the consideration agreed to be paid for the services rendered under the contract, it raises a doubt at once as to whether the party would have assented to such a liability had it been called to his attention at the making of the contract unless the consideration to be paid was also raised so as to correspond in some respect to the liability assumed.[256]

However, the disproportion between the fee and size of the loss is 'merely one possible pointer' against an assumption of responsibility and is by itself not normally enough.[257]

(ii) The Way the Defendant Appears to Have Priced the Contract

Pricing points to another difference between carriage and sale cases. As Lord Hoffmann has observed, extra-judicially,

> In a contract of carriage, the price will be based on such matters as size, weight and distance rather than the value or importance of the goods to the owner. The price may be relatively trivial in relation to the consequential loss which the owner may suffer from later or non-delivery. So, in the absence of express terms, the courts have been very reluctant to make the carrier liable for consequential loss unless he clearly had the opportunity to decide whether to accept such liability or not and, if necessary, stipulate for higher payment.[258]

In the Arkansas case of *Morrow v First National Bank of Hot Springs*, the bank's delay in notifying the plantiffs when they had safety-deposit boxes available so that the plaintiffs could move their coin collection there led to the coins being at the

---

[255] Lord Hoffmann in *The Achilleas* [2009] AC 61 at paras 13 and 20. See also *Stuart Property v Condor Commercial Property* [2006] NSWCA 334 (New South Wales CA) para 97; *Out of the Box Pte Ltd v Wanin Industries Pte Ltd* [2013] SGCA 15 (Singapore CA) at para 54 (although expressly applying a policy, not assumption of responsibility, approach to remoteness); *John Grimes Partnership Ltd v Gubbins* [2013] EWCA Civ 37 Sir David Keene at para 30; US Restatement (Second) of Contracts §351(3) and cmt (f).

[256] *Hooks Smelting Co v Planters' Compress Co* 79 SW 1052 (1904) (SC of Arkansas).

[257] *John Grimes Partnership Ltd v Gubbins* [2013] EWCA Civ 37 Sir David Keene at para 30.

[258] Lord Hoffmann, 'The Achilleas: custom and practice or foreseeability?' (2010) *Edinburgh L Rev* 47 at 57. See further above at n 46.

plaintiffs' house when it was burgled, and the coins were taken.[259] The bank was held not to be liable for over US$32,000 value of the coins, there having been no additional consideration paid for the promise to notify as to the boxes' availability (above the US$75 rental for the boxes when they became available).

E. Is there a Market Understanding or Custom or General Expectation as to the Allocation of Responsibility?

Although none of the other judges in the House of Lords placed any weight on the point, Lord Hoffmann in *The Achilleas* was in part persuaded by a market understanding, as found by the arbitrators, that a charterer's liability on late redelivery was limited to the market loss for the period of the overrun.[260] Lord Hoffmann might have gone so far as to say that the market understanding in *The Achilleas* meant that there was a term (effectively an exclusion clause) implied in law into charterparties covering the point,[261] although if that is correct (and it is not the majority decision of the House) then *The Achilleas* is not a remoteness case at all.

F. Is the Loss a Result of Fraud of the Defendant?

However foreseeable the fraud or deliberate breach of the defendant is, it may be that the claimant nevertheless can rarely be taken to have assumed responsibility for its consequences. This is the approach the law takes, or is sometimes said to take, when construing exclusion clauses.[262]

G. Physical Damage, Personal Injury and Non-Pecuniary Loss

Similarly, as discussed above in section 14.3H(i), in many situations the reasonable person may more easily understand the defendant to have undertaken responsibility for physical damage or personal injury than economic loss (or, to look at it another way, the reasonable person may less easily understand the *claimant* to have taken the risk upon themselves of physical damage and personal injury).

Applying remoteness to non-pecuniary loss other than physical damage and personal injury is the subject of the entirety of chapter nineteen, especially section 19.1E.

---

[259] *Morrow v First National Bank of Hot Springs* 550 SW 2d 429 (1977) (SC of Arkansas). The 'tacit agreement' test of remoteness prevails in Arkansas.

[260] *Transfield Shipping Inc v Mercator Shipping Inc (The Achilleas)* [2009] AC 61 (HL) at paras 6–7 and 9; Lord Hoffmann, 'The Achilleas: custom and practice or foreseeability?' (2010) *Edinburgh L Rev* 47 at 59.

[261] *Transfield Shipping Inc v Mercator Shipping Inc (The Achilleas)* [2009] AC 61 (HL) at para 11 and Lord Hoffmann, 'The Achilleas: custom and practice or foreseeability?' (2010) *Edinburgh L Rev* 47 at 61.

[262] *HIH Casualty and General Insurance Ltd v Chase Manhattan Bank* [2003] UKHL 6; *Astrazeneca UK Ltd v Albemarle International Corp* [2011] EWHC 1574 (Comm).

14.7 The Interaction of Scope of Duty with Contribution and Contributory Negligence

A. Contributory Negligence

The question arose for the House of Lords in *Platform Home Loans Ltd v Oyston Shipways Ltd*[263] as to how the scope of a valuer's duty fits in with the assessment of contributory negligence. It was held by the majority of the House that the reduction for contributory negligence (in that case 20 per cent due to imprudent lending by the bank) would be applied to the full or 'basic' loss, not to the loss after it had been limited to the *SAAMCo* cap.

Thus in a valuer's negligence case, if the loss far exceeds the cap amount of the overvaluation, it will be unnecessary to assess the claimant's contributory negligence, since only if it is very large will it have an effect on recovery (by reducing the actual loss by so much that it falls below the limit that would in any case be imposed by the *SAAMCo* cap).

The rationale of their Lordships in *Platform v Oyston* was that the scope of duty principle is an exercise in attribution and there would be double counting to apply the further attribution under the 1945 Act on top of that;[264] the 'damage' suffered that is apportioned under the Act is the loss, not the mathematically calculated but separate amount of the overvaluation;[265] and the claimant's own fault contributed to its loss, not merely to the part of the loss falling within the valuer's scope of duty.[266]

The applicability of this reasoning may depend upon the nature of the contributory negligence in the particular case. As Lord Millett observed:

> Where the lender's negligence has caused or contributed directly to the overvaluation, then it may be appropriate to apply the reduction to the amount of the overvaluation as well to the overall loss. Where, however, the lender's imprudence was partly responsible for the overall loss but did not cause or contribute to the overvaluation, it is the overall loss alone which should be reduced, possibly but not necessarily leading to a consequential reduction in the damages. When the consequences of the lender's imprudence cannot be calculated, the judge will have to do the best he can to assess the parties' respective contributions. But the court should not speculate when it can calculate.[267]

The result is not particularly surprising as a practical and policy matter, and given that the *SAAMCo* cap is a rough and ready cap rather than a logical application of the remoteness/scope of duty principle. However it is difficult to justify as a general approach: it cannot be right in every case of a remoteness or scope of duty argument to which contributory negligence applies that the claimant has to calculate the basic loss prior to the application of the remoteness and scope of duty principles

---

[263] *Platform Home Loans Ltd v Oyston Shipways Ltd* [2000] 2 AC 190 (HL).
[264] Ibid Lord Hobhouse at 211–12.
[265] Ibid Lord Millett at 214.
[266] Ibid Lord Millett at 214.
[267] Ibid at 215.

and apply contributory negligence to that, rather than to the otherwise recoverable loss after the application of remoteness and/or scope of duty.

B. Contribution

In *Ball v Banner*,[268] the author of an investment prospectus containing misstatements brought contribution proceedings against the valuer whose information led to the misstatement. Hart J confirmed that the *SAAMCo* cap is only to be applied after responsibility has been allocated between the parties under the Civil Liability (Contribution) Act 1978: the contribution allocation was based (by section 2(1)) on the extent of responsibility for the 'damage' parties have suffered, whereas the *SAAMCo* cap only limits the amount of 'damages' recoverable.[269]

[268] *Ball v Banner* [2000] Lloyd's Rep PN 56 (Hart J), appeal allowed on a different point: (CA), 30 June 2000.
[269] Para 12.

15

Legal Causation and Mitigation and the Breach Position

The principle of legal causation, and its sub-principle of mitigation, provide that unconnected or unreasonable acts or omissions of the claimant or supervening events break the chain of causation: their consequences are disregarded when calculating damages, and they are deemed not to have occurred. Also, the reduction of damages for contributory negligence pursuant to statute.

15.1. Introduction
15.2. Legal Causation
15.3. The Principle of Mitigation
15.4. Burdens of Proof
15.5. Contributory Negligence
15.6. Applying Legal Causation to What Would Have Happened but for the Breach

15.1 Introduction

A S DISCUSSED IN chapters eleven to thirteen above, recovery requires factual causation, in other words that, but for a breach by the defendant, a harm would not have occurred or a gain would have occurred. This is necessary but not sufficient to found liability. Two further interlocking principles (remoteness including the scope of duty principle, and the chain of causation principle including the mitigation principle) ask whether the loss that the defendant in fact caused fell within the scope of the defendant's responsibility, and determine what needs to be added or taken away from harm that was factually caused—the breach position—to reach the measure of damages for recoverable loss.

Remoteness is discussed above in chapter fourteen. That principle applies both to the breach position (things that actually happened to cause harm may be too remote) and the non-breach position (gains that would have been made may be too remote).

The legal causation and mitigation principles, however, are primarily directed to the breach position. These are discussed in this chapter (as to principles) and the next chapter (as to the cases).[1] Their main effect is to require legal editing of the

---

[1] The relatively minor role in relation to the non-breach position is discussed at the end of this chapter in section 15.6.

actual proven breach position to alter it (before working out the loss) to how it would be if certain acts, omissions or events had not occurred.

A. Introduction to the Principles of Legal Causation and Collaterality (Including Mitigation)

Even where the breach of contract has caused (in a 'but for' sense) the relevant loss, some events, actions or omissions subsequent to the breach may be sufficiently important that the law treats them as exculpating the breach of contract, such that the defendant will not be held responsible for the loss resulting from those events or actions, nor need the claimant give credit for the benefit accruing to it from them.

At first sight this may seem to interfere with the basic compensatory principle of contract law, and in a sense it does. Superficially at least, the exhortation to place the claimant 'in the same situation, with respect to damages, as if the contract had been performed'[2] simply requires a comparison between the position the claimant is in and the position it would have been in, ie it simply requires the principle of factual or 'but for' causation. However, a moment's reflection indicates that this has the potential to work injustice and go beyond compensation as anyone would understand that term, because the test of simple factual causation alone makes the defendant responsible for all the things that happened to the claimant after the breach that would not otherwise have happened, including, to take an extreme example, losses resulting from the claimant's own deliberate or reckless increasing of its loss. Just because I wrongfully sacked an employee and gave him a lot of free time, should I really compensate him because during that free time he took up gambling and frittered away his money? Or because took a walk and was struck by lightning? Or if he passed up an even better job the next day?

We will turn in more detail to a discussion of labels in a moment, but the law has developed various concepts under the heading of 'legal causation' to mark its judgement that although the harm or gain was factually (but for) caused by the defendant, legally it is not treated as the defendant's responsibility.

A final point to note at this stage is that, other than the mitigation cases, the majority of the cases on legal causation arise under the law of tort and not contract. Remoteness has a greater role in contract law than legal causation does, although the mitigation and collateral benefit aspects of legal causation are still important in contract cases, as the number of cases discussed in the next chapter shows. The legal causation principles are, in any event, the same in both contract and tort law,[3] and various tort cases are referred to in these chapters when the legal principles are being described.

---

[2] *Robinson v Harman* (1848) 1 Exch 850.
[3] *Dimond v Lovell* [2002] 1 AC 384 (HL) Lord Hoffmann at 402.

(i) Mitigation

The most important causation principle to contract law has its own label, 'mitigation'. Nevertheless, mitigation is little more than the application of this general concept of legal causation to action or, more frequently, inaction, of the claimant (as opposed to actions or omissions of the defendant or third parties and non-human events). This means that where the claimant acts reasonably in trying to avoid loss, then no principle of legal causation applies and the costs, losses and benefits resulting from those actions are treated as caused by the breach. However, where the claimant acts unreasonably in trying to avoid loss or (more frequently) failing to try to avoid loss, the consequences of so doing are not treated as caused by the breach for the purposes of the damages calculation.

Despite it being a part of the doctrine of causation, it remains useful to consider mitigation separately, since particular considerations operate in relation to acts and omissions of the *claimant* that do not operate for other supervening acts and omissions, and because of the unusual focus in mitigation cases on an *omission* breaking the chain of causation. Mitigation is discussed further below at section 15.3.

15.2 Legal Causation

A. The Principle

(i) Metaphorical Labels Focusing on Causation

Many different labels are applied to the principle of legal causation. Where events that increase losses are concerned, it is often said that the later cause is a 'novus actus interveniens', or new intervening act, which 'breaks the chain of causation'[4] between the breach and the harm or benefit, or that the later cause is legally the 'sole cause' or a 'supervening cause' or the 'independent cause',[5] or 'obliterates' or 'wholly supplants' the breach,[6] or the breach is a 'remote' and not sufficiently 'proximate cause' of the harm or gain.[7] As Lord Sumner put it:

> It is hard to steer clear of metaphors. Perhaps one may be forgiven for saying that B. snaps the chain of causation; that he is no mere conduit pipe through which consequences flow from A. to C., no mere moving part in a transmission gear set in motion by A.; that, in a word, he insulates A. from C.[8]

---

[4] *Vinmar International Ltd v Theresa Navigation SA* [2001] EWHC 497 (Comm) (Tomlinson J) at para 42; *Petroleo Brasileiro SA v ENE Kos 1 Ltd* [2012] UKSC 17 Lord Sumption at para 14.

[5] *Zodiac Maritime Agencies Ltd v Fortescue Metals Group Ltd (The Kildare)* [2011] 2 Lloyd's Rep 360 (Steel J) at para 70; *Petroleo Brasileiro SA v ENE Kos 1 Ltd* [2012] UKSC 17 Lord Sumption at para 14.

[6] *Great Elephant Corporation v Trafigura Beheer BV* [2013] EWCA Civ 905 per Longmore LJ at para 45 and the cases cited therein.

[7] *Petroleo Brasileiro SA v ENE Kos 1 Ltd* [2012] UKSC 17 Lord Mance throughout.

[8] *Weld-Blundell v Stephens* [1920] AC 956 (HL) Lord Sumner at 986.

(ii) Labels When Discussing Credits or Benefits

Where the question is whether a benefit (rather than a harm) is to be taken into account, similar labels are used. Some were listed by the Court of Appeal in the tort case of *Burdis v Livsey*:

> In our judgment, the authorities to which we have so far referred establish that subsequent events which are not referable in a causative sense to the commission of the tort [*or the breach of contract*], that is to say events which, on a true analysis, are *collateral*[9] to the commission of the tort, or *res inter alios acta*,[10] or *too remote*—we regard these expressions as interchangeable—do not affect the measure of a direct loss suffered when the tort was committed. (Emphasis added)[11]

Or the benefit or advantage is said to be 'wholly independent of the relation between the plaintiff and the defendant'[12] rather than 'part of a continuous transaction' with the breach.[13]

(iii) Labels When Discussing Mitigation

All it means to say that there is a 'duty' to take a mitigatory step is that failure to take that step is an unreasonable omission that breaks the chain of legal causation.[14] Thus Toulson J (as he then was) explained that: 'The orthodox view is that the rule as to avoidable loss is merely an aspect of the fundamental principle of causation that a plaintiff can recover only in respect of damage caused by the defendant's wrong'.[15] This view was approved on appeal by Potter LJ:

> [I]n truth, causation and mitigation are two sides of the same coin ... In every case where an issue of failure to mitigate is raised by the defendant it can be characterised as an issue of causation in the sense that, if damage has been caused or exacerbated by the claimant's unreasonable conduct or inaction, then to that extent it has not been caused by the defendant's tort or breach of contract.[16]

All the familiar language of legal causation applies here: a failure to act in accordance with the duty to mitigate is thus said to be independent of the breach[17] and

---

[9] Also eg *Famosa Shpping Co Ltd v Armada Bulk Carriers Ltd (The Fanis)* [1994] 1 Lloyd's Rep 633 (Mance J) at 636; *Rubenstein v HSBC Bank plc* [2012] EWCA Civ 1184 Rix LJ at para 134.

[10] Short for 'res inter alios acta, aliis nec nocet nec prodest', Latin for 'a thing done between others neither harms nor benefits others'.

[11] *Burdis v Livsey* [2003] QB 36 (CA) at para 91.

[12] *British Westinghouse Manufacturing and Electric Co v Underground Electric Railways Co of London* [1912] AC 673 (HL) Viscount Haldane LC at 690 (a contract case).

[13] *Rubenstein v HSBC Bank plc* [2012] EWCA Civ 1184 Rix LJ at paras 134 and 136 (a contract and tort case).

[14] *Activa DPS Europe Sarl v Pressure Seal Solutions* [2012] EWCA Civ 943 Patten LJ at para 36. Cf *Mobil North Sea Ltd v PJ Pipe and Valve Co (t/a PJ Valve Ltd)* [2001] EWCA Civ 741 Rix LJ at para 30.

[15] *Standard Chartered Bank v Pakistan National Shipping Corp (No 3)* [1999] 1 Lloyd's Rep 747 (Toulson J) at 758 (deceit).

[16] *Standard Chartered Bank v Pakistan National Shipping Corp (No 3)* [2001] EWCA Civ 55 Potter LJ at para 41.

[17] *Glory Wealth Shipping Pte Ltd v Korea Line Corp* [2011] EWHC 1819 (Comm) (Blair J) at para 16; *Zodiac Maritime Agencies Ltd v Fortescue Metals Group Ltd (The Kildare)* [2011] 2 Lloyd's Rep 360 (Steel J) at para 65.

so not caused by it;[18] *res inter alios acta*;[19] a choice,[20] decision[21] or speculation;[22] and any benefit thereby earned is a collateral benefit that need not be taken into account.[23] '[A]lthough phrased in terms of a duty to mitigate, this is really another aspect of causation'.[24]

As for reasonable mitigatory actions actually taken by the claimant (as opposed to the mitigatory actions that should have been taken but were not), Viscount Haldane LC in *British Westinghouse* expressly tied the result in that case (that the claimant's reasonable mitigatory actions were to be taken into account) in with the general rules of legal causation and collateral advantages, alongside a discussion of cases on insurance or post-breach transactions which do not 'aris[e] out of the consequences of the breach and in the ordinary course of business' or out of 'the transactions the subject-matter of the contract' and were 'independent' and 'res inter alios acta'.[25] Mitigatory actions are taken into account if they 'formed part of a continuous dealing between the parties' rather than being 'an independent or disconnected transaction'[26] and 'collateral'.[27]

(iv) Fairness and Responsibility

Turning back to causation generally, rather than mitigation specifically: of course, as a matter of logic, and despite talk of 'breaks' and the like, there remains a chain of necessary factual causation between the breach and the event/harm/credit, because these questions would not even arise if it had not already been demonstrated that but for the breach the event/harm/benefit would not have occurred. There is therefore a chain, or continuous transaction in at least one sense, and the later event is never literally the 'sole cause'.

---

[18] *Habton Farms (an unlimited company) v Nimmo* [2003] EWCA Civ 68 Clarke LJ at para 66; *Downs v Chappell* [1996] 1 WLR 426 (CA) Hobhouse LJ at 437; *South Australia Asset Management Corp v York Montague Ltd* [1997] 1 AC 191 (HL) Lord Hoffmann at 221; *Burdis v Livsey* [2003] QB 36 (CA) Aldous LJ at para 88; *Transfield Shipping Inc v Mercator Shipping Inc (The Achilleas)* [2007] 2 Lloyd's Rep 555 (CA) Rix LJ at para 105. See further below in section 15.3D.
[19] *British Westinghouse Electric & Manufacturing Co Ltd v Underground Electric Railways Co of London Ltd* [1912] AC 673 (HL) Lord Haldane at 691; *Transfield Shipping Inc v Mercator Shipping Inc (The Achilleas)* [2007] 2 Lloyd's Rep 555 (CA) Rix LJ at para 102.
[20] *Downs v Chappell* [1996] 1 WLR 426 (CA) Hobhouse LJ at 437.
[21] *Zodiac Maritime Agencies Ltd v Fortescue Metals Group Ltd (The Kildare)* [2011] 2 Lloyd's Rep 360 (Steel J) at para 65.
[22] *Glencore Energy UK Ltd v Transworld Oil Ltd* [2010] EWHC 141 (Comm) (Blair J) at para 75.
[23] *Jamal v Moolla Dawood Sons & Co* [1916] 1 AC 175 (PC) Lord Wrenbury at 180.
[24] *British Midland Tool Ltd v Midland International Tooling Ltd* [2003] 2 BCLC 523 (Hart J) at para 186(j) (breach of fiduciary duty).
[25] *British Westinghouse Electric & Manufacturing Co Ltd v Underground Electric Railways Co of London Ltd* [1912] AC 673 (HL) at 690–91. See also the discussion *Compania Financiera Soleada SA v Hamoor Tanker Corp Inc (The Borag)* [1981] 1 WLR 274 (CA) Denning MR at 280–81 and Shaw LJ at 283 and Templeman LJ at 283–85, to the effect that the label of causation/mitigation/remoteness does not matter much, the test is reasonableness in any case.
[26] *R Pagnan & Fratelli v Corbisa Industrial Agropacuaria Limitada* [1970] 1 WLR 1306 (CA) at 1315; *Mobil North Sea Ltd v PJ Pipe and Valve Co (t/a PJ Valve Ltd)* [2001] EWCA Civ 741 Rix LJ at para 30.
[27] *Pankhania v London Borough of Hackney* [2004] EWHC 323 (Ch) (Vos QC) at para 37; *Mobil North Sea Ltd v PJ Pipe and Valve Co (t/a PJ Valve Ltd)* [2001] EWCA Civ 741 Rix LJ at para 30.

Closer to the mark might be to say that the defendant's *responsibility* is oblit-erated by the intervening cause, which eliminates 'any efficacy of the breach'.[28] As Laws LJ put it: 'The real question is whether on the proved or admitted facts the respondents should or should not be held responsible for the appellants' loss'.[29] As Lord Bingham explained:

> The rationale of the principle that a *novus actus interveniens* breaks the chain of causation is fairness. It is not fair to hold a tortfeasor liable, however gross his breach of duty may be, for damage caused to the claimant not by the tortfeasor's breach of duty but by some independent, supervening cause (which may or may not be tortious) for which the tortfeasor is not responsible.[30]

(v) The Test

As Mance J (as he then was) explained, the question is

> whether any profit or loss arose out of or was sufficiently closely connected with the breach to require [it] to be brought into account in assessing damages. Resolution of that issue involves taking into account all the circumstances, including the nature and effects of the breach and the nature of the profit or loss, the manner in which it occurred and any intervening or collateral factors which played a part in its occurrence, in order to form a commonsense overall judgment on the sufficiency of the causal nexus between breach and profit or loss.[31]

Much ink has been spilled on trying to define the circumstances in which the chain of causation is broken. Ultimately, the question is not simply a factual one, but rather is an evaluative question,[32] ie a moral or perhaps even a policy question. It is a 'common sense judgment'.[33] In reaching this judgement, it certainly matters whether the action taken can be said to be 'ordinary',[34] or 'natural' and/or 'reasonable'.[35] Beyond that, it is best to look at the decisions in the cases similar to the one at hand (see chapter sixteen below), rather than rely on general formulations.

---

[28] *Vinmar International Ltd v Theresa Navigation SA* [2001] EWHC 497 (Comm) (Tomlinson J) at para 42.

[29] *Six Continents Retail Ltd v Carford Catering Ltd* [2003] EWCA Civ 1790 at para 19.

[30] *Corr v IBC Vehicles Ltd* [2008] 1 AC 884 (HL) Lord Bingham at para 15; *Chubb Fire Ltd v Vicar of Spalding* [2010] EWCA Civ 981. Of course, Lord Bingham's language is not quite accurate; the point is that the damage is not caused *only* by the tortfeasor's breach but is *also* caused by some independent, supervening cause.

[31] *Famosa Shipping Co Ltd v Armada Bulk Carriers Ltd (The Fanis)* [1994] 1 Lloyd's Rep 633 (Mance J) at 636–37.

[32] *Sayce v TNT (UK) Ltd* [2011] EWCA Civ 1583 Moore-Bick LJ at para 18.

[33] *Famosa Shpping Co Ltd v Armada Bulk Carriers Ltd (The Fanis)* [1994] 1 Lloyd's Rep 633 (Mance J) at 636.

[34] *British Westinghouse Electric & Manufacturing Co Ltd v Underground Electric Railways Co of London Ltd* [1912] AC 673 (HL) at 689–90. The general thesis of leading causation scholars HLA Hart and T Honoré, *Causation in the Law*, 2nd edn (Oxford, OUP, 1985) focuses on whether an intervening event is 'normal' or 'abnormal'.

[35] *The Oropesa* [1943] P 32 Lord Wright at 38–40.

B. How the Legal Causation Principle Operates

(i) *Where No Break in the Chain is Found the Actual Loss is Recoverable*

The first aspect or effect of the principle of legal causation, and perhaps the most obvious but most often forgotten, is that where the principle does not apply the actual loss is recoverable, ie all harms and credits that would not have resulted but for the breach are taken into account.[36] This is worth noting, however, because it is sometimes said in the mitigation context that there is a principle that the costs and consequences of reasonable action by the claimant are taken into account,[37] whereas in fact this is merely the result of the basic measure (the comparison between the breach position and the non-breach position) and the *non*-application of the legal causation principle to alter what is taken as the breach position. It is not a rule of legal causation or mitigation that such consequences are taken account of, save in the same sense that it is a rule of remoteness that losses that are not too remote are recoverable.

(ii) *Where a Break in the Chain is Found the Breaking Event is Deemed Not to Have Happened*

In many cases in which something breaks the chain of causation between the breach and a harm or benefit, the harm or benefit can simply be ignored. The calculation of the recoverable harms and benefits can simply omit the particular harm or benefit that occurred after the break in the chain.

Sometimes, however, the effect of an intervening cause on the calculation of damages is more complicated. This arises where, had the intervening cause not occurred, there would still have been harm or a benefit after the date of that cause, just in a different amount to that which actually occurred. In such cases the law does not prevent account being taken of all harms and benefits after the date of the cause by imposing a guillotine at that date, but rather allows such harms and benefits to be taken into account as would have occurred but for the intervening cause which is being disregarded, even though they did not in fact occur. The effect of this is that, for the purposes of the damages calculation, the law *deems* the cause not to have happened and then carries out the ordinary calculation of damages on the basis of that alternative breach position that would have occurred but for the intervening cause (instead of the actual breach position the claimant finds itself in).

This is most obvious in mitigation cases. If the claimant omits to take steps to prevent harm, the claimant can still recover for the loss that would have been suffered after the date of the omission if it had taken those steps. And if the claimant spends too much on a repair or replacement, the claimant can still recover the reasonable cost that it should have spent. These points are discussed further below in section 15.3B(iv).

---

[36] See further below in section 15.3C.
[37] McGregor's second rule: see n 47 below.

Similarly, moving away from cases of claimant action or inaction in response to the breach (and particularly cases of mitigation), another good example is the claimant's sale of property following defective construction or other works by the defendant. In many cases the sale will be *res inter alios acta*, in which case the claimant is entitled to 'the damages which would, but for the assignment and the transfer of property, have been recoverable',[38] which can include the cost of cure the claimant would have incurred even though the claimant will not (because of the sale) be incurring it.[39] Likewise, where a claimant is able to reduce its actual loss by using spare property it happened to have, or performing work in-house, that is disregarded and the claimant can recover the market cost of cure or repair even though that cost was not in fact incurred.[40] Again, in these cases the principle of legal causation does not merely act as a guillotine to a benefit or harm, but deems to have been incurred a harm (cost) that was in fact not incurred.

This can be illustrated by a variation of the illustration above in chapter one, section 1.3B:

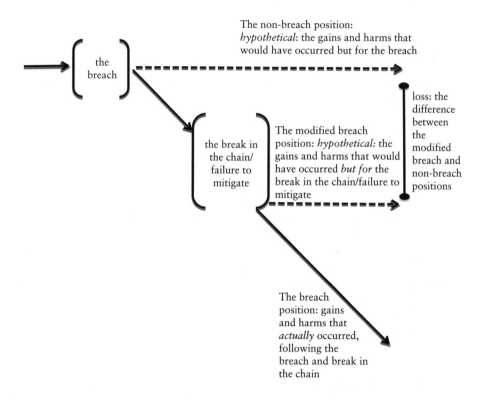

The non-breach position:
hypothetical: the gains and harms that would have occurred but for the breach

the breach

loss: the difference between the modified breach and non-breach positions

the break in the chain/ failure to mitigate

The modified breach position: *hypothetical*: the gains and harms that would have occurred *but for* the break in the chain/failure to mitigate

The breach position: gains and harms that *actually* occurred, following the breach and break in the chain

---

[38] *Linden Gardens Trust Ltd v Lenesta Sludge Disposals Ltd* (1992) 30 Con LR 1 (CA) Staughton LJ at 28.

[39] See further below in section 15.3B(iv)(d).

[40] See further below in chapter sixteen, section 16.7A.

(iii) The Principles Cut Both Ways: Harms and Gains

It is also important to realise that the principles of legal causation apply to both harms and gains. In other words, they can decrease or increase a loss. If an event, action or inaction is treated as robbing the defendant of responsibility for its consequences, then all of those consequences must be disregarded, whether positive or negative. If my sacking an employee causes him to have more spare time and he gets hit by lightning in a place he would not have been in but for the breach, I will not be held to have caused any personal injury resulting from the lightning, but nor will the claimant have to give credit for the money he made selling his story to the newspaper. If my sacked employee takes up gambling, I will not be held responsible for the gambling losses but nor must the claimant give credit for the gains. If a claimant buyer fails promptly to go to the market to purchase replacement goods, but instead speculates on the market falling, the defendant is not held responsible for the additional cost of purchasing the replacement later on the market if it rose, nor need the claimant give credit for the saving made if the claimant's speculation paid off and the market did in fact drop.[41]

(iv) Interaction with Remoteness/Scope of Duty

That remoteness and causation are closely related is often observed upon,[42] but the relationship between remoteness and legal causation and mitigation is somewhat obscure.

Where a harm positively falls outside the scope of responsibility/duty because of the purpose or nature of the duty, that harm will not be legally caused. As Lord Hoffmann has said extra-judicially of the mountaineer example:

> The reason why we say that [the doctor] did not cause the mountaineer's injury is because of the view which we have formed about the scope of duty ... the reason why the negligence of the valuer had not caused the additional loss was because of the limited way in which the House construed the scope of the rule imposing liability.[43]

It might be better to say, however, that the question of legal causation does not arise in such cases. Similarly, if the purpose of a duty was to protect against a third party-caused or natural event-caused harm then the third party action or natural event will not be too remote and nor will it break the chain of causation.[44]

Otherwise, the foreseeability of the intervening event will weigh against it breaking the chain of causation but not be conclusive.[45]

---

[41] The various cases on harms and collateral benefits are discussed in the next chapter.

[42] See for example *Platform Home Loans Ltd v Oyston Shipways Ltd* [2000] 2 AC 190 (HL) Lord Hobhouse at 208 and the authorities cited there; *Kuwait Airways Corp v Iraqi Airways Co (No 6)* [2002] 2 AC 883 (HL) Lord Nicholls at para 70 (conversion).

[43] Lord Hoffmann, 'Common Sense and Causing Loss' (Lecture to the Chancery Bar Association, 15 June 1999).

[44] See further below in chapter sixteen, section 16.8D and 16.13D(iv). See especially *Calvert v William Hill Credit Ltd* [2009] 1 Ch 330 (CA), where the defendant was liable for the loss embraced by the scope of duty even though otherwise it would not have been recoverable (para 46).

[45] *Iron and Steel Holding and Realisation Agency v Compensation Appeal Tribunal* [1966] 1 WLR 480 (CA) Winn LJ at 492; *Royscot Trust Ltd v Rogerson* [1991] 2 QB 297 (CA) Balcolme LJ at 307–8;

(v) The Case Law

The case law on legal causation (including collateral benefits and mitigation) is set out in some detail in chapter sixteen. Key examples of situations involving third party intervening acts are set out in chapter sixteen sections 16.10 and 16.13, key examples of situations involving natural events in sections 16.13, and key examples of situations involving claimant action or inaction in sections 16.2–16.5 and 16.8.

15.3 The Principle of Mitigation

A. Summary

As introduced above,[46] there are no separate principles of mitigation. Mitigation is merely the name given to the principle of legal causation when applied to the actions and inactions of the claimant in response to the breach (rather than natural events, or the actions or inactions of the defendant or third parties). It is, however, normal and not inconvenient to refer to the principles of mitigation as a separate body of rules, and they can be summarised as follows:

(1) Unreasonable conduct will break the chain of causation and will be deemed by the principle of legal causation not to have happened:
   a. Omissions: If the claimant unreasonably fails to take steps, ie fails to take steps all reasonable people would have taken—referred to as 'prescribed' conduct below, that omission will break the chain of causation, and the claimant will be deemed by the principle of legal causation to have taken them (and any costs or benefits that would have resulted from them are taken into account, and any that would not are not).
   b. Actions: If the clamant takes steps that were out of the ordinary course, speculative or otherwise to be treated as collateral and not part of the continuous chain from the breach, ie unreasonable steps, the steps will be deemed by the principle of legal causation not to have occurred for the purposes of assessing damages (and any costs or benefits resulting from the steps ignored).

(2) Otherwise, the actual loss—the net of all actual costs or benefits—is recoverable. The claimant has acted reasonably, whether or not its steps were prescribed (ie, it would have been unreasonable not to have taken the steps) or not (ie, the steps were reasonable but it would also have been reasonable not to have taken them). Here no legal rule has been engaged; rather the principle of legal causation has *not* been engaged because nothing the claimant

---

Banque Bruxelles Lambert SA v Eagle Star Insurance Co Ltd [1995] QB 375 (CA) Bingham MR at 420 (appeal allowed [1997] 1 AC 191 (HL)). See also *Monarch Steamship Co Ltd v Karlshamns Oljefabriker (A/B)* [1949] AC 196 (HL); *Mahony v Kruschich* (1985) 156 CLR 522 (HC of Australia) (tort).

[46] See section 15.1A(i).

did or failed to do was unreasonable so as to break the chain of causation: point (1) above was not engaged.[47]

B. Omissions by the Claimant and the 'Duty' to Mitigate

(i) The 'Duty' is Not a Duty

As has often been observed, the 'duty' to mitigate is not a duty in the sense of an obligation that can be enforced by the defendant.[48] A claimant

> is not under any actual obligation to adopt the cheaper method: if he wishes to adopt the more expensive method, he is at liberty to do so and by doing so he commits no wrong against the defendant or anyone else.[49]

Nevertheless, the law implicitly recognises a duty, at least in the limited sense that an omission by the claimant to act will break the chain of causation where the omission is treated as significant to the responsibility of the defendant, and it is convenient shorthand to identify the significance of the omission by saying that in such cases there was a duty of some sort to act. (Not all relevant conduct of the claimant that can break the chain of causation will consist of omissions—for example positively using or supplying to others goods known to be defective or dangerous will break the chain—but it is one of the distinctive features of the mitigatory part of the legal causation rule that often a claimant's omission to act will break the chain of causation whereas a third party's omission to act rarely would do so.[50])

---

[47] It will be apparent that this author parts company with those commentators who prefer to see mitigation governed by separate principles from causation, and who prefer to present mitigation as comprising multiple principles, eg *McGregor on Damages*, 18th edn (3rd Supp) (London, Sweet & Maxwell, 2012) at ch 7, summarised at paras 7-002 to 7-007 and fn 1; *Chitty on Contracts*, 31st edn (London, Sweet & Maxwell, 2012) at para 26-077. McGregor's first rule (the claimant cannot recover for avoidable loss) is a reflection of the rule of legal causation, although it is unhelpful merely to say (as McGregor does) that unavoidable loss is irrecoverable (because in fact the claimant is deemed to have taken the steps and so, eg, can recover for the cost of the steps that it was deemed to have taken). McGregor's second and third rules (the claimant can recover the harm suffered following reasonable mitigatory steps, and is limited to such loss) are merely the non-application of any rule, ie the actual loss is recoverable where McGregor's first rule does not apply and the principle of legal causation is not engaged.

[48] *Darbishire v Warran* [1963] 1 WLR 1067 (CA) Pearson LJ at 1075; *Satef-Huttenes Albertus SpA v Paloma Tercera Shipping Co SA (The Pegase)* [1981] 1 Lloyd's Rep 175 (Goff J) at 188; *Sotiros Shipping Inc v Samiet Solholt (The Solholt)* [1983] 1 Lloyd's Rep 605 (CA) Donaldson MR at 608; *Sealace Shipping Co Ltd v Oceanvoice Ltd (The Alecos M)* [1991] 1 Lloyd's 120 (CA) McCowan LJ at 124; *Arkin v Borchard Lines Ltd (No 4)* [2003] EWHC 687 (Comm) (Colman J) at para 536; *Golden Strait Corp v Nippon Yusen Kubishika Kaisha (The Golden Victory)* [2007] 2 AC 353 (HL) Lord Bingham at para 10.

[49] *Darbishire v Warran* [1963] 1 WLR 1067 (CA) Pearson LJ at 1075. Also *Sotiros Shipping Inc v Samiet Solholt (The Solholt)* [1983] 1 Lloyd's Rep 605 (CA) Donaldson MR at 608.

[50] Generally speaking, positive action will more usually constitute a 'new cause' than inaction: *Knightley v Johns* [1982] 1 All ER 851 (CA) (tort). Cf *R v Cheshire* [1991] 3 All ER 670 (CA) (crime).

(ii) The 'Duty' Only Applies Post-Breach

The duty to mitigate can only apply to post-breach acts or omissions.[51] Accordingly a claimant's failure to register an option will not affect the legal causation of damages for the defendant's subsequent wrongful sale of land defeating the option.[52] Similarly an employee cannot be criticised for failure to mitigate before his dismissal,[53] for example by accepting the offer of a new role which offer itself constituted the constructive dismissal.[54] Pre-breach actions can, however, render loss too remote or amount to contributory negligence (where that doctrine is applicable).

An anticipatory breach of contract (including a renunciation) does not give rise to an expectation that the claimant will mitigate[55] unless the anticipatory breach is repudiatory and is accepted, thereby bringing the contract to an end and triggering the duty to mitigate.[56] (An actual non-repudiatory breach or unaccepted repudiatory breach, such as a breach of warranty in a contract of sale, does, however, give rise to the duty to mitigate.)

(iii) The Standard of Mitigation Expected of the Claimant

At the heart of the mitigatory principle, then, is a so-called 'duty' to mitigate loss, which prescribes or expects certain conduct. Without this rule, a claimant who needed a widget to fix its factory machinery would, upon non-delivery of the widget by a seller or carrier, be able to claim (subject to the rule of remoteness) for all the consequences of the machinery being thenceforth and forever at a standstill. By the same token, without the rule a sacked employee could sit at home and claim his pay as damages for the remainder of his working life.

As to the standard of behaviour expected of the claimant, the following quotation of Lord Macmillan, explaining that the duty to mitigate is not an exacting one, is often repeated and approved:

> Where the sufferer from a breach of contract finds himself in consequence of that breach placed in a position of embarrassment the measures which he may be driven to adopt in

---

[51] *Sotiros Shipping Inc v Samiet Solholt (The Solholt)* [1981] 2 Lloyd's Rep 580 (Staughton J) at 580, affirmed [1983] 1 Lloyds' Rep 605 (CA); *UBC Chartering Ltd v Liepaya Shipping Co Ltd (The Liepaya)* [1999] 1 Lloyd's Rep 649 (Rix J) at 671–72. For discussion of the separate but related issue as to the importance of whether the claimant *knew* of the breach or not, see below in section 15.3B(iii)(c).

[52] *Wright v Dean* [1948] Ch 686 (Wynn-Parry J).

[53] *F&G Cleaners Ltd v Saddington* (EAT), 16 August 2012, Burke QC at paras 27(3) and 37 ff and the cases cited therein in relation to the statutory action for unfair dismissal.

[54] *Whittaker v Unisys Australia Pty Ltd* [2010] VSC 9 (SC of Victoria) at paras 166–67.

[55] *Brown v Muller* (1872) LR 7 Ex 319 (contract of sale affirmed by buyer); *Anglo-African Shipping Co of New York, Inc v J Mortner Ltd* [1962] 1 Lloyd's Rep 81 (appeal allowed [1962] 1 Lloyd's Rep 610 (CA)); *Phoebus D Kyprianou Coy v Wm H Pim Jnr & Co Ltd* [1977] 2 Lloyd's Rep 570 (Kerry J) (contract of sale affirmed by sellers); *Shindler v Northern Raincoat Co Ltd* [1960] 1 WLR 1038 (Diplock J); *Bulkhaul Ltd v Rhodia Organique Fine Ltd* [2009] 1 Lloyd's Rep 353 (CA) Smith LJ at para 24; *Parbulk AS v Kristen Marine SA* [2011] 1 Lloyd's Rep 220 (Burton J) at para 28. Also *Clea Shipping Corp v Bulk Oil International Ltd (The Alaskan Trader)* [1984] 1 All ER 129 (Lloyd J). But compare Uniform Commercial Code s 2-610a.

[56] *Roth & Co Ltd v Taysen Townsend & Co* (1896) 12 TLR 211 (CA); *Garnac Grain Co Inc v HMF Faure & Fairclough Ltd* [1968] AC 1130 (HL) at 1140; *Melachrino v Nicholl & Knight* [1920] 1 KB 693 (Bailhache J); *Gebruder Metelmann GmbH & Co KG v NBR (London) Ltd* [1984] 1 Lloyd's Rep 614 (CA); *Kaines (UK) Ltd v Osterreichische Warenhandelsgesellschaft Austrowaren GmbH* [1993] Lloyd's Rep 1 (CA).

order to extricate himself ought not to be weighed in nice scales at the instance of the party whose breach of contract has occasioned the difficulty.[57]

See further the comments of Roskill J:

> The defendants broke this contract. It is they who put the plaintiffs in this difficulty. Of course, a plaintiff has always to act reasonably, and of course he has to do what is reasonable to mitigate his damages. But he is not bound to nurse the interests of the contract breaker, and so long as he acts reasonably at the time it ill lies in the mouth of the contract breaker to turn round afterwards and complain, in order to reduce his own liability to a plaintiff, that the plaintiff failed to do that which perhaps with hindsight he might have been wiser to do.[58]

And in the context of tortiously caused property damage, Lord Loreburn CJ has observed:

> Now I think a Court of justice ought to be very slow in countenancing any attempt by a wrong-doer to make captious objections to the methods by which those whom he has injured have sought to repair the injury. When a road is let down or land let down, those entitled to have it repaired find themselves saddled with a business which they did not seek, and for which they are not to blame. Errors of judgment may be committed in this as in other affairs of life. It would be intolerable if persons so situated could be called to account by the wrong-doer in a minute scrutiny of the expense, as though they were his agents, for any mistake or miscalculation, provided they act honestly and reasonably. In judging whether they have acted reasonably, I think a Court should be very indulgent and always bear in mind who was to blame.[59]

To put the matter in Potter LJ's more straightforward language: 'the court or tribunal deciding the issue must not be too stringent in its expectations of the injured party'.[60] As Tomlinson J explained, the law takes a 'tender approach to those who have been placed in a predicament by a breach of contract'.[61] And as the US Restatement (Second) of Contracts puts it, the claimant is not expected to do anything requiring 'undue risk, burden or humiliation'.[62]

Perhaps the most important point to remember in practice is that the innocent party 'will not be held disentitled to recover the cost of such [reasonable remedial] measures merely because the party in breach can suggest that other measures less burdensome to him might have been taken',[63] or as Sedley LJ has put it:

> [I]t is not enough for the wrongdoer to show that it would have been reasonable to take the steps he has proposed: he must show that it was unreasonable of the innocent party not to take them. This is a real distinction. It reflects the fact that if there is more than one reasonable response open to the wronged party, the wrongdoer has no right to determine his choice. It is where, and only where, the wrongdoer can show affirmatively that the other party has acted unreasonably in relation to his duty to mitigate that the defence will succeed.[64]

---

[57] *Banco de Portugal v Waterlow & Sons Ltd* [1932] AC 452 (HL) at 507.
[58] *Harlow & Jones Ltd v Panex (International) Ltd* [1967] 2 Lloyd's Rep 509 (Roskill J) at 530.
[59] *Lodge Holes Colliery Co Ltd v Wednesbury Corp* [1908] AC 323 (HL) at 325.
[60] *Wilding v British Telecommunications plc* [2002] IRLR 524 (CA) at para 37.
[61] *Britvic Soft Drinks Ltd v Messer UK Ltd* [2002] 1 Lloyd's Rep 20 (Tomlinson J) at para 114 affirmed [2002] 2 Lloyd's Rep 368 (CA).
[62] § 350(1).
[63] *Banco de Portugal v Waterlow & Sons Ltd* [1932] AC 452 (HL) Lord Macmillan at 506.
[64] *Wilding v British Telecommunications plc* [2002] IRLR 524 (CA) at para 55.

(a) Prudent Uninsured: Ignore Right against the Defendant

It may be useful to consider what the claimant would have done if it did not expect compensation from the defendant. In other words, a claimant's mitigatory duty is similar to that owed by an insured to an insurer to conduct matters and minimise loss as if it were a 'prudent uninsured', ie not to be frivolous merely because it is someone else's money at stake.[65]

(b) The Relevance of the Claimant Acting on Advice

Acting on advice can never be conclusive as to reasonableness but does support it.[66]

(c) The Importance of Knowledge of the Breach

Whether the claimant's failures (by action or inaction) absolve the defendant depends largely, although not wholly, on whether or not the claimant's failures occurred after it had knowledge of the defendant's breach.

In the Court of Appeal decision in *Schering Agrochemicals Ltd v Resibel NV SA*,[67] Scott LJ observed that he would prefer to confine the principle of mitigation to situations where there is

> actual knowledge on the part of the plaintiff of the loss or of the wrongful act and where, with that knowledge, the plaintiff has done something wrong whereby the loss sought to be recovered has been increased or has omitted to do something which, if done, would have reduced or eliminated the loss.

Philips J was of the same view in the *Superhulls* case, emphasising that the mitigation principle depends upon 'deliberate' and 'voluntary conduct' and so requires knowledge of the breach.[68]

To this might be added constructive knowledge, ie the duty to mitigate can also apply '[o]nce facts have come to the knowledge of the plaintiff which suffice to disclose that a breach of contract has occurred', Hobhouse LJ in *County Ltd v Girozentrale Securities*.[69]

The test of mitigation (or, more broadly, legal causation) applied to the claimant absent such actual or constructive knowledge is less strict. As Hobhouse LJ observed in the same case:

> Where a plaintiff does not know of a defendant's breach of contract and where he is entitled to rely upon the defendant having performed his contract, it will only be in the most exceptional circumstances that conduct of the plaintiff suffices to break the causal relationship between the defendant's breach and the plaintiff's loss.

---

[65] *Archbold Freightage Ltd v Wilson* [1974] IRLR 10 (National Industrial Relations Court); *Sharif v Garrett & Co* [2002] 3 All ER 195 (CA) Tuckey LJ at para 29.

[66] *Youell v Bland Welch & Co Ltd (The Superhulls Cover Case) (No 2)* [1990] 2 Lloyd's Rep 423 (Phillips J) at 461. See also the discussion above in chapter four, section 4.3B(ii)(a).

[67] *Schering Agrochemicals Ltd v Resibel NV SA* (CA), 26 November 1992.

[68] *Youell v Bland Welch & Co Ltd (The Superhulls Cover Case) (No 2)* [1990] 2 Lloyd's Rep 423 (Phillips J) at 461–62. Also *UBC Chartering Ltd v Liepaya Shipping Col Ltd (The Liepaya)* [1999] 1 Lloyd's Rep 649 (Rix J) at 672.

[69] *County Ltd v Girozentrale Securities* [1996] 3 All ER 834 (CA) at 858. But see *Youell v Bland Welch & Co Ltd* [1990] 2 Lloyd's Rep 423 (Phillips J) at 462.

The plaintiffs' conduct was not voluntary in the sense of being undertaken with a knowledge of its significance. Conduct which is undertaken without an appreciation of the existence of the earlier causal factor will normally only suffice to break the causal relationship if the conduct was reckless. It is the character of reckless conduct that it makes the actual state of knowledge of that party immaterial. If the conduct of the plaintiffs had been so exceptional as to take it outside the contemplation of the parties, then it might have made the consequent loss too remote.[70]

Although the sense of this recklessness explanation holds good and is useful, recklessness is not an absolute legal test.[71] Failure to discover a defect can break the chain of causation in appropriate cases.[72]

In short, where the claimant's failures occurred without knowledge of the defendant's breach, they will be judged according to the doctrines of legal causation (ie whether they were a break in the chain) or remoteness, and the defendant is unlikely to be absolved if the claimant's failings fall short of recklessness. Where they occurred with knowledge of the defendant's breach, the defendant is held to the stricter, although still not very exacting, standard of the prudent claimant who must act to mitigate its loss.

Practically speaking, the knowledge of the claimant can be very important. Eg with latently defective goods the claimant cannot be expected to do anything until the defect is discovered or reasonably discoverable. However, in other cases, eg lending following a negligent valuation, the mitigatory steps taken following the borrower's default will be exactly the same whether or not the lender knows that the valuer's wrongdoing induced the transaction.

(iv) The Claimant's Omissions: Failure to Mitigate and Breach of the 'Duty'

(a) Deem that Reasonable Mitigation Performed

When addressing the 'events which have actually happened' (what I earlier refer to as the breach position), so as to work out the difference between what happened and what would have happened, 'unreasonable failure to mitigate does alter the equation, for then what must be looked at is not the existing situation, but that which would have obtained had reasonable steps to mitigate been taken'.[73]

Thus in goods cases where there is an available market the principle of mitigation normally requires that 'the conventional market loss' rather than 'the actual loss suffered' is recoverable, the claimant being 'assumed to have mitigated his loss by buying in substitute goods at the market price. It does not matter that he chooses not to buy in or delays his purchase'.[74] As Lord Bingham has explained:

> Thus where, as here, there is an available market for the chartering of vessels, the injured party's loss will be calculated *on the assumption that he has*, on or within a reasonable

---

[70] [1996] 3 All ER 834 at 857.

[71] *Borealis AB v Geogas Trading SA* [2011] 1 Lloyd's Rep 482 (Gross LJ) para 46; *Trebor Bassett Holdings Ltd v ADT Fire and Security plc* [2011] EWHC 1379 (TCC) (Coulson J) at para 547.

[72] Eg *Bostock & Co Ltd v Nicholson & Sons Ltd* [1904] 1 KB 725 (Bruce J).

[73] *Stephenson Blake (Holdings) Ltd v Streets Heaver Ltd* [2001] Lloyd's Rep PN 44 (Hicks QC) at para 159.

[74] *Transfield Shipping Inc v Mercator Shipping Inc (The Achilleas)* [2007] 2 Lloyd's Rep 555 (CA) Rix LJ at paras 102 and 109; *Air Studios (Lyndhurst) Ltd v Lombard North Central plc* [2012] EWHC 3162 (QB) (Males J).

time of accepting the repudiation, taken reasonable commercial steps to obtain alternative employment for the vessel for the best consideration reasonably obtainable. This is the ordinary rule whether in fact the injured party acts in that way or, for whatever reason, does not. *The actual facts are ordinarily irrelevant.* The rationale of the rule is one of simple commercial fairness. The injured party owes no duty to the repudiator, but fairness requires that he should not ordinarily be permitted to rely on his own unreasonable and uncommercial conduct to increase the loss falling on the repudiator. (Emphasis added)[75]

Of course, in many cases it is harmless to treat a failure to mitigate or break in the chain of causation as operating a guillotine which prevents recovery of losses that would have been avoided, but the true position is more complex: the law *edits* the breach position not merely to cut out certain consequences (both benefits and harms) from account, but also to bring others that were not suffered into account. In other words, the law *deems* (ie fictionally assumes) the claimant to have taken the steps that the duty to mitigate prescribes, *replacing* in the damages calculation the part of the breach position that should not have occurred with that which should. Thus, unlike under the guillotine approach, a claimant is not only debarred from recovering the costs and losses that were suffered but would have been avoided had it mitigated properly, but the claimant may recover the attendant costs and losses that would have been suffered if it had done so even though they were not suffered because it did not do so.

A few examples should assist the reader in understanding that the deeming applies for better or worse, and both debars recovery of losses that would have been avoided if the claimant had reasonably mitigated, and allows the claimant to recover the losses that would have been suffered if it had reasonably mitigated:

In *Jones v Just*, the claimant bought Manilla hemp, discovering that it was defective at the date of delivery. It was entitled to damages as if it had sold the hemp immediately upon delivery, and entitled to retain the benefit it in fact received by holding the hemp for a time and then selling it at auction after a market rise.[76]

In *Downs v Chappell*, the claimants were fraudulently induced to purchase a bookshop business in 1988, discovered the deceit in late 1989, and sold the business between the date of trial in 1994 and appeal in 1996 for less than £60,000.[77] The Court of Appeal found that they should have sold the business in 1990 in mitigation of their loss, and when assessing the loss, credited (in the defendants' favour) the sum the claimants would have recovered at that date (which was greater than the sum actually received by the claimants when they sold the property).

In *Habton Farms v Nimmo*, the claimant seller recovered the full value of a horse which it would have sold but for the defendant's breach, and which died before it had the reasonably opportunity to sell it.[78] Had the claimant learned before the death of the horse that the buyer it was pressing to perform was not in fact bound

---

[75] *Golden Strait Corp v Nippon Yusen Kubishika Kaisha (The Golden Victory)* [2007] 2 AC 353 (HL) at para 10; *Zodiac Maritime Agencies Ltd v Fortescue Metals Group Ltd (The Kildare)* [2011] 2 Lloyd's Rep 360 (Steel J) at para 65.

[76] *Jones v Just* (1868) LR 3 QB 197.

[77] *Downs v Chappell* [1997] 1 WLR 426 (CA). A dictum of Hobhouse LJ in *Downs v Chappell* in relation to the measure of loss was disapproved in *Smith New Court Securities Ltd v Scrimgeour Vickers (Asset Management) Ltd* [1997] AC 254 (HL) but the decision of *Downs v Chappell* remains intact.

[78] *Habton Farms (an unlimited company) v Nimmo* [2003] EWCA Civ 68.

to buy (the defendant had breached a warranty of authority), and had the claimant had reasonable time to sell, it would have recovered nothing as it would have been deemed to have sold the horse before it died.[79]

In *Bulkhaul Ltd v Rhodia Organique Fine Ltd*,[80] the Court of Appeal held that damages for repudiation by a lessee of some chemical tanks required credit to be given for the price that could have been recovered on sale of the tanks, as the claimant should have sold the tanks in mitigation of its loss, although the claimant could also set off as a loss the costs of such sales even though it did not in fact incur them.

In the builder's negligence case of *McGlinn v Waltham Contractors Ltd*,[81] the claimant recovered (by judgment in March 2007) the £380,000 cost of repairs as at 31 March 2005, which was the date on which the claimant should have conducted the repairs, plus, importantly, interest on those costs (which had not actually been expended) from that date.

In solicitor's negligence case *Herrmann v Withers LLP*,[82] the claimant recovered the £25,000 cost of an 80-year assignable licence, plus negotiating costs. These were not actually incurred, the claimant not in fact taking these steps in reasonable mitigation, but were recoverable nevertheless. (The claimant also recovered £65,000 diminution in value, as reflecting the value in the property that would have remained after taking those steps had they been taken, plus £2,000 for loss of amenity.)

(b) Which is the Reasonable Action from a Range?

Frequently there is 'more than one reasonable response open to the wronged party'.[83] In a particular case, a reasonable claimant may, for example, purchase a replacement one hour after learning of the non-delivery, or two hours afterwards, or perhaps the next day. Where the claimant takes any of the reasonable responses within the range, it is not in breach of the duty to mitigate, ie has not performed an omission which breaks the chain of causation. However, where the claimant does not make any of the reasonable responses (and does not purchase a replacement at all, to continue the above example) then the court must select one of the reasonable possibilities and will deem that to have been made. There is no clear authority that this author could find as to how the law selects which of the range of responses the claimant is deemed to have made, but by analogy with the way the law identifies which of the non-breach possibilities a defendant would have taken if it had not breached a duty,[84] the likelihood is that the law will select the middle of the range.

---

[79] *Habton Farms (an unlimited company) v Nimmo* [2003] EWCA Civ 68 Clarke LJ at para 100, also Auld LJ at para 128.

[80] *Bulkhaul Ltd v Rhodia Organique Fine Ltd* [2009] 1 Lloyd's Rep 353 (CA).

[81] *McGlinn v Waltham Contractors Ltd* [2007] EWHC 149 (TCC) (Coulson QC) at paras 875–80 and [2007] EWHC 698 at paras 5–9.

[82] *Herrmann v Withers LLP* [2012] EWHC 1492 (Ch) (Newey J).

[83] *Wilding v British Telecommunications plc* [2002] IRLR 524 (CA) Sedley LJ at para 55, quoted above more fully at text to n 64.

[84] *Lion Nathan Ltd v C-C Bottlers Ltd* [1996] 1 WLR 1438 (PC) at 1445–47 and *South Australia Asset Management Corp v York Montague Ltd* [1997] 1 AC 191 (HL) at 221–22, discussed above in chapter thirteen, section 13.3B(ix).

(c) The Effects of Deeming: Credit for Income the Claimant Would
Have Received (But Didn't)

First, as is well known, the award following a failure to mitigate must take account of income that the claimant would have received if it had acted reasonably (but did not in fact receive), and which would have reduced the loss. This may be the price that would have been received from the market,[85] or on an alternative development,[86] or revenue that would have been received in a deal with the defendant or a third party. Thus in a claim for wrongful dismissal where the claimant failed to take reasonable steps to secure an alternative job, the claimant recovers its lost income from the job with the defendant less the amount that would have been received from the alternative job the claimant could have been expected to secure.

The loss of chance principle applies here. Where, even if the claimant had acted reasonably, a certain income might but would not definitely have been earned, the allowance for that deemed income in the damages measure must be reduced for it being the chance only of such an income.[87]

(d) The Effects of Deeming: Recovery of the Costs the Claimant
Would Have Incurred (But Didn't)

Secondly, the deeming involves taking into account costs that the claimant would have incurred if it had acted reasonably (but did not in fact incur), and which would have increased the loss, although incurred with a view ultimately to minimising it. This may involve awarding damages for types of loss that would have been incurred but were not. The most obvious example is the attendant costs of the steps the claimant should have taken in reasonable mitigation, which are costs not in fact incurred, such as the legal costs the claimant would have incurred if it had pursued mitigatory steps to secure what the defendant cost it,[88] or the costs of improving their alarm and safety systems.[89] These are recoverable, and indeed in cases of sale of goods the costs (whether or not actually incurred) of the reasonable resort to the market to purchase replacement goods form the majority of the damages award in most cases.[90] Similarly in cases of non-acceptance by a buyer, where the seller is deemed to have sold the goods but did not, the costs that would have been incurred in selling them will be deducted.[91] And where the claimant should have carried out an alternative development, it is the profit that would have been

---

[85] Hence the difference in market value measure presumed by sections 50(3) and 53(3) of the Sale of Goods Act 1979 involves the implicit assumption that the seller would have received the market value for the property that the claimant wrongfully did not accept, or that the buyer would have received the market value for the defective goods. See also eg *Downs v Chappell* [1997] 1 WLR 426 (CA), a deceit case where the claimant should have sold property earlier than it did.

[86] *Joyce v Bowman Law Ltd* [2010] EWHC 251 (Ch) (Vos J).

[87] *Houndsditch Warehouse Co Ltd v Waltex Ltd* [1944] KB 579 (Stable J) where it was not clear that the seller would have done the relevant deal if the buyer had pursued it.

[88] *Herrmann v Withers LLP* [2012] EWHC 1492 (Ch) (Newey J).

[89] *Schering Agrochemicals Ltd v Resibel NV SA* 4.5.91, Hobhouse J.

[90] Hence the difference in market value measure presumed by sections 51(3) and 53(3) of the Sale of Goods Act 1979 involves the implicit assumption that the seller would have paid the market price for the property that the seller wrongfully did not deliver, or that was defective due to the seller's breach.

[91] *Bulkhaul Ltd v Rhodia Organique Fine Ltd* [2009] 1 Lloyd's Rep 353 (CA), where the chemical tanks should have been sold for £20,000 but the costs of sale of £2,000 must be deducted from that

earned that is deducted from the actual loss, ie the revenue is deducted but the costs of earning it are added as a deemed expense.[92] The cost of repairs that should have been performed will be recoverable as priced at the date when they should have been incurred,[93] including where the claimant did perform repairs but took the opportunity to perform a refurbishment (the claimant's claim being limited to the cost of repairs that would have been incurred if the claimant had not performed the refurbishment).[94] Also recoverable are the costs of re-cartoning damaged goods even though that was not done;[95] likewise the costs of steps an employee should have taken to find a replacement job.[96]

(e) The Effects of Deeming: Interest

Similarly, the claimant can recover interest from the date when a cost should have been incurred, even if it was not in fact incurred.[97]

(f) The Effects of Deeming: Recover Income the Claimant Would Have Foregone

Thirdly, it must also include taking account of foregone income that the claimant would not have earned if it had acted reasonably (but as it did not so act, it did not in fact forego), and which would have increased the loss with a view to reducing it overall. In *Schering Agrochemicals Ltd v Resibel NV SA*,[98] Hobhouse J awarded lost profits that would have been incurred on its defective bottle-capping line supplied by the defendant, had the claimant taken the line out of action for repairs, rather than unreasonably run the line leading to a fire that destroyed it. As Hobhouse J observed:

> [T]he Plaintiffs are entitled to recover damages from the Defendants for breach of contract but that such damages must be limited to those which would not have been avoided if reasonable steps to mitigate their loss had been taken by the Plaintiffs following the 8th September incident. Thus the Plaintiffs are entitled to recover the cost of bringing the alarm and safety system up to specification and the loss of profit etc that would result from the line being out of production meanwhile ... The assessment will have to be on a hypothetical basis assuming that reasonable steps had been taken to avoid the loss that the Plaintiffs did in fact suffer.

The point was not mentioned in the Court of Appeal, where the judgment was upheld.[99]

---

deemed receipt; *Ali Reza-Delta Transport Co Ltd v United Arab Shipping Co SAG* [2003] 2 Lloyd's Rep 450 (CA) as to shipping costs.

[92] Eg *Joyce v Bowman Law Ltd* [2010] EWHC 251 (Ch) (Vos J).

[93] *McGlinn v Waltham Contractors Ltd* [2007] EWHC 149 (TCC) (Coulson QC); *Tomlinson v Wilson*, 11 May 2007 (Langan).

[94] *Gagner Pty Ltd v Canturi Corporation Pty Ltd* [2009] NSWCA 413 (CA of New South Wales) at paras 105–7 and 109. Also the cases at chapter four n 262.

[95] *Commercial Fibres (Ireland) Ltd v Zabaida* [1975] 1 Lloyd's Rep 27 (Donaldson J).

[96] *Christianson v North Hill News Inc* (1993) 106 DLR (4th) 747 (Ontario CA), obiter at para 20 (the costs were in fact incurred in that case).

[97] *McGlinn v Waltham Contractors Ltd* [2007] EWHC 698 (TCC) (Coulson QC) at paras 5–9.

[98] *Schering Agrochemicals Ltd v Resibel NV SA*, 4 May 1991 (Hobhouse J); 26 November 1992 (CA).

[99] See discussion of this point in *Beoco Ltd v Alfa Laval Co Ltd* [1995] QB 137 (CA) Stuart-Smith LJ at 152–53.

However, a different result was reached in *Beoco Ltd v Alfa Laval Co Ltd*.[100] In that similar case the defendant negligently failed properly to repair the heat exchanger in the claimant's seed-oil plant but the claimant recklessly put the exchanger into operation despite failing a test administered by the claimant, which broke the chain of causation, and an explosion destroyed the plant. The defendant was not liable for the explosion but was held liable for the cost of making good the heat exchanger (had the claimant not recklessly put it into operation and it then been destroyed). It was not held liable for the lost profits that would have been suffered during the repair that would have taken place (again, had the claimant not passed the heat exchanger for use and it then been destroyed). *Schering* was not followed by the Court of Appeal in *Beoco* on this point on the basis that the point was not properly argued before Hobhouse J, and so *per incuriam*, and was not mentioned by the Court of Appeal in *Schering*.[101] Nevertheless, the approach of *Schering* is to be preferred.

(g) If Things Would Have Been No Different

Of course, even if there is a failure to mitigate, if the outcome would have been the same then the mitigatory/causation principle does not alter the measure of recovery and the actual loss is recoverable.[102]

C. The Claimant's Post-Breach Actions: Where the Claimant Acts Reasonably

The basic principle is that where the claimant acts reasonably, the actual gains and losses are measured and the rule of mitigation has no role to play.[103] This is so whether the loss is avoided or reduced, increased, or unaffected by the actions of the claimant. There is no deeming taking place here, and the intervention of no legal rule, and so the default position applies: as no supervening cause (including failure to mitigate) has been shown to break the chain of causation, the actual conduct and the actual harms and benefits that resulted are not ignored for causation or remoteness reasons and so no rule applies to make the recovery anything other than the actual losses. 'It is apparent that actual attempts to mitigate, if successful or reasonable, do not affect the rule that it is the existing situation which must be compared with what would have happened but for the breach'.[104]

---

[100] *Beoco Ltd v Alfa Laval Co Ltd* [1995] QB 137 (CA).

[101] Ibid Stuart-Smith LJ at 153. This is unconvincing: the same result would obtain whether *Schering* was a mitigation case or a causation case, ie the claimant must be deemed to have acted reasonably, and the majority of the Court of Appeal in *Schering* did not uphold the judgment on a 'different basis' of causation; rather they said that it did not matter whether the principle of causation or mitigation was applied.

[102] *RP Explorer Master Fund v Chilukuri* [2013] EWHC 103 (Ch) (Leslie Blohm QC) obiter at para 132.

[103] See the quotation below from *British Westinghouse Electric & Manufacturing Co Ltd v Underground Electric Railways Co of London Ltd* [1912] AC 673 (HL) at text to n 117, which emphasises that the reasonable conduct (and the costs and benefits of it) is taken into account where the claimant is 'bound' to take it as well as where he is not.

[104] *Stephenson Blake (Holdings) Ltd v Streets Heaver Ltd* [2001] Lloyd's Rep PN 44 (Hicks QC) at para 159. This is correct as regards reasonable actions, but successful unreasonable actions will not be taken until account: see below in section 15.3BD.

The short of it is that

> [w]here steps have been taken to mitigate the loss which would otherwise have been caused by a breach of contract that principle requires the benefits obtained by mitigation to be set against the loss which would otherwise have been sustained. To fail to do so would put the claimant in a better position than he would have been in had the contract been performed,[105]

and the only exception is where the steps taken broke the chain of causation or were *res inter alios acta*, as discussed in section 15.3D below.

(i) Two Types of Reasonable Action

There are two types of action that, along with inaction absent a duty to act, the claimant might take but that will not break the chain of causation. The first is actions that are prescribed by the duty to mitigate, and which, had the claimant not taken them, the claimant would nevertheless have been deemed to have done (as the failure to do so would have broken the chain of causation). The second is other reasonable actions, the taking of which is not prescribed such that failure would break the chain of causation, but which are nevertheless not treated as themselves so disconnected with the breach as to break the chain of causation.

1: Actions Complying with the 'Duty' to Mitigate

Actual actions that are taken, and would have been prescribed by the duty to mitigate if not taken, will be taken into account along with their consequences. Thus in sale of goods cases where the claimant did in fact reasonably resort to the market promptly to mitigate losses, the 'actual loss suffered' will be recoverable ('rather than the conventional market loss').[106] Similarly, in non-acceptance cases, where the seller acts reasonably, the actual resale price will be the measure of damages 'because it shows what loss the seller has suffered, uncomplicated by issues of remoteness or failure to mitigate'.[107] Likewise if repairs are reasonably engaged but cost more than expected, the claimant can still recover the larger cost.[108]

2: Actions Going Beyond the Duty But Not Breaking the Chain

Further, although in some cases there is prescribed conduct that all reasonable people would have performed, such that any other conduct breaks the chain of causation and the claimant will be deemed to have taken the prescribed conduct for the purposes of the damages calculation, in many cases there will not be such prescribed conduct.

In such cases, the claimant's conduct will fall into one of the two categories: they are either reasonable acts which are taken into account in the ordinary way, or

---

[105] *Omak Maritime Ltd v Mamola Challenger Shipping Co* [2010] EWHC 2026 (Comm) (Teare J) at para 65.

[106] *Transfield Shipping Inc v Mercator Shipping Inc (The Achilleas)* [2007] 2 Lloyd's Rep 555 (CA) Rix LJ at para 109.

[107] *Hooper v Oates* [2013] EWCA Civ 91 Lloyd LJ at para 38.

[108] See the tort case of *The Sivand* [1998] 2 Lloyd's Rep 97 (CA).

unreasonable acts which are deemed not to have occurred, as they broke the chain of causation. The former category is considered here, and the latter is discussed below in section 15.3D.

The former category—reasonable actions—consists of acts treated as 'attempts to mitigate' which 'go beyond his obligation [to mitigate]' (the prescribed conduct preferred to above) but are still a 'reaction to the problem caused by the breach' and as a result of which the claimant 'is entitled to bring his loss into account but must give credit for any benefit'.[109] These actions 'formed part of a continuous dealing between the parties'[110] or a 'continuous transaction' from the breach.[111]

In case of such reasonable actions, the actual loss will be recoverable, including the costs of taking this course of conduct.[112] This is because, as Lord Hoffmann has explained, a claimant's reasonable attempt to cope with the consequences of the defendant's breach of duty does not negative the causal connection between that breach of duty and the ultimate loss.[113]

This was the category into which the actions of the claimants in the famous *British Westinghouse* decision, the leading case on mitigation, probably fall.[114] Viscount Haldane LC observed that the claimants 'were doubtless not bound to purchase machines of a greater kilowatt power than those originally contracted for, but they in fact took the wise course in the circumstances of doing so' and 'it was reasonable and prudent to take the course they actually did in purchasing the more powerful machines'[115] and

> when in the course of his business he has taken action arising out of the transaction, which action has diminished his loss, the effect in actual diminution of the loss he has suffered may be taken into account even though there was no duty on him to act ... provided the course taken to protect himself by the plaintiff in such an action was one which a reasonable and prudent person might in the ordinary conduct of business properly have taken, and in fact did take whether bound to or not, a jury or an arbitrator may properly look at the whole of the facts and ascertain the result in estimating the quantum of damage.[116]

---

[109] *Mobil North Sea Ltd v PJ Pipe and Valve Co (t/a PJ Valve Ltd)* [2001] EWCA Civ 741 Rix LJ at para 30.

[110] *R Pagnan & Fratelli v Corbisa Industrial Agropacuaria Limitada* [1970] 1 WLR 1306 (CA) at 1315.

[111] *Westlake v JP Cave and Co*, 14 January 1998 (Ebsworth J); *Pankhania v London Borough of Hackney* [2004] EWHC 323 (Ch) (Vos QC) at para 37.

[112] The judge in *Jewelowski v Propp* [1944] KB 510 (Lewis J) failed to recognise this category, appearing to believe that any conduct that was not prescribed would be ignored as collateral.

[113] *South Australia Asset Management v York Montague* [1997] 1 AC 191 (HL) Lord Hoffmann at 221, citing with approval *The Oropesa* [1943] P 32 (CA) (master reasonably boating with crew after a tortious collision, so death of one of them was caused by the initial collision).

[114] *British Westinghouse Electric & Manufacturing Co Ltd v Underground Electric Railways Co of London Ltd* [1912] AC 673 (HL). And see the discussion in *Cockburn v Trusts and Guarantee Co* (1917) 55 SCR 264 (SC of Canada) at 268; *Westlake v JP Cave and Co*, 14 January 1998 (Ebsworth J).

[115] [1912] AC 673 at 688.

[116] Ibid at 689–90. However, A Dyson, '*British Westinghouse* Revisited' [2012] *LMCLQ* 412 argues that purchasing the replacement turbine was prescribed behaviour and that had the claimant not done so it would have been deemed by the mitigatory principle to have done.

(ii) Thus in Either Case, the Recovery is of Actual Loss

Any conduct that is not collateral, ie either of these two types of reasonable action (prescribed and unprescribed), is taken into account, in other words the court will simply 'look at what actually happened, and ... balance loss and gain'.[117] 'Any gains which flow must be brought into account' and the defendant is entitled to 'credit for that profit' earned by the claimant.[118] In those circumstances there is no rule of law operating to deem anything contrary to reality, and the actual loss is recoverable.[119]

(a) Actual Costs and Harms are Recoverable, Even if the Steps
     Increased the Harm

Thus if the claimant acts reasonably the actual loss is recoverable, whether greater or smaller than if the claimant had taken the steps. If a claimant incurs expense to avoid harm, the expense is recoverable as the measure of loss.[120] The recoverable expenses will include the costs of seeking a replacement[121] and the costs of litigating with third parties,[122] and will be recoverable even where the mitigation was unsuccessful.[123]

It will also include whatever harm is suffered, even if the actions taken in a reasonable attempt to mitigate loss actually led to the harm being increased. As Lord Scott has observed

> If the mitigating steps do not succeed in reducing the loss but were, nonetheless, reasonable steps in all the circumstances for the injured party to take for the purpose of mitigation, the injured party can add to his damages claim the cost of taking the steps in question ... Unsuccessful attempts at mitigation may, therefore, increase the damages payable by the guilty party.[124]

---

[117] [1912] AC 673 at 691.

[118] *Westlake v JP Cave and Co*, 14 January 1998 (Ebsworth J).

[119] This is a much simpler way of putting things than, for example, *Koch Marine Inc v D'Amica Societa di Navigazione Arl (The Elena D'Amico)* [1980] 1 Lloyd's Rep 75 (Goff J) at 89: 'where the plaintiff does take reasonable steps to mitigate the loss to him consequent upon the defendant's wrong he can recover for loss incurred in so doing; this is so even although the resulting damage is in the event greater than it would have been had the mitigating steps not been taken. Put shortly, the plaintiff can recover for loss incurred in reasonable attempts to avoid the loss ... where the plaintiff does take steps to mitigate the loss to him consequent upon the defendant's wrong and these steps are successful, the defendant is entitled to the benefit accruing from the plaintiff's action and is liable only for the loss as lessened ... Put shortly, the plaintiff cannot recover for avoided loss'.

[120] *Dimond v Lovell* [2002] 1 AC 384 (HL) Lord Hobhouse at 406.

[121] See eg *Westwood v Secretary of State for Employment* [1985] AC 20 (HL) where the costs of finding a replacement job were recovered by an employee, and *Christianson v North Hill News Inc* (1993) 106 DLR (4th) 747 (Ontario CA) where the costs of further training to make the employee more employable were recovered.

[122] See chapter twenty.

[123] *Harling v Eddy* [1951] 2 KB 739 (CA), where the veterinary fees of an unsuccessful attempt to cure a tubercular heifer were recoverable; *Lloyds and Scottish Finance Ltd v Modern Cars and Caravans (Kingston) Ltd* [1966] 1 QB 764 (Edmund Davies J).

[124] *Lagden v O'Connor* [2004] 1 AC 1067 (HL) (tort) at para 78. See also *Harling v Eddy* [1951] 2 KB 739 (CA). See also: *Lloyds and Scottish Finance Ltd v Modern Cars and Caravans (Kingston) Ltd* [1966] 1 QB 764 (Edmund Davies J) at 782; *The World Beauty* [1970] P 144 (CA) (tort) Winn LJ at 120; *Downs v Chappell* [1996] 1 WLR 426 (CA) Hobhouse LJ at 437 (deceit).

This is simply a consequence of the correct application of the rule: the claimant acted reasonably, and therefore none of the legal principles exclude anything that occurred or deem anything contrary to reality to have occurred, and so the actual loss is recoverable whatever that may be (providing the rule of causation does not cut in).

A good example can be found in the Court of Appeal's decision in *Hoffberger v Ascot International Bloodstock Bureau Ltd*.[125] The defendant reneged on a promise to purchase the claimant's horse for £6,000 in October 1973. The claimant could have sold the horse in December 1973, possibly for £4,000 or £5,000, but the claimant reasonably chose to keep the horse because she was ill and sell her in December 1974 when recovered. At that sale the claimant recovered only £1,690 for the mare and her foal, having spent £1,404 during the year. The claimant accordingly recovered from a unanimous Court of Appeal the cost expended plus the lost profit,[126] Lord Denning MR observing that it was an exceptional case where the cost of mitigating the damages had increased the damages a great deal but, in law, that cost was recoverable because the claimant had acted reasonably.

The same applies in the cases where the claimant reasonably and promptly resorts to the market for a replacement and the market in fact then rises (so the claimant could have done better had it waited).[127]

Similarly, upon its sub-buyer rejecting contaminated naphtha supplied by the defendant, a claimant reasonably hedged its exposure to a falling market and recovered the cost of so doing even though the market rose and so the mitigation did not reduce loss.[128]

A final neat example is the tort case of *The Metagama*, where after a vessel was holed it was reasonably beached although unluckily (and without negligence on the claimant's part) this led to the vessel sinking and being lost.[129]

(b) Benefits Received are Taken Into Account

Similarly, the actual benefits that accrued from the mitigatory act will be taken into account. This was the essence of *British Westinghouse* itself, where the House of Lords decided that the savings and profits that accrued from purchasing replacement machines should be taken into account (along with the cost of the replacement machines), allowing the appeal in that respect. As Lord Hoffmann explained in a later case, *British Westinghouse* is authority for 'the rule that requires additional benefits obtained as a result of taking reasonable steps to mitigate loss to be brought into account in the calculation of damages'.[130]

---

[125] *Hoffberger v Ascot International Bloodstock Bureau Ltd* (1976) 120 *Sol Jo* 130 (CA).
[126] Although the report does not give enough information to work out how the sum awarded of £7,215 was reached. Logic would suggest an award of £5,714 (= £6,000 + £1,404 - £1690) plus interest.
[127] Eg *Gebruder Metelmann GmbH & Co KG v NBR (London) Ltd* [1984] 1 Lloyd's Rep 614 (CA).
[128] *Choil Trading SA v Sahara Energy Resources Ltd* [2010] EWHC 374 (Comm) (Clarke J) at para 161.
[129] *Canadian Pacific Railway Co v Kelvin Shipping Co Ltd* (1927) 29 Ll L Rep 253 (HL).
[130] *Dimond v Lovell* [2002] 1 AC 384 (HL) at 401–2.

D. The Claimant's Post-Breach Actions: Where the Actions Break the Chain

If the claimant does not act reasonably, and instead performs acts that are an 'entirely independent and collateral matter arising not in the context of mitigation at all', they will be ignored and deemed not to have happened, with only the deemed loss recoverable.[131] These acts are 'an independent or disconnected transaction'[132] and 'collateral'.[133] They are a 'break in the causal chain' between the negligence and the harm or benefit, so any resulting benefit will be treated as collateral and 'for [the claimant's] own benefit' and need not be taken into account, and likewise any loss caused by the acts will cannot be recovered from the defendant.[134]

The relevant case law on whether the claimant's actions are reasonable and taken into account or unreasonable and ignored is set out below in chapter sixteen. Particular examples include the claimant in the misrepresentation case of *Hussey v Eels* who, rather than selling defective land, sought and eventually obtained planning permission thus increasing the value of the property;[135] the claimant in the surveyor's negligence case of *Gardner v Marsh & Parsons* procuring its landlord's payment of necessary repairs;[136] and claimants who speculated by delaying resort to the market to sell or replace defective or missing property or services.[137]

It is difficult to summarise the effect of those decisions, but where the claimant takes a gamble or goes far beyond what would have been expected then the courts will often treat any costs and benefits accruing to the claimant from that conduct as collateral and not to be taken into account.[138]

Further, if the claimant performs repairs or acquires a replacement going beyond what is necessary, then that is not for the account of the defendant, although the claimant can recover the reasonable cost.[139]

---

[131] *Mobil North Sea Ltd v PJ Pipe and Valve Co (t/a PJ Valve Ltd)* [2001] EWCA Civ 741 (CA) per Rix LJ at para 30. See also *British Westinghouse Electric & Manufacturing Co Ltd v Underground Electric Railways Co of London Ltd* [1912] AC 673 (HL) at 690–92, and *Dimond v Lovell* [2002] 1 AC 384 (HL) Lord Hoffmann at 402.

[132] *R Pagnan & Fratelli v Corbisa Industrial Agropacuaria Limitada* [1970] 1 WLR 1306 (CA) at 1315.

[133] *Pankhania v London Borough of Hackney* [2004] EWHC 323 (Ch) (Vos QC) at para 37.

[134] *Westlake v JP Cave and Co*, 14 January 1998 (Ebsworth J).

[135] *Hussey v Eels* [1990] 2 QB 227 (CA), discussed above at text to chapter three fn 40.

[136] *Gardner v Marsh & Parsons* [1997] 1 WLR 489 (CA), discussed below at text to chapter sixteen fn 287.

[137] See below in chapter sixteen, section 16.5.

[138] It is noteworthy that in *British Westinghouse Electric & Manufacturing Co Ltd v Underground Electric Railways Co of London*, the claimant at arbitration sought to argue that its actions in acquiring replacement machines and so reducing its loss were independent and must be disregarded as collateral, and therefore sought the increased costs it would have suffered if it had not acquired the replacement, although that argument was dropped at first instance (see [1912] 3 KB 128 (CA) pt 13 at 131).

[139] See above in chapter four, text to n 262.

15.4 Burdens of Proof

A. Remoteness

The burden of proving that a loss is not too remote falls on the claimant.[140] Remoteness is a mixed question of fact and law.[141]

B. Mitigation

The burden of proving (i) a failure of a duty to mitigate, and (ii) that this increased the harm suffered, falls on the defendant.[142] The question of whether there is a failure to mitigate is one of fact and not law.[143]

C. Causation

It is said that the legal burden falls on the claimant to show both factual causation (which is unsurprising) and legal causation (which is more surprising),[144] although the evidential burden of raising a case that the chain of causation was broken must fall on he who asserts it, leaving the other party to then disprove that.[145] In truth, and for consistency with the burden in mitigation cases (given that mitigation is part of legal causation), the legal burden too must fall on he who asserts a break in the chain.

15.5 Contributory Negligence

A. To Which Types of Contractual Breach Does it Apply?

Section 1 of the Law Reform (Contributory Negligence) Act 1945 gives a court the power to reduce the claimant's damages to 'such extent as the court thinks just

---

[140] Most of the cases on this are tort cases: See the discussion in *The Guildford* [1956] P 364 (Merriman P) at 370; *The Oropesa* [1943] P 32 (CA) at 40. And see for example *Bank of Credit & Commerce International SA v Ali (No 2)* [1999] 4 All ER 83 (Lightman J) at para 88.

[141] *Mehmet Dogan Bey v Abdeni* [1951] 2 KB 405 (McNair J) at 411.

[142] *Roper v Johnson* (1873) LR 8 CP 167; *Garnac Grain Co Inc v HMF Faure & Fairclough Ltd* [1968] AC 1130 (HL); *Red Deer College v Michaels* [1976] 2 SCR 324 (SC of Canada); *Kaines (UK) Ltd v Osterreichische Warenhandelsgesellschaft Austrowaren GmbH* [1993] Lloyd's Rep 1 (Steyn J) at 8; *Levy v Lewis* (CA), 26 November 1993, where the point was not properly pleaded and put by the breaching party; *Standard Chartered Bank v Pakistan National Shipping Corp* [1999] 1 Lloyd's Rep 747 (Toulson J) at 764 ff, affirmed [2001] EWCA Civ 55 Potter LJ at paras 38–39 and 41 (there the defendant proved a failure to mitigate but not the effect on the loss); *Geest plc v Lansiquot* [2002] 1 WLR 3111 (PC).

[143] *Payzu v Saunders* [1919] 2 KB 581 (CA) at 588 and 589; *The Solholt* [1983] 1 Lloyd's Rep 605 (CA) at 608; *Standard Chartered Bank v Pakistan National Shipping Corp* [2001] EWCA Civ 55 Potter LJ at para 47; *Wilding v British Telecommunications plc* [2002] IRLR 524 (CA) at para 36; *Welford v EDF Energy Networks (LPN) Ltd* [2007] EWCA Civ 293 at para 36.

[144] *Borealis AB v Geogas Trading SA* [2011] 1 Lloyd's Rep 482 (Gross LJ) para 43.

[145] Ibid. It will usually be the defendant asserting the break in the chain, but it may be the claimant where seeking to argue that certain benefits received were collateral.

and equitable having regard to the claimant's share in the responsibility for the damages', but only where the damage suffered results from the defendant's 'fault'.

(i) Applicable in Concurrent Contract/Tort Negligence Claims Only

The Act primarily applies to tort claims, and generally does not apply to contract claims. However, the limited circumstances in which the Act can apply to contract claims was established by the 1987 decision of the Court of Appeal in *Forsikringsaktieselskapet Vesta v Butcher*.[146] In the High Court, Hobhouse J had identified three categories of case, namely:

(1) Where the defendant's liability arises from some contractual provision which does not depend on negligence on the part of the defendant.
(2) Where the defendant's liability arises from a contractual obligation which is expressed in terms of taking care (or its equivalent) but does not correspond to a common law duty to take care which would exist in the given case independently of contract.
(3) Where the defendant's liability in contract is the same as his liability in the tort of negligence independently of the existence of any contract.[147]

Hobhouse J found that the Act did apply to the third category of case, as this counted as a case in which the claimant suffers damage as a result of the 'fault' of the defendant,[148] and his conclusion was approved by the Court of Appeal.[149] It has since been confirmed that, consistently with this approach, the Act does not apply to the other two categories.[150] The question arises on an obligation-by-obligation, not a contract-by-contract, basis, ie whether contributory negligence arises depends upon the particular obligation the breach of which gives rise to the damages claim.[151]

This means that the damages in a contractual claim can be reduced for the claimant's own fault only where the claim is for breach of a contractual duty of care *and* there is also a tortious duty of care concurrent with the contractual one (whether or not the claimant relies upon the latter duty in the action).[152]

Although such duties can arise in many types of case, typically they arise in personal injury cases (where there is a contract, eg employment) and in professional negligence cases.

---

[146] *Forsikringsaktieselskapet Vesta v Butcher* [1989] AC 852 (CA), affirmed [1989] UKHL 5.
[147] *Forsikringsaktieselskapet Vesta v Butcher* [1986] 2 All ER 488 (Hobhouse J) at 508.
[148] Within the meaning of section 1 of the Law Reform (Contributory Negligence) Act 1945.
[149] *Forsikringsaktieselskapet Vesta v Butcher* [1989] AC 852 (CA). (The House of Lords' decision is on a different point.) The approach in *Vesta v Butcher* was rejected in Australia in *Astley v Austrust Ltd* (1999) 197 CLR 1 (HC of Australia), prompting New South Wales' Law Reform (Miscellaneous Provisions) Amendment Act 2000 which allows contributory negligence reductions in tort cases and for 'breach of a contractual duty of care that is concurrent and co-extensive with a duty of care in tort'.
[150] *Barclays Bank plc v Fairclough Building Ltd* [1995] QB 214 (CA).
[151] Eg *Bank of Nova Scotia v Hellenic Mutual War Risks Association (Bermuda) Ltd (The Good Luck)* [1988] 1 Lloyd's Rep 514 (Hobhouse J) at 555.
[152] However, such a reduction can be made in all unfair dismissal awards by the Employment Rights Act 1996 s 123(6).

This means that, in a concurrent liability case, while there may be good reasons for choosing to sue in contract rather than tort, avoiding a reduction for contributory negligence is not one of them.

(ii) No Reduction in Contractual Claims Not Based on Carelessness

Accordingly, there can be no reduction for contributory negligence where the contractual duty was not a duty of care (Hobhouse J's first category in *Vesta v Butcher*). Thus there can be no reduction in case of a failure to deliver goods complying with the contractual description, or failure to pay on time, or the many other strict duties expressly or impliedly agreed in contracts (whether or not there is a concurrent tortious duty[153]).

Because of the importance the issue can have to the amount of damages payable, there are several professional liability cases where claimants have worked hard to identify and prove breach of a strict duty, in addition to the professional's duty of care. The proper approach to the question was set out in the valuer case of *Platform Funding Ltd v Bank of Scotland plc*:[154]

> [A]lthough there is a presumption that those who provide professional services normally do no more than undertake to exercise the degree of skill and care to be expected of a competent professional in the relevant field ... there is nothing to prevent them from assuming an unqualified obligation in relation to particular aspects of their work. Whether a professional person has undertaken an unqualified obligation of any kind in any given case will depend on the terms of the contract under which he has agreed to provide his services ... although the court should be cautious about holding that a professional person has undertaken an unqualified obligation in the absence of clear words to that effect, there is no reason not to give effect to the language of the contract where it is clear.

In that case the majority found that the obligation to value a particular property (rather than, as in that case, the wrong property) was strict, although the obligation in relation to the actual valuation process was a duty to take care. In *Barclays Bank plc v Fairclough Building Ltd*, the duty to clean a roof to a specified standard was found to be strict and not a duty of care.[155] Likewise there are many insurance broker cases confirming their strict duties to follow instructions and obtain cover on the terms instructed,[156] and there are solicitor cases finding that duties to obtain

---

[153] See *Banque Keyser Ullmann SA v Skandia (UK) Insurance Co Ltd* [1990] 1 QB 665 (Steyn J) at 720–21.

[154] *Platform Funding Ltd v Bank of Scotland plc (formerly Halifax plc)* [2009] 2 All ER 344 (CA) Moore-Bick LJ at para 30.

[155] *Barclays Bank plc v Fairclough Building Ltd* [1995] QB 214 (CA). See also *Mueller Europe Ltd v Central Roofing (South Wales) Ltd* [2013] EWHC 237 (TCC) (Stuart-Smith J) at paras 116–19, where the employer avoided a 40% reduction because the contractor had breached some strict express duties (to take precautions, inspect etc).

[156] See *Jackson & Powell on Professional Liability*, 7th edn at para 16-012.

good title[157] or to notify the lender client of matters known by the solicitor which might prejudice the security are strict.[158]

In contrast, in *Trebor Basset Holdings Ltd v ADT Fire and Security plc*,[159] the Court of Appeal confirmed that the bespoke fire protection system designed by the defendant for the claimant's popcorn plant did not amount to goods which gave rise to implied warranties of quality (or if it did that warranty could not be said to be breached because the system could only be assessed against the specific design objectives of the claimant). Further, the express contract properly construed did not include such warranties or other absolute obligations, and therefore the only breach was that of a duty of care and damages could therefore be reduced for contributory negligence. The reduction was 75 per cent.

(iii) Not Applicable to Claims Based on a Contractual Duty of Care without a Concurrent Tortious Duty

Similarly, there can be no reduction for contributory negligence in a case where there is a claim for breach of a contractual duty of care but no concurrent duty of care exists in tort (Hobhouse J's second category in *Vesta v Butcher*).

This situation arises relatively rarely as compared with the other two categories. Examples include *Raflatac Ltd v Eade,*[160] where a contractor was contractually but not tortiously liable for the negligence of its sub-contractor. See also *Haugesund Kommune v Depfa ACS Bank,*[161] where there was a contractual duty of care but (because governed by Norwegian law) no tortious duty.

There have been proposals for legislation applying the doctrine of contributory negligence to this second Hobhousian category of the purely contractual duty of care.[162]

B. Other Matters

(i) Does Contributory Negligence Only Apply to Pre-Breach Actions?

Although it is most usually applied to pre-breach conduct (with the legal mind turning to the principle of mitigation in cases post-breach conduct), it may well

---

[157] *Zwebner v The Mortgage Corp Ltd* [1998] PNLR 769 (CA) and *The Mortgage Corp Ltd v Mitchells Roberton* 1997 SLT 1305 (OH). But see the contrasting decisions to the effect that the duty is only one to take reasonable care: *Barclays Bank plc v Weeks Legg & Dean* [1999] QB 309 (CA); *Midland Bank plc v Cox McQueen (a firm)* [1999] PNLR 593 (CA); *UCB Corporate Services Ltd v Clyde & Co (a firm)* [2000] Lloyd's Rep PN 653 (CA).

[158] *Bristol & West Building Society v A Kramer & Co (a firm)* (unreported, 26 January 1995, Blackburne J). Further, many of the duties owed by solicitors to lenders under the CML Handbook are strict duties to the breach of which contributory negligence does not apply: *Mortgage Express v Iqbal Hafeez Solicitors* [2011] EWHC 3037 (Ch) (Randall QC) at para 74.

[159] *Trebor Basset Holdings Ltd v ADT Fire and Security plc* [2012] EWCA Civ 1148.

[160] *Raflatac Ltd v Eade* [1999] 1 Lloyd's Rep 506 (Colman J).

[161] *Haugesund Kommune v Depfa ACS Bank* [2012] QB 549 (CA).

[162] Law Commission, *Contributory Negligence as a Defence in Contract* (Report No 219, 1993).

be that contributory negligence can be applied to post-breach conduct. Certainly nothing in the Act provides otherwise, and tort case law indicates that it can.[163]

(ii) The Amount of the Reduction

The court has the power to reduce damages by such amount as is 'just and equitable'.[164] The two factors of particular relevance to the judge's exercise of this discretion are 'causative potency' and 'blameworthiness',[165] albeit that ultimately the statutory discretion is unfettered.

'Blameworthiness' focuses on the degree of fault of the claimant and defendant. Thus there is a scale from deliberate wrongful actions, through reckless and then grossly negligent actions, to merely negligent actions. Criminal acts are worse than non-criminal. Continuing dangerous conduct is worse than a momentary lapse. It is worse when a person should know better because they are older, or because they have been warned.

'Causative potency' is a difficult concept. In essence, it asks, given that both parties' conduct was a 'but for' cause of the harm or loss, which played a greater part in the chain of events leading to it? To look at it another way, was it the blameworthy part of a party's conduct that was central to the chain of causation?[166]

Determining the amount of reduction is a difficult one: how does one put a figure on the relative causative potency and blameworthiness of not wearing a seat belt/ hard hat as against an employer not having protective systems in place, for example? The case law varies according to the specific type of case. More specific works (such as on employers' liability, or professional negligence) should be consulted.

(iii) Interaction of Contributory Negligence with Scope of Duty

The House of Lords in *Platform Home Loans Ltd v Oyston Shipways Ltd*[167] confirmed that where a valuer's liability is limited by the principle of the scope of duty[168] to the amount by which the lender over-valued the property, rather than the total harm suffered by the lender, a reduction for contributory negligence is to be applied to the latter total loss figure and not the former attributable loss figure.[169]

(iv) Unfair Dismissal

The statutory action for unfair dismissal does routinely involve reductions for contributory fault.[170]

---

[163] *Spencer v Wincanton Holdings* [2009] EWCA Civ 1404. Also *Corr v IBC Vehicles* [2008] 1 AC 884 (HL).

[164] Section 1 of the Law Reform (Contributory Negligence) Act 1945.

[165] Denning LJ in *Davies v Swan Motor Co (Swansea) Ltd* [1949] 2 KB 291 (CA) at 326. Approved by the House of Lords in *Fitzgerald v Lane* [1989] AC 328 at 345 and by numerous successive appellate decisions. See also G Williams, *Joint Torts and Contributory Negligence* (London, Stevens & Son, 1951).

[166] For a useful illustration of the two concepts, see Hale LJ's formulation in the road traffic personal injury decision of *Eagle v Chambers* [2003] EWCA Civ 1107 at paras 17–18.

[167] *Platform Home Loans Ltd v Oyston Shipways Ltd* [2000] 2 AC 190 (HL).

[168] Following *South Australia Asset Management Corp v York Montague Ltd* [1997] AC 191 (HL).

[169] See further above in chapter fourteen, section 14.7.

[170] Employment Rights Act 1996 ss 122(2) and 123(6). See further discussion of this statutory action above in chapter thirteen, section 13.3B(iv)(b).

15.6 Applying Legal Causation to What Would Have Happened but for the Breach

The principle of legal causation (including mitigation) is almost entirely relevant only to the breach position and so to actions, omissions and events that actually occurred between the breach and the harm. Accordingly the next chapter is devoted to these many actions, omissions and events that actually take place but may be disregarded as *res inter alios acta*. It is necessary, however, to consider whether such principles of legal causation have anything to say when considering the non-breach position.

A. The Non-Breach Position and the Claimant

Plainly the principle of mitigation has nothing to say about the non-breach position, as it is concerned with the steps taken and not taken by the claimant to minimise the loss following the breach (whereas but for the breach the need for mitigation plainly would not have arisen). However, the general principle of legal causation must have some relevance to the non-breach position. Imagine an employer guilty of wrongful dismissal that was able to show that the employee would have deliberately injured himself at work if he had not been sacked, merely because (through no fault of the employer) the place of work provided the tools to assist the employee in doing so. Just as an employee would not be able to increase recoverable loss by showing that wrongfully dismissing the employee gave him the opportunity to self-harm at home and so the breach caused the harm (which as a matter of factual causation it did), similarly the employer should not be able to decrease the recoverable loss by showing that although the dismissal caused the employee to lose wages and other benefits, it saved the employee from the self-harm. The self-harm in either case is *res inter alios acta*.

B. The Non-Breach Position and the Defendant

The principle of legal causation can also be said to have something to say about what the defendant would have done but for the breach, in the limited sense that the defendant will be assumed to have acted lawfully[171] and in some cases to have performed only the minimum obligation.[172] To that extent any unlawful action of the defendant that would have taken place is nevertheless disregarded, arguably because it is *res inter alios acta*, as is any step the defendant would have taken that helps the claimant but that the defendant was not obliged to do (to the extent that it falls within the limited minimum obligation rule).

---

[171] See above in chapter thirteen, section 13.3A(i).
[172] See above in chapter thirteen, section 13.3B.

C. The Non-Breach Position and Third Parties and External Events

As regards third parties and external events, it does appear that certain things that would but for the breach have occurred will be disregarded as *res inter alios acta*. Recoverable loss against a wrongfully dismissing employer cannot be increased by proof that the employee unsuccessfully gambled in the spare time that followed dismissal, or decreased by proof that the employee had some success with a lottery ticket following dismissal.[173] Equally the employee should not be able to increase its recoverable loss by showing that that the dismissal meant that the employee ceased participation in an office lottery-ticket syndicate that won a fortune shortly after the dismissal (nor should the recoverable loss be reduced because the employee saved the costs of participation in an unsuccessful office lottery-ticket syndicate). Some of these results are explicable by remoteness or scope of duty (the duty not to dismiss an employee is aimed at ensuring the employee has a job and wage, not the incidental opportunity to gamble[174]), but there still appears to be a principle of legal causation at play, with its principles of collaterality, connectedness and intervening cause.

A difficult question arose in the employment dispute *Ministry of Defence v Cannock*.[175] The discriminatorily dismissed employee had a claim for lost wages, from which had to be netted off childcare costs which were saved by the employee being off work. However, the truth was that while working for the defendant the claimant had received half of its childcare free from family members and so had not had to make that deduction from its wages. The claimant therefore argued that it had lost its wages gross of childcare, ie it had not actually saved any childcare cost by being off work. The Employment Appeal Tribunal dismissed this argument, on the basis that the free childcare 'is *res inter alios acta*', and deducted the full cost of childcare from the lost wages to come to the awarded loss figure.[176] Had the breach caused the need for childcare (rather than eliminated the need for it), the free childcare would have been disregarded as a collateral benefit and the claimant able to recover the cost of childcare (as occurs in personal injury cases where a partner or other family member provides care to the injured party).[177] It is therefore logical, if harsh, to disregard the free childcare when it is part of the non-breach position and where the result operates in favour of the employer.

---

[173] See chapter sixteen, n 133.

[174] And so in *Jones v Lingfield Leisure plc* (EAT), 21 January 1998, approved (CA) 20 May 1999, the private earnings which a leisure centre employee made through running classes while working at the leisure centre were held to be too remote to be recoverable under the statutory action for unfair dismissal. See similarly *Schlesinger v Swindon and Marlborough NHS Trust* (EAT), 24 August 2004.

[175] *Ministry of Defence v Cannock* [1995] 2 All ER 449 (EAT).

[176] Ibid at 471.

[177] See below in chapter sixteen, section 16.10.

16

Intervening Acts and Events by Category

Categorisation of the various intervening acts and events with discussion of whether each act or event breaks the chain of causation or is too remote.

16.1 Introduction to this Chapter

THIS CHAPTER GATHERS together under practical headings the results of the voluminous case law on post-breach acts, omissions and events. The legal principles behind these decisions are principally those of legal causation and mitigation (discussed in chapter fifteen above), although some turn on remoteness (chapter fourteen above), and many turn on more than one principle or fail to specify the relevant principle. The essential question in all the cases, however, is whether despite the claimant suffering a harm that would not have taken place but for the breach, or foregoing a gain that would have been earned but for the breach, the breach position is nevertheless modified to ignore certain post-breach acts, omissions or events and thereby alter the measure of loss recoverable. This book does not seek to formulate a general principle or set of factors that govern all of these cases, beyond the observations made in chapter fifteen that whether something is *res inter alios acta*/collateral will depend, among other things, upon whether it was normal or unusual/idiosyncratic, reasonable or unreasonable, likely/foreseeable or unlikely/unforeseeable.

16.2 Claimant Failure to Avoid the Danger

A. Failing to Discover the Danger/Second-Guess the Defendant

Generally, a person is not expected to guard against the failure of another person to carry out their legal obligations.[1]

(i) Physical Defects and Danger

Failure to discover a danger will rarely break the chain of causation. Thus in *Mowbray v Merryweather*, although the dangerous defect in an (actual, not metaphorical) chain was reasonably discoverable on inspection, the claimant stevedores' failure to inspect the chain did not prevent the defendant shipowner from being liable for the chain's failure and the resulting injury to the claimant's employee.[2] It was important in that case that the defendant had been contractually obliged to provide a chain that was fit for purpose and the claimant had no duty to examine the chain. A similar approach was taken to a cargo owner which put its ethylene into a defendant carrier's vessel that was said to be obviously dirty and to have contaminated the cargo.[3] In another case a claimant's failure to heed a rather vague warning of fire and to protect against fire did not absolve the defendant, who had negligently installed a rotisserie on the wrong surface, which installation led to just such a fire.[4] And in another case, although a contractor had an obligation to satisfy itself as to all matters of design, it was entitled to rely on the defendant geotechnical consultants, and so the contractor's adoption of the consultants' unsuitable design did not break the chain of causation.[5]

A similar approach is taken in cases in which a third party, rather than the claimant, could or would ordinarily have discovered but did not discover the danger.[6]

The modern view is therefore probably that little short of recklessness will break the chain of causation in the case of an undiscovered defect.[7] However, in *Bostock & Co Ltd v Nicholson & Sons Ltd* the failure by the claimant or its chemists to discover the arsenic in the sulphuric acid purchased from the defendant, before selling glucose made with the acid to brewers, did prevent the claimant recovering dam-

---

[1] *Barclays Bank plc v Fairclough Building Ltd* [1995] QB 241 (CA) per Beldam LJ at 226.
[2] *Mowbray v Merryweather* [1895] 2 QB 640 (CA). Similarly *Pinnock Bros v Lewis & Peat Ltd* [1923] 1 KB 690 (Roche J); *Borealis AB v Geogas Trading SA* [2011] 1 Lloyd's Rep 482 (Gross LJ).
[3] *Vinmar International Ltd v Theresa Navigation SA* [2001] EWHC 497 (Comm) (Tomlinson J).
[4] *Six Continents Retail Ltd v Carford Catering Ltd* [2003] EWCA Civ 1790.
[5] *Linden Homes South East Ltd v LBH Wembley Ltd* (2003) 87 Con LR 180 (TCC) (Aylen QC).
[6] *Heskell v Continental Express Ltd* [1950] 1 All ER 1033 (Devlin J) at 1049 (although it may have been significant that the defendant's duty was a continuing one throughout the period of the delay); *East Ham Corp v Bernard Sunley & Sons Ltd* [1966] AC 406 (HL). And see *Pearson Education Ltd v The Charter Partnership Ltd* [2007] EGLR 89 (CA), where the third party did discover the danger but did not pass that on and the chain of causation was not broken.
[7] *County Ltd v Girozentrale Securities* [1996] 3 All ER 834 (CA) at 857 (quoted above at text to chapter fifteen n 70); *Trac Time Control Ltd v Moss Plastic Parts Ltd* [2004] EWHC 3298 (TCC) (Grenfell J) at para 182; *Borealis AB v Geogas Trading SA* [2011] 1 Lloyd's Rep 482 (Gross LJ) para 46 (quoted below at text to n 24 *Flanagan v Greenbanks Ltd* [2013] EWCA Civ 1702). See further above in chapter fifteen, section 15.3B(iii)(c). And see *Pearson Education Ltd v The Charter Partnership Ltd* [2007] EGLR 89 (CA), especially at para 32.

ages to cover its liability to on-buyers.[8] The damages were limited to the loss of sale profits from the glucose.[9]

(ii) Insurance Placements

Where a claimant signs without checking an insurance proposal that fails accurately to record the insured's instructions, that can sometimes break the chain of causation between the broker's carelessness in completing the form and the loss caused by the insurer refusing cover, given that the insured has (and should know it has) the primary duty of utmost good faith to the insurer to make sure the proposal is accurate.[10] However, an insured is generally entitled to rely on the insurer as having performed its duties and carried out the insured's instructions and the insured need not examine the documents to check that this is the case, to the point where courts will often even refuse to make a reduction for contributory negligence.[11]

(iii) Other Cases

Where a defendant is responsible for failing to advise on something, a claimant will rarely be held to have caused or contributed to the loss by failing to make its own enquiries.[12]

B. Knowingly Risking the Danger Created by the Defendant

As a general principle, 'if a buyer becomes aware of a defect in goods, but continues to use the goods notwithstanding this knowledge, there is a break in the chain of causation from that point on'.[13] Thus, if a claimant knows its goods (bought from the defendant) are defective, it would break the chain of causation for the claimant nevertheless to supply them to a sub-buyer without telling the sub-buyer, or not to pass on the information to the sub-buyer if they had already been on-sold but the communication may minimise the damage.[14] Where the claimant's agents were

---

[8] *Bostock & Co Ltd v Nicholson & Sons Ltd* [1904] 1 KB 725 (Bruce J).

[9] Because of the way the claim had been formulated, the award actually made was the claimant's price paid to the defendant for the goods, plus the cost of the goods mixed with the acid to make glucose and thereby rendered useless by it. These are best seen as a fair, if low, estimate of the difference in value between sellable glucose and worthless glucose. The crucial point, however, is that they were losses that would have been incurred even if the defect had been discovered.

[10] *O'Connor v BDB Kirby & Co* [1972] 1 QB 90 (CA). But see *Dunbar v A & B Painters Ltd* [1985] 2 Lloyd's Rep 616 (Pratt QC), affirmed [1986] 2 Lloyd's Rep 38 (CA) (proposal form was inaccurate as to a matter that related to prior placements and insurance premiums); *Youell v Bland Welch & Co Ltd (The Superhulls Cover Case) (No 2)* [1990] 2 Lloyd's Rep 431 (Phillips J) (as to the terms of the policy); *Samani v Walia* (CA), 22 April 1994 (broker knew the proposal form was inaccurate but failed to draw this to the insured's attention).

[11] *Dickson & Co v Devitt* (1916) 86 LJKB 315 (Atkin J) at 317-8, *Youell v Bland Welch (The Superhulls Cover No 2)* [1990] 2 Lloyd's Rep 431 (Phillips J), *Bollom v Byas Mosley* [1999] Lloyd's LR 598 (Moore-Bick J) at 614.

[12] Eg *AW Group Ltd v Taylor Walton* [2013] EWHC 2610 (Ch) (Hodge QC) obiter at para 254.

[13] *Trac Time Control Ltd v Moss Plastic Parts Ltd (t/a Rowan Plastic Parts Centre)* [2004] EWHC 3298 (TCC) (Grenfell J) at para 182.

[14] *Dobell (GC) & Co Ltd v Barger and Garratt* [1931] 1 KB 219 (CA) at 238; *Biggin & Co Ltd v Permanite Ltd* [1951] 1 KB 422 (Devlin J) at 435.

aware of a defect in soya meal that could have been put right at no cost, but did nothing, this prevented the claimants from recovering against the sellers.[15]

In *Lexmead (Basingstoke) Ltd v Lewis*[16] the farmer purchaser's continued use of a defective towing coupling to tow a trailer, once it became apparent that the coupling was defective, exonerated the vendor from liability for the subsequent harm. In *Commercial Fibres (Ireland) Ltd v Zabaida*, a seller was liable for the cost of repackaging yarn delivered in damaged cartons, but not the subsequent devaluation of the yarn caused by shipping the yarn in the damaged cartons (which came apart, rendering the yarn all but valueless).[17] But in another case Amstrad was found to have acted reasonably in still selling its computers despite discovering that the hard drives supplied by the defendant and incorporated into the computers had problems.[18] These issues are discussed more generally above in relation to patent defects, the measure of loss usually being based on the claimant replacing or repairing the defective goods.[19]

In *Schering Agrochemicals Ltd v Resibel NV SA*,[20] a claimant failed to replace the defendant's defectively designed fire safety device despite a small fire having revealed defects (although not that they were the defendant's fault). A subsequent fire would have been avoided but for the claimant's failure and the defendant was not liable for it.[21] Although the claimant was not aware of the breach, it was fully aware of the danger, which had become patent, and should have discovered the breach. Failure to act on its knowledge of the danger was a failure to mitigate,[22] else a break in the chain of causation.[23]

As Gross LJ observed in the *Borealis AB v Geogas Trading SA* case,

> the more the Claimant has actual knowledge of the breach, of the dangerousness of the situation which has thus arisen and of the need to take appropriate remedial measures, the greater the likelihood that the chain of causation will be broken. Conversely, the less the Claimant knows the more likely it is that only recklessness will suffice to break the chain of causation.[24]

---

[15] *Toepfer v Warinco AG* [1978] 2 Lloyd's Rep 569 (Brandon J) at 579.

[16] *Lexmead (Basingstoke) Ltd v Lewis* [1982] AC 225 (HL).

[17] *Commercial Fibres (Ireland) Ltd v Zabaida* [1975] 1 Lloyd's Rep 27 (Donaldson J).

[18] *Amstrad plc v Seagate Technology Inc* (1998) 86 BLR 34 (Lloyd QC) at numbered section 20.

[19] See above in chapter four, section 4.2B(v).

[20] *Schering Agrochemicals Ltd v Resibel NV SA* (CA), 26 November 1992.

[21] Ibid. Distinguished on closely similar facts in *Trebor Bassett Holdings Ltd v ADT Fire and Security plc* [2011] EWHC 1379 (TCC) (Coulson J).

[22] This is the explanation of Hobhouse J at first instance in *Schering Agrochemicals* (above n 17) (4 June 1991), and of Nolan LJ in the Court of Appeal (26 November 1992), Purchas LJ not deciding between failure to mitigate and a break in the chain of causation. This failure to mitigate explanation was preferred by the Court of Appeal in *County Ltd v Girozentrale Securities* [1996] 3 All ER 834, especially Hobhouse LJ (as he then was) at 858–59. See further the discussion in *Trebor Basset Holdings Ltd v ADT Fire and Security plc* [2012] EWCA Civ 1148 Tomlinson LJ at paras 66–67, where, obiter, *Schering* was distinguished on the facts, as in *Trebor Basset* the knowledge of the earlier fire did not go to a high enough level in the claimant company.

[23] Scott LJ in the Court of Appeal in *Schering*. See further *Beoco Ltd v Alfa Laval Co Ltd* [1995] QB 137 (CA).

[24] *Borealis AB v Geogas Trading SA* [2011] 1 Lloyd's Rep 482 (Gross LJ) para 46. Contrary to the suggestion in this quotation, for these purposes (unlike, eg, the starting time to run for limitation purposes), knowledge of the danger must be enough to potentially break the chain of causation, without

In *Quinn v Burch Bros (Builders) Ltd*,[25] when the defendant head contractor failed to supply a step-ladder, the claimant plastering sub-contractor used an unsuitable unfooted trestle and fell and injured his heel. The Court of Appeal upheld dismissal of the claim on the basis that the claimant's careless decision to use the trestle broke the chain of causation from the defendant's breach. Similarly, in another case a local authority landlord was held not responsible for a slipped disc caused by the lack of a working lift as the resident had acted unreasonably in carrying all her shopping up the stairs in one trip and without help.[26]

Accordingly, the claimant was lucky to succeed in *Parsons (Livestock) Ltd v Uttley Ingham & Co Ltd*,[27] discussed above.[28] In that case the defendant was responsible for a food hopper that, due to defective installation, made the nuts stored in it mouldy. The claimant, who was a pig-farmer and so presumably knew more about pigs than the defendant hopper supplier, knowingly fed the mouldy nuts to his pigs believing there to be only a very slight possibility of illness from mouldy nuts.[29] In those circumstances one might have thought that the claimant's actions, voluntarily taking the risk of feeding mouldy nuts to the pigs, would break the chain of causation. Here the damage caused by the hopper (to the nuts) and the danger to the pigs (of illness) were patent, and one might have expected the defendant's damages to be limited to the costs of buying replacement nuts, but not the loss which actually resulted from feeding the pigs the nuts anyway, namely the illness and subsequent death of pigs from being fed mouldy pignuts. Surprisingly, the Court of Appeal was not concerned that the claimant's actions in knowingly feeding the pigs mouldy nuts had any effect on the chain of causation,[30] and decided the case in favour of the claimant solely on the basis of remoteness, ie foreseeability.

C. Claimant Actions in the Heat of the Crisis

A failure of a claimant in the heat of a crisis, including if the claimant panics, will not be treated as a failure to mitigate or a break in the chain of causation, at least if the claimant acted reasonably in the circumstances.[31] As Lord Shaw memorably observed, when rejecting the argument that the claimant's employee acted too slowly and so caused or contributed to the loss resulting from the defendant's collision, 'we are not dealing with the psychology of a superman but simply that of a ship's captain'.[32] Thus although a claimant's master was worried as to the safety of the port notified by the defendant charterer (and so aware of the danger), he was on the 'horns of a dilemma' and had not been negligent in nevertheless sailing to that

---

there being a need for knowledge that it was caused by the breach (which is irrelevant to the steps the claimant could be expected to take).

[25] *Quinn v Burch Bros (Builders) Ltd* [1966] 2 QB 370 (CA).
[26] *Berryman v Hounslow London Borough Council* [1997] PIQR P83 (CA).
[27] *Parsons (Livestock) Ltd v Uttley Ingham & Co Ltd* [1978] QB 791 (CA).
[28] Text to chapter fourteen n 81.
[29] [1978] QB 791 at 799.
[30] Ibid at 801.
[31] Eg *The Oropesa* [1943] P 32 (CA) (tort causing death).
[32] *United States of America Shipping Board v Laird Line Ltd* [1924] AC 286 (HL) at 292.

port, and the defendant was therefore liable for damage resulting from nomination of an unsafe place for loading.[33] Even negligence in the face of a danger caused by the defendant may not break the chain of causation.[34]

D. The Claimant's Failure to Protect against the Loss

In one case, the claimant's failure to fit a protective device that would have prevented a fire did not absolve the defendant of responsibility for a pump with a defective electrical cable and the electrical fire it caused.[35] And where the purposes of the defendant's duty were to guard against the very thing that happened by virtue of the claimant's conduct, there will only be a break in the chain in the most rare and extreme case.[36] Accordingly, in *Mueller Europe Ltd v Central Roofing (South Wales) Ltd*, even a concurrent breach of contract by an employer in failing to isolate its heaters (which caused a fire) did not break the chain of causation from the roofing contractor's breach in failing to operate safely, the contractor having primary responsibility for safety and this including avoiding danger if the employer failed to isolate the heaters.[37]

16.3 Failing to Terminate the Contract with the Defendant

A. The Duty to Mitigate and Termination of the Contract

Once the defendant has breached, the duty to mitigate arises.[38] This means that (despite some dicta to the contrary), for the purposes of calculating the damages payable by the defendant, a claimant can be deemed to have terminated the contract and sought a replacement on the market if (and this will be rare) all reasonable claimants would have done so and/or failure to do so is treated as a speculative or independent action of the claimant, even if the claimant in fact affirmed the contract and, perhaps unsuccessfully, pursued specific relief remedies against the defendant to trial.

This question of whether the claimant acted reasonably is raised by the principles of mitigation and legal causation, and so it is only relevant to a claim for damages, ie only relevant where specific performance or the action for an agreed sum is either

---

[33] *Compania Naviera Maropan S/A v Bowaters Lloyd Pulp and Paper Mills Ltd* [1955] 2 QB 58 (Devlin J). The same conclusion was reached a fortiori when the master had no reason to doubt the defendant's nomination: *Reardon Smith Line Ltd v Australian Wheat Board* [1956] AC 266 (HL), also *Gard Marine & Energy Ltd v China National Chartering Co Ltd (The Ocean Victory)* [2013] EWHC 2199 (Comm) (Teare J).

[34] *Gard Marine & Energy Ltd v China National Chartering Co Ltd (The Ocean Victory)* [2013] EWHC 2199 (Comm) (Teare J) obiter at para 174.

[35] *Hi-Lite Electrical Ltd v Wolseley UK Ltd* [2011] EWHC 1379 (TCC) (Ramsey J), obiter as the defendant was not in fact found liable.

[36] *Mueller Europe Ltd v Central Roofing (South Wales) Ltd* [2013] EWHC 237 (TCC) (Stuart-Smith J) at paras 124 and 127 and see below in section 16.13E(vii).

[37] Ibid at paras 126–27.

[38] See above in chapter fifteen, section 15.3B(ii).

refused or not sought. (Contrast *White and Carter* and similar cases where specific relief was awarded and so the there was no damages question for the court, discussed below in section 16.3B(ii).)

The Canadian position can be found in the decision of the Supreme Court of Canada in *Asamera Oil Corporation Ltd v Sea Oil & General Corporation*.[39] In 1958 Mr Brook of Asamera Oil contracted to return to Baud Corporation by the end of 1959 (extended by agreement to the end of 1960) the 125,000 of shares in Asamera that Baud had loaned him. Mr Brook did not do so. At the end of 1960, when the shares should have been returned, the market value of the shares was 29¢ per share. In July 1960, Baud injuncted Mr Brook from disposing of the shares, and required him to at all times hold that amount of shares, which he did. The specific shares loaned had been sold by Mr Brook in 1958, although Baud did not know this until July 1967, by which time the shares were trading at about CAN$4.30 per share (having risen since 1966 when Asamera struck oil in Sumatra). Baud never terminated the agreement and at trial sought specific performance, which was refused. By the date of the opening of the trial in 1969 the shares were trading at CAN$46.50 per share, but this declined to about CAN$22 per share by the date of judgment in 1972. By Estey J's judgment of the Supreme Court in 1978, it was held that Baud could reasonably have been expected to purchase replacement shares during the period from autumn 1966 to autumn 1967 at a median price of CAN$6.50 per share and 'thereafter the loss is of its own making', and that even if this were not the case the claimant had not prosecuted its claim with reasonable promptness.

Estey J correctly explained both that the principle of mitigation does not apply to the remedy of specific performance, and further that it is not disapplied to the claim for damages merely because the claimant had an injunction. Where the claimant has a 'a substantial and legitimate interest in seeking performance as opposed to damages, then a plaintiff will be able to justify his inaction', ie failure to resort to the market for a replacement, 'and on failing in his plea for specific performance might then recover losses which in other circumstances might be classified as avoidable and thus unrecoverable'. However, the claimant

> may not merely by instituting proceedings in which a request is made for specific performance and/or damages, thereby shield himself and block the court from taking into account the accumulation of losses which the plaintiff by acting with reasonable promptness in processing his claim could have avoided.[40]

Here the judge developed Lord Reid's novel 'legitimate interest' test from *White and Carter* regarding when a claimant is able to affirm a contract and claim an agreed sum (where previously there had been no restriction),[41] but applied it to the more ordinary context of mitigation and its effect on contract damages (where reasonableness is the normal test).[42] The outcome in *Asamera* suggests that for Estey J the test of whether damages will be reduced for failure to terminate and seek a

---

[39] *Asamera Oil Corporation Ltd v Sea Oil & General Corporation* [1979] 1 SCR 633 (SC of Canada).
[40] Ibid at 667–69.
[41] Below at 16.3B(ii).
[42] See *Jervis v Harris* [1996] Ch 195 (CA) Millet LJ at 201.

replacement is stricter on the claimant than Lord Reid's legitimate interest test in *White and Carter*, and more in line with the general approach to mitigation, which does not expect a high a standard from claimants, but is more demanding than Lord Reid's test of legitimate interest, of which a claimant would only fall foul in exceptional circumstances. Estey J did confirm that the sorts of reasons that would justify pursuing specific remedies rather than terminating the contract include that the property is of unique importance (key real estate or a controlling block of shares), or that if the claimant were to discontinue performance there might be aggravation of losses.

This approach was applied obiter in Saskatchewan in *Kopec v Pyret*.[43] The judge pointed out that

> As a practical matter, the utility of the remedy of specific performance would be greatly impaired if the plantiff could not rely on his right to seek specific performance as a justification for not purchasing alternate land in mitigation of the losses occasioned by the defendant's breach of contract,[44]

but also confirmed that the *Asamera* test applied, although in the instant case the claimant had pursued 'his remedy of specific performance with reasonable diligence and where his claim to specific performance holds out a reasonable likelihood of success'.[45] Most recently, the Supreme Court of Canada again applied this approach in *Southcott Estates Inc v Toronto Catholic District School Board* in the context of a contract of sale of land.[46] As Karakantasis J put it, a claimant with a substantial and legitimate interest in specific performance who pursues it is not excused from the duty to mitigate: rather 'such a claim for specific performance informs what is reasonable behaviour for the plaintiff in mitigation'.[47] The court found, however, that the claimant had failed to mitigate when the defendant school board failed to deliver the land for a development, and rather than simply seeking specific performance (which is more rarely available in land sale cases in Canada than in England) it should have spent its money on an alternative development property.

The *Asamera* case has not been discussed in the English cases. However, it does appear that the rule of mitigation applicable to a claim for damages will deem a claimant to have terminated and sought a replacement, where reasonable (in the sense of that word as applied to mitigation). In other words, the rule of mitigation can bring forward the date on which market value is taken to before the actual date of termination of the contract, because a replacement should have been sought.

Although in the leading English case of *Johnson v Agnew*[48] (where an order for specific performance was actually made and then discharged) the damages were assessed by reference to the value of the promised property at the date of trial, the issue of the date of assessment was, despite the claimant having pursued specific performance, considered to be at large. In particular, although the contract was affirmed

---

[43] *Kopec v Pyret* (1983) 146 DLR (3d) 242 (Saskatchewan QB), affirmed (1987) 36 DLR (4th) 1 (Saskatchewan CA).

[44] Ibid at 258.

[45] Ibid.

[46] *Southcott Estates Inc v Toronto Catholic District School Board* 2012 SCC 51 (SC of Canada).

[47] Ibid at para 36.

[48] *Johnson v Agnew* [1980] AC 367 (HL).

and only came to an end at judgment when the claimant had to elect to claim damages, Lord Wilberforce justified the award on the basis (accepting counsel's submissions) that the claimant had 'reasonably' continued to press for performance and seek specific performance.[49] This indicates that in England too the mitigation principle does apply to the claimant's decision whether to affirm the contract rather than to seek a replacement in the market, and that if the claimant in *Johnson v Agnew* had not acted reasonably (ie had no substantial and legitimate interest in seeking specific performance, to use Estey J's terms from *Asamera*) the loss may have been measured as if the claimant had terminated the contract at an earlier date.

This means that the claimant has a difficult decision to make when considering whether to terminate the contract or whether to seek specific performance. The latter, if awarded, may well provide a better remedy than damages when the market has moved upwards, but that is merely a consequence of the fact that specific performance delivers the property whereas damages compensate for unavoidable loss resulting from not having the property at and from the date of delivery (rather than necessarily not having the property at the date of trial[50]). Auld LJ in the Court of Appeal's decision in *Habton Farms v Nimmo* has suggested that, as regards a damages claim, at some stage a seller may become obliged by the mitigatory principle to stop pressing the buyer and 'to mitigate its damages by accepting the notional buyer's repudiation and seeking another buyer'.[51] There are many other cases where a failure to act reasonably has been found in circumstances in which the claimant does not appear to have terminated the contract,[52] although it should be noted that there are dicta suggesting incorrectly that the duty to mitigate does not apply to the decision as to termination.[53]

Of course, one would expect the courts not to be too astute to find that a claimant unreasonably pursued the defendant for performance rather than terminating and cutting its losses, and being refused specific performance certainly doesn't prove that it was unreasonable to pursue it. Yet it does appear that the test of mitigation nevertheless does apply to the question of whether to accept a repudiation, terminate, mitigate and claim damages, or to affirm the contract and seek specific remedies and/or press for performance all the way to trial. (Just to be clear, however,

---

[49] Ibid at 401, apparently accepting submissions by Mr Millet QC as he then was (recorded [1980] AC 367 at 387) that 'Where the remedy of specific performance is available and is properly sought, there is no basis for treating the plaintiff as acting unreasonably in refusing to accept the breach as a repudiation. Accordingly, there is no reason to fix an earlier date than the date on which he abandons the claim for specific performance. Normally that would be the date of the hearing but here it is the date after which specific performance was no longer possible'. See also *Suleman v Shahsavari* [1988] 1 WLR 1181 (Park QC) at 1183–84 where the reasonableness test was applied and passed by a claimant who affirmed the contract and sought but was refused specific performance.

[50] See further chapters four and six.

[51] *Habton Farms (an unlimited company) v Nimmo* [2004] 1 QB 1 (CA) at para 128.

[52] Eg *Payzu v Saunders* [1919] 2 KB 581 (CA). Or consider the claimant who purchases patently defective goods and nevertheless supplies them without warning to the sub-buyer, who then suffers harm for which it claims against the claimant: in such a case the claimant has not terminated the contract but still cannot, because of the mitigatory/legal causation principle, recover from the defendant the costs of compensating the sub-buyer—*Dobell (GC) & Co Ltd v Barger and Garratt* [1931] 1 KB 219 (CA) at 238; *Biggin & Co Ltd v Permanite Ltd* [1951] 1 KB 422 (Devlin J) at 435.

[53] *Sotiros Shipping Inc v Samiet Solholt (The Solholt)* [1983] 1 Lloyd's Rep 605 (CA) Donaldson MR at 608, says that mitigation only arises upon cancellation in relation to *further* actions.

this is only relevant for a damages award. If the claimant is awarded an agreed sum or specific performance, the issue does not arise, although the legitimate interest rule discussed below may be relevant to whether a claimant should be awarded an agreed sum.[54])

The reasoning in earlier decisions suggesting that damages in lieu of specific performance are subject to different principles,[55] while not without sense given that if specific performance were granted the claimant would get the property at trial not damages for its loss, must be doubted in the light of *Johnson v Agnew* in which the House of Lords confirmed that the same principles apply to damages in lieu of specific performance as to common law damages.[56]

(i) Failure to Terminate the Contract with a Third Party

The same principle applies in relation to a contract with a third party. Thus a claimant seller cannot indefinitely delay the day at which property it is left with due to the defendant's breach of warranty of authority is to be valued and credited to the loss calculation, as 'at some stage … the claimant would be taken to have had a duty, as against the warrantor, to mitigate its damages by accepting the notional buyer's repudiation and seeking another buyer'.[57]

B. 'Mitigation', Legitimate Interest and the Action for an Agreed Sum

The issue of mitigation proper, and whether for the purposes of calculating damages the claimant should be treated as having broken the chain of causation by not terminating, only arises on a claim for damages. If the claimant seeks and is awarded specific performance or an agreed sum under an action for a debt, there is no question of loss and therefore of avoidable loss. This simple fact almost completely explains the controversial case of *White and Carter v McGregor*[58] (which is discussed here for completeness, even though it concerns the action for an agreed sum and not the remedy of damages).

In that well-known case McGregor, a garage proprietor, engaged White and Carter to advertise the garage for three years at a weekly rental on the sides of rubbish bins in the Clydebank area of Scotland, renewing a prior three year contract that had just expired. On the same day as the renewal McGregor renounced the contract (ie asked to cancel it), on the basis that the garage sales manager should never have entered into it, but White and Carter affirmed the contract and, when the McGregor refused to pay the sums as they became due,[59] performed their advertising duties

---

[54] This caveat is of little practical importance. It would be very rare indeed, however, for it to be unreasonable (for the purposes of damages) for a claimant to pursue specific performance (usually because the claimant has no realistic prospect of succeeding) or an agreed sum, and for it yet to succeed.

[55] *Wroth v Tyler* [1974] Ch 30 (Megarry J); *Malhotra v Choudhury* [1980] Ch 52 (CA).

[56] See further above in chapter one, section 1.2B(iii).

[57] *Habton Farms (an unlimited company) v Nimmo* [2003] EWCA Civ 68 Auld LJ at para 128.

[58] *White and Carter v McGregor* [1962] AC 413 (HL).

[59] There was initially an unaccepted anticipatory breach but, as Lord Keith explained [1962] AC 413 at 435, this case was really about the unaccepted actual repudiatory breach that arose at the date the first payment became due.

and pursued McGregor for the full sum payable for the three years, there being an express term that if any payment is missed, the full sum shall become payable.[60]

The bare majority of the House of Lords found that the advertiser was entitled to its debt. This is an entirely correct application of the law that has been followed in subsequent cases.[61]

(i) The Practical Effect of a Need for the Defendant's Cooperation

Of course, as Lord Reid explained in *White and Carter*, 'In most cases by refusing co-operation the party in breach can compel the innocent party to restrict his claim to damages'.[62] This is because in most cases the obligation of the defendant to pay does not arise until certain performance by the claimant, and the claimant cannot perform in that way without the cooperation of the defendant.

As Salmon LJ has observed,

> you cannot claim money as payable under a contract if you have not earned it under the contract. The fact that the contract-breaker has prevented you from earning it by his breach cannot entitle you to claim it as due under the contract,[63]

to which the following riders must be added: if the claimant can force the cooperation by specific performance or an injunction, then it can then earn the money;[64] and even if the money is not earned and cannot be claimed as a debt, it can still be claimed as loss, but subject to the duty to mitigate and other principles.

Thus in most cases, such as where the claimant's right to the price only arises upon the defendant accepting delivery of the goods, the claimant will in practice although not in law have to break the stalemate by terminating the contract and seeking damages, as the defendant's obligations to pay anything (here, damages) will otherwise never arise.[65] Likewise under a demise charter the defendant giving

---

[60] As this was an accelerated payment clause, not a liquidated damages clause, it was not susceptible to challenge under the rule against penalties: see Lord Reid, ibid at 427.

[61] *Anglo-African Shipping Co of New York, Inc v J Morntner Ltd* [1962] 1 Lloyd's Rep 81 (Mega J), affirmed [1962] 1 Lloyd's Rep 610 (CA); *Gator Shipping Corp v Trans-Asiatic Oil Ltd (The Odenfeld)* [1978] 2 Lloyd's Rep 357 (Kerr J); *Abrahams v Performing Rights Society Ltd* [1995] ICR 1028 (CA); *Ministry of Sound (Ireland) Ltd v World Online Ltd* [2003] EWHC (Ch) 2178 (Strauss QC); *Reichman v Beveridge* [2007] 1 EGLR 37 (CA); *Isabella Shipowner SA v Shagang Shipping Co Ltd* [2012] EWHC 1077 (Comm) (Cooke J). Cf *McLaughlin v Governor of the Cayman Islands* [2007] UKPC 50.

[62] Lord Reid [1962] AC 413 at 428–29 and Lord Keith at 437.

[63] *Decro-Wall International SA v Practioners in Marketing Ltd* [1971] 2 All ER 216 (CA) at 224.

[64] This failed in *Hounslow London Borough Council v Twickenham Garden Developments* [1971] Ch 413 (Megarry J).

[65] See eg *Hounslow London Borough Council v Twickenham Garden Developments* [1971] Ch 413 (Megarry J) where building contractors could not build without the repudiating defendant's consent to their entry to the property, and if they did not build the obligation to pay would never arise; *Attica Sea Carriers Corp v Ferrostaal Poseidon Bulk Reederei (The Puerto Buitrago)* [1976] 1 Lloyd's Rep 250 (CA), where Orr LJ and Browne LJ held that owners' right to charter hire did not arise until the charterers had repaired the vessel; *Telephone Rentals plc v Burges Salmon* (CA), 9 April 1987, where the provision of telephony services required the defendant to consent to hire and to allow installation on their premises. Most employment cases will also fall into this category, and the employee will be confined to damages: see the discussion in *Masood v Zahoor* [2008] EWHC 1034 (Ch) (Smith J) at para 279, but see *Geys v Société Générale, London Branch* [2012] UKSC 23, where it was decided that even in employment cases the contract does not automatically come to an end, Lord Sumption dissenting on the grounds that where cooperation was required the contract did automatically terminate upon repudiation

up possession puts an end to the right to hire, in contrast with a time charter.[66] In a case of telephone answering machine supply, where the defendant repudiated before the machine had been installed and just a few days after order, the claimant was, unsurprisingly, restricted to claiming damages.[67]

(ii) The Legitimate Interest Rule

Although not strictly a matter of the law of contract damages, it should be observed that, as foreshadowed above, although Lord Reid in *White and Carter* rejected the suggestion that 'a person is only entitled to enforce his contractual rights in a reasonable way, and that a court will not support an attempt to enforce them in an unreasonable way',[68] he did, obiter, identify a possible exception. The claimant cannot continue to perform and claim under the action for an agreed sum (or, presumably, specific performance) if the claimant has no 'no legitimate interest, financial or otherwise' in performance of the contract because terminating will be 'equally advantageous to him' and therefore cannot insist on the alternative remedy of the agreed sum.[69]

This suggestion of a 'legitimate interest' test for specific remedies was taken up and applied in subsequent case law, but is very narrow and the burden falls on the defendant to prove its application in a particular case.[70] In foreign jurisdictions, however, there is a broader mitigation-type of rule applicable to whether a claimant can affirm that applies even to an action for an agreed sum.[71]

16.4 The Claimant Sourcing or Not Sourcing a Replacement or Repair

A. Market Replacement and Repair

Where there is an available market that can minimise the claimant supplier or buyer's losses, the claimant will be deemed where reasonable to have had prompt

---

by the defendant. See also *Brown v Southall & Knight* [1980] IRLR 130 (EAT) and *Attica Sea Carriers Corp v Ferrostaal Poseidon Bulk Reederei (The Puerto Buitrago)* [1976] 1 Lloyd's Rep 250 (CA) Lord Denning MR at 255.

[66] *Isabella Shipowner SA v Shagang Shipping Co Ltd (The Aquafaith)* [2012] EWHC 1077 (Comm) (Cooke J) at paras 37 and 40.

[67] *Robophone Facilities Ltd v Blank* [1966] 1 WLR 1428 (CA).

[68] [1962] AC 413 at 430.

[69] [1962] AC 413 at 431. Discussed in *Stocznia Gdanska SA v Latvian Shipping Co* [1995] 2 Lloyd's Rep 592 (Clarke J) at 600–602; *Ocean Marine Navigation Ltd v Koch Carbon Inc (The Dynamic)* [2003] 2 Lloyd's Rep 693 (Simon J).

[70] See especially *Isabella Shipowner SA v Shagang Shipping Co Ltd (The Aquafaith)* [2012] EWHC 1077 (Comm) (Cooke J) for discussion and demonstration of how limited the exception is. The exception was successfully applied in *Attica Sea Carriers Corp v Ferrostaal Poseidon Bulk Reederei (The Puerto Buitrago)* [1976] 1 Lloyd's Rep 250 (CA) by Denning MR and Browne LJ (Orr LJ and Browne LJ relied on an alternative basis); and in *Clea Shipping Corp v Bulk Oil International Ltd (The Alaskan Trader)* [1984] 1 All ER 129 (Lloyd J) at 136 ff.

[71] See *Clarke v Marsiglia* (1845) 1 Denio 317 (NY), and see the Uniform Commercial Code s-709(1) (b) in relation to the seller's action for the price.

recourse to the market in finding a replacement customer or supplier. This arises out of the mitigatory principle, and is the basis of the prima facie measure in non-supply, defective supply and non-acceptance sale of goods cases, as well as repudiation of charterparty and other cases.[72] Similarly, the damages in an employee dismissal claim must take account of the alternative employment that the claimant either did or could have been expected to (or will) secure,[73] and in claims for loss of use of money the court will presume that the claimant suffered loss equal to but not greater than the cost of borrowing alternative money.[74]

Sometimes, unconventional or unobvious resort to the market will still be taken into account as mitigatory action caused by the breach. In one case a claimant was able to cure its short-fall in delivery of coal because a later vessel ran aground in mud and the authorities therefore permitted its being made lighter by the offloading from that vessel of replacement coal. This was taken into account in the calculation of damages.[75]

And in the leading case of *British Westinghouse Co v Underground Electric Rys Co of London*,[76] where a buyer of deficient turbines replaced them, after a few years, with a new model better even than the turbines initially promised, and the savings made by the new turbines' additional efficiency meant that they paid for themselves, the continuing loss was, from the date of the replacement, avoided.[77]

B. Delaying the Replacement or Repair

Waiting beyond the date of breach where reasonable in the circumstances, and not for independent commercial reasons, will be causally insignificant and not prevent recovery of actual losses.[78] However, if it is not a reasonable mitigatory act, then it will be disregarded as a speculation (see below in section 16.5).

C. Squandering the Replacement or Repair

An employee who obtains a replacement job and then loses it through his or her own fault cannot claim for wages lost that would have been avoided if the replacement job had been kept, as his or her own unreasonable actions break the chain of causation.[79]

---

[72] See chapter four, section 4.2C; chapter five, section 5.1A; and chapter seventeen, section 17.1B for a full discussion.

[73] See above chapter five n 50 and accompanying text.

[74] *Equitas Ltd v Walsham Bros & Co Ltd* [2013] EWHC 3264 (Comm) (Males J) at para 123.

[75] *Montevideo Gas and Drydock Co Ltd v Clan Line Steamers Ltd* [1921] 6 Ll L Rep 539 (Roche J), decision affirmed [1921] 8 Ll L Rep 192 (CA)

[76] *British Westinghouse Electric & Manufacturing Co Ltd v Underground Electric Railways Co of London Ltd* [1912] AC 673 (HL).

[77] The issue of betterment is discussed above in chapter four, section 4.4B.

[78] See chapter seventeen.

[79] *Courthaulds Northern Spinning Ltd v Moosa* [1984] ICR 218 (EAT); *Mabey Plant Hire Ltd v Richens* (CA), 6 May 1993.

D. Spending Too Much or Making an Unnecessary Replacement

The tort cases of car damage and temporary replacements have explored this point at the highest level. Where a car owner pays additional costs to obtain a replacement hire vehicle on finance, those additional costs are irrecoverable[80] (unless the car-owner could not afford to do it any other way[81]). However, provided the replacement vehicle is reasonable and the repairer carefully selected, the claimant's recovery is not restricted merely because the repairs ended up taking a long time.[82] (Conversely, if a car-owner in fact does not incur the cost of repair, it is often still recoverable: see sections 16.7A and 16.10E(ii).) For cases in other areas on spending too much on repairs, see above.[83]

E. Non-Market Solutions

Often the mitigatory act will not involve a mere market replacement. Sometimes, the claimant will have had an opportunity to get something from a specific third party that was almost as good as it should have had. In *Joliffe v Charles Coleman & Co*,[84] the claimant failed to mitigate when it rejected an offer from the landlord of a tenancy not much worse than the statutory tenancy the defendant solicitor should have procured. Similarly, in *Herrmann v Withers LLP*,[85] the claimants could have significantly mitigated the problem of not having a statutory right of access to the communal garden near their new £6.8m Knightsbridge home by obtaining an 80-year licence assignable to occupiers for a little over £25,000. (Something a little less than this had been offered to the claimants, and it was found that these terms would have been available if the price had been met by the claimants.) The claimants were therefore awarded the £25,000 they would have paid for the licence if they had pursued that option, plus the £10,000 legal costs they would have incurred to proceed down that route and the £65,000 difference in property value there would have been between the licence and the statutory right.[86] This course would have significantly increased the value of the property, and therefore decreased the loss suffered (the difference between the price paid and the value of property obtained).[87]

Alternative sources of income (other than simple market replacement) are discussed below at section 16.6.

---

[80] *Dimond v Lovell* [2002] 1 AC 384 (HL).
[81] See below in section 16.7B.
[82] *Daily Office Cleaning Contractors Ltd v Shefford* [1977] RTR 361 (Stabb QC).
[83] Chapter four n 262.
[84] *Joliffe v Charles Coleman & Co* (1971) 219 EG 1608 (Browne J).
[85] *Herrmann v Withers LLP* [2012] EWHC 1492 (Ch) (Newey J).
[86] Although actually the comparison should have been between the rice paid and the value with the licence.
[87] See also *Dent v Davis Blank Furniss* [2001] Lloyd's Rep PN 534 (Blackburne J), where the claimant was in fact able to eliminate some of the unwanted commons registration status of the land.

16.5 Speculation by the Claimant

The concept of speculation is fundamental to a number of actions that are treated as breaking the chain of causation, and to having a more sophisticated understanding of what the law means by a reasonable (non-chain-breaking) and unreasonable (chain-breaking) action.

A. Delaying Sale of Defective/Unwanted Goods or Purchase of a Replacement

(i) Contract of Sale Cases[88]

Where there is no good reason for delaying sale of defective property, and/or purchase of replacement property/sale to a replacement purchaser (such good reasons including that the defect was latent, the claimant was pressing the defendant for performance, there was no available market etc[89]), the claimant will be deemed to have gone to the market promptly whether or not it did so, because any delay is or would be 'speculation' or 'speculative',[90] *res inter alios acta* and the claimant's 'own change of mind'.[91] As Goff J put it, this is the claimant's 'own business decision independent of the wrong; and the consequences of that decision are his. If he judges the market correctly, he reaps the benefit; if he judges it incorrectly, then the extra cost falls upon him'.[92] Such speculation is therefore at the claimant's 'own risk' and 'to his account',[93] and it is 'down to him'[94] and 'of its own making'.[95]

Crucially (Goff J again) 'It does not matter ... that his decision was a reasonable one, or was a sensible business decision, taken with a view of reducing the impact upon him of the legal wrong committed by the shipowners'.[96] Thus when asking whether an action was reasonable and so does not break the chain of causation, a special sense of 'reasonable' is meant. It does not mean sensible or having a reason,

---

[88] See Michael G Bridge, 'Market damages in sale of goods cases—anticipatory repudiation and mitigation' [1994] *JBL*152.

[89] See below in chapter seventeen, section 17.3.

[90] *Transfield Shipping Inc v Mercator Shipping Inc (The Achilleas)* [2007] 2 Lloyd's Rep 555 (CA) Rix LJ at para 102 respectively. Also *Glencore Energy UK Ltd v Transworld Oil Ltd* [2010] EWHC 141 (Comm) (Blair J) at para 75 (although the step to be taken there was promptly closing out a hedge, not resorting to a goods market).

[91] *South Australia Asset Management Corp v York Montague Ltd* [1997] 1 AC 191 (HL) Lord Hoffmann at 221.

[92] *Koch Marine Inc v D'Amica Societa di Navigazione Arl (The Elena D'Amico)* [1980] 1 Lloyd's Rep 75 (Goff J) at 89 and *Glory Wealth Shipping Pte Ltd v Korea Line Corp* [2011] EWHC 1819 (Comm) (Blair J) at para 16.

[93] *Golden Strait Corp v Nippon Yusen Kubishika Kaisha (The Golden Victory)* [2007] 2 AC 353 (HL) per Lord Brown at para 79.

[94] *Kaines (UK) Ltd v Osterreichische Warenhandelsgesellschaft Austrowaren GmbH* [1993] Lloyd's Rep 1 (CA) Bingham LJ at 11, quoted with approval by Lord Brown in *Golden Strait Corp v Nippon Yusen Kubishika Kaisha (The Golden Victory)* [2007] 2 AC 353 (HL) at para 79.

[95] *Asamera Oil Corporation Ltd v Sea Oil & General Corporation* [1979] 1 SCR 633 (SC of Canada).

[96] *Koch Marine Inc v D'Amica Societa di Navigazione Arl (The Elena D'Amico)* [1980] 1 Lloyd's Rep 75 (Goff J) at 89; *Habton Farms v Nimmo* [2003] EWCA Civ 68 (CA) per Clarke LJ at para 92.

rather it means acting sensibly *in response to and not independently of the wrong.* As Toulson J has observed:

> Whether the innocent party thereafter in fact enters into a substitute contract is a separate matter. He has, in effect, a second choice whether to enter the market similar to the choice which first existed at the time of the original contract, but at the new prevailing rate instead of the contract rate (the difference being the basis of the normal measure of damages). The *option* to stay out of the market arises from the breach, but it does not follow that there is a causal nexus between the breach and a *decision* by the innocent party to stay out of the market, so as to make the guilty party responsible for that decision and its consequences. The guilty party is not liable to the innocent party for the effect of market changes occurring after the innocent party has had a free choice whether to re-enter the market, nor is the innocent party required to give credit to the guilty party for any subsequent market movement in favour of the innocent party.[97]

Thus, eg, in *Jones v Just* the claimant was entitled to have disregarded the profits made by deferring sale of defective goods after discovery of the defect and therefore benefiting from a rise in the market for hemp.[98]

(ii) Misrepresentation, Deceit and Negligent Advice Cases

The same approach is applied to the similar question of when the claimant could be expected to sell property it was induced to purchase by the claimant's wrongful advice or representations. Hobhouse LJ in *Downs v Chappell* in the Court of Appeal found that the claimant's decision not to sell the property at a particular point after the deceit or misrepresentation had been discovered, even if acting 'reasonably', was 'their choice, freely made, and they cannot hold the defendants responsible if the choice has turned out to have been commercially unwise' because by that point 'The causative effect of the defendants' faults was exhausted'.[99]

Thus it has been held that when buyers claim damages in the United States for securities fraud, they are entitled to damages measured at the date of discovery of the fraud whether or not they actually sold their securities then:

> The plaintiff will not be able to avail himself of any further decrease in the value of the security after that date. So also the defendant should not be able to avail itself of any increase in the value of the stock after that date.[100]

> By continuing to hold the stock after that date [the buyer] has, in effect, made a second investment decision unrelated to his initial decision to purchase the stock … what happens after this second decision has no bearing whatsoever on the measure of plaintiff's damages.[101]

---

[97] *Dampskibsselskabet 'Norden' A/S v Andre & Compagnie SA* [2003] 1 Lloyd's Rep 287 (Toulson J) at para 42.

[98] *Jones v Just* (1868) LR 3 QB 197.

[99] *Downs v Chappell* [1997] 1 WLR 426 (CA) at 437. A dictum of Hobhouse LJ in *Downs v Chappell* in relation to the measure of loss was disapproved in *Smith New Court Securities Ltd v Scrimgeour Vickers (Asset Management) Ltd* [1997] AC 254 (HL) but the decision of *Downs v Chappell* remains intact. Cf *Watts v Morrow* [1991] 1 WLR 1421 (CA) Bingham LJ at 1445.

[100] *Cant v AG Becker & Co, Inc* 379 F Supp 972 (1974) (Northern District of Illinois), in relation to an action under rule 10-5(b) of the Securities Exchange Act of 1974 (US).

[101] *Harris v American Investment Co* 523 F 2d 220 (1975) (US Court of Appeals 8th Circuit). See also *Kerr v Danier Leather Inc* (2004) CanLII 8186 (Ontario Superior Court of Justice) (appeal allowed on

And in the negligent misadvice case of *Gestmin SGPS SA v Credit Suisse (UK) Ltd*, Leggatt J held (obiter, as breach was not found) that where there is market on which to sell the property the claimant was induced to buy, even if the claimant did not in fact sell the property 'this can be seen as the claimant's free choice and any subsequent gain or loss can properly be regarded as a consequence of the claimant's trading decision to retain the property rather than the defendant's wrong'.[102]

(iii) Property Damage

This approach to speculation has also been applied following property damage in the important tort case of *Blue Circle Industries v Ministry of Defence*.[103] In that case, from the date by which the claimant had cleaned up its radioactively contaminated land and could have sold it, the decision not to do so was a 'speculation' and any loss or gain resulting from it was not part of a 'continuous transaction' with the tort: on the date on which a sale could have been expected the risk 'switch[es] back' to the claimant.[104]

B. Delaying Making a Replacement Sale

Exactly the same principle applies in cases of non-acceptance by buyers, where it is the seller who has to go into the market to sell. Waiting, rather than promptly procuring a replacement buyer, where one is available, is an 'independent market decision',[105] and a 'speculation' and the positive or negative consequences for the seller will be ignored,[106] unless the claimant had a good reason that was related to the defendant's breach.[107] In each case there will

> come a time at which it could properly be held that the decision not to sell ... was a market decision independent of the breach of warranty. Once that moment [is reached], the correct approach would in my opinion be to deduct the market value at that time from the contract price and to award the difference (if any) as damages for breach of warranty of authority.[108]

---

liability (2005) 77 OR (3d) 321 (Ontario Court of Appeal), further appeal dismissed [2007] 3 SCR 331 (Supreme Court of Canada), both appellate courts declining to consider the damages issues).

[102] *Gestmin SGPS SA v Credit Suisse (UK) Ltd* [2013] EWHC 3560 (Comm) (Leggatt J) at para 186.
[103] *Blue Circle Industries plc v Ministry of Defence* [1989] 2 Ch 289 (CA).
[104] Ibid at 321–22.
[105] *Habton Farms (an unlimited company) v Nimmo* [2003] EWCA Civ 68 (CA) Clarke LJ at para 92, also paras 62, 86, 89–90, 95 and 97, and Auld LJ at para 129. (Breach of warranty of authority by a purported agent of the buyer, but damages correctly measured as if the case were one of non-acceptance).
[106] *Jamal v Moolla Dawood Sons & Co* [1916] 1 AC 175 (PC) Lord Wrenbury at 179, discussed and quoted above in chapter five, section 5.1A(iv).
[107] See below in chapter seventeen, section 17.3.
[108] *Habton Farms (an unlimited company) v Nimmo* [2003] EWCA Civ 68 Clarke LJ at para 100, also Auld LJ at para 128.

As in cases of making a market decision not to buy a replacement,

> it would be irrelevant whether the decision [whether or not] to sell at that time was reasonable or unreasonable because ... the decision whether or not to sell would not be caused by the breach but would be independent of it.[109]

C. Not Selling Readily Marketable Goods

With highly marketable and disposable goods, it will sometimes be found that holding those goods after the date of acquisition is per se an independent market decision at the claimant's own risk, and so breaks the chain of causation. In this minority of cases, if the property then manifests a latent defect later, or is harmed for some other reason, the loss will not be recoverable, as the decision to hold the property rather than trade it immediately broke the chain of causation. This is discussed further below,[110] and is rare. For example, ordinarily it is only after a defect has become patent that holding goods will be treated as a speculation that breaks the chain of causation (as discussed in the following section).

D. Selling before Discovery of the Defect or Misstatement

Whilst a failure to sell until the buyer has discovered the defect or misstatement will rarely break the chain of causation, an actual sale before the date of discovery will usually be taken into account as fixing the claimant's loss. Such an act, in ignorance of the problem affecting the property, is not an act in mitigation per se, because the claimant does not know that there is anything to mitigate, and might arguably be said to be an independent speculative action of the claimant. Nevertheless, the likelihood is that such a sale will be taken into account and the claimant will not be able to measure loss by reference to a notional sale at the later date of discovery of the problem. (Indeed, at least under certain North American statutory securities causes of action, if the claimant sells shares before the misrepresentation is discovered by the market, ie both buys and sells on the artificial market, then the claimant cannot recover any damages.[111])

16.6 Money Made by the Claimant Post-Breach

A. Immediate Income through the Transaction Induced by the Defendant

Plainly a claimant who complains of being induced to part with money in a transaction cannot claim the loss of the money without giving credit for the (albeit unwanted)

---

[109] Ibid Clarke LJ at para 100.
[110] See below at text to chapter seventeen, section 17.2B(ii).
[111] *Pearson v Boliden Ltd* (2002) 222 DLR (4th) 453 (British Columbia CA) at para 92, approved in *Kerr v Leather Inc* (2004) CanLII 8186 (Ontario Superior Court of Justice) at paras 322 and 345 (appeal allowed on liability (2005) 77 OR (3d) 321 (Ontario Court of Appeal), further appeal dismissed [2007] 3 SCR 331 (Supreme Court of Canada), both appellate courts declining to consider the damages issues).

benefits received in the transaction itself, most obviously the property purchased or business acquired. Thus the usual measure of loss on a 'no transaction' case (a case where but for the breach the claimant would not have entered into the transaction) is the difference between the expenditure incurred and the property, savings or other value received.[112] A claimant induced to make a sale must give credit for money received, and a lender induced to lend must give credit for repayments made.

Such income from the transaction includes tax advantages or credits received as a result of a purchase,[113] or (in one case) a payment of £3,000 made by a bank to the claimant on sale of the claimant's home in a case where but for the defendant solicitor's wrong the bank would not have had any right to repossess the home (and would therefore not have made the payment).[114]

(i) A Loan Advance is Credited against Any Loss[115]

As a result, being induced to take out a loan does not of itself give rise to any loss at all, as the amount of the liability is offset by the amount of the advance.[116] Any loss results from the costs of extrication from the loan (eg early repayment charges) or the costs of borrowing until redemption of the loan is permitted (if not immediate). Any loss of the loan monies by the claimant by spending them unwisely, even if the claimant would not have done so if it had not taken out the loan, will rarely be the responsibility of the defendant valuer or other professional who caused the loan, as the defendant will rarely have a duty to protect the claimant from itself and it is the claimant's choice whether it spends the money (which, after all, it had and could have kept, and instead had value from).[117]

The opposite position is not so simple: a *lender* may but will not necessarily suffer a loss upon advancing funds, even though it receives the debtor's debt in return. Whether the lender suffers a loss upon making the loan depends upon whether the bundle of rights acquired by the lender, in particular the value of the borrower's covenant to repay (the debt) and the value of rights to any security, are greater than the sum advanced. It may be that a loss is only suffered at a later date than the date of advance (eg after the borrower's covenant has become less valuable or the value of the security has reduced).[118]

---

[112] See further above in chapter three, section 3.1B(i).

[113] *Levison v Farin* [1978] 2 All ER 1129 (Gibson J); *Capita Alternative Fund Services (Guernsey) Ltd v Drivers Jonas (a firm)* [2012] EWCA Civ 1407.

[114] *Jarvis v T Richards & Co*, 30 July 1980, 124 *Sol Jo* 793 (Nourse J).

[115] As the general point of whether a debt must be credited as an asset when calculating loss, see below in section 16.10G(iii).

[116] *Galoo v Bright Grahame Murray* [1994] 1 WLR 1360 (CA); *MacMahon v Hamilton* [2002] Lloyd's Rep PN 33 (Northern Ireland HC); *Moore v Zerfahs* [1999] Lloyd's Rep PN 144 (CA).

[117] *Saddington v Colleys Professional Services* [1995] EGCS 109, [1999] Lloyd's Rep PN 140 (CA); *Moore v Zerfahs* [1999] Lloyd's Rep PN 144 (CA). Also *R v Investors Compensation Scheme Ltd, ex parte Bowden* [1996] AC 261 (HL). For the converse point as to whether a defendant can complain that a claimant would have spent money even but for the breach, see chapter eleven, section 11.2D and following.

[118] *Nykredit Mortgage Bank plc v Edward Erdman Group Ltd (No 2)* [1997] WLR 1627 (HL). Compare *Axa Insurance Ltd v Akther & Darby* [2010] 1 WLR 1662 (CA). The relevant principles are summarised in *Arrowhead Capital Finance Ltd v KPMG LLP* [2012] EWHC 1801 (Comm) (Males QC) at paras 75–80.

B. Later Income through the Unwanted Transaction Induced by the Defendant

Generally speaking, where a claimant seeks to recover for losses on a transaction it must give credit for receipts.

Thus, if the defendant's supplying defective goods leads to the claimant making profit from supplying spares (to those who bought the claimant's product incorporating the defendant's defective goods), such profit should be taken into account.[119]

In *Needler Finance v Taber*, a claimant who had been mis-sold a pension transfer did not have to give credit for the shares he'd received on demutualisation of the new pension holding.[120] It is difficult to see why this was a collateral benefit and not to be taken into account. Similarly doubtful, is a Canadian Supreme Court decision by which a claimant, who would have sold his old property within six months had the defendant vendor of a new property completed, was not required to give credit for the value increase on the old property between the date of breach and the date of judgment, even though his damages included the value increase on the new property between the same dates.[121]

Easier to justify is *Jewelowski v Propp*, where the claimant was fraudulently induced to lend £1,000 on a debenture and only received £257 out of the liquidation of the borrower, but did not have to give credit for the £600 profit made buying the debtor company's assets cheaply from the receiver and selling them on.[122] This latter step was speculative and an independent commercial decision of the claimant, albeit the opportunity was afforded by circumstances resulting from the defendant's breach. Likewise in *Hussey v Eels* the claimant purchaser of a defective property who instead of selling it, sought and obtained planning permission increasing its value, did not have to give credit for his profit.[123]

A similar result was reached by the Court of Appeal in *Primavera v Allied Dunbar Assurance plc*.[124] Bad tax advice led a claimant to fail to take sufficient money from his business as salary rather than dividends, and so he did not have a particular tax-free lump-sum remaining available from his pension at a certain date in 1995 (the remainder having to be taken by taxable annuity). The claimant then discovered the correct position, including as to the true effect of the relevant legislation, and was able to make the tax-free withdrawal, albeit in 2000, five years later than

---

[119] *GKN Centrax Gears Ltd v Matbro Ltd* [1976] 2 Lloyd's Rep 555 (CA), although no award was made here because the profit was found to have been offset by loss due to inconvenience and interruption.

[120] *Needler Financial Services Ltd v Taber* [2002] 3 All ER 501 (Morritt VC). But see *Rubenstein v HSBC Bank plc* [2012] EWCA Civ 1184, discussed below in n 294.

[121] *Semelhago v Paramadevan* [1996] 2 SCR 415 (SC of Canada). Nor was the claimant required to give credit for the savings in mortgage costs that were made by non-delivery of the property. The court's rationale was that the damages were in lieu of specific performance, and if specific performance had been ordered the claimant would have obtained the property at trial without having to give credit for anything. This approach differs from that in English law, where damages in lieu of specific performance are not made on any different measure to common law damages. See further chapter one, section 1.2B(iii), above.

[122] *Jewelowski v Propp* [1944] KB 510 (Lewis J). Cf *Komercni Banka AS v Stone and Rolls Ltd* [2003] 1 Lloyd's Rep 383 (Toulson J) obiter at para 167: a 'smart later purchase' must be disregarded. Contrast *Cockburn v Trusts and Guarantee Co* (1917) 55 SCR 264 (SC of Canada).

[123] *Hussey v Eels* [1990] 2 QB 227 (CA), discussed above at chapter three n 40.

[124] *Primavera v Allied Dunbar Assurance plc* [2002] EWCA Civ 1327.

planned. In the meantime, the value of the fund had had almost doubled from nearly £800,000 to nearly £1.5m, the claimant having only made a further £140,000 of contributions. The claimant nevertheless claimed £101,000, the amount by which the fund was worth less (after tax) than it would have been in 1995, when he had planned to make the withdrawal, plus £140,000 for the additional contributions made that would not have been made. It is clear that damages should be assessed as at no later date than 2000, because all reasonable claimants would mitigate their loss by taking the lump sum then, and so the claimant's retention of the fund after that date without taking the lump sum should be at his own risk. However, that the Court of Appeal chose the 1995 date and awarded £101,000[125] requires some explanation.

The central question is whether failure to take a lump sum in 1995 broke the chain of causation and should be treated as putting the risk of future consequences (good or bad) on the claimant. Otherwise, failing to take a lump sum in 1995 was a reasonable act of mitigation and part of the continuous run of events with the breach, and so damages should be assessed as in 2000. As Mance LJ explained,[126] had there been no misrepresentation as to the legislative cap on the lump sum, it might be said that all reasonable claimants would have foregone a lump sum in 1995 and preferred the relatively easy cure of taking the necessary amounts of salary out of the company for the necessary period of years. Accordingly, damages would have been assessed on the basis of the later date when the reasonable claimant would have successfully taken enough salary out and then drawn the lump sum tax free. However, given the misrepresentation as to the cap (the truth as to which was only learned in 1997), a reasonable claimant would not have thought in 1995 that taking further salary from the company would solve the problem, would have seen the problem as insoluble, and could be expected to take the lower lump sum in 1995, with any other course of action being a speculation at his own risk as to the value going up or down. The 1995 date was therefore correct.

However although a claimant induced by breach to sell something must give credit for the money received, it need not give credit for profits made by investing that money in a further venture, as that is the product of an independent decision.[127]

(i) Return of the Money Paid Out by the Claimant

Of course, as in lender cases, if a claimant is induced to part with money and the money is returned, the claimant must give credit for that. However, there are limits to this principle. Certainly in the deceit context, it has been noted that if a defendant obtains money from the claimant and uses it to repay a debt to the claimant that it would otherwise have defaulted upon, nevertheless the claimant need not give credit for the receipt and can recover the full amount paid out/stolen.[128] Repayment of

---

[125] Given that the 1995 date was adopted, the court property disregarded the further £140,000 of contributions made after that date, because if they were to be taken into account then the benefit made during that period would also have to be taken into account (and that benefit wiped out the contributions).

[126] Ibid at paras 39–45.

[127] *Komercni Banka AS v Stone and Rolls Ltd* [2003] 1 Lloyd's Rep 383 (Toulson J) obiter at para 167.

[128] Ibid at paras 170–71.

an otherwise bad debt owed by the defendant itself is not treated as a value to be credited. The same may be true where the bad debt is owed by a third party and discharged by the defendant.[129]

C. Income through Other Transactions Induced by the Defendant's Breaches

Difficult questions arise where the defendant's breach is responsible for the claimant entering into several transactions, only some of which were loss-making. Where the transactions are all connected, the court will sometimes require the profitable transactions to be taken into account.[130] However, there is clear authority in *Brown v KMR Services Ltd*, concerning different breaches by negligent advice from members' agents in different years under different contracts, that where there are separate breaches of contract, the claimant is entitled to bring into account the results of one particular breach and not the results of other breaches for which no claim is made (or which may indeed be time barred).[131]

D. Making Money in Alternative Ways

(i) Collateral Earnings

Where a claimant has found other ways to make money, that money will often not have to be taken into account in assessing loss. Thus, although a dismissed employee's alternative employment must be taken into account, his profiting from investments in equities unrelated to that new employment need not (even though such investments had been forbidden under the defendant's employment and so in that sense they only arose from the dismissal).[132] Eg a dismissed employee with spare time who then buys a lottery ticket cannot claim the cost of the ticket but need not account in the damages calculation for the winnings.[133] Similarly, a charterer was not required to bring into account bunker profits made on the substitute charter it took to replace that breached by the defendant shipowner.[134]

In one case a claimant's ship lost passengers due to the defendant's delay in discharging its vessel, but most of the passengers fortuitously ended up travelling

---

[129] Ibid obiter at para 171.

[130] *Bartlett v Barclays Bank Trust Co Ltd* [1980] 1 Ch 515 (Brightman J) at 538 (breach of trust) and *Hulbert v Avens* [2003] EWHC 76 (Ch) (Richard Seymour QC) at para 56 (breach of trust). And cf *Van Wagner UK Ltd v Brown* [2005] EWHC 1505 (Ch) (David Kitchin QC) at para 79 (breach of fiduciary duty).

[131] *Brown v KMR Services Ltd* [1995] 4 All ER 598 (CA) Hobhouse LJ at 641 (Peter Gibson LJ agreeing), Stuart-Smith LJ dissenting at 623 and agreeing with the first instance decision at [1994] 4 All ER 385 (Gatehouse J) at 411. And see *Attorney General of Zambia v Meer Care & Desai (a firm)* [2007] EWHC 1540 (Ch) (Peter Smith J) at paras 27–33.

[132] *Lavarack v Woods of Colchester Ltd* [1967] 1 QB 278 (CA).

[133] The same point is made as to a lottery ticket purchased after personal injury in the Law Commission's, *Damages for Personal Injury: Medical, Nursing and Other Expenses; Collateral Benefits* (Law Com No 262) (November 1999) at 100–101.

[134] *Famosa Shpping Co Ltd v Armada Bulk Carriers Ltd (The Fanis)* [1994] 1 Lloyd's Rep 633 (Mance J).

on another ship part-owned by some of the claimants. The court found that the claimant can still claim for the lost profit and needn't bring this additional revenue into account.[135] It may well be that the claimants did not receive the same benefit from the passengers travelling on the other vessel, either because they did not own the second vessel (although some of them owned some of it), or because the supply exceeded demand (ie the vessels were full) so the claimants overall lost a volume of profitable carriage.[136] Alternatively, this may be explicable on the same basis that spares are often ignored as *res inter alios acta*.[137]

(ii) Not a Break in the Chain of Causation

In contrast, where a lessor deprived a trader of trade to its retail kiosk in Goodge Street London Underground station (by closing the exit next to it), and consequently trade at the trader's bureau de change kiosk in the same station picked up, that *did* have to be taken into account when calculating the net loss.[138] Similarly, a property developer whose finance was sabotaged by the defendant in breach of contract probably would have had to take into account the profit from a contract with a housing trust entered into as an alternative means of realising the property's development potential.[139] And a shipowner was required to take into account profits it made by substituting the vessel that should have been chartered to the defendant into a pre-existing charter with a different charterer.[140]

In one case, the claimant was also able partially to mitigate its loss in relation to the non-delivered gas coal by using the wrongly delivered steam coal, and this was taken into account.[141] In another case, the claimant was able to mix wet sugar into dry sugar to make it more saleable, and this was taken into account in assessing the damage suffered.[142] And where a supplier refused to supply gas and the buyer set up in production itself, then if the gas works project ended up being profitable because of its ultimate sale value, this was to be taken into account and so the buyer had suffered no loss.[143]

A personal injury case is also instructive: the claimant driving instruction business owner was injured and so reduced his business expansion, but a few years later was able cheaply to buy a driving simulator he would have taken more expensively on hire-purchase. When claiming for lost profits through not having the simulator, the

---

[135] *Jebsen v East and West India Dock Co* (1875) LR 10 CP 300, approved in *British Westinghouse Electric & Manufacturing Co Ltd v Underground Electric Railways Co of London* [1912] AC 673 (HL).

[136] See above chapter five, section 5.2.

[137] See below in section 16.7A(ii).

[138] *Platt v London Underground Ltd* [2001] 2 EGLR 121 (Ch) (Neuberger J).

[139] *Red River UK Ltd v Sheikh* [2010] EWHC 1100 (Ch) (Henderson J) obiter at para 168.

[140] *Zodiac Maritime Agencies Ltd v Fortescue Metals Group Ltd (The Kildare)* [2011] 2 Lloyd's Rep 360 (Steel J) at paras 67 ff.

[141] *Montevideo Gas and Drydock Co Ltd v Clan Line Steamers Ltd* (1921) 6 Ll L Rep 539 (Roche J), decision affirmed (1921) 8 Ll L Rep 192 (CA).

[142] *Redpath Industries Ltd v The Cisco* (1993) 110 DLR (4th) 583. Similar steps were not reasonable or expected in *CHS Inc Iberica SL v Far East Marine SA (M/V Devon)* [2012] EWHC 3747 (Comm) (Cooke J).

[143] *Erie County Natural Gas and Fuel Co Ltd v Samuel S Carroll* [1911] 1 AC 105 (PC), approved in *British Westinghouse Electric & Manufacturing Co Ltd v Underground Electric Railways Co of London Ltd* [1912] AC 673 (HL).

claimant was required to bring into account the profits later made from the simulator, the purchase merely being that of a prudent business man.[144]

(iii) Duty to Mitigate

In some cases, there may even be a duty to pursue an alternative means of profit. In one case, a developer who did not get an option to purchase neighbouring land should have proceeded promptly with a smaller development on the land it already had.[145]

E. Non-Alternative Income

Where the claimant makes money in a way that is not an alternative means of obtaining performance, and that money would therefore have been earned even if the defendant had not breached, the income need not be taken into account as it was not factually caused by the breach. Thus a claimant who opens a new business but would have done so alongside the old business need not deduct its profits from its claim for lost profits on the old business.[146] This is the issue of supply and demand discussed above.[147]

16.7 Impecuniosity and Other Special Characteristics of the Claimant

A. The Claimant Doing Work In-house or 'Making Do'

In the same way that additional cost resulting from particular circumstances of the claimant (eg impecuniosity) will be irrecoverable if too remote or *res inter alios acta*, similarly a reduction in costs resulting from particular circumstances will also not be taken into account if *res inter alios acta*. The test is that 'if the plaintiff has been able to avoid suffering a particular head of loss by a process which is not too remote (as is insurance), the plaintiff will not be entitled to recover in respect of that avoided loss'[148] and conversely if the plaintiff has avoided loss by a remote or collateral process (such as insurance), the avoidance is ignored.

(i) Doing Work In-house

If a claimant performs repair work in-house, and so avoids the full costs of a third party repairer, the claimant can nevertheless recover the market cost of third party

---

[144] *Bellingham v Dhillon* [1973] QB 304 (CA).
[145] *Joyce v Bowman Law Ltd* [2010] EWHC 251 (Ch) (Vos J).
[146] *Karas v Rowlett* [1944] SCR 1 (SC of Canada).
[147] See chapter five, section 5.2.
[148] Lord Hobhouse in *Dimond v Lovell* [2002] 1 AC 384 (HL) at 406. The term 'remote' here encompasses legal causation generally: the disregarding of insurance is usually explained by the latter and not the former principle.

repairs,[149] unless the claimant being able to do this was within the contemplation of the parties and/or is not *res inter alios acta*.

(ii) Having Spares

Similarly, a claimant's replacement vehicles will usually be irrelevant and the claimant will still be entitled to recover damages for loss of use while a vehicle is out of action.[150] And if a claimant charterer, upon the defendant shipowner failing to charter a particular type of vessel to it, decided to reorganise its fleet so as not to operate a vessel of that type rather than engaging a replacement, that is to be disregarded and the claimant can still recover the normal costs of chartering a replacement, although those costs were not in that case incurred.[151]

(iii) Selling on at Cost Price

Often, where a claimant for its own reasons sells goods on at cost price, that is *res inter alios acta* and the claimant can nevertheless recover from the defendant additional sums it had to pay for replacement goods (even though that additional cost was recouped from the claimant's customers and no profits were lost).[152]

B. Impecuniosity

Often some loss is caused by the claimant's lack of funds, in circumstances in which if the claimant were more pecunious the damage resulting from the defendant's breach could have been halted early or otherwise lessened or prevented. The modern approach, after the House of Lords decision in the tort case of *Lagden v O'Connor*,[153] is simply to apply the rules of causation, remoteness and mitigation in the ordinary way: a claimant will recover its actual loss provided it acted reasonably (ie has not failed to mitigate) given the circumstances including the impecuniosity, and provided any impecuniosity is foreseeable (ie not too remote), as will usually be the case.

The general principles as regards the duty to mitigate are therefore that 'A plaintiff who is obliged to mitigate is not obliged, in order to reduce the damages, to do

---

[149] *Jones v Stroud District Council* [1986] 1 WLR 1141 (CA); *Coles v Hetherton* [2012] EWHC 1599 (Comm) (Cooke J) at para 31.

[150] See above text to chapter six, section 6.5B(i), and *Jebsen v East and West India Dock Co* (1875) LR 10 CP 300. Of course, *not* having a spare may well render a resulting loss too remote: *Hadley v Baxendale* (1854) 9 Exch 341.

[151] *Koch Marine Inc v D'Amica Societa di Navigazione Arl (The Elena D'Amico)* [1980] 1 Lloyd's Rep 75 (Goff J) at 90.

[152] *Diamond Cutting Works Federation Ltd v Triefus & Co* [1956] 1 Lloyd's Rep 216 (Barry J) and *Clark v Macourt* [2013] HCA 56 (HC of Australia), both discussed in relation to this point in chapter four, section 4.4C.

[153] *Lagden v O'Connor* [2004] 1 AC 1067 (HL), replacing the earlier rule from *Dredger Liesbosch (Owners) v SS Edison (Owners) (The Liesbosch)* [1933] AC 449 (HL) against recovery for losses resulting from impecuniosity in many circumstances. See also *Alcoa Minerals of Jamaica Inc v Broderick* [2002] 1 AC 371 (PC).

that which he cannot afford to do'[154] and as regards causation the principle is that 'The wrongdoer must take his victim *talem qualim* and if the position of the latter is aggravated because he is without the means of mitigating it, so much the worse for the wrongdoer'.[155]

(i) Paying on Credit

By the *Lagden* decision, an impecunious claimant who needs a temporary car after an accident can recover the additional costs of hiring one on credit if he or she cannot afford to do so otherwise[156] (but not if he or she can afford not to use credit or it is otherwise unreasonable,[157] and not to the extent that the finance charges are unreasonably high[158]). And a company that needed to buy a replacement machinery part, after the defendant supplier's raw material damaged the machine, acted reasonably in purchasing on hire purchase, and so the hire purchase cost, including financing charges, was recoverable.[159]

(ii) Having to Sell Up

If the defendant's breach means that the claimant cannot afford to continue with a building project and so sells the property, the consequences must all be taken into account.[160] Similarly, if a buyer of defective property cannot afford to repair and then sells the property instead, but at a higher price, that must be taken into account.[161]

(iii) Not Being able to Pay for Repair or Replacement

A claimant who lost the opportunity to buy goods worth nearly £40,000 at auction for £2,500 recovered the entirety of the lost profit as damages because he did not have the money to buy replacement goods and the defendant solicitors were well aware of his impecuniosity.[162] In a solicitor's negligence case the defendant failed to secure a flat for the claimant on her divorce, which she would have sold to purchase another, and the defendant was liable for a replacement at the date of trial.[163] However, in one case where a solicitor's negligence led a client to buy (and live in) an unworkable business, the rental and other living expenses incurred after the client had sold the business, caused because the client's family couldn't afford

---

[154] *Dodd Properties (Kent) Ltd v Canterbury City Council* [1980] 1 WLR 433 (CA) Megaw LJ at 453.
[155] *The Liesbosch* [1933] AC 449 (HL) Lord Wright at 452. See also *Robbins of Putney Ltd v Meek* [1971] RTR 345 (Stephenson J) at 349, where the defendant buyer had to take the claimant seller as it found him 'with the maximum limit foxed for their overdraft and with their lack of liquid capital'.
[156] Also *W v Veolia Environmental Services (UK) plc* [2011] EWHC 2020 (QB) (Mackie QC).
[157] *Dimond v Lovell* [2002] 1 AC 384 (HL) at 402 and 406–7; *Opoku v Tintas* (CA), 5 July 2013.
[158] *Compania Financiera Soleada SA v Hamoor Tanker Corp Inc (The Borag)* [1981] 1 WLR 274 (CA).
[159] *Bacon v Cooper (Metals) Ltd* [1982] 1 All ER 397 (Cantley J). And see *Wroth v Tyler* [1974] Ch 30 (Megarry J) in relation to the purchase of land.
[160] *Doran v Delaney* [1999] 1 IR 303 (Irish High Court).
[161] Obiter Mustill LJ in *Hussey v Eels* [1990] 2 QB 227 (CA) at 240–41.
[162] *Thomas Eggar Verrall Bowles (a firm) v Rice*, 21 December 1999 (Rimer J).
[163] *Jarvis v T Richards & Co*, 30 July 1980, 124 *Sol Jo* 793 (Nourse J).

to buy what they wanted, were held to be unforeseeable and outside the solicitor's responsibility and too remote.[164]

It will often be reasonable for an impecunious claimant to await acceptance of liability by the defendant's insurers[165] or the outcome of the trial and the resulting payment from the defendant before incurring repair costs, even though they will be greater by then[166] and this will lead to a greater period of hire of a replacement.[167] Where the accruing losses are great, however, the claimant may be expected to scrimp and save to afford the repairs or other rectification work.[168]

Where impecuniosity means that a claimant could not proceed with works until the insurer paid up, and the insurer wrongfully delayed, the impecuniosity will not turn what is a bad case for damages (because the nature of insurance means that there can be no damages for late payment by an insurer) into a good one.[169]

(iv) Other Cases

In a contract claim against an insurance broker, the damage to the business caused by the lack of responding insurance cover, but exacerbated by the claimant's poor cash flow, was recoverable.[170] Where a claimant had limited finances, and it was reasonable for it not to borrow money, its damages were not limited on the basis that it should have pressed on with its development without awaiting the outcome of the litigation against the defendant construction contractor or designer.[171] And where the lost profits caused by the defendant led a claimant to default on a mortgage and lose its land, the lost profits were recoverable but the consequences of not earning them were held to be too remote.[172]

(v) The Claimant Being Out of Funds to the Defendant

Even if, strictly speaking, the claimant can afford to purchase a replacement or cure, it may be reasonable, where the claimant has pre-paid the defendant, for the claimant to await the outcome of the dispute with the defendant rather than be doubly out of pocket for the same goods or on the same transaction. It seems that

---

[164] *Scott & Kennedys Law LLP v Vertex Law LLP* [2011] EWHC 3808 (Ch) (Vos J).

[165] *Martindale v Duncan* [1973] 1 WLR 574 (CA).

[166] *Cory & Son Ltd v Wingate Investment (London Colney) Ltd* (1980) 17 BLR 104 (CA); *Dodd Properties (Kent) Ltd v Canterbury City Council* [1980] 1 WLR 433 (CA); *Burns v MAN Automotive (Aust) Pty Ltd* (1986) 161 CLR 653 (HC of Australia); *Syrett v Carr & Neave (a firm)* [1990] 2 EGLR 161 (Bowsher QC); *Leahy v Rawson* [2004] 3 IR 1 (Irish High Court). Also *Alcoa Minerals of Jamaica Inc v Herbert Broderick* [2002] 1 AC 371 (PC) (tort of nuisance).

[167] *Mattocks v Mann* [1993] RTR 13 (CA). (*Ramwade Ltd v WJ Emson & Co Ltd* [1987] RTR 72 (CA) must now be considered wrong in the light of *Lagden v O'Connor* [2004] 1 AC 1067 (HL).)

[168] *Opoku v Tintas* (CA), 5 July 2013.

[169] *Sprung v Royal Insurance (UK) Ltd* [1999] Lloyd's Rep IR 111 (CA) Evans LJ at 118.

[170] *Arbory Group Ltd v West Craven Insurance Services (a firm)* [2007] PNLR 23 (Grenfell J).

[171] *Bevan Investments Ltd v Blackhall and Struthers (No 2)* [1978] 2 NZLR 97 (NZCA); *Aldgate Construction Co Ltd v Unibar Plumbing & Heating Ltd* (2010) 130 Con LR 190 (Akenhead J). Cf *Zakrzewski v Chas J Odhams & Sons* [1981] 2 EGLR 15 (Rougier QC); *Attorney General v Geothermal Produce New Zealand Ltd* [1987] 2 NZLR 348 (New Zealand CA).

[172] *Freedhoff v Pomalift Industries Ltd* (1971) 19 DLR (3d) 153 (Ontario CA). As to whether insolvency caused by the claimant will be too remote, see above in chapter seven, section 7.4.

this argument was accepted in some early nineteenth-century cases[173] and supported by some comments of Atkin LJ in the early twentieth century that are on point,[174] but rejected in the case of *Startup v Cortazzi*.[175] The proper approach nowadays is probably that having pre-paid is a relevant consideration as to what is reasonable but does not automatically justify not resorting to the market with fresh money for a replacement.[176]

(vi) The Claimant Having Ear-marked Funds

A further step on from the point set out in the previous sub-section is the argument that it is much more reasonable to expect a disappointed buyer who has not pre-paid to purchase a replacement promptly than to expect an owner whose property has been damaged or destroyed to do so. The buyer has money set aside for the purchase and clearly has access to the market. The owner of damaged or destroyed property may be able to afford a replacement but will not have earmarked funds for the purpose, and it will not be such an obvious and affordable step. Accordingly, the courts will less automatically look to market replacement in destruction than non-delivery cases.[177]

16.8 Unreasonable Claimant Conduct

A. Generally

As Lord Reid has observed in the context of tortiously caused personal injury:

> if the injured man acts unreasonably, he cannot hold the defender liable for injury caused by his own unreasonable conduct. His unreasonable conduct is novus actus interveniens. The chain of causation has been broken and what follows must be regarded as caused by his own conduct and not by the defender's fault or the disability caused by it.[178]

The majority of unreasonable claimant conduct is discussed in the sections above in this chapter in relation to the failure to mitigate by going to the market or repairing property or similar. Further miscellaneous types of claimant carelessness/recklessness are discussed in this section.

---

[173] See the reasoning in *Shepherd v Johnson* (1802) 2 East 211; *Gainsford v Carroll* (1824) 2 B & C 624; *Shaw v Holland* (1846) 15 M & W 136.

[174] *Aronson v Mologa Holzindustrie AG* (1927) 32 Com Cas 276 (CA) Atkin LJ at 289–91. In that case the claimant had pre-paid and indeed property had passed but had then been converted by the seller selling it another. Cf *Wroth v Tyler* [1974] Ch 30 (Megarry J) at 57.

[175] *Startup v Cortazzi* (1835) 2 CM & R 165.

[176] See the discussion in *Industria Azucarera Nacional SA v Empresa Exportadora de Azucar*, 29 February 1980 (Mustill J).

[177] This point is made by H McGregor, *McGregor on Damages*, 18th edn (London, Sweet & Maxwell, 2009) at para 7-038.

[178] *McKew v Holland, Hammond & Cubitts (Scotland) Ltd* [1969] 3 All ER 1621 (HL).

B. Claimant Mismanagement and Trading Losses

If the claimant's mismanagement of its business and intransigence contributed to a loss of value and therefore a lower sum being earned upon the sale of the business after a delay, the loss is irrecoverable to that extent from the defendant who caused the delay.[179] Nevertheless, trading losses during a delay will not break the chain of causation or be too remote if the defendant was responsible for the lack of profitability (for example because it induced the purchase by a misrepresentation as to profitability[180]), or the decrease in the value of the business is otherwise not too remote.[181]

C. Failing to Prosecute the Claim against the Defendant Promptly

In cases of continuing loss it may be said that failure to prosecute the claim promptly is a failure to mitigate and should lead to disallowance of a period of losses that wouldn't have been suffered if the claimant had pursued its rights more promptly. In one sense this is a difficult argument where the losses could also have been avoided by the defendant satisfying its liability earlier;[182] there is a clear analogy with cases of interest awards which effectively compensate for loss of use of money and which (under the statutory award) can be reduced for delay.[183]

D. Intentional or Reckless Self-harm

Ordinarily the deliberate self-harm of the claimant, following breach, will breach any chain of causation. 'The law does not generally treat us as our brother's keeper, responsible for what he may choose to do to his own disadvantage. It is his choice'.[184] However, if the defendant's duty was to protect the claimant against that harm, the defendant will be responsible and it would in such cases be 'self-contradictory to say that the breach could not have been a cause of the harm because the victim caused it to himself'.[185] The same was true where the defendant employer's breach caused a workplace accident that led to the claimant suffering from depression, which six years later led to the claimant committing suicide. The defendant was held liable to the administrator of the deceased's estate.[186] Likewise if the defendant had been the

---

[179] *British & Commonwealth Holdings plc v Quadrex Holdings Inc* (CA), 10 April 1995. See also *Galoo v Bright Grahame Murray* [1994] 1 WLR 1360 (CA).

[180] *Esso Petroleum Co Ltd v Mardon* [1976] QB 801 (CA), discussed and distinguished in *Intervention Board for Agricultural Produce v Leidig* [2000] Lloyd's Rep PN 144 (CA) Simon Brown LJ at 148.

[181] *Tom Hoskins plc v EMW Law (a firm)* [2010] EWHC 479 (Ch) (Floyd J) at paras 143–56.

[182] See eg the comments of Ormrod LJ in *Esso Petroleum Co Ltd v Mardon* [1976] 1 QB 801 (CA) at 829. However there is no legal obligation to pay damages before judgment: see text to chapter one, section 1.2C(i), above.

[183] See above chapter seven n 93. See also Toulson LJ in the deceit case of *Parabola Investments Ltd v Browallia Cal Ltd* [2011] 1 QB 477 (CA) at para 59.

[184] Lord Bingham in *Corr v IBC Vehicles Ltd* [2008] 1 AC 884 (HL) at 901.

[185] *Reeves v Commissioner of Police of the Metropolis* [2000] 1 AC 360 (HL) Lord Hoffmann at 368 (tort).

[186] *Corr v IBC Vehicles Ltd* [2008] 1 AC 884 (HL).

only gambling outlet it would have been liable in *Calvert v William Hill Credit Ltd* for letting the claimant gamble after agreeing not to.[187] (As it was, there were other gambling outlets which had not made such a promise, so the claim failed as even but for the breach the claimant would still have lost his money gambling elsewhere and the defendant had no duty to prevent such gambling with third parties.) Obtaining a loan therefore cannot be loss even if the claimant spends the money it would not otherwise have had and therefore spent, unless the defendant has a duty to protect the claimant from itself.[188]

E. Other Conduct

Where a lender of money carelessly fails to investigate the status of indicative commitments of the borrowing company's chairman, that will not break the chain of causation[189] (although it may lead to a reduction for contributory negligence, where applicable). However, where a claimant time charterer's agent released a bill of lading following the defendant shipowner's master's wrongly marking the bill of lading, in breach of charter, this might have broken the chain of causation.[190] A bank that fails to close out third party swaps promptly upon the default of the fixed rate borrower whose borrowing the swaps are hedging has acted unreasonably and damages will be calculated as if it closed out promptly.[191]

16.9 Post-Breach Dealings with the Defendant

A. Delaying Other Recourse While Seeking a Deal with the Defendant

In many cases, even if not all claimants would have sought to do a deal with the defendant (such that the claimant is deemed to have done so whether it did or not), it will be reasonable for a claimant to do so such that if the claimant does that will be taken into account for the purpose of calculating damages and not treated as a collateral matter to be disregarded. Thus where the claimant reasonably delays its resort to the market while pressing the defendant for performance or seeking to do a deal, losses will be assessed as at the date when those attempts are proven unsuccessful and the claimant should have gone to the market or sought alternative mitigation (and not at any earlier date such as the date of breach).[192]

---

[187] *Calvert v William Hill Credit Ltd* [2009] 1 Ch 330 (CA).
[188] See above section 16.6A(i).
[189] *County Ltd v Girozentrale Securities* [1996] 3 All ER 834 (CA).
[190] *Cosemar SA v Marimarna Shipping Co Ltd (The Mathew)* [1990] 2 Lloyd's Rep 323 (Steyn J) at 326: the arbitrators found a break in the chain but Steyn J did not rule on the point.
[191] Conceded by the bank in *Mortgage Agency Services Number One Ltd v Edward Symmons LLP* [2013] EWCA Civ 1590.
[192] See the discussion below in chapter seventeen, section 17.2C(i).

B. Actual Dealings with the Defendant

Similarly, if actual deals are done with the defendant or the defendant provides a benefit of some sort because of the breach, that will usually be taken into account. Thus if a buyer ends up buying the same goods from the same defendant seller but for a price lower than the market price (although higher than the contract price), this act is connected to the original contract and breach, and damages must be calculated on the basis of this price actually paid.[193] In *Esso Petroleum Co Ltd v Mardon*,[194] the claimant in fact accepted an offer from the defendant to reduce its rent, which partially mitigated the claimant's loss after purchasing a poor petrol station business in breach of the defendant's warranty and induced by the defendant's negligent representations. Other cases on payments or help from the defendant are discussed below in section 16.10.

C. Being Expected to Do a Deal with the Defendant

In some cases, the claimant does not do a deal with the defendant and that is held to be a failure to mitigate.

(i) Sale of Goods[195]

Where a buyer has rejected goods for a reason other than defective quality, and they are cheaper than the market replacement, the buyer may unreasonably fail to mitigate by not then buying those same goods from the seller.[196] In the leading case of *Payzu v Saunders*,[197] it was held unreasonable of the claimant buyer to refuse in a rising market to pay the cash that the seller was demanding in breach of the contract which provided for delivery on credit. In *The Solholt*,[198] a shipbuyer who terminated for late delivery on a rising market should have sought to purchase the ship from the breaching seller at the original (sub-market) price. In another sale case the buyer should have allowed the seller to cure the defect in a yacht.[199] And in a case of a dispute between a cotton seller and its financing bank, in which the latter converted the cotton, the claimant seller had failed to mitigate by unreasonably rejecting the

---

[193] *R Pagnan & Fratelli v Corbisa Industrial Agropacuaria Limitada* [1970] 1 WLR 1306 (CA). Further discussed by Mustill LJ in *Hussey v Eels* [1990] 2 QB 227 (CA) at 239, and by *Mobil North Sea Ltd v PJ Pipe and Valve Co (t/a PJ Valve Ltd)* [2001] EWCA Civ 741 Rix LJ at para 31 where he emphasised that in *Pagnan & Fratelli* 'The self-same goods and the self-same parties were involved'.

[194] *Esso Petroleum Co Ltd v Mardon* [1976] QB 801 (CA) at 816, 821 and 829.

[195] See further on this point MG Bridge, 'Mitigation of damages in contract and the meaning of avoidable loss' (1989) 105 LQR 398.

[196] *Heaven & Kesterton Ltd v Etablissements Francois Albiac & Compagnie* [1956] 2 Lloyd's Rep 316 (Devlin J) obiter at 321 (in that case the goods were defective).

[197] *Payzu v Saunders* [1919] 2 KB 581 (CA).

[198] *Sotiros Shipping Inc v Samiet Solholt (The Solholt)* [1983] 1 Lloyd's Rep 605 (CA).

[199] *Clegg v Andersson (t/a Nordic Marine)* [2002] EWHC 943 (QB) (Seymour QC) at para 61, appeal allowed as in fact the goods had been rejected [2003] EWCA Civ 320, [2003] 2 Lloyd's Rep 32 (CA).

bank's offer to sell the goods and keep the proceeds safe pending resolution of the dispute between them.[200]

In *Houndsditch Warehouse Co Ltd v Waltex Ltd*, had the offer been without prejudice to the right to damages, the buyer of men's braces should have accepted the offer to return the goods in return for the price,[201] although it could not be expected (or deemed) to have done so if the offer was in full and final settlement and therefore required the buyer to give up the right to damages.[202] However, courts have expressed the view that a buyer will rarely be expected in mitigation to agree to return the goods in exchange for the money paid for them, as this would not merely mitigate loss but would give up the right to the goods and to damages,[203] although this concern seems overstated and ultimately the question is fact-dependant.

Further, 'there may be cases where as a matter of fact it would be unreasonable to expect a plaintiff to consider any offer made in view of the treatment he has received from the defendant'.[204] Sometimes it will be reasonable to refuse the defendant's offer,[205] as when the offer to adjust the property to make it more suitable for the claimant was vague.[206]

(ii) Employment

It was unreasonable for the claimant to refuse the offer of re-engagement by his partners on the same terms as those prior to his technical wrongful dismissal in *Brace v Calder*,[207] and the Court of Appeal held the employee in *Wilding v BT plc*[208] to have acted unreasonably in refusing an offer of part-time re-employment (without compromising his claim for damages) following a discriminatory dismissal after a back injury.[209]

---

[200] *Uzinterimpex JSC v Standard Bank plc* [2008] 2 Lloyd's Rep 456 (CA).

[201] *Houndsditch Warehouse Co Ltd v Waltex Ltd* [1944] KB 579 (Stable J). It was held unreasonable not to pursue the negotiations and seek to clarify the offer and the claimants were deemed to have done so, although the savings that would have been made from such a deal and which fell to be deducted from the damages sum fell to be reduced because of the chance that the deal would not in fact have been done or would not have been reached for all the goods. *Strutt v Whitnell* [1975] 1 WLR 870 (CA) is more difficult for the reasons discussed below at text to n 202.

[202] *Houndsditch Warehouse Co Ltd v Waltex Ltd* [1944] KB 579 (Stable J). Compare the non-acceptance by a buyer case of *Velmore Estates Ltd v Roseberry Homes Ltd* [2006] EWHC 3061 (Rich QC) where for this reason there was no failure to mitigate in refusing a buyer's offer to complete. Also *Shindler v Northern Raincoat Co Ltd* [1960] 1 WLR 1038 (Diplock J) and *Bunge SA v Nidera BV* [2013] EWHC 84 (Comm) (Hamblen J). And see also the charterparty dispute of *UBC Chartering Ltd v Liepaya Shipping Co Ltd (The Liepaya)* [1999] 1 Lloyd's Rep 649 (Rix J) at 671, where the fact that the offer was not without prejudice was significant. And cf the employment case of *Shindler v Northern Raincoat Co Ltd* [1960] 1 WLR 1038 (Diplock J).

[203] *Strutt v Whitnell* [1975] 1 WLR 870 (CA); *Activa DPS Europe SARL v Pressure Seal Solutions Ltd (t/a Welltec Systems UK)* [2012] EWCA Civ 943 obiter.

[204] Bankes LJ in *Payzu v Saunders* [1919] 2 KB 581 (CA) at 588, also Scrutton LJ at 589.

[205] Eg *Golden Strait Corp v Nippon Yusen Kubishika Kaisha* [2006] 1 WLR 533 (CA). This issue was not disputed in the House of Lords. Also *Truk (UK) Ltd v Tokmakidis GmbH* [2000] 1 Lloyd's Rep 543 (Jack QC).

[206] *Albury Asset Rentals Ltd v Ash Manor Cheese Company Ltd* [2013] EWCA Civ 548.

[207] *Brace v Calder* [1895] 2 QB 253 (CA).

[208] *Wilding v British Telecommunications plc* [2002] IRLR 524 (CA).

[209] And see *Edwards v Society of Graphical and Allied Trades* [1971] Ch 354 (CA), where a union re-admitted its member after wrongfully excluding him.

However, it may be reasonable to refuse such employment where the re-employment offered is inferior to the previous employment in role, status or wage,[210] the employee no longer has any confidence in the employer,[211] the relationship has been irreparably damaged,[212] the employee can no longer do the job,[213] or the employee injured himself in the job and has no assurance that the system of work and supervision which prevailed at the time of the accident has changed.[214] Moreover, a claimant will not be expected to accept an offer of alternative employment from an employer where a condition of that offer is that all claims to unavoided damages are abandoned,[215] although the fact that the claimant is in litigation with the employer is not itself sufficient reason to refuse re-employment.[216]

(iii) Construction

The same principles have been applied in construction cases. As a general rule, 'the mere fact that an employer does not give the contractor an opportunity to rectify defects in the works will not always amount to a failure to mitigate the losses'[217] and the question will often depend upon 'whether it is reasonable for the Claimants now to say that in the light of the past events they do not want the Defendant to come back to the property to undertake any work at all'.[218] Indeed, in relation to residential works, Coulson QC observed that

> it would take a relatively extreme set of facts to persuade me that it was appropriate to deny a homeowner financial compensation for admitted defects, and leave him with no option but to employ the self-same contractor to carry out the necessary rectification works.[219]

---

[210] *Clayton-Greene v De Courville* (1920) 36 TLR 790 (McCardie J) (reasonable for an actor engaged to play the lead in a play to refuse a secondary part on artistic, suitability and career-development grounds); *Basnett v J & A Jackson Ltd* [1976] IRLR 154 (Crichton J); *F & G Cleaners Ltd v Saddington* (EAT), 16 August 2012 (reasonable to refuse engagement on a self-employed basis where entitled to employment transfer under TUPE regulations); *Whittaker v Unisys Australia Pty Ltd* [2010] VSC 9 (SC of Victoria). See also *Parker v Twentieth Century Fox Film Corp* 474 P 2d 689 (1970) (SC of California): the film studio cancelled the Los Angeles musical film 'Bloomer Girl' that it had engaged actress Shirley Maclaine (then Shirley Maclaine Parker) for, and she reasonably refused to appear instead in the Australian western they offered her 'Big Country, Big Man' for the same fee.

[211] *Jackson v Hayes Candy & Co Ltd* [1938] 4 All ER 353 (Du Parcq LJ); *Yetton v Eastwoods Froy Ltd* [1967] 1 WLR 104 (Blain J).

[212] *Payzu v Saunders* [1919] 2 KB 581 (CA) obiter Bankes LJ at 588–89; *Whittaker v Unisys Australia Pty Ltd* [2010] VSC 9 (SC of Victoria) obiter at para 174.

[213] *Emblem v Ingram Cactus Ltd* (CA), 5 November 1997.

[214] Ibid.

[215] *Shindler v Northern Raincoat Co Ltd* [1960] 1 WLR 1038 (Diplock J).

[216] *Wilding v British Telecommunications plc* [2002] IRLR 524 (CA); *F&G Cleaners Ltd v Saddington* (EAT), 16 August 2012, at para 27.

[217] *Woodlands Oak Ltd v Conwell* [2011] EWCA Civ 254 May J at para 22. Also *Connaught Restaurants Ltd v Indoor Leisure Ltd* [1992] 2 EGLR 252 (Bowsher QC), appeal allowed on a different point [1994] 4 All ER 834 (CA).

[218] *Iggleden v Fairview New Homes (Shooters Hill) Ltd* [2007] EWHC 1573 (TCC) (Coulson QC) at para 77.

[219] Ibid at para 79; *Melhuish & Saunders Ltd v Hurden* [2012] EWHC 3119 (TCC) (Havelock-Allen QC) at paras 104–6.

The builder's case will be all the weaker if it did not promptly offer to rectify the works, but rather merely raises the argument at trial of the homeowner's failure to mitigate by allowing him to cure the defects.[220]

However, in some cases, particularly where the defects were merely snagging items, failure to give the defendant the opportunity to rectify the defects will amount to a failure to mitigate and bar recovery of the third party cost of cure.[221] Indeed in some cases there will be an express contractual requirement that the customer give the contractor an opportunity to rectify the defects.[222] In one such case[223] the claimant was limited to recovery of what it would have cost the defendant to do the work, although that is best understood as a particular consequence of the express obligation to give the defendant the opportunity to do the work.[224]

(iv) Other Cases

In a charterparty case it was reasonable for the owner to reject the defendant's offer to re-hire,[225] although it won't always be reasonable to do so.[226] And in a share warranty and deceit case it was reasonable to reject an offer from the defendant after it had proved to be untrustworthy.[227]

In the tort cases of car damage it has been held reasonable to refuse the defendant's offer of a free car when the defendant does not sufficiently 'make clear the cost of hire to the Defendant for the purpose of enabling the Claimant to make a realistic comparison with the cost which he is incurring or about to incur',[228] although it will sometimes be unreasonable to refuse such an offer, especially where it is of a reasonable replacement and the claimant knows that to refuse 'will increase the ultimate burden on the defendant, regardless of the effect on his own position'.[229] Save in

---

[220] *Melhuish & Saunders Ltd v Hurden* [2012] EWHC 3119 (TCC) (Havelock-Allen QC) at para 106.

[221] *City Axis Ltd v Daniel P Jackson* (1998) 64 Con LR 84 (HHJ Toulmin); *Woodlands Oak Ltd v Conwell* [2011] EWCA Civ 254.

[222] *Pearce & High Ltd v Baxter* (1999) 66 Con LR 110 (CA). See also *Iggleden v Fairview New Homes (Shooters Hill) Ltd* [2007] EWHC 1573 (TCC) (Coulson QC) at para 76.

[223] *Pearce & High Ltd v Baxter* (1999) 66 Con LR 110 (CA).

[224] This is explicable on the basis that the express obligation displaces the ordinary application of the rule of mitigation, so the claimant is not debarred from recovering the cost of cure from a third party, but the defendant may counterclaim for the entire amount for which it is liable to the claimant (but would not have been had the claimant got the defendant to do the work) less the cost to the defendant of doing the work (saved by the claimant not having re-engaged the defendant), leaving a net recovery in the amount of the cost to the defendant of doing the work: ibid at 115–16 and 118.

[225] *UBC Chartering Ltd v Liepaya Shipping Co Ltd (The Liepaya)* [1999] 1 Lloyd's Rep 649 (Rix J) at 671. Likewise *Golden Strait Corp v Nippon Yusen Kubishika Kaisha (The Golden Victory)* [2007] 2 AC 353 (HL) Lord Carswell at para 52, summarising the arbitrator's decision (the owner had refused to rehire to the charterer unless the operation of the war clause was excluded and this was not found to have been unreasonable) which had not been appealed.

[226] *Sous Secretaire d'Etat au Ministaire des Travaux Publiques Charge de la Marine Marchande v W & R Barnet* (1924) 19 Ll L Rep 120 (Roche J).

[227] *Great Future International Ltd v Sealand Housing Corp* [2002] EWHC 2454 (Ch) (Lightman J) at para 149, appeal allowed on an evidential point [2002] EWCA Civ 1183, although the court also held that the offer was not a genuine and credible one.

[228] *Copley v Lawn* [2009] EWCA Civ 580 Longmore LJ at para 32(i).

[229] *Sayce v TNT (UK) Ltd* [2011] EWCA Civ 1583 Moore-Bick LJ at para 21, applying *Copley v Lawn* [2009] EWCA Civ 580. See also the discussion in *Albury Asset Rentals Ltd v Ash Manor Cheese Company Ltd* [2013] EWCA Civ 548 at paras 37–38.

the special situation in which there is an express obligation to give the defendant a second chance,[230] the cost to the defendant should be irrelevant: the claimant's obligation is to minimise its loss, including the cost of cure, but not to minimise the defendant's cost.

However, in the tort cases of replacement cars, the Court of Appeal has said, obiter, that where it is unreasonable to refuse the defendant's offer of a free replacement vehicle, the clamant can still recover the reasonable cost of repair as reflected by the cost to the defendant of doing the repairs,[231] although this has been doubted, again obiter, in a later Court of Appeal decision.[232] If it was unreasonable to refuse the offer of a free replacement, the claimant should not be able to recover any cost (as it would not have incurred one if it had taken the offer), and the fact that the defendant would have incurred a cost if the claimant had accepted the offer and has therefore saved money should be irrelevant to the claim for contract damages, which compensate for the claimant's loss.

Finally, and unsurprisingly, in one tort collision case, the victim's refusal of offers of assistance from the vessel which caused the accident *and* from a third party broke the chain of causation.[233]

D. Payments or Help from the Defendant

Payments made or care provided by the defendant (in contrast to many of those furnished by third parties, discussed in the next section) are to be taken into account. It has been said that at least part of the purpose of the rule permitting recovery despite third party voluntary care is to provide funds to pay the carer, which is unnecessary where the carer is the defendant himself,[234] and that payments by the defendant are treated in law as the defendant reducing its liability *pro tanto* by voluntary provision.[235]

Such voluntary payments are exemplified by payments made by defendant employers following wrongful injury to the claimant[236] or upon (or prior to) wrongful or unfair dismissal of the claimant.[237] Similarly, where a trade union re-admitted a

---

[230] See above at n 221 and accompanying text.
[231] *Copley v Lawn* [2009] EWCA Civ 580 Longmore LJ at para 30 and 32(ii).
[232] *Sayce v TNT UK Ltd* [2011] EWCA Civ 1583 Moore-Bick LJ at paras 27–29.
[233] *MV Mitera Marigo v MV Fritz Thyssen (The Fritz Thyssen)* [1967] 2 Lloyd's Rep 199 (CA). There does not seem to have been a claim for losses that would have occurred if the claimant had not unreasonably refused assistance, but in principle such losses should have been recoverable.
[234] *Hunt v Severs* [1994] 2 AC 350 (HL) Lord Bridge at 363.
[235] Ibid at 358.
[236] *Colledge v Bass Mitchells & Butlers Ltd* [1988] 1 All ER 536 (CA); *Hussain v New Taplow Paper Mills Ltd* [1988] 1 AC 514 (HL); *Williams v BOC Gases Ltd* (CA), 29 March 2000; *Gaca v Pirelli General plc* [2004] 1 WLR 2683 (CA). For non-employment cases, see *Hayden v Hayden* [1992] 1 WLR 986 (CA) (care provided by father after he caused injury); *Hunt v Severs* [1994] 2 AC 350 (HL) (care provided by defendant, who also recovered the costs of itself visiting the claimant).
[237] *Stocks v Magna Merchants Ltd* [1973] 1 WLR 1505 (Arnold J) (redundancy payment must be deducted from a wrongful dismissal award); approved *Aspden v Webbs Poultry and Meat Group (Holdings) Ltd* [1996] IRLR 521 (Sedley J); but see *Basnett v J & A Jackson Ltd* [1976] IRLR 154 (Crichton J). Awards for *unfair dismissal* would only be deducted from a claim for damages for *wrongful dismissal* if and to the extent that they cover the same loss: they did not in *O'Laoire v Jackel International*

wrongfully excluded member, the loss suffered was treated as having been reduced,[238] as it was where the seller of a business reduced the rent the claimant had to pay.[239]

(i) Payments by Third Parties for or on Behalf of the Defendant

In a contract case in which an employer had promised to insure the claimant geologist's life and did not do so but its parent company did, and the claimant was abducted and killed by Angolan rebels, the £123,000 payment by the insurer, although stated to be 'ex gratia', was properly to be taken into account as reducing the defendant's liability.[240] If a third party were to contribute to the claimant with the stated intention of benefiting the tortfeasor, the gift should be taken into account as in effect being made on account of the defendant.[241]

16.10 Receipt by the Claimant of Payments or Help from Third Parties (Including Insurance and State Assisstance)

There are often said to be two exceptions to the rule that benefits received must be taken into account, namely benevolence and insurance.[242] In truth the law is more complicated and broader than that would suggest, and these are just the main examples.[243]

A. Charity and Benevolence

Charity and other voluntary assistance by third parties will rarely be taken into account as reducing the claimant's loss. This rule evolved in personal injury cases, where there was an undisguised policy motivation of not deterring charity,[244] which

---

Ltd (No 2) [1991] ICR 718 (CA) or *Shove v Downs Surgical plc* [1984] 1 All ER 7 (Sheen J); they did in *Aspden v Webbs Poultry and Meat Group (Holdings) Ltd* [1996] IRLR 521 (Sedley J).

[238] *Edwards v Society of Graphical and Allied Trades* [1971] Ch 354 (CA).

[239] *Esso Petroleum Co Ltd v Mardon* [1976] QB 801 (CA).

[240] *Pope v Energem Mining (IOM) Ltd* [2011] EWCA Civ 1043 Rix LJ at para 38.

[241] *Zheng v Cai* (2009) 239 CLR 446 (HC of Australia), the majority at para 20 obiter. Cf the approach to payments by an insurer under a policy taken out by the defendant, below in section 16.10B(ii) and accompanying text.

[242] *Hunt v Severs* [1994] 2 AC 350 (HL) Lord Bridge at 358; *Dimond v Lovell* [2002] 1 AC 384 (HL) Lord Hoffmann at 400; *Gaca v Pirelli General plc* [2004] 1 WLR 2683 (CA) at para 11.

[243] Thus the discussion of NHS care in *Hunt v Severs* [1994] 2 AC 350 (HL) is explicable not merely as failing to fall within one of those two exceptions, as Lord Hoffmann says in *Dimond v Lovell* [2002] 1 AC 384 (HL) at 400, but because of the way state assistance is treated in the case law generally, as discussed below in section 16.10C. See further the comments of Staughton LJ in *Linden Gardens Trust Ltd v Lenesta Sludge Disposals Ltd* (1992) 30 Con LR 1 (CA) at 21.

[244] See the personal injury cases of *Liffen v Watson* [1940] 1 KB 556 (CA) (accommodation provided father, which may or may not ultimately be paid for); *Redpath v Belfast & County Down Railway* [1947] NI 167 (Northern Ireland KB, approved in *Hussain v New Taplow Paper Mills Ltd* [1988] 1 AC 514 (HL)) (a public subscription); *Parry v Cleaver* [1970] AC 1 (HL) at 14 and 29–31 (not a charity/benevolence case but these dicta are on the point); *Cunningham v Harrison* [1973] QB 942 (CA) (ex gratia payments by employer); *Donnelly v Joyce* [1974] QB 454 (CA) (mother providing care); *Hunt v Severs* [1994] 2 AC 350 (HL) (assistance from friends and relatives).

leads to a focus on the donor's intention. As one Australian judge pointed out, 'they are given for the benefit of the sufferer and not for the benefit of the wrongdoer'.[245] The fact that a third party 'out of kindness were to repair the injury and make no charge for it' is irrelevant and does not mean the claimant cannot claim for the cost of those repairs or the other loss suffered.[246] Thus if the claimant

> himself repairs the car[247] or a friend does so without charge, the Claimant is still entitled to recover the amount it would have cost him to have the car repaired had he gone out into the market for that purpose. If he can get a knock-down price for repairs by virtue of a particular relationship that he has, it is still open to him to claim the diminution in value of the car by reference to the market cost of repair.[248]

As Neill LJ observed, in a case of a council negligently approving plans that led to a property being dangerously defective,

> if property ... has been damaged to an extent which is proved and the court is satisfied that the property has been or will be repaired I do not consider that the court is further concerned with the question whether the owner has had to pay for the repairs out of his own pocket or whether the funds have come from some other source.[249]

(However, this may well go too far: it is certainly correct where the motivation is benevolence, or where there is some intra-group arrangement, but may not be where the third party had some other reason for helping, as the cases in the following sections show.)

Where the assistance is non-financial, leaving it out of account will mean that the claimant will be deemed to have paid the reasonable cost on the market of such assistance, and is entitled to recover that sum.[250] The same applies to cases of assistance provided to claimants who have suffered personal injury.[251]

---

[245] *Zheng v Cai* (2009) 239 CLR 446 (HC of Australia) the majority at para 19 quoting from *National Insurance Company of New Zealand Ltd v Espagne* (1961) 105 CLR 569 (HC of Australia) Windeyer J (and see further Dixon CJ at para 4 in *Espagne*, quoted with approval in *Parry v Cleaver* [1970] AC 1 (HL) at 29 and 37). In *Zheng*, a church made benevolent payments to the claimant voluntary worker and, allowing the appeal, they were held by the High Court of Australia not to be wages to be deducted from the claim. But things are different where the payment is deliberately for the benefit of the wrongdoer: see section 16.9D above.

[246] *The Endeavour* (1890) 6 Asp MC 511, 48 LTNS 636 (Sir James Hannen) obiter, approved by Neill LJ in *Jones v Stroud District Council* [1986] 1 WLR 1141 (CA) at 1150.

[247] Doing the work in-house is discussed above in section 16.7A.

[248] *Coles v Hetherton* [2012] EWHC 1599 (Comm) (Cooke J) at para 31, although the explanation given (that the cost of repairs is merely a measure of diminution in value) is wrong and the better explanation is that such particular circumstances are *res inter alios acta*. And compare *Daily Office Cleaning Contractors Ltd v Shefford* [1977] RTR 361 (Stabb QC), where the claimant only sought and only recovered the actual cost of a replacement car, which was at a reduced rate due to a good customer relationship.

[249] *Jones v Stroud District Council* [1986] 1 WLR 1141 (CA) at 1150–51.

[250] Eg *Donnelly v Joyce* [1974] QB 454 (CA); *Coles v Hetherton* [2012] EWHC 1599 (Comm) (Cooke J) at para 31.

[251] Although not affecting this underlying principle, since section 8 of the Administration of Justice Act 1982 was enacted, in Scotland in cases of family members providing necessary services to injured claimants the liability of the defendant to pay the claimant has been set out in statute, which imposes a liability on the claimant which did not previously exist to pass the cost of the services reimbursed by the defendant on to the third party. See the discussion in *Hunt v Severs* [1994] 2 AC 350 (HL) Lord Bridge at 363.

The rule also applies in the contractual damages context and has been correctly explained in that context in the following terms:

> In essence, it seems to me that the principle can be said to be based on the proposition that the gratuitous payment of money by third parties to the claimant is res inter alios acta, as between the claimants and the defendants.[252]

Thus a grant from the Department of the Environment indemnifying the claimant for its construction costs was disregarded in one claim against an architect for increasing the cost of the housing project, as being collateral and *res inter alios acta*.[253] And as Lord Griffiths observed in a construction negligence dispute,

> A very common example occurs in personal injury cases where the cost of medical treatment is borne by a relative; but that has never been seen as a reason why that sum should not ultimately be paid by the defendant if he is found liable for the injuries. The law regards who actually paid for the work necessary as a result of the defendant's breach of contract as a matter which is res inter alios acta so far as the defendant is concerned[254]

B. Insurance and Pension Pay-outs

(i) The Claimant's Insurance or Pension

Following the majority of the House of Lords' decision in the leading (tort) case of *Parry v Cleaver*,[255] which concerned a police disability pension which paid out after severe injury by the defendant, the general rule is that an insurance or pension policy paid for by the claimant is to be ignored. Although the reasoning in that decision has a large dose of policy in it, the fact that the claimant (or another linked to the claimant) has purchased this independent protection is nevertheless generally treated as too remote/collateral/*res inter alios acta*[256] (even though in personal injury cases the contract of employment between the claimant and the third party, by which the claimant suffered a loss of earnings, is of course not unconnected, because the claimant himself brings that into account to make his claim). The essence of this exception appears to be that the premium is paid by or on behalf of the claimant[257] and the insurance is the fruit of the claimant's own thrift and contracting.

---

[252] *Hamilton Jones v David & Snape (a firm)* [2004] 1 WLR 924 (Neuberger J) at para 74.

[253] *Design 5 v Keniston Housing Association Ltd* (1986) 10 Con LR 122 (HHJ David Smout). See also *Treml v Ernest W Gibson & Partners* [1984] 2 EGLR 162 (Popplewell J). And cf *Palatine Graphic Arts Co Ltd v Liverpool City Council* [1986] QB 335 (CA) on disregarding a development grant when calculating the compulsory purchase price.

[254] Lord Griffiths in *Linden Gardens Ltd v Lenesta Sludge Disposals Ltd* [1994] 1 AC 85 (HL) at 98.

[255] *Parry v Cleaver* [1970] AC 1 (HL), especially at 14. See also *Bradburn v Great Western Railway Co* (1874) LR 10 Exch 1; *Hobbs v Marlowe* [1978] AC 16 (HL); *Smoker v London Fire and Civil Defence Authority* [1991] 2 AC 502 (HL). But see *Ironield v Eastern Gas Board* [1964] 1 All ER 544 (Streatfield J) where the insurer did not participate through subrogation and the claimant (on behalf of the insured) recovered only for the insurance excess and loss of no-claims bonus.

[256] *Coles v Hetherton* [2013] EWCA Civ 1704 (CA) at para 36. An indemnity insurer (which the pension fund in *Parry v Cleaver* was not) will acquire subrogated rights against the defendant, and therefore there will be no double recovery.

[257] *Gaca v Pirelli General plc* [2004] 1 WLR 2683 (CA) Dyson LJ at paras 50–53.

Similarly in lender claims for professional negligence, the lender's recovery under a mortgage indemnity policy is not to be taken into account in calculating the damages payable by the professional.[258] A similar approach was reached where a central Lloyd's fund made payments to the claimant Lloyd's names to discharge the managing agents' liability to the names.[259] And a post-damage arrangement with an insurer, by which the insurer would pay for repairs if it was given all damages recovered in an (ultimately unsuccessful) action against a third party, was not taken into account.[260]

This means that where an insurer provides a car owner's replacement hire vehicle under the insurance policy for which the insured paid a premium before the accident damaging his car, the insurer's provision must be disregarded and, in effect, the court has to ask what the car owner's loss of use was without taking a replacement vehicle. This was made clear in *Bee v Jenson*.[261] The measure of loss of use applied in these cases is discussed below,[262] but will often (as in *Bee v Jenson*) be the spot hire cost of a replacement (thus allowing the insurer to recover its actual costs of a replacement but by the back door). Moreover, where reasonable repair costs are being ascertained, the court should look to the reasonable cost that the claimant, not its insurer, would pay.[263]

The principle has been applied in contract cases, such as wrongful dismissal cases where a disability or retirement pension will usually not be taken into account in a damages calculation, even if the pension was funded partly or wholly by the employer.[264] Thus in one case an ex-IBM employee claiming for wrongful dismissal did not have to give credit for the payments in fact received from his pension scheme during the reasonable notice period, when but for the wrongful dismissal he would still have been employed but not yet receiving his pension.[265] In that case the pension was a defined benefit retirement or termination pension plan entirely funded by the employer as part of his employment benefits, but the court nevertheless held

---

[258] *Bristol and West Building Society v May May & Merrimans (No 2)* [1997] 3 All ER 206 (Chadwick J); *Arab Bank plc v John D Wood Commercial Ltd* (11.11.99, CA); *Portman Building Society v Bevan Ashford* [2000] 1 EGLR 81 (CA). The difference between these policies and most insurance policies is that these are taken out in relation to the specific transaction (eg induced by the professional) and so might be said to be part and part of it (and further the premium is often paid by the borrower as a condition of the lending). Where, as is usual, the insurer is subrogated to the lender's claim then there is no room for double recovery or taking the insurance pay-out into account, but if for some reason there is no subrogation then it could be argued that the insurance is part and parcel of the relevant transaction and should be taken into account. Ultimately such arguments should be rejected. The premium (if paid by the lender) should not be recoverable in the ordinary case as the insurance is a speculation by the lender and should still be treated as *res inter alios acta*, and thus the benefits and costs of the insurance should not be for the defendant's account.

[259] *Deeny v Gooda Walker Ltd (No 3)* [1995] 1 WLR 1206 (Philips J) at 1210. The finding was obiter as the names in any event were found to have an obligation to reimburse the Lloyd's fund.

[260] *Naumann v Ford* [1985] 2 EGLR 70 (Price QC).

[261] *Bee v Jenson* [2007] 4 All ER 791 (CA). The insurer then (by subrogation) recovers the claimant's recovery for itself. See also *McAll v Brooks* [1984] RTR 99 (CA) and the discussions in *W v Veolia Environmental Services (UK) plc* [2011] EWHC 2020 (QB) (Mackie QC) and *Coles v Hetherton* [2012] EWHC 1599 (Comm) (Cooke J).

[262] See chapter six, section 6.5.

[263] *Coles v Hetherton* [2013] EWCA Civ 1704 (CA) at paras 42 and 44.

[264] *Hopkins v Norcross* [1993] 1 All ER 565 (David Latham QC).

[265] *Waterman v IBM Canada Ltd* 2011 BCCA 337 (British Columbia CA) and the other Canadian cases cited therein.

that it was not intended only to be a substitute for wages (and it was significant that the pension was a defined benefit and not, like some disability pensions, calculated as an indemnity of lost wages). If the disability pension is wholly funded by the employer and indemnifies for the lost income (ie is intended as salary *replacement*), it may well not be *res inter alios acta* to the wrongful dismissal.[266]

Likewise, an international sugar trader's pay-out from its insurance of its goods was *res inter alios acta* in a claim against the carrier for damage.[267]

A further consequence of this approach, by which any insurance pay-out is usually treated as *res inter alios acta*, is that a claimant will not be held to have failed to mitigate or broken the chain of causation by failing to take out insurance or to claim under it.

Of course, this is all subject to what the contract says. Where the contract expressly contemplates the operation of insurance, it will not be *res inter alios acta*.[268]

(ii) The Defendant's Insurance

However, where the defendant has caused injury to the claimant employee and the *defendant's* own health insurance scheme pays the claimant an equivalent of sick pay, those payments are to be taken into account.[269] But such insurance[270] or pension[271] is not to be taken into account where the claimant contributed to it.

(iii) Insurance Settlements

If a claimant is insured against a car accident or cargo loss and his insurer pays for a replacement vehicle or cargo, the insurer is subrogated to the claimant's rights against the defendant and can recover the costs as if the claimant had paid them and were seeking to recover them. The positions of the insured and insurer are conflated for these purposes.[272]

Provided the insurer settled the claimant's insurance claim in good faith, it will be able to recover from the defendant the payment it made to the claimant, using the claimant's rights to which it is subrogated, and the defendant is not entitled to 'rip up the settlement' and examine it in detail (by arguing that the claimant's loss is not reflected by the amount the insurer paid).[273] Even if the insurer might technically have refused the claim as not being within the policy limits, it can nevertheless

---

[266] *Sylvester v British Columbia* [1997] 2 SCR 315 (SC of Canada).

[267] *Redpath Industries Ltd v The Cisco* (1993) 110 DLR (4th) 583.

[268] *Bunge SA v Kyla Shipping Company Ltd* [2012] EWHC 3522 (Comm) (Flaux J) at para 78.

[269] *Hussain v New Taplow Paper Mills Ltd* [1988] 1 AC 514 (HL); *Page v Sheerness Steel plc* [1996] PIQR Q26 (CA) (the relevant part of the judgment is not included in the [1997] 1 WLR 652 and [1997] 1 All ER 673 reports, as to which see further the discussion in *Gaca v Pirelli General plc* [2004] 1 WLR 2683 (CA) at paras 47–48); *Gaca v Pirelli General plc* [2004] 1 WLR 2683 (CA); *Pope v Energem Mining (IOM) Ltd* [2011] EWCA Civ 1043 (contract claim). *McCamley v Cammell Laird Shipbuilders Ltd* [1990] 1 WLR 963 (CA) is wrongly decided in the light of *Hussain*, as was confirmed by the Court of Appeal in *Williams v BOC Gases Ltd* (CA), 29 March 2000, and in *Gaca v Pirelli*.

[270] See the discussion in *Gaca v Pirelli General plc* [2004] 1 WLR 2683 (CA) at para 50.

[271] *Smoker v London Fire and Civil Defence Authority* [1991] 2 AC 502 (HL).

[272] See eg *Bee v Jenson* [2007] 4 All ER 791 (CA) Longmore LJ at para 9.

[273] *King v Victoria Insurance Co Ltd* [1896] AC 250 (PC) Lord Hobhouse at 254.

recover the settlement if it acted reasonably in paying it, and the law will not treat it as a voluntary payment the loss of which must fall on the claimant (or, in this case, its insurers).[274] However, where the insurers have paid more than their policy limit (with a view to recovering the same from the defendant), the additional amount may be irrecoverable as a gratuitous payment that should not have been made.[275]

C. State Assistance

In contrast to private insurance schemes or benevolence, state social security benefits will usually be deducted from a damages award, especially where they are intended to replace the benefit that the defendant should have provided, such as unemployment benefit in a wrongful dismissal claim, and especially where the defendant has contributed to the benefit to protect against just the loss that forms part of the claim.[276] Such a benefit is not too remote or collateral,[277] and the state is not to be considered as equivalent to a private insurer.[278] (In personal injury and employee dismissal cases the position has been adjusted by legislation by which, although the benefits usually reduce the compensation payable by the defendant to the claimant, the defendant is obliged to reimburse the state for those benefits.[279])

Similarly, although private care and medical assistance provided by charity is ignored,[280] state medical assistance under the National Health Service or state-provided accommodation and care are to be taken into account.[281] However, a claimant will not be held to have failed to mitigate its loss by opting to pay privately rather than taking a freely available state-funded solution, as cases and legislation on care and accommodation following personal injury show.[282]

Sick pay or incapacity benefit paid by the state to an employee after dismissal will not affect the amount of the award by the employer if the sick pay would have been paid in addition to any wages if the employee had still been employed, but not otherwise.[283] Similarly, invalidity benefit will not be deducted if the invalidity was

---

[274] Ibid Lord Hobhouse at 255.

[275] *W v Veolia Environmental Services (UK) plc* [2011] EWHC 2020 (QB) (Mackie QC) at para 40.

[276] *Parsons v BNM Laboratories Ltd* [1964] 1 QB 95 (CA); *Westwood v Secretary of State for Employment* [1985] AC 20 (HL); *Hodgson v Trapp* [1989] AC 807 (HL). In unfair dismissal cases, the statutory discretion means that a tribunal need not adopt the all or nothing approach and can make a deduction for half the social security benefit received: *Rubenstein v McGloughlin* [1996] IRLR 557 (EAT).

[277] *Parsons v BNM Laboratories Ltd* [1964] 1 QB 95 (CA), Pearson LJ at 143–44.

[278] Lord Bridge in *Westwood v Secretary of State for Employment* [1985] AC 20 (HL) at 43. See also *Hodgson v Trapp* [1989] AC 807 (HL).

[279] Social Security (Recovery of Benefits) Act 1997; Employment Protection (Recoupment of Jobseeker's Allowance and Income Support) Regulations 1996 (SI 1996/2349) and the Employment Tribunals Act 1996 ss 16–17.

[280] See above section 16.10A.

[281] *Cunningham v Harrison* [1973] QB 942 (CA) at 952; *Hunt v Severs* [1994] 2 AC 350 (HL) obiter Lord Bridge at 360–61; *Sowden v Lodge* [2003] EWHC 588 (QB) (Andrew Smith J) at para 47.

[282] *Peters v East Midlands Strategic Health Authority* [2010] QB 48 (CA). And s 2(4) of the Law Reform (Personal Injuries) Act 1948 provides that it is not a failure to mitigate to 'go private' rather than opt for free NHS care.

[283] *Sun and Sand Ltd v Fitzjohn* [1979] ICR 268 (EAT) at 269 and see *Puglia v C James & Sons* [1996] IRLR 70 (EAT).

caused by the dismissal and but for the dismissal the employee would have been earning wages.[284]

D. Other Payments

(i) Payments or Assistance by a Group Company

If a group company covers the cost of repairs necessitated by the defendant's breach of contract, that is irrelevant to the calculation of the defendant's liability to the claimant.[285]

(ii) Payments or Assistance by a Joint Venture Company

The same is true if a joint venture agreement means that the claimant is part funded by a third party.[286]

(iii) Payments or Assistance by a Landlord

In *Gardner v Marsh & Parsons*, a surveyor was liable for the claimant having bought a property with undisclosed structural defects even though the claimant managed to get the landlord to pay for the repairs at no cost to the claimant.[287] This was because the landlord's paying, several years later after protracted negotiations, was not 'part of a continuous transaction' running from the negligence and purchase. However, in another case the claimant secured a substantial contribution from its landlord to remedial works necessitated by the defendant's negligent construction.[288] That sum was taken into account as reducing the builder's liability (the judge noting that it was 'neither gratuitous nor made out of love or affection'[289]).

(iv) Payments or Assistance by a Tenant

Where leased property is damaged by a third party to the lease, repairs to the property performed or paid for by the lessee will be factored into the damages calculation, as the lessor is only entitled to damage to its reversion and the lease must therefore be taken into account.[290] However, a lessor will not usually be treated as failing to mitigate by not pursing the lessee third party for repair costs if it did not in fact do so.[291]

---

[284] *Hilton International Hotels (UK) Ltd v Faraji* [1994] ICR 249 (EAT). But see *Puglia v C James & Sons* [1996] IRLR 70 (EAT) and *Morgans v Alpha Plus Security Ltd* [2005] ICR 125 (EAT).
[285] *Jones v Stroud District Council* [1986] 1 WLR 1141 (CA) (the company was owned by the claimant); *St Martin's Property Corp Ltd v Sir Robert McAlpine Ltd*, reported with *Linden Gardens Ltd v Lenesta Sludge Disposals Ltd* [1994] 1 AC 85 (HL).
[286] See also *John Harris Partnership v Groveworld Ltd* (1999) 75 Con LR 7 (Thornton QC) at para 71.
[287] *Gardner v Marsh & Parsons (a firm)* [1997] 1 WLR 489 (CA) at 503.
[288] *Linklaters Business Services v Sir Robert McAlpine Ltd* [2010] EWHC 2931 (TCC) (Akenhead J).
[289] At para 165.
[290] Eg *HSBC Rail (UK) Ltd v Network Rail Infrastructure Ltd* [2005] EWCA Civ 1437.
[291] *Prudential Assurance Co Ltd v McBains Cooper*, 27 June 2000 (Havery QC).

And if the claim is against the defendant tenant for breach of the covenant of repair, that a local authority or later tenant paid for repairs will be *res inter alios acta* the defendant tenant's breach of covenant.[292]

(v) Other Third Party Payments or Assistance

Certain types of recovery will stand to be taken into account. Where faulty software caused a local authority to undercharge its residents but it recouped the money the following year by adding the charge on to that year's charge, the authority could only recover interest to compensate for a year of being without the money.[293] However, a doctor who bought an assisted fertility practice with unusable sperm stocks, and then had to purchase replacement sperm, did not have to give credit for the fact that she was able to pass the cost on to her patients.[294]

Similarly where a bad investment was made on the misadvice of the defendant, an ex gratia payment made by the investment vehicle (AIG) was properly taken into account as being part of a continuous transaction with the investment itself.[295]

However, in another case a residential purchaser of land, who would not have gone through with the purchase had the surveyor advised of the use of 'mundic' (metalliferous mine waste) in construction of the property, managed (with the assistance of his local MP) to get his re-mortgage lender to drop the mortgage debt in exchange for assignment of the property. The claimant had therefore suffered no loss (the original loan being funded 100 per cent by mortgage), but the lapse of 11 years and the unusualness of the arrangement reached with a third party lender made the steps too remote to be taken into account, and so the claimant recovered substantial damages.[296]

And a claimant will not usually be expected to embark upon litigation against a third party, ie will not be in breach of the duty to mitigate for not doing so.[297]

E. Credit Agreements with Third Parties

(i) Simple Unconditional Credit

Simple credit agreements entered into by claimants, where the claimant actually incurs expenses by paying out money on repairs or similar, but then is reimbursed by a third party in return for an absolute liability to repay the third party, can be disregarded (unless the claimant wishes also to claim the costs of the credit as not

---

[292] *Smiley v Townshend* [1950] 2 KB 311 (CA) Denning LJ at 320; *Haviland v Long* [1952] 2 QB 80 (CA) Denning LJ at 84.

[293] *St Albans City and District Council v International Computers Ltd* [1996] 4 All ER 481 (CA).

[294] *Clark v Macourt* [2013] HCA 56 (HC of Australia), discussed in chapter 4 section 4.4C.

[295] *Rubenstein v HSBC Bank plc* [2012] EWCA Civ 1184 Rix LJ at paras 133–36, distinguishing *Needler Financial Services Ltd v Taber* [2002] 3 All ER 501 (Morritt VC) which is discussed above at n 120.

[296] *Devine v Jefferys* [2001] Lloyd's Rep PN 301 (Jack QC). The re-mortgage lender had also recovered damages from its surveyor.

[297] See below in section 16.10G(ii).

too remote[298]). They are equivalent to a simple loan. In this situation 'the loss [the claimant] has sustained remains the same irrespective of whether he has actually paid the expenses from his own pocket or converted them into a liability to a third party'.[299]

(ii) Credit Hire and Similar Agreements

In tortious car damage cases, a claimant will often not pay for the hire of a replacement car itself. Where the car hire is covered by insurance, the insurance must be disregarded as *res inter alios acta* and the claimant is treated as having paid for the care hire itself.[300]

Frequently, however, the claimant enters into a post-collision credit hire agreement with a third party under which the claimant is granted a hire car but liability to pay for it is deferred until after determination of the claim against the defendant. Although in practice the credit hire company treats the liability as contingent and does not pursue the hirer if the claim against the defendant fails,[301] the liability is still a legal liability.[302] It will often be reasonable for claimants to enter into such agreements.[303] It was held by the House of Lords in *Dimond v Lovell* that such agreements are distinguishable from insurance[304] and should be taken into account (ie are not *res inter alios acta*) in assessing damages. Accordingly, where the agreement is unenforceable (as in *Dimond v Lovell* itself), and the claimant has therefore got away without paying any hire costs or incurring any liability for hire costs, it cannot claim anything from the defendant for hire.[305] Where the agreement is enforceable the claimant can recover the hire component of the hire costs it has to pay the credit hire company (which is usually the same as the market rate for hire), ie excluding the part attributable to additional benefits, but the defendant is not liable to pay interest on the hire costs because the claimant is not out of pocket on the hire costs and has no interest liability to the credit hire provider.[306]

The Court of Appeal in *Burdis v Livsey* considered a similar unenforceable credit agreement, this time in relation to repair costs rather than temporary car hire.[307]

---

[298] See below in 16.7B(i).

[299] *Browning v The War Office* [1963] QB 750 (CA) Diplock LJ at 770. Cf *The Endeavour* (1890) 6 Asp MC 511, 48 LTNS 636 (Sir James Hannen).

[300] *McAll v Brooks* [1984] RTR 99 (CA); *Bee v Jenson* [2007] 4 All ER 791 (CA). See further above at text to n 260 and following.

[301] *Dimond v Lovell* [2002] 1 AC 384 (HL) Lord Nicholls at 390 and Lord Hoffmann at 395.

[302] *Giles v Thompson* [1994] 1 AC 142 (HL) Lord Mustill at 166–67.

[303] See further *Lagden v O'Connor* [2004] 1 AC 1067 (HL).

[304] *Dimond v Lovell* [2002] 1 AC 384 (HL) Lord Hobhouse at 406.

[305] *Dimond v Lovell* [2002] 1 AC 384 (HL); *Burdis v Livsey* [2003] QB 36 (CA) obiter at paras 58 and 86.

[306] *Giles v Thompson* Lord Mustill [1994] 1 AC 142 at 168. See also *Pattni v First Leicester Buses Ltd* [2011] EWCA Civ 1384 esp at para 61 ff, where interest was payable to the hire company by the claimant as that was the price of the credit the claimant received (since without the arrangement the claimant would have had to pay upfront). Save for impecunious claimants, this credit was not necessary to the mitigation and so not a cost the claimant was entitled to recover, and the Court refused to disregard the hire agreement and treat the claimant as if he had paid for the hire himself, in which case he would have been entitled to interest for loss of use of his money.

[307] *Burdis v Livsey* [2003] QB 36 (CA).

Dimond v Lovell was distinguished. The repair costs were recoverable. First, the agreement was held to be collateral/*res inter alios acta*[308] and so to be disregarded, meaning the claimant must be deemed to have incurred the repair costs itself and could recover them. This is suspect, however, as there was no basis for distinguishing *Dimond v Lovell*, and so the decision must be doubted. Moreover, the reasoning of the court is not followed through in all its conclusions, as it illogically disallowed the claim for interest,[309] whereas such an award of interest should follow from the ignoring of the credit agreement and the deeming the claimant to have paid the repair costs itself and was therefore out of pocket. Secondly, it was held that the rule against double recovery and rule of *res inter alios acta* do not apply in the same way to the cost of repairs—which cost (the court said) is mitigation of the immediately suffered diminution in value loss—as they do to the cost of temporary car hire—which cost (the court said) is mitigation of the consequential loss of use of the vehicle; and the cost of repairs is a measure of the immediately suffered harm and so recoverable irrespective of the credit agreements.[310] This is problematic, indeed wrong, for the reasons explained above.[311] The cost of repairs is recoverable irrespective of the credit agreements if the decision that it is *res inter alios acta* is right, for that very reason, and not because the principle of *res inter alios acta* does not apply to such costs.

(iii) *Costs that Won't be Payable Unless the Claimant Wins against the Defendant*

Difficult questions can arise when the liability of the claimant is not only practically but legally conditional. In one sale of goods case the claimant supplier agreed to pay its supplier's storage charges only if it could recover them from the defendant, from whom they were prima facie payable. The court found that this conditional arrangement did not prevent the claimant recovering from the defendant the charges it would then have to pass on to the third party.[312] A similar arrangement was reached between the shipowners and a cargo owner as to expenses that were for the time charterer's account with the same result.[313] Likewise an arrangement between the claimant and his mother-in-law in relation to alternative accommodation while damping problems caused by the defendant were resolved[314] (although the latter accommodation may have been *res inter alios acta* in any case[315]).

---

[308] Ibid at para 104.
[309] Ibid at para 161.
[310] Ibid [2003] QB 36 at paras 84–95.
[311] See chapter four, section 4.5B(vi).
[312] *Harlow & Jones Ltd v Panex (International) Ltd* [1967] 2 Lloyd's Rep 509 (Roskill J) at 531.
[313] *Cosemar SA v Marimarna Shipping Co Ltd (The Mathew)* [1990] 2 Lloyd's Rep 323 (Steyn J) at 328.
[314] *Steuerman v Dampcoursing Ltd* [2002] EWHC 939 (TCC) (Bowsher QC).
[315] See above at text to n 250 and surrounding.

F. Hedging

Hedging contracts, entered into with third parties to minimise or eliminate the risks of interest rate or market movements, are commercially similar to insurance.

In cases of oil sales, however, hedging is an inevitable adjunct of every such sale and accordingly the hedging contract and reasonable action under it (including closing it out when the contract of sale it was to hedge fell through, rather than keeping it open as a market speculation) are to be taken into account in measuring loss and is not *res inter alios acta*.[316] Break costs of interest rate swaps have also been found not to be too remote a consequence of non-delivery under a ship sale and leaseback contract.[317]

In other cases, of copper trading[318] and hedging by lenders under fixed-rate loans,[319] hedging may well be collateral and properly to be disregarded, although much will depend upon how normal and expected hedging is as a part of the industry and how involved the defendant is in that industry.

G. Third Parties Liable to the Claimant

(i) Usually Take Recovery from Third Parties into Account if Received

If the claimant does pursue a claim against third parties such steps may be treated as collateral/*res inter alios acta* and the costs and benefit from them not taken into account,[320] although if recovery is made from a third party in relation to the same damage then that will go to reduce the claimant's loss and so be taken into account.[321] Most obviously, a lender suing a valuer or other professional must give credit in that claim for any recovery made against the borrower, and an insured suing a broker must give credit for any recovery made against the insurer.[322] Other payments or help by third parties not elicited by litigation may or may not fall to be taken into account when assessing damages, as discussed above in section 16.10.

---

[316] *Addax Ltd v Arcadia Ltd* [2000] 1 Lloyd's Rep 493 (Morison J), obiter at 496 in relation to a hedge that reduced losses and emphasising the foreseeability of hedging in the oil trading industry; *Glencore Energy UK Ltd v Transworld Oil Ltd* [2010] EWHC 141 (Comm) (Blair J) at para 78, in which the hedge and actions under it reduced the loss; *Choil Trading SA v Sahara Energy Resources Ltd* [2010] EWHC 374 (Comm) (Clarke J) at para 161, where the hedge was taken out after breach and was a reasonable cost of mitigation and increased the loss.

[317] *Parbulk AS v Kristen Marine SA* [2011] 1 Lloyd's Rep 220 (Burton J).

[318] *Trafigura Beheer BV v Mediterranean Shipping Co SA (The MSC Amsterdam)* [2007] EWHC 944 (Comm) (Aikens J) (conversion and breach of contract by carrier of goods), affirmed [2007] 2 Lloyd's Rep 622 (CA).

[319] See above in chapter seven, section 7.1B(i).

[320] Eg *Jack L Israel Ltd v Ocean Dynamic Lines SA (The Ocean Dynamic)* [1982] 2 Lloyd's Rep 88 (Goff J), as explained in *Union Discount Co Ltd v Zoller* [2002] 1 WLR 1517 (CA) at para 16; *Vision Golf Ltd v Weightmans (a firm)* [2005] EWHC 1675 (Ch) (Lewison J) at paras 53–54 (the claimant pursued a hopeless late attempt for relief against forfeiture).

[321] See below in chapter twenty-four, section 24.2.

[322] On the latter point, see n 324 below and section 16.10H.

(a) Repayments of a Loan

A lender claimant may end up suffering no loss if the original loan to the third party, which it complains of, is extinguished. Most obviously, this will occur when the borrower repays the loan in the ordinary course, such receipts having to be credited to the loss calculation, but it may also occur where the lender later makes a further advance to the same borrower by way of a re-mortgage entailing a redemption of the original mortgage.[323] Likewise it may occur where there are several advances protected by a security and the lender makes the mistake of appropriating the funds recovered from enforcing its security to the particular advance caused by the defendant.[324]

(b) Settlement with the Third Party

As with settlements with third parties where the claimant is liable to the third party (see the more detailed discussion below in chapter twenty), similarly where the claimant settles a claim it has against a third party, the determining question is whether the settlement was reasonable. Provided it was, the claimant is entitled to recover any shortfall against the defendant.

This most commonly arises in cases where the broker's negligence has given an insurer an argument that it is not liable to the insured by reason of material non-disclosure or breach of warranty, and the insured then settles with the insurer. The settlement must be objectively reasonable, ignoring hindsight and given what the claimant knew at the time. Legal advice the claimant had is therefore relevant although not conclusive.[325] Essentially, the shortfall between the amount that would have been paid by the insurer and the settlement is recoverable loss unless the broker can show that the claimant insured acted unreasonably so as to break the chain of causation.

(c) Settlement with a Co-Claimant

Where a claimant reorganises the terms of its own and a third party's rights against the defendant by a settlement agreement, that was found to be collateral and *res inter alios acta*.[326]

(ii) *Rarely Unreasonable Not to Pursue Third Parties*

Even though a claimant may have a claim against a third party which is not *res inter alios acta*, such that any recovery under the claim would fall to be taken into account in measuring the claimant's loss, that does not mean that the claimant's

---

[323] *Preferred Mortgages Ltd v Bradford & Bingley Estate Agencies Ltd* [2002] EWCA Civ 336.

[324] *Capital Home Loans Ltd v Countrywide Surveyors Ltd* [2011] 3 EGLR 153 (HHJ Hazel Marshall in the Central London CC).

[325] On these points and the reasonableness of settlement in this context see: *Unity Insurance Brokers Pty Ltd v Rocco Pezzano Pty Ltd* (1998) 192 CLR 603 (HC of Australia); *Mander v Commercial Union Assurance Co plc* [1998] Lloyd's Rep IR 93 (Rix J) at 148–49; *BP Plc v Aon Ltd* [2006] EWHC 424 (Comm) (Colman J) at paras 282–83; *Ground Gilbey Ltd v Jardine Lloyd Thomson UK Ltd* [2011] EWHC 124 (Comm) (Blair J) at paras 102–3 and 109.

[326] *Mobil North Sea Ltd v PJ Pipe and Valve Co Ltd (t/a PJ Valve Ltd)* [2001] EWCA Civ 741.

failure to pursue the third party will break the chain of causation as a failure to mitigate. (And in this context, it must be remembered that the defendant will often be able itself to seek a contribution against the third party under the Civil Liability (Contribution) Act 1978 if it thinks that the claimant has a good claim that it is not pursuing.[327])

The first rule, sometimes called the rule from *Pilkington v Wood* after the leading case by that name in which it was formulated, is that a claimant cannot be expected to embark upon 'complicated and difficult' litigation against a third party.[328] In that case the defendant conveyancing solicitor's argument that the claimant property purchaser should have sued the vendor was rejected.[329]

However, where the litigation would be relatively simple the courts will sometimes find a failure to mitigate. Thus a residential lender will often be expected to enforce its security by a possession action even if its security is only over half the property (because of a co-owner the bank did not know about), and not merely rely on its claim against the negligent conveyancing solicitor.[330] Similarly, where a negligently drafted will can be rectified, the beneficiary should usually try that before suing the solicitor,[331] unless it has particular complications or difficulties.[332]

Similarly, even where a claimant has a contractual right to an indemnity or partial indemnity from a third party, there may be good commercial reasons why it is not unreasonable not to exercise that right. In *London and South of England Building Society v Stone*,[333] the building society claimant (which had sued the defendant surveyor) was entitled to waive its right to pass on part of its losses (resulting from subsidence) to the borrowers, given that the building society thought it would be unfair to do so and bad for public relations. Similarly, a buyer may elect not to pursue a sub-buyer where to do so may harm its commercial relationship.[334]

But where a claimant actually has a judgment against a third party, it can usually be expected to apply for satisfaction and take basic enforcement steps, although not to go to extreme lengths to attempt to enforce.[335]

(iii) Must Credit a Right under a Third Party Debt but Not a Right to Damages

A related question is whether the unpursued claim against the third party is of itself a value that must be credited when calculating the damages against the defendant.

---

[327] Discussed below in chapter twenty-four, at 24.2D.

[328] *Pilkington v Wood* [1953] Ch 770 (Harman J) at 777. See also *Haugesund Kommune v Depfa ACS Bank* [2010] 2 Lloyd's Rep 323 (Tomlinson J) at para 21 (overturned on other points at [2012] QB 549 (CA)); *Olafsson v Foreign & Commonwealth Office* [2009] EWHC 2608 (QB) (Eady J).

[329] And see *Williams v Glyn Owen & Co* [2003] EWCA Civ 750.

[330] *Eagle Star Insurance Co Ltd v Gale & Power* (1955) 166 EG 37 (Devlin J); *Western Trust & Savings Ltd v Cliver Travers & Co* [1997] PNLR 295 (CA).

[331] *Walker v Geo H Medlicott & Son (a firm)* [1999] 1 All ER 685 (CA).

[332] *Horsfall v Haywards* [1999] 1 FLR 1182 (CA).

[333] *London and South of England Building Society v Stone* [1983] 1 WLR 1242 (CA).

[334] Cf *James Finlay & Co Ltd v NV Kwik Hoo Tong Handel Maatschappij* [1929] 1 KB 400 (CA), where it was held that the mitigation rule did not require a buyer to rely on a conclusive evidence clause to force goods with an incorrectly dated bill of lading through onto his sub-buyers because it would damage his commercial reputation to do so.

[335] *Shuman v Coober Pedy Tours Pty Ltd* [1994] SASC 4401 (SC of South Australia) King CJ at para 29.

As a general rule, a claimant's loss against a defendant is not reduced merely because the claimant has a cause of action against a third party[336] (or indeed even if the claimant has a judgment against a third party[337]). If this were not so, then the question of whether a claimant fails to mitigate by not pursuing the third party (discussed in the immediately preceding section) would be academic; the claim against the defendant would be reduced merely by the fact of the cause of action against the third party. And, as Rix LJ observed in the contract claim of *Haugesund Kommune v Depfa ACS Bank*,

> [i]f it were otherwise, no claimant with remedies against more than one defendant could ever get judgment against either, for each defendant could play off the claim against him by referring to the claim against the other. And where the claimant has sued only one out of a number of possible defendants, the litigation before the court would become embroiled in satellite litigation involving the alleged position relating to other parties. It is rather for the defendants involved to bring contribution or other similar proceedings against each other, or for the sole defendant to implead other parties if it is thought prudent to do so.[338]

However, as the *Nykredit* decision shows, where the claimant lender is owed the loan debt by the borrower (known as the borrower's 'covenant'), this does have to be factored in so as to work out, as against a valuer, when the lender suffers loss for limitation purposes and also, therefore, the amount of that loss. If the borower's debt, albeit unsatisfied, is more valuable than the costs and harms suffered by the lender, the lender has no loss to claim against the valuer.[339]

Longmore LJ has explained the result in *Nykredit* on the basis of an

> essential difference between a claim for repayment of a debt (to which there can ordinarily be no substantive defence and in respect of which a claimant does not have to prove a loss) and a claim for damages for breach of contract (to which there may be many defences and in respect of which the claimant must prove his loss).[340]

Whether or not this is the full explanation,[341] clearly the uncertainty in liability and in quantum of a right to damages, as compared with the certainty in both of a valid loan debt, and the increased difficulty in trading the damages claim as compared with the loan, are important in explaining the result in *Nykredit* and why it differs from the general rule that a claim against a third party does not reduce the claimant's damages against a defendant. Where the claim against the third party is simple

---

[336] *The Liverpool (No 2)* [1963] *P 64 (CA) (negligence); International Factors v Rodriguez [1979] QB 351 (CA) (conversion); Peters v East Midlands Strategic Health Authority [2010] QB 48 (CA) (negligence); Eastgate Group Ltd v Lindsey Morden Group Inc [2002] 1 WLR 642 (CA) (professional negligence).

[337] See below, chapter twenty-four, section 24.2A.

[338] *Haugesund Kommune v Depfa ACS Bank* [2012] QB 549 (CA) at para 40.

[339] *Nykredit Mortgage Bank plc v Edward Erdman Group Ltd (No 2)* [1997] WLR 1627 (HL). See further *Paratus AMC Ltd v Countrywide Surveyors Ltd* [2011] EWHC 3307 (Ch) (Keyser QC) at para 62(1).

[340] *Eastgate Group Ltd v Lindsey Morden Group Inc* [2002] 1 WLR 642 (CA) at para 14.

[341] The debt/damages distinction was doubted in *Marlborough District Council v Altimarloch Joint Venture Ltd* [2012] NZSC 11 (SC of New Zealand) by Blanchard J at para 70 (and by Tipping J at para 104, dissenting).

and marketable then it can, and should, be valued as an asset for which credit must be given.

The issue was explored, obiter, in *Haugesund Kommune v Depfa ACS Bank*, where (as in *Nykredit*) a lender was induced by the defendant professional to grant a loan but (unlike in *Nykredit*) the loan was void and the lender was left only with an unjust enrichment claim and not a debt as intended.[342] Any loss was held to be outside the defendant solicitor's scope of duty, but Rix LJ was of the view (obiter) that the right to restitution for unjust enrichment *could* go to reduce the lender's loss against the solicitor who induced the loan, at least where the borrower did not dispute and was intending to satisfy the duty to make restitution, although probably not where the borrower is determined to keep the money and throw up any defences it could.[343] Gross LJ was inclined to disagree, emphasising the difference between a remedial cause of action against a third party (which probably did not reduce the loss) and a borrower's covenant (which does).[344] A New Zealand decision confirms that a right to restitution against a vendor following rescission would not reduce a damages claim against a professional who induced the transaction.[345]

H. Recovery by Exercise of the Claimant's Security Rights

A lender who is claiming against the defendant for the losses suffered as a result of entering into a loan, eg which would not have been advanced but for the negligence of the defendant solicitor or valuer, must give credit for the property rights it has under a security interest even before exercising them,[346] and must give credit for the money received from the sale in exercise of those security rights.

Furthermore, where the recovery is reduced as a result of a drop in the value of the security due to a market fall, the lender may not be able to pass that fall on to the defendant (ie recover the amount by which the actual loss is increased by the market fall) even though the claimant would not have been exposed to it but for the negligence. By the *SAAMCo* principle, an implied limit on the scope of the claimant's duty may restrict recoverability of such losses. Thus the risk of a fall in the market is usually treated as accepted by the lender who employs a valuer to value the property that is to be used as security for a loan, and not by

---

[342] *Haugesund Kommune v Depfa ACS Bank* [2012] QB 549 (CA) at para 63.
[343] At paras 84–86 and 94.
[344] At para 98. Peter Smith J did not express a view on the point, merely agreeing with both other judges (although they themselves disagreed). For further authority that a right to restitution of the price pursuant to a voidable contract does not automatically reduce the damages claim against a third party who induced the transaction, see *Shuman v Coober Pedy Tours Pty Ltd* [1994] SASC 4401 (SC of South Australia) King CJ at para 25 and Olsson J at para 40 (purchase of a dinosaur bone that was not a dinosaur bone).
[345] *Marlborough District Council v Altimarloch Joint Venture Ltd* [2012] NZSC 11 (SC of New Zealand) Blanchard J at para 71 and McGrath J at para 200 (Anderson J agreeing), relying on Lord Nicholls in *Nykredit* [1997] WLR 1627 at 1630 and the inference that in Lord Nicholls' example there was also a cause of action against the vendor which did not prevent an actionable loss against the defendant.
[346] *Nykredit Mortgage Bank plc v Edward Erdman Group Ltd (No 2)* [1997] WLR 1627 (HL).

the valuer (where the valuer's duty is to provide information rather than advice). Even if the lender would not have lent at all had the valuer taken reasonable care (a no transaction case) the valuer's liability will be limited to the amount of the overvaluation, rather than the total amount of the lender's shortfall caused by the negligence after the lender had to call in the security upon non-payment of the loan.[347]

16.11 Payments by the Claimant to Third Parties

A. Costs and Liabilities

In many cases the majority of the loss constitutes payments made by the claimant to third parties. These include costs of repair or replacement costs,[348] or sums paid by the claimant to third parties as a result of a liability the defendant caused the claimant to have, or the costs of fighting the third party.[349]

B. Gratuitous Payments Made by the Claimant

The law takes a lenient view of claimants who make payments in mitigation of their loss or for other reasons that as a matter of strict law they did not have to make. As Judge Mackie QC has summarised: 'A Claimant who pays a charge for goods or services which he has enjoyed is not failing to mitigate even if it is likely or even probable that he will not have to pay if he takes the matter to court'.[350] Thus a landlord recovered against a supermarket tenant who had withdrawn from the development the costs of rebates voluntarily paid to other tenants.[351]

However, if a claimant incurs liability for hire charges for a replacement vehicle under an irredeemably unenforceable credit hire agreement (which agreements are not *res inter alios acta*[352]), the claimant cannot recover those hire charges from the defendant, as it will not be liable to pay them itself,[353] and offering an undertaking to do so will not change the position.[354] But if the claimant has already paid the hire charges, even though perhaps not strictly required to do so as a matter of law, the hire charges will be recoverable unless it was unreasonable to pay them.[355]

---

[347] *South Australia Asset Management Corp (SAAMCo) v York Montague Ltd* [1997] 1 AC 191 (HL), discussed above in chapter fourteen, section 14.5.

[348] See chapters four and six.

[349] See below in chapter twenty.

[350] *W v Veolia Environmental Services (UK) plc* [2011] EWHC 2020 (QB) (Mackie QC).

[351] *Transworld Land Co Ltd v J Sainsbury plc* [1990] 2 EGLR 255 (Knox J).

[352] See above in section 16.10E(ii) and *Dimond v Lovell* [2002] 1 AC 384 (HL), but see *Burdis v Livsey* [2003] QB 36 (CA).

[353] *Dimond v Lovell* [2002] 1 AC 384 (HL).

[354] *Burdis v Livsey* [2003] QB 36 (CA) at para 58.

[355] *W v Veolia Environmental Services (UK) plc* [2011] EWHC 2020 (QB) (Mackie QC).

In one case of back-to-back insurance and reinsurance, the Court of Appeal found that an insurer paying out on the insurance when it was not liable and without having sought the views of reinsurers, or already knowing that reinsurers disputed liability, broke the chain of causation between the brokers' breach of duty in failing to draw certain post-placement matters to the insurer's attention and the reinsurers' refusal to pay on the reinsurance.[356]

C. Claimant Insolvency

If the claimant becomes insolvent and so never pays the third party for a relevant cost (eg repair), the claimant (or the liquidator of the claimant) may still recover the cost as damages against the defendant.[357] The third party will retain a right to prove in the insolvency, albeit that the third party's recovery will be less than the amount of the liability.

16.12 Passing on Risk or Selling the Property to Third Parties

A. Risk

Insurance is not the only way of off-loading risk to third parties,[358] and other forms arise particularly in the context of commercial lending.

In *Interallianz Finanz AG v Independent Insurance Co Ltd*[359] the claimant lent on the strength of the defendant's negligent valuation. The claimant then passed on 87 per cent of the risk of the loan to other lenders by sub-participation agreements by which the other lenders lent to the claimant and shared in the risk and reward of the loan but had no contract with the borrower or rights against the valuer (in contrast with a syndication where there is a direct contract of loan between each syndicated lender and the borrower and usually a direct cause of action against a valuer). The claimant still suffered the full loss, albeit that it had indemnities from the sub-participating lenders. The sub-participation agreements were not taken into account in measuring recovery as they were *res inter alios acta* and not within the contemplation of the valuer.[360]

In *Legal & General Mortgage Services Ltd v HPC Professional Services*[361] the lender borrowed the funds for the loan by a back-to-back loan from another lender, and it may be that the funds were paid directly by that lender to the ultimate

---

[356] *HIH Casualty and General Insurance Ltd v JLT Risk Solutions Ltd* [2007] 2 Lloyd's Rep 278 (CA) at paras 104 and 115.

[357] *The Endeavour* (1890) 6 Asp MC 511, 48 LTNS 636 (Sir James Hannen).

[358] Insurance is discussed above in section 16.10B.

[359] *Interallianz Finanz AG v Independent Insurance Co Ltd*, 18 December 1997 (Thomas J).

[360] Although it was the judge's view that if the sub-participation had been entered into in knowledge of the defendant's negligence as a way of passing on the risk in mitigation then the sub-participation agreements should be taken into account.

[361] *Legal & General Mortgage Services Ltd v HPC Professional Services* [1997] PNLR 567 (Langan QC).

borrower (although the evidence on that point was unclear). In an action by the intermediate lender against the valuer, the court (obiter because negligence was not found) held that the back-to-back loan did not prevent the intermediate having a proper cause of action against the borrower. The point also arose later in *VTB Capital plc v Nutritek*,[362] another case in which the lender took a back-to-back loan on the same date from an associated company under a participation agreement. This was merely the source of its funds for the loan, and, even though the head-lender had a direct cause of action against the defendant misrepresentor, this was found to be an independent transaction and *res inter alios acta* as regards the claimant lender's loss.

Another method of off-loading risk is securitisation. By this means a lender, after making various loans, packages them up and passes on the risk and reward in the loan package to investors. This is often done by assigning the rights in the loans and often those against valuers to a special purpose vehicle, which may effect the securitisation by issuing notes to investors giving them rights against the single purpose vehicle to participation in the income of the loan package, or to fixed returns, with the loans themselves as security. In *Paratus AMC Ltd v Countrywide Surveyors*[363] it was held, obiter, that the fact that the lender had offloaded its risk and been paid for doing so did not mean that it had not suffered loss.

All of these methods are in effect forms of insurance and are disregarded under the same principle as that by which insurance is disregarded.[364] The lender enters into a contractual arrangement with a third party by which the third party agrees to indemnify against or contribute to certain losses suffered by the claimant, thus passing the risk on to the third party, in return for a premium which in the lender cases usually takes the form of a right to participation in the income stream of the transaction (the loan), in contrast to a more traditional fixed premium in the case of straightforward insurance.

These decisions must be contrasted with the situation where the claimant has actually passed on the *loss* to third parties because it has shared out the rights against the borrower to the syndicate by novation or assignment of its own rights so as to reduce its own legal loss and putting the other bank in its place (in contrast with passing on risk by engaging someone to indemnify it for part of a loss it suffers). Accordingly, no lender can claim to have suffered the full loss and each syndicated lender can only claim (directly against the relevant professional) for the amount of its loss.[365]

---

[362] *VTB Capital plc v Nutritek International Corp* [2011] EWHC 3107 (Ch) (Arnold J), affirmed [2012] EWCA Civ 808 Lloyd LJ at paras 111–19, affirmed on different grounds [2013] UKSC 5.

[363] *Paratus AMC Ltd v Countrywide Surveyors Ltd* [2011] EWHC 3307 (Ch) (Keyser QC) at para 62(4)–(5).

[364] See above in section 16.10B.

[365] *Banque Bruxelles Lambert SA v Eagle Star Insurance Co Ltd* [1995] 2 All ER 769 (Phillips J) at 802 (reversed [1995] QB 375 (CA), that decision reversed [1997] AC 191 (HL), on a different point), distinguished in *VTB Capital plc v Nutritek International Corp* [2011] EWHC 3107 (Ch) (Arnold J) at para 157.

B. Sale of the Property after Breach or Damage

(i) Where the Terms or Result of the Sale are Affected by the Breach

Where a sale by the claimant of property affected by the defendant's breach is at arm's length, and the property defect, or failure to repair or improve, is patent and so affects the price received on such a sale,[366] the claimant's loss comprises and is confined to the amount of the reduction in the sale price or the liability to the purchasers (or any pre-sale cost of cure[367]), provided the sale itself was not too remote and did not break the chain of causation. The same is true if the defect is latent but the purchaser obtains a cause of action against the seller (for damage arising when the defect comes to light).[368] The claimant cannot recover any post-sale cost of cure, as it will not be incurring that cost, and the sale must be taken into account;[369] with a latent defect the claimant's claim against the defendant will often be for an indemnity of liability to the purchaser.

(ii) Where the Sale is Unaffected by the Breach

Where the property is sold by an internal group reorganisation at full book value[370] or for nothing or nominal consideration,[371] the sale is *res inter alios acta*.[372] The same often applies where the property is sold at arm's length at market value but the defect was latent and so the sale price unaffected, and the buyer could *not* recover from the seller for the damage.[373] Thus a person 'can maintain a claim for loss notwithstanding the transfer of the underlying property, whether for full value

---

[366] *GUS Property Management Ltd v Littlewoods Mail Order Stores Ltd* 1982 SLT 533 (HL) obiter Lord Keith at 538 (tortious damage); *Calabar Properties Ltd v Stitcher* [1984] 1 WLR 287 (CA) at 299 (landlord's failure to repair and its effect on the sale price of the tenancy). This is also reflected by the usual sale of goods measure of recovery in cases of patent defects, namely the difference between the market sale price as is and that as would have been. In such cases, of course, the actual or deemed market sale is taken into account.

[367] *Linden Gardens Trust Ltd v Lenesta Sludge Disposals Ltd* (1992) 30 Con LR 1 (CA) in relation to the £22,205.02 of works already done by the assignor before the assignment; *Tinseltime Ltd v Roberts* [2011] EWHC 1199 (TCC) (HHJ Stephen Davies) at paras 57 and 65.

[368] *Bence Graphics International Ltd v Fasson UK Ltd* [1998] QB 87 (CA) (sale), discussed above in chapter four, section 4.2B(v).

[369] Cf *Dodd Properties (Kent) Ltd v Canterbury City Council* [1980] 1 WLR 433 (CA) Donaldson J at 456–57; *Birse Construction Ltd v Eastern Telegraph Co Ltd* [2004] EWHC 2512 (TCC) (Humphrey Lloyd QC) at para 53.

[370] *GUS Property Management Ltd v Littlewoods Mail Order Stores Ltd* 1982 SLT 533 (HL) (delict); *IMI Cornelius (UK) Ltd v Bloor* (1991) 57 BLR 108 (Newey QC) (construction contract).

[371] *GUS Property Management Ltd v Littlewoods Mail Order Stores Ltd* 1982 SLT 533 (HL) obiter Lord Keith at 538; *Pegasus v Ernst & Young* [2012] EWHC 738 (Ch) (Mann J).

[372] *Offer-Hoar v Larkstore Ltd sub nom Technotrade Ltd v Larkstore Ltd* [2006] EWCA Civ 1079 Rix LJ at para 73, also *Linden Gardens Trust Ltd v Lenesta Sludge Disposals Ltd* (1992) 30 Con LR 1 (CA) at 21 and 36; and *Pegasus v Ernst & Young* [2012] EWHC 738 (Ch) (Mann J) at para 35.

[373] See *Linden Gardens Trust Ltd v Lenesta Sludge Disposals Ltd* (1992) 30 Con LR 1 (CA); *Offer-Hoar v Larkstore* [2006] 1 WLR 2926 (CA). In both cases it appears that the buyer could not (and certainly did not) claim against the seller, but instead took an assignment of such rights against the builder as the seller had.

or not',[374] the court awarding the loss the claimant would have suffered as if the transfer had never taken place.[375] (Although it should be noted that although the question is as to the transferor's claim and loss, in most of these cases the transfer was accompanied by an assignment of the cause of action and so in practice it is the transferee making the claim.)

The quantum of the loss may be the cost of cure[376] or diminution in value,[377] or liability to third parties[378] or tax authorities.[379] It will be the loss the transferor would have suffered, and the cost of cure the transferee in fact incurred is only relevant as evidence of the transferor's loss.[380] This principle has been applied in cases of damage to property,[381] defective construction,[382] and negligent tax advice.[383]

If, however, the subsequent owner has its own claim by a direct cause of action, in addition to that of the original owner (which may or may not have been assigned to the subsequent owner), the law must consider a way of avoiding double recovery.[384]

As the judges in the above cases have emphasised, there is a powerful inclination of the courts to prevent issues of transfers and assignments allowing loss to fall into a 'black hole', and to therefore treat transfers as *res inter alios acta* where not so to do would have this effect.[385]

(a) The *Albazero* Principle

The interaction between this principle and the *Albazero* principle of similar scope is uncertain. By that principle, discussed below in chapter twenty-one section 21.1, the claimant can recover substantial damages even after it has transferred property, but that principle only applies where the sale of the property was contemplated at the time of contracting and it was intended that the claimant would be able to claim for that loss, and under that principle the claimant must hold the damages for that third party.

---

[374] *Pegasus v Ernst & Young* [2012] EWHC 738 (Ch) (Mann J) at para 22.

[375] See in particular *Linden Gardens Trust Ltd v Lenesta Sludge Disposals Ltd* (1992) 30 Con LR 1 (CA) Staughton LJ at 28; *Offer-Hoar v Larkstore* [2006] 1 WLR 2926 (CA) Rix LJ at para 87.

[376] The cost of cure was considered to be a possibility in *GUS Property Management Ltd v Littlewoods Mail Order Stores Ltd* 1982 SLT 533 (HL); rejected in *IMI Cornelius (UK) Ltd v Alan J Bloor* (1991) 57 BLR 108 (Newey QC) as the transferor would not in fact incur it; apparently approved of in *Linden Gardens Trust Ltd v Lenesta Sludge Disposals Ltd* (1992) 30 Con LR 1 (CA) at 28; approved obiter in *A Meredith Jones & Co Ltd v Vangemar Shipping Co Ltd (The Apostolis) (No 2)* [2000] 2 Lloyd's Rep 337 (CA) at 348.

[377] *GUS Property Management Ltd v Littlewoods Mail Order Stores Ltd* 1982 SLT 533 (HL).

[378] Part of the loss in *Offer-Hoar v Larkstore* [2006] 1 WLR 2926 (CA).

[379] *Pegasus v Ernst & Young* [2012] EWHC 738 (Ch) (Mann J).

[380] *Linden Gardens Trust Ltd v Lenesta Sludge Disposals Ltd* (1992) 30 Con LR 1 (CA) at 28 and 33.

[381] *GUS Property Management Ltd v Littlewoods Mail Order Stores Ltd* 1982 SLT 533 (HL).

[382] *IMI Cornelius (UK) Ltd v Alan J Bloor* (1991) 57 BLR 108 (Newey QC), *Linden Gardens Trust Ltd v Lenesta Sludge Disposals Ltd* (1992) 30 Con LR 1 (CA)

[383] *Pegasus v Ernst & Young* [2012] EWHC 738 (Ch) (Mann J).

[384] *Linden Gardens Trust Ltd v Lenesta Sludge Disposals Ltd* (1992) 30 Con LR 1 (CA) Staughton LJ at 27.

[385] Eg *Offer-Hoar v Larkstore* [2006] 1 WLR 2926 (CA) Mummery LJ at para 44 to 46 and Rix LJ at paras 67 and 85 to 86; *Pegasus v Ernst & Young* [2012] EWHC 738 (Ch) (Mann J) at para 30.

(b) Property Damage

In property damage or destruction cases, recovery is not prevented by the claimant having sold the goods and passed the risk to the purchaser.[386] Thus:

> The fact that the claimant or plaintiff has contracts of sale or purchase which enable him to collect the price from his buyer or obtain reimbursement of the price or other compensation from a seller do not disentitle him from recovering full damages. Full damages assessed by reference to the sound arrived value of the goods are not affected by the fact that the owner of the goods has sold them on at a higher or lower price. All the cases demonstrate the principle that it is the loss to the proprietary or possessory interest that is compensated, not some other or different economic loss.[387]

This result is informed by the focus in damage cases upon harm being suffered instantly and not depending upon subsequent events. At the very least, this means that far more is too remote or *res inter alios acta* in damage cases than in sale or construction or other ordinary contract cases.

16.13 Events External to the Claimant

A. Legislation

In *Kennedy v KB Van Emden & Co* the negligence of solicitors led to the purchase of a lease that could not be assigned at a premium.[388] After purchase but before trial, and before the purchaser wanted to assign the lease, this restriction was removed by legislation. The Court of Appeal confirmed that such a happy evaporation of the problem should be taken into account and no loss was found to have been suffered as a result of that issue.[389]

B. War

In *Monarch Steamship Co Ltd v Karlshamns Oljefabriker (AB)*[390] a charterer succeeded in claims for delay and extra cost when the shipowner failed to provide a seaworthy vessel, which meant that the voyage could not be completed before WWII

---

[386] *The Charlotte* [1908] P 206 (CA); *R & W Paul Ltd v National Steamship Co Ltd* (1937) 59 Ll L Rep 28 (Goddard J); *Obestain Inc v National Mineral Development Corp Ltd (The Sanix Ace)* [1987] 1 Lloyd's Rep 465 (Hobhouse J). Also *GUS Property Management Ltd v Littlewoods Mail Order Stores Ltd* 1982 SLT 533 (HL).

[387] *Obestain Inc v National Mineral Development Corp Ltd (The Sanix Ace)* [1987] 1 Lloyd's Rep 465 (Hobhouse J) at 468–69.

[388] *Kennedy v KB Van Emden & Co* [1997] 2 EGLR 137 (CA).

[389] The particular decision was a case in which but for negligent advice the claimants would not have bought the lease. Ordinarily the measure of loss is the price paid less the value of the property acquired, assessed at the date of acquisition, since after that date it is the claimant's speculation whether it sells or retains the property. However, given that the lease had no market value at the time of acquisition (because of the restriction on assignment at a premium) it cannot be reasonably expected that any purchaser would sell it and so events occurring after that date are properly taken into account.

[390] *Monarch Steamship Co Ltd v Karlshamns Oljefabriker (AB)* [1949] AC 196 (HL).

broke out and so the vessel had to travel by a longer route. It was relevant that at the time of contracting there was a serious risk of war, and so the parties could be taken to have contemplated the possibility of outbreak.[391] A fortiori, war will not be disregarded where the contract expressly provides for it: in *The Golden Victory* the charterparty included a war cancellation clause, and the outbreak of war (and what the defendant would have done upon that outbreak) was taken into account when calculating the gains that would have been made in the non-breach position.[392]

However, where unexpected war destroys property that is already damaged by the defendant, that is usually treated as a supervening cause that is to be disregarded, meaning that recovery can be made against the defendant as if the destruction had not occurred.[393] Likewise, if war leads to destruction of property the defendant induced the claimant to purchase, the destruction must be ignored and that further loss of value due to it cannot be laid at the claimant's door.[394] And the fact that a warship would probably have been destroyed anyway cannot absolve the claimant of responsibility as, although the war could not be said to be unexpected (as this case concerned a warship), use and loss of the ship in war was the purpose for which the claimant wanted the vessel and could not count as a harm.[395]

C. Market Movements

Because of the well-recognised remoteness of losses due to market movements in lender/valuer cases, where the claim is restricted to the amount of the overvaluation even though the valuer's breach caused the lender to make the loan and therefore expose itself to the risk of market movements,[396] it is often wrongly thought that losses due to market movements are too remote.

In fact, the opposite is true. Outside the limited context of the professional whose duty is to provide information and not advice,[397] losses due to market movements form a central part of recoveries in a huge range of cases. Most businesses depend upon market prices, and so the loss resulting from many breaches of most services and goods contracts will obviously be affected by market movements. The simplest example is probably delayed delivery of commodities. Where a carrier delays in delivery, it was confirmed in the leading House of Lords authority of *The Heron II* that the profits lost due to a drop in the market price that the claimant can obtain on delivery are recoverable: 'He must have known that the price in a market may fluctuate. He must have known that if a price goes down someone whose goods are

---

[391] Ibid, Lord Wright at 222, Lord Du Parcq at 233–34 and, in more emotive terms, Lord Morton at 234–35.

[392] *Golden Strait Corp v Nippon Yusen Kubishika Kaisha (The Golden Victory)* [2007] 2 AC 353 (HL).

[393] *The Glenfinlas* [1918] P 363 (Roscoe R); *The Kingsway* [1918] P 344 (CA) Pickford LJ at 358–59. And see below in section 16.13D(ii).

[394] *Twycross v Grant* (1877) 2 CPD 469 (CA) Cockburn CJ at 544.

[395] *Clydebank Engineering Co v Don Jose Ramos Ysquierdo y Castaneda* [1905] AC 6 (HL) Halsbury LC at 13, discussed above in chapter four, section 4.5C(iv). Cf *The Admiralty Commissioners v Owners of The Chekiang (The Chekiang)* [1926] AC 637 (HL) as to the value of warships in a time of war.

[396] *South Australia Asset Management Corp v York Montague Ltd* [1997] 1 AC 191 (HL).

[397] See above in chapter fourteen, section 14.5B.

late in arrival may be caused loss'.[398] Similarly, the basic measure in non-delivery or non-acceptance of goods cases turns on the difference between the contract price and the market price, or the cost of repairs, at the date on which the claimant could reasonably have been expected to resort to the market (which may be long after the date of breach and may lead to much greater loss than there was at the date of breach).[399] And the loss permitted in *The Achilleas* was the difference between the rate the shipowner could have obtained on the charter market and the contract rate, for the period of the charter overrun.[400]

Similarly, property developments are obviously dependent upon the market value of the units at the date at which they are ready for market sale. Professionals causing delay to such developments will often be liable for profits lost due to the market fall during the delay.[401] Thus in *John Grimes Partnership Ltd v Gubbins*, the Court of Appeal awarded the claimant damages for the 15-month drop in the value of its property development caused by delays resulting from breaches of the defendant consultant engineering and geological services.[402] As Sir David Keene observed in that case, 'the fact that a loss is suffered because of a change in market values during the period of wrongful delay does not of itself in any way render the case out of the ordinary'.[403]

However, such losses were held to be collateral/*res inter alios acta* in the delayed construction case of *Earl's Terrace Properties Ltd v Nilsson Design Ltd*.[404] In that case it was held that although the claimant could recover for loss of use of the money that would have been earned earlier from sale of the developed houses, the subsequent market movements were 'not sufficiently close to' the breach and 'unconnected' and/or too remote, and so to be disregarded: the market had in fact risen, and this benefit was to be disregarded, but it was also confirmed that had the market fallen the additional lost profits would have been irrecoverable.[405]

Further, it may be that unusually volatile markets may weigh in favour of losses being too remote, ie the defendant not incurring responsibility for losses due to market movements.[406]

The non-remoteness of market movements can work for or against the claimant. In one case, if the defendant had performed the alleged contractual duty to sell the investment site within 18 months, the claimant would have received its share of the proceeds after the market crash, and so damages would have been (had they been awarded) much lower than if an earlier date was taken.[407]

---

[398] *C Czarnikow Ltd v Koufos (The Heron II)* [1969] 1 AC 350 (HL) at 400.

[399] See chapter seventeen, below.

[400] *Transfield Shipping Inc v Mercator Shipping Inc (The Achilleas)* [2009] AC 61 (HL).

[401] See above chapter three n 146 and chapter seven n 30 and accompanying text.

[402] *John Grimes Partnership Ltd v Gubbins* [2013] EWCA Civ 37.

[403] Ibid at para 27.

[404] *Earl's Terrace Properties Ltd v Nilsson Design Ltd* [2004] EWHC 136 (TCC) (Thornton QC).

[405] Ibid at paras 103 and 106. Compare the solicitor's negligence decision in *Kirkton Investments Ltd v VMH LLP* [2011] CSOH 200 (Court of Session, Outer House) where there was a market drop that was not too remote.

[406] As in *Transfield Shipping Inc v Mercator Shipping Inc (The Achilleas)* [2009] AC 61 (HL). And see *John Grimes Partnership Ltd v Gubbins* [2013] EWCA Civ 37 Sir David Keene at para 27 and Tomlinson LJ at paras 33–34.

[407] *Abbar v Saudi Economic & Development Co (SEDCO) Real Estate Ltd* [2013] EWHC 1414 (Ch) (David Richards J) obiter at paras 217 and 221 (in fact no contractual obligation and so no breach found).

D. Unrelated Works to, Damage to, or Destruction of Property

(i) Pre-booked Works and the Prior Condition of the Property

The general principle is that the defendant can take a situation as it finds it. If the defendant is a secondary cause of damage or destruction, it is entitled to take the property as it found it, ie as already damaged or destroyed, and is only liable for damage, repairs (or other expenses such as docking dues) or loss of use that goes beyond the first cause. Although supervening events are often treated as *res inter alios acta* (see below in section 16.13D(ii)), pre-existing conditions or post-breach events that were inevitable or planned prior to the breach (eg works that had to be done due to prior incidents or damage) are usually taken into account and not *res inter alios acta*.

(a) Prior Damage

This is demonstrated by the Court of Appeal's decision in *Performance Cars v Abraham*.[408] Two parties in separate incidents caused minor damage to a Rolls Royce Silver Cloud necessitating the same partial re-spray, the action before the court being a claim against the cause of the second incident (judgment having already been obtained against the cause of the first incident, although it was unlikely to be satisfied). The cause of the first incident was held liable and the cause of the second incident was not held liable because at the time of the second incident the car was 'in a condition which already required that it should be resprayed in any event'.[409]

(b) Pre-planned or Inevitable Works or Loss of Use

Thus if a vessel is already out of use through prior damage or other incident, the defendant's damage or destruction did not cause the loss of use (which would have happened anyway) until such time as the previously inevitable loss of use would have finished. 'If [the vessel] ceases to be a profit-earning machine it follows that she can sustain no damage from being detained until she again becomes capable of earning profit'.[410] The unrelated reason for taking the property out of use and requiring the work may (for example) be a third party wrongdoer (ie another defendant or

---

[408] *Performance Cars Ltd v Abraham* [1962] 1 QB 33 (CA).

[409] Ibid, Evershed MR at 39. See also *The Haversham Grange* [1905] P 307 (CA). In that case the Court of Appeal made the first in time cause solely liable for the lost profit during the period of delay, ie demurrage charges, but made both defendants liable for the costs of docking and repair, ie dock dues. The decision was overruled on the latter point by the House of Lords in *Carslogie Steamship Co Ltd v Royal Norwegian Government* [1952] AC 292 (HL), which confirmed that the first in time cause is liable for both the loss of profit and the costs. The principle was applied by the Supreme Court of Canada in *Sunrise Co Ltd v The Ship 'Lake Winnipeg'* (1991) 77 DLR (4th) 701 (SC of Canada), although the minority refused to apply the rule and preferred to split the overlapping period between the two causes. And see *Beoco Ltd v Alfa Laval Co Ltd* [1995] QB 137 (CA) at 149 (contract). And cf the approach in *Smith New Court Securities Ltd v Scrimgeour Vickers (Asset Management) Ltd* [1997] AC 254 (HL) to a pre-existing condition, discussed in section 16.13E(ii).

[410] *Carslogie Steamship Co Ltd v Royal Norwegian Government* [1952] AC 292 (HL) obiter Viscount Jowitt at 300–301, see also at 306 (although in that case the defendant's tort did not cause immediate repairs).

possible defendant);[411] damage from a natural event such as a storm[412] or fire;[413] detention by ice;[414] or the vessel simply being worn out.[415]

The same applies where the period of loss of use was already inevitable due to the claimant's own decision or activity, such as by contracting to sell the property in terms requiring a period out of use for a pre-sale inspection,[416] or by booking the property in for other works anyway,[417] although not if the booking is tentative or reversible and so the period of loss of use was not (until the defendant's breach) inevitable.[418]

Likewise where a replacement had already been ordered for property at the time of its destruction,[419] or it had already been planned that the property would be destroyed,[420] or redeveloped or refurbished[421] no damages for the diminution in the value of the property or its repair will be recoverable.[422] In such cases, the defendant will only be liable for the amount by which the cost of the total works is increased by reason of the second incident,[423] and by which the loss of use was increased by the defendant.

(c) Not Immediately Essential Work that is Slotted
in to Deal with Prior Damage or Condition

Where, however, the defendant causes damage that does require essential repairs or otherwise forces a particular period of loss of use and repair, the claimant need not

---

[411] Obiter in *Beoco Ltd v Alfa Laval Co Ltd* [1995] QB 137 (CA) Stuart-Smith LJ at 149.

[412] *Carslogie Steamship Co Ltd v Royal Norwegian Government* [1952] AC 292 (HL): the defendant's tort caused damage requiring 10 days in dock but before the vessel reached the dock a storm caused damage requiring 30 days in dock, and the repairs resulting from the defendant's tort were carried out at the same time.

[413] Obiter in *Beoco Ltd v Alfa Laval Co Ltd* [1995] QB 137 (CA) Stuart-Smith LJ at 149.

[414] Obiter in *The York* [1929] P 178 (CA) Scrutton LJ at 185.

[415] *Segontian v Cornouaille* (1922) 10 Ll L Rep 242 (Hill J) at 243.

[416] *The York* [1929] P 178 (CA).

[417] *Galbraith, Pembroke & Co Ltd v Regent Stevedoring Co Ltd* (1946) 79 Ll L Rep 292 (Atkinson J), where the inessential repairs had already been booked in and committed to; *The Hassel* [1962] 2 Lloyd's Rep 139 (Hewson J).

[418] *Carslogie Steamship Co Ltd v Royal Norwegian Government* [1952] AC 292 (HL), see especially Viscount Jowitt at 301. See also the discussion in *The Acanthus* [1902] P 17 (Jeune P), where a deposit had been paid but there was apparently no binding engagement to continue with the repairs.

[419] *Southampton Container Terminals Ltd v Schiffahrts-Gesellschaft 'Hansa Australia' mbH & Co (The Maersk Colombo)* [2001] 2 Lloyd's Rep 275 (CA).

[420] *The London Corporation* [1935] P 70 (CA) Greer LJ at 77; *Taylor Wholesale Ltd v Hepworths Ltd* [1977] 1 WLR 659 (May J) at 669–70.

[421] Section 18(1) of the Landlord and Tenant Act 1927, discussed above in chapter four, 4.3B(iii)(d). It is notable that this section makes the same distinction as the common law: by the doctrine of supercession, the cost of repairs will not be awarded in relation disrepair that was to be obliterated by redevelopment that the landlord had already made up his mind to do, but redevelopment that has not then been decided on but is later nevertheless performed will be ignored as a *res inter alios acta* supervening event. Also *Gagner Pty Ltd v Canturi Corporation Pty Ltd* [2009] NSWCA 413 (CA of New South Wales) obiter at para 110: in that case the refurbishment had not already been planned and would not have taken place but for the damage, so the reasonable costs of repair (but not the greater costs of the refurbishment) were recovered.

[422] But compare *Tradebe Solvent Recycling Ltd v Coussens of Bexhill Ltd* [2013] EWHC 3786 (QB) (Andrews J), where the pre-ordered replacement tanks that had been intended to replace those that were damaged were reasonably used elsewhere to minimise losses to the business, so the claimant was still able to recover for the cost of replacing the damaged tanks.

[423] *Organic Research Chemicals v Ricketts* (CA) 16 November 1961, *Times Law Reports*.

give credit if it takes the opportunity while the vessel is out of use to do other works that *could have waited*, ie where but for the defendant's wrong the loss of use would not necessarily have taken place *at that time*.

Here the claimant is entitled to retain the 'windfall benefit'[424] of the saving of the costs of docking[425] and period of loss of use[426] even though it would, but for the defendant's wrong, have been suffered by the claimant at a later date when it had eventually to do the other works. Thus in *The Ruabon* a shipowner had nine months left to run on its vessel's Lloyd's classification (like a car's MOT roadworthiness certificate) but took the opportunity to have it reclassified early, while the vessel was in dock for essential repairs made necessary by the damage tortiously caused by the defendant, the reclassification not extending the period of docking for repairs in any way.[427] No reduction was made for the claimant's having avoided a later period of docking that would have been necessitated.

The crucial question is whether the other work done would, even but for the defendant's wrong, have required the vessel to be out of use 'at or about the time'[428] when it was in fact out of use, or whether that work would have required it to be out of use only at a later date (ie the claimant could have waited for a more opportune moment). If the defendant's wrong brings forward the loss of use even by a few weeks, the defendant is liable for the loss of use and no credit need be given for the saving of the loss of use that would otherwise have been suffered those few weeks later.[429] Of course, the defendant is not liable for any *additional* costs of repair or period of loss of use that would not have been needed had the only damage been that caused by the defendant and which was necessitated by the bringing forward of the not immediately essential works.[430]

Assuming it can be proven that the loss of use would in fact have been suffered later (which is not always the case[431]), the law's refusal to give credit for the loss of use and (eg) costs of docking that would otherwise have been incurred anyway, but a few weeks later, can seem harsh. It is, however, consistent with the rule of betterment:[432] the cure for the damage dictating the period of stoppage and/or repairs necessarily leads to the claimant making a saving by reason of the repairs

---

[424] *Elpidoforos Shipping Corp v Furness Withy (Australia) Pty Ltd (The Oinoussian Friendship)* [1987] 1 Lloyd's Rep 258 (Hirst J) at 265.

[425] *Ruabon Steamship Co Ltd v London Assurance Co (The Ruabon)* [1900] AC 6 (HL); *The Acanthus* [1902] P 17 (Jeune P): taking the opportunity to install 'a luxury', namely bilge keels.

[426] *Admiralty Commissioners v Owners of SS Chekiang (The Chekiang)* [1926] AC 637 (HL): taking the opportunity to perform an annual refit; *The Ferdinand Retzlaff* [1972] 2 Lloyd's Rep 120 (Brandon J): taking the opportunity to perform a special survey and some other repairs. Obiter in *Vitruvia Steamship Co Ltd v Ropner Shipping Co Ltd* [1925] SC (HL) 1.

[427] *Ruabon Steamship Co Ltd v London Assurance Co (The Ruabon)* [1900] AC 6 (HL). See also *Admiralty Commissioners v Owners of SS Chekiang (The Chekiang)* [1926] AC 637 (HL); *The Ferdinand Retzlaff* [1972] 2 Lloyd's Rep 120 (Brandon J).

[428] *The Hassel* [1962] 2 Lloyd's Rep 139 (Hewson J).

[429] *The Ferdinand Retzlaff* [1972] 2 Lloyd's Rep 120 (Brandon J). See also the discussion in *Elpidoforos Shipping Corp v Furness Withy (Australia) Pty Ltd (The Oinoussian Friendship)* [1987] 1 Lloyd's Rep 258 (Hirst J) at 264–65.

[430] *The Ferdinand Retzlaff* [1972] 2 Lloyd's Rep 120 (Brandon J).

[431] Lord Brampton in *Ruabon Steamship Co Ltd v London Assurance Co (The Ruabon)* [1900] AC 6 (HL) at 17; *Gagner Pty Ltd v Canturi Corporation Pty Ltd* [2009] NSWCA 413 (CA of New South Wales) at paras 105–9.

[432] See above in chapter four, section 4.4B.

also repairing the other damage, or by reason of the claimant reasonably taking the opportunity to do such works; however, it is not possible or practical to provide a cure that does not provide this betterment and accordingly the claimant need not make any deduction for it (as regards a claim against whoever did dictate the period of stoppage or the works).

(ii) Supervening Damage or Destruction is Usually Res Inter Alios Acta

The huge number of damage or destruction cases, mainly tort cases of ship collisions, are not easy to reconcile, dealing as they do with diminution in value, costs of repairs, and lost profits while the property is out of use, not always entirely consistently.

However, the general rule is that supervening damage or destruction of property subsequent to the defendant's breach and unrelated to it, whether caused by another wrongdoer or by an external event, is treated as *res inter alios acta*[433] as regards the earlier breach of the defendant, ie 'accidental to the plaintiffs [and] of which the defendants have no knowledge'.[434]

As with all things that are *res inter alios acta*, this means that the law does not ask whether but for the defendant's first damage or destruction the property would in any case have been damaged/needed repairs/been out of use. (As a matter of 'but for' causation, the answer is yes it would and therefore the first damage or destruction was not a factual cause of the loss). Rather (i) whatever the supervening event did to make things worse is not laid at the door of the earlier event, thus if the supervening event increased costs or destroyed the vessel the earlier cause is not responsible even if but for that cause the supervening event would not have happened;[435] and also, crucially, (ii) the supervening damage or destruction is ignored and the law deems it not to have occurred. The claimant can therefore recover against the defendant first cause of harm the damages it would have been able to recover if the supervening event had never occurred, ignoring the further damage or destruction that the supervening event caused.

Thus claimants have recovered damages for diminution in value where after the defendant harms the property it is destroyed,[436] given away,[437] or sold to shipbreakers or for scrap.[438] Likewise for the cost of repairs where the property damaged

---

[433] *Smiley v Townshend* [1950] 2 KB 311 (CA), obiter Denning LJ at 320.

[434] *The London Corporation* [1935] P 70 (CA) Greer LJ at 77.

[435] *Twycross v Grant* (1877) 2 CPD 469 (CA) Cockburn CJ at 544.

[436] *The Glenfinlas* [1918] P 363 (Roscoe R), discussed in *The York* [1929] P 178 (CA) Scrutton LJ at 184–85 (where the cost of repairs and diminution in value are not clearly distinguished); *Smiley v Townshend* [1950] 2 KB 311 (CA), obiter Denning LJ at 321 (example of car destroyed by fire); *Intervention Board for Agricultural Produce v Leidig* [2000] Lloyd's Rep 144 (CA) obiter Robert Walker LJ at 149, quoting *Alexander v Cambridge Credit Corporation* (1987) 9 NSWLR 310 (example of an earthquake). See also *Texaco Ltd v Arco Technology Inc*, 31 July 1989 (Phillips J) and then 1 October 1989 (Phillips J) (destroyed by claimant, but no diminution in value prior to that).

[437] *The London Corporation* [1935] P 70 (obiter Bateson J at 74), affirmed [1935] P 70 (CA).

[438] *The London Corporation* [1935] P 70 (CA). Compare *The Argonaftis* [1989] 2 Lloyd's Rep 487 (Sheen J), where scrapping the vessel was reasonable and this scrap value was taken as the value after the harm, so this was not a supervening event that was ignored but a reasonable action that was taken into account.

by the defendant was then sunk by a mine,[439] or hit by a second tortfeasor,[440] or destroyed by the claimant's negligence,[441] before the repairs could be carried out. The same principle should apply to the loss of use of property during repairs necessitated by the first cause, and indeed has been,[442] although as set out below, there are cases in which the court has resisted carrying this principle through to loss of use that was caused by the defendant but where a supervening event in fact destroyed the property.[443]

Similarly, where an unusual flood or similar event has occurred while the claimant's property was left somewhere due to the defendant's delay, the defendant will not be held responsible providing the delay did not increase the risk of the flood or similar damage.[444]

(a) Cases Not Following These Principles

However, not all the cases are consistent on this point. Contrary to the previous two paragraphs, in some cases the courts decide that the later action broke the chain of causation and rather than being *res inter alios acta* to be disregarded, leaving the loss that would have occurred anyway, actually ends the defendant's responsibility. Where the supervening event is destruction of the damaged property by the claimant's own carelessness, the courts correctly do not lay the destruction at the door of the defendant's earlier wrong, as the claimant must be deemed to have acted carefully.[445] However, even where the claim is made for the costs of repairs and loss of use that would have resulted from the earlier damage if the claimant had taken care and the property not been destroyed (and such a claim is not always made), the courts sometimes refuse such a claim, failing to realise that the claimant should be deemed to have acted carefully and so that loss should be recoverable. Indeed in two cases the court permitted the claim for the cost of repairs that were never carried out but would have been if the claimant had taken care, but refused the claim

---

[439] *The Glenfinlas* [1918] P 363 (Roscoe R), although loss of use was not awarded.

[440] *The Haversham Grange* [1905] P 307 (CA). In that case the Court of Appeal made the first in time cause solely liable for the lost profit during the period of delay, ie demurrage charges (although the first in time did not dispute that liability), but made both defendants liable for the costs of docking and repair, ie dock dues. The decision was overruled on the latter point by the House of Lords in *Carslogie Steamship Co Ltd v Royal Norwegian Government* [1952] AC 292 (HL), which confirmed that the first in time cause is liable for both the loss of profit and the costs. The principle was applied by the Supreme Court of Canada in *Sunrise Co Ltd v The Ship 'Lake Winnipeg'* (1991) 77 DLR (4th) 701 (SC of Canada), although the minority would have preferred to split the overlapping period between the two causes.

[441] *Schering Agrochemicals Ltd v Resibel NV SA*, 4 May 1991 (Hobhouse J); 26 November 1992 (CA) (contract; discussed above at fn 20); *Beoco Ltd v Alfa Laval Co Ltd* [1995] QB 137 (CA) (contract), where the point was not disputed by the defendant.

[442] *The Haversham Grange* [1905] P 307 (CA), approved in *Carslogie Steamship Co Ltd v Royal Norwegian Government* [1952] AC 292 (HL), both discussed above at n 441; *Schering Agrochemicals Ltd v Resibel NV SA*, 4 May 1991 (Hobhouse J); 26 November 1992 (CA) (contract).

[443] See the next sub-section.

[444] *Toledo & Ohio Central Railroad Co v Kibler & Co* 199 NE 733 (1918) (Ohio). But compare *Green-Wheeler Shoe Co v Chicago, Rock Island & Pacific Railroad Co* 130 Iowa 123 (1906).

[445] *MV Mitera Marigo v MV Fritz Thyssen (The Fritz Thyssen)* [1967] 2 Lloyd's Rep 199 (CA); *Texaco Ltd v Arco Technology Inc*, 31 July 1989 (Phillips J) and then 1 October 1989 (Phillips J); *Beoco Ltd v Alfa Laval Co Ltd* [1995] QB 137 (CA).

for loss of use that would have resulted from those repairs.[446] A similar incorrect approach has been applied to disallow damages for loss of use but not repair, or for both repairs and loss of use, where the property was destroyed by an external event such as war[447] or a third party tortfeasor.[448]

(b) Where the Supervening Act is Not *Res Inter Alios Acta*

Of course, not all subsequent events will break the chain. Where they were related to, or the risk of them was increased by, the defendant's breach, or were ordinary occurrences, they will not prevent the defendant being liable. For example, where seawater enters a ship after it has been holed in war or scuttled, the perils of the sea do not break the chain of causation from the earlier cause;[449] similarly, where the defendant's duty was to prevent the successive act.[450] Likewise where a storm aggravates the loss caused to the claimant by the defendant landlord's failure to repair, the full losses will still be recoverable.[451]

(iii) Successive Causes in Personal Injury Cases

Broadly speaking, the same principle applies to personal injury cases.[452] Post-breach incidents (especially where tortiously caused) will usually be disregarded as supervening unrelated causes, and pre-existing conditions (including where caused by tortfeasors) will usually be taken into account in assessing damages. This approach from physical damage case *Performance Cars Ltd v Abraham*[453] was followed in *Steel v Joy* where the first and not second tortfeasor was liable.[454] In a claim against a tortfeasor responsible for the first incident, supervening events that break the chain of causation are ignored and deemed not to have occurred for the purpose of the calculation of damages.[455] Thus in *Baker v Willoughby* the defendant caused a

---

[446] *Beoco Ltd v Alfa Laval Co Ltd* [1995] QB 137 (CA); *Texaco Ltd v Arco Technology Inc*, 31 July 1989 (Phillips J) and then 1 October 1989 (Phillips J). In *MV Mitera Marigo v MV Fritz Thyssen (The Fritz Thyssen)* [1967] 2 Lloyd's Rep 199 (CA) no claim was made for the losses that would have resulted if the vessel had not been sunk by the claimant's negligence.

[447] *The Glenfinlas* [1918] P 363 (Roscoe R), although the cost of repairs was allowed. See also obiter comments in *The Kingsway* [1918] P 344 (CA) Pickford LJ at 358–59 ('Suppose that after the collision damage she had been torpedoed or sunk by perils of the sea'); and *The York* [1929] P 178 (CA) Scrutton LJ at 184–85.

[448] *Salcon Ltd v United Cement Pte Ltd* [2004] 4 SLR 353 (Singapore CA), where a defective cement silo collapsed due to a third party's negligence in operating it beyond 70% of its capacity against advice. The arbitrator had allowed damages for the 'notional' cost of repairs and loss of use that would have been suffered had the supervening event not taken place, but the Court of Appeal (incorrectly) allowed the appeal and refused such an award.

[449] *Leyland Shipping Co Ltd v Norwich Union Fire Insurance Society Ltd* [1918] AC 350 (HL); *P Samuel & Co Ltd v Dumas* [1924] AC 431 (HL).

[450] See below in section 16.13D(iv).

[451] *Loria v Hammer* [1989] 2 EGLR 249 (Lindsay QC) at 258.

[452] Although L'Heureux-Dubé J in *Sunrise Co Ltd v The Ship 'Lake Winnipeg'* (1991) 77 DLR (4th) 701 (SC of Canada) has warned against the possibility of 'meaningful comparison' between personal injury and other types of losses in this context. See also the comments of Lord Reid in *Baker v Willoughby* [1970] AC 467 (HL) at 493.

[453] *Performance Cars Ltd v Abraham* [1962] 1 QB 33 (CA) discussed above in text to n 407.

[454] *Halsey v Milton Keynes General NHS Trust, Steel v Joy* [2004] 1 WLR 3002 (CA).

[455] *Nolan v Dental Manufacturing Co Ltd* [1958] 2 All ER 449 (Paull J) (claimant's subsequent act ignored).

collision injuring the claimant's leg. An armed robber later shot the claimant's leg, necessitating amputation, and the defendant remained liable for pain and suffering after the amputation.[456]

Similarly, any tortfeasor is entitled to take a victim as he finds him, and will only be liable for making things worse. Thus where a pre-existing condition would have caused harm in any event, the supervening cause is only liable for the additional amount of harm. In *Jobling v Associated Dairies Ltd*, the claimant's pre-existing but dormant medical condition meant that his working life would have been cut short even if the defendant employer had not negligently injured him, and so the defendant was only liable for the additional period of pain and suffering that would not have occurred but for the accident.[457] And lost earnings during medical treatment and/or recovery following injury caused by the defendant's wrong will not be recoverable if those earnings would have been lost anyway, albeit at a later date, due to a pre-existing condition.[458]

Events that do not break the chain of causation are taken into account and actual loss is recovered, whether the events increased the loss[459] or, because they would have happened anyway, reduce the loss (for example death cutting short pain and suffering).

(iv) Where the Purpose of the Defendant's Duty Was to Guard against the Event or Damage

Where the defendant was engaged to prevent the particular type of harm, that loss will inevitably fall within the scope of the defendant's duty and assumption of responsibility however unlikely it is, and other intervening actions of third parties[460] or external events will not break the chain of causation to absolve the defendant. As Rix LJ put it in *Rubenstein v HSBC*:

> Where the obligation of a defendant is not merely to avoid injuring his claimant but to protect him from the very kind of misfortune which has come about, it is not helpful to make fine distinctions between foreseeable events which are unusual, most unusual, or of negligible account.[461]

In that case the bank was held liable for an unexpected market crash because the very breach of the defendant was in exposing the claimant to market fluctuations.[462]

---

[456] *Baker v Willoughby* [1970] AC 467 (HL). Heavily criticised in *Jobling v Associated Dairies* [1982] AC 794 (HL). Approved in *Halsey v Milton Keynes General NHS Trust, Steel v Joy* [2004] 1 WLR 3002 (CA), where Dyson LJ explained at para 70 that 'In *Baker*, the issue was whether the tortfeasor who had caused the first injury was liable for its consequences after they had arguably become merged in the consequences of the second injury' and that there was a necessary modification of the 'but for' test in that case.

[457] *Jobling v Associated Dairies Ltd* [1982] AC 794 (HL).

[458] *Cutler v Vauxhall Motors Ltd* [1971] 1 QB 418 (CA)—pre-existing varicose veins necessitated an operation but the defendant was responsible for a graze that brought forward the need for the operation by four or five years. Also *Tickner v Glen Line Ltd* [1958] 1 Lloyd's Rep 468 (Devlin J).

[459] *Wilkins v William Cory & Son Ltd* [1959] 2 Lloyd's Rep 98 (Gorman J).

[460] Third party actions that the claimant's duty was to protect against are discussed below in section 16.13E(vii).

[461] *Rubenstein v HSBC Bank plc* [2012] EWCA Civ 1184 at para 124.

[462] Ibid at para 124.

Similarly, in *Siemens Building Technologies FE Ltd v Supershield Ltd* a defendant was responsible for flood losses resulting from failure of a flood protection device (a ball valve) installed by it, which losses clearly fell within its responsibility (the avoidance of the flood being the very purpose of the flood protection mechanism), and the (albeit highly unlikely) failure of a second flood protection device (drains and a 60cm-high wall) did not absolve the defendant.[463] The whole point of the valve was to protect against flood and the fact that there was also a drain did not mean that the maker of the valve (or the maker of the drain) would not be liable if they failed. This decision was largely resolved under the remoteness heading, where the purpose of the valve meant that the loss, however unlikely (dependent as it was on the failure of the drains), was within the defendant's assumption of responsibility and so not too remote, with the Court of Appeal also confirming (without any difficulty) that the chain of causation had not been broken.[464] The principle was explained earlier in *The Achilleas* by Lord Walker as follows:

> If a manufacturer of lightning conductors sells a defective conductor and the customer's house burns down as a result, the manufacturer will not escape liability by proving that only one in a hundred of his customers' buildings had actually been struck by lightning.[465]

And plainly the distress and losses resulting from an unwanted pregnancy are within the scope of responsibility of a doctor who was negligent in performing a vasectomy.[466]

---

[463] *Siemens Building Technologies FE Ltd v Supershield Ltd* [2010] EWCA Civ 7).

[464] See also *Sea Harvest Corp (Pty) Ltd v Duncan Dock Cold Storage (Pty) Ltd* [2000] 1 SALR 827 (SCA of S Africa). A harbour cold store was set on fire by a flare, fired from the harbour during New Year celebrations, landing on the flammable fiberglass gutters on the roof. The building had fire extinguishers and hose-reels but not sprinklers, which would have stopped the fire. Streicher JA assumed negligence (ie that reasonable protection against all fires would have required a sprinkler) but found that the way the fire started made it too remote, being unforeseeable. The majority of the Court preferred to conflate the issue of negligence with that of scope of duty/legal causation (following South African scholar Boberg's 'relative approach' to negligence), and found that there had been no breach of the duty of care as the particular way the fire started was not reasonably foreseeable. The English approach would be to determine breach of duty separately, asking whether precautions against fires generally would require sprinklers (as Streicher JA did), and then to consider remoteness. The view of this author is that the decision would probably be decided differently in England: there is no logical reason to think that the defendant's assumption of responsibility extended to some fires but not to fires caused externally even though highly unlikely/unforeseeable. The defendant should have protected against fire (cf *Siemens Building Technologies FE Ltd v Supershield Ltd*) and failed to do so. See also *Mueller Europe Ltd v Central Roofing (South Wales) Ltd* [2013] EWHC 237 (TCC) (Stuart-Smith J) discussed above at text to n 36 and surrounding.

[465] *Transfield Shipping Inc v Mercator Shipping Inc (The Achilleas)* [2009] AC 61 (HL) at para 78. See also the ceiling example and Lord Hoffmann's explanation of it, above at text to chapter fourteen nn 66 and 68.

[466] *McFarlane v Tayside Health Board* [2000] 2 AC 59 (HL) (tort, although many of the previous cases discussed were concurrent contractual and tort liability cases). The costs of raising the child were irrecoverable for policy reasons. Cf the tort case of *Reeves v Commissioner of Police of the Metropolis* [2000] 1 AC 360 (HL), where the police's duty to protect the claimant from self-harm in custody meant that that harm was not too remote and did not break the chain of causation.

E. Third Party Wrongs and Actions

> In general … even though A. is in fault, he is not responsible for injury to C. which B., a stranger to him, deliberately chooses to do. Though A. may have given the occasion for B.'s mischievous activity, B. then becomes a new and independent cause.[467]

Thus in *Wiseman v Virgin Atlantic Airways plc*,[468] although the defendant airline's breach caused the claimant to be stuck in Nigeria, the claimant's being robbed was held to have been a supervening cause of loss for which the defendant was not responsible.[469]

(i) Omissions

Third party omissions are fairly unlikely to break the chain of causation. Where the defendant solicitor and a subsequently instructed third party solicitor both failed to obtain relief from forfeiture, the latter's failure did not break the chain of causation from the defendant's failure.[470]

(ii) Third Party Fraud

Where a valuer negligently valued a property but, unbeknownst to the valuer (who could not have been expected to discover it) there was a price-inflation fraud being perpetrated on the claimant lender by the seller, buyer, and buyer and lender's solicitors, the loss was not caused by the valuer and was outside the valuer's responsibility.[471] However, in the *Smith New Court Securities* deceit case an unrelated fraud on Ferranti prior to the purchase of shares meant that the shares were bought on a false market (the market not being aware of true facts) and were already 'pregnant' with that fraud and 'doomed to collapse'.[472] The House of Lords found that the crash in the share value when the fraud came to light did not break the chain of causation and, given that the claimant's holding the shares long enough for that fraud to come to light also did not break the chain, the fraud was taken into account. The logic of the reasoning (and emphasis on the pregnancy of the shares with the fraud) indicates that the fraud would be more likely to have broken the chain of causation had it occurred after the shares were purchased.[473]

---

[467] *Weld-Blundell v Stephens* [1920] AC 956 (HL) obiter Lord Sumner at 986.

[468] *Wiseman v Virgin Atlantic Airways plc* [2006] EWHC 1566 (QB) (Eady J). See similarly *Cobb v Great Western Railway Co* [1894] AC 419 (HL).

[469] See also the cases discussed in HLA Hart and T Honoré, *Causation in the Law*, 2nd edn (Oxford, OUP, 1985) at 136–42.

[470] *Vision Golf Ltd v Weightmans* [2005] EWHC 1675 (Ch) (Lewison J) at para 36. See also the cases cited at n 6 above.

[471] *Platform Funding Ltd v Anderson & Associates Ltd* [2012] EWHC 1853 (QB) (Thornton QC) at paras 109–10. In this case although negligently prepared, the valuation would in any case have been the same had reasonable care been taken.

[472] *Smith New Court Securities Ltd v Scrimgeour Vickers (Asset Management) Ltd* [1997] AC 254 (HL) Lord Browne-Wilkinson at 268, Lord Steyn at 279 and 285.

[473] See especially Lord Steyn's discussion at 285 and 279 of the diseased horse example.

(iii) Surprising Third Party Conduct

And in the unusual case of *Bates v Barrow Ltd*, a respectable insurer denying liability on the basis of its own unlawful conduct in conducting insurance business while unauthorised was held to be too remote from the defendant broker's breach of duty in placing the claimant's insurance with that insurer,[474] as would be any spurious argument put forward by an insurer.[475]

In *Weld-Blundell v Stephens*, the bare majority found that an accountant who negligently left the claimant's libellous letter at the claimant's office was not liable for the harm caused to the claimant when it was sued for libel, someone having read the letter and passed it on to the libel victims.[476]

(iv) Not Wholly Surprising Third Party Conduct

In *Chagger v Abbey National plc*[477] the Court of Appeal confirmed that third party employers' unlawful refusal to employ the claimant because he had sued his former employer (the defendant) did not prevent the claimant recovering against the defendant for the lost wages it had been unable to replace on the job market with such employers.

In contrast, a bank was held liable in *Jackson v RBS* for the consequences of carelessly allowing the claimant customer's own customer to see documents showing how much profit the claimant was making, those consequences being that the customer broke off its supply relationship with the claimant.[478]

(v) Public Authority Intervention

In one case although it was foreseeable and did not break the chain of causation that damaged maize would be confiscated by a public authority and sold at a low price, losses resulting from the same thing happening to undamaged maize were irrecoverable as too remote and the confiscation did break the chain of causation.[479] In another, government interference leading to a delay in port was not too remote.[480] As one judge put it, 'If every arbitrary exercise of power in any country in the world

---

[474] *Bates v Barrow Ltd* [1995] 1 Lloyd's Rep 680 (Gatehouse J).

[475] Cf *Standard Life Assurance Ltd v Oak Dedicated Ltd* [2008] EWHC 222 (Comm) (Tomlinson J) at para 102; *Ground Gilbey Ltd v Jardine Lloyd Thomson UK Ltd* [2011] EWHC 124 (Comm) (Blair J) at para 104.

[476] *Weld-Blundell v Stephens* [1920] AC 956 (HL). The decision may be criticised on the basis that the whole point of a duty not to leave something confidential lying around is that others might find it and disseminate it.

[477] *Chagger v Abbey National plc* [2010] ICR 397 (CA), discussed above at text to chapter eighteen n 64.

[478] *Jackson v Royal Bank of Scotland plc* [2005] 1 WLR 377 (HL).

[479] *Empresa Cubana Importadora de Alimentos v Octavia Shipping Co SA (The Kefalonia Wind)* [1986] 1 Lloyd's Rep 273 (Bingham J) at 288.

[480] *Islamic Republic of Iran Shipping Lines v Ierax Shipping Co of Panama (The Forum Craftsman)* [1991] 1 Lloyd's Rep 81 (Hobhouse J). However, a large part of the delay was either not a result of the defendant's breach or was too remote.

where ships come and go were sufficient to displace serious breaches of contract, that might be to encourage lawlessness'.[481]

(vi) Strike

A strike that exacerbated repairs will often not break the chain of causation.[482]

(vii) Where the Defendant's Duty Was to Prevent the Third Party Conduct

Just as in the case of external events[483] or claimant actions[484] that the defendant's duty was to prevent, third party conduct that conduct will not break the chain of causation. As Hobhouse LJ has observed, obiter,

> If a defendant is under a duty to protect the plaintiff against the consequences of the conduct of others, such conduct will not break the causal relationship between the defendant's conduct and the plaintiff's loss; indeed, it provides the necessary causal link.[485]

Thus, in *London Joint Stock Bank v Macmillan*, the defendant bank's customer was liable for the loss to the bank resulting from the bank's employee fraudulently altering the defendant's cheque, given that the defendant's duty not to draw cheques that might facilitate fraud was directed at preventing exactly this sort of occurrence.[486] A solicitor who should not have exposed its lender customer to the risk of lack of security could not complain that the loss only happened because the other side breached its undertaking to put security in place.[487] Likewise in *Stansbie v Troman* the defendant decorator's negligently leaving the door unlocked rendered the defendant liable for the loss caused by third party theft, that being 'the very thing' that the defendant was contractually obliged to guard against by locking the door.[488] And in another case the chain of causation between the defendant's careless recommendation of a stockbroker and the stockbroker's stealing from the claimant was not broken by the criminal acts of the broker.[489]

---

[481] *Great Elephant Corporation v Trafigura Beheer BV* [2013] EWCA Civ 905 per Longmore LJ at para 47.

[482] *HMS London* [1914] P 72 (Sir Samuel Evans); *Moore v DER Ltd* [1971] 1 WLR 1476 (CA); *Candlewood Navigation Corp Ltd v Mitsui OSK Lines Ltd (The Mineral Transporter)* [1986] AC 1 (PC).

[483] See above at section 16.13E(vii).

[484] See above at section 16.13D(iv).

[485] *County Ltd v Girozentrale Securities* [1996] 3 All ER 834 (CA) at 858.

[486] *London Joint Stock Bank Ltd v Macmillan* [1918] AC 777 (HL).

[487] *ACC Bank plc v Johnston* [2011] IEHC 376 (Irish High Court) at para 7.15.

[488] *Stansbie v Troman* [1948] 2 KB 48 (CA) Tucker LJ at 52. Likewise where the theft was due to the landlord's failure to install security measures or keep the front door in proper repair: *Marshall v Rubypoint Ltd* [1997] 1 EGLR 69 (CA). And see also the tort cases of *Home Office v Dorset Yacht Co Ltd* [1970] AC 1004 (HL) (borstal officers liable for damage caused when they lost control of the boys under their care); *Smith v Littlewoods Organisation Ltd* [1987] AC 241 (HL) (owner of a cinema liable for damage caused by trespassers to neighbouring property after the cinema was not secured properly); *Attorney General of the British Virgin Islands v Hartwell* [2004] 1 WLR 1273 (PC) (police liable for giving an unsafe officer access to a gun). But compare *Morrow v First National Bank of Hot Springs* 550 SW 2d 429 (1977) (SC of Arkansas), discussed above at text to chapter fourteen n 260.

[489] *De La Bere v Pearson Ltd* [1908] 1 KB 280 (CA).

F. Disease

Cockburn CJ in *Twycross v Grant*[490] gave the example of a horse with a latent disease where the purchase was induced by the defendant's wrong unrelated to that disease. That judge was of the view that if the disease was latent at the time of purchase it would not break the chain of causation, whereas if the disease was caught after the purchase then it would, and this was endorsed by Lord Steyn in the *Smith New Court Securities* case.[491] In contrast, in *Habton Farms v Nimmo*, the defendant's breach of warranty of authority prevented the seller from selling the horse before it then died from peritonitis.[492] There was no deemed sale at any earlier date (the claimant not having acted independently in keeping the horse, but rather having reasonably pursued the initial buyer because of the defendant's breach, and it in any event taking several weeks to sell a racehorse), and even though the death was not reasonably foreseeable,[493] it was taken into account and so the claimant was entitled to recover the full price, as the horse it was left with was treated (because of the death) as worthless.

---

[490] *Twycross v Grant* (1877) 2 CPD 469 (CA) Cockburn CJ at 544.

[491] *Smith New Court Securities Ltd v Scrimgeour Vickers (Asset Management) Ltd* [1997] AC 254 (HL) Lord Steyn at 286, also at 279. Some care must be taken when seeking to apply fraud decisions on causation to other contexts, because the causation rules are more relaxed in fraud cases.

[492] *Habton Farms (an unlimited company) v Nimmo* [2003] EWCA Civ 68.

[493] Ibid at paras 83, 88 and 102.

17

The Date of Assessment[1]

Determining the date as at which market value or cost of cure is to be assessed or other damages questions are to be answered.

17.1. The Principles
17.2. The Different Dates of Purchase of a Replacement on the Market
17.3. The Different Dates of Sale to the Market
17.4. Where there is No Opportunity to Resort to the Market

17.1 The Principles

A. Introduction

The supposed 'breach date rule' will be discussed in the sections below. In summary, however, the correct analysis is that of Oliver J in *Radford v De Froberville*: 'the proper approach is to assess the damages at the date of the hearing unless it can be said that the plaintiff ought reasonably to have mitigated by seeking an alternative performance at an earlier date'.[2]

The points made here are general, but the majority of the cases concern one of three fact situations. First, a claimant is deprived of property or has defective or damaged property (and so can often use the market to replace it). Secondly, a claimant has defective or damaged property or an unwanted business or property (and so can often use the market to sell the property or business). Thirdly, a claimant has defective or damaged property (and so can use the services market to purchase a repair).

(i) The Right to Damages Vests at the Date of Breach

The right to damages vests at the date of breach, but the amount is then 'unsettled' and is affected by mitigatory steps and other post-breach events.[3]

---

[1] See further A Dyson and A Kramer, 'There is No "Breach Date Rule": Mitigation, Difference in Value and Date of Assessment' (2014) 130 *LQR* 259.

[2] *Radford v De Froberville* [1977] 1 WLR 1262 (Oliver J) at 1286.

[3] See the discussion in *Kwei Tek Chao v British Traders and Shippers* [1954] 2 QB 459 (Devlin J) at 496–97.

(ii) Losses May Continue Up to and Beyond Judgment

Losses and gains will continue to occur after judgment, but the court has to fix damages at judgment. When considering post-judgment events, the court has to make predictions or evaluate chances, and must make a discount for accelerated receipt of damages.[4]

(iii) Take into Account all Evidence Available at Trial

Evidence of events occurring after breach but before judgment is admissible to prove the loss caused to the claimant. As Lord Macnaughten famously explained:

> It is [the judge's] duty, I think, to avail himself of all information at hand at the time of making his award ... Why should he listen to conjecture on a matter which has become an accomplished fact? Why should he guess when he can calculate? With the light before him, why should he shut his eyes and grope in the dark?[5]

In the professional negligence dispute *Kennedy v KB Van Emden & Co*,[6] Schiemann LJ explained that:

> The overriding rule governing the awards of damages is that the party who has been injured should be awarded by the court a sum of money which, in so far as money can do this, will, when it is paid, fairly compensate him for the wrong which the defendant has inflicted upon him. That will often involve looking at what happened or might have happened shortly after the defendant's breach of duty, what has happened between breach and trial and what is likely to happen in the future ... The court, when making its award, will look at all factors known to it at the time of judgment.

> In the present cases all the relevant facts were known by the date of trial. By contrast, in many cases judgment will be before the wrongful act ceases to have a deleterious effect on the plaintiff ... Even in such cases, no one suggests that the court should add to the uncertainties by putting itself notionally into the position it would have been in had it tried the case the day after the wrongful act started to inflict damage.

> The present case is devoid of all such uncertainties. There is no advantage in the court, sitting at a time when all the facts are known, putting itself notionally into the position of ignorance it would have been in had it been assessing the damages on the day after the wrong was inflicted. This would be to add pointless and avoidable uncertainties. In a personal injury case, no one would dream of submitting that the court should at trial assess damages by putting itself notionally into the position it would have been in had it been hearing the case on the day after the accident ...

---

[4] See chapter one, section 1.2C(v), above.

[5] *Bwyllfa and Merthyr Dare Steam Collieries (1891) Ltd v Pontypridd Waterworks Co* [1903] AC 426 (HL) at 431. This was recently repeated (and affirmed) by Lord Brown in *Golden Strait Corp v Nippon Yusen Kubishika Kaisha (The Golden Victory)* [2007] 2 AC 353 (HL) at para 78. See also Halsbury LJ in *Bwyllfa* at 429: 'It is, of course, only an accident that the true sum can now be ascertained with precision; but what does that matter?', quoted with approval by Ward LJ in *Kennedy v KB Van Emden & Co* [1997] 2 EGLR 137 (CA) at 140; and see further *South Australia Asset Management Corp (SAAMCo) v York Montague Ltd* [1997] 1 AC 191 (HL) Lord Hoffmann at 220–21.

[6] *Kennedy v KB Van Emden & Co* [1997] 2 EGLR 137 (CA) at 141.

I fully accept that, had these cases come on for trial, say, six months after completion, at a time when the statutory prohibition on assignments with a premium was still in force, the court might well have awarded compensation for the unforeseen restraint on charging premiums on any assignment. That is because, at that notional date of trial, the court would have been faced with the task of putting compensation figures on the plaintiffs' then existing disabilities in relation to future assignments or using the property as security for a loan and so on.

In that case the court took into account the change of law between the breach and trial which meant that the claimant could sell its lease at a premium and so had suffered no loss. And similarly it was observed in the Supreme Court of Canada in a claim for the profits that would have been made if a partnership had not been repudiated:

> Where future damages are claimed, future conditions must necessarily be considered, and what better evidence of conditions, which were in the future at the date of the breach, can be made than by shewing, at the date of the trial, what has actually occurred since the breach of contract?[7]

The leading case on the point is *The Golden Victory*, where the House of Lords considered the point at length and held by a majority that the court did not need to speculate as to the chances of war breaking out and cutting a charter short (because of a charterer's lawful option to terminate upon war) where the court knew at the date of trial that war had in fact broken out and precisely when.[8]

The same approach was applied in the tortious property damage case of *Re-Source America International Ltd v Platt Site Services Ltd*,[9] where the Court of Appeal refused to disregard a collapse in the market for fibre optics and closure of the claimant's plant, both of which took place after breach but before judgment. Similarly, where proof of the lost profits on a development can be informed by evidence of the profit actually made on the development after breach, that evidence is of course to be taken into account.[10] In *McKinnon v e.surv Ltd*, where the defendant surveyor failed to spot that the residential property purchased was still subject to subsidence movement, the court took into account the fact that by the time of trial the property had settled and movement had ceased.[11] And in *AW Group Ltd v Taylor Walton*, the court took into account the fact that the claimant had found tenants and made improvements as evidence of the true value of the property at the earlier date of acquisition.[12]

---

[7] *Findlay v Howard* (1919) 58 SCR 516 (SC of Canada) Mignault J at 544.

[8] *Golden Strait Corp v Nippon Yusen Kubishika Kaisha (The Golden Victory)* [2007] 2 AC 353 (HL). The consequences of that for the defendant's choice to terminate are discussed above in chapter thirteen, section 13.3B(iv).

[9] *Re-Source America International Ltd v Platt Site Services Ltd* [2005] 2 Lloyd's Rep 50 (CA), a bailment claim for profits consequential upon property damage.

[10] *William Aitchison v Gordon Durham & Co Ltd* (CA), 30 June 1995.

[11] *McKinnon v e.surv Ltd (formerly known as GA Valuation & Survey Ltd)* [2003] EWHC 475 (Ch) (Gaunt QC). See also *Techno Land Improvements Ltd v British Leyland (UK) Ltd* [1979] 2 EGLR 27 (Goulding J); *Murfin v Campbell* [2011] EWHC 1475 (Ch) (Pelling QC).

[12] *AW Group Ltd v Taylor Walton* [2013] EWHC 2610 (Ch) (Hodge QC) obiter at para 243.

(iv) Appeal and Post-Trial Events

On appeal the court may take post-trial events into account when assessing a loss of chance.[13]

B. The Supposed 'Breach Date Rule' and Why there Isn't One

(i) The Supposed 'Breach Date Rule'

The calculation of damages awards is bedevilled by mistaken reliance on a supposed rule that damages are to be assessed as at the date of breach. The conventional view is that there is such a rule in both contract and tort, but that it is to be applied flexibly and not mechanistically, and departed from when justice or the compensatory principle requires.[14] Accordingly, a market measure at the date of delivery is rebuttably presumed by the Sale of Goods Act in relation to non-delivery, non-acceptance and defective goods case.[15]

Yet it is also orthodox to explain the date of assessment principles, and the cases in which the date of breach is departed from, by reference to the principle of mitigation, such that if the claimant did not and could not have been expected to have recourse to the market at the date of breach by way of mitigation (to replace the performance not provided by the defendant) then the date of breach will not apply. This is the true position.

(ii) The Magic of the Market and the Rebuttable Presumption of the Date of Breach Where there is a Market

The existence of a market for goods or services can provide a clean way of avoiding and thereby eliminating from the damages calculation most complex and case-specific losses. This is because if the claimant can purchase replacement goods or services then it can go on and do whatever it would have done with the promised goods and services. All the losses consequent upon not having the goods or services, which can be as varied as businesses and particular businesses' plans, are thereby avoided. Moreover, the market is such a large and available means of avoiding loss that where a suitable market exists it will usually be the case that all reasonable claimants would use it to avoid these losses, and accordingly the principle of mitigation will usually deem the claimant to have done so whether or not she in fact did.[16]

---

[13] *Whitehead v Hibbert Pownall & Newton (a firm)* (CA), 4 March 2008.

[14] *Miliangos v George Frank (Textiles) Ltd* [1976] AC 443 (HL) Lord Wilberforce at 468; *Johnson v Agnew* [1980] AC 367 (HL) Lord Wilberforce at 401; *Dodd Properties (Kent) Ltd v Canterbury City Council* [1980] 1 WLR 433 (CA) Megaw LJ at 451 and Donaldson LJ at 457; *County Personnel (Employment Agency) Ltd v Alan R Pulver & Co* [1987] 1 WLR 916 (CA) Bingham LJ at 925–26; *Smith New Court Securities Ltd v Citibank NA* [1997] AC 254 (HL) Lord Browne-Wilkinson at 265–26; *Golden Strait Corp v Nippon Yusen Kubishika Kaisha (The Golden Victory)* [2007] 2 AC 353 (HL) Lord Bingham at paras 9, 11 and 13 and Lord Scott at para 33; *Parabola Investments Ltd v Browallia Cal Ltd* [2011] QB 477 (CA) Toulson LJ at para 33.

[15] See above in chapter four, section 4.2C.

[16] See above in chapter sixteen, section 16.4A.

Further, because the market is usually quick and easy to access, in cases where there *is* a market it becomes normal to measure losses by reference to the difference between the contract price and the market price *at the date of breach*, because it is at the date of breach that the claimant either went to the market or was deemed to have done so.

This therefore gives rise to a perfectly sensible rebuttable presumption that where there is a market it provides the measure of loss, at the date of breach. The Sale of Goods Act 1979 records such a rule as a set of rebuttable presumptions (which on the whole apply if, and only if, there is an available market). But these are only rebuttable presumptions. As one judge has observed of the date of breach 'rule' in a case of non-delivery of land,

> what is called the general rule, that is to say the rule whereby damages are assessed as at the date of the breach, is in reality no more than the commonest answer *in fact* to the question what method of assessment will put the plaintiff in the same position as if the breach had not occurred. It is a rule, therefore, of circumstance rather than law, and where on the facts, either proved or for the purposes of this particular decision postulated, the application of that general rule would not put the plaintiff in the same position as if the breach had not occurred, for a variety of reasons, including those where he was unable to mitigate through circumstances beyond his control, then I ought not to follow that general rule and I ought to hold that the situation amounts to another exception.[17]

In short, 'Where there is a market in which the injured party can buy a replacement, the date of non-delivery is usually deemed the appropriate date. But where there is no such market, a later date may be appropriate'.[18] All depends upon the date on which the claimant could be expected to mitigate. This mitigation explanation of the 'difference in value at the date of breach' measure, and the authorities for it, are discussed in some detail above in relation to goods.[19]

(iii) There is No Date of Breach 'Rule'

It is important to realise that therefore there is no 'date of breach rule' (in contrast with a date of breach presumption applicable in certain circumstances), for the following reasons:

i) <u>The need for a market</u>: as Toulson LJ observed in the 2013 Court of Appeal non-acceptance decision in *Hooper v Oates*, 'the breach date is the right date for assessment of damages only where there is an immediately available market for the sale of the relevant asset or, in the converse case, for the purchase of an equivalent asset'.[20] Where there is no market, there is no reason to fix anything at the date of breach, and all loss is recoverable under ordinary principles, up to and beyond trial. This is self-evidently correct for, eg, personal injury cases: if the claimant is injured he or she can recover all the losses resulting from the injury. The claimant cannot (at least with present technology)

---

[17] *Zakrzewski v Chas J Odhams & Sons* [1981] 2 EGLR 15 (Rougier QC) at 17.
[18] *Johnson v Perez* (1988) 166 CLR 351 (HC of Australia) Mason CJ at para 7.
[19] See chapter four, section 4.2, especially sub-section C.
[20] *Hooper v Oates* [2013] 3 All ER 211 (CA) Lloyd LJ at para 38.

replace his arm on any market, and so the mitigatory principle has nothing to say and the claimant recovers all its lost earnings and amenity up to trial and beyond. The same is true of all cases in which so-called 'consequential losses' are awarded by the courts: they were unavoidable through a market or otherwise, so are recoverable, whenever they occurred or will occur.

ii) <u>The need for it to be reasonable to go to the market</u>: there are many cases in which it is not reasonable to expect the claimant to use the market, at least for a time. These include where the claimant pressed the defendant for specific performance, or where the defect was latent and so the claimant did not know it needed to replace the property. These are discussed further below in sections 17.2 and 17.3.

iii) <u>The date is not always the date of breach</u>: even where the market measure applies, the applicable date will not always be the date of breach: for example the relevant date will be later where it reasonably takes time to access the market. This is most obvious in cases of land, where it may take months or years, but may also apply in certain cases of goods. See further below section 17.2C(ii).

iv) <u>The measure only replaces some losses with others</u>: the market measure at first sight appears to restrict damages to the difference between the contract price and the market price. This is because the act of market replacement avoids all the consequential losses that would have arisen from not having the goods or service (such as losses on a sub-sale, losses from use of goods in a factory, etc). Any losses suffered during the period up to the date of accessing the market are still recoverable. The date of accessing the market only puts an end to further losses.

Moreover, on closer analysis, it does not put an end to all further losses. Frequently the claimant will pay more on the market than it was obliged to pay under the contract, and therefore will suffer a net additional cost at the date of going to the market.

Thus access to the market may crystallise the loss in the sense of eliminating the messy and bespoke damages for subsequent loss of use of goods or similar, but will replace it with a claim for loss of use of money (the extra spent on the market as compared with what would have been payable under the contract), from the date of accessing the market forwards. Such a loss of use of money will usually be compensated for by an award of statutory interest, which many lawyers have forgotten is a type of compensation, but it is now also clear that loss of use of money can be compensated for by a properly pleaded claim for contract damages.[21] Of course, usually such a claim will be fairly simple and general—a rate of interest to reflect the costs of borrowing or the income that would have been made with the money—but this will not always be the case and, besides, should not prevent us realising that the damages continue after the date of access to the market.

Thus the market replacement merely allows the claimant to swap the harm from loss of use of property up until trial and beyond, which would have been

---

[21] *Sempra Metals Ltd (formerly Metallgesellschaft Ltd) v Inland Revenue Commissioners* [2008] 1 AC 561 (HL), and see chapter seven.

suffered without the replacement, for harm from loss of use of money up until trial, following the replacement.

v) <u>There is no restriction on using post-breach events and evidence</u>: Even where the market measure does apply, there is no rule that post-breach events or evidence cannot be taken into account.

By way of example, where there is an available market, evidence of post-breach events affecting the intended use of the property will be irrelevant in a claim for non-supply. However, as regards loss of use of the money needed to purchase a replacement, post-breach events are still relevant.

Furthermore, even with a replacement, there may be situations where it is necessary to look at what happened or would have happened after the market date in order to calculate damages.[22]

It is important to recognise that there is no breach date rule, only the legal rules (especially mitigation), because only then can we give sensible answers to the relevant questions of whether there was an available market, and on what date if any a market measure should be taken. The breach date rule/market measure rule is merely an ossified form of a sensible rebuttable presumption as to a particular mitigatory step. The ossification is natural enough in sale of goods cases, where the presumption is (save in latent defect cases) relatively rarely rebutted, but it is a rebuttable presumption nonetheless, and is much less frequently applicable in sale of land or professional negligence cases.

(iv) Capital Value as a Measure of Future Income

Before discussing the general rules of date of assessment and mitigation, it is important to note that a diminution in market value at the date of breach may also be taken as a measure of the loss of income after that date, where the market value of the asset (property or business) itself reflects the future income stream, the acceleration of the receipt, and any suitable discount for the risks of not achieving that income. This is discussed below in chapter eighteen, section 18.1B.

17.2 The Different Dates of Purchase of a Replacement on the Market

This section considers cases where the claimant is deprived of property, or has defective property, that can be replaced. The market measure applies to such cases, but not always at the date of breach.

---

[22] Thus in *Golden Strait Corp v Nippon Yusen Kubishika Kaisha (The Golden Victory)* [2007] 2 AC 353 (HL) it was necessary to look at post-breach events to calculate what would have been earned under the breached charter, because it contained a profit share provision such that the charter fee paid depended upon how well the charterer did, and so even though the damages were assessed by comparing the actual charter with a replacement charter, there was still a need to look past the breach date. See Lord Brown at para 81, and also the Court of Appeal decision [2006] 1 WLR 533 Lord Mance at paras 13 and 25.

A. Date Prior to Delivery

(i) Termination for Anticipatory Breach

Where the claimant has accepted an anticipatory breach and terminated prior to the date of delivery, the market value will be taken at the date of termination, or the date thereafter when the claimant could be expected to or did reasonably have recourse to the market for a replacement.[23] Thus in *Kaines (UK) Ltd v Osterreichische Warenhandelsgesellschaft* the claimant buyer's damages upon non-delivery of crude oil were fixed by the market rate on the day following the day on which (at 5.28pm) the seller's anticipatory repudiatory breach was accepted, rather than the date 10 days later when the buyer actually bought a replacement.[24] If that is the date upon which a reasonable person would have purchased a replacement, it is irrelevant that the market in fact moves in the claimant's favour between that date and the date due for performance.[25]

(ii) The Claimant Has Not Terminated

Even if the claimant has not terminated, in rare cases it may be that it should (if properly mitigating its loss) have resorted to the market and terminated. If that is the case, and if the claimant is ultimately awarded damages (rather than specific performance or an agreed sum), it is open to the court to restrict the award on the basis of a deeming that the claimant had terminated and resorted to the market earlier.[26]

B. The Date of Delivery/Breach

A usual (at least in sale of goods contracts) date when the claimant will resort or will be deemed to have resorted to the market will be the date of delivery,[27] or so shortly thereafter as to make no difference, hence the presumption in the Sale of Goods Act 1979.[28] The cases applying this date are those where the breach date presumption has not been rebutted, and those that support the (flawed) argument that there is a breach date rule.

---

[23] *Melachrino v Nickoll and Knight* [1920] 1 KB 693 (Bailhache J), obiter. See further chapter fifteen, section 15.3B(ii) above.

[24] *Kaines (UK) Ltd v Osterreichische Warenhandelsgesellschaft Austrowaren Gesellschaft mbH* [1993] Lloyd's Rep 1 (CA).

[25] *Gebruder Metelmann GmbH & Co KG v NBR (London) Ltd* [1984] 1 Lloyd's Rep 614 (CA).

[26] See chapter sixteen, section 16.3 above.

[27] *Johnson v Agnew* [1980] 1 AC 367 (HL) Lord Wilberforce at 401.

[28] Eg *AKAS Jamal v Moolla Dawood Sons & Co* [1916] 1 AC 175 (PC); *Campbell Mostyn (Provisions) Ltd v Barnett Trading Co* [1954] 1 Lloyd's Rep 65 (CA). See further the cases cited at n 14 above.

C. A Date between Breach and Trial

There are numerous situations in which there is a market that the claimant reasonably accessed or should have accessed for a replacement at some date after breach but before trial.

(i) The Claimant Pressed the Defendant for Performance for a Time

In non-delivery, defective delivery, or non-acceptance cases, the innocent party may have reasonably pressed the defendant for performance after the date for delivery, only giving up or being expected to give up on the defendant later.[29] Thus in *Bear Stearns Bank plc v Forum Global Equity*,[30] it was reasonable of the buyer of shares to press for a year before finally terminating and buying replacements, and the market price at the end of that year (not the earlier date for delivery) was applied for the purpose of calculating damages. Or the breaching party may have requested further time, delaying the date on which the claimant should have sought or did reasonably seek a replacement.[31]

And so in *Habton Farms v Nimmo* it was reasonable for the claimant to pursue its initial seller because the defendant's breach of warranty of authority was still acting on it (ie was still latent), but

> There would of course come a time at which it could properly be held that the decision not to sell the horse was a market decision independent of the breach of warranty. Once that moment came, the correct approach would in my opinion be to deduct the market value at that time from the contract price and to award the difference (if any) as damages for breach of warranty of authority.[32]

(ii) It Takes a Little Time to Arrange the Replacement

Such a later date will also be reasonable, and therefore applicable under the mitigatory principle, where it takes time to effect a replacement purchase (in a non-delivery case) or sale (in a non-acceptance case) or both (in a defective delivery case). As Steyn J observed 'it is [often] reasonable to allow the aggrieved party a little time to measure the impact of what has happened' but commercial parties can be expected

---

[29] *Asamera Oil Corp Ltd v Sea Oil & General Corp* [1979] 1 SCR 633 (SC of Canada); the discussion in *Johnson v Agnew* [1980] 1 AC 367 (HL) of Lord Wilberforce at 401; *Johnson Matthey Bankers Ltd v The State Trading Corp of India Ltd* [1984] 1 Lloyd's Rep 427 (Staughton J); *Habton Farms (an unlimited company) v Nimmo* [2003] EWCA Civ 68 (pressed a third party because of the defendant's breach of warranty of authority); *Carbopego-Abastecimento de Combustiveis SA v AMCI Export Corp* [2006] 1 Lloyd's Rep 736 (Aikens J); *Bear Stearns Bank plc v Forum Global Equity* [2007] EWHC 1576 (Comm) (Andrew Smith J); *Greenglade Estates Ltd v Chana* [2012] EWHC 1913 (Ch) (Donaldson QC). But see *Janred Properties Ltd v Ente Nazionale Italiano per il Turismo* [1989] 2 All ER 444 (CA) at 457. See also the discussion in chapter sixteen, section1 6.3. Likewise where the claimant seeks recovery of property tortiously taken from it: *City of Calgary v Costello* 1997 ABCA 281 (CA of Alberta).

[30] *Bear Stearns Bank plc v Forum Global Equity* [2007] EWHC 1576 (Comm) (Andrew Smith J).

[31] *Ogle v Earl Vane* (1867) LR 2 QB 275; *Hickman v Haynes* (1875) LR 10 CP 598; *Toprak Mahsulleri Ofisi v Finagrain Compagnie Commerciale Agricole et Financière* [1979] 2 Lloyd's Rep 98 (CA).

[32] *Habton Farms v Nimmo* [2003] EWCA Civ 68 Clarke LJ at para 100, also Auld LJ at para 128.

to act with reasonable alacrity.[33] Devlin J has also referred to the claimant being expected to act 'within a reasonable time' of discovery of the defect:

> [I]f one bears in mind the principle that the buyer is bound to mitigate his damage, then as soon as he knows of his rights he must sell the goods. He cannot do so before he does know his rights, and 'as soon as' means within a reasonable time thereafter.[34]

Lord Brown has pointed out that the expectation is at its strictest with goods or shares, whereas in other cases 'time may well be needed before the injured party can reasonably be required to re-enter the market'.[35] In the case of a racehorse, it may take four or five weeks.[36] Indeed, in land cases the claimant will almost always need and be allowed several months.[37] An even longer time may be needed in the case of a business.[38]

Accordingly the wording of the non-binding UNIDROIT Principles of International Commercial Contracts, asking whether the buyer went to the market 'within a reasonable time and in a reasonable manner',[39] reflects the English common law approach, which recognises that it will often take at least some hours or a day if not longer to effect a replacement, and will rarely look to an earlier date if the claimant in fact did resort to the market a short time after delivery.[40] A simple example arose in a case of tortious destruction of a lorry, which took some time to replace and then to adapt so as to be useable in the claimant's business (and lost profits were recovered in the meantime).[41]

(iii) A Latent Defect that Was Discovered

In defective delivery cases, a post-breach date will be applicable where a defect was initially latent and was not reasonably discovered until some time after delivery, such as upon rejection by a sub-buyer. In that situation the date upon which the claimant is expected to have gone to the market, and therefore the date on which the market value is taken, will be the date of actual discovery or when the claim-

---

[33] *Kaines (UK) Ltd v Osterreichische Warenhandelsgesellschaft Austrowaren Gesellschaft mbH* [1993] Lloyd's Rep 1 (Steyn) at 8, his approach approved on appeal (same citation). The same point was made and applied in *C Sharpe & Co Ltd v Nosawa & Co* [1917] 2 KB 814 (Atkin J) at 821, where a few weeks were allowed; *Owners of Dredger Liesbosch v Owners of SS Edison (The Liesbosch)* [1933] AC 449 (HL) Lord Wright at 465; *Golden Strait Corp v Nippon Yusen Kubishika Kaisha (The Golden Victory)* [2007] 2 AC 353 (HL) Lord Scott at para 34.

[34] *Kwei Tek Chao v British Traders and Shippers Ltd* [1954] 2 QB 459 (Devlin J) at 494.

[35] *Golden Strait Corp v Nippon Yusen Kubishika Kaisha (The Golden Victory)* [2007] 2 AC 353 (HL) Lord Brown at para 80.

[36] *Habton Farms (an unlimited company) v Nimmo* [2003] EWCA Civ 68 Auld LJ at para 128–29.

[37] *Hooper v Oates* [2013] 3 All ER 211 (CA) Lloyd LJ at paras 34 and 38.

[38] See *British & Commonwealth Holdings plc v Quadrex Holdings Inc* (CA), 10 April 1995.

[39] Article 7.4.5(1).

[40] *Asamera Oil Corp Ltd v Sea Oil & General Corp* [1979] 1 SCR 633 (SC of Canada); *Kaines (UK) Ltd v Osterreichische Warenhandelsgesellschaft Austrowaren Gesellschaft mbH* [1993] Lloyd's Rep 1 (CA) (where the day *after* the pre-delivery termination for anticipatory breach was the relevant date). See also non-acceptance cases where it reasonably took a little time to find a replacement buyer: *Stewart v Cauty* (1841) 8 M & W 160; *Techno Land Improvements Ltd v British Leyland (UK) Ltd* [1979] 2 EGLR 27 (Goulding J); *Shearson Lehman Hutton Inc v Maclaine Watson & Co Ltd (No 2)* [1990] 3 All ER 723 (Webster J).

[41] *Jones v Port of London Authority* [1954] 1 Lloyd's Rep 489 (Devlin J) at 490.

ant should have discovered the defect, if earlier. The cases in this area are discussed above at section chapter four, section 4.2B(v) (and see the dictum of Devlin J quoted in the previous paragraph),[42] and fit with the general idea that mitigatory steps are only expected once the claimant is aware of the breach.[43] Of course, if the claimant has already used or sold the property it may be that no recourse to the market is expected or indeed possible.[44]

(iv) Other Reasons

It may have taken time to discover the breach, or there may not immediately be an available market. The claimant's impecuniosity may reasonably prevent the claimant resorting to the market immediately,[45] or it may need governmental approvals before returning to the market.[46] In the *British Westinghouse* case the turbines were replaced three years after purchase and the replacement taken into account, with losses in the interim being recoverable.[47]

And in the Canadian case of *Asamera Oil Corporation Ltd v Sea Oil & General Corporation*, the relevant date was calculated by allowing a reasonable time for negotiations with the defendant, then a reasonable time for arranging finance for a replacement, and then a time to carefully acquire replacement shares in blocks (and, given the size of the purchase, allowance was also made for the upward pressure on price that the first parts of the purchase itself would have had), although the date of deemed replacement was still some 10 years before trial.[48]

(v) Reasonable to Speculate?

Note that the relevant date will not be deferred because it is a sensible commercial decision to speculate on the market. Although that conduct may be reasonable in one sense, it is outside the defendant's responsibility and treated as being for the claimant's account.[49]

---

[42] The same point applies to the date at which repairs to a latent defect should be carried out: *East Ham Corp v Bernard Sunley & Sons Ltd* [1966] AC 406 (HL).

[43] Above in chapter fifteen, section 15.3B(iii)(c).

[44] See chapter four, section 4.2A(v).

[45] Obiter in the preliminary issue hearing of *Zakrzewski v Chas J Odhams & Sons* [1981] 2 EGLR 15 (Rougier QC). As to impecuniosity generally, see chapter sixteen, section 16.7, above.

[46] *Empresa Cubana Importada de Alimentos (Alimport) v Iasmos Shipping Co SA (The Good Friend)* [1984] 2 Lloyd's Rep 586 (Staughton J) at 596.

[47] *British Westinghouse Electric & Manufacturing Co Ltd v Underground Electric Railways Co of London Ltd* [1912] AC 673 (HL).

[48] *Asamera Oil Corporation Ltd v Sea Oil & General Corporation* [1979] 1 SCR 633 (SC of Canada) at 674–75. As to these points on the date of assessment, see further chapter sixteen section 16.3A above, where this decision is discussed in more detail.

[49] See chapter sixteen, section 16.4A, above.

D. The Date of Judgment

The same factors that may make it reasonable for the claimant not to have resorted to the market until a post-breach date may in other cases justify the claimant not having done so at any time prior to judgment. If the claimant has not resorted to the market, the proper approach is to award the actual loss, including any market costs assessed at the date of judgment, 'unless it can be said that the plaintiff ought reasonably to have mitigated by seeking an alternative performance at an earlier date'.[50]

(i) Impecuniosity

The most common situation in which a claimant will reasonably not have resorted to the market until trial, even where such resort is possible (ie a market is available), is where the claimant could not afford to do so. Provided such impecuniosity is not on the particular facts too remote, and the claimant acted reasonably, the claimant is entitled to the market cost at the date of judgment even if higher than at an earlier date.[51]

(ii) Pressed the Defendant for Performance Up to Trial

A specific reason that may justify an assessment at the date of trial is a version of the point made above about the claimant reasonably pressing the claimant for performance.[52] In some cases, the innocent party may have reasonably sought specific performance, and therefore not sought a replacement from the market, and only ended up with a damages award (assessed at the date of trial) because specific performance was refused at trial,[53] withdrawn at trial,[54] or ordered but then dissolved upon non-observance by the party subject to the order.[55] In these instances, the relevant time when the claimant should seek a replacement (and at which the cost of doing so will be fixed) is the date of judgment, albeit that in practice it may make more sense to quantify the damages at the slightly earlier date of trial.[56]

---

[50] *Radford v De Froberville* [1977] 1 WLR 1262 (Oliver J) at 1286.

[51] See further chapter sixteen section 16.7B above, and *Wroth v Tyler* [1974] Ch 30 (Megarry J); *Dodd Properties (Kent) Ltd v Canterbury City Council* [1980] 1 WLR 433 (CA) Megaw LJ at 451, as discussed in *Kennedy v KB Van Emden & Co* [1997] 2 EGLR 137 (CA) Ward LJ at 140; *Jarvis v T Richards & Co*, 30 July 1980 (Nourse J); *Forster v Silvermere Golf & Equestrian Centre Ltd* (1981) 42 P & CR 255 (Dillon J); *Syrett v Carr & Neave (a firm)* [1990] 2 EGLR 161 (Bowsher QC).

[52] Above in section 17.2C(i).

[53] *Wroth v Tyler* [1974] Ch 30 (Megarry J); *Malhotra v Choudhury* [1980] Ch 52 (CA); *Kopec v Pyret* (1983) 146 DLR (3d) 242 (Saskatchewan QB), affirmed (1987) 36 DLR (4th) 1 (Saskatchewan CA); *Suleman v Shahsavari* [1988] 1 WLR 1181 (Park QC); *Duffy v Ridley Properties Ltd* [2008] 4 IR 282 (SC of Ireland). Contrast *Asamera Oil Corp Ltd v Sea Oil & General Corp* [1979] 1 SCR 633 (SC of Canada). See further the discussion in relation to unreasonably seeking specific performance in chapter sixteen, section 16.3.

[54] *Semelhago v Paramadevan* [1996] 2 SCR 415 (SC of Canada).

[55] *Johnson v Agnew* [1980] AC 367 (HL).

[56] *Semelhago v Paramadevan* [1996] 2 SCR 415 (SC of Canada) Sopinka J at para 18: 'Technically speaking, the date of assessment should be the date of judgment. That is the date upon which specific performance is ordered. For practical purposes, however, the evidence that is adduced which is relevant

An earlier date will be fixed, however, in the relatively rare case that specific performance was sought unreasonably (ie with little realistic chance of success), in which case the market measure will be taken at the earlier date on which the claimant should have ceased to press the defendant and terminated the contract.[57] Similarly, even if seeking specific performance was reasonable, if the claimant's unreasonably tardy pursuit of its claim leads to judgment being given at a later date than it would otherwise have been, the earlier date when it should have got judgment will be taken in quantifying any damages.[58]

17.3 The Different Dates of Sale to the Market

A. The Applicable Principles: No 'Breach Date Rule', Just the Rules of Mitigation and Legal Causation

In the cases discussed in the previous section, the continuing losses to the claimant can only be stopped by purchasing a replacement or cure to give the claimant the equivalent property or position to that it would otherwise have had.

The other use of a market is to sell unwanted property. This is something the claimant will want (and be expected) to do where it has damaged or defective property that is replaced not repaired, or otherwise is of no use. The same applies where the breach consists of inducing the claimant to enter into a transaction which, but for the breach, it never would have entered into, typically by a professional giving negligent advice.[59] The primary element of the claim will consist of losses on the transaction, the claimant seeking to be put in the position it would have been in had it never entered the transaction. (This is essentially the tort measure, as applicable to misrepresentation and deceit,[60] and many of the cases below are tort cases.)

As with purchase of a replacement, so with the question of sale of unwanted property, there has traditionally been considered to be a prima facie breach date rule that the property acquired is to be valued for the purposes of giving credit in the claim for damages at the date of breach. However, as Lord Browne-Wilkinson explained in the leading deceit case of *Smith New Court Securities*,

> in assessing such damages it is not an inflexible rule that the plaintiff must bring into account the value as at the transaction date of the asset acquired: although the point is not adverted to in the judgments, the basis on which the damages were computed shows that there can

to enable damages to be assessed will be as of the date of trial. It is not usually possible to predict the date of judgment when the evidence is given'.

[57] See above in chapter sixteen, section 16.3.

[58] *Malhotra v Choudhury* [1980] Ch 52 (CA). See also *McGrath v Stewart*, 11 November 2008 (Irish High Court), and see also the discretion to alter the date from which interest runs, discussed above in chapter seven n 93.

[59] See also cases of breach by the other party to the transaction of a collateral contractual duty of care by the giving of pre-contractual representations, as in *Esso Petroleum Co Ltd v Mardon* [1976] QB 801 (CA).

[60] For discussion of the measure of recovery in professional negligence cases, see above in chapter three.

be circumstances in which it is proper to require a defendant only to bring into account the actual proceeds of the asset provided that <u>he has acted reasonably in retaining it</u>.

The old 'inflexible rule' is both wrong in principle and capable of producing manifest injustice. The defendant's fraud may have an effect continuing after the transaction is completed, e.g. if a sale of gold shares was induced by a misrepresentation that a new find had been made which was to be announced later it would plainly be wrong to assume that the plaintiff <u>should have sold the shares</u> before the announcement should have been made. Again, the acquisition of the asset may, as in *Doyle v. Olby (Ironmongers) Ltd.* itself, <u>lock the purchase into continuing to hold the asset until he can effect a resale</u>. To say that in such a case the plaintiff has obtained the value of the asset as at the transaction date and must therefore bring it into account flies in the face of common sense: <u>how can he be said to have received such a value if, despite his efforts, he has been unable to sell</u> ... ?

In the light of these authorities the old 19th century cases can no longer be treated as laying down a strict and inflexible rule. In many cases, even in deceit, it will be appropriate to value the asset acquired as at the transaction date if that truly reflects the value of what the plaintiff has obtained. Thus, <u>if the asset acquired is a readily marketable asset and there is no special feature (such as a continuing misrepresentation or the purchaser being locked into a business that he has acquired) the transaction date rule may well produce a fair result. The plaintiff has acquired the asset and what he does with it thereafter is entirely up to him, freed from any continuing adverse impact of the defendant's wrongful act</u> ...

So long as he is not aware of the fraud, no question of a duty to mitigate can arise. But once the fraud has been discovered, if the plaintiff is not locked into the asset and the fraud has ceased to operate on his mind, a failure to take reasonable steps to sell the property may constitute a failure to mitigate his loss requiring him to bring the value of the property into account as at the date when he discovered the fraud or shortly thereafter ...

(4) as a general rule, the benefits received by him include the market value of the property acquired as at the date of acquisition; but such general rule is not to be inflexibly applied where to do so would prevent him obtaining full compensation for the wrong suffered; (5) although the circumstances in which the general rule should not apply cannot be comprehensively stated, it will normally not apply where either (a) the misrepresentation has continued to operate after the date of the acquisition of the asset so as to induce the plaintiff to retain the asset or (b) the circumstances of the case are such that the plaintiff is, by reason of the fraud, locked into the property; (6) In addition, the plaintiff is entitled to recover consequential losses caused by the transaction; (7) the plaintiff must take all reasonable steps to mitigate his loss once he has discovered the fraud. (Emphasis added)[61]

Lord Steyn also emphasised that the date of transaction was 'only prima facie the right date' and 'the date of transaction rule is simply a second order rule' and 'valuation at the transaction date is simply a method of measuring loss which will satisfactorily solve many cases'.[62]

---

[61] *Smith New Court Securities Ltd v Scrimgeour Vickers (Asset Management) Ltd* [1997] AC 254 (HL) at 265–67 (these pages deserve to be read in their entirety).
[62] Ibid at 284.

As Nourse LJ explained in the surveyor's negligence case of *Patel v Hooper & Jackson*:[63]

> The house never having been sold, the real difficulty in the case is to decide by what date the plaintiffs were able to sell it or, to put it objectively, by what date they ought reasonably to have sold it. If, as the recorder correctly held, the plaintiffs' duty was to act reasonably in attempting to mitigate their loss, sooner or later they ought to have sold the house, not just in order to avoid the risk of a further depreciation in its value but also to put a term to the period during which the defendants would be liable to compensate them for the costs of their alternative accommodation.

And in a solicitor's negligence case, Bingham LJ explained that the date of breach rule should not be 'mechanistically applied in circumstances where assessment at another date may more accurately reflect the overriding compensatory rule'.[64] Lord Hoffmann in the valuer's negligence case *SAAMCo* confirmed that a post-acquisition date for selling property is taken where 'the claimant had reacted reasonably to his predicament'.[65] Toulson J has explained that all depends upon when there is an available market and the knowledge that makes it fair to expect the claimant to access it.[66] The Irish High Court has carefully explained that

> If the party decides to keep the impaired asset, for whatever reason, then it seems to me that unless it can be demonstrated that there was some good reason for keeping it, rather than selling it, then it is difficult to see how the negligent defendant can be fixed with any knock-on consequences that would not have occurred had the asset been disposed of.[67]

As is clear from these dicta and the cases below, the correct rule in sale to the market cases is that the claimant must give credit for the value of the property received at the date on which the claimant reasonably sold the property or the date on which the claimant could have been expected to sell the property in mitigation of its loss, if earlier, and the claimant can recover continuing losses from holding that property up to that date. In other words, the so-called breach date rule in the sale to the market context, like the market replacement context, is just a useful presumption as to the correct application of the mitigatory principle.

Of course, as in cases of replacement where there is no market, if there was no market upon which the property could have been sold at fair value then the mitigatory/causational principles are not engaged and the date of trial is the correct date for assessment of loss.[68]

---

[63] *Patel v Hooper & Jackson (a firm)* [1999] 1 WLR 1792 (CA) at 1802.

[64] *County Personnel (Employment Agency) Ltd v Alan R Pulver & Co* [1987] 1 WLR 916 (CA) at 926. Approved and applied in *Portman Building Society v Bevan Ashford* [2000] 1 EGLR 81 (CA) Otton LJ at 84.

[65] *South Australia Asset Management Corp (SAAMCo) v York Montague Ltd* [1997] 1 AC 191 (HL) at 219.

[66] *Standard Chartered Bank v Pakistan National Shipping Corp* [1999] 1 Lloyd's Rep 747 (Toulson J) at 760. Also *Gestmin SGPS SA v Credit Suisse (UK) Ltd* [2013] EWHC 3560 (Comm) (Leggatt J) at para 186.

[67] *Kelleher v O'Connor* [2010] IEHC 313 (Irish High Court) at para 10.5.

[68] *Gestmin SGPS SA v Credit Suisse (UK) Ltd* [2013] EWHC 3560 (Comm) (Leggatt J) obiter at para 190.

B. Cases Fixing a Post-Breach Date for Sale to the Market

As for the purchase of a replacement, discussed in section 17.2 above, the cases are grouped together here under the different reasons why the date on which the value of the property for which the claimant must give credit will be deferred beyond the date of breach.

(i) Misrepresentation (ie Latent Problems)

In latent defect cases, it will usually not be reasonable to expect the claimant to sell the property until the defect (ie breach of warranty) has been discovered,[69] but losses after that date on which the property should have been sold will be irrecoverable.[70]

The same principle applies to transactions induced by misadvice or misrepresentation, in which the claimant is not usually expected to seek to extricate itself from the transaction until it knows about the misadvice or misrepresentation.[71] As Toulson J explained in the deceit case of *Standard Chartered Bank v Pakistan National Shipping Corp*, 'a person is not likely to be in a position to make a fair evaluation of the benefit which he has received if he continues to be under a distorted perception by reason of the defendant's fraud', and so is not reasonably expected to sell the property until that distortion is removed.[72] Similarly, a claimant who does not know a surveyor's negligence has induced her to purchase a property with severe defects does not, until she discovers this, 'have an opportunity of cutting her losses'.[73] And

---

[69] *Naughton v O'Callaghan* [1990] 3 All ER 191 (Waller J).

[70] *Salford City Council v Torkington* [2004] EWCA Civ 1546 discussed below in chapter eighteen, section 18.4D.

[71] *Esso Petroleum Co Ltd v Mardon* [1976] QB 801 (CA) (also a breach of a warranty that took reasonable care); *Naughton v O'Callaghan* [1990] 3 All ER 191 (Waller J) (breach of warranty); *Doyle v Olby (Ironmongers) Ltd* [1969] 2 QB 158 (CA); *Downs v Chappell* [1997] 1 WLR 426 (CA); *Smith New Court Securities Ltd v Scrimgeour Vickers (Asset Management) Ltd* [1997] AC 254 (HL); *Slough Estates plc v Welwyn Hatfield District Council* [1996] 2 EGLR 219 (May J) (deceit); *Standard Chartered Bank v Pakistan National Shipping Corp* [1999] 1 Lloyd's Rep 747 (Toulson J) (deceit); *Dent v Davis Blank Furniss (a firm)* [2001] Lloyd's Rep PN 534 (Blackburne J) (misadvice by a solicitor); *Beary v Pall Mall Investments (a firm)* [2004] EWHC 1608 (Ch) (Sir Donald Rattee) (misadvice by a financial adviser); *4 Eng Ltd v Harper* [2009] Ch 91 (Richards J) (deceit); *Joyce v Bowman Law Ltd* [2010] EWHC 251 (Ch) (Vos J) (solicitor negligence, where the solicitor himself continued to tell the claimant that the problem could be sorted out) at para 98. *Gardner v Marsh & Parsons (a firm)* [1997] 1 WLR 489 (CA) Hirst LJ at 496 should be doubted on this point, the error probably resulting from overreliance on the discredited *Philips v Ward* [1956] 1 WLR 471 (CA) formulation (see chapter three text to note 19 and following).

[72] *Standard Chartered Bank v Pakistan National Shipping Corp* [1999] 1 Lloyd's Rep 747 (Toulson J) at 760.

[73] *Syrett v Carr & Neave (a firm)* [1990] 2 EGLR 161 (Bowsher QC) at 165. (This was doubted obiter by Gibson LJ in *Watts v Morrow* [1991] 1 WLR 1421 (CA) at 1434–38 but it is clear from the decision and reasoning in *Patel v Hooper & Jackson (a firm)* [1999] 1 WLR 1792 (CA) that Gibson LJ's approach that the date of acquisition was always the correct date is wrong.) See also: *Hayes v Dodd* [1990] 2 All ER 815 (CA), where the defendant did not confirm the lack of a right of way for a year; *Portman Building Society v Bevan Ashford* [2000] 1 EGLR 81 (CA) Otton LJ at 84; *Joyce v Bowman Law Ltd* [2010] EWHC 251 (Ch) (Vos J) at para 98 (solicitor negligence), where the claimant did not discover for some time that he did not have the option he thought he had, and was encouraged in this belief by the defendant solicitor. See also the obiter discussion of Bingham MR in *Reeves v Thrings & Long* [1996] PNLR 265 (CA). *Wapshott v Davis Donovan & Co (a firm)* [1996] PNLR 361 (CA), where the value at acquisition (zero) was taken in a solicitor's negligence action, must therefore be doubted.

in *SAAMCo* Lord Hoffmann explained that a lender could not be criticised for failing to sell its rights under the mortgage immediately on the date of the advance, in part because the lender did not know about the over-valuation at that date.[74]

As to identification of the date of discovery, where a fraud or other latent problem comes to light gradually, the date will often be taken at the end of the period of disclosures, not at the beginning.[75]

An important example of deferral of the date of assessment for latency is *Naughton v O'Callaghan*.[76] The claimant bought a chestnut colt called Fondu for 26,000 guineas, which is what it would have been worth if as described. Had the breach of warranty as to its pedigree (and accompanying misrepresentation) been known about earlier, the claimant could and would have sold the horse immediately for 23,500 guineas,[77] but they were not known about and the claimant instead trained and raced the horse, which was always its intention and what the defendant would have expected: 'their decision to keep Fondu and race it was precisely what the sellers would have expected. Fondu was not a commodity like, for example, rupee paper, which it would be expected that the defendants would go out and sell'.[78] (The reference to rupee paper is to a readily marketable asset to which special rules sometimes apply, as discussed in the next section.[79]) The court found that it was not reasonable to expect the claimant to sell the defective property until the latent defect had been discovered, after the horse had been raced for a season or two, by which time the horse was worth only £1,500 (although had it been as described it may have had more success and retained its value much better).

The correct measure of contract damages in such a case of property that was intended to be held is the difference between the value the property would have had at the date of discovery (plus all net profits that would have been earned to that date), less the value the property actually had at that date. In fact, although correctly taking the date of assessment at the date of discovery, the court awarded the orthodox *tort* measure (this also being a claim for negligent misrepresentation) of the difference between the price paid and the market value of £1,500 upon discovery of the breach, plus costs of upkeep up to that date and for a short period afterwards until the horse could be disposed of.[80] This is the correct tort/misadvice measure, putting the claimant in the position as if the horse had never been bought. As a contract measure (which received little discussion by the judge), it is best explained on the basis that, given the limited evidence put forward by the claimant, the court had to infer that but for the breach the horse would at the date of judgment have entirely held its value since purchase, as well as at least breaking even by earning revenue equal to the costs of upkeep of the horse;[81] or alternatively that

---

[74] *South Australia Asset Management Corp v York Montague* [1997] 1 AC 191 (HL) at 222.
[75] *4 Eng Ltd v Harper* [2007] EWHC 1568 (Ch) (Briggs J) at para 53.
[76] *Naughton v O'Callaghan* [1990] 3 All ER 191 (Waller J).
[77] Waller J (ibid) at 195 and 197.
[78] Waller J (ibid) at 198, also 192.
[79] And in particular, the rupee paper is a reference to *Waddell v Blockey* (1879) 4 QBD 678 (CA).
[80] [1990] 3 All ER 191 Waller J at 198.
[81] The presumption is entirely orthodox (see above in chapter six, section 6.5A(i), and below in chapter eighteen, section 18.3) and is hinted at by claimant counsel as Waller J notes at 196 and 198, although the costs of upkeep should, according to the presumption, run all the way up to judgment.

no separate contract measure was pressed and the claimant was entitled to elect for the tort measure.

(ii) *The* Waddell v Blockey *Rule: No Deferral of the Date with Readily Marketable Assets, Even in Cases of Latent Problems*

However, in cases of 'disposable' property,[82] 'readily marketable asset'[83] or a 'commodity ... which it would be expected that the defendants would go out and sell',[84] sometimes any retention of the property after the date of acquisition will be treated as a *novus actus interveniens* making loss too remote, and therefore being at the claimant's own risk.[85] This was the result in *Waddell v Blockey*, where the court would not take into account events after the date of acquisition of highly tradeable rupee paper even though the acquisition was induced by a fraud of which the claimant was unaware and the claimant did not actually sell the paper until four months later. The decision not to sell was regarded as a commercial one and the claimant's 'own voluntary act' and loss after the date of the deemed sale 'flowed from' the decision to retain.[86] This decision and the principle behind it have been affirmed at the highest level.[87]

The *Waddell*-type of case has been distinguished from other cases where the purchase is of a 'long term investment in a form which is not readily realisable or not contemplated to be realised at the date of the transaction'[88] or an investment bought 'to hold'[89] such as a business,[90] a race horse,[91] a loan and security,[92] shares bought as a market-making risk to hold for a comparatively long period of time,[93] or collateralised debt obligations.[94] In these cases, the ordinary rules will apply such that holding the property will not break the chain of causation until the date upon

---

[82] *Alliance & Leicester Building Society v Edgestop Ltd*, 13 June 1994 (Knox J).

[83] *Smith New Court Securities Ltd v Scrimgeour Vickers (Asset Management) Ltd* [1997] AC 254 (HL) per Lord Browne-Wilkinson at 266; *Gestmin SGPS SA v Credit Suisse (UK) Ltd* [2013] EWHC 3560 (Comm) (Leggatt J) at para 184.

[84] *Naughton v O'Callaghan* [1990] 3 All ER 191 (Waller J) at 198.

[85] See the comments in *Standard Chartered Bank v Pakistan National Shipping Corp* [1999] 1 Lloyd's Rep 747 (Toulson J) at 760. As to the general concept of a speculative decision breaking the chain of causation, see above in chapter sixteen, section 16.5.

[86] *Waddell v Blockey* (1879) 4 QBD 678 (CA) Bramwell LJ at 681 and Baggallay LJ at 682.

[87] *Naughton v O'Callaghan* [1990] 3 All ER 191 (Waller J) at 198; *Alliance & Leicester BS v Edgestop*, 13 June 1994 (Knox J); *Smith New Court Securities Ltd v Scrimgeour Vickers (Asset Management) Ltd* [1997] AC 254 (HL) Lord Browne-Wilkinson at 266; *South Australia Asset Management Corp (SAAMCo) v York Montague Ltd* [1997] 1 AC 191 (HL) Lord Hoffmann at 221; *Cassa di Risparmio della Repubblica di San Marino SpA v Barclays Bank Ltd* [2011] EWHC 484 (Comm) (Hamblen J) at para 557.

[88] *Alliance & Leicester Building Society v Edgestop Ltd*, 13 June 1994 (Knox J).

[89] *Cassa di Risparmio della Repubblica di San Marino SpA v Barclays Bank Ltd* [2011] EWHC 484 (Comm) (Hamblen J) obiter at para 553.

[90] Obiter in *Alliance & Leicester Building Society v Edgestop Ltd*, 13 June 1994 (Knox J).

[91] *Naughton v O'Callaghan* [1990] 3 All ER 191 (Waller J) at 198.

[92] *South Australia Asset Management Corp (SAAMCo) v York Montague Ltd* [1997] 1 AC 191 (HL) Lord Hoffmann at 221.

[93] *Smith New Court Securities Ltd v Scrimgeour Vickers (Asset Management) Ltd* [1997] AC 254 (HL) Lord Browne-Wilkinson at 260 and Lord Steyn at 285.

[94] *Cassa di Risparmio della Repubblica di San Marino SpA v Barclays Bank Ltd* [2011] EWHC 484 (Comm) (Hamblen J) obiter at paras 553 to 561.

which the defect or fraud or misstatement are discovered or for some other reason a sale could be expected to take place.

(iii) When it Takes Time to Repair

In a construction case where it took some years to cure the defects by repairing the residential properties the residual diminution in value after the repairs had to be assessed at the date of completion of the repairs and not the date of damage, as no question of resale could arise until the repairs had been completed, although market fluctuations after the date of trial were to be disregarded.[95]

(iv) When it Takes Time to Sell

It may take time to sell defective property. Thus in deceit case *Doyle v Olby*[96] the claimant, upon discovering the fraud,

> had burnt his boats and had to carry on with the business as best he could. He tried to sell it, but there were difficulties. One was that the landlord, Mr. Cecil Olby, would not give him a licence to assign, and so forth. After three years he did manage to sell it for a sum of some £3,700

and, there being no failure to mitigate,[97] the claimant only had to give credit for the £3,700 received years after the date of acquisition. Likewise in the surveyor negligence case *Hayes v James and Charles Dodd*[98] the claimant reasonably, and on advice, waited five years until the lease obligations on a workshop had expired before selling both that and the attached maisonette. In another deceit case, there was no immediate available market for the particular bitumen, and credit only had to be given for the value obtained on a later sale by the claimant.[99]

In a case where there was a market the claimant was expected to sell promptly but not hastily and to have a reasonable time to do so.[100]

In the case of a lender's claim against a valuer for negligence, it will not usually be expected that the lender will crystallise loss by selling on the rights under the loan,

---

[95] *Shepherd Homes Ltd v Encia Remediation Ltd* [2007] EWHC 1710 (TCC) (Jackson J) at paras 722 and 725.

[96] *Doyle v Olby (Ironmongers) Ltd* [1969] 2 QB 158 (CA), result approved (but some of the reasoning doubted) in *Smith New Court Securities Ltd v Scrimgeour Vickers (Asset Management) Ltd* [1997] AC 254 (HL).

[97] Winn LJ in *Doyle v Olby* [1969] 2 QB 158 at 169.

[98] *Hayes v James and Charles Dodd (a firm)* [1990] 2 All ER 815 (CA). And see also *County Personnel (Employment Agency) Ltd v Alan R Pulver & Co* [1987] 1 WLR 916 (CA) where it took five years to negotiate an exit from an onerous underlease and the damages were measured as at the end of that five years, and *East v Maurer* [1991] 1 WLR 461 (CA) where the claimant had behaved reasonably in trying to sell the business although it ultimately took three years to do so.

[99] *Standard Chartered Bank v Pakistan National Shipping Corp (Assessment of Damages)* [2001] EWCA Civ 55. Potter LJ there referred at para 37 to the claimant being 'locked in' by the lack of an available market.

[100] *Waddell v Blockey* (1879) 4 QBD 678 (CA) Bramwell LJ at 681, but see Baggallay LJ at 682 who preferred the very day of the acquisition.

at least where the loan is to a development site, because there will not usually be a market for single mortgage loans on development sites.[101]

In contrast, in some cases claimants have failed to act with alacrity. In *Downs v Chappell* the claimants were fraudulently induced to purchase a bookshop business for £120,000 in 1988, discovered the deceit in late 1989, sought to sell the business, and refused offers of around £76,000 in spring 1990. They then later sold the business between the date of trial in 1994 and appeal in 1996 for less than £60,000.[102] The Court of Appeal found that

> Even accepting that they acted reasonably, the fact remains that it was their choice, freely made, and they cannot hold the defendants responsible if the choice has turned out to have been commercially unwise. They were no longer acting under the influence of the defendants' representations. The causative effect of the defendants' faults was exhausted; the plaintiffs' right to claim damages from them in respect of those faults had likewise crystallised.

and damages were measured by the difference between the price paid and the price they would have received if they had sold in spring 1990. And in the surveyor negligence case of *Patel v Hooper & Jackson*, the claimant did not sell the property but was deemed to do so at the time a reasonable claimant would have done so (and so alternative accommodation costs were only recoverable up to that date).[103]

(v) Negotiating with the Defendant

Where the claimant negotiated with the defendant rather than immediately selling the property, the delay in selling may well be reasonable and the sale price taken at the date when the negotiations broke down and the claimant could have been expected to sell the property.[104]

(vi) Reasonable to Hold the Property or 'Locked In'

One of the features of the *Smith New Court Securities* deceit case was that the fraud 'locked' the claimant into holding the shares 'having bought them for a purpose and at a price which precluded them from sensibly disposing of them'.[105]

---

[101] *South Australia Asset Management Corp (SAAMCo) v York Montague Ltd* [1997] 1 AC 191 (HL) Lord Hoffmann at 222.

[102] *Downs v Chappell* [1997] 1 WLR 426 (CA). A dictum of Hobhouse LJ in *Downs v Chappell* in relation to the measure of loss was disapproved in *Smith New Court Securities Ltd v Scrimgeour Vickers (Asset Management) Ltd* [1997] AC 254 (HL) but the decision of *Downs v Chappell* remains intact.

[103] *Patel v Hooper & Jackson (a firm)* [1991] 1 WLR 1792 (CA) (surveyor negligence). The diminution in value appears to have been incorrectly taken at the date of completion, not the date of the putative sale, but that is presumably because the point was not focused on and the evidence of value at that date was not available on appeal.

[104] Ibid, where the claimant did not in fact sell but should have done. See also *Esso Petroleum Co Ltd v Mardon* [1976] QB 801 (CA).

[105] *Smith New Court Securities Ltd v Scrimgeour Vickers (Asset Management) Ltd* [1997] AC 254 (HL) Lord Browne-Wilkinson at 268. Toulson J understood the phrase 'locked in' in *Smith New Court* as referring to the fraud having meant that there was no available market: *Standard Chartered Bank v Pakistan National Shipping Corp* [1999] 1 Lloyd's Rep 747 (Toulson J) at 760. See also the appellate judgment at [2001] EWCA Civ 55 Potter LJ at para 37.

Induced by the deceit as to there being other interested bidders, the claimant bought the 28m Ferranti shares in July 1989 at a price of 82¼p that necessarily made them 'a market-making risk', ie a long-term purchase speculating on the market, as opposed to a 'bought deal' purchase for immediate resale in smaller parcels to clients of the client. The latter type of purchase could only have worked at a price under the 78p market price at which the shares could have been disposed of immediately.[106] Accordingly, the claimant acted reasonably (and indeed predictably) in retaining them beyond September 1989 when the Guerin fraud perpetrated on Ferranti prior to the purchase of the shares was discovered and caused the value to crash, and around which time the claimant discovered the deceit that had induced it to purchase the shares.[107] The claimant acted reasonably in realising the shares gradually in late 1989 and the early part of 1990 for between 30p and 49p.[108] Given that the crash in the share price was caused by a pre-existing fraud, the shares were when bought by the claimant already 'pregnant' with the earlier fraud and 'doomed to collapse', ie they were bought on a false market because the market was unaware of the true facts, and so that fraud did not break the chain of causation and the claimant therefore only had to give credit for the low prices it actually received for the shares.[109]

In the solicitor's negligence case of *Scott v Vertex Law*, the claimants bought a guesthouse business that due to planning permission problems could never be made to work.[110] The claimants acted reasonably in pursuing planning appeals and the business for five years before selling it.

(vii) Adopting the Unwanted Transaction and Never Selling

In some cases it may be reasonable to never sell the property (at least for the foreseeable future) that, but for the breach, the claimant would not have had, but instead make the most of it and incur ongoing losses or costs. Thus in the surveyor case *Farley v Skinner* the House of Lords rejected the argument that the claimant should have sold the property within a year and should be confined to the costs of so doing (as the market value was the same as the price), holding that the claimant had expended in the region of £100,000[111] in modernising and renovating before moving in and learning of the defect (aircraft noise) and that the expenses of selling and buying a new house would have been considerable (over £10,000[112]), and therefore it was reasonable to put up with the house and continue to suffer the discomfort.[113]

---

[106] Lord Browne-Wilkinson [1997] AC 254 at 260 and 268 and Lord Steyn at 285.

[107] Lord Steyn (ibid) at 273.

[108] Lord Browne-Wilkinson (ibid) at 260 and 268, Lord Steyn at 285. Contrast the approach taken in *Great Future International Ltd v Sealand Housing Corp* [2002] EWHC 2454 (Ch) (Lightman J), discussed above in chapter four text to n 62.

[109] Lord Browne-Wilkinson [1997] AC 254 at 268, Lord Steyn at 279 and 285.

[110] *Scott v Kennedys Law LLP and Vertex Law LLP* [2011] EWHC 3808 (Ch) (Vos J).

[111] *Farley v Skinner* [2002] 2 AC 732 (HL). See the judge's findings quoted at para 11. See further the Court of Appeal decision (2000) 73 Con LR 70 (CA) at 86 pt 9.

[112] *Farley v Skinner* (2000) 73 Con LR 70 (CA) at para 69.

[113] *Farley v Skinner* [2002] 2 AC 732 (HL), Lord Steyn at para 26 and Lord Hutton at paras 55–56. See also Lord Scott at para 108. And see *Zeneca Ltd v King Sturge & Co*, 19 September 1996 (Jackson

Thus in *Dent v Davis Blank Furniss*[114] the claimants bought at auction a paddock for £94,000 and built their dream home on it at a cost of nearly four times the price they paid for the land. Three years after the purchase, and after the claimants had built their house, it was discovered that the land was commons land, a matter undiscovered due to the defendant solicitor's negligence. The claimants remained on the property and at a cost of £20,000 were able to de-register part of the land. Blackburne J correctly refused to award the difference in value at the time of purchase, as the claimants did not know of the problem then and could not have been expected to extricate themselves from the sale at that time. Further, the claimants acted reasonably in engaging new solicitors and securing release from the commons registration at a cost of £20,000. Accordingly the correct date for assessment of damages was immediately after the commons de-registration was effected.

Similarly, in *Hipkins v Jack Cotton*, the claimant paid £17,400 for property that was in fact worth £8,500 due to structural problems which the defendant surveyor failed to warn the claimant of.[115] It was held that the claimant acted reasonably in staying in the property and, on professional advice, waiting to see what happened when the problems started to materialise, and then three years after purchase paying around £14,000 for the repairs, and those costs were awarded in damages. In *Keydon Estates Ltd v Eversheds LLP* the claimant could not sell the investment reversion it had been induced into buying and recovered the loss of income it would have made on an alternative transaction.[116]

In the solicitor's negligence case of *Braid v WL Highway & Sons* the claimant may be said to have been locked into the lease he purchased, as he was sued by the landlady within two weeks of the acquisition and had then to resolve that dispute.[117] The claimant recovered the cost of buying out the reversion.

And in *Esso Petroleum Co Ltd v Mardon*[118] the claimant was held to have acted reasonably in retaining the garage business even after discovering the contractually and tortiously negligent representations as to its throughput, and taking a reduced lease with the defendant on its encouragement, discussing with it the possibility of also taking a prime site to balance out the losses, and making a go of the business, in part because he was 'trapped' by his losses. This was not speculation breaking the chain of causation, or an unreasonable failure to mitigate.

But in the Irish case of *Kelleher v O'Connor*, it was not reasonable to hold the property so the date of a deemed sale was taken, but it was clear that if it had

---

QC) (the claimant had commenced works on the property, so the cost of repairs was recoverable) and *Joyce v Bowman Law Ltd* [2010] EWHC 251 (Ch) (Vos J) at paras 98–99. And see *Syrett v Carr & Neave (a firm)* [1990] 2 EGLR 161 (Bowsher QC) at 165, where the claimant only discovered the problems with the property after 'she was so heavily involved with the property that it was reasonable for her to keep it and repair it'.

[114] *Dent v Davis Blank Furniss (a firm)* [2001] Lloyd's Rep PN 534 (Blackburne J). See also *Herrmann v Withers LLP* [2012] EWHC 1492 (Ch) (Newey J) (solicitor's negligence), discussed above in chapter three, text to n 92, and chapter sixteen, text to n 85.
[115] *Hipkins v Jack Cotton Partnership* [1989] 2 EGLR 157 (Baker J).
[116] *Keydon Estates Ltd v Eversheds LLP* [2005] EWHC 972 (Ch) (Evans-Lombe J) (solicitor's negligence).
[117] *Braid v WL Highway & Sons* (1964) 191 EG 433 (Roskill J).
[118] *Esso Petroleum Co Ltd v Mardon* [1976] QB 801 (CA) esp at 829.

reasonably appeared at the time that 'persevering with the impaired asset was likely to be a better course of action than selling it (or even that there was not much to choose between the two)' then the damages award may have been different.[119]

(viii) Subsequent Disasters

Any damage to the property caused by a disaster or event which would have been avoided if the claimant had sold on the property when it should have will be irrecoverable. Even if the claimant reasonably retains the property, however, the courts, at least in deceit cases, draw a distinction between disasters or diseases that pre-date the purchase (even if unrelated to the deceit) and those post-dating it. Where the defect was inherent at the time of the purchase (such as a diseased horse or a company 'pregnant with disaster') it will probably not break the chain of causation, but where it arises later, and so is a 'supervening cause', it may do.[120]

17.4 Where there is No Opportunity to Resort to the Market

Where there is no question of a resorting to the market for purchase of a replacement or for sale of property, for example because the promised property is delivered but merely late, or the goods were latently defective and the defect is only discovered after the goods have been on-sold, an entirely different set of issues arises. The date of assessment cannot be fixed by the claimant's need for the price of a cure, or the date when the claimant could be expected to obtain such a cure. Mitigation does not arise. The cost of cure or replacement does not arise.

In these cases the question is simply one of the loss suffered and the governing principles of remoteness and legal causation. The prima facie position is that the date of judgment governs, not because of the claimant pressing for performance or similar (which is only relevant in cases where the claimant would have been expected to purchase a replacement), but because the true prima facie rule is always that loss is measured up to judgment (and beyond), subject—and this is an important qualification—to the rules of remoteness and legal causation.

---

[119] *Kelleher v O'Connor* [2010] IEHC 313 (Irish High Court) at para 10.9, also para 10.5.

[120] *Twycross v Grant* (1877) 2 CPD 469 (CA) Cockburn CJ at 544 (shares already worthless at time of purchase); *Waddell v Blockey* (1879) 4 QBD 678 (CA) obiter Thesiger LJ at 683; *Smith New Court Securities Ltd v Scrimgeour Vickers (Asset Management) Ltd* [1997] AC 254 (HL) Lord Steyn at 286, also at 279 (company already pregnant with disaster).

Part 5

Particular Types of Loss Requiring Separate Examination

18

Proving Business Loss: Revenue, Profit and Costs

The level of particularity of pleading and evidence required to prove lost profits, the type of evidence relied upon, and the different ways of calculating such losses (including loss of a chance). Detailed discussion of the important presumption that the claimant would have broken even and its operation.

18.1 Revenue, Profit and Capital Loss

A. Revenue and Profit

The basic rule that the claimant is to be put in the position it would have been in but for the breach means that, as regards pecuniary loss, the claimant should be awarded the total of revenue (less costs) that would have been earned, less the total of revenue (less costs) actually earned. Or to put it another way, the claim is for the amount by which the revenue was decreased by the breach, plus any increase in costs as a result of the breach, less any cost savings as a result of the breach.[1] If the expenditure that would have been incurred was all incurred and so is the same in the breach and non-breach positions, but the breach merely prevented or reduced the receipt of revenue, then only the difference in revenue need be measured, but in most cases the breach will have affected costs as well as revenue, and the two must be netted off for both the breach and non-breach positions in order properly to measure the loss. The damages award puts the claimant in the financial position it would have been in but for the breach. If the claimant would have made a net profit,

---

[1] In relation to this cost savings point, by way of example an employer who is liable for discriminatorily dismissing an employee need only compensate for her lost earnings net of childcare costs which she saved by being sacked: *Ministry of Defence v Cannock* [1995] 2 All ER 449 (EAT).

the award will make good that position; if the claimant would have made a net loss smaller than the actual loss, the award will make good that position.[2]

Non-breach position (but for the wrong)	Breach position (actual)	Net loss caused by the breach
revenue earned – costs incurred = profit	revenue earned – costs incurred = profit	profit 'but for' – actual profit = lost profit

This simple table illustrates the calculation. Sometimes the breach will reduce the revenue (eg by reducing sales) and increase the costs (eg where the breach causes problems for the claimant's business), and these two changes added together make up the net loss. Sometimes the breach will reduce the revenue but also reduce the costs (eg where the breach causes the claimant to abort a business venture part-way through, or prevents the claimant pursuing profitable litigation), in which case the savings made must be deducted from the lost revenue to give the full picture. Sometimes the breach will not affect the revenue but will merely increase the costs.[3] In some cases the breach may even increase the revenue but increase the costs by a greater sum, in which case the increased revenue must be taken from the increased costs to work out the net loss.

As Flaux J explains,

> as a matter of first principle, placing the company in the position it would have been in if the contract had not been broken requires the court to assess whether the net income of the company without the franchise has been and will be less than what the net income would have been had the Franchise Agreement continued for the rest of its duration. In other words, in shorthand, the measure of damages is the loss of profits suffered as a consequence of the breach.

> If that assessment demonstrated that the net income is and will be less than it would have been if the Franchise Agreement had not been repudiated by Antal London, the amount of that diminution in income (or loss of profits) would be the measure of damages awarded, subject to an appropriate discount for early receipt of money. Equally, if that assessment failed to demonstrate any diminution in income (because for example the company had continued or was expected to continue to be as profitable without the franchise as it had been with the franchise) or demonstrated that with or without the franchise the business would have been loss making, the company would not establish any loss of profits and the damages awarded would be nominal.[4]

---

[2] If the claimant would have made a greater loss than it did, then no substantial damages are awarded, and in fact the breach has done the claimant a favour.

[3] In *British Westinghouse Electric & Manufacturing Co Ltd v Underground Electric Railways Co of London Ltd* [1912] AC 673 (HL) a railway company recovered several years of increased coal costs that resulted from the turbines supplied by the claimant being less efficient than promised (during the years before the defendant replaced the turbines).

[4] *MMP GmbH v Antal International Network Ltd* [2011] EWHC 1120 (Comm) (Flaux J) at paras 81–82.

B. Timing, and Measuring the Capital Value or Lost Profit Stream

Where lost profits would have been made up to and beyond the date of trial, in principle they should be calculated at the date of trial and cover the entire period when they should have been made, including the future.[5]

However, where the entire business or property is concerned (rather than a particular project or part of its profits), a more accurate route to the same result may be to take the market capital value of the business or property at a particular date,[6] together with any relevant lost profits up to but not beyond that date.[7] The profits part of the calculation must stop at that date, since the capital value is in effect a capitalised value of the future profit stream from that date forward, once the market has allowed for risks etc, so to award profits after that date would double count. In any event taking the capital value at a particular date usually assumes a putative sale of the business or property, after which time no further profits would have been earned.

This approach will allow for the market perception of all profit streams and their risks: 'An approach which seeks to arrive at the price which a willing third party negotiating at arms-length would pay for Limited or for the benefit of the agreement will fully reflect the uncertainties of the business'.[8] Thus in *Crehan v Inntrepreneur Pub Co (CPC)*, the judge at first instance (in a claim for breach of European law) took projected profits of an aborted pub business up to the date of trial, discounted by 15 per cent for contingencies, and added the residual value of the pub at the date of trial.[9] The Court of Appeal rejected that in favour of an award of the lost profits up until 1993, when the business was aborted, plus the market value at that date, as the market value would more realistically assess the risks of the business than a speculative discount of 15 per cent.[10]

The same approach was applied in *Cullinane v British 'Rema' Manufacturing Co Ltd*, where a claimant claimed lost profits up to trial on a machine that did not meet the warranted specification, and then claimed the difference in market value at trial rather than seeking to estimate future profits thereafter. The value at trial would merely be 'a method of computing profit for the possible profit-earning period after

---

[5] As to awards of future losses, see above in chapter twelve, section 12.2, and chapter thirteen, section 13.6.

[6] *Owners of Liesbosch Dredger v Owners of SS Edison (The Liesbosch)* [1933] AC 449 (HL) at 463; *The Llanover* [1947] P 80 (Pilcher J); *ELO Entertainments Ltd v Grand Metropolitan Retailing Ltd* [1999] 1 All ER (Comm) 473 (CA); *Jenmain Builders v Steed & Steed* (CA) 20 February 2000; *Vision Golf Ltd v Weightmans* [2005] EWHC 1675 (Ch) (Lewison J) at paras 51–52.

[7] *Plummer v Tibsco Ltd*, 9 March 2001 (Neuberger J); *Salford City Council v Torkington* [2004] EWCA Civ 1546; *Crehan v Inntrepreneur Pub Co (CPC)* [2004] EWCA Civ 637 at paras 172 ff.

[8] *Total Spares & Supplies Ltd v Antares SRL* [2004] EWHC 2626 (Ch) (David Richards J) at paras 222 ff.

[9] *Crehan v Inntrepreneur Pub Co* [2003] EWHC 1510 (Ch) (Park J).

[10] *Crehan v Inntrepreneur Pub Co* [2004] EWCA Civ 637 at paras 172 ff, which was overturned on a different point at [2007] 1 AC 333 (HL). *Crehan* followed *UYB Ltd v British Railways Board*, 16 April 1999 (Jack QC), affirmed 20 October 2000 (CA), and was explained in *Total Spares & Supplies Ltd v Antares SRL* [2004] EWHC 2626 (Ch) (David Richards J) at paras 222 ff. See also *ELO Entertainments Ltd v Grand Metropolitan Retailing Ltd* [1999] 1 All ER (Comm) 473 (CA) Stuart Smith LJ at 478; *Vision Golf Ltd v Weightmans (a firm)* [2005] EWHC 1675 (Ch) (Lewison J) at paras 51–52.

the date of the hearing'.[11] The trial date is suitable in such cases because at that date the claimant can go and buy an alternative business if necessary.[12] However, if the difference in value is taken at an earlier date, the claimant should recover lost profits up to that earlier date. The lost capital value will include the lost profits from that date forward.[13]

In *Plummer v Tibsco Ltd*,[14] the defendant landlord's alleged misrepresentation induced the claimants to swap their five-year pub tenancy with an option to renew (which, it was found, would probably have run until 2010) for a 20-year lease (to 2012) on different repairing and assignability conditions. The claimant was held by Neuberger J to be entitled to net additional costs incurred up to the date of the trial (in 2001), plus *either* the difference in the value of the tenancy and the lease in 2001 *or* the lost revenue to 2010 discounted to 2001, although

> In principle, these two alternative approaches should produce roughly the same figure: the value of the lease or tenancy is the present day value of the likely benefits and likely disadvantages in the future for the tenant if he takes the relevant interest.[15]

It should be noted that, especially where the difference in capital value is taken at a date before trial, the difference in value may not as fully capture the lost income stream as a calculation of lost profits would do. This is because an assessment of a pre-trial difference in value fails to take account of the facts between the assessment and trial dates, which may mean that the income was greater than the market would have given credit for in its earlier valuation.[16] The market will always allow for risk and the onerousness of, eg carrying out a development, which is why developers can still make money from buying property (ie when it works out, the income is greater than the market price of the property).[17]

---

[11] *Cullinane v British 'Rema' Manufacturing Co Ltd* [1954] 1 QB 292 (CA) Evershed MR at 307. See also Jenkins LJ at 308 explaining that the difference in capital value of goods is a measure of their profitability.

[12] *4 Eng Ltd v Harper* [2009] Ch 91 (Richards J).

[13] *Voaden v Champion (The Baltic Surveyor and The Timbuktu)* [2001] 1 Lloyd's Rep 739 (Colman J) at paras 75–76, appeal allowed in part [2002] 1 Lloyd's Rep 623 (CA). The actual decision is difficult to justify because the claimant did not have money to replace the vessel for some time, and so should have recovered damages for loss of use up to, and the cost of replacement at, the date of trial. In professional negligence action *Earl of Malmesbury v Strutt & Parker (a partnership)* [2007] EWHC 999 (QB) (Jack J), the defendant's negligence led to the claimant leasing its carpark property for worse terms than would otherwise be the case. The judge reluctantly felt obliged to award the difference in value of the freehold reversion at the date of breach, rather than the actual lost income stream or the difference in value at the date of trial, which therefore ignored the massive increase in income the claimant would have had if the lease terms had been as they should have been (due to increased use of the carpark) but which was not predictable at the date of breach. This must be doubted, unless the claimant's decision not to sell the reversion is treated as its own speculation, and therefore there is a deemed sale at the date of breach.

[14] *Plummer v Tibsco Ltd*, 9 March 2001 (Neuberger J), appeal allowed in relation to the part of the case concerning breach of contract to grant a tenancy and not the misrepresentation case, at [2002] 1 EGLR 29 (CA).

[15] There was a discussion of which measure should apply. Neuberger J observed that it would not be a breach of the duty to mitigate not to sell, and that the claimants in fact did not want to sell, although those points are largely irrelevant: the decision to retain the business breaks the chain of causation (provided that there is a market for it), as discussed above in chapter sixteen, section 16.5, and so the difference in value measure should have been adopted (although the judge did not have the evidence to do so and it would not have made any material difference to the measure).

[16] Eg *Earl of Malmesbury v Strutt & Parker* [2007] EWHC 999 (QB) (Jack J).

[17] See *Watts v Bell & Scott WS* [2007] CSOH 108 (Court of Session, Outer House).

For these reasons, a difference in value approach should only be taken at a date prior to trial where the claimant could have been expected to buy an alternative property or business, and/or the claimant's retaining the relevant property or business is treated as its own commercial decision and *res inter alios acta*. Where the claimant should have sold its business at a particular date and cut its losses then the capital value approach is the only appropriate approach, since it is what the claimant would have received if it had acted reasonably.[18] But the difference in value approach should not be adopted where it fails properly to measure the lost profits, for example because there is no market for the business.[19]

Flaux J has made the following observations in a case where the claimant was put out of business:

> If the effect of the breach of contract had been to put the company out of business then since, by definition, there are no future profits (or losses) against which to compare the profits (or losses) which the company would have made had the breach not occurred, then it is not possible for the court to assess damages on the basis of loss of profits in the normal way. It seems to me that it is only in such situations that the court will fall back on what Mr Clarke in his closing submissions described as a 'proxy for ... loss of profits' of seeking to value the company as at the date of the breach, both because it is that value of which the Claimant has been deprived by the breach and because it is only by such valuation that the court can arrive at a 'proxy' for the loss of profits. However where it is possible to assess the loss of profits in the normal way, that should be the measure of damages.[20]

Flaux J stated in that quotation that it is not possible to award profits in the ordinary way as there are no actual profits. This is correct in the mundane sense that there cannot be a comparison between actual and future profits, but the principle of awarding a diminution in profits can still apply. To put it another way, the actual profits are zero and so the entire amount of profits as they would have been is awarded. The capital value will, however, correctly measure the discounted future cash flows, allowing for accelerated receipt and the market assessment of the risks of non-recovery.

These same issues arise where the claimant is not put out of business but rather is prevented from acquiring a business.[21]

18.2 Pleading, Proof and Evidence

A. The Burden of Proof and Evidence

In general terms the burden of proof falls on the claimant as to the amount of loss and its causation. The task is essentially a jury (factual) question (although without a jury).[22]

---

[18] As in *Salford City Council v Torkington* [2004] EWCA Civ 1546.

[19] *Stewart v Scottish Widows and Life Assurance Society plc* [2005] EWHC 1831 (QB) (Eccles QC) at para 138, appeal allowed in part on a different point [2006] EWCA Civ 999.

[20] *MMP GmbH v Antal International Network Ltd* [2011] EWHC 1120 (Comm) (Flaux J) at para 83.

[21] See below in section 18.4A.

[22] *Capita Alternative Fund Services (Guernsey) Ltd v Drivers Jonas (a firm)* [2012] EWCA Civ 1407 Moore-Bick LJ at para 80.

(i) The Claimant Must Bring Forward all Available Evidence

It is for the claimant to bring forward the necessary evidence: 'where precise evidence is obtainable, the court naturally expects to have it. Where it is not the court must do the best it can'.[23] As Moore-Bick LJ has observed in the context of proof of loss by proof of value:

> The court's task is to make whatever findings it can on the evidence before it, although an obvious failure to obtain better evidence may result in its being unpersuaded of the claimant's case. Having said that, the court cannot conjure facts out of the air. There must be some evidence to support its finding.[24]

And in the same case Lloyd LJ observed:

> [T]he court requires as good evidence as can reasonably be obtained, and should only be forced to do the best it can, in the absence of evidence, if the evidence is not reasonably obtainable ... it is not for the court to embark on what could be no more than guesswork to make good the failure of the Claimant's attempt to adduce evidence on which the court could rely in order to prove the amount of their loss.[25]

For the court to make an award, it is necessary that the claimant put forward such evidence as is reasonably available to it, as otherwise the court may find the loss unproven, particularly if the defendant had objected to the inadequacy of evidence (eg documentation) at suitable moments.[26]

(ii) The Court Will Tolerate a Level of Uncertainty as to the Evidence

More generally, where the profits that would have been made are not 'capable of ... precise calculation' the law does not impose the burden of proof on the balance of probabilities to the specific pleaded figure of the loss and the judge is entitled to make a 'reasonable assessment'.[27] Difficult questions may arise and the fact that the loss of profits may depend upon many speculative factors is not a sufficient reason for denying an assessment.[28] The court will do the best it can and examine the evidence in a realistic manner[29] and 'the fact that damages cannot be assessed with certainty does not relieve the wrongdoer of the necessity of paying damages for his breach of contract'.[30]

---

[23] *Biggin & Co Ltd v Permanite Ltd* [1951] 1 KB 422 (Devlin J) at 438.

[24] *Capita Alternative Fund Services (Guernsey) Ltd v Drivers Jonas (a firm)* [2012] EWCA Civ 1407 Moore-Bick LJ at para 80.

[25] Ibid Lloyd LJ at paras 122–23. See also *White Arrow Express Ltd v Lamey's Distribution Ltd* [1995] 15 Tr L 69 (CA); *Abbar v Saudi Economic & Development Co (SEDCO) Real Estate Ltd* [2013] EWHC 1414 (Ch) (David Richards J) at para 223.

[26] *Hawkins v Woodhall* [2008] EWCA Civ 932 Arden LJ at para 53.

[27] *Parabola Investments Ltd v Browallia Cal Ltd* [2011] 1 QB 477 (CA) Toulson LJ at paras 22–23 (deceit claim for lost profits on alternative trades). Applied in *Vasiliou v Hajigeorgiou* [2010] EWCA Civ 1475 (negligence action against landlord) Patten LJ at para 25. See also *Hall v Ross* (1813) 1 Dow 201 (HL), approved in *C Czarnikow Ltd v Koufos (The Heron II)* [1969] 1 AC 350 (HL); *Canlin Ltd v Thiokol Fibres Canada Ltd* (1983) 142 DLR (3d) 450 (Ontario CA) Cory J at para 14.

[28] *Simpson v London and North Western Railway Co* (1876) 1 QBD 274 Cockburn CJ at 277; *Durham Tees Valley Airport Ltd v bmibaby Ltd* [2011] 1 Lloyd's Rep 68 (CA) Toulson LJ at para 93.

[29] Eg *Fera v Village Plaza Inc* 242 NW 2d 372 (1976) (SC of Michigan).

[30] *Chaplin v Hicks* [1911] 2 KB 786 (CA) Vaughan Williams LJ at 792; *IRT Oil and Gas Ltd v Fiber Optic Systems Technology (Canada) Inc* [2009] EWHC 3041 (QB) (Tugenhat J) at paras 108 and 110; *Yam Seng Pte Ltd v International Trade Corp Ltd* [2013] 1 Lloyd's Rep 526 (Leggatt J) at para 188.

As was observed in the employment law context,

> If an employee suffers career loss, it is incumbent on the tribunal to do its best to calculate the loss, albeit that there is a considerable degree of speculation. It cannot lie in the mouth of the employer to contend that because the exercise is speculative, the employee should be left with smaller compensation than the loss he actually suffers. Furthermore, the courts have to carry out similar exercises every day of the week when looking at the consequences of career shattering personal injuries.[31]

(iii) Where the Lack of Evidence is Caused by the Defendant, the Claimant Will Get the Benefit of the Doubt

In specific cases (such as valuing property or evaluating a lost chance) there is authority for a presumption that uncertainties are resolved against the defendant so as to give the claimant a 'fair wind',[32] and this has been applied to the evaluation of lost profits.[33] There is a trend to distinguish, doubt and disapply the fair wind principle, including in lost profit claims;[34] however, recently, it was said that the court will apply 'the principle of reasonable assumptions' such that

> it is fair to resolve uncertainties about what would have happened but for the defendant's wrongdoing by making reasonable assumptions which err if anything on the side of generosity to the claimant where it is the defendant's wrongdoing which has created those uncertainties.[35]

Moreover, the claimant will, at least where there are difficulties of proof, usually have the very considerable assistance of the presumption that it would have broken even.[36]

(iv) However, the Court Will Not Guess

Yet it is important 'not to depart from the task of estimating probable loss and cross over into the realm of pure guesswork'.[37]

---

[31] *Wardle v Crédit Agricole Corporate and Investment Bank* [2011] IRLR 604 (CA) Elias LJ at paras 50 and 52.

[32] See above in chapter thirteen, section 13.5B(iv).

[33] *Wilson v Northampton and Banbury Junction Railway Co* (1873–74) LR 9 Ch App 279 (CA); *Double G Communications Ltd v News Group International Ltd* [2011] EWHC 961 (QB) (Eady J) at para 5.

[34] *Porton Capital Technology Funds v 3M UK Holdings Ltd* [2011] EWHC 2895 (Comm) (Hamblen J) at paras 243–44 as to lost profits (and see also the doubts in *Zabihi v Janzemini* [2009] EWCA Civ 851 in the context of valuing property).

[35] *Yam Seng Pte Ltd v International Trade Corp Ltd* [2013] 1 Lloyd's Rep 526 (Leggatt J) at para 188, citing *Wilson v Northampton and Banbury Junction Railway Co* (1873–74) LR 9 Ch App 279 (CA). And in construction delay cases, so-called 'global claims' are permissible where it is impratical precisely to separate out losses and their separate causes: *Walter Lilly & Co Ltd v Mackay* [2013] EWHC 1773 (TCC) (Akenhead J).

[36] See below in section 18.3.

[37] *Double G Communications Ltd v News Group International Ltd* [2011] EWHC 961 (QB) (Eady J) at para 15. Also *White Arrow Express Ltd v Lamey's Distribution Ltd* [1995] 15 Tr L 69 (CA); *Capita Alternative Fund Services (Guernsey) Ltd v Drivers Jonas (a firm)* [2012] EWCA Civ 1407 Moore-Bick LJ at para 80 and Lloyd LJ at paras 122–23; *Abbar v Saudi Economic & Development Co (SEDCO) Real Estate Ltd* [2013] EWHC 1414 (Ch) (David Richards J) at para 223.

B. Pleadings, 'Jackpot Damages' and Changes of Case

Although the claim form must set out a statement of the value claimed, this does not limit the power of the court to give judgment for a larger or smaller amount.[38] Nevertheless, in some circumstances, judges will not go beyond the claimant's pleading.

First, any loss of profits must be pleaded and proven, and a mere pleading of 'damages' may not be sufficient to give the defendant warning of the claim it has to meet, save perhaps if lost profits are the necessary and immediate consequence of the breach.[39] Ultimately the question will be whether the defendant had been unfairly surprised.[40]

Secondly, assuming lost profits have been pleaded, if a claimant pleads an 'all or nothing' claim on the basis that particular damage was caused entirely by one cause, with no alternative claim that it was caused partly by that cause and partly by another, it is open to the court, if it rejects the allegation that the damage was entirely caused in the way pleaded, to award nothing even if as a matter of law some damages might if claimed be recoverable.[41] Likewise if a claimant pleads damages on a particular basis, an award on alternative basis will often be refused even if there is evidence to support it.[42] And claimants should therefore be cautioned by the following dictum of Stuart-Smith LJ from *Senate Electrical Wholesalers Ltd v Alcatel Submarine Networks Ltd*, referring to the 'high risk policy' of 'aiming at jackpot damages':

> [W]hile we sympathise with the judge's view that having found that there was a breach of warranty and thinking that some modest loss should be attributed to it, he was anxious not to send the plaintiff away empty handed, we think that he should have resisted the temptation to do so. The plaintiff deliberately adopted a high risk policy of aiming at jackpot damages. We have little doubt that it was part of that policy not to offer the judge a much more modest alternative.[43]

In that case the warranty claim on sale of a business ultimately failed for lack of timely notice, but (obiter) the Court of Appeal would have allowed the appeal against the judge's assessment of damages at £5m because that assessment was on a basis not pursued by the claimant and with which the defendant therefore did not have fair opportunity to deal in evidence, submissions, and by settlement negotiations.

---

[38] Civil Procedure Rules, r 16.3(7).

[39] *Perestrello e Companhia Limitada v United Paint Co Ltd* [1969] 1 WLR 570 (CA). In that case a shift to an unpleaded claim for over £250,000 lost profits, rather than a pleaded claim for £4,000 wasted expenditure, came too late.

[40] See the discussion in *Whalley v PF Developments Ltd* (CA), 14 February 2013 (trespass).

[41] *Latvian Shipping Co v Russian People's Insurance Co (ROSNO) Open Ended Joint Stock Co* [2012] EWHC 1412 (Comm) (Field J).

[42] *Anglo-Cyprian Trade Agencies Ltd v Paphos Wine Industries Ltd* [1951] 1 All ER 873 (Devlin J) at 875; *White Arrow Express Ltd v Lamey's Distribution Ltd* [1995] 15 Tr L 69 (CA). See also *Credit Suisse AG v Arabian Aircraft & Equipment Leasing Co EC* [2013] EWCA Civ 1169 (alternative damages measures set down in different clauses of the contract).

[43] *Senate Electrical Wholesalers Ltd v Alcatel Submarine Networks Ltd* [1999] 2 Lloyds Rep 423 (CA) Stuart-Smith LJ at para 54, contrary to the view at first instance at *Senate Electrical Wholesalers Ltd v STC Submarine Systems Ltd*, 20 December 1996 (May J).

However, provided the defendant is not unfairly taken by surprise and the evidence is before the court (unlike in *Senate v Alcatel*), a judge is entitled to make an award that does not reflect either of the positions adopted by the parties (and often will be somewhere in between), especially where the question is one of valuation of property or a business.[44] And where the claimant has incorrectly formulated the damages measure the court will often correct it provided the defendant is not unfairly prejudiced.[45] Similarly, if the claimant has failed to plead a head of loss but has put it clearly in issue in evidence, the court will often allow that head of loss provided, again, that the defendant has not been unfairly surprised.[46]

C. Types of Evidence

The evidence used to prove lost profits will vary depending upon the type of business in issue and the type of contract and breach. As Cardozo J observed in the New York Court of Appeal, a court must be flexible and realistic:

> It is true, of course, that the conditions of a business affect the possibilities of proof and thus the measure of recovery. No formula can be framed, regardless of experience, to tell us in advance when approximate certainty may be attained. The rule of damages must give true expression to the realities of life.[47]

(i) Proof of Specific Custom Lost?

There is no requirement that the claimant prove that specific customers or contracts were lost. As was observed in a Canadian decision:[48]

> In my view, the law may be summarized as follows. The basic rule is that damages for lost profits, like all damages for breach of contract, must be proven on a balance of probabilities. Where it is shown with some degree of certainty that a specific contract was lost as a result of a breach with the consequent loss of profit, that sum should be awarded. However, damages may also be awarded for loss of more conjectural profits where the evidence demonstrates the possibility that contracts have been lost because of the breach and also establishes that it is probable that some of these possible contracts would have materialized had the breach not occurred. In such a case, a court should make a moderate award recognizing that some of the contracts may not have materialized had there been no breach.

---

[44] *Great Future International Ltd v Sealand Housing Corp* [2002] EWHC 2454 (Ch) (Lightman J) at paras 39 and 42; *Capita Alternative Fund Services (Guernsey) Ltd v Drivers Jonas (a firm)* [2012] EWCA Civ 1407.

[45] *Doyle v Olby (Ironmongers) Ltd* [1969] 2 QB 158 (CA) (deceit).

[46] *Whalley v PF Developments Ltd* [2013] EWCA Civ 306 (trespass).

[47] *Broadway Photoplay Co v World Film Corp* 225 NY 104 (1919) (NYCA). In that case the claimant cinema failed to prove that the promised first run feature films were more profitable than the later run feature films actually provided by the defendant.

[48] *Houweling Nurseries Ltd v Fisons Western Corp* (1988) 49 DLR (4th) 205 (British Columbia CA) McLachlin J at 210, quoted with approval in *Sharab Developments Ltd v Zellers Inc* [1999] SCC 192 (SC of Canada).

The matter may be put another way. Even though the plaintiff may not be able to prove with certainty that it would have obtained specific contracts but for the breach, it may be able to establish that the defendant's breach of contract deprived it of the opportunity to obtain such business. The plaintiff is entitled to compensation for the loss of that opportunity but it would be wrong to assess the damages for that lost opportunity as though it were a certainty.

Of course, if the claimant can prove loss of specific custom, such as

> from evidence given by customers of a plaintiff as to what orders they would have given had the product not been defective over a period of time in the future which is deemed by the Court to be reasonable and proper',[49]

that will help its case, and loss of general custom can be inferred from such evidence of loss of specific custom.[50]

(ii) Historical Trading Figures

Historical trading figures will often be important in proving lost profits. They provide important evidence of what would have happened but for the breach where a business has been interrupted or altered,[51] or property taken out of use.[52] Thus, where a claimant is deprived of the opportunity to earn commission, previous earnings by the claimant or actual earnings by a replacement will be good evidence of what the claimant would have earned.[53] It may be necessary, however, to make a deduction to allow for contingencies by which profits may fall.[54]

The approach to evidence is set out in the official comments to the US Restatement (Second) of Contracts[55] (which is the same as the approach applied in England):

> If the breach prevents the injured party from carrying on a well established business, the resulting loss of profits can often be proved with sufficient certainty. Evidence of past performance will form the basis for a reasonable prediction as to the future.

> However, if the business is a new one or if it is a speculative one that is subject to great fluctuations in volume, costs or prices, proof will be more difficult. Nevertheless, damages may be established with reasonable certainty with the aid of expert testimony, economic and financial data, market surveys and analyses, business records of similar enterprises, and the like.

Where bad customer service by the defendant was proven to have had a significant effect on the claimant's business, the 'portfolio method' was used of taking a portfolio of 30 of the claimant's customers, rather than each customer separately, and applying a counterfactual model of tonnage and margins to estimate what profits

---

[49] *Canlin Ltd v Thiokol Fibres Canada Ltd* (1983) 142 DLR (3d) 450 (Ontario CA) Cory J at para 14.
[50] See the text to n 73 below.
[51] *Canlin Ltd v Thiokol Fibres Canada Ltd* (1983) 142 DLR (3d) 450 (Ontario CA) Cory J at para 14; *Leche Pascual SA v Collin & Hobson plc* [2004] EWCA Civ 700; *Parabola Investments Ltd v Browallia Cal Ltd* [2011] 1 QB 477 (CA).
[52] See above in chapter six.
[53] *Devonald v Rosser& Sons* [1906] 2 KB 728 (CA); *Addis v Gramophone Company Ltd* [1909] AC 488 (HL).
[54] *Leche Pascual SA v Collin & Hobson plc* [2004] EWCA Civ 700.
[55] Restatement (Second) of Contracts §352 Comment b.

would have been made from all customers.[56] In other cases, evidence of actual sales and the fact that the claimant would have fallen short of its forecasts even but for the breach is highly relevant.[57]

(iii) Allowing Best Evidence of Costs

In construction and other large project cases, it is often impractical to retain sufficiently detailed records enabling proof at the dispute stage of exactly which employee's work, or which materials bought in which consignment from which supplier, were necessitated by the breach of the employer's contract. The standard approach, accepted in practice but not discussed in case law, is to use a 'rate book' by which a sensibly weighted average of actual expenditure on all employees of that grade in that year (say), or all materials of that type at that time, is produced and (after being agreed by the experts) recoverable as the best estimate of the actual expenditure on the particular employee or material. A less desirable alternative is to use an external rate book published by a professional body as to rates used by that profession, which is little more than an estimate of market rates rather than the claimant's actual paid rates.

(iv) Inferring Loss in Reputation Cases

(a) Credit Rating and Financial Reputation

Damages to a company or individual's credit or financial reputation (such as a credit rating) will often have financial consequences, such as in loss of custom or higher debt interest rates charged or loan facilities, but such damages are often difficult to prove. Courts have shown a willingness to award substantial damages in such cases without direct proof, most usually in cases of wrongful dishonour by banks of customer cheques,[58] failure to advance promised funds,[59] or a bank's failure leading to a customer's bankruptcy.[60] In these cases 'the inference arises that pecuniary loss will necessarily ensue'.[61]

(b) Bad Publicity and Employee Reputation

Likewise where an employer damaged an employee's (or independent contractor's) reputation in breach of contract, the employee could recover for the financial consequences, such as where the BCCI bank's widespread fraudulent and corrupt operations tarnished the reputation of the innocent employees and prevented them

---

[56] *Tullis Russell Papermakers Ltd v Inveresk plc* [2010] CSOH 148 (Court of Session, Outer House).
[57] *Yam Seng Pte Ltd v International Trade Corp Ltd* [2013] 1 Lloyd's Rep 526 (Leggatt J).
[58] The modern leading case is *Kpohraror v Woolwich Building Society* [1996] 4 All ER 119 (CA), where it was held that, contrary to the prior understanding in some courts, the rule applied to all customers and not only 'traders'. See also *Rolin v Steward* (1854) 14 CB 595.
[59] *Larios v Bonany y Gurety* (1873) LR 5 PC 346 (PC).
[60] *Wilson v United Counties Bank Ltd* [1920] AC 102 (HL).
[61] Obiter Sir Wilfrid Green MR in *Groom v Cocker* [1939] 1 KB 194 (CA) at 205.

gaining employment in the financial services industry[62] (ie they were 'handicapped in the labour market'[63]).

A difficult question arose in *Chagger v Abbey National plc*.[64] An employee was unfairly and discriminatorily dismissed and brought an action for damages, in which he succeeded. However, part of his claim for damages was for stigma damages on the basis that his future earnings had been decreased because some employers were, unlawfully and contrary to anti-victimisation legislation, discouraged from employing him because it was known that he had lawfully and successfully sued his previous employer, the defendant. The Court of Appeal held that third parties' unlawful victimisation was not too remote and provided the claimant had acted reasonably in seeking to mitigate his loss, and the evidence indicated that he would not be able to obtain replacement employment, he could recover his actual loss even if exacerbated by the unlawful action of third parties.

(c) Failure to Confer Good Publicity on Employees

Similarly, 'financial loss' is recoverable where the defendant failed to provide publicity to the claimant, which deprived the claimant of an opportunity to enhance its reputation or (for example by being out of work) damaged the claimant's existing reputation.[65] This is typical in cases of actors or performers (it is a curiosity of this area that many of the cases concern 'music hall artistes'),[66] and of writers who not only lose their income but also the screen credit from a screenplay[67] or the chance of reputational increase as an expert from publication of an article or book.[68]

Similarly, where a trade union wrongfully expelled the claimant member in breach of contract the claimant recovered damages for loss of earnings and of earning prospects (non-membership having excluded the claimant from the possibility of employment by union-only employers), although the period of this loss was confined in that case by the union readmitting the claimant to membership.[69]

---

[62] *Malik v Bank of Credit & Commerce International SA* [1998] 1 AC 20 (HL). In that case the breach was of the mutual duty of trust and confidence, and the question of how the financial losses would be proven was not addressed, the issue being dealt with only in principle as a preliminary issue. This type of damages was referred to in the case as 'stigma compensation' (see throughout Lord Steyn's judgment).

[63] Ibid Lord Nicholls at 37.

[64] *Chagger v Abbey National plc* [2010] ICR 397 (CA).

[65] *Marbé v George Edwardes (Daly's Theatre) Ltd* [1928] 1 KB 269 (CA); *Withers v General Theatre Co Ltd* [1933] 2 KB 536 (CA). These two decisions conflict as to whether financial losses for damage to existing reputation (rather than failure to enhance reputation) are recoverable, but the former case, determining that they are, is to be preferred: *Malik v BCCI SA* [1998] 1 AC 20 (HL) Lord Nicholls at 41 and Lord Steyn at 51–52.

[66] Ibid and *Bunning v The Lyric Theatre Ltd* (1894) 71 LT 396 (Stirling J) (classical music director and conductor at a theatre) and *Herbert Clayton and Jack Waller Ltd v Oliver* [1930] AC 209 (HL) (actor in theatre musicals).

[67] *Tolnay v Criterion Film Productions Ltd* [1936] 2 All ER 1625 (Goddard J).

[68] *Joseph v National Magazine Co Ltd* [1959] Ch 14 (Harman J) (article); *Sadler v Reynolds* [2005] EWHC 309 (QB) (Slade QC) (ghost-writing of an autobiography). cf *Malcolm v The Chancellor, Masters and Scholars of the University of Oxford (t/a Oxford University Press)* [1994] EMLR 17 (CA) (confirming the principle as regards a philosophy book but ordering an enquiry as to damages).

[69] *Edwards v Society of Graphical and Allied Trades* [1971] Ch 354 (CA).

(d) Failure to Train an Employee

Similarly, an employee may lose prospects of future employment if an employer prevents him from completing his apprenticeship and gaining qualifications.[70] A vivid example of how an apprenticeship might assist a career was given by one judge:

> Take, for example, the case where a young and gifted performer agrees to work for a famous impresario at a nominal salary and for a period of years on the express terms that the latter should advertise the former and should endeavour in all proper ways to secure his publicity and success. In such a case I deem it clear that substantial damages might be obtained if the impresario wrongfully repudiated his agreement with the artiste. If the law were otherwise, grave injustice might be inflicted, for loss of advertisement may involve a serious financial injury.[71]

(e) Lost Customers and Repeat Orders

Subject to remoteness, if the defendant's breach causes the claimant to breach a contract with a third party, the claimant can recover not only for the losses on the particular sub-sale or other contract with the third party, but also for losses of past or future sales to the same third party or others. As Denning LJ observed in *GKN Centrax Gears Ltd v Matbro Ltd*,

> Centrax knew as well as anybody the purpose for which these axles were required. It must have been within the contemplation of the parties that if these axles failed, it would cause much damage to the goodwill of Matbro. Customers would be disappointed and would not order any more. It seems to me that the arbitrator was entirely correct. Loss of repeat orders from existing customers can be recovered [for] where that is naturally within the contemplation of the parties as a consequence of the breach.[72]

Sometimes it will be difficult for a business to show the amount of custom lost. The approach of the courts is a flexible one, summarised by Stephenson LJ in the same case:[73]

> It is contrary to common sense to require that pecuniary loss under this head should be limited to loss proved by customers actually called to swear that they would have given further orders to Matbro but for Centrax's breaches of warranty regarding their axles' fitness. When there are none called, no damages will be given: *Foaminol Laboratories v British Plastics*[74] to which my Lord has referred. When some are called and there is evidence of a

---

[70] *Dunk v George Waller & Son* [1970] 2 QB 163 (CA). See also *Cronin v Eircom Ltd* [2007] 3 IR 104 (Irish High Court).

[71] *Turpin v Victoria Palace Ltd* [1918] 2 KB 539 (McCardie J).

[72] *GKN Centrax Gears Ltd v Matbro Ltd* [1976] 2 Lloyd's Rep 555 (CA) at 574. See also *Cointat v Myham & Son* [1913] 2 KB 220 (Coleridge J) (unfit meat supplied to a butcher causing public health prosecutions); *Anglo-Continental Holidays Ltd v Typaldos Lines (London) Ltd* [1967] 2 Lloyd's Rep 61 (CA) (cancellation of ship accommodation harming a travel agent's goodwill); *Amstrad plc v Seagate Technology Inc* (1998) 86 BLR 34 (Lloyd QC) at section 21. Cf *Foaminol Laboratories Ltd v British Artid Plastics Ltd* [1941] 2 All ER 393 (Hallett J) where lost profits from lack of cooperation with magazine editors who had been messed around in relation to a product that was never produced were not recovered.

[73] *GKN Centrax Gears Ltd v Matbro Ltd* [1976] 2 Lloyd's Rep 555 (CA) Stephenson LJ at 578. See also *Canlin Ltd v Thiokol Fibres Canada Ltd* (1983) 142 DLR (3d) 450 (Ontario CA).

[74] [1941] 2 All ER 393 (Hallett J) (failure to supply containers for a summer cream that had been advertised to the market).

drop in subsales, damages will be given not limited in amount to the loss of custom actually proved by the customers called: *Aerial Advertising v. Batchelor's Peas*,[75] to which my
Lord has also referred. The Court can and should draw inferences from the evidence called
as to the probable extent of the total loss of business resulting from the original seller's
breach of contract and must make its own moderate estimate without attempting perfect
compensation.

Stephenson LJ confirmed that even though the claimant had pleaded that particular
customers had been lost, that lost custom could be proven without necessarily calling all of those customers.[76]

In one case the claimant fizzy drinks supplier failed to prove that any lost profit
resulted from damage to its reputation, given that it handled the public relations
of the recall of the defective drinks very well and that its competitors were also
affected, and that the internal reports of the year's figures did not refer to the incident as having affected profits.[77]

D. Loss of Chance?[78]

(i) Making Profits from a Particular Third Party

Where profits derive from a particular transaction or trading relationship with a
particular third party, the 'loss of chance' approach will apply. This is exemplified
by *Chaplin v Hicks* (the beauty competition)[79] and *Jackson v RBS* (the dog-chew
supply relationship with a particular buyer).[80] Thus the questions of whether a
particular third party would have agreed to buy or sell something, and what price
it would have agreed, must be determined as loss of a chance.[81]

(ii) General Lost Profits/Sales

(a) Where the Only Question is 'How Much?'

Where the claim is for general loss of profits, a loss of chance approach is in principle applicable, with a discount for the chance that the claimant would not have
made a profit or would indeed have made a loss. However, in the ordinary case the

---

[75] *Aerial Advertising Co v Batchelors Peas Ltd (Manchester)* [1938] 2 All ER 788 (Atkinson J) (advertising pulled by a plane was flown over a city centre during the armistice services, causing negative impact
to reputation). See also *Marcus v Myers and Davis* (1895) 11 TLR 327 (Kennedy J) (failure to print in the
Jewish Chronicle newspaper the claimant ladies' tailor's advertisements, there being no rival publication
to advertise to the same clientele in, and custom being proven to have dropped off, with no new Jewish
customers after the advertisements stopped).

[76] [1976] 2 Lloyd's Rep 555 at 578. See also *Amstrad plc v Seagate Technology Inc* (1998) 86 BLR 34
(Lloyd QC) at section 18; *Tullis Russell Papermakers Ltd v Inveresk Ltd* [2010] CSOH 148 (Court of
Session, Outer House) where lost reputation and customer order profits were quantified and proven.

[77] *Britvic Soft Drinks Ltd v Messer UK Ltd* [2002] 1 Lloyd's Rep 20 (Tomlinson J) at paras 131 ff,
affirmed [2002] 2 Lloyd's Rep 368 (CA).

[78] See above in chapter thirteen, section 13.5, for more detailed discussion of loss of a chance.

[79] *Chaplin v Hicks* [1911] 2 KB 786 (CA), discussed above in chapter thirteen, section 13.5A(i).

[80] *Jackson v Royal Bank of Scotland* [2005] 1 WLR 377 (HL), discussed above in chapter thirteen,
section 13.5B(viii) . See also *4 Eng Ltd v Harper* [2009] Ch 91 (Richards J) (deceit).

[81] *Stovold v Barlows* [1996] PNLR 91 (CA).

loss of chance aspect vanishes because the probability element disappears: there is no need for multiplication of an amount of profit by a particular probability because it is found as a fact that the claimant would definitely have made a profit and the only question is as to how much.[82] Thus in one such case the judge 'decided that he was assessing the profits of a successful restaurant. The only issue was how successful'.[83]

This was most clearly explained by Anthony Clarke MR in the case of the *Vicky 1* as to the profits a vessel would have made by being chartered out:

> There are many cases in which courts or arbitrators have to determine what rate of profit would have been earned but for a tort or breach of contract. As I see it, in a case of this kind, where the court has held that the vessel would have been profitably engaged during the relevant period, where there is a relevant market and where the court can and does make a finding as to the profit that would probably have been made (and has been lost), there is no place for a discount from that figure to reflect the chance that the vessel would not have been employed.

> ... This situation is to be contrasted with a case in which it is not shown that the vessel would have been profitably employed but she might have been. It may be that in those circumstances it would be possible to approach the problem as a loss of a chance.[84]

Thus as regards anything being sold or chartered to a 'readily available market like a commodity market or a well-developed property market',[85] the finding that there is a market is a finding that the thing would definitely have been sold or chartered, and the only question then is as to the (market) price,[86] which is merely the valuer's opinion of the most likely or average of all the range of possible prices that the property might go for.[87] A valuation of property is 'no more than an estimate of what a property would [*not might*] fetch on a given date'.[88]

For example, in *Matlaszek v Bloom Camillin*,[89] the defendant solicitor's negligence in failing to explain the limit of credit-worthiness checks performed led the claimant to sell a company to an uncreditworthy buyer and so receive only £7,000 of the £77,000 cash price. (The non-cash part of the price was the discharge of debts owed by the claimant to the buyer.) But for the negligence, the claimant would not have sold to this buyer.[90] Accordingly, the defendant was liable for the price the

---

[82] *Parabola Investments Ltd v Browallia Cal Ltd* [2011] 1 QB 477 (CA) Toulson LJ at paras 22–23 (deceit claim, trading profits); *Vasiliou v Hajigeorgiou* [2010] EWCA Civ 1475 Patten LJ at paras 25–26 (negligent by landlord, profits from Greek restaurant).

[83] *Vasiliou v Hajigeorgiou* [2010] EWCA Civ 1475 Patten LJ at para 28.

[84] *Owners of the 'Front ACE' v Owners of the 'Vicky 1'* [2008] EWCA Civ 101 at paras 71 ff.

[85] *Equitable Life Assurance Society v Ernst & Young* [2003] EWCA Civ 1114 Brooke LJ (giving the judgment of the court) at para 87.

[86] See further *Skipton Building Society v Stott* [2001] QB 261 (CA) (as to the price that could have been obtained on selling a property) Evans LJ at para 11; *Equitable Life Assurance Society v Ernst & Young* [2003] EWCA Civ 1114 Brooke LJ (giving the judgment of the court) at para 87 (citing *Skipton Building Society v Stott* on this point). Cf *Law Debenture Trust Corp plc v Elektrim SA* [2010] EWCA Civ 1142.

[87] *Lion Nathan Ltd v C-C Bottlers Ltd* [1996] 1 WLR 1438 (PC).

[88] Ibid Lord Hoffmann at 1444.

[89] *Matlaszek v Bloom Camillin (a firm)* [2003] EWHC 2728 (Ch) (Park J).

[90] This is clear from the decision on liability: *Matlaszek v Bloom Camillin (a firm)*, 15 February 2001 (Hart J), [2001] All ER (D) 188.

business would have realised for the claimant on the open market (ie the profit that would have been made if another buyer had been found), with credit given for the £7,000 received.[91] There was no question of a loss of a chance.

(b) Where there is Also a Question of Whether any Profit Would Have Been Made

Where, however, it is proven that the claimant would have tried to make a sale but might not have been successful (because the market was difficult or there was no clear market to speak of), then the question is not merely at what price a sale would have been made but whether it would have been made at all. Depending as it does on third parties, this is determined as a question of loss of a chance.[92]

And where the defendant deprived the claimant of a racehorse, the claimant was entitled to damages for the lost chance of profits from racing prize money, given that it was not a certainty that any such profits would have been made.[93]

(iii) Discount for Contingencies

In many cases it will be convenient for the judge to reach an all-in figure that allows for the risks that profits would have been lower or higher, but in some cases it is useful to break-down the losses according to the particular chances that particular events would have happened.[94] However, in some cases it may be useful to calculate the most likely sum of profits that would have been earned if things went well and then make a deduction to allow for the chances, 'contingencies', that things had gone less well.[95]

18.3 The Presumption of Breaking Even

A. Introduction to Wasted Expenditure Awards

In some cases the damages measure will (at least at first sight: see the discussion below) be measured by the claimant's expenditure wasted by the defendant's breach. It is important to distinguish this from an award of expenditure *caused* by the breach, which is recoverable under ordinary principles; here we are talking only about expenditure that, even but for the breach, would still have been incurred although not (it is said by the claimant) wasted.

---

[91] *Matlaszek v Bloom Camillin* [2003] EWHC 2728 (Ch) (Park J).
[92] *First Interstate Bank of California v Cohen Arnold & Co* [1996] PNLR 17, (1996) 5 Bank LR 150 (CA); *Equitable Life Assurance Society v Ernst & Young* [2003] EWCA Civ 1114 Brooke LJ (giving the judgment of the court) at paras 83–88.
[93] *Howe v Teefy* (1927) 27 SR (NSW) 301 (Federal Court of Australia). And see also text to nn 122 to 125.
[94] Eg *Jackson v Royal Bank of Scotland* [2005] 1 WLR 377 (HL).
[95] Obiter in *Salford CC v Torkington* [2004] EWCA Civ 1546 Potter LJ at paras 53–55.

B. Where it is Impossible to Prove Profits

The presumption being discussed in this section was first developed in cases of profit-making ventures where it was impossible to prove the profits that would have been made but for the breach because the particular venture was speculative and/or had no history. Many of these cases arise in cases of provision of services or diversion of staff efforts, and are discussed in some detail above (chapter two, especially section 2.2B).

Thus in *Anglia TV v Reed*[96] the claimants could recover £2,750 for the pre- and post-contractual expenditure that was wasted as a result of the planned film being cancelled when the defendant actor (Robert Reed, star of 1970s TV sitcom 'The Brady Bunch') pulled out due to a double-booking. In that case the claimant could not 'say what their profit would have been on this contract if Mr. Reed had come here and performed it'.[97] Similarly, in the Australian case of *McRae v Commonwealth Disposals Commission*,[98] the purchaser bought the rights to salvage a non-existent sunken oil-tanker on a particular reef, the risk of that non-existence falling on the vendor. It was impossible to value the non-existent oil-tanker (certainly by reference to any market), or even to prove that it would have had some value,[99] but the purchaser recovered instead its wasted expenditure because the vendor could not prove that the expenditure would have been *wasted* even if the tanker had been there, the burden shifting to it.[100] Again, in a Canadian case the defendant refused, in breach of contract, to permit the claimant to operate its travel agency in certain of the defendant's department stores, and in the absence of evidence to disprove that the claimant would have broken even the claimant was permitted to recover its wasted expenditure.[101]

In *Dataliner Ltd v Vehicle Builders & Repairers Association*,[102] the car repairers could not show how much business they would have earned at a trade show, had the show been organised and advertised properly, but were awarded their expenditure (the award upheld by the Court of Appeal) because there was a justifiable assumption that the repairers would have earned enough new business to recoup their expenditure. The question in that case was not as to profits of the business as a whole, but the profitability of the trade show as a way of increasing the claimants' business.

And in *Commonwealth v Amann Aviation Pty Ltd*, while it was in theory possible to prove the lost profits from Amann's operation of the contract to provide aerial surveillance of Australia's northern coastline, this was particularly difficult because it was hard to estimate the chances of the employer terminating before the end of the first term, and the chances of the employer securing a renewal of the contract, and

---

[96] *Anglia Television Ltd v Reed* [1972] 1 QB 60 (CA).
[97] Ibid at 63.
[98] *McRae v Commonwealth Disposals Commission* (1951) 84 CLR 377 (HC of Australia).
[99] Ibid at paras 22–23.
[100] Ibid at para 26. And see *Seal Rocks Victoria (Australia) Pty Ltd v State of Victoria* [2003] VSC 85 (SC of Victoria).
[101] *Sunshine Vacation Villas Ltd v Governor and Co of Adventurers of England Trading Into Hudson's Bay* (1984) 13 DLR (4th) 93 (British Columbia CA).
[102] *Dataliner Ltd v Vehicle Builders & Repairers Association* (CA), 27 August 1995.

the value of the renewal (the terms of the renewal tender) were hard to estimate.[103] Accordingly, Amann recovered in the High Court of Australia its wasted expenditure on the unrebutted presumption that it would have broken even.

C. The Rebuttable Presumption: There is No Separate 'Reliance' Basis

Despite these awards, it is important to understand that there is in contract law no 'reliance' measure of loss that the claimant can 'elect' to recover instead of the usual expectation measure, seeking to be put in the position the claimant would have been in had there been no contract.[104]

That there is no separate reliance measure, but rather that it is a proxy for the expectation measure where profits are hard to prove, is clear from the Court of Appeal's decision in *C&P Haulage v Middleton*,[105] in which the claimant could not recover damages for expenses it incurred but which it would not have recovered through trading its vehicle repair business had the contract not been breached. Expenditure damages cannot be used to put the claimant in a better position than it would have been in had the contract been performed, and so it all comes down to expectation in the end.

The reason why expenditure is a useful proxy (for the minimum revenue that would have been earned) is that it is easy to prove. Whereas it may be difficult to prove the total amount of revenue that would have been received—ie that a profit would have been recovered and how much it would have been—the claimant will be able to prove the historical fact of how much expenditure it has incurred.

Because the claimant's predicament was caused by the defendant's breach, the law reverses the onus of proof: it is assumed that the claimant would have broken even

> where money has been spent in that expectation [of making a profit] but the defendant's breach of contract has prevented that expectation from being put to the test, it is fair to

---

[103] *Commonwealth of Australia v Amann Aviation Pty Ltd* (1992) 174 CLR 64 (HC of Australia).

[104] The now discredited separate 'reliance loss' theory stems from LL Fuller and WR Perdue, 'The Reliance Interest in Contract Damages' (1936) 46 *Yale Law Journal* 52. See also *Cullinane v British Rema Manufacturing Co* [1954] 1 QB 292 (CA) Evershed MR at 303; *Anglia Television Ltd v Reed* [1972] 1 QB 60 (CA). Of course, in contract cases where the wrong consists of inducing a transaction (eg misadvice or contractual misrepresentation cases) the measure of loss is essentially the reliance measure, not because the principles have changed but because the promise was to take reasonable care and therefore the expectation measure requires that damages be measured as if that promise had been honoured and therefore the transaction had not been entered into. In those cases the expectation measure requires that damages put the claimant in the position as if there had been no transaction, which is the same as the tort measure for deceit and negligent misstatement, and not dissimilar to the award received on restitution for unjust enrichment where the contract has been terminated or rescinded and there has been a total failure of consideration.

[105] *C&P Haulage Co Ltd v Middleton* [1983] 1 WLR 1461 (CA), approved by the Court of Appeal in *Dataliner Ltd v Vehicle Builders & Repairers Association* (CA), 27 August 1995. See also *CCC Films (London) Ltd v Impact Quadrant Films Ltd* [1985] QB 16 (Hutchinson J); *PJ Spillings (Builders) Ltd v Bonus Flooring Ltd* [2008] EWHC 1516 (QB) (Forbes J); *Commonwealth of Australia v Amann Aviation* (1992) 174 CLR 64 (HC of Australia). See further M Owen, 'Some Aspects of the Recovery of Reliance Damages in the Law of Contract' (1984) 4 *OJLS* 393; D McLauchlan, 'Reliance Damages for Breach of Contract' [2007] *NZL Rev* 417.

assume that the claimant would at least have recouped its expenditure had the contract been performed unless and to the extent that the defendant can prove otherwise.[106]

To break even, the claimant would have had to receive revenue that matched the expenditure, and so the claimant is permitted to recover its expenditure as the amount the law has presumed it would have received in revenue from the relevant contract, if that presumption is not rebutted.[107] As Deane J has observed in the High Court of Australia in *Amann*:

> [The] plaintiff may rely on a presumption that the value of [the benefits which the plaintiff would have derived from performance by the defendant] would have been at least equal to the total detriment which has been or would have been sustained by the plaintiff in doing whatever was reasonably necessary to procure and perform the contract.[108]

This echoes the approach of US judge Learned Hand CJ in *L Albert & Son v Armstrong Rubber* in 1949:

> In cases where the venture would have proved profitable to the promisee, there is no reason why he should not recover his expenses. On the other hand, on those occasions in which the performance would not have covered the promisee's outlay, such a result imposes the risk of the promisee's contract upon the promisor. We cannot agree that the promisor's default in performance should under this guise make him an insurer of the promisee's venture; yet it does not follow that the breach should not throw upon him the duty of showing that the value of the performance would in fact have been less than the promisee's outlay. It is often very hard to learn what the value of the performance would have been; and it is a common expedient, and a just one, in such situations to put the peril of the answer upon that party who by his wrong has made the issue relevant to the rights of another. On principle therefore the proper solution would seem to be that the promisee may recover his outlay in preparation for the performance, subject to the privilege of the promisor to reduce it by as much as he can show that the promisee would have lost, if the contract had been performed.[109]

These points were carefully explained by Teare J in the 2010 High Court decision in *Omak Maritime Ltd v Mamola Challenger Shipping Co*,[110] confirming that 'The Claimant's expenditure should only be recoverable where the likely gross profit would at least cover that expenditure'[111] and further:

---

[106] *Yam Seng Pte Ltd v International Trade Corp Ltd* [2013] 1 Lloyd's Rep 526 (Leggatt J) at paras 188 and 190.

[107] *CCC Films v Impact Quadrant Films Ltd* [1985] QB 16 (Hutchinson J) at 39–40; *McRae v Commonwealth Disposals Commission* (1951) 84 CLR 377 (HC of Australia) at para 26; *Commonwealth of Australia v Amann Aviation* (1992) 174 CLR 64 (HC of Australia) Mason CJ and Dawson J at para 42 and Brennan J at 14–15; *AC Daniels & Co Ltd v Jungwoo Logic* (Hicks QC), 14 April 2000, at paras 39 ff. Although note that in *Dataliner Ltd v Vehicle Builders & Repairers Association* (CA), 27 August 1995, the Court of Appeal required it to be demonstrated that the claimant's expectation of recovering its expenditure was 'well-founded' and not 'aleatory', and would not rely on a shifted burden of proof.

[108] *Commonwealth of Australia v Amann Aviation* (1992) 174 CLR 64 (HC of Australia) Deane J at para 11.

[109] *L Albert & Son v Armstrong Rubber* 178 F 2d 182 (2d Cir 1949), quoted with approval in *Omak Maritime Ltd v Mamola Challenger Shipping Co* [2010] EWHC 2026 (Comm) (Teare J).

[110] *Omak Maritime Ltd v Mamola Challenger Shipping Co* [2010] EWHC 2026 (Comm) (Teare J). The decision was approved in *Yam Seng Pte Ltd v International Trade Corp Ltd* [2013] 1 Lloyd's Rep 526 (Leggatt J).

[111] Ibid para 45.

In some cases a contract can be shown to be a bad bargain. In other cases it may not be possible to show one way or the other whether the likely gross profits would at least equal the expenditure. In that latter type of case the question arises as to which party should bear the evidential burden of proof. Should the burden be on the Claimant to show that the likely profits would at least equal his expenditure or on the Defendant to show that the likely profits would not at least equal the Claimant's expenditure? The authorities to which I have referred, in particular *L Albert & Son v Armstrong Rubber* and *CCC Films (London) Ltd v Impact Quadrant Films Ltd* provide a rational and sensible explanation for the view that that burden should be on the Defendant.[112]

In *Omak* this was important, because the charterer had terminated at a time when the owner was able to make more on the market than it had under the charter, ie the owner suffered no loss as a result of the breach. The owner sought to circumvent this obvious truth by claiming its expenditure towards the terminated charter on (it said) a reliance basis, and succeeded before the arbitrators, who awarded US$86,534. The High Court allowed the appeal from this award as there was no separate reliance basis and but for the breach, the claimant would have been in a worse, not a better overall position.

The principle was most fully explained by the High Court of Australia in the important decision of *Commonwealth v Amann Aviation Pty Ltd* (which was approved in *Omak*):

> The manner in which a plaintiff frames his or her claim for damages will be dictated ... according to whether the contract, if fully performed, would have been and could be shown to have been profitable (even if the actual amount of profit is not readily ascertainable). If this can be demonstrated, a plaintiff's expectation of a profit, objectively made out, will be protected by the award of damages. Otherwise, subject to it being demonstrated that a plaintiff would not even have recovered any or all of his or her reasonable expenses, a plaintiff's objectively determined expectation of recoupment of expenses incurred will be protected by the award of damages.

> An award of damages for expenditure reasonably incurred under a contract in which no net profit would have been realized, while placing the plaintiff in the position he or she would have been in had the contract been fully performed, also restores the plaintiff to the position he or she would have been in had the contract not been entered into. In this particular situation it will be noted that there is a coincidence, but no more than a coincidence, between the measure of damages recoverable both in contract and in tort.[113]

Thus in one case of a breach of a commercial landlord's covenant to repair, Staughton LJ in the Court of Appeal interpreted and upheld the first instance judge's award of two months' rent on the basis that it was a 'reasonable inference' that 'The tenant must have been making at least sufficient profit to pay his rent; otherwise he would not be doing it at all' and therefore that during the two months of the business being closed down the claimant had lost revenue equal to the amount of the rent.[114] In another case of breach of a contract to supply various Manchester United Football Club products, the claimant recovered the wasted expenditure on

---

[112] Ibid para 47.
[113] *Commonwealth of Australia v Amann Aviation* (1992) 174 CLR 64 (HC of Australia) Mason CJ and Dawson J at paras 36–37.
[114] *Savva v Hussein* [1996] 2 EGLR 65 (CA) Staughton LJ at 67.

the basis of an unrebutted presumption that it would at least have broken even,[115] as did a claimant in a case of an aborted contract to provide a new island tourist attraction,[116] and one of wrongful eviction of a restaurant business.[117]

A useful illustration of the way the presumption should operate is provided by the case of *Sapwell v Bass*.[118] In that case the defendant repudiated a contract to allow the claimant to use a particular stallion (Cyllene) to breed with the claimant's mare (Dear Mary) for one season for a price of £315. There were many contingencies that would determine whether this led to a surviving foal that grew into a valuable horse. After the repudiation, the claimant never paid this price, and instead found an alternative stallion (Cicero, Cyllene's son) at a cost of £100, and this produced a foal. The court refused damages on the ground that they were too speculative. Had this not been the case, the court should have presumed that the claimant would have broken even on its expenditure of £315, and so ended up not out of pocket. Damages would be payable, therefore, if the claimant's actual position was that it was out of pocket because it had not in fact recouped its actual revenue of £100. As there was no evidence of this, the presumption would not have assisted the claimant even had it sought to rely on it.

D. The Claimant can Rebut the Presumption and Prove it Would Have Made a Profit

Obviously, if the claimant can prove that it not only would have broken even but would have made a profit, it can recover that profit in addition to any unrecovered expenditure/reduction in his assets.[119] Where the claimant proves lost profits then it has rebutted the presumption, although the presumption need not be, and rarely is, discussed in such cases.

E. The Defendant can Rebut the Presumption and Prove that the Claimant Would Have Made a Loss

Similarly, it is open to the defendant to prove that the claimant would have made a loss.[120] This is illustrated by the Supreme Court of British Columbia case of *Bowlay Logging Ltd v Domtar Ltd*[121] where the defendant timber hauliers were able to

---

[115] *Yam Seng Pte Ltd v International Trade Corp Ltd* [2013] 1 Lloyd's Rep 526 (Leggatt J).

[116] *Seal Rocks (Victoria) Pty Ltd v State of Victoria* [2003] VSC 84 (SC of Victoria).

[117] *Ontario Inc v Select Restaurant Plaza Corp* 2006 CanLII 44266 (Ontario Superior Court), although damages for half of the lost value of the lease were also awarded on a not entirely clear basis.

[118] *Sapwell v Bass* [1910] 2 KB 486 (Jelf J).

[119] Cf *JP Morgan Chase Bank v Springwell Navigation Corp* [2006] EWCA Civ 161.

[120] Thus the US Restatement (Second) of Contracts §349 requires that there be a deduction from any claim for net expenditure of 'any loss that the party in breach can prove with reasonable certainty the injured party would have suffered had the contract been performed', ie (as in English law) the burden falls on the defendant of proving that the claimant would have made a loss and the amount of that loss. See also *Yam Seng Pte Ltd v International Trade Corp Ltd* [2013] 1 Lloyd's Rep 526 (Leggatt J) obiter at para 190.

[121] *Bowlay Logging Ltd v Domtar Ltd* (1978) 87 DLR (3d) 325 (British Columbia SC), affirmed (1982) 135 DLR (3d) 179. Approved in *C&P Haulage Co v Middleton* [1983] 1 WLR 1461 (CA) and *Omak Maritime Ltd v Mamola Challenger Shipping Co* [2010] EWHC 2026 (Comm) (Teare J).

show that the claimant's timber business, by which it had contracted with the defendant to cut, skid and load logs onto the defendant's trucks, was loss-making and the defendant effectively did the claimant a favour by stopping providing its trucks so that the contract was terminated.

Certain ventures will be speculative and/or as likely to make a loss as a profit. Gambling is one example.[122] Marketing a new beverage,[123] or pharmaceuticals in a new market,[124] or racing a horse,[125] are others. In these cases any presumption of breaking even is rebutted. However, where there is specific evidence (eg a history) of profit-making in such ventures, the lost revenue (including profit where appropriate) is recoverable as proven (but without the assistance of any presumption).[126] There may also be factual situations where the presumption is rebutted in the light of the inferences that can be drawn from the unconvincingness of the claimant's own evidence as to its lost revenue,[127] but the burden on the defendant is a real one, and the court will not lightly conclude that the claimant would not have recouped its expenditure.[128]

Thus in *Ampurius Nu Homes Holdings Ltd v Telford Homes (Creekside) Ltd*[129] the defendant construction company repudiated its contract but was able to demonstrate (only the defendant calling expert evidence on the point) that, although the claimant genuinely thought it would profit from the contract, but for the breach the claimant developer would have made a loss on the development and would not have recovered its wasted expenditure. Accordingly, following *Omak Maritime*, no substantial damages were awarded in relation to expenditure or profits.

Where it is proved that the claimant would have made a loss, the claimant's recovery is therefore limited to the amount of its expenditure that it would have recouped.[130]

F. Interest

One concrete effect of the recoverability of wasted expenditure as a proxy for lost revenue, rather than as a loss in its own right, is that where interest is recovered it should date from the day when the revenue (in the amount of the wasted expenditure) would have been received, not from the day when the wasted expenditure was

---

[122] See the commodities trading case of *E Bailey & Co Ltd v Balholm Securities Ltd* [1973] 2 Lloyd's Rep 404 (Kerr J).

[123] Although *Out of the Box Pte Ltd v Wanin Industries Pte Ltd* [2013] SGCA 15 (Singapore CA) was decided on remoteness grounds, a further ground implicit in much of the reasoning was that the claimant had not shown that it would have recovered its huge marketing costs of the new product in revenues (which marketing was wasted by the defendant's faulty manufacture causing a public relations disaster).

[124] *Apotex Inc v Global Drug Ltd* (Ontario CA), 2 October 2010.

[125] *Howe v Teefy* (1927) 27 SR (NSW) 301 (Federal Court of Australia).

[126] Cf the deceit case *Parabola Investments Ltd v Browallia Cal* [2010] 3 WLR 1266 (CA).

[127] This is the best explanation for the obiter conclusions in *Filobake Ltd v Rondo Ltd* [2005] EWCA Civ 563 at paras 58–68 that it could not even be presumed that the claimant would have broken even.

[128] *Grange v Quinn* [2013] EWCA Civ 24.

[129] *Ampurius Nu Homes Holdings Ltd v Telford Homes (Creekside) Ltd* [2012] 144 Con LR 72 (Roth J) app allowed on repudiation [2013] 4 All ER 377 (CA).

[130] See the discussion in *Sunshine Vacation Villas Ltd v Hudson's Bay Co* (1984) 13 DLR (4th) 93 (British Columbia CA).

actually incurred (since if the defendant had performed the contract the claimant would still have been without the use of the money between those two dates).[131]

There is a separate question as to whether the revenue presumed should include not only the wasted expenditure but also a return on the expenditure, on the basis that no commercially sensible person would employ money without receiving a return at least equal to inflation or to the rate recoverable on deposit. However, this is a question of what revenue should be presumed,[132] and is not an award of interest per se.

G. Other Situations in Which the Presumption of Breaking Even Applies

Elsewhere in this book the reader can find discussions of the application of the presumption of breaking even to service claims (chapter two, section 2.2B), lost management time claims (chapter two, section 2.2B(iii)), property sale claims (chapter four, section 4.5A(ii)(b)), non-acceptance claims (chapter five, section 5.3), loss of use of property claims (chapter six, section 6.4D) and non-pecuniary loss claims (chapter nineteen, section 19.2C).

H. The Alternative Presumption that the Claimant Would Have Recovered the Value to the Claimant of the Promise?

As discussed below, where the claimant cannot prove lost profits and the presumption of breaking even cannot help (for example, because the breach does not lead to loss of a venture and it is impossible to separate out the costs relating to the particular breached obligation), the claimant can sometimes recover lost hypothetical bargain damages under the *Wrotham Park* measure. This measure is discussed below in chapter twenty-two, alongside this author's view that they are best explained on the basis of a presumption that but for the breach the claimant would have earned (in money or otherwise) the value of the promise to the promisee, ie the amount the claimant would accept to waive the obligation.

18.4 Examples of Lost Profit Awards

Although the principles of recovery are the same whatever the factual situation, it can sometimes be useful (and more persuasive to judges) to look at case law that covers the same fact pattern as the case being litigated.[133]

---

[131] The point was not argued, but it appears (although not clearly) that an incorrect approach to the period of interest was applied in *CCC Films (London) Ltd v Impact Quadrant Films Ltd* [1985] QB 16 (Hutchinson J).

[132] See eg chapter six, section 6.5A(ii).

[133] Of course, profits from such types of business as buying and selling goods or chartering out vessels are dealt with at length elsewhere in this book and not covered in this section.

A. Profits on a Business the Claimant Did Not Get to Operate[134]

The cases on the purchase of an unwanted business where the claimant proves it would have bought an alternative business began with *Esso Petroleum Co Ltd v Mardon*,[135] a case of breach of a collateral warranty that reasonable care had been taken in describing the petrol station bought by the claimant (ie the contractual equivalent of a negligent misstatement case, with exactly the same damages award). The Court of Appeal awarded the claimant damages to be assessed for the profits that would have been made on a generic similar alternative business, at least up until such time as the claimant was in fact or should have been able to restore himself after selling the petrol station to the position he would have been in if he had never bought it.[136] And in the deceit case of *East v Maurer*[137] the claimants recovered for the profit they would have made in an alternative hairdressing business. The Court of Appeal rejected the judge's approach of estimating the loss from the profits that were previously made by the defendant vendor on the unwanted business actually bought, as the claimant was new to the area and the clientele, but found that some figure had to be reached and a starting point was to presume a reasonable return on capital.[138]

However, in another deceit case in relation to a public house the Court of Appeal upheld the judge's finding that the claimant would in the alternative business have merely broken even, and so awarded the capital losses but no lost profit.[139]

In the deceit case of *4 Eng Ltd v Harper*[140] the claimant actually identified the specific alternative business it would have bought. Accordingly the lost profits awarded were reduced to an 80 per cent figure to correspond to the chance that the owners of the particular business would have sold it to the claimant. That percentage was multiplied by the lost profits for the period up to trial, plus the capital value that the business would have had at trial.

In the negligence case of *Vasiliou v Hajigeorgiou*, the landlord's breaches prevented the claimant from opening a Greek restaurant on the leased premises.[141] The Court of Appeal upheld the judge's factual finding that the claimant was an experienced restaurant owner and would have run a profitable business. And in a Singaporean case of sale of a business that was not completed by the seller, the buyer recovered for a loss of profits that would have been made from the business, allowing for various contingencies.[142]

---

[134] See also above at text to n 20.
[135] *Esso Petroleum Co Ltd v Mardon* [1976] 1 QB 801 (CA).
[136] Lord Denning MR ibid at 821–22.
[137] *East v Maurer* [1991] 1 WLR 461 (CA).
[138] Beldam LJ (ibid) at 467.
[139] *Davis v Churchward Brook Haye & Co* (CA), 6 May 1993.
[140] *4 Eng Ltd v Harper* [2009] Ch 91 (Richards J).
[141] *Vasiliou v Hajigeorgiou* [2010] EWCA Civ 1475.
[142] *Straits Engineering Contracting Pte Ltd v Merteks Pte Ltd* [1996] 4 LRC 259 (Singapore CA).

B. Profits on a Business Cut Short

The defendant's breach may cut short the claimant's business, as in the franchise case of *MMP GmbH v Antal International Network*.[143] Alternatively, the breach may delay the business getting up and running, as in the tort case of damage to the claimant's first crop of roses.[144]

C. Profits on a Trading Relationship Cut Short

Where a trading relationship is cut short, it may be difficult to prove how long the relationship would have continued. In *Jackson v RBS*, the court evaluated the increasing year-on-year chance that a trading relationship would, because of competition or similar, have been broken off.[145]

D. Profits Lost Due to Competition

Where there has been a warranty that the claimant would not face competition and it has done so, the claimant is entitled to the additional profits that would have been earned had there not been competition. Such an award was made in *Salford City Council v Torkington*.[146] The trial judge held that but for the breach of warranty the claimants would have kept the grocer's shop it first leased in 1981 until 1994, when it would have sold it for a total (including stock) of £62,000, and awarded that figure plus the lost profits to one claimant from 1981 to 1994 and the other from 1981 to 1988 (that claimant having been found to have failed to mitigate then) of around £120,000, plus 10 years of interest on that sum to the trial date of 2004. In fact, because of the competition of which the breach of warranty consisted, the claimants ceased trading in February 1988 but did not in fact sell up then, the business having no value. The Court of Appeal held that the damages should be assessed in March 1988 at £65,000, being the difference between the value the business had at that date (nil) and the value it would have had at that date but for the breach, plus the lost profits up to that date of around £46,000, plus interest to trial. No award was made for lost profits from March 1988 to 1994 or beyond, because the claimants should have sold the business in March 1988 and cut their losses and gone elsewhere to try to earn their money (as they in fact did), and any lost profits after that date were reasonably avoidable.[147] It is worth noting that had there been no failure to mitigate, and so the lost profits measured to 1994, the court would have had to have taken into account the profits the claimants made from 1988 working

---

[143] *MMP GmbH v Antal International Network Ltd* [2011] EWHC 1120 (Comm) (Flaux J). See also *Bank of America NA v CD Smith Motor Co* 106 SW 3d 425 (2003) (SC of Arkansas).

[144] *Attorney General v Thermal Produce New Zealand Ltd* [1987] 2 NZLR 348 (New Zealand CA).

[145] *Jackson v Royal Bank of Scotland* [2005] 1 WLR 377 (HL). See also *Take Ltd v BSM Marketing Ltd* [2007] EWHC 3513 (QB) then [2009] EWCA Civ 45.

[146] *Salford City Council v Torkington* [2004] EWCA Civ 1546.

[147] Esp Potter LJ (ibid) at paras 40 and 48 and Mance LJ at paras 62–64.

in their other businesses,[148] but these sums were not taken into account by the judge, making his approach inconsistent.[149]

E. Loss of Employment on a Project

In *VK Mason Construction Ltd v Bank of Nova Scotia*[150] the claimant construction company would not have worked on a particular construction project if the defendant had not negligently misrepresented the financial position of the employer. The Supreme Court of Canada 'assume[d] that Mason would have found a profitable means of employing itself had it not been induced to work on the Courtot project by the Bank's misrepresentation', and used the anticipated profit in the unwanted transaction as an estimate of what would have been made otherwise.

F. Reduced Profitability

In *British Westinghouse Co v Underground Electric Rys Co of London*, the claimant recovered lost profits to the railway business caused by deficient turbines.[151] In another case, damages were recoverable for lost profits to a high performance car repair business, caused by the landlord's installation of speed bumps.[152] Similarly, where the claimant would but for the breach have obtained its building materials cheaper[153] or sold its products for more.[154]

G. Farming

Farming provides a common setting for contract damages disputes. *Parsons (Livestock) Ltd v Uttley Ingham & Co Ltd* concerned lost pigs and the profits therefrom.[155] Similarly, lost profits have been sought by buyers or sub-buyers in in cases of defective seeds.[156]

H. Financial Trading

In *Parabola Investments Ltd v Browallia Cal Ltd*[157] the claimant (the vehicle of trader Mr Gill), induced by the defendant's repeated deceitful statements that trading

---

[148] As to these other businesses, see Potter LJ at para 12.
[149] On cases of wrongful competition, see also chapter ten, section 10.4.
[150] *VK Mason Construction Ltd v Bank of Nova Scotia* [1985] 1 SCR 271 (SC of Canada) at 285–86.
[151] *British Westinghouse Co v Underground Electric Rys Co of London* [1912] AC 673 (HL).
[152] *Stewart v Scottish Widows and Life Assurance Society plc* [2005] EWHC 1831 (QB) (Eccles QC), appeal allowed in part on a different point [2006] EWCA Civ 999.
[153] *Clef Aquitaine SARL v Laporte Materials (Barrow) Ltd* [2001] QB 488 (CA).
[154] *Jackson v Royal Bank of Scotland plc* [2005] 1 WLR 377 (HL).
[155] *Parsons (Livestock) Ltd v Uttley Ingham & Co Ltd* [1978] QB 791 (CA).
[156] *Randall v Raper* (1858) EB & E 84; *Wagstaff v Short-horn Dairy Co* (1884) Cab & El 324.
[157] *Parabola Investments Ltd v Browallia Cal Ltd* [2011] 1 QB 477 (CA).

was going well, made disastrous trades in contracts for difference from June 2001 until the fraud was discovered in 2002. The claimant recovered not only for the £3.2m depletion of the fund up until 2002, but the lost profits it would have made on alternative trades up to May 2009 using its June 2001 fund of £4.25m had the deceit not taken place. Extrapolating from the very high trading profit percentages from the claimant's pre- and post-fraud track record of trading with smaller sums, the court awarded £1.6m for the lost profits up to 2002 and £12m for the lost trading profits from 2002 up until March 2008, far higher than any interest award that would have been made in lieu of proof of lost alternative transactions. It is no bar to recovery that the profits would have been lost not through putting money into a single business venture but through a succession of one-off unspecified trades.[158] The speculative nature of the trading did not matter where the judge was convinced that the profits would have been made, although some Indian trades were too speculative and not proven. In other cases, such financial trading may be too speculative for a loss of profits to be proven.[159]

I. Lost Profits on a New Product

It is difficult to quantify lost profits on a new product. In one contract damages case the court had to consider whether a new board game based around *The Sun* newspaper's Page 3 stripper feature would have been profitable, and considered evidence of the marketing, how successful the game could be expected to be relative to other board games, and what its realistic shelf-life would be (it was not likely to be a 'hardy perennial' and had a maximum life of three years) before estimating units sold and prices for each of the years it would be sold.[160] A simpler calculation as to the net profit and amount of likely sales was made in the case of a face cream which the defendant's non-supply prevented the claimant from ever selling.[161]

J. Lost Income from Leasing Commercial Property

In *Keydon Estate Ltd v Eversheds LLP* the solicitor's negligence induced purchase of an office building reversion with a view to securing the income stream from the tenant.[162] Upon the claimant being unable to sell or let the property except at a much reduced rent, the judge awarded the lost income on an alternative office building reversion, being 'not the loss of the income stream from the Property itself but

---

[158] Toulson LJ (ibid) at para 44.
[159] *E Bailey & Co Ltd v Balholm Securities Ltd* [1973] 2 Lloyd's Rep 404 (Kerr J), obiter; *ATA v American Express Bank Ltd* (17.6.98, CA).
[160] *Double G Communications Ltd v News Group International Ltd* [2011] EWHC 961 (QB) (Eady J).
[161] *Foaminol Laboratories Ltd v British Artid Plastics Ltd* [1941] 2 All ER 393 (Hallett J). An award was also made for wasted expenditure of advertising which, in light of the legal developments set out in section 18.3 above, must be on the implicit basis that the claimant would at least have recovered the cost of such advertising through its future sales.
[162] *Keydon Estate Ltd v Eversheds LLP* [2005] EWHC 972 (Ch) (Evans-Lombe J).

the loss of a similar alternative income stream',[163] the claimant having led evidence of specific alternative properties that were available.

K. Lost Property Development

It is common for a claimant to recover the lost profits that would have been made on a development that, due to the defendant's breach, the claimant lost[164] or had retained but on less profitable terms,[165] providing not too remote,[166] And that they wouldn't have been suffered anyway.[167]

---

[163] Para 31.

[164] *Cottrill v Steyning and Littlehampton Building Society* [1966] 1 WLR 1083 (Elwes J); *Farmer Giles Ltd v Wessex Water Authority* [1990] 1 EGLR 177 (CA) (effectively a tort case); *William Aitchison v Gordon Durham & Co Ltd* (CA) (breach of a joint venture); *Jenmain Builders v Steed & Steed* (20.2.00, CA) (solicitor's negligence), although the development profit was held to be built into the capital value of the property lost and any further loss was avoidable had the claimant pursued an alternative development; *Watts v Bell & Scott WS* [2007] CSOH 108 (Scot Outer House).

[165] *Finley v Connell Associates* (Ouseley J); *Joyce v Bowman Law Ltd* [2010] EWHC 251 (Ch) (Vos J) (solicitor's negligence, the claimant should have gone ahead with a smaller development). As to cases where the defendant delayed the development, see *Marshall v Mackintosh* (1898) 14 TLR 458 (Kennedy J); *Finley v Connell Associates* (27.7.01, Ouseley J); *Earl's Terrace Properties Ltd v Nilsson Design Ltd* [2004] EWHC 136 (TCC) (Thornton QC); *Kirkton Investments Ltd v VMH LLP* [2011] CSOH 200 (Scot Outer House).

[166] *Diamond v Campbell-Jones* [1961] Ch 22 (Buckley J).

[167] *Reeves v Thrings & Long* (19.11.93, CA).

19

Non-Pecuniary Loss

Damages awards for non-pecuniary loss

19.1. The Evolution of the Legal Test
19.2. Specific Issues in Non-Pecuniary Loss Awards
19.3. (Physical) Inconvenience and Disturbance
19.4. Personal Injury

T
HE EVOLUTION OF contract damages for non-pecuniary loss (which includes both the infliction of distress, anxiety and disappointment etc, and the failure to confer enjoyment, happiness and satisfaction etc) has lagged some way behind that for pecuniary loss. This is for perfectly understandable practical reasons, such as that non-pecuniary loss is often small and so uneconomic to litigate; consumer losses in goods cases are usually reduced or avoided altogether by the provision of a replacement (which turns the loss into a financial loss); and statutory or informal redress often satisfies the consumer's complaint. Moreover, it is plainly easier to measure and so compensate for pecuniary than non-pecuniary loss. Despite significant developments in recent decades, most especially by the House of Lords' decisions in *Ruxley Electronics and Construction Ltd v Forsyth*[1] and *Farley v Skinner*,[2] further consolidation and expansion of the law of non-pecuniary loss can be expected in the coming years.

19.1 The Evolution of the Legal Test

A. The Old Starting Point: A Basic Rule of Non-Recoverability

(i) Introduction

As Bingham LJ has observed, 'a contract-breaker is not in general liable for any distress, frustration, anxiety, displeasure, vexation, tension or aggravation which his breach of contract may cause to the innocent party'.[3] Any breach of contract (and litigation) will be distressing, but damages are not available where the claimant

---

[1] *Ruxley Electronics and Construction Ltd v Forsyth* [1996] AC 344 (HL).
[2] *Farley v Skinner* [2002] 2 AC 732 (HL).
[3] *Watts v Morrow* [1991] 1 WLR 1421 (CA) at 1443.

merely suffers anguish or vexation as a result of the manner in which a contract is broken, for example as a result of an unpleasant dismissal from employment, as was confirmed by the majority of an extended panel of the House of Lords in the 1909 decision usually treated as laying down a rule against general recovery of contract damages for non-pecuniary loss, *Addis v Gramophone Company Ltd*.[4] In truth, although injured feelings of the claimant were mentioned,[5] *Addis* focused on whether the motive and conduct of the defendant might permit a jury to award additional essential exemplary or punitive damages, and the answer was (and remains) 'No'.

Nevertheless, *Addis* has long been treated at the highest level as having laid down a general rule preventing recovery for injury to feelings, although subject to various exceptions. That approach is exemplified by Lord Lloyd's comments in the *Ruxley* case discussed below, '*Addis v. Gramophone Co. Ltd* established the general rule that in claims for breach of contract, the plaintiff cannot recover damages for his injured feelings. But the rule, like most rules, is subject to exceptions',[6] and also the similar observations of Lord Bingham,

> The general rule laid down in *Addis v Gramophone Co Ltd* [1909] AC 488 was that damages for breach of contract could not include damages for mental distress. Cases decided over the last century established some inroads into that general rule.[7]

The law of non-pecuniary losses is, however, moving towards abandonment of any special rules, leaving recovery to depend (as in financial loss cases) solely on ordinary general requirements of proof, remoteness, mitigation and legal causation. One obstacle to this step has been the conclusion that non-pecuniary losses are often irrecoverable even where foreseeable as not unlikely, ie even where (it was assumed) they are not too remote, suggesting an additional exclusionary rule must be in operation.[8] As explained below, this involves something of a misunderstanding of the remoteness rule, which is in fact able to distinguish those cases where non-pecuniary loss is recoverable and those where it is not, and does not merely apply a foreseeability test. Nevertheless, at present the approach is still one of a general rule of non-recoverability of non-pecuniary loss, save in cases of (still evolving) exceptions to that rule.

(ii) Compare with the Tort of Negligence

What must be noted at the outset, however, is that the test for recovery of non-pecuniary loss for breach of contract is, quite properly, different to the test in the tort law of negligence. There the law proscribes who can sue for what it calls 'nervous shock', partly for policy reasons, given that a tortious negligent action can give rise

---

[4] *Addis v Gramophone Company Ltd* [1909] AC 488 (HL). As to dismissal claims, see further chapter five, section 5.4.
[5] Lord Loreburn LC (ibid) at 491, with whose judgment a majority of the court agreed.
[6] *Ruxley Electronics and Construction Ltd v Forsyth* [1996] 1 AC 344 (HL) at 374.
[7] *Johnson v Gore Wood & Co* [2002] 2 AC 1 (HL) at 37, also Lord Goff at para 42. See also *Bliss v South East Thames Regional Health Authority* [1987] ICR 700 (CA) Dillon LJ at 717.
[8] See eg Bingham LJ in *Watts v Morrow* [1991] 1 WLR 1421 (CA) at 1443–45.

to liability to very large number of claimants.[9] There is no such problem in contract law: first because policy has little role to play as the question is ultimately what injury the contract—which is the parties' private set of laws—recognises, and not what injury the law recognises; and secondly because in any case the only people able to claim under a contract will be the determinate and small class of co-contractors or those rare third parties with rights to enforce the contract.

B. The Main Traditional Exception: the 'Major or Important Object' Test

This general approach of non-pecuniary losses being irrecoverable subject to a category of exceptional cases has been principally formulated in a series of Court of Appeal cases. Thus in *Bliss v South East Thames Regional Health Authority*, Dillon LJ confined claims for such losses to contracts 'to provide peace of mind or freedom from distress'.[10] Such damages were held in the solicitor's negligence case of *Hayes v James and Charles Dodd* by Staughton LJ to be irrecoverable where 'the object of the contract was not comfort or pleasure, or the relief of discomfort, but simply carrying on a commercial activity with a view to profit',[11] and by Bingham LJ in *Watts v Morrow* to be recoverable where 'the very object of a contract is to provide pleasure, relaxation, peace of mind or freedom from molestation'.[12]

That test has been deliberately relaxed from the test of 'the very object' of the contract by the 2001 House of Lords' decision in *Farley v Skinner*,[13] discussed below, which confirmed the requirement as being that 'a major or important object of the contract is to give pleasure, relaxation or peace of mind'.[14] In a solicitor's negligence case, this has been formulated as requiring that 'a significant part of the purpose of the claimant's instructing the defendants ... was ... to protect the claimant's peace of mind'.[15]

(i) Holidays and Consumer Services

The traditional category of cases in which such damages have historically been awarded is that of contracts for provision of a holiday.[16] Such contracts are all

---

[9] Eg *White v Chief Constable of South Yorkshire Police* [1999] 2 AC 455 (HL), which concerned the 1989 Hillsborough football stadium tragedy, Lord Steyn at 494.

[10] *Bliss v South East Thames Regional Health Authority* [1987] ICR 700 (CA) at 718.

[11] *Hayes v James and Charles Dodd (a firm)* [1990] 2 All ER 815 (CA) at 824. But see Lord Scott in *Farley v Skinner* [2002] 2 AC 732 (HL) at para 97.

[12] *Watts v Morrow* [1991] 1 WLR 1421 (CA) at 1445.

[13] *Farley v Skinner* [2002] 2 AC 732 (HL).

[14] Lord Steyn para 24. Lords Browne-Wilkinson and Scott agreed. Surprisingly, Ward LJ in *Milner v Carnival plc* [2010] 3 All ER 701 (CA) at para 31 seemed to view *Farley v Skinner* as a case about physical inconvenience (see below). That does not seem to be the view their Lordships in *Farley v Skinner* took, and at heart no special principles apply to that field in any event.

[15] *Hamilton Jones v David & Snape (a firm)* [2004] 1 WLR 924 (Neuberger J) at para 47.

[16] *Stedman v Swan's Tours* (1951) 95 Sol Jo 727 (CA); *Jarvis v Swan's Tours Ltd* [1973] QB 233 (CA); *Jackson v Horizon Holidays Ltd* [1975] 1 WLR 1468 (CA); *Baltic Shipping Co v Dillon* (1993) 176 CL 344 (HC Australia); *Peninsular & Oriental Steam Navigation Co (P&O) v Youell* [1997] 2 Lloyd's Rep 136 (CA); *Milner v Carnival plc* [2010] 3 All ER 701 (CA). And similarly for an award of such damages upon delay by an airline of luggage, see *O'Carroll v Ryanair* [2008] Scot SC 23 (Sh Ct).

about peace of mind and enjoyment. It is natural that they would provide the setting for the development of this rule, as holidays (along with residential leases) are some of the only expensive services contracted for by consumers that do not also lead to property improvement or other financial gain. The same would apply to other cases for leisure and entertainment, such as receiving a three-course meal instead of a five-course meal,[17] although such services are cheaper and so rarely litigated. Likewise such damages are awarded in purely sentimental contracts such as the Scottish case of the wedding photographer, *Diesen v Samson*,[18] or a contract for a burial plot.[19]

An even longer-standing category was that of breaches of the promise to marry, although the enforceability of such promises as contracts was abolished by statute.[20] And awards for non-pecuniary loss have been confirmed as available for breach of a contractual duty of confidence.[21] Likewise awards have been made where medical negligence in relation to a vasectomy gave rise to damages for the distress of the unwanted pregnancy and birth.[22] One can imagine other cases such as contracts for cosmetic or other surgery designed not to cure an ailment but merely to improve the claimant's body, which fails to do so but does not cause any damage or pain,[23] contracts to store the claimant's sperm or sentimental property,[24] or 'contracts for status such as membership of a trade union or a club'.[25] Another major category, so far barely litigated in the civil courts, is that of contracts (with schools and higher education establishments) to provide education.[26]

Finally, it should be noted that personal injury and employment discrimination cases recognise a non-pecuniary loss of the satisfaction and enjoyment gained from

---

[17] An example given in *Giedo Van der Garde BV v Force India Formula One Team Ltd* [2010] EWHC 2373 (QB) (Stadlen J) at para 458. Note also that part of the award in the holiday case of *Jarvis v Swan's Tours Ltd* [1973] QB 233 (CA) was for getting 'desiccated biscuits and crisps' rather than 'delicious Swiss cakes', for the lack of a 'yodler evening' etc.

[18] *Diesen v Samson* 1971 SLT (Sh Ct) 49. See also the Canadian wedding disc jockey case of *Dunn v Disc Jockey Unlimited Co* (1978) 87 DLR (3d) 408 (Ontario Small Claims Court).

[19] *Reed v Madon* [1989] Ch 408 (Morritt J). See also the County Court decision in *Raw v Croydon London Borough Council* [2002] CLY 941 where the defendant's breach led to the claimant and his family paying their respects for 18 months at the wrong burial site.

[20] Law Reform (Miscellaneous Provisions) Act 1970, section 1.

[21] *Cornelius v De Taranto* [2001] EWCA Civ 1511.

[22] *McFarlane v Tayside Health Board* [2000] 2 AC 59 (HL) (tort, although many of the previous cases discussed were concurrent contractual and tort liability cases. The costs of raising the child were irrecoverable for policy reasons.)

[23] Cf *Taylor Flynn v Sulaiman* [2006] IEHC 150 (Irish High Court), where the only damage caused was a rash, but (with little discussion) the claimant was awarded a refund of the costs of the procedure and significant general damages for distress and inconvenience that resulted from an operation that should not have happened.

[24] See *Yearworth v North Bristol NHS Trust* [2010] QB 1 (CA), a bailment case on loss of sperm decided on contractual principles.

[25] *Johnson v Gore Wood & Co* [2002] 2 AC 1 (HL) Lord Cooke at 49. See also *Graham v Ladeside of Kilbirnie Bowling Club* 1994 SLT 1295 (Court of Session, Outer House), where a £500 'solatium' (a principally Scottish/Civil Law term for an award of damages for distress) was awarded for eight years of wrongful suspension from the club.

[26] Such awards were approved obiter in *Gunasinghe v Henley Management College* [2006] EWHC 346 (Admin) (Underhill J) at paras 5 and 9. And see Bingham MR's violin lesson example at the text to chapter two nn 60 and 65 above, and the driving instruction facts and examples in *Giedo Van der Garde BV v Force India Formula One Team Ltd* [2010] EWHC 2373 (QB) (Stadlen J).

pursuing a chosen career, although this has not been considered in contract law cases (and will rarely arise there).[27]

(ii) Professional Negligence Cases

Awards of non-pecuniary loss have also been made in professional services cases where the service was to provide freedom from distress. This is not uncommon in solicitor cases, where the impact of the solicitor's advice or assistance is often felt other than in money. Thus such awards have been made in cases of a solicitor failing to obtain a non-molestation order,[28] failing to avoid its client's bankruptcy[29] or to advise of deadlines for using an IVA to annul bankruptcy,[30] failing to prevent its client's criminal conviction[31] (but refused in a case of failure to prevent civil judgment against the client[32]), failing to protect a mother's custody of two children,[33] and mishandling ancillary relief proceedings leading to a much lower award,[34] but are generally unavailable in solicitor negligence cases where no particular feature of the retainer was to protect from distress or disappointment.[35]

(iii) Cases where Awards Have Been Refused

The award has been disallowed in cases arising out of breach of loan and employment contracts,[36] breach of a marine insurance contract by failure to pay out on a good claim,[37] breach of a bank's contract with its customer by making phantom deductions from the account[38] or wrongfully dishonouring a cheque,[39] which are not contracts for which freedom from distress was an important object; likewise most solicitor negligence cases.[40] A contract for a flight, even though part of a

---

[27] See chapter two n 74 above and accompanying text.

[28] *Heywood v Wellers* [1976] QB 446 (CA).

[29] *Rey v Graham & Oldham* [2000] BPIR 354 (McKinnon J). See also *Wilson v United Counties Bank Ltd* [1920] AC 102 (HL) as regards the inferred financial losses resulting from the damage to credit and reputation caused by bankruptcy.

[30] *Demarco v Perkins* [2006] EWCA Civ 188. The Court of Appeal increased the award from the judge's award of £2,000.

[31] *McLeish v Amoo-Gottfried & Co* (1993) 10 PN 102 (Scott Baker J).

[32] *Groom v Cocker* [1939] 1 KB 194 (CA).

[33] *Hamilton Jones v David & Snape (a firm)* [2004] 1 WLR 924 (Neuberger J).

[34] *Dickinson v Jones Alexander & Co* [2002] EWCA Civ 353, but contrast *Channon v Lindley Johnstone (a firm)* [2002] EWCA Civ 353.

[35] See *Smyth v Huey & Co* [1993] NI 236 (Macdermott J) in relation to ordinary conveyancing; *Channon v Lindley Johnstone* [2002] EWCA Civ 353, in relation to a bad outcome of an ancillary relief dispute. See also the comments in *Cook v Swinfen* [1967] 1 WLR 457 (A) Bridge LJ at 463, and *Hartle v Laceys* [1999] Lloyd's Rep PN 315 (CA) in relation to solicitor negligence on a commercial conveyance.

[36] *French v Barclays Bank plc* [1998] EWCA Civ 1092.

[37] *Ventouris v Trevor Rex Mountain (The Italia Express (No 2))* [1992] 2 Lloyd's Rep 281 (Hirst J). And in relation to insurance contacts of indemnity see above in chapter nine, section 9.5B(i). In Canada, awards for mental distress are made upon non-payment of insurance: *Warrington v Great-West Life Assurance Co* (1996) 139 DLR (4th) 18.

[38] *McConville v Barclays Bank plc* (1993) 12 LDAB 520, [1993] 2 Bank LR 211 (Hicks QC).

[39] *Rae v Yorkshire Bank plc* [1988] FLR 1 (CA), although an action for defamation or for damage to reputation will frequently lie in wrongful dishonour cases: see further *Kpohraror v Woolwich Building Society* [1996] 4 All ER 119 (CA).

[40] See n 35 above and accompanying text.

holiday booking, was held by the Court of Appeal judge not to be a contract within this category.[41] Likewise an ordinary contract to repair a Rolls Royce car was held not to sound in distress damages (although in the particular case there was in any case no distress).[42]

However, the Supreme Court of Canada has awarded such damages for wrongful refusal to pay out under a disability insurance policy, peace of mind being held by that court to be the very object of such a contract of insurance,[43] although such damages would not currently be available in England for reasons specific to English insurance law.[44] Damages for non-pecuniary loss are also available in Canada but not in England for distress caused where the manner of dismissal from employment breaches the duty of good faith (the English equivalent of which is the duty of mutual trust and confidence).[45]

(iv) Summary of the Cases

The test is whether a 'major or important object' of the relevant obligations in the contract was non-financial. Leisure activities (broadly conceived) include holidays, family matters (including custody of children), protection from molestation, consumer goods (clothes, cars, food, albeit that some of these may also be in part a financial investment). If there is a breach of a contract to provide one of these leisure activities, or to provide professional advice in relation to securing them, then it will sound in distress/amenity damages if such loss is caused. As Lord Steyn has summarised:

> non-pecuniary damages are regularly awarded on the basis that the defendant's breach of contract deprived the plaintiff of the very object of the contract, viz pleasure, relaxation, and peace of mind. The cases arise in diverse contractual contexts, e g the supply of a wedding dress or double glazing, hire purchase transactions, landlord and tenant, building contracts, and engagements of estate agents and solicitors.[46]

C. Residential Property and a Broader Approach

Many major consumer expenditures relate to residential property. People purchase or improve residential property for both commercial and non-commercial purposes because a residential building

> has a number of qualities. It is a capital asset which can be turned to account by sale. It is a habitation which protects the occupants from the elements. It may be an amenity with attributes of location or facilities particularly congenial to the owner.[47]

---

[41] *Graham v Thomas Cook Group* [2012] EWCA Civ 1355 Toulson LJ at para 25; also *Cowden v British Airways* [2009] 2 Lloyd's Rep 653 (HHJ Orrell, Stoke on Trent County Court), obiter.
[42] *Alexander v Rolls Royce Motor Cars Ltd* [1996] RTR 95 (CA).
[43] *Fidler v Sun Life Assurance Co of Canada* [2006] 2 SCR 3 (SC of Canada) at paras 38–41 and 45.
[44] See above in chapter seven, sections 7.6D and F, and chapter nine, section 9.5B(i).
[45] Ibid.
[46] *Farley v Skinner* [2002] 2 AC 732 (HL) at para 20.
[47] Seymour QC in *Cox v Sloane*, 19 July 2000.

Further, the renting of residential property for occupation is, of course, solely for non-commercial purposes.

It is no surprise therefore that much of the development of the law of non-pecuniary loss has arisen in residential property cases. The striking thing about such cases, however, is that both in the body of case law on landlords' breaches, and in the leading decision in *Ruxley Electronics v Forsyth* on defective construction of a swimming pool, there is little or no discussion of whether non-pecuniary gains or losses are a major or important object of the contract, usually considered to be the legal test for non-pecuniary loss in all other cases.

(i) Ruxley Electronics v Forsyth *and Domestic Building Works*

Historically, in the domestic building context the non-pecuniary value ascribed by residents to their homes has found expression in consideration of whether the cost of cure is reasonable and whether the defendant has substantially performed the contract.[48] However, since the 1995 decision of the House of Lords in *Ruxley Electronics v Forsyth*,[49] it has been orthodox to award damages for non-pecuniary loss in domestic building work cases under the label 'loss of amenity'.[50] The choice between a pecuniary only 'difference in value' award and an award of the cost of cure has been revealed to be an incomplete menu for the judge.

In *Ruxley*, Ruxley Electronics Ltd was contracted to build a swimming pool at a residential home. The pool was to have a diving area 7 feet 6 inches deep. The pool as built had a diving area only 6 feet deep, although still suitable for diving. The market value of the home with the pool was the same with the actual pool as it would have been with the promised pool. It would have cost £21,560 to rebuild the pool to the promised depth. The cost of cure was awarded by the majority of the Court of Appeal, but the House of Lords overturned this result, finding the cure disproportionately expensive and so unreasonable, and instead awarding the customer £2,500 damages for loss of amenity.

Building works to residential properties are clearly intended by the customer both for financial benefit (the increase in the value of the property) and for non-financial benefit (enjoyment while the claimant is living in the property). The building works in *Ruxley* were for a swimming pool, and as the first instance judge in the *Ruxley*

---

[48] Eg *Jacob & Youngs v Kent* 230 NY 239 (1921) (NYCA); *O'Grady v Westminster Scaffolding Ltd* [1962] 2 Lloyd's Rep 238 (Edmund Davies J); *Ward v Cannock Chase District Council* [1986] Ch 546 (Scott J). Thus until the decision of the House of Lords in *Ruxley*, the choice in building cases had been falsely understood to be between cost of cure and difference in financial value. Non-financial matters had encouraged a finding of reasonableness of cure, rather than being treated as sounding in damages on their own account. Thus in the High Court of Australia in *Bellgrove v Eldridge* (1954) 90 CLR 613 the Court observed at para 5: 'Departures from the plans and specifications forming part of a contract for the erection of a building may result in the completion of a building which, whilst differing in some particulars from that contracted for, is no less valuable. For instance, particular rooms in such a building may be finished in one colour instead of quite a different colour as specified. Is the owner in these circumstances without a remedy? In our opinion he is not; he is entitled to the reasonable cost of rectifying the departure or defect so far as that is possible'.

[49] *Ruxley Electronics and Construction Ltd v Forsyth* [1996] AC 344 (HL). See also the slightly earlier decision in *GW Atkins Ltd v Scott* (1996) 46 Con LR 14 (CA).

[50] This is a term from personal injury law, where it denotes the loss of enjoyment and use resulting from impairment to the claimant's body (eg through loss of an arm).

Electronics case put it: 'Swimming pools are not necessities, they are for fun'.[51] However, in many such works there are personal preferences expressed in the work specification, the ignoring of which by the builder would have no negative effect on the financial value. A house with a door will be worth more than one with no door, and may be worth more than one with an old door, but it will be worth the same whether the door is painted the colour the customer chose or the colour of paint that the builder preferred (or already had in its garage left over from a previous job).[52] If no amenity damages were available then, as Lord Mustill explained in *Ruxley*,

> in order to escape unscathed the builder has only to show that to the mind of the average onlooker, or the average potential buyer, the results which he has produced seem just as good as those which he had promised

and that would render part of the promise (eg a personal preference for a particular colour) 'illusory'.[53] Indeed some things contracted for may, if the contract is performed, actually harm the value of the claimant's property, such as 'lurid bathroom tiles' or a 'grotesque folly' to be erected in the grounds, and yet the 'eccentric' claimant should still be able to recover the loss of amenity for non-performance in such cases.[54]

This reflects the approach described in the New York case of *Smith v Brady*[55] in 1858 (albeit in that case the issue was whether there had been substantial performance so as to give rise to an obligation to make payment):

> I suppose it will be conceded that everyone has a right to build his house, his cottage or his store after such a model and in such style as shall best accord with his notions of utility or be most agreeable to his fancy. The specifications of the contract become the law between the parties until voluntarily changed. If the owner prefers a plain and simple Doric column, and has so provided in the agreement, the contractor has no right to put in its place the more costly and elegant Corinthian. If the owner, having regard to strength and durability, has contracted for walls of specified materials to be laid in a particular manner, or for a given number of joists and beams, the builder has no right to substitute his own judgment or that of others. Having departed from the agreement, if performance has not been waived by the other party, the law will not allow him to allege that he has made as good a building as the one he engaged to erect.

In these situations the English courts will either award damages to reflect the loss caused by the dissatisfaction of the aesthetic or other preference (as occurred in *Ruxley*), or go a step further and award the cost of cure (discussed above in chapter four, section 4.3B(iii)(a)).

The importance of *Ruxley* lies in the House of Lords providing a sensible general conceptual foundation for the rule permitting distress or amenity damages, namely that it was needed to protect the 'consumer surplus' by which consumers' valuation of goods or services exceeds the financial or third party valuation of the

---

[51] The first instance judge was Diamond QC, quoted by Lord Lloyd in [1996] AC 344 (HL) at 363.

[52] Cf the example of a contract for second-hand rather than new bricks: *Bellgrove v Eldridge* (1954) 90 CLR 613 (HC of Australia) at 618–19.

[53] Lord Mustill in *Ruxley* [1996] AC 344 at 360.

[54] Lord Mustill (ibid) at 361, Lord Lloyd at 370–71. See also the comments of Megarry V-C in *Tito v Waddell (No 2)* [1977] Ch 106 at 331–32.

[55] *Smith v Brady* 17 NY 173 (1858) (NY CA).

service.[56] In *Ruxley* the shallower pool added no less financial value to the house than the deeper pool. The depth was, therefore, a matter of personal preference or amenity. The House of Lords awarded £2,500 (and refused the cost of cure as being disproportionate).

Similarly in *Freeman v Niroomand* (construction of a porch and extension) an award of £130 for loss of amenity was upheld by the Court of Appeal.[57] And in another case a claimant's pristine period-decorated home was not returned to its prior condition after use by the defendant film production company as a set, and £1,000 was awarded for non-pecuniary loss because the claimant's pride in and enjoyment of his home was impaired.[58] An award would also now be made on the facts of *Knott v Bolton*,[59] where, prior to *Ruxley*, the Court of Appeal refused to make an award in a claim against an architect who failed to design the imposing staircase requested for the claimants' new home, but that failing did not affect the financial value of the house. The House of Lords in *Farley v Skinner* overruled the *Knott* decision.[60]

Not all failures to comply with contractual instructions or specifications will necessarily lead to non-financial loss. As Cardozo J has observed, 'Substitution of equivalents [by the builder] may not have the same significance in fields of art on the one side and in those of mere utility on the other'.[61] If, although specified, the claimant in fact did not have any particular preference for what was promised over what was provided, then no non-financial loss will in fact be caused by the substitution by the builder.

(ii) Other Professionals and Residential Property

The House of Lords in *Ruxley* did not place any real reliance on the narrow rule of mental distress damages that evolved from the holiday cases, nor did it explain how its decision fitted in with that rule.[62] However, the House readdressed the issue in *Farley v Skinner*,[63] relying heavily on both the holiday cases and *Ruxley* and finding that £10,000 damages for distress or loss of amenity were recoverable against a surveyor who failed carefully to survey for aircraft noise when specifically asked to do so, because 'a major or important object of the contract is to give pleasure,

---

[56] Lord Mustill in *Ruxley* [1996] AC 344 at 360. See further the seminal article Harris, Ogus and Phillips, 'Contract Remedies and the Consumer Surplus' (1979) 95 *LQR* 581, cited by Lord Mustill in *Ruxley* at 360, Lord Millet in *Alfred McAlpine Construction Ltd v Panatown Ltd* [2001] 1 AC 518 (HL) at 589, and by Lord Steyn in *Farley v Skinner* [2002] 2 AC 732 (HL) at para 21. This use of the term 'consumer surplus' deserves care. In economics the consumer surplus is often understood to be the amount a claimant would have been willing to *pay* above the *price* actually paid, whereas for Lord Mustill it is the amount by which the claimant *values* the performance over the financial *value* of the performance, which may be different.

[57] *Freeman v Niroomand* (1996) 52 Con LR 116 (CA). See also *Rowlands v Collow* [1992] 1 NZLR 178 (NZ HC).

[58] *Haysman v Mrs Rogers Films Ltd* [2008] EWHC 2494 (QB) (Derek Sweeting QC).

[59] *Freeman v Niroomand* (1995) 45 Con LR 127 (CA).

[60] *Farley v Skinner* [2002] 2 AC 732 (HL) at paras 24, 41, 52 and 93.

[61] *Jacob & Youngs v Kent* 230 NY 239 (1921) (NYCA).

[62] Only Lord Lloyd referred to the holiday cases and to the swimming pool being a pleasurable amenity.

[63] *Farley v Skinner* [2002] 2 AC 732 (HL).

relaxation or peace of mind'.[64] This was a small relaxation of the test from the holiday and other cases requiring that 'the very object' of the contract be peace of mind or similar, rather than an abandonment of that test, as the approach in *Ruxley* seemed to be.

See also *Herrmann v Withers LLP*,[65] where £2,000 was awarded against a conveyancing solicitor for the enjoyment that would have been received from use of a communal garden in an alternative home, had the defendant properly advised the claimants (and therefore had they not bought this home).[66] However, in another case damages for non-pecuniary loss were refused where the claimants were already tenants of their home but due to the solicitors' negligence lost the right to buy, even though having ownership (rather than tenancy) was designed to bring comfort after a bereavement.[67]

(iii) Residential Landlord's Failure to Repair

(a) Non-Pecuniary Loss Suffered by the Tenant

Where the tenant was, or would but for the breach have been, in occupation, recovery is for 'the difference in value to the tenant',[68] which the Court of Appeal has explained merely means the 'loss of comfort and convenience which results from living in a property which was not in the state of repair it ought to have been'[69] and moreover has noted that 'Distress and inconvenience caused by disrepair are not free-standing heads of claim, but are symptomatic of interference with the lessee's enjoyment of that asset', ie symptomatic of this loss of comfort and convenience.[70]

In other words, the award is for non-pecuniary loss of amenity, as with the shallow swimming pool in *Ruxley Electronics* and the holiday cases.[71] Indeed, such awards are very important to any general account of non-pecuniary loss,[72] although as landlord and tenant law is a specialist field of practice many general practitioners are not familiar with the relevant case law.

For an unusual case, see *Verrall v Great Yarmouth BC*[73] where, following the council's refusal to honour a licence of a town hall for the National Front political party's annual conference, the Master ordered an inquiry for damages, although

---

[64] Lord Steyn (ibid) para 24. Lords Browne-Wilkinson and Scott agreed. *Watts v Morrow* [1991] 1 WLR 1421 (CA) was distinguished on the basis that there was no specific request or undertaking in relation to the feature that led to the distress: see *Farley v Skinner* [2002] 2 AC 732 at paras 15 and 42.

[65] *Herrmann v Withers LLP* [2012] EWHC 1492 (Ch) (Newey J).

[66] And in *Jarvis v T Richards & Co* (Nourse J) an award was made on a solicitor's failure to secure the claimant's home for her on a divorce, although the non-pecuniary award was by consent and the judge expressed no view as to its correctness.

[67] *Blackwood v Saunders & Co* [2007] EWHC 3504 (QB) (Hawkesworth QC) at paras 46–47.

[68] *Hewitt v Rowlands* (1924) 93 LJKB 1080 (CA) Bankes LJ at 1082.

[69] *Wallace v Manchester City Council* [1998] 3 EGLR 38 (CA) Morritt LJ at 40 and 42. Also *Earle v Charalambous* [2006] EWCA Civ 1090 Carnwath LJ at paras 18–32 and *Electricity Supply Nominees Ltd v National Magazine Co Ltd* [1999] 1 EGLR 130 (Hicks QC).

[70] *Earle v Charalambous* [2006] EWCA Civ 1090 Carnwath LJ at para 32.

[71] Pecuniary losses in residential lease cases are discussed above in chapter eight, section 8.3C.

[72] Cf the quotation at text to n 46 above.

[73] *Verrall v Great Yarmouth Borough Council* [1981] QB 202 (CA).

on appeal specific performance was granted. And non-pecuniary loss awards have also been recognised outside the lease context in negative covenant cases, eg where there was a promise not to operate a business in the houses neighbouring the claimant's residential property that was breached by operation of a school.[74] Awards have, however, been refused in cases of a landlord's breach of the covenant of quiet enjoyment.[75]

(b) Using Market Rent to Measure Non-Pecuniary Loss

In assessing the loss of amenity and/or physical inconvenience, the court may just fix a 'global' award.[76] However, the court may also, and will often, measure the loss by a proportion of the rent, used to indicate the amount by which the property was worth less to the tenant than it would have been had the repairs been done.[77] As the Court of Appeal has explained in some careful judgments, this measure is best understood as simply being a measure of the tenant's non-pecuniary loss by a convenient means.[78] As one judge has noted, 'In an open market rack-rents are evidence not only of the return available to investors but also of the value that prospective tenants attach to that enjoyment' and so 'consideration of diminution of that value can properly start from there and may often helpfully be approached in terms of its proportional reduction'.[79] Thus the award of difference in market rent value is made on the basis of a presumption that the claimant receives at least as much non-pecuniary benefit from proper repair as the additional amount it costs to rent a home in that condition.[80] This is partly because the distress is related to the reasonable expectations engendered by the rent,[81] and tenants of more expensive properties are entitled to expect higher standards and will value amenities at a higher level.[82]

As the Court of Appeal has confirmed, the reduction in rent is 'likely to be the most appropriate starting point'[83] and is a useful 'cross-check' on the award.[84]

---

[74] *Kemp v Sober* (1851) 61 ER 200 at 200 (actually an injunction case but anxiety damage was recognised). Negative covenant cases are discussed further above in chapter ten.

[75] *Branchett v Beaney* [1992] 3 All ER 910 (CA), obiter (as the damages were in any event justified as exemplary damages for the tort of trespass).

[76] Discussed by *Wallace v Manchester City Council* [1998] 3 EGLR 38 (CA) Morritt LJ at 42. See *Sturolson & Co v Mauroux* [1988] 1 EGLR 66 (CA); *Calabar Properties Ltd v Stitcher* [1984] 1 WLR 287 (CA); *Brent London Borough Council v Carmel* (1995) 28 HLR 203 (CA); *Wallace v Manchester City Council* [1998] 3 EGLR 38 (CA). See also n 150 below.

[77] *Hewitt v Rowlands* (1924) 93 LJKB 1080 (CA) at 1082; *McCoy & Co v Clark* (1982) 13 HLR 87 (CA).

[78] *Wallace v Manchester City Council* [1998] 3 EGLR 38 (CA) Morritt LJ at 41 and 42; *Earle v Charalambous* [2006] EWCA Civ 1090. Also *English Churches Housing Group v Shine* [2004] EWCA Civ 434. See further chapter eight, section 8.3B.

[79] *Electricity Supply Nominees Ltd v National Magazine Co Ltd* [1999] 1 EGLR 130 (Hicks QC) at 133 and 136 (the case is a commercial tenancy decision but discussing residential cases).

[80] See further below as to the presumption of breaking even and its application to non-pecuniary loss: section 19.2C(ii).

[81] *English Churches Housing Group v Shine* [2004] EWCA Civ 434 Wall LJ at para 105.

[82] *Niazi Services Ltd v Van der Loo* [2004] 1 EGLR 62 (CA) at para 31. Cf the holiday case of *Milner v Carnival plc* [2010] 3 All ER 701 (CA) Ward LJ at paras 37 and 47, also the discussion at para 35.

[83] *Earle v Charalambous* [2006] EWCA Civ 1090 Carnwath LJ at para 32.

[84] *Wallace v Manchester City Council* [1998] 3 EGLR 38 (CA) Morritt LJ at 42. See also the useful comments of *Langham Estate Management Ltd v Hardy* [2008] 3 EGLR 125 (Central London County

Further, although the presumption that non-pecuniary loss matches the notional reduction in rent must be rebuttable, and so damages may exceed the difference in market rent, there is nevertheless said to be a basic rule of thumb that the market rent differential provides a maximum for the award.[85]

(c) Commercial Leases

As discussed above in chapter eight, section 8.3B, commercial tenants can, where unable to prove lost profits, recover a general award that may either be for non-pecuniary loss or on a presumption that revenue was lost.

D. Property and Goods Cases

The vast majority of non-pecuniary loss awards have been made in cases of either pure services (such as holidays) or services related to property value (such as domestic building works or surveying). Nevertheless, the principles of non-pecuniary loss should apply equally to goods and property cases.[86]

E. Assimilation of the Non-Pecuniary Loss Test into the New Remoteness Test

It used to be said that the test for mental distress/loss of amenity damages (the 'very object' test) was a narrower test than the remoteness test.[87] This was when remoteness was understood solely in terms of foreseeability. Given the development of the remoteness test in *The Achilleas*[88] into a test of implied assumption of responsibility, the mental distress/loss of amenity test can now be seen as really only a specific application of the remoteness test.[89] The correct question should be whether the defendant implicitly assumed responsibility for the non-financial

---

Court, Marshall QC) at para 166: 'There are two ways of arriving at a logical figure for the assessment of such damage. One is to put a global figure on the loss and damage suffered; the other is to make an appropriate allowance against the rent paid for the relevant period, usually as a percentage. The former places more emphasis upon valuing the loss suffered and the latter upon valuing the value not received. They ought to amount to the same thing, but one approach may feel more natural than the other, depending upon the facts. It is entirely a matter for the trial judge which approach it is more appropriate to adopt, and it is even permissible to combine the two, although care must be taken to avoid double-counting. It is also advisable to cross-check the result of either approach against the other as a reality check'.

[85] *English Churches Housing Group v Shine* [2004] EWCA Civ 434 especially Wall LJ at para 109, where a judge's finding that the loss was more than 50% more than the total rent payable for the period was set aside. The non-pecuniary loss/notional rental value interaction is further confused by the fact that in cases where the rent is fixed by the relevant statutory authority in part on the basis of the state of the property (and so its disrepair), the claimant may have to give credit for the additional rent that would have been payable if the landlord had performed its obligations: see the discussion in *Sturolson & Co v Mauroux* [1988] 1 EGLR 66 Taylor LJ at 68.

[86] See chapter four, section 4.5C(iv).

[87] See above in section 19.1A(i).

[88] *Transfield Shipping Inc v Mercator Shipping Inc (The Achilleas)* [2009] AC 61 (HL).

[89] A Kramer, 'An Agreement-Centred Approach to Remoteness and Contract Damage' in Cohen and McKendrick (eds), *Comparative Remedies for Breach of Contract* (Oxford, Hart Publishing, 2005).

consequences of breach, and in the case of an obligation to comply with a personal preference (a yellow rather than white wall, a holiday etc) the answer will be yes, in part because the parties must have known that no (or not only) financial loss would result from breach, that the obligation was oriented towards non-financial interests, and those interests were the purpose of the claimant's paying for the obligation. In cases of ordinary contracts and ordinary disappointment from a breach, the answer will be no, the defendant did not assume responsibility for these non-financial consequences.

The implied assumption of responsibility test (before it had been identified in *The Achilleas*) is what Ralph Gibson LJ was getting at in *Watts v Morrow* when he said that there was no express or implied 'promise for the provision of peace of mind or freedom from distress' in that case.[90]

The Supreme Court of Canada's decisions on mental distress, especially *Fidler v Sun Life Assurance Co of Canada* (also before *The Achilleas*) already recognise that the 'very object of the contract' test is no more than an application of the remoteness rule:

> In normal commercial contracts, the likelihood of a breach of contract causing mental distress is not ordinarily within the reasonable contemplation of the parties. It is not unusual that a breach of contract will leave the wronged party feeling frustrated or angry. The law does not award damages for such incidental frustration. The matter is otherwise, however, when the parties enter into a contract, an object of which is to secure a particular psychological benefit. In such a case, damages arising from such mental distress should in principle be recoverable where they are established on the evidence and shown to have been within the reasonable contemplation of the parties at the time the contract was made. The basic principles of contract damages do not cease to operate merely because what is promised is an intangible, like mental security.
>
> Principle suggests that as long as the promise in relation to state of mind is a part of the bargain in the reasonable contemplation of the contracting parties, mental distress damages arising from its breach are recoverable. This is to state neither more nor less than the rule in *Hadley v. Baxendale* ... It follows that there is only one rule by which compensatory damages for breach of contract should be assessed: the rule in *Hadley v. Baxendale*. The *Hadley* test unites all forms of contract damages under a single principle. It explains why damages may be awarded where an object of the contract is to secure a psychological benefit, just as they may be awarded where an object of the contract is to secure a material one ... *Hadley v. Baxendale* is the single and controlling test for compensatory damages in cases of breach of contract.[91] (Emphasis added)

Similarly, Lord Millett, in the important House of Lords decision on non-pecuniary loss of *Johnson v Unisys*, applied, again before *The Achilleas*, the assumption of responsibility test of remoteness in the mental distress context, explaining the test of recovery and non-recovery of damages for mental distress as based on the implied

---

[90] *Watts v Morrow* [1996] 1 WLR 1421 (CA) at 1442.

[91] *Fidler v Sun Life Assurance Co of Canada* [2006] 2 SCR 3 (SC of Canada) at paras 45, 48, 54–55. See also *Vorvis v Insurance Corp of British Columbia* (1989) 58 DLR (4th) 193 (SC of Canada), and *Honda Canada Inc v Keays* [2008] 2 SCR 362 (SC of Canada) at paras 54–55. In relation to personal injury and more generally, see also *Mustapha v Culligan of Canada* [2008] 2 SCR 114 (SC of Canada) at para 19.

assumption of risk and incorporating the 'major object of the contract' rule into that rationale:

> [In] ordinary commercial contracts entered into by both parties with a view of profit ... non-pecuniary loss such as mental suffering consequent on breach is <u>not within the contemplation of the parties and is accordingly too remote</u>. The ordinary feelings of anxiety, frustration and disappointment caused by any breach of contract are also excluded, but seemingly for the opposite reason: they are so commonly a consequence of a breach of contract that the parties must be regarded not only as having foreseen it but <u>as having agreed to take the risk of its occurrence</u>: see *Treitel, The Law of Contract* 10th ed, p 923. Contracts which are not purely commercial but which have as their object the provision of enjoyment, comfort, peace of mind or other non-pecuniary personal or family benefits (as in *Jarvis v Swans Tours Ltd* [1973] QB 233, [1973] 1 All ER 71 and similar cases) are usually treated as exceptions to the general rule, <u>though in truth they would seem to fall outside its rationale</u>. Such injury is not only within the contemplation of the parties but is the direct result of the breach itself and not the manner of the breach. <u>Indeed the avoidance of just such non-pecuniary injury can be said to be a principal object of the contract</u>.[92] (Emphasis added)

And in Arkansas, where a tacit agreement test like that from *The Achilleas* has governed remoteness for a long time, this also determines when non-pecuniary losses are recoverable.[93]

However, as yet the English courts have not yet consistently made this connection between *The Achilleas* development and damages for mental distress, and so subsumed the mental distress test into the general remoteness principle (now rather more sophisticated than a rule of mere foreseeability). This is expected as the next logical and proper development, and the next piece in the remoteness jigsaw.

F. Contracts for the Benefit of Third Parties

There is a clear convergence between the development of the law of recovery of non-pecuniary loss and the development of the law of recovery for damages on failure to confer a benefit on a third party. As discussed below in chapter twenty-one, even where the failure to confer a benefit on the third party does not lead to any expense on the part of the claimant (in paying for a replacement conferral of benefit), the law is moving in the direction of an award for the loss suffered by the claimant, such damages to be retained by the claimant and not merely held by the claimant for the third party.

Such awards make sense as awards of non-pecuniary loss suffered by the claimant. If the true question is whether the claimant valued the performance in a non-pecuniary way, ie a way that meant that it would count itself as disadvantaged by non-performance other than by being out of pocket, and that non-pecuniary valuing is not too remote, the loss should be recovered, and in third party benefit cases this test will often be satisfied. As Lord Scarman has observed in this context: 'Whatever the reason, he must have desired the payment to be made to [the third

---

[92] *Johnson v Unisys Ltd* [2003] 1 AC 518 (HL) at 547.
[93] *Stifft's Jewelers v Oliver* 678 SW 2d 372 (1984) (SC of Arkansas).

party] and he must have been relying on [the promisor] to make it'.[94] And as Lord Millett has said in the leading case of *Alfred McAlpine v Panatown*, 'the fact that a contracting party has required services to be supplied at his own cost to a third party is at least prima facie evidence of the value of those services to the party who placed the order'.[95]

Lord Millett further explained that there are several reasons why the promisee may wish the service to be provided. There may be a 'family or commercial relationship', or the promisee may be a 'charitable donor [who] ... has a legitimate interest in the object of his charity'.[96] However, (as he observed) it is not necessary to identify any legitimate interest in order to identify a loss: the fact of the promise proves that there is some value to the promisee. As Lord Jauncey explained in the same case, quoting Oliver J in *Radford v De Froberville*, a person 'contracts for the supply of that which he thinks serves his interests—be they commercial, aesthetic or merely eccentric'.[97]

In the academic literature, the award of such damages for failure to confer a benefit on third parties and the awards for non-pecuniary loss have been collectively described as protection of the 'performance interest'.[98] This term was adopted in the third party benefit context in the leading House of Lords decision of *Alfred McAlpine Construction Ltd v Panatown Ltd*,[99] although it has rarely been used in the context of non-pecuniary loss cases not involving third parties.[100] Its usefulness lies in focusing attention on the claimant's non-pecuniary interest in performance, and the law's protection of that interest where non-pecuniary loss results.

19.2 Specific Issues in Non-Pecuniary Loss Awards

A. Is There a Limit to Recoverable Types of Non-Pecuniary Loss?

Although the case law inevitably describes the loss being compensated, using labels such as 'peace of mind', 'mental distress' and 'loss of amenity', these should not be treated as a limit on the types of non-pecuniary loss that can be recovered. There is no principled reason for restricting the non-pecuniary loss that can be recovered, save by the test of remoteness (the further test of the 'major or important object' as discussed above, if that is a separate test at all). Courts should resist the sort of exercise that Neuberger J believed he had to perform in *Hamilton Jones v David &*

---

[94] Lord Scarman in *Woodar Investment Development v Wimpey Construction UK Ltd* [1980] 1 WLR 277 (HL) at 300.

[95] Lord Millett in *Alfred McAlpine Construction Ltd v Panatown Ltd* [2001] 1 AC 518 (HL) at 592.

[96] Ibid at 592.

[97] Ibid at 551, quoting *Radford v De Froberville* [1977] 1 WLR 1262 Oliver J at 1270.

[98] See eg B Coote, 'Contract Damages, *Ruxley*, and the Performance Interest' (1997) 56 *CLJ* 537; E McKendrick, 'Breach of Contract and the Meaning of Loss' (1999) 48 *CLP* 37.

[99] Lord Goff at 546, 549 and 553, Lord Browne-Wilkinson at 577–78 and Lord Millett at 588–91 and 595–96. See also *And So To Bed Ltd v Dixon*, 21 November 2000 (Donaldson QC) at paras 52–54; *Bovis Lend Lease Ltd v RD Fire Protection Ltd* (2003) 89 Con LR 69 (Thornton QC) *passim*; *SmithKline Beecham plc v Apotex Europe Ltd* [2007] Ch 71 (CA) Jacob LJ at paras 94–95.

[100] But see *Giedo Van der Garde BV v Force India Formula One Team Ltd* [2010] EWHC 2373 (QB) (Stadlen J) at para 212.

Snape,[101] the case of the solicitors who failed to take steps to protect against their client's children being abducted. The judge asked the question

> whether it can fairly be said that the contract between the claimant and the defendants in the present case can be said to have had as its object the provision of 'pleasure, relaxation, peace of mind or freedom from molestation', or something akin thereto

and in doing so said:

> For a relatively altruistic parent, the claimant's primary concern could be said to have been the children; a more selfish parent would have had her own interests in the forefront. However, on any view, it appears to me that both the claimant and the defendants would have had in mind that a significant reason for the claimant instructing the defendants was with a view to ensuring, so far as possible, that the claimant retained custody of her children for her own pleasure and peace of mind. It would, I think, be a relatively unusual parent who, in the position of the claimant in the present case, would not have had, and would not be perceived by her solicitors to have had, her own peace of mind and pleasure in the company of her children as an important factor.

The short point is that this inquiry is unnecessary. An altruistic parent should also make a recovery in this situation. The solicitor knew the client valued the custody of the children as an important advantage provided by the contract, and that it would therefore be a non-pecuniary loss to the client not to retain custody, and so whatever label is put on that non-pecuniary loss, it is not too remote and is recoverable.

Thus non-pecuniary loss should be recoverable under the general tests regardless of the type of non-pecuniary loss. The key is merely that the claimant values the performance of the promise in a non-pecuniary way. Lord Mustill explained in *Ruxley* that the law recognises situations where 'the value of the promise to the promisee exceeds the financial enhancement of his position which full performance will secure'.[102] As the discussions in that judgment make clear, this can include aesthetic preferences and not merely distress, peace of mind or enjoyment save in any narrow senses of those words. Lord Lloyd was similarly general in his view that the law is able to award a 'sum, not based on difference in [financial] value, but solely to compensate the buyer for his disappointed expectations'.[103] The value being satisfied in *Ruxley* was described later by Millett LJ simply as 'the personal and intangible loss which arises from the fact that [the claimant] has not obtained what he wanted and what he expressly contracted for'.[104] And in *Farley v Skinner*, Lord Steyn explained the principle as recognising that there are contractual promises 'which, although not of economic value, have value to' the promisee.[105]

Accordingly, the law will award non-pecuniary loss of any type, providing it satisfies the general tests. 'Peace of mind' or freedom from 'distress' are merely some common types of non-pecuniary loss for which recovery is granted, not tests as to recoverability.

---

[101] *Hamilton Jones v David & Snape (a firm)* [2004] 1 WLR 924 (Neuberger J) at para 61.
[102] *Ruxley Electronics and Construction Ltd v Forsyth* [1996] AC 344 (HL) at 360.
[103] Ibid at 374.
[104] *Freeman v Niroomand* (1996) 52 Con LR 116 (CA).
[105] At para 21.

B. Corporate Claimants and Commercial Contracts

The question then arises as to whether companies are entitled to recover non-pecuniary loss.

It has been stated by Hirst J and by the Court of Appeal (obiter), that a company can never recover damages for distress, discomfort or inconvenience.[106] However, the proper approach is probably to look at the contemplated purposes of the contract, not merely the identity of the claimant. It is not the corporate nature of the claimant that is important, but the commercial nature of most contracts entered into by such claimants, under which contracts non-pecuniary losses will usually be too remote and not a major or important object.[107]

In *Hayes v James and Charles Dodd*, Staughton LJ suggested that damages for non-pecuniary loss would not be recoverable in cases where the object of the contract was 'simply carrying on a commercial activity with a view to profit'.[108] Lord Millett explains that 'ordinary commercial contracts entered into by both parties with a view of profit ... non-pecuniary loss such as mental suffering consequent on breach is not within the contemplation of the parties and is accordingly too remote'.[109] In *GKN Centrax Gears Ltd v Matbro Ltd*, a defective goods case, the arbitrator refused to require credit to be given for an incidental profit arising out of the breach because it was offset by inconvenience. The Court of Appeal did not disapprove of the award of damages for inconvenience as a matter of principle, but disallowed it as not having been pleaded or sought by the claimant.[110]

In another case, many (largely elderly) investors sought to release capital from flawed home income plans, by which equity was released by a re-mortgage and that equity invested in bonds providing an income. The investors were held not to have suffered recoverable mental distress.[111] Mann LJ and Tuckey J ruled as follows:

> Income is enjoyable. However, the enjoyment is consequent upon the achievement of the contract and is not the object of the contract. The object was that of releasing capital. Any contract relating to personal investment has an inherent capacity to result either in happiness or distress and we do not regard such contracts whatever the puffery which preluded them, as being within the exceptional class identified by Bingham L.J. [in *Watts v Morrow*].[112]

---

[106] *Ventouris v Trevor Rex Mountain (The Italia Express No 2)* [1992] 2 Lloyd's Rep 281 (Hirst J) at 293; *Regus (UK) Ltd v Epcot Solutions Ltd* [2008] EWCA Civ 361 at paras 31 and 32.

[107] Cf *Rowlands v Collow* [1992] 1 NZLR 178 (NZ HC) at 207.

[108] *Hayes v James and Charles Dodd* [1990] 2 All ER 815 (CA) at 824. Lord Scott in *Farley v Skinner* [2002] 2 AC 732 (HL) at para 97 did not want the commercial/non-commercial distinction to be considered to be a rule, instead explaining that the commercial character of the contract in *Hayes* meant that distress was outside the parties' reasonable contemplation.

[109] *Johnson v Unisys Ltd* [2003] 1 AC 518 (HL) at 547, quoted at length above at text to n 92. See also *Fidler v Sun Life Assurance Co of Canada* [2006] 2 SCR 3 (SC of Canada) at para 45, quoted above at text to n 91.

[110] *GKN Centrax Gears Ltd v Matbro Ltd* [1976] 2 Lloyd's Rep 555 (CA) at 566.

[111] *R v Investors Compensation Scheme Ltd, ex parte Bowden* [1994] 1 WLR 17 (Mann LJ and Tuckey J).

[112] Ibid para 28. This decision and the irrecoverability of mental distress damages in cases of investment of money was approved by Lord Scott in *Farley v Skinner* [2002] 2 AC 732 (HL) at para 101, although the narrow 'very object' test of Bingham LJ identified in the quotation was disapproved by the House in *Farley*, including by Lord Scott at para 101.

Moreover, it is clear that in cases of failure to provide covenanted-for benefits to a commercial tenant (such as working lifts, air-conditioning and non-leaky roofs), where particular financial losses cannot be shown, the claimant is still entitled to recover a general sum for inconvenience, that being the diminution in value of the property to that tenant.[113] There is no special rule at play here, and the general law will in due course have to accommodate this and recognise that commercial claimants can suffer non-pecuniary losses.

C. Quantification and Presumptions

The quantification of non-pecuniary loss awards is necessarily rough, as with those for loss of amenity in personal injury cases (eg the lost amenity of having a finger missing). In *Farley v Skinner* it was observed by the House of Lords that £10,000 awarded in 1999 was at the top end of the range of suitable awards.[114] The award in *Ruxley* in 1995, it will be remembered, was £2,500. It must be rare that the harm would exceed the 11 years of a mother's loss of custody of her two children, who were brought up in a foreign country, for which £20,000 was awarded in 2003 against the solicitors whose negligence caused the harm.[115] Some assistance can be gleaned from the price of the service, or even the amount the defendant saved by skimping performance, as is explained below in section 19.2C.

(i) Objective or Subjective

The question arises as to whether the lost amenity award is objective or subjective. This is similar to the question in personal injury cases of whether a loss of amenity award should be made in cases where the claimant is unaware of the injury because, eg, in a coma,[116] and whether by the 'thin skull' rule, a claimant with a particular susceptibility can recover for it. It is also similar to the question of whether an unjust enrichment award should be based on the value the defendant put on the service received, known as the principle of 'subjective devaluation'.[117]

The answer is not wholly clear. In *Ruxley* it was pointed out that the pool was contracted to be safe for diving, although Mr Forsyth had no intention or desire to fit a diving board[118] (and it does not seem that even at the promised depth one would have been safe and therefore appropriate). In *Farley v Skinner* the judge

---

[113] See above in chapter eight, section 8.3B. But see the discussion in *Electricity Supply Nominees Ltd v National Magazine Co Ltd* [1999] 1 EGLR 130 (Hicks QC) at 134 in relation to corporate claimants and these awards.

[114] *Farley v Skinner* [2002] 2 AC 732 (HL) Lord Steyn at para 28, also Lord Hutton at para 61 and Lord Scott at para 110.

[115] *Hamilton Jones v David & Snape (a firm)* [2004] 1 WLR 924 (Neuberger J).

[116] As confirmed in *West & Son Ltd v Shephard* [1964] AC 326 (HL) and *Lim Poh Choo v Camden Islington Area Health Authority* [1980] AC 174 (HL), the answer in personal injury cases is that unconsciousness does not prevent the award being made.

[117] The answer is that the subjective value of an enrichment can reduce the award below the market value ('subjective devaluation'), but the subjective value probably cannot increase the award above the market value ('subjective revaluation'): *Benedetti v Sawiris* [2013] UKSC 50.

[118] *Ruxley Electronics and Construction Ltd v Forsyth* [1996] AC 344 (HL) at 362.

thought it important enough to note that the claimant was not a man of excessive susceptibility to aircraft noise.[119] This latter point provides a clue to the proper approach of contract law, in line with the general run of remoteness cases: the question to be asked is whether the loss suffered by the claimant is one for which the defendant impliedly took responsibility. If the loss is due to a particular susceptibility not disclosed to the defendant then it may be too remote and/or the claimant may be limited to the more usual amount of such loss.[120] Likewise, where the purpose of the defendant's performance is *apparently* profitable, the fact that the claimant business person had an undisclosed sentimental reason for it (eg had a preference for finishing all projects on a Tuesday) cannot give rise to a mental distress recovery, as that would be too remote.[121]

(ii) Proxies and Presumptions

Financial loss may be difficult to prove, but is easy to quantify in terms of money: loss of £1 should be compensated by damages of £1.

Non-financial loss is more difficult. However, the case law shows that there are various methods and proxies that can be used to assist in valuing non-financial loss, all of which can confuse the unwary into thinking that something else is going on than an award of damages for the non-financial loss suffered by the claimant. (Indeed these methods can also be used in financial cases where it is difficult either to prove causation between the breach and the financial bottom line or to quantify what that financial bottom line would have been but for the breach.[122])

(a) The Price and Presumption of Breaking Even

The first method is to start from an assumption, or presumption, that a claimant's non-financial loss resulting from the breach was at least as much as the defendant was paid for the promise. This is the non-financial analogue of the important presumption in financial cases that the claimant would have made financial revenue equal to the expenditure (including the price) incurred to get it.[123]

The claimant may in fact have misjudged the promise and paid too much, because it would not have yielded as much non-financial value (loss) as estimated at the time of contracting (just as a claimant may in fact make less monetary revenue from a performance than estimated). And in many cases a claimant would have got more non-pecuniary benefit than the price.[124] Thus in *Jarvis v Swan's Tours* the Court

---

[119] *Farley v Skinner* [2002] 2 AC 732 (HL) Lord Clyde at 754.

[120] See holiday case *Kemp v Intasun Holidays Ltd* [1987] 2 FTLR 234, (1988) 6 Tr L 161 (CA). And see the capping principle discussed above in chapter fourteen, section 14.4.

[121] Although by the capping principle, the claimant could recover actually suffered non-pecuniary loss up to the amount of the contemplated, but not suffered, financial loss. See chapter fourteen, section 14.4 below.

[122] See chapter eighteen, section 18.3, also 18.2.

[123] Discussed above in chapter eighteen, section 18.3.

[124] This surplus is what is referred to as the 'consumer surplus' in *Ruxley Electronics and Construction Ltd v Forsyth* [1996] AC 344 (HL). See above n 56 as to this term.

of Appeal awarded £125 in damages for non-pecuniary loss on a holiday that had cost £63.50.[125]

However, absent such evidence, the price paid is a sensible starting place. As Edmund-Davies LJ explained on appeal, the first instance judge in *Jarvis v Swan's Tours*

> held that the value of the plaintiff's loss was what he paid under the contract for his holiday; that as a result of the defendants' breaches of contract he has lost not the whole of what he has paid for, but broadly speaking a half of it; and what he has lost and what reduces its value by about one half includes such inconvenience as the plaintiff suffered from the holiday he got not being, by reason of the defendants' breaches, as valuable as the holiday he paid for.[126]

Thus that judge started from the presumption that the holiday was worth to the claimant what it cost, and awarded half of that (£31.72). The Court of Appeal in *Jarvis* increased the award to £125, finding that 'the entertainment and enjoyment which [Mr Jarvis] was promised, and which he did not get' was worth far more to Mr Jarvis than it cost,[127] which is not at all surprising. The presumption that the holiday was worth the price paid was rebutted; it was found to be worth more.

This approach is also used in landlord's failure to repair cases when calculating the non-pecuniary loss suffered: the law takes a notional reduction in rent as a starting point.[128]

It is important to realise, though, that this is a compensatory award. First, it is not a restitutionary award of the price or part of the price. As the Court of Appeal explained of holiday cases awards based on the price paid, 'that does not render the first part of the award a restitutionary claim, but simply a yardstick by which the damages are assessed'.[129] Accordingly, there can be no damages awarded for the price per se, because but for the breach the claimant would still have paid it; rather the price is used as a proxy to measure the non-financial loss suffered by the claimant. Failure to get this point across in the *White Arrow* case is what led the claim to be rejected, as the Court of Appeal saw the claim of a portion of the price (where there was no rational way of so apportioning it) as being a disguised attempt to get restitution (although note that that case was about pecuniary and not non-pecuniary loss).[130] Secondly, the award in landlord and tenant cases is not for the difference in market value of the property per se; rather the market value is used as a proxy

---

[125] *Jarvis v Swans Tours Ltd* [1973] QB 233 (CA).

[126] Ibid at 240.

[127] Ibid at 238.

[128] See above in chapter eight, section 8.3.

[129] *Peninsula & Oriental Steam Navigation Co (P&O) v Youell* [1997] 2 Lloyd's Rep 136 (CA) Potter LJ at 141.

[130] *White Arrow Express Ltd v Lamey's Distribution Ltd* (1995) 15 Tr L 69 (CA). It appears from Morritt LJ's comments that counsel for the claimants also accepted that if there is a market it is necessary to value by reference to it. In my view this concession should not have been made.

for the part of the price paid for the particular obligation, which is a proxy for the non-pecuniary loss.[131]

(b) Gain Made by the Defendant

In *Freeman v Niroomand* the trial judge was given no assistance in measuring the loss of amenity, and awarded £130, which was the amount the defendant saved by skimping on his performance. The Court of Appeal upheld this award whilst nevertheless making it clear that the award was of compensation for loss of amenity and not restitution or restitutionary damages (the defendant's savings merely being a useful figure where there was no other evidence as to the amount of the claimant's loss of amenity).[132]

(c) What Would the Claimant Have Taken to Consent to the Breach?

The next method is slightly different and perhaps more accurate. It is to do broadly what economists would do, and ask how much the claimant would have been willing to pay to forego the benefit. This, the reader will recognise, is in fact the well-established 'hypothetical bargain' approach from the *Wrotham Park* line of cases, by which the court asks what the claimant (if willing) would have accepted prior to the breach to agree to consent to it.[133] Such awards are usually considered to be either an odd sort of compensation or even a measure of partial restitution or disgorgement, but are best understood as compensation, with the measure being a rebuttable presumption as to the value of the service to the claimant, where other evidence is difficult to obtain.[134] The amount a person is willing to pay for something will, of course, usually be more than the amount they actually paid, and the amount they would accept to forego the performance is a pretty good measure of the value they ascribed to it.[135]

---

[131] *Wallace v Manchester City Council* [1998] 3 EGLR 38 (CA) Morritt LJ at 41 and 42; *Earle v Charalambous* [2006] EWCA Civ 1090, and see chapter eight, section 8.3B–C above.

[132] *Freeman v Niroomand* (1996) 52 Con LR 116 (CA).

[133] As to whether such awards in restrictive covenant cases are really compensation for non-pecuniary loss, see below text to chapter ten n 6 and surrounding.

[134] Of course, it may be that, like in *Wrotham Park* itself, the claimant never would have agreed to forego the performance if asked. In reality this will often be the case, and in a personal injury case a loss of an ear may be economically and/or legally equivalent for the claimant to a certain amount of money and yet the claimant would never willing make the trade. Economic equivalence assuming, contrary to fact, a certain willingness to compromise (unless the reasons for not being willing to compromise are within the defendant's responsibility) is still a legitimate means of valuing the non-financial advantages.

[135] What someone actually pays is sometimes called the 'revealed willingness to pay' by economists, and the amount above this actual price that they were willing to pay, the 'consumer surplus'. This use of the term is different to that employed in *Ruxley*, where the concept of the 'consumer surplus' was used to indicate the amount by which a consumer values what is bought over and above the financial value the consumer receives (not the price the consumer paid). Of course, these concepts all refer to what the claimant was willing to pay for the service itself. Asking what the claimant was willing to pay to consent to the breach is a slightly different question (the willingness may not have been there had this actually occurred), but is more precise in focusing on the breach itself rather than the entire service which is valued by the claimant compendiously.

Such an award was made in the *Van der Garde* case[136] as an alternative to Stadlen J's award of the difference in market value, but in exactly the same amount.

(d) Market Value

The final method is to look to what third parties generally would have paid for the promise (ie the difference between what would have been paid by another for the service provided and that promised). This is the market measure, and may be more or less than the price in fact paid by the claimant (depending upon whether the claimant got a good or bad deal as compared with the market). Stadlen J in the *Van der Garde* case saw this as the primary measure, and was of the view that the price paid should yield to this.[137] As discussed above,[138] the better view is that this goes too far, and that, as is clear from the breach of landlord covenant to repair cases, the market measure is just a useful proxy for the non-pecuniary loss.[139]

Thus the true measure is personal to the claimant, but the market value will be especially useful where the breach is of a non-pro-rateable part of the contract, as in such cases there is no way of working out what part of the *price* accords with the particular performance withheld, but market evidence can be led to show how the market views the promised performance as against that delivered.[140] A typical example is that of a residential property in disrepair; the so-called notional reduction in rent, assessed by reference to the market, is used as a proxy for the non-pecuniary loss suffered by the tenant.[141]

Of course, the market value will often be less than the non-pecuniary loss, and so a not particularly helpful proxy, especially where the breach consists not of skimping on the services in any objective sense, but rather disappointing a preference. One meal in a restaurant will have the same market value as another, as will films in a cinema or colours of bedroom wall paint, but that does not mean that the disappointed claimant has not suffered non-pecuniary loss and will not be awarded damages for it. Similarly a bad service may cause more non-pecuniary loss than the market value of the entire service.[142]

---

[136] *Giedo Van der Garde BV v Force India Formula One Team Ltd* [2010] EWHC 2373 (QB) (Stadlen J). Discussed above in chapter two, section 2.2C.

[137] Ibid paras 438–87. And the Court of Appeal in *White Arrow Express Ltd v Lamey's Distribution Ltd* (1995) 15 Tr L 69 (CA) saw it as 'usually' the right measure.

[138] See chapter two, section 2.2C(ii) above.

[139] See chapter eight, section 8.3B(iii) and C above.

[140] In *Van der Garde* the price was fairly easy to pro rate as a numerical proportion of the total homogenous service (a certain number of laps) was not supplied, and so this was the measure of the loss awarded. In *White Arrow* the market value would have been a more sensible starting point as pro rating was not easily available (the difference between a basic and premier service being qualitative not quantitative).

[141] See above in section 19.1C(iii).

[142] Eg the holiday case of *Jarvis v Swan's Tours* [1973] QB 233 (CA). See the discussion of this point in landlord and tenant cases in *English Churches Housing Group v Shine* [2004] EWCA Civ 434 and above at text to n 85.

(e) Tariff/Precedent

Despite the dangers of doing so, judges will often compare awards with other cases in order to ensure that the award is in line with other non-pecuniary loss awards. This is particularly common in landlord breach cases, holiday cases and cases of physical inconvenience from construction.[143]

19.3 (Physical) Inconvenience and Disturbance

A claimant who suffers 'physical inconvenience and discomfort caused by breach and mental suffering directly related to that inconvenience and discomfort' is entitled to compensation for that harm if it is not too remote,[144] although awards should be 'restrained'.[145] A sensible gloss that has been added by Lord Scott in *Farley v Skinner* is that the word 'physical' is misleading. The real question is whether the cause of inconvenience or discomfort is 'sensory experience' (including eg being kept awake by noise, or irritated by darkness) rather than mere disappointment at the contract being broken.[146]

Such awards are typical, even routine, in building cases (including during the period of rectification works),[147] cases of negligent surveyors,[148] landlord's (or other's) covenant to repair[149] and landlord's covenant to provide facilities[150] or wrongful eviction[151] cases. There are also examples of transport failure causing the inconvenience of walking,[152] and a solicitor failing to obtain repossession of the claimant's house (requiring him and his family to live in one room at his parent's house).[153]

---

[143] See eg *Milner v Carnival plc* [2010] 3 All ER 701 (CA) Ward LJ at paras 32–41, and section 19.3A below.

[144] *Watts v Morrow* [1991] 1 WLR 1421 (CA) Bingham LJ at 1445.

[145] Ibid.

[146] *Farley v Skinner* [2002] 2 AC 732 (HL) at para 85. And note Lord Clyde's observation that the word 'physical' was unnecessary: *Farley v Skinner* [2002] 2 AC 732 (HL) at para 35.

[147] In *Ruxley*, £750 was awarded, in addition to the £2,500 for loss of amenity. See also *Batty v Metropolitan Property Realisations Ltd* [1978] QB 554 (CA); *Boynton v Willers* [2003] EWCA Civ 904; *Melhuish & Saunders Ltd v Hurden* [2012] EWHC 3119 (TCC) (Havelock-Allen QC).

[148] *Perry v Sidney Phillips & Son* [1982] 1 WLR 1297 (CA) (this was interpreted as an award for physical inconvenience, rather than a mental distress, by the Court of Appeal in *Hayes v James and Charles Dodd (a firm)* [1990] 2 All ER 815 (CA)). See also, for example, *Bigg v Howard Son & Gooch* [1990] 1 EGLR 173(Hicks QC); *Watts v Morrow* [1991] 1 WLR 1421 (CA); *Patel v Hooper & Jackson (a firm)* [1999] 1 WLR 1792 (CA); *Ezekiel v McDade* [1995] 2 EGLR 107 (CA); *Wapshott v Davis Donovan & Co* [1996] PNLR 361 (CA); *Hoadley v Edwards* [2001] PNLR 964 (Evans-Lombe J).

[149] Eg *Chiodi v De Marney* [1988] 2 EGLR 64 (CA); *Wallace v Manchester City Council* [1998] 3 EGLR 38 (CA) and the cases cited therein; *Long v Southwark London Borough Council* [2002] EWCA Civ 403; *English Churches Housing Group v Shine* [2004] EWCA Civ 434 Wall LJ at para 105. See also *Haysman v Mrs Roger Films Ltd* [2008] EWHC 2494 (QB) (Derek Sweeting QC), a case of a film production company's failure to restore a house that had been used for filming and damaged.

[150] *McCall v Abelesz* [1976] QB 585 (CA): no gas supply. *Newman v Framewood Manor Management Co Ltd* [2012] EWCA Civ 159: no internal route of access to the swimming pool, sauna instead of jacuzzi, also failure to keep the gym in good repair.

[151] *Perera v Vandiyar* [1953] 1 WLR 672 (CA).

[152] *Hobbs v London and South Western Railway Co* (1875) LR 10 QB 111.

[153] *Bailey v Bullock* [1950] 2 All ER 1167 (Barry J).

The loss must have actually been suffered: an employer kept out of a property that is to be rented out and not lived in anyway cannot recover damages under this head.[154]

In 'successful transaction cases'[155] such loss will usually be irrecoverable because it would have been suffered even but for the breach, although this will not always be the case (eg where a tenant's over-payment meant the claimant could not afford to do the repairs when he would have done them had he paid less[156]).

A. Quantum

Examples of awards from the 1990s include £4,000 for the claimant's family having to live in assorted council accommodation for a year and a half because undiscovered defects prevented them from selling their home property when they wanted (and needed) to,[157] and £5,000 for two or three years of aggravation.[158] In the absence of particular physical symptoms or illnesses, one judge has said that this type of damages would rarely exceed £2,500 per person per year at 2007's prices,[159] with £7,000, £5,000 and £2,000 awarded to the mother, father and son dislocated for nearly two years as a result of damp for which the defendant architect was responsible.[160] Comparison with personal injury and discrimination awards can be useful.[161] Holiday cases usually run from tens to a few thousands of pounds.[162]

B. Basis and Relation with Mental Distress/Diminution in Value

Physical inconvenience damages often run together with mental distress damages, and are often considered compendiously.[163] There is no real harm in this.

---

[154] *Hutchinson v Harris* (1978) 10 BLR 19 (CA) at 37 and 46.

[155] Ie where but for the breach the transaction would have still gone ahead but on different terms: see above at chapter three, section 3.1B, as to this term.

[156] *Perry v Sidney Phillips & Son*[1982] 1 WLR 1297 (CA).

[157] *Ezekiel v McDade* [1995] 2 EGLR 107 (CA).

[158] *Hoadley v Edwards* [2001] PNLR 964 (Evans-Lombe J).

[159] *Axa Insurance UK plc v Cunningham Lindsey United Kingdom (an unlimited company)* [2007] EWHC 3023 (TCC) (Akenhead J) at 275, referred to and broadly applied in *West v Ian Finlay & Associates (a firm)* [2013] EWHC 868 (TCC) (Edwards-Stuart J). See also *Wallace v Manchester City Council* [1998] 3 EGLR 38 (CA) at 42–43, where Morritt LJ discussed but did not approve a tariff running up to £2,750 per annum in 1998.

[160] *West v Ian Finlay & Associates (a firm)* [2013] EWHC 868 (TCC) (Edwards-Stuart J). But see the much lower awards in *Hunt v Optima (Cambridge) Ltd* [2013] EWHC 681 (TCC) (Akenhead J) at paras 256–59.

[161] See *Milner v Carnival plc* [2010] 3 All ER 701 (CA) per Ward LJ at paras 38–40.

[162] *Milner v Carnival plc* [2010] 3 All ER 701 (CA) Ward LJ at para 37.

[163] Eg *Hutchinson v Harris* (1978) 10 BLR 19 (CA); *Channon v Lindley Johnstone (a firm)* [2002] EWCA Civ 353; *Milner v Carnival plc* [2010] 3 All ER 701 (CA). See also the comment of Lord Steyn in *Farley v Skinner* [2002] 2 AC 732 (HL) at para 20 as to 'a tendency of the court sometimes not to distinguish between the cases presently under consideration [mental distress cases] and cases of physical inconvenience and discomfort'.

The 'major or important object of the contract' test thought to govern mental distress awards is rarely applied to physical inconvenience awards,[164] even where the inconvenience falls short of personal injury (which is discussed below) and is essentially anxiety and loss of enjoyment just like in many of the mental distress awards. The reason the main mental distress test is rarely applied to physical inconvenience cases is probably that physical inconvenience is less a type of anxiety or loss of enjoyment than a particular way of causing it, and any contract that can cause physical *inconvenience* can usually (although perhaps not always) be said to have physical *convenience* as a major object or not too remote consequence. Certainly this is true in the typical cases such as domestic building works and landlords' covenants to repair. Accordingly the 'major object' test does not need to be considered because it is easily satisfied and/or the losses fall within the defendant's assumption of risk.

19.4 Personal Injury

Personal injury can arise in contract cases (especially sale of goods, employment, and medical care cases) but is primarily a matter for tort law, especially the law of negligence. For detailed discussion of damages for personal injury, the reader is referred to specialist texts on the subject.[165]

Where contract breach *does* cause personal injury, damages will be recoverable, subject to the test of remoteness. Examples include a breach by a carpet-cleaner which led to the claimant tripping up,[166] a breach by a theatre which led to the collapse of the theatre ceiling,[167] and a breach by a holiday-provider which led to a diving injury.[168] Such damages have been refused on remoteness grounds, eg where a train did not go to the intended destination and the claimants had to walk (the wife got ill and that was unrecoverable as too remote, although some damages for physical inconvenience were recovered)[169] and where a solicitor mishandled a divorce causing the client to have a nervous breakdown.[170]

---

[164] See eg Lord Steyn in *Farley v Skinner* [2002] 2 AC 732 (HL) at paras 15–16.

[165] Eg *Kemp & Kemp: Personal Injury Law, Practice & Procedure* (looseleaf) (London, Sweet & Maxwell).

[166] *Kimber v William Willett Ltd* [1947] KB 570 (CA).

[167] *Pope v St Helen's Theatre Ltd* [1947] KB 30 (Sellers J).

[168] *Evans v Kosmar Villa Holidays plc* [2008] 1 WLR 297 (CA), although no liability was found in that case.

[169] *Hobbs v London and South Western Railway Co* (1875) LR 10 QB 111.

[170] *Cook v Swinfen* [1967] 1 WLR 457 (CA).

Employees frequently recover damages for psychiatric conditions caused by the employer's lack of a safe system of work or other breach, including in cases of excessive stress or workload.[171] Tenants often recover where a landlord's disrepair leads to hand injuries, pneumonia etc from ceiling collapses, unsafe steps, dampness etc.[172] Personal injury in sale of goods cases is discussed above.[173] And private medical negligence actions will, of course, often include damages for personal injury, including general damages and consequential losses of profits.[174]

---

[171] *Barber v Somerset County Council* [2004] 1 WLR 1089 (HL); *Walker v Northumberland County Council* [1995] 1 All ER 737 (Colman J).

[172] *Griffin v Pillet* [1926] 1 KB 17 (Wright J); *Porter v Jones* [1942] 2 All ER 570 (CA); *Summers v Salford Corp* [1943] AC 283 (HL); *McCoy & Co v Clark* (1982) 13 HLR 87 (CA); *Marshall v Rubypoint Ltd* [1997] 1 EGLR 69 (CA) (injury caused by assault by a burglar where front door left unrepaired). Refused in *Berryman v Hounslow London Borough Council* [1997] PIQR P83 (CA) on remoteness/causation grounds.

[173] See chapter four, section 4.2A(v)(b) and (e).

[174] See eg *Johnson v Fourie* [2011] EWHC 1062 (QB) (Owen J).

20

Indemnity for Liability to Third Parties and Compensation for Litigation Costs

Damages to indemnify the claimant for liability it has to third parties as a result of the defendant's breach; damages for the costs of litigation or arbitration against the defendant or third parties.

20.1. Indemnity for Third Party Liability
20.2. Costs in Relation to the Breach of Contract Dispute Itself
20.3. Costs in Previous Proceedings against the Defendant
20.4. Costs in Third Party Proceedings

20.1 Indemnity for Third Party Liability

A. Service Cases

THE BREACH OF service or employment contracts will often give rise to vicarious or other liability on the part of the claimant employer to third parties, especially where the defendant has injured a third party[1] or damaged property belonging to the third party,[2] and the defendant is liable to indemnify in such cases.

The same applies in professional negligence cases. Thus in the tort case of *Law Society v Sephton & Co*,[3] the defendant accountant's negligence exposed the claimant to possible claims for compensation by the former clients of a solicitor's firm.[4] Similarly in *Axa v Akhtar & Darby*[5] the defendant solicitor negligently approved

---

[1] Eg *Lister v Romford Ice and Cold Storage Co Ltd* [1957] AC 555 (HL), where the claimant's employee drove into another employee (in fact, his father).

[2] Eg *Parallel Productions Ltd v Goss Contracting Co* (1968) 69 DLR (2d) 609 (British Columbia SC), where the claimant had promised to restore the third party's land after use for a film shoot, and the defendant gravel supplier to the claimant had caused a bridge collapse on the property.

[3] *Law Society v Sephton & Co* [2006] 2 AC 543 (HL). Also *Braid v WL Highway & Sons* (1964) 191 EG 433 (Roskill J) (solicitor's negligence led claimant to run business on property that made it liable to the owner of the reversion).

[4] See also construction cases, eg *Sims v Foster Wheeler Ltd* [1966] 1 WLR (CA); *Shepherd Homes Ltd v Encia* [2007] EWHC 1710 (TCC) (Jackson J), and other professional negligence cases *Woods v Martins Bank Ltd* [1959] 1 QB 255 (Salmon J); *Braid v WL Highway & Sons* (1964) 191 EG 433 (Roskill J) (solicitor); *Deeny v Gooda Walker Ltd (No 3)* [1995] 1 WLR 1206 (Philips J) (Lloyd's managing and underwriting agents); *Redbus LMDS Ltd v Jeffrey Green & Russell (a firm)* [2006] EWHC 2938 (Behrens J).

[5] *Axa Insurance Ltd v Akhtar & Darby Solicitors* [2010] 1 WLR 1662 (CA).

the acceptance of various personal injury claims into an after-the-event insurance scheme and the damage suffered was the claimant insurer's liability to the personal injury claimants.

And routinely a breach of a construction sub-contract or supply contract, especially a breach which causes delay, may lead a head contractor to be liable in liquidated or unliquidated damages to the customer. Remoteness will rarely be a problem in sub-contract breach cases,[6] although it was as to the extent of the head contractor's liability in the Piper Alpha disaster case, where the defendant would never have foreseen that the contractor could be liable to third parties for punitive damages awards in Texan courts.[7]

An insurance broker's breach may give rise to a duty to indemnify more indirectly. The broker may not cause the claimant to be liable to the third party, but it may well cause the claimant to be uninsured in relation to that liability.[8]

Where the liability to the third party has not yet been quantified, the court may order an indemnity to be assessed, or may seek to estimate the liability that will be incurred to the third party in the future.[9]

Analogously to the liability discussed in the above cases, where the defendant printers' breach led to the circulation of false currency, payments to the holders of the currency to buy it back were recoverable in damages.[10]

B. Goods Cases

Damages indemnifying the claimant for its liability to its buyer are available when not too remote. This can be where the defendant seller's non-delivery or patent defect, or the defendant non-seller's destruction or damage, caused the claimant's sale to fall through (in damage or defect cases, often because the claimant's buyer rejected the property),[11] or where a defect, damage or late delivery does not cause the loss of the sub-sale but does give rise to liability under it,[12] but frequently the unavoidable losses on the sub-sale will be too remote.[13]

---

[6] See eg *PPG Industries (Singapore) Pte Ltd v Compact Metal Industries Ltd* [2013] SGCA 23 (Singapore CA) esp at para 20.

[7] *Elf Enterprise Caledonia Ltd v London Bridge Engineering Ltd* [1997] Scot CS 1 (Court of Session, Outer House), discussed above at text to chapter fourteen n 109.

[8] Eg *Pennant Hills Restaurants Pty Ltd v Barrell Insurances Pty Ltd* (1981) 55 ALJR 258 (HC of Australia); *Unity Insurance Brokers Pty Ltd v Rocco Pezzano Pty Ltd* (1998) 192 CLR 603 (HC of Australia).

[9] See above in chapter one, section 1.1C(ii).

[10] *Banco de Portugal v Waterlow & Sons Ltd* [1932] AC 452 (HL).

[11] *Grébert-Borgnis v J & W Nugent* (1885) 15 QBD 85 (CA) (non-delivery of skins); *Re Hall (R and H) Ltd and WH Pim Junior & Co's Arbitration* [1928] All ER Rep 763 (HL) (non-delivery of corn); *Household Machines Ltd v Cosmos Exporters Ltd* [1947] KB 217 (Lewis J) (non-delivery of cutlery and tableware); *Garside v Black Horse Ltd* [2010] EWHC 190 (QB) (King J) (car rejected by hire purchaser as a result of defect).

[12] *Contigroup Companies Inc v Glencore AG* [2005] 1 Lloyd's Rep 241 (Glick QC) (late delivery of butane).

[13] *Borries v Hutchinson* (1865) 18 CB (NS) 445, and see above in chapter four more generally. Alternatively, even if liability on the sub-sale is not too remote, it may be that specific features of the sub-sale or liability are out of the ordinary and therefore those aspects are too remote and only the ordinary measure of such liability can be recovered. See further above in chapter 14, section 14.4A.

Such liability of the claimant to its buyer is more common, however, in cases of latent defects or damage, where the claimant's sale proceeds but the buyer later has a claim for damages against the claimant as a result of the defect.[14] This is because liability on any such sale is an ordinary consequence of a latent defect,[15] whereas in non-delivery, destruction and patent defect cases the liability will only arise if the claimant's sale is entered into prior to the date of delivery under the main contract with the defendant (in sale cases) and the sub-sale liability cannot be avoided by purchase of a market replacement. For example, if a defendant manufacturer's fur coat is latently defective so as to cause skin disease, the claimant retailer will incur unavoidable liability if it sells the coat on to almost any buyer on almost any terms.[16]

C. Quantifying the Liability

A liability to a third party is a purely contingent loss: it may not materialise if the third party does not sue or loses when it does. The date of damage in such cases (relevant for the purposes of calculating interest, as well as for limitation purposes in a tort but not contract claim) will often be the date on which the contingency occurs and the damage is suffered, because a legal liability, even unsatisfied, amounts in law to a loss.[17] However, at the date of judgment the liability on the sub-sale may not yet have crystallised through a judgment or settlement.

Where the liability is more than speculative but has not yet arisen by the date of judgment, the court may instead: make a declaration that the defendant will be liable to indemnify the claimant when the third party liability eventuates;[18] possibly make an award reflecting the chance of a liability to the third party;[19] or where appropriate, defer dealing with the issue.[20] However, where the liability is only conditional and by the time of trial it has become clear that the condition will not

[14] Eg *Randall v Raper* (1858) EB & E 84; *Hammond v Bussey* (1888) 20 QBD 79 (CA); *Pinnock Bros v Lewis & Peat Ltd* [1923] 1 KB 690 (Roche J); *Sidney Bennett Ltd v Kreeger* (1925) 41 TLR 609 (Branson J); *Kasler & Cohen v Slavouski* [1928] 1 KB 78 (Branson J); *Biggin & Co Ltd v Permanite Ltd* [1951] 2 KB 314 (CA); *Hendry Kendall & Sons v William Lillico & Sons Ltd* [1969] 2 AC 31 (HL); *Ashington Piggeries Ltd v Christopher Hill Ltd* [1972] AC 441 (HL); *GKN Centrax Gears Ltd v Matbro Ltd* [1976] 2 Lloyd's Rep 555 (CA); *Britvic Soft Drinks Ltd v Messer UK Ltd* [2002] 1 Lloyd's Rep 20 (Tomlinson J), affirmed [2002] 2 Lloyd's Rep 368 (CA); *Bacardi-Martini Beverages Ltd v Thomas Hardy Packaging Ltd* [2002] 1 Lloyd's Rep 62 (Tomlinson J), affirmed [2002] 2 Lloyd's Rep 379 (CA); *McSherry v Coopers Creek Vineyard Ltd* (2005) 8 NZBLC 101 (Panckhurst J); *Britestone Pte Ltd v Smith & Associates Far East Ltd* [2007] SGCA 47 (Singapore CA) at para 66. Cf *Butterworth v Kingsway Motors Ltd* [1954] 2 All ER 694 (Pearson J).

[15] See above discussion of remoteness in this context: chapter four, section 4.2B(v).

[16] *Sidney Bennett Ltd v Kreeger* (1925) 41 TLR 609 (Branson J) and *Kasler & Cohen v Slavouski* [1928] 1 KB 78 (Branson J).

[17] *Randall v Raper* (1858) EB & E 84; *Total Liban SA v Vitol Energy SA* [2001] QB 643 (Peter Gross QC); *Law Society v Sephton & Co* [2006] 2 AC 543 (HL) (tort). But see *Axa Insurance Ltd v Akhtar & Darby Solicitors* [2010] 1 WLR 1662 (CA).

[18] *Household Machines Ltd v Cosmos Exporters Ltd* [1947] KB 217 (Lewis J) (a non-delivery case); *Hydrocarbons Great Britain Ltd v Cammell Laird Shipbuilders Ltd* (1991) 53 BLR 84 (CA); *Shepherd Homes Limited v Encia* [2007] EWHC 1710 (TCC) (Jackson J) at paras 734 to 743 and the cases cited.

[19] *Alucraft Pty Ltd v Grocon Ltd (No 2)* [1996] 2 VR 386 (SC of Victoria).

[20] See the discussion above in chapter one, section 1.2C(ii).

be satisfied, then no loss has been suffered.[21] Similarly where for whatever reason there is no liability to the sub-buyer or the sub-buyer is not pursuing any claim, and so the seller has, in effect, 'got away with it', in those circumstances the claimant has suffered no loss and can get only nominal damages.[22]

There can be no recovery, however, where although there is a legal liability, it is clear it will never give rise to an actual payment (because the legal liability was to an insolvent company which owed more than it was owed).[23]

Even if the liability does not lead to an award against the claimant, the defendant may be responsible for the dispute and so liable to pay the claimant's costs of litigating when it would not have had to do so but for the breach, as discussed in the following sections.

D. Indemnity for the Cost of Settlement of a Third Party Claim

(i) Reasonable Settlements

A defendant will be liable to the claimant to indemnify it for a settlement made with a third party if that falls within the defendant's responsibility under the usual rules of mitigation, remoteness and causation.

The essential principle, deriving from *Biggin & Co Ltd v Permanite Ltd*,[24] is that if the defendant's breach exposes the claimant to a claim by a third party and that claim is not too remote, then the defendant will usually be liable to reimburse the claimant for any 'reasonable' settlement of that claim. If the claim is not too remote a reasonable settlement will also not be.[25] The evidential burden of proving unreasonableness of the settlement falls on the defendant,[26] at least where the settlement was made on legal advice.[27]

As Toulson LJ's recent explanation in the Court of Appeal decision in *Siemens Building Technologies FE Ltd v Supershield Ltd* shows, the defendant will have an uphill battle in seeking to show that the claimant's settlement was unreasonable, and a fair amount of deference is given to the parties (on the fair assumption that they are doing the best they can in the light of what is known at the time):

> Megarry J once described the law reports as charts of the wrecks of unsinkable cases. Because of its uncertainty and expense, prudent parties usually try to avoid litigation

---

[21] *Murfin v Campbell* [2011] EWHC 1475 (Ch) (Pelling QC).

[22] *McSherry v Coopers Creek Vineyard Ltd* (2005) 8 NZBLC 101 (Panckhurst J): mis-labelled inferior wine sold on to a further merchant and by that merchant to retail customers, with no complaints.

[23] *Biffa Waste Services Ltd v Maschinenfabrik Ernst Hese GmbH* [2009] PNLR 5 (Ramsey J).

[24] *Biggin & Co Ltd v Permanite Ltd* [1951] 2 KB 314 (CA).

[25] *Biggin & Co Ltd v Permanite Ltd* [1951] 2 KB 314 (CA) Somervell LJ at 321–22; *P&O Developments Ltd v Guys and Thomas' National Health Service Trust and others* (1998) 62 Con LR 38 (Bowsher QC) at paras 38–39; *General Feeds Inc Panama v Slobodna Plovidba Yugoslavia* [1999] 1 Lloyd's Rep 688 (Colman J) at 691.

[26] *Mander v Commercial Union Assurance Co plc* [1998] Lloyd's Rep IR 93 (Rix J) at 148; *P&O Developments Ltd v Guys and Thomas' National Health Service Trust and others* (1998) 62 Con LR 38 (Bowsher QC) at para 38. See further above inchapter four, section 4.3B(i)(b), and chapter fifteen, section 15.4.

[27] *BP plc v AON Ltd (No 2)* [2006] 1 Lloyds Rep IR 577 (Colman J) at paras 281–82.

where possible. It has to be borne in mind that the 'settlement value' of a claim is not an objective fact (or something which can be assessed by reference to an available market) but a matter of subjective opinion, taking account of all relevant variables. Often parties may have widely different perceptions of what would be a fair settlement figure without either being unreasonable. The object of mediation or negotiation is then to close the gap to a point which each finds acceptable. When a judge is considering the reasonableness of a settlement he will have in mind these factors and another: that he is likely to have a less complete understanding of the relative strengths of the settling parties than they had themselves (unless he is to embark on a disproportionately detailed investigation), and especially so in complex litigation. The issue which the judge has to decide is not what assessment he would have made of the likely outcome of the settled litigation, but whether the settlement was within the range of what was reasonable. If he decides that it was, an appellate court will not interfere with his decision unless persuaded that he erred in principle or (which is intrinsically unlikely) that his decision was incapable of justification on any reasonable view.[28]

As Colman J has explained, it is not necessary for the claimant to show that on the balance of probabilities it was even liable to the third party:

> There may be many claims which appear to be intrinsically weak but which common prudence suggests should be settled in order to avoid the uncertainties and expenses of litigation ... unless it appears on the evidence that the claim is so weak that no reasonable owner or club would take it sufficiently seriously to negotiate any settlement involving payment, it cannot be said that the loss attributable to a reasonable settlement was not caused by the breach.[29]

It may be reasonable to settle even where there is no liability.[30]

As to the amount of the settlement,[31] the question is not whether it is the best the claimant could have done, but whether it is within the range of settlements reasonable people in the position of the claimant might have made,[32] considering the strength of the claim, and uncertainties and expenses of litigation, and the benefits of settling rather than disputing. This reasonableness is evaluated as at the date of the settlement and in the light of the chances in the litigation as seen at that time, and without the benefit of hindsight (which may allow more to be known about the issues between the parties and the strength of the claim).[33] It has been explained that

> the test of reasonableness [is] a generous one appropriate to a party placed in an awkward situation by another's breach, where the law recognizes that he is not expected to act in a manner which will imperil his existing business relationships.[34]

---

[28] *Siemens Building Technologies FE Ltd v Supershield Ltd* [2010] EWCA Civ 7 at para 28.

[29] *BP plc v AON Ltd (No 2)* [2006] 1 Lloyds Rep IR 577 (Colman J) at para 281.

[30] *John F Hunt Demolition Ltd v ASME Engineering Ltd* [2008] 1 All ER 180 (Coulson QC) at paras 60–63.

[31] Although the two questions of reasonableness to settle and the amount of the settlement are really only one question: *Comyn Ching & Co Ltd v Oriental Tube Co Ltd* (1979) 17 BLR 47 (CA) Goff LJ at 89.

[32] *BP plc v AON Ltd (No 2)* [2006] 1 Lloyds Rep IR 577 (Colman J) at para 283; *Ground Gilbey Ltd v Jardine Lloyd Thompson UK Ltd* [2011] EWHC 124 (Comm) (Blair J) at para 119.

[33] *Mander v Commercial Union Assurance Co plc* [1998] Lloyd's Rep IR 93 (Rix J) at 148–49.

[34] *Britvic Soft Drinks Ltd v Messer UK Ltd* [2002] 1 Lloyd's Rep 20 (Tomlinson J) at para 126, affirmed [2002] 2 Lloyd's Rep 368 (CA).

The fact that the claimant had legal advice is important.[35] Although it has been said that it will rarely be necessary to call evidence from the legal advisors who advised on settlement,[36] it has also be said that the claimant will be expected to lead such evidence,[37] and such evidence is as a matter of fact often called.[38] The fact that notice of the settlement process had been given to the defendant and its views sought, may be relevant but will not prevent the need nevertheless to assess the reasonableness of the settlement.[39]

Settlement may not merely be a matter of paying money. In a trademark case a claimant reasonably delivered up goods to a third party as part of a compromise of an arguable case for trade mark infringement with that third party.[40]

(ii) Unreasonable Settlements

If it can be shown that the claim was so weak that it was unreasonable to make a settlement, the settlement sum is irrecoverable from the defendant. There are not many cases in which this has been found.[41] It may be unreasonable to settle if the key point is one which can be speedily and easily determined by a court, for example as a preliminary issue.[42]

If making a settlement was reasonable but the sum was not, the claimant will still be able to recover damages to the extent of a reasonable settlement.[43] It is only the excess over the reasonable sum that was not caused by the claimant or was not reasonable mitigation which is irrecoverable. However, there is also authority for the view that the unreasonable settlement must be disregarded entirely and a general measure of loss found.[44] In one case a lessee agreed with its landlord to incur the huge cost of reinstatement of property damaged by the defendant's contract breach even though the diminution in value was much smaller. This was found to have been unreasonable and the reinstatement sum was not recoverable.[45] Generally speaking, the former approach of allowing recovery of the reasonable sum is more in keeping with the law of mitigation and causation generally.

---

[35] *Biggin & Co Ltd v Permanite Ltd* [1951] 2 KB 314 (CA) Singleton LJ at 325. *Comyn Ching & Co Ltd v Oriental Tube Co Ltd* (1979) 17 BLR 47 (CA) Goff LJ at 89. See also the analogous situation of expending money in cure of a defect on advice, discussed above in chapter four, section 4.3B(ii)(a).

[36] *Biggin & Co Ltd v Permanite Ltd* [1951] 2 KB 314 (CA) Singleton LJ at 325.

[37] *Britestone Pte Ltd v Smith & Associates Far East Ltd* [2007] SGCA 47 (Singapore CA) at para 66.

[38] Eg *BP plc v AON Ltd (No 2)* [2006] 1 Lloyds Rep IR 577 (Colman J) at para 284; *Ground Gilbey Ltd v Jardine Lloyd Thompson UK Ltd* [2011] EWHC 124 (Comm) (Blair J) at para 105.

[39] *Britestone Pte Ltd v Smith & Associates Far East Ltd* [2007] SGCA 47 (Singapore CA).

[40] *Azzurri Communications Ltd v International Telecommunications Equipment Ltd (t/a SOS Communications)* [2013] EWPCC 17 (Birss QC).

[41] See *Kiddle v Lovett* (1885) 16 QBD 605, approved in *Biggin & Co Ltd v Permanite Ltd* [1951] 2 KB 314 (CA) and discussed in *General Feeds Inc Panama v Slobodna Plovidba Yugoslavia* [1999] 1 Lloyd's Rep 688 (Colman J).

[42] *Comyn Ching & Co Ltd v Oriental Tube Co Ltd* (1979) 17 BLR 47 (CA) Goff LJ at 89.

[43] *BP plc v AON Ltd (No 2)* [2006] 1 Lloyds Rep IR 577 (Colman J) at para 283; *John F Hunt Demolition Ltd v ASME Engineering Ltd* [2008] 1 All ER 180 (Coulson QC) at paras 60–63.

[44] *John F Hunt Demolition Ltd v ASME Engineering Ltd* [2008] 1 All ER 180 (Coulson QC) at paras 66–67.

[45] *Stow (George) & Co Ltd v Walter Lawrence Construction Ltd* (1992) 40 Con LR 57 (Hicks QC) at para 330.

(iii) Waiver by the Third Party

Unsurprisingly, where a defendant is responsible for a claimant being liable to pay a particular tax, the authorities' later waiver of that tax is properly to be brought into account in determining whether the claimant suffered loss.[46]

20.2 Costs in Relation to the Breach of Contract Dispute Itself

The costs of the litigation disputing the breach of contract itself (including lawyers' fees, disbursements to experts, and expenses) are a loss caused by the breach. But for the breach the claimant would not have had to embark upon the litigation against the defendant. However, under English law the costs of proceedings are dealt with by the Civil Procedure Rules 43 to 48. These procedural rules have exclusive jurisdiction over the costs of the dispute before the court (including of lawyers, expert reports etc) and mean that the ordinary rules of contract damages do not apply.[47]

As for these procedural rules, in brief summary:[48] although subject to overall discretion,[49] and subject to special rules in cases of certain types of cost and certain types of smaller claim (especially so-called 'fast-track' claims and 'small claims'),[50] there are two basic measures of assessment applied. Under the 'indemnity basis' the court will award all costs other than those unreasonably incurred or unreasonable in amount. Under the 'standard basis' the court will only award costs that are proportionate to the matters in issue, as well as disregarding unreasonable costs.[51]

20.3 Costs in Previous Proceedings against the Defendant

Costs incurred by the claimant in previous proceedings are recoverable on ordinary damages principles (ie like all other costs and harms), save where those previous proceedings were in England under the English system and between the same parties and therefore there has already been an application of the English costs rules to the question.[52] The costs of foreign proceedings considered here include satellite litigation in support of English litigation, including arresting a vessel in foreign proceedings as security for the present proceedings against the defendant.[53]

---

[46] *Intervention Board for Agricultural Produce v Leidig* [2000] Lloyd's Rep 144 (CA).

[47] See *Hutchinson v Harris* (1978) 10 BLR 19 (CA) at 39–40; *Seavision Investment SA v Evennett (The Tiburon)* [1992] 2 Lloyd's Rep 26 (CA); *ENE Kos v Petroleo Brasilero SA* [2009] EWHC 1843 (Comm) (Andrew Smith J) at para 65; and Louise Merrett, 'Costs as Damages' (2009) 125 *LQR* 468. As to the dividing line between the costs of litigation and other costs caused by the wrong, see L Merrett, 'Costs as Damages' (2009) 125 *LQR* 468 and, as to expert reports, *Bolton v Mahadeva* [1972] 1 WLR 1009 (CA) at 1014.

[48] See further the textbooks on costs and the notes in *The White Book*.

[49] And see the matters listed in CPR r 44.5.

[50] See CPR rr 27 and 45–46.

[51] CPR r 44.4.

[52] See *Berry v British Transport Commission* [1962] 1 QB 306 (CA); *Carroll v Kynaston* [2011] QB 959 (CA).

[53] *CHS Inc Iberica SL v Far East Marine SA (M/V Devon)* [2012] EWHC 3747 (Comm) (Cooke J) at para 93(iv).

As regards foreign proceedings and the application of the damages rules, all depends upon whether the defendant's breach caused the particular litigation (not uncommon in cases of negligence by defendant professionals[54] or breach of anti-suit, exclusive jurisdiction and arbitration clauses[55]) and that it was not too remote or avoidable. One particular feature deserves note, which is reasonableness. It was held in *Nat West v Rabobank (No 3)*[56] that the award of damages under ordinary principles (there, the costs of defending proceedings in California and bringing a claim for breach of the anti-suit injunction) is equivalent to the 'indemnity' measure of costs award applied to determining the amount of costs recoverable upon success in an English procedure, not the narrower 'standard' measure.[57] In other words ordinary rules of causation, mitigation and remoteness (like the indemnity and standard bases for costs) prevent recovery of unreasonable costs[58] but not of disproportionate costs (which are irrecoverable under the standard but not indemnity basis of costs).

20.4 Costs in Third Party Proceedings

The claimant's costs of proceedings against third parties will be recoverable where caused by the defendant's breach. This is most common in cases of latent defects where the defect is only discovered after the goods have been on-sold, or cases of non-delivery or patent defects where there is a string contract or minimal time before delivery is due under the sub-sale, so the loss cannot be avoided.[59] Likewise, a buyer could recover from the seller the costs of unsuccessfully *resisting* a claim by the true owner of goods.[60] And similarly where the defendant's negligent advice has caused the claimant litigation costs. These are recoverable, if reasonable.[61] Where the claimant did recover some costs in the third party proceedings, it can still recover the remainder (subject to the usual damages principles) from the defendant.[62]

---

[54] See above in chapter three.

[55] See above in chapter ten, section 10.3.

[56] *National Westminster Bank plc v Rabobank Nederland (No 3)* [2007] EWHC 1742 (Comm) (Colman J) especially at para 26, departing from the earlier approach under different costs rules in *British Racing Drivers' Club Ltd v Hextall Erskine & Co* [1996] 3 All ER 667 (Carnwath J). Followed in a professional negligence context in *Herrmann v Withers LLP* [2012] EWHC 1492 (Ch) (Newey J).

[57] See further above at text to n51.

[58] Eg *Baxendale v London, Chatham & Dover Railway Co* (1873) LR 10 Exch 35; *Hammond v Bussey* (1888) 20 QBD 79 (CA) at 92.

[59] *Pinnock Bros v Lewis & Peat Ltd* [1923] 1 KB 690 (Roche J); *Sidney Bennett Ltd v Kreeger* (1925) 41 TLR 609 (Branson J); *Kasler & Cohen v Slavouski* [1928] 1 KB 78 (Branson J); *Comyn Ching & Co Ltd v Oriental Tube Co Ltd* (1979) 17 BLR 47 (CA) Goff LJ at 91.

[60] *Lloyds and Scottish Finance Ltd v Modern Cars and Caravans (Kingston) Ltd* [1966] 1 QB 764 (Edmund Davies J).

[61] For sale of goods cases see eg *Hammond v Bussey* (1888) 20 QBD 79 (CA); *Sidney Bennett Ltd v Kreeger* (1925) 41 TLR 609 (Branson J); *Kasler & Cohen v Slavouski* [1928] 1 KB 78 (Branson J); *Comyn Ching & Co Ltd v Oriental Tube Co Ltd* (1979) 17 BLR 47 (CA) Goff LJ at 92–93. For professional cases see chapter three, section 3.2C(iii) above.

[62] *Agius v Great Western Colliery Co* [1899] 1 QB 413 (CA).

Part 6

Other Matters

21

Third Parties and Loss

Damages in contracts for the benefit of third parties. Including recovery by the claimant of damages that must be passed to the third party, recovery by the claimant of damages to be kept for itself, and recovery of the third party of damages under the Contracts (Rights of Third Parties) Act 1999.

21.1. Recovery by the Claimant of the Third Party's Loss for the Benefit of the Third Party ('Transferred Loss' and the *Albazero* Principle)
21.2. Recovery by a Claimant of its Own Loss
21.3. Third Party Claims under the Contracts (Rights of Third Parties) Act 1999

OFTEN A CONTRACT will be entered into for the benefit of a third party. One family member may pay for work to be done on property wholly or partly in another family member's name, or for a holiday or other service benefiting the whole family. A company may, often for accounting or tax reasons, engage a service or purchase property that is to benefit another associated company. In these cases, difficult issues arise as to whether damages can be recovered in relation to the third party's loss. (We leave aside situations in which, on the proper analysis, the third party is in fact not a third party but as a result of the rules of agency a party to the contract,[1] or otherwise has a right to sue under the contract.[2])

The basic rule remains that the claimant cannot recover damages for the third party's loss.[3]

21.1 Recovery by the Claimant of the Third Party's Loss for the Benefit of the Third Party ('Transferred Loss' and the *Albazero* Principle)

In certain situations the law treats a third party's loss as 'transferred loss', transferred to the contracting party and with the contracting party thus able to sue for it, and liable to account for the recovery to the third party.[4]

---

[1] Where the claimant is the agent of another then the principal is in fact a party to the contract, and not really a third party, and so is entitled to sue for damages in his own right.

[2] For example under the Contracts (Rights of Third Parties) Act 1999 briefly touched on at section 21.3 below.

[3] *Woodar Investment Development Ltd v Wimpey Construction UK Ltd* [1980] 1 WLR 277 (HL).

[4] *White v Jones* [1995] 2 AC 207 (HL) Lord Goff at 264–68, Lord Mustill at 281–82; *Alfred McAlpine Construction Ltd v Panatown Ltd* [2001] AC 518 Lord Clyde at 529, Lord Goff at 527.

A. Trusts

If the claimant had contracted as trustee then it can recover damages for losses to the beneficiary, provided it was known to both parties at the time of contracting that the beneficiary had an interest in the contract.[5] The claimant will be obliged to the third party to pass on any recovery.

B. The *Albazero* principle

(i) History of the Rule[6]

(a) Carriage of Goods and *The Albazero*

After the House of Lords' obiter comments in *The Albazero*,[7] interpreting the nineteenth-century decision in *Dunlop v Lambert*,[8] it became well-established that if a breach of contract for the carriage of goods causes damage to or destruction of goods after the transfer of the goods to a third party to the contract, the claimant transferor may sue the defendant and recover damages for the benefit of the third party.

The interpretation of *Dunlop v Lambert* itself in *The Albazero* may well be wrong (that case probably turned on the claimant having retained risk over the damaged goods, and therefore having a liability to the purchaser for which the defendant was liable to indemnify the claimant),[9] and was in any case obiter in *The Albazero* (the principle not applying there because the third party had a direct cause of action against the defendant by reason of the Bills of Lading Act 1855).

However, the rule was confirmed by their Lordships in *Alfred McAlpine Construction Ltd v Panatown Ltd*.[10] It is justified by the need to avoid a legal 'black hole', which arises where (as a result of the privity rule) a claimant has a cause of action but not substantial loss, and a third party a substantial loss but no cause of action.[11]

See also H Unberath, *Transferred Loss: Claiming Third Party Loss in Contract Law* (Oxford, Hart Publishing, 2003).

[5] *Lloyd's v Harper* (1880) 16 Ch D 290 (CA); *Rolls Royce Power Engineering Plc v Ricardo Consulting Engineers Ltd* [2003] EWHC 2871 (HHJ Seymour) at para 116; *Darlington Borough Council v Wiltshier Northern Ltd* [1995] 1 WLR 68 (CA) Dillon LJ obiter at 75.

[6] See further N Palmer and G Tolhurst, 'Compensatory and Extra-compensation Damages: The Role of "The Albazero" in Modern Contract Damages Claims: Parts I and II' (1997) 12 *Journal of Contract Law* 1 and 97.

[7] *Albacruz v Albazero (The Albazero)* [1977] AC 774.

[8] *Dunlop v Lambert* (1839) 6 Cl & Fin 600, 7 ER 824 (HL).

[9] *Alfred McAlpine Construction Ltd v Panatown Ltd* [2001] AC 518 Lord Clyde at 523–28, Lord Goff at 539, Lord Jauncey at 565, Lord Millett at 582, and see below at text to n75. Lord Diplock in *The Albazero* said [1977] AC 774 at 843 that he found the reasoning in *Dunlop v Lambert* 'baffling'.

[10] *Alfred McAlpine Construction Ltd v Panatown Ltd* [2001] AC 518.

[11] The phrase was first used in *GUS Property Management Ltd v Littlewoods Mail Order Stores Ltd* 1982 SC (HL) 157 at 166 Lord Stewart, and Lord Keith on appeal at 177. It was adopted by Lord Browne-Wilkinson in *St Martin's Property Corp Ltd v Sir Robert McAlpine Ltd* [1994] 1 AC 85 at 109, and by various of their Lordships in *Alfred McAlpine Construction Ltd v Panatown Ltd* [2001] AC 518 (HL) at 529, 568–69, 573–75. One judge has noted in passing that it may not be wholly apt: 'I am not

In addition, the *Albazero* principle has, in the carriage of goods by sea context, been codified in section 2(4) of the Carriage of Goods by Sea Act 1992. By that section the lawful holder of the bill of lading (who therefore has direct contractual rights against the carrier) may exercise his contractual rights 'for the benefit of the person who sustained the loss or damage'.[12] As in the common law *Albazero* principle, the claimant (consignee of the bill of lading) is suing under his own cause of action but for someone else's loss.[13] The Law Commission explained that this was necessary because sometimes the bank or forwarding agent, rather than the property owner, was the lawful holder of the bill of lading.[14] The claimant will then have a duty to account for the damages recovered in respect of the third party's loss to that third party.[15]

(b) The Extension of the *Albazero* Principle to Defective or Incomplete Construction

The *Albazero* principle was extended by the House of Lords in *St Martin's Property Corporation Ltd v Sir Robert McAlpine Ltd*[16] to cover construction contracts where the land on which the construction was to be performed was transferred by the claimant to a third party after the contract had been entered into. In that case at the time of contracting the builder could have foreseen that parts of the development might be sold to third parties,[17] and that those third parties would not have a direct cause of action against the builder (not least because there was a non-assignment term in the main contract).[18] The claimant was permitted to recover the cost of cure (in contrast to compensation arising out of damage or destruction of which the principle permitted recovery in the carriage of goods cases).

Because Lord Griffiths based his decision in *St Martin's Property* on a broader principle of recovery for loss suffered by the claimant itself (discussed below in section 2.1D), the application of the *Albazero* principle in this context has come also to be known as the 'narrow ground' of the decision in *St Martin's Property*, viz recovery of damages on behalf of a third party that must then be accounted for to the third party.

---

wholly convinced that it is helpful to compare the situation of a person who finds himself out of pocket on account of the breach of a contract to which he was not a party with the extraordinary gravitational pull of the dense collections of mass in outer space that are colloquially known as black holes but, one way or another, that is how they have come to be known', *Gordon v Turcan Connell* 2009 SCLR 336 (Court of Session, Outer House).

[12] This section of the Carriage of Goods by Sea Act appears to have no requirement that it was foreseeable that the goods would be sold after the contract was entered into, unlike the common law rule from *The Albazero*.

[13] *Pace Shipping Co Ltd v Churchgate Nigeria Ltd (The Pace) (No 2)* [2010] EWHC 2828 (Comm) (Burton J) at para 28.

[14] Ibid at para 22.

[15] Ibid at para 30.

[16] *St Martin's Property Corporation Ltd v Sir Robert McAlpine Ltd*, reported with *Linden Gardens Trust Ltd v Lenesta Sludge Disposals Ltd* [1994] 1 AC 85 (HL).

[17] Ibid at 114.

[18] Ibid at 114–15.

A further extension was made by the Court of Appeal in *Darlington BC v Wiltshier Northern Ltd*.[19] In that case finance company Morgan Grenfell engaged a construction company to build a leisure centre on council land (this being a preferable arrangement, as a result of restrictions on councils' borrowing, to the council borrowing the money and engaging the builders itself). The finance company excluded in its contract with the council liability to the council for defect or incompletion, but did assign to the council the rights to sue under the construction contract. The assignment, of course, could only give the council the same rights as the finance company had had, but the Court of Appeal held that those rights included the right to recover substantive damages on behalf of the council.

The extension in the *Darlington* case was approved, obiter, by a majority of the House of Lords in *Alfred McAlpine Construction Ltd v Panatown Ltd*,[20] where at the time of contracting (and thereafter) the employer of the building contractor did not own the land on which the offices and car park were to be built, that land being owned by another company in the group (the contracts being arranged this way for VAT-saving reasons).[21]

(c) No Need for the Claimant to Have Owned the Property at the Time of Contracting

The significance of the *Darlington* extension, approved by the majority in *McAlpine v Panatown*, is that as a result of that case, the principle permitting recovery on behalf of a third party is no longer restricted to cases in which the claimant at the time of contracting was owner of the property that was to be carried or built upon. *Darlington* permits recovery in cases such as itself and *McAlpine v Panatown*, where the claimant never owned the property, and so could never have suffered the loss itself. It should apply, for example, in the case of a husband engaging a builder to repair the roof of the house that is in his wife's name.[22] It has also been applied to a case where a claimant aircraft lessee's loss had been covered by a third party under a maintenance agreement (the claimant recovering for the third party).[23]

---

[19] *Darlington Borough Council v Wiltshier Northern Ltd* [1995] 1 WLR 68 (CA). See also *John Harris Partnership v Groveworld Ltd* (1999) 75 Con LR 7 (Thornton QC) obiter; *Earl's Terrace Properties Ltd v Nilsson Design Ltd* [2004] EWHC 136 (TCC) (Thornton QC) at paras 67 ff; *Catlin Estates Ltd v Carter-Jonas (a firm)* [2005] EWHC 2315 (TCC) (HHJ Toulmin); *Mirant Asia-Pacific Construction (Hong Kong) Ltd v Ove Arup and Partners International Ltd* [2007] EWHC 918 (TCC) (HHJ Toulmin) obiter; and in Scotland, *McLaren Murdoch & Hamilton Ltd v Abercromby Motor Group Ltd* (2002) 100 Con LR 63 (Lord Drummond Young) obiter.

[20] *Alfred McAlpine Construction Ltd v Panatown Ltd* [2001] AC 518 (Lord Millett at 585 disapproved). See also *John Harris Partnership v Groveworld*, 3 March 1999 (HHJ Thornton) at para 82.

[21] Lord Millett, in the minority on this, was of the view that the extension was not justified and *Darlington v Wiltshier* should be explained as an application of Lord Griffiths' broad ground, discussed below.

[22] Lord Griffiths' example in *St Martin's Property* [1994] 1 AC 85 at 96–97, although Lord Griffiths employed the example to support a substantial award to the husband for his own loss, not damages to be held for the benefit of the third party wife.

[23] *Sabena Technics SA v Singapore Airlines Ltd* [2003] EWHC 1318 (Comm) (Colman J).

(d) The Claimant Must Account to the Third Party for the Damages Recovered

The claimant who recovers under this principle is then required to account to the third party for the damages recovered in respect of the third party's loss.[24]

(e) The Third Party Cannot Compel the Claimant to Bring the Action

The third party is not able to compel the claimant to bring the action if it does not want to do so.[25]

(f) Requirement of Contemplation that the Third Party May Suffer Harm

The fundamental requirement of *The Albazero* principle appears to be that the parties contemplated at that time of contracting that the third party might suffer harm (or, in other words, that the contract might benefit the third party).[26] One judge has interpreted the principle as applying whenever

> it was in the contemplation of the parties to the relevant contract that an identified third party, or at least a third party falling within an identified class, would or might suffer damage in the event that there was a breach of the contract.[27]

Thus although *Darlington v Wiltshier* was not a case of property that the parties contemplated would pass to the third party, as in the carriage of goods cases from which the *Albazero* principle originated, it was still important that 'It was plainly obvious to Wiltshier throughout that the Dolphin Centre was being constructed for the benefit of the council on the council's land'.[28]

(g) Requirement of Intention that the Claimant Have a Right to Claim?; Inapplicability of the Principle where the Third Party has a Direct Cause of Action

Foreseeing that the third party may suffer harm cannot itself be enough; otherwise the *Albazero* principle would apply to all third party cases. The relevance of foreseeing that the contract will or may benefit the third party is probably that the foresight that the contract benefits the third party is evidence and raises a rebuttable presumption that the claimant is intended to have a right to sue for the third party's loss.[29]

---

[24] *The Albazero* Lord Diplock [1977] AC 774 at 844–45. See also *McAlpine v Panatown* Lord Jauncey [2001] AC 518 at 573, Lord Browne-Wilkinson at 575, Lord Millett at 594.

[25] *The Albazero* Lord Diplock [1977] AC 774 at 845; *White v Jones* [1995] 2 AC 207 (HL) Lord Goff at 267; *McAlpine v Panatown* Lord Clyde [2001] AC 518 at 536, Lord Browne-Wilkinson at 575.

[26] *The Albazero* Lord Diplock [1977] AC 774 at 847; *Rolls Royce Power Engineering plc v Ricardo Consulting Engineers Ltd* [2003] EWHC 2871 (Seymour QC) obiter at para 124; *McAlpine v Panatown* Lord Goff [2001] AC 518 at 540.

[27] HHJ Seymour obiter in *Rolls Royce Power Engineering plc v Ricardo Consulting Engineers Ltd* [2003] EWHC 2871 at para 121, also para 124. That test was held not to have been satisfied in the *Rolls Royce* case itself.

[28] Dillon LJ [1995] 1 WLR 68 at 75.

[29] This is similar to the test in section 1 of the Contracts (Rights of Third Parties) Act 1999, where the contract purporting to confer a benefit on a third party gives rise to a rebuttable presumption that the parties intend the contract to be enforceable by the third party.

It is certainly clear that some sort of intention test applies, although the courts are not always precise as to what it is. The House of Lords in *St Martin's Property* justified the applicability of the *Albazero* principle on the basis that there was a prohibition against assignment of the claimant's rights against the defendant, and therefore the contract was made 'on the footing' that the claimant would be able to claim on behalf of the third party.[30] This logic is imperfect, as the existence of a right to assign would only be of significance if the claimant already had a right to recover damages upon the third party suffering loss (which right could then be assigned).[31] However the test of whether the contract was made 'on the footing' that the claimant would be able to claim on behalf of the third party appears nevertheless to be the applicable test, as applied in *Darlington v Wiltshier* (where the defendant knew that the third party had a right to call for assignment of the claimant's rights).[32]

And in *St Martin's Property*, Lord Browne-Wilkinson justified the rule as based on an imputed intention that the third party will benefit from the contract,[33] which presumably includes benefiting through recovery of damages even if the defendant breaches (although only if the claimant chooses to enforce the *Albazero* right). The Court of Appeal in *McAlpine v Panatown* relied directly on an intention test, requiring (and finding) an intention that the claimant had a right to recover substantial damages,[34] and Lord Millett in *McAlpine v Panatown* confirmed that the *Albazero* rule rested on imputed intention.[35]

It is clearly established that the rule does not apply where the third party has (or is contemplated to have) a direct contractual right against the defendant,[36] especially when that direct right will be in different terms to the claimant and defendant's contract.[37] In such a case there is no 'black hole' that needs filling by the rule.[38] This may well be because the direct cause of action affects whether the parties intended the claimant to be able to recover for the third party's loss, ie that this is part of the intention principle.[39] Thus in *McAlpine v Panatown*, there was no black hole, as the employer company had procured that the third party entered into a duty of care deed directly with the third party company (although on slightly different terms to the main contract and without an arbitration clause). Structuring the contracts in

---

[30] *St Martin's Property* Lord Browne-Wilkinson [1994] 1 AC 85 at 114–15. Lord Goff has subsequently observed that the non-assignment clause would appear to mean that the parties plainly did not intend that the contract was entered into for the benefit of the third parties, although that case dealt with a slightly different point: *White v Jones* [1995] 2 AC 207 (HL) at 267. Lord Clyde has questioned the relevance of the prohibition on assignment: *McAlpine v Panatown* [2001] AC 518 at 531.

[31] *Darlington v Wiltshier* Dillon LJ [1995] 1 WLR 68 at 74.

[32] *Darlington v Wiltshier* Dillon LJ ibid at 74, also Steyn LJ at 79–80. As to the assignability of the claimant's contract with the defendant not barring the application of the *Albazero* principle, see also *McAlpine v Panatown* Lord Clyde [2001] AC 518 at 531 (and in that case the rights were assignable with the consent of the defendant, such consent not to be unreasonably withheld).

[33] *St Martin's Property* Lord Browne-Wilkinson [1994] 1 AC 85 at 114.

[34] *Alfred McAlpine Construction Ltd v Panatown Ltd* (1998) 58 Con LR 46 at 96.

[35] *McAlpine v Panatown* [2001] AC 518 at 594.

[36] *The Albazero* Lord Diplock [1977] AC 774 at 847–48; *St Martin's Property* Lord Browne-Wilkinson [1994] 1 AC 85 at 115; *McAlpine v Panatown* Lord Clyde [2001] AC 518 at 530–32, Lord Jauncey at 568, Lord Browne-Wilkinson at 575 and 577, Lord Millett at 594.

[37] *McAlpine v Panatown* Lord Clyde [2001] AC 518 at 531.

[38] *McAlpine v Panatown* Lord Browne-Wilkinson ibid at 575 and 577.

[39] *McAlpine v Panatown* Lord Clyde [2001] AC 518 at 530–31. Cf *The Albazero* Lord Diplock [1977] AC 774 at 847–48.

this way, such that the third party had a direct cause of action, evidenced an intention that the claimant should not itself have a right to claim damages on behalf of the third party.[40] (In contrast, the Court of Appeal in *McAlpine v Panatown* had been of the view that the duty of care deed, which provided more limited cover than the claimant had, did not as a matter of construction evidence such an intention.[41]) A direct tort action under the Defective Premises Act 1972 has been held, however, not to bar the right under *The Albazero*.[42]

Since 1855, there will usually be a direct contractual right in carriage of goods by sea (but not land) cases, where the lawful holder of a bill of lading has a statutory right to sue the carrier (as was the case in *The Albazero* itself).[43]

Finally, it should be noted that although the majority of judges rely on the intention of the parties, the need for such foresight or intention was doubted in *McAlpine v Panatown* by Lords Clyde and Millett, who preferred to see the rule as imposed by law (although excludable by contrary intention).[44]

(h) The Measure of Damages

The principle applies to recovery of damages for property damage or destruction where the claimant contracts with a carrier (or probably any other bailee) of goods and then transfers the goods to a third party, who then suffers the harm.[45]

The principle also applies to recovery of damages for cost of cure (where reasonable and genuinely intended) as a result of defective or incomplete construction on land, either initially owned by the claimant employer but then transferred to a third party,[46] or never owned by the claimant as the defendant knew at the time.[47] It probably also applies to damages for consequential loss.[48]

It is not clear whether the principle permits recovery of other damages for defective or incomplete construction in the above situations, eg damages for the difference in value and/or loss of amenity where paying for a cure is unreasonable. Logically there is no reason why it should not, such loss in the usual way being suffered by the third party and the claimant being liable to account to that third party for any damages.

---

[40] Lord Clyde [2001] AC 518 at 531–32, Lord Goff at 545, but see Lord Millett at 584.

[41] (1995) 58 Con LR 46 at 99.

[42] *Catlin Estates Ltd v Carter-Jonas (a firm)* [2005] EWHC 2315 (TCC) (HHJ Toulmin) at para 304.

[43] By the Bills of Lading Act 1855, replaced by the Carriage of Goods by Sea Act 1992. Accordingly, there is little case law in the carriage context in which the *Albazero* principle has been applied. The situation does sometimes arise where there is no direct cause of action: see *Pace Shipping Co Ltd v Churchgate Nigeria Ltd* [2010] EWHC 2828 (Comm) (Burton J) and the point made by the Law Commission referred to above at text to n 14.

[44] *McAlpine v Panatown* [2001] AC 518 at 530–31 and 582–83 respectively.

[45] *The Albazero* obiter. Also, for carriage at sea, s 2(4) Carriage of Goods by Sea Act 1992.

[46] *St Martin's Property.*

[47] *Darlington v Wiltshier*; *McAlpine v Panatown* obiter.

[48] *McAlpine v Panatown* Lord Clyde [2001] AC 518 at 530–31.

(i) Other Service Cases

It is not clear whether the principle applies to contracts other than carriage and construction.[49] It cannot apply to all third party contracts, because it is clear from the House of Lords decision of *Beswick v Beswick* that a claimant cannot recover substantial damages on behalf of a third party where the defendant breaches an obligation to pay the third party,[50] even though in such a case it must have been contemplated that the third party would suffer loss and the promisee claimant would not.

In *Jackson v Horizon Holidays Ltd*[51] the Court of Appeal upheld an award of £500 damages for mental distress caused by defective holiday accommodation that the claimant had engaged for himself, his wife and their two children. James LJ appeared to regard this as damages for the claimant's own distress,[52] but Denning MR was clear that the recovery was both for the claimant and for the benefit of his family.[53] Denning MR gave the following example:

> A host makes a contract with a restaurant for a dinner for himself and his friends. The vicar makes a contract for a coach trip for the choir. In all these cases there is only one person who makes the contract. It is the husband, the host or the vicar, as the case may be. Sometimes he pays the whole price himself. Occasionally he may get a contribution from the others. But in any case it is he who makes the contract ... the real truth is that in each instance, the father, the host or the vicar, was making a contract himself for the benefit of the whole party. In short, a contract by one for the benefit of third persons ... Suppose the holiday firm puts the family into a hotel which is only half built and the visitors have to sleep on the floor? Or suppose the restaurant is fully booked and the guests have to go away, hungry and angry, having spent so much on fares to get there? Or suppose the coach leaves the choir stranded half-way and they have to hire cars to get home? None of them individually can sue. Only the father, the host or the vicar can sue. He can, of course, recover his own damages. But can he not recover for the others? I think he can.

Denning MR concluded:

> I consider it to be an established rule of law that where a contract is made with A. for the benefit of B., A. can sue on the contract for the benefit of B. and recover all that B. could have recovered if the contract had been made with B. himself.[54]

---

[49] See also *John Harris Partnership v Groveworld Ltd* (1999) 75 Con LR 7 (Thornton QC) at para 81, confirming that the principle applied to property-related contracts other than building contracts.

[50] *Beswick v Beswick* [1968] AC 58. However, Lord Pearce at 88 was of the view that substantial damages were recoverable. See also *Woodar Investment Development Ltd v Wimpey Construction Co Ltd* where Fox J and then the Court of Appeal awarded substantial damages 'for the use and benefit of' the third party when the defendant failed in breach to make a payment to that third party. However, the House of Lords by a majority allowed the appeal on the basis that there had not been repudiation: [1980] 1 WLR 277 (HL). Lord Wilberforce (with whom Lord Scarman, dissenting, agreed) reserved his view on whether substantial damages would have been available. Lord Scarman at 300 thought that some award for substantial damages should have been available for the claimant's own loss (not for the use or benefit of the third party). Lord Russell at 293, dissenting, would have allowed the appeal on the award, and awarded only nominal damages.

[51] *Jackson v Horizon Holidays Ltd* [1975] 1 WLR 1468 (CA).

[52] Ibid at 1474. This approach was approved by Lord Russell and Lord Keith in *Woodar v Wimpey* [1980] 1 WLR 277 at 293–94 and 297 respectively.

[53] [1975] 1 WLR at 1472.

[54] Ibid at 1473.

As *Beswick v Beswick* shows, this goes too far, and it has been expressly disapproved (obiter).[55] There has been (obiter) judicial approval for James LJ's explanation of the result in *Jackson*,[56] although Lord Wilberforce has stated that Lord Denning may be correct as regards a narrower principle applicable to cases such as 'family holidays, ordering meals in restaurants for a party, hiring a taxi for a group'.[57] (There has also been a suggestion that a claimant in a case such as *Jackson* may recover substantial damages for his own loss resulting merely from a failure to confer a benefit on a third party.[58] This principle is discussed below.[59])

In *White v Jones* a direct cause of action (in tort) was found between the third party beneficiary and the defendant, and (the promisee not having sued) the House of Lords did not decide either way whether the promisee could have recovered substantial damages under the *Albazero* principle,[60] although doubts were expressed on the basis that the loss suffered by the third party was not a loss that could ever have been suffered by the claimant (unlike in the *Albazero* line of cases or *St Martin's Property* where if the claimant had owned the property it would have suffered the loss).[61]

21.2 Recovery by a Claimant of its Own Loss

Where a defendant breaches a contract that benefits a third party, it may be that the claimant has itself suffered loss for which it can recover.

A. Shareholder Claims where the Loss to the Third Party Company Causes a £ for £ Loss to the Claimant

Where a company and its shareholder both have a cause of action, and the shareholder's loss merely reflects (by way of diminution in the value of the shareholder's shareholding) the loss to the company, only the company and not the shareholder may sue, by the company law principle of 'no reflective loss'.[62]

---

[55] *Woodar Investment Development Ltd v Wimpey Construction Co Ltd* [1980] 1 WLR 277 (HL) Lords Wilberforce and Russell at 284 and 293–94. Denning MR's approach was not taken in the construction case of *Forster v Silvermere Golf & Equestrian Centre Ltd* (1981) 42 P & CR 255 (Dillon J) where the claimant and her children suffered loss of their home.

[56] *Woodar v Wimpey* Lord Russell [1980] 1 WLR 277 at 293–94 and Lord Keith at 297. Lord Wilberforce also said this *may* be correct at 284.

[57] Ibid at 284. See also Lord Keith's similar but vaguer statements at 297.

[58] *McAlpine v Panatown* Lord Goff [2001] AC 518 at 552 and 543, and Lord Millett at 588.

[59] See section 21.2, especially sub-section D.

[60] *White v Jones* [1995] 2 AC 207 (HL) Lord Goff at 267.

[61] Ibid Lord Mustill at 282, also Lord Goff at 267. Cf See also *John Harris Partnership v Groveworld Ltd* (1999) 75 Con LR 7 (Thornton QC) at para 71.

[62] This is the rule from *Foss v Harbottle* (1843) 2 Hare 461, explained in *Johnson v Gore Wood & Co (a firm)* [2002] 2 AC 1 (HL). But see the exception in *Perry v Day* [2005] 2 BCLC 405 (Rich QC) disapplying the principle where the company has been disabled from suing by the defendant's own actions.

Save in such cases, a shareholder may claim damages in contract (or under other causes of action) where it has suffered loss as a result of damage primarily suffered by the company.

This arises most frequently where there is a corporate group whereby the claimant company happens to have contracted with the defendant although the contract primarily affects a different company in the group. Thus in *George Fischer (Great Britain) Ltd v Multi Construction Ltd and Dexion Ltd*, the claimant parent company recovered substantial damages from the defendant construction contractor who installed defective equipment at the storage and distribution centre of the group.[63] The cost of repairs was borne by the claimant. The lost profits were borne initially by the two wholly-owned manufacturing subsidiaries of the claimant and the wholly-owned distribution and sales subsidiary of the claimant (the latter being the company occupying and operating the distribution centre). However, it was proven that 'a £1 loss to the subsidiary company as a result of a breach of contract would result in a £1 loss to the balance sheet or profits of the holding company' and so the parent company indirectly suffered loss by diminution in value of its shareholding in the subsidiaries (there being no loss of dividends proven), and this loss was not too remote. It remains for the claimant to prove that the subsidiary's loss amounts (pound-for-pound or otherwise) to a loss to the parent or other shareholder.[64] (In corporate group cases, the claimant company may, despite having a contractual right against the defendant builder (for example), not have suffered a loss in the value of its shareholding or otherwise. In such cases the claimant may nevertheless suffer loss, either under the *Albazero* principle or the broad ground by which it can demonstrate that it has suffered a financial or non-financial loss.[65])

Other examples include a shareholder recovering substantial damages for breach of an inter-shareholder agreement by misuse of confidential information and diversion of lucrative business from the company.[66] Likewise, a claim under a share purchase agreement is a claim by a shareholder against the seller of the shares, but will often take the form (in a breach of warranty claim) of a complaint as to defects or other matters in the underlying company in which the claimant bought shares.[67]

(A similar issue arises where the claim is by the company for its own loss, but where that loss (eg the costs of borrowing or entering a swap) are primarily suffered by a different company in the group, such as a treasury entity. In such cases it is necessary to show that by contracts or accounting or other arrangements the treasury entity in fact passes on its costs pound-for-pound to the claimant company.[68])

---

[63] *George Fischer (Great Britain) Ltd v Multi Construction Ltd and Dexion Ltd* [1995] 1 BCLC 260 (CA).

[64] The majority found that this was not proven in the patent case of *Gerber Garment Technology Ltd v Lectra Systems Ltd* [1997] RPC 443 (CA).

[65] This was the situation in *Alfred McAlpine Construction Ltd v Panatown Ltd* [2001] AC 518 (HL), although the company who directly suffered the loss had a direct cause of action by a collateral warranty deed and so the findings as to recovery by the contracting customer company were obiter. See also *Earl's Terrace Properties Ltd v Nilsson Design Ltd* [2004] EWHC 136 (TCC) (Thornton QC) at paras 67 ff. See further section 21.2 below, also chapter 16, section 16.12B above.

[66] *Giles v Rhind* [2003] Ch 618 (CA).

[67] See further chapter nine above.

[68] *Bank of Scotland v Dunedin Property Investment Co Ltd* (Court of Session, Outer House), 14 March 1997, obiter, appeal allowed on a different point but affirming on this point: 1998 SCLR 531

A simpler example arose in *De Jongh Weill v Mean Fiddler Holdings*.[69] The defendant breached a contractual promise to the claimant to issue shares to a third party company representing the claimant's family interests, to be nominated. No such company was nominated, but nevertheless it was not difficult for the court to find that the loss was the claimant's (ie the payment to the company was to compensate him and would benefit him) and/or that every pound of loss to the company would be a loss to the claimant.

B. Where the Sale of Property to the Third Party is *Res Inter Alios Acta*

In some cases the claimant contracting party has not suffered loss because the loss arises in relation to property that it no longer owns. In some such cases the court will treat the alienation of the property as *res inter alios acta* and to be disregarded, and therefore the claimant is permitted to recover as if it were still the property owner.[70] This principle has an uneasy fit with the *Albazero* principle.

C. Where the Claimant is Liable to the Third Party as a Result of the Defendant's Breach

It is uncontroversial that where a claimant is liable to a third party as a result of the defendant's breach, the claimant can recover from the defendant an indemnity for that liability, subject to the ordinary rules of remoteness.[71] A sub-contractor who breaches its contract with the main contractor will be liable to compensate the main contractor in the amount of the main contractor's consequent liability to the employer. Similarly, where an employer of works on a third party's land has undertaken liability to the third party for the works, the employer will be able to pass on that liability to the contractor.[72] Sale of goods cases also commonly lead to recovery for an indemnity of the liability the claimant has incurred to a third party as a result of the defendant's breach.[73]

Indeed, the origin of *The Albazero* rule, the case of *Dunlop v Lambert*, is probably merely an application of this principle: in the latter case, as is not unusual, risk did not pass with the property, such that the seller of goods/consignor of the bill of lading (the claimant) remained at risk, ie liable to the third party buyer for damage to the goods, even though no longer the owner. Where the consignor (claimant) had

(Court of Session, Inner House); *ACC Bank plc v Johnston* [2011] IEHC 376 (Irish High Court) at paras 3.7–3.8.

[69] *De Jongh Weill v Mean Fiddler Holdings Ltd*, 22 July 2005 (Coles QC) [2005] All ER (D) 331 at paras 24–30.
[70] See above in chapter sixteen, section 16.12B.
[71] See the dictum of Lord Keith in *Woodar Investment Development Ltd v Wimpey Construction Co Ltd* [1980] 1 WLR 277 (HL) at 297. See further chapter twenty below.
[72] The difficulty in *Darlington v Wiltshier* and *McApline v Panatown* was that in neither case had the employer undertaken such liability to the third party land owner (and indeed in *Darlington* the liability had been expressly excluded).
[73] See above in chapter four.

539

a special contract with the carrier even though no longer the lawful holder of the bill of lading, it could sue under that contract for damages indemnifying him for his liability to the third party.[74]

Likewise, it may be the case that a contractor for works on a third party's land would, as an implied part of its licence to engage works on that third party's land, also have an obligation to seek to complete the works.[75]

D. Lord Griffiths' Broad Ground: The Claimant is Not Liable to the Third Party but Has Paid or Will Pay the Cost of Cure

(i) The Principle Permitting Recovery of the Cost of Cure

In the *St Martin's Property Corporation Ltd v Sir Robert McAlpine Ltd* case, in which (as explained above) the House of Lords extended the *Albazero* principle (of recovery of a third party's losses for benefit of the third party) to contracts for construction on land, Lord Griffiths also sought to rely upon a broader ground. The broader ground was not supported by the rest of the House,[76] but did gain majority support of the House of Lords in *Alfred McAlpine Construction Ltd v Panatown Ltd*,[77] albeit obiter, and therefore is now good law.

Lord Griffiths gave the following example in the *St Martin's* case:

> the matrimonial home is owned by the wife and the couple's remaining assets are owned by the husband and he is the sole earner. The house requires a new roof and the husband places a contract with a builder to carry out the work. The husband is not acting as agent for his wife, he makes the contract as principal because only he can pay for it. The builder fails to replace the roof properly and the husband has to call in and pay another builder to complete the work.[78]

In Lord Griffiths' view, the husband can recover 'the cost of putting it right', and has himself suffered the financial loss 'because he has to spend money to give him the benefit of the bargain which the defendant had promised but failed to deliver'.[79]

An example of this principle in action may well be *Radford v De Froberville*,[80] where (as Lord Millett explained in *McAlpine v Panatown*[81]), the landlord suffered

---

[74] See the explanation of Lord Clyde in *Alfred McAlpine Construction Ltd v Panatown Ltd* [2001] AC 518 at 523–28.

[75] Lord Goff in *Alfred McAlpine Construction Ltd v Panatown Ltd* [2001] AC 518 at 560. This raises a circular argument: if there is an implied obligation, as Lord Goff suggests, to use damages recovered from a defendant to complete the works, can that be enough of a liability to the third party to found the right to recover those damages from the defendant? On Lord Goff's view, there is no need for such a liability to found the right of recovery, as the claimant can recover substantial damages anyway, as discussed below.

[76] Lords Keith and Bridge [1994] 1 AC 85 at 95 and 96 were sympathetic to Lord Griffiths' view but did not express a concluded opinion.

[77] Lord Goff [2001] AC 518 at 546 ff, Lord Jauncey at 574, Lord Millett at 590–91. Steyn LJ, in a minority of one, also relied on this ground in *Darlington v Wiltshier* [1995] 1 WLR 68 at 80, and Lord Millett in *McAlpine v Panatown* [2001] AC 518 at 585 agreed that *Darlington v Wiltshier* was best explained on this ground.

[78] [1994] 1 AC 85 at 96.

[79] Ibid at 97.

[80] *Radford v De Froberville* [1977] 1 WLR 1262 (Oliver J).

[81] *McAlpine v Panatown* Lord Millett [2001] AC 518 at 589–90, but see Lord Jauncey at 572.

no loss of amenity or financial difference in value but still obtained the cost of cure in relation to the covenanted wall so as to replace it for the exclusive benefit of the tenants.

(ii) The Claimant Must Intend to Do the Work

It appears to be essential to this principle that the claimant has incurred or will incur the cost of cure,[82] although it may do so indirectly (eg another incurs the cost but the claimant will reimburse for it[83]).

(iii) No Need to Account to the Third Party

Under this rule, the claimant recovers for his own loss, and it is not yet clear whether the claimant is liable to account to anyone for his recovery, although the better view is probably that he is not (given that the claimant is recovering for his own loss and not a third party's).[84]

(iv) Excluded by the Existence of a Direct Cause of Action?

The existence of an independent cause of action between the third party and defendant may show that the claimant does not have an intention to do the work, and in *McAlpine v Panatown* the duty of care deed between the defendant and third party was what convinced the judges who supported Lord Griffiths' broad ground that it nevertheless could not apply in that case.[85] However, for Lord Millett this was because of double recovery (and the building employer's action should usually be stayed pending the building owner's action) and not because a direct cause of action by the third party affected the claimant's claim in relation to its own loss.[86] (Lord Goff was of the view that despite the duty of care deed there should be substantial recovery, as is discussed in the next section.) Indeed, in another case, where it was expected that there would be a direct cause of action by a direct warranty, but the intermediate party failed to procure one, it was held that the broad ground was nevertheless excluded because the parties expected and contemplated the direct right of recovery.[87]

---

[82] Lord Griffiths [1994] 1 AC 85 at 97. *McAlpine v Panatown* Lord Clyde [2001] AC 518 at 532, Lord Jauncey at 569–71 and 574–75, but see Lord Millett at 592. *Bovis Lend Lease Ltd v RD Fire Protection Ltd* (2003) 89 Con LR 69 (Thornton QC) at paras 178, 183 and 191–94, where the lack of an intention was one of the grounds for refusal of the claim.

[83] *Bovis Lend Lease Ltd v RD Fire Protection Ltd* (2003) 89 Con LR 69: the important thing, Thornton QC at para 183 obiter, is that the damages 'will find their way to the person who is thereby out of pocket'.

[84] *St Martin's Property* Lord Griffiths [1994] 1 AC 85 at 97 (the claimant need account to the third party); *Darlington v Wiltshier* Steyn LJ [1995] 1 WLR 68 at 80 (the claimant need not account); *McAlpine v Panatown* Lord Clyde [2001] AC 518 at 532 (the claimant need not account), Lord Jauncey at 572 (the claimant need not account), Lord Browne-Wilkinson at 577 (did not express a view but summarised the point), Lord Millett at 592 (the claimant need not account).

[85] *McAlpine v Panatown* Lord Jauncey ibid at 574.

[86] *McAlpine v Panatown* Lord Millett ibid at 594–95.

[87] *Bovis Lend Lease Ltd v RD Fire Protection Ltd* (2003) 89 Con LR 69 (Thornton QC) at 185–90.

(v) Commentary

On proper analysis, this is only an incremental extension from ordinary contract law. The defendant's breach causes a foreseeable cost to the claimant in making good the benefit to the third party—the cost of cure. True the claimant is not liable to make the payment to the third party, but the payment is nevertheless a direct and proximate consequence, and falls within the ordinary rules of causation, remoteness and mitigation permitting all reasonable payments to be recovered.[88]

The difficulty is not so much with Lord Griffiths' broad ground, but with how it fits in with the *Albazero* principle. As has been shown above, Lord Griffiths' example of a husband engaging a roof contractor for the home held in his wife's name should also give rise to damages for the benefit of the wife under that principle. But the husband cannot recover both cost of cure damages for the benefit of the wife, and substantial damages for his own costs in choosing to cure the damage. The answer should be that where the *Albazero* principle applies, the husband cannot recover under Lord Griffiths' broader ground because (as in the case where the wife has a direct cause of action) the husband is not in fact going to perform the cure (the wife having recovered, through the husband, just the monies needed to do so).

A further difficulty is in rationalising this approach with the decision of the House of Lords in *Beswick v Beswick*.[89] Lord Clyde stated in *McAlpine v Panatown* that:

> It can cover the case where A contracts with B to pay a sum of money to C and B fails to do so. The loss to A is in the necessity to find other funds to pay to C and provided that he is going to pay C, or indeed has done so, he should be able to recover the sum by way of damages for breach of contract from B. If it was evident that A had no intention to pay C, having perhaps changed his mind, then he would not be able to recover the amount from B because he would have sustained no loss, and his damages would at best be nominal.[90]

This seems logical, but is directly inconsistent with the result in *Beswick v Beswick*, where the majority held that only nominal damages were available and therefore specific performance was awarded. It might be said that on the facts of *Beswick v Beswick* the promisee estate, which had no money, did not therefore intend to cover for the third party the maintenance the defendant had promised to pay (which is supported by comments of Lord Upjohn[91]), although in general terms this is somewhat surprising, as in many cases of a cost of cure the genuine intention to pay for the cure *if damages are recovered* is sufficient to justify the award of those damages. It might be that Lord Griffiths' broad ground (like the *Albazero* principle) does not apply to such contracts and is, for example, limited to contracts for construction or other services.[92]

The better answer is probably that the law has moved on since *Beswick v Beswick*, and that the court did not have benefit of being able to consider the deci-

---

[88] See eg *Banco de Portugal v Waterlow & Sons Ltd* [1932] AC 452.
[89] *Beswick v Beswick* [1968] AC 58.
[90] [2001] AC 518 at 533. See also the comments of Lord Scarman in *Woodar Investment Development Ltd v Wimpey Construction Co Ltd* [1980] 1 WLR 277 (HL) at 300 ff.
[91] [1968] AC 58 at 102.
[92] Lord Millett limited the principle to contracts of work and materials in *McAlpine v Panatown* [2001] AC 518 at 591.

sions in *St Martin's Property* and *McAlpine v Panatown*. That the claimant could not recover substantial damages was probably obiter in *Beswick v Beswick*, since although that assumed inadequacy of damages was one reason for the award of specific performance (which on any view removes the need or justification for any damages award), Lord Pearce took the view that substantial damages would have been available but that specific performance was nevertheless justified as more appropriate.[93] Accordingly, in a *Beswick v Beswick* case where specific performance is not available, on the current state of the law substantial damages are.[94]

E. Lord Goff's Even Broader Ground: the Claimant Suffering Loss per se, Even if Not Spending Anything on the Third Party

The question arises whether the claimant can recover even if it is not liable to spend, and does not intend to spend, its own money paying for a cure or paying the third party. In other words, can it be said that the claimant has suffered a loss recognisable by law merely because it engaged the defendant to do something (which is most directly of benefit to a third party) and the defendant did not do it? This was described by many of the judges in *Alfred McAlpine Construction Ltd v Panatown Ltd* (borrowing from the academic literature) as a claim for simple loss of bargain or of the claimant's 'performance interest'.[95] Lord Millett also emphasised the promisee's 'defeated expectations'.[96]

It seems doubtful whether Lord Griffiths in the *St Martin's* case intended his principle to stretch to this situation. As set out above, he focused on the claimant recovering the financial loss of the cost of cure and only recovering if he was intended to spend the damages on that cure.[97] He sought to distinguish cases where a carrier damages what is by then a third party's property (ie the *Albazero* situation). In those cases the claimant has suffered no financial loss as a result of the damage to or destruction of the cargo.[98]

However, the minority of Lords Goff and Millett in *Alfred McAlpine Construction Ltd v Panatown Ltd* were clear that they supported a broader rule permitting the claimant to recover substantial damages whether or not they would in a particular case reflect a cost of cure (ie whether or not such a cure was possible or reasonable) or be passed to a third party.[99] This would include damages for diminution in value,[100] delay in building something for a third party (where no cure would

---

[93] *Beswick v Beswick* [1968] AC 58 (HL) at 88.

[94] See also Edwin Peel (ed), Treitel, *The Law of Contract*, 13th edn (London, Sweet & Maxwell, 2011) at 634–35.

[95] Lord Goff [2001] AC 518 at 556, Lord Browne-Wilkinson at 577.

[96] Ibid at 588.

[97] And see Lord Clyde's discussion of this point in *McAlpine v Panatown* [2001] AC 518 at 533, where he calls it the 'second formulation' of Lord Griffiths' approach, and disapproves it.

[98] *St Martin's Property* [1994] 1 AC 85 at 97.

[99] Lord Goff [2001] AC 518 at 547–54. Lord Millett at 591–92 and 594.

[100] *Bovis Lend Lease Ltd v RD Fire Protection Ltd* (2003) 89 Con LR 69 (Thornton QC) at para 183.

be possible, or for delay prior to the effecting of a cure)[101] or other consequential loss.[102] It would probably also include damages for failure to provide a pleasurable amenity to a third party, and in this way may explain Lord Denning MR's approval of an award in *Jackson v Horizon* for the family's loss of amenity.[103]

The starting point would be that 'the fact that a contracting party has required services to be supplied at his own cost to a third party is at least prima facie evidence of the value of those services to the party who placed the order'.[104] As Lord Scarman has observed,

> in the absence of evidence to show that he has suffered no loss, A, who has contracted for a payment to be made to C, may rely on the fact that he required the payment to be made as prima facie evidence that the promise for which he contracted was a benefit to him and that the measure of his loss in the event of non-payment is the benefit which he intended for C but which has not been received. Whatever the reason, he must have desired the payment to be made to C and he must have been relying on B to make it.[105]

This value would be easier to demonstrate where the contracting party had a demonstrable legitimate interest in ordering services for a third party, such as a family or commercial relationship, or a charitable intention, but this legitimate interest would not be a separate requirement.[106]

Lord Millett would have limited this ground to contracts for the supply of work and materials.[107] In his view, the rule was not needed in goods cases because property passed to the buyer even if it then went to a third party, whereas in services cases the buyer could not point to such intermediate ownership of property so as to fix a loss.[108]

In this case, on Lord Goff's view, it is irrelevant if the third party has a direct cause of action against the defendant. The claimant is suing for its own, entirely separate, loss.[109] Lord Millett agreed that the loss was separate, but was of the view that the performance interest reflects and could not exceed the interest of the third party property owner and would be reduced by its being satisfied, and so it was necessary to know whether the building owner could pursue its own claim before allowing the contracting party to recover its performance interest.[110]

There is as yet no binding authority for Lords Goff and Millett's approach. It was disapproved by others of their Lordships in *McAlpine v Panatown*, expressing concerns about possible double recovery and the unfairness of the claimant being able to recover substantial damages and keep them himself.[111] In one case the possibility

---

[101] Lord Goff [2001] AC 518 at 554–56, Lord Millett at 587 and 591. Lord Goff notes at 554–55 that this would mean that a liquidated damages clause for delay would not automatically be a penalty, as it would if no damages were recoverable at common law.

[102] Lord Millett ibid at 587.

[103] See *McAlpine v Panatown* Lord Goff [2001] AC 518 at 552–53 and Lord Millett at 588.

[104] *McAlpine v Panatown* Lord Millett ibid at 592.

[105] *Woodar Investment Development Ltd v Wimpey Construction Co Ltd* [1980] 1 WLR 277 (HL) at 300. However, Lord Scarman went on to discuss the need for A to find the money itself.

[106] *McAlpine v Panatown* Lord Millett [2001] AC 518 at 592.

[107] Ibid at 592.

[108] Ibid at 586 and 588–89.

[109] Lord Goff at 558–59. But see Lord Browne-Wilkinson, contra, at 577–78.

[110] Ibid at 595–96.

[111] Lord Clyde ibid at 534.

was considered but rejected on the facts without the need to decide if it did apply.[112] In another it was rejected on the basis that the contract at hand was not one for supply of services.[113] There is a High Court dictum of Thornton QC in the *Bovis* case indicating that the recovery is

> not confined to remedial work costs but, as is clear from the *Ruxley Electronics ...* case, these principles can be extended to any other direct loss arising from an interference such as loss of value or loss arising from an impairment of expectation,

the example given in that case being the sum payable under a settlement agreement to a third party.[114]

It therefore seems that in the right case, the broader ground of allowing recovery of the claimant's own loss where a benefit is not conferred on a third party, even though the claimant will not be put out of pocket by it, is likely to be applied. Moreover, this reference to *Ruxley Electronics* is apposite, as the development of the award of non-pecuniary loss goes very much hand-in-hand with the development of an award of damages for a claimant's (non-pecuniary) loss upon a benefit the claimant paid for not being conferred upon a third party.[115]

Further, in *Fox v British Airways plc*,[116] the Court of Appeal held that a claimant could recover for unfair dismissal and discrimination (or under general tort principles[117]) for his or her estate's loss of the right that the deceased's family be paid death-in-service benefits, following cases cited therein in which the loss of life cover for family was treated as a loss suffered by the claimant dismissed employee or injured party.[118] The contingent diminution in value of the benefits is treated as a pecuniary loss suffered by the claimant notwithstanding that the benefits were never to be paid to the claimant himself.[119] Where an alternative could be obtained in the market, that was the measure of loss, but where it was too late to do so (because the claimant died very shortly after the dismissal) the full value of the benefits that would have paid out to the family was recovered.[120]

---

[112] *And So To Bed Ltd v Dixon*, 21 November 2000 (Donaldson QC). The case concerned a franchise agreement in which the benefit of the franchise's continuation inured both to the franchisor (through franchise payments) and the franchisor's sister company (through the purchase of goods by the franchisee), and in those circumstances the court would not have found any performance interest loss to the franchisor over and above its own financial loss, so as to reflect the benefits the sister company would have earned through supply of goods.

[113] *DRC Distributions Ltd v Ulva Ltd* [2007] EWHC 1716 (QB) (Flaux J) at para 70.

[114] *Bovis Lend Lease Ltd (formerly Bovis Construction Ltd) v RD Fire Protection Ltd* (2003) 89 Con LR 69 (Thornton QC) at paras 183 and 194.

[115] See below in chapter nineteen. And see *McAlpine v Panatown* Lord Millett [2001] AC 518 at 588–89. See B Coote, 'The Performance Interest, *Panatown* and the Problem of Loss' (2001) 117 *LQR* 81; E McKendrick, 'The Common Law at Work: The Saga of Alfred McAlpine Construction Ltd v Panatown Ltd' (2003) 3 *Oxford University Commonwealth Law Journal* 145 and the articles cited above at chapter 19 n 98.

[116] *Fox v British Airways plc* [2013] EWCA Civ 972.

[117] Underhill LJ ibid at para 10.

[118] Ibid para 24.

[119] Ibid paras 25, 28 and 31.

[120] Ibid paras 34–38.

21.3 Third Party Claims under the Contracts (Rights of Third Parties) act 1999

A. The General Rules

The Contracts (Rights of Third Parties) Act 1999 gives a person the right in certain circumstances to enforce a contract to which it is not a party. Section 1(5) of the Act provides that the third party shall have available

> any remedy that would have been available to him in an action for breach of contract if he had been a party to the contract (and the rules relating to damages, injunctions, specific performance and other relief shall apply accordingly).

Accordingly, subject to the next section, damages are recoverable for the third party's loss on ordinary principles of contract damages.

The 1999 Act is excluded by most standard form and commercial contracts, rarely litigated, and so there is no relevant case law concerning the measure of damages under the Act of which this author is aware.

B. Double Recovery

Section 5 of the 1999 Act does provide that the award to the third party shall be reduced to the extent the court thinks appropriate to take account of a sum already recovered by the promisee in respect of 'the third party's loss' or 'the expense to the promisee of making good to the third party the default of the promisor'. In other words, if the promisee recovers damages under the other principles set out in this chapter, the third party's damages will be reduced accordingly. (The opposite would presumably also be true: if the third party has recovered under the Act, a court would be likely to reduce the promisee's damages under common law principles where it felt that otherwise there would be double recovery.)

An analogous double recovery problem arose in *Corbett v Bond Pearce*.[121] This was not a 1999 Act claim, but rather a contractual claim by the personal representative of the deceased against the solicitors responsible for a will, and a concurrent tortious claim by disappointed beneficiaries against the same solicitors under the *White v Jones*[122] principle. The personal representative brought proceedings successfully challenging the second of two wills, and recovered the costs of so doing. The beneficiaries sued the solicitors for failing to procure that the second will was effective, and settled with full recovery. In a subsequent action by the solicitors, the court construed the contractual and tortious duties as complementary and so not covering the same loss.

---

[121] *Corbett v Bond Pearce* [2001] 3 All ER 769 (CA).
[122] *White v Jones* [1995] 2 AC 207 (HL).

22

Wrotham Park *Hypothetical Bargain Damages*

The unusual damages measure of hypothetical bargain damages from the *Wrotham Park* line of authorities. These are compensatory but bear some resemblance to restitutionary damages and have special features.

THERE IS A special type of award of what are often called *Wrotham Park* damages,[1] after the decision in *Wrotham Park Estates Ltd v Parkside Homes Ltd*.[2] The award is also known as 'hypothetical bargain' or 'reasonable licence fee' damages. On their proper analysis and in the light of the weight of modern authority, these are compensatory damages albeit on an unorthodox basis, but they have superficial similarities with and are often confused with restitutionary damages, a non-compensatory award discussed in the next chapter.

22.1 The *Wrotham Park* Decision

The award grew out of property disputes such as the *Wrotham Park* case itself. There the defendant property developers, in building their Kentish housing estate of 14 houses and a road, breached a restrictive covenant, which had been entered into in 1935 by predecessors in title and provided that the defendant's land could only be developed in accordance with a particular written planned layout.[3] The claimant sought and was refused a mandatory injunction to force the defendant to knock down the development, and could not prove any loss of financial value of its own property (the Wrotham Park estate). Drawing an analogy with the reasonable

---

[1] Pronounced 'Root-um' Park.
[2] *Wrotham Park Estates Ltd v Parkside Homes Ltd* [1974] 1 WLR 798 (Brightman J).
[3] Although essentially contractual, a restrictive covenant is also a proprietary interest and runs with the land, therefore binding successors in title to the two neighbouring tenements in modification of the ordinary rules of privity.

licence fee damages ('wayleave rent') awarded in tortious trespass cases (and also contractual cases of unauthorised use of property[4]), where damages can be measured by the reasonable fee that would have been payable for the trespass even if greater than the damage to the property,[5] Brightman J awarded damages measured by 'such a sum of money as might reasonably have been demanded by the plaintiffs from Parkside as a quid pro quo for relaxing the covenant'—ie a reasonable licence fee. This award was made even though, had the defendant in fact approached the claimant to seek to pay for a relaxation of the covenant, 'On the facts of this particular case the plaintiffs, rightly conscious of their obligations towards existing residents, would clearly not have granted any relaxation' (and would have obtained a prohibitory injunction).[6] Thus even though the hypothetical negotiation would not have resulted in a deal had the defendant sought to pay for a waiver of its obligation, Brightman J held that for the purposes of the calculation of damages he must assume the opposite, and awarded £2,500 as the sum the parties would have agreed as the fee for such a waiver, being five per cent of the defendant's 'anticipated profit' (anticipated at the time of the hypothetical negotiation, in advance of the breach and construction).[7]

22.2 The Principles

A. Assess a Hypothetical Bargain Assuming Willing Negotiators

It has already been observed that the award is made assuming willing negotiators even if in reality the claimant never would have consented to waive the obligation or license the breach.[8] However, this is not where the hypothesis ends, and the courts take seriously the task of evaluating what price might have been paid in such a negotiation. It is *not* a broad equitable assessment and misconduct is irrelevant.[9]

A good illustration is that of Mann QC in the High Court in another restrictive covenant case, *AMEC Developments Ltd v Jury's Hotel Management (UK) Ltd* in 2000, where the defendant's hotel development had breached the covenant by the

---

[4] Eg *Penarth Dock Engineering Co Ltd v Pounds* [1963] 1 Lloyd's Rep 359 (Denning MR).

[5] *Wrotham Park Estates Ltd v Parkside Homes Ltd* [1974] 1 WLR 798 (Brightman J) at 812–14. The links with the award in property claims were discussed in *Pell Frischmann Engineering Ltd v Bow Valley Iran Ltd* [2011] 1 WLR 2370 (PC) Lord Walker at para 48.

[6] *Wrotham Park Estates Ltd v Parkside Homes Ltd* [1974] 1 WLR 798 (Brightman J) at 815.

[7] There is no reason why the percentage need always be so low, as was confirmed in *Lane v O'Brien Homes Ltd* [2004] EWHC 303 (QB) (Clarke J) at para 18; it merely depends upon the circumstances.

[8] As in *Wrotham Park Estates Ltd v Parkside Homes Ltd* [1974] 1 WLR 798 (Brightman J) at 815. And see *Pell Frischmann Engineering Ltd v Bow Valley Iran Ltd* [2011] 1 WLR 2370 (PC) Lord Walker at para 49. For this reason it is surprising that *Wrotham Park* damages were not claimed in *Attorney General v Blake* [2001] AC 268 (HL) (discussed below in chapter twenty-three, section 23.2), although it may be because, as Chadwick LJ observed in *WWF—World Wide Fund for Nature v World Wrestling Federation Entertainment Inc* [2008] 1 WLR 445 (CA) at para 46, 'the concept of a notional bargain between the Crown (as employer) and a double agent—under which the Crown was to be taken as having agreed (for a suitable sum) to release the agent from an undertaking not to publish official secrets—was, perhaps, too bizarre to contemplate'.

[9] *AMEC Developments Ltd v Jury's Hotel Management (UK) Ltd* (2000) 82 P & CR 286 (Mann QC) at para 33.

hotel's footprint crossing a line by 4m, and the award was £375,000 (rather than over £1m as contended for by the claimant).[10] In that case the judge set out the features that were relevant to his decision as to how the negotiation would have gone:[11]

(a) On'the one side Amec is a willing seller, but only at a proper price.[12]

(b) On the other side, Jury is a willing buyer, wanting to acquire the right to cross the A-B line and prepared to pay a proper price but not a large ransom.[13]

(c) In such a negotiation the parties would proceed on common ground, put forward their best points and take into account the other side's best points.

(d) The negotiations are deemed to take place before any transgression occurs.

(e) The basis of the negotiation would be a split of the perceived gain to Jury. That gain would not be obvious, and would be the subject of debate within the sort of variables that I have described above.

(f) The parties are to be taken to know the hotel's actual figures for the purposes of assessing gain.

(g) In this case, the extent to which Jury would have been able to build more than 240 rooms if they had to confine their hotel to the proper footprint is not clear. I have already held that they might be able to get a small number more, but beyond that the picture is much more murky, and I treat the negotiation as taking place with no clearer a picture than was presented to me. The parties would have, at those negotiations, the case that I had which demonstrates that while Jury could *design* a hotel of more than 260 or 265 rooms on the proper footprint, but which did not clearly demonstrate that such a hotel would or could be built. One should not assume that it would; it has not even been proved clearly enough that Jury would have found Mr Stevens' design (or any particular alternative design) acceptable. Jury would be able to make a case for extracting some extra rooms from the proper footprint, that case declining in strength as the number rises. This factor is one of the unresolvable points that would be canvassed in the negotiation with no final conclusion being reached on it in terms of deciding an actual number; but it can be said that Jury would not advance a completely convincing case for 265 rooms.

(h) The numbers arising from these calculations are also debatable because of a genuine difference of view as to discount factors and yields.

(i) Amec cannot pray in aid any damage to its own property. It is simply trying to extract a benefit from its right to prevent Jury from earning some more money from a larger hotel.

---

[10] Ibid.

[11] Ibid at para 35.

[12] See further Bingham MR's comments in *Jaggard v Sawyer* [1995] 1 WLR 269 (CA) at 282–83: 'In situations of this kind a plaintiff should not be treated as eager to sell, which he very probably is not. But the court will not value the right at the ransom price which a very reluctant plaintiff may put on it'.

[13] It seems that uncertainty as to the bindingness of the right may be disregarded: *Lane v O'Brien Homes Ltd* [2004] EWHC 303 (QB) (Clarke J) at para 26. The approach in *Tito v Waddell (No 2)* [1977] Ch 106 (Megarry V-C) at 335–36 must be doubted. There the court decided that given that the cost of replacement was irrecoverable and only the much smaller diminution in value of the land was recoverable, the defendant would not have agreed to pay anything for a release from its obligation to replant the trees on the island. The judge held, wrongly, that the court need not take into account the uncertainty as to the measure of loss and the assumed desire to legalise the action in advance and can assume that the defendant knows it will ultimately be ordered to pay very little in damages and so is bargaining from an unrealistic position of extreme strength.

(j)   The additional land which Jury were seeking was not just a few inches—it was almost 4 metres wide, and in area was 11% of the area of the hotel. That is a significant amount of extra building.

(k)   While militating against any sort of de minimis figure (at least), the preceding factor also imposes a restraint on very high figures. For example, it shows why Jury would never pay (and Amec could never expect) Mr Uglow's £2.3m figure. Mr Uglow may be able to get there as a matter of logic, but as a matter of common sense Jury would never pay a sum approaching £2.3m for the right to build on a 4m strip of land when they had only paid £2.65m for the whole plot in the first place.

(l)   Jury's costs figures, while perhaps generally in the right area, have not been proved as cleanly and as clearly as one would expect.

(m)   Jury would be fairly keen, though not overwhelmingly anxious, to have the right to build over the A-B line.

(n)   As important as any of the above factors is this. In any negotiation science and rationality gets one only so far. At the end of the day the deal has to feel right. Some of the numbers that have been suggested by Amec in the course of this litigation, while perhaps intellectually justifiable, seem to me to be way over the top of what Jury would be prepared to pay, when set in the context of the rest of the cost of this hotel.

To this should be added that if the defendant could have circumvented the need for the claimant's agreement at a cost, that cost will be a factor in the hypothetical negotiations.[14] Similarly, if the parties would at the time of the negotiation have understood there to be chance that the claimant's right was defeasible, that must be taken into account.[15] Further, if the hypothetical bargain would have made payment to the claimant conditional upon a particular bid succeeding and that bid did not or would not have succeeded, then the award will be zero.[16]

B. Assess as at the Date of Breach

One of the crucial features of the award is that although the hypothetical bargain often has one eye on the anticipated profits the defendant seeks to make—pursuant to which paying off the claimant is one cost on the way—the bargain is considered as if it took place at the time of breach and not later when actual profits are known.[17] It may be more precise to say that the bargain is considered at 'the time at which the Defendants would have sought to be released from their contractual commitment',[18] although that will often be the date of breach. Ordinarily it would be illegitimate to take account of later events because they would not have affected

---

[14] *Giedo Van der Garde BV v Force India Formula One Team Ltd* [2010] EWHC 2373 (QB) (Stadlen J) at paras 549 and 552; *Force India Formula One Team Ltd v 1 Malaysia Racing Team SDN BHD* [2012] EWHC 616 (Ch) (Arnold J) at para 427.

[15] *Lunn Poly Ltd v Liverpool & Lancashire Properties Ltd* [2006] EWCA Civ 430, where it was held (Neuberger LJ at para 15) that any lawyer could have told the parties that the claimant was very likely to obtain relief from forfeiture (as it in fact did).

[16] *Jones v IOS (RUK) Ltd* [2012] EWHC 348 (Ch) (Hodge QC), obiter at para 102.

[17] *AMEC Developments Ltd v Jury's Hotel Management (UK) Ltd* (2000) 82 P & CR 286 (Mann QC) at para 35(d); *Lunn Poly Ltd v Liverpool & Lancashire Properties Ltd* [2006] EWCA Civ 430 Neuberger LJ at para 17; *WWF v World Wrestling Federation Entertainment Inc* [2008] 1 WLR 445 (CA) Chadwick LJ at para 53.

[18] *Lane v O'Brien Homes Ltd* [2004] EWHC 303 (QB) (Clarke J) at para 24.

the minds of the parties at the time of the hypothetical bargain.[19] This is a matter of logic, and is the general approach.[20] Thus in *Pell Frischmann Engineering Ltd v Bow Valley Iran Ltd* the Privy Council rooted the hypothetical negotiation as to the anticipated profits of the oil deal in the understanding of the parties at the time, and not the actual profits ultimately earned, which were much lower.[21]

That said, and while emphasising its exceptional character, the courts have confirmed a residual right to depart from this rule 'either by selecting a different valuation date or by directing that a specific post-valuation-date event be taken into account', given the 'quasi-equitable nature' of the award.[22] If the award is truly compensatory and based on a presumption but otherwise on orthodox principles, as is argued below, then this residual right should be rejected.

22.3 Scope of the Principles

A. Not Only if in Lieu of an Injunction

In *Wrotham Park* itself the damages were awarded under Lord Cairns' Act in lieu of an injunction.[23] Despite some later attempts to explain the awards by reference to that special feature,[24] and to emphasise that feature as the central basis of the award,[25] it is not a condition to the making of the award nor an explanation for it. The House of Lords has confirmed that damages under that Act are on the ordinary contractual basis[26] and the Privy Council has confirmed that it is not a condition for the award of *Wrotham Park* damages that an injunction was sought or available,[27] and further there are decisions awarding this type of damages even when there was no injunction sought.[28]

---

[19] *Lunn Poly Ltd v Liverpool & Lancashire Properties Ltd* [2006] EWCA Civ 430 Neuberger LJ at paras 19 and 29.

[20] Ibid, Neuberger LJ at paras 19 and 29; *Pell Frischmann Engineering Ltd v Bow Valley Iran Ltd* [2011] 1 WLR 2370 (PC) Lord Walker at paras 50–51. See also *AMEC Developments Ltd v Jury's Hotel Management (UK) Ltd* (2000) 82 P & CR 286 (Mann QC) at para 13.

[21] *Pell Frischmann Engineering Ltd v Bow Valley Iran Ltd* [2011] 1 WLR 2370 (PC).

[22] *Lunn Poly Ltd v Liverpool & Lancashire Properties Ltd* [2006] EWCA Civ 430 Neuberger LJ at para 29, approved in *Pell Frischmann Engineering Ltd v Bow Valley Iran Ltd* [2011] 1 WLR 2370 (PC) Lord Walker at paras 50–51. In *Lunn Poly* the fact that the claimant's lease was ultimately not forfeited was taken into account, although this was unimportant as the parties would have anticipated just that result (Neuberger LJ at para 15).

[23] See above in chapter one, section 1.2B(iii) in relation to such awards.

[24] *Jaggard v Sawyer* [1995] 1 WLR 269 (CA) Millett LJ at 291–92.

[25] *Pell Frischmann Engineering Ltd v Bow Valley Iran Ltd* [2011] 1 WLR 2370 (PC) Lord Walker at para 46.

[26] *Johnson v Agnew* [1980] 1 AC 367 (HL), discussed above in chapter one, text to n 16.

[27] *Pell Frischmann Engineering Ltd v Bow Valley Iran Ltd* [2011] 1 WLR 2370 (PC) Lord Walker at para 48. See also *WWF v World Wrestling Federation Entertainment Inc* [2008] 1 WLR 445 (CA) Chadwick LJ at paras 41 and 54.

[28] Eg *Giedo Van der Garde BV v Force India Formula One Team Ltd* [2010] EWHC 2373 (QB) (Stadlen J) especially at para 533; *Pell Frischmann Engineering Ltd v Bow Valley Iran Ltd* [2011] 1 WLR 2370 (PC). *Surrey County Council v Bredero Homes Ltd* [1993] 1 WLR 1361 (CA) depended upon this point and is therefore wrong: see further the discussion of that decision in *Jaggard v Sawyer* [1995] 1 WLR 269 (CA) Bingham MR at 281–82 and the disapproval of *Surrey County Council v Bredero Homes Ltd* in *Attorney General v Blake* [2001] AC 268 (HL) Lord Nicholls at 283 and Lord Hobhouse at 298.

B. Not Only in Property Cases

Although very many of the cases in which this award has been made involve the invasion of property rights (such as the restrictive covenant in *Wrotham Park*), or breach of agreements relating to property rights (such as the intellectual property dispute in *WWF v Worldwide Wrestling Federation Entertainment*),[29] it is clear that the *Wrotham Park* award is a general contractual common law remedy and does not require invasion of a property right or any proprietary element.[30] This was made clear by the discussion in *Attorney General v Blake*,[31] 'decisively' so in the view of Lord Walker in the Privy Council in *Pell Frischmann*.[32]

C. Negative Promises Only?

A serious difficulty therefore arises as to whether there is *any* limit to the award of *Wrotham Park* damages. Can a claimant in any case (careless advice by a surveyor? late delivery of goods?) claim that had the defendant come to negotiate with the claimant in advance of the breach the claimant would have been able to exact a price for a waiver and that is the measure of loss?[33] As Stadlen J has observed in the *Van der Garde* case:

> This prompts the question why the principle has not been more widely applied to cases not involving property rights and not involving a breach of a restrictive covenant. Is it merely because it is predominantly in such cases that conventional compensatory damages for breach of contract are likely to prove an inadequate remedy? Or is it, as Mr Tregear would submit, because its wider application to claims for breach of a positive covenant not involving invasion of property rights or breach of a restrictive covenant would subvert the long established framework of compensatory damages for breach of contract?[34]

See also the discussion below of restitutionary damages, which are most likely to be available only in circumstances where an injunction would have been available if applied for sufficiently promptly: see chapter twenty-three, section 23.2B.

[29] See the cases at chapter ten nn 4 and 8–9.

[30] *Giedo Van der Garde BV v Force India Formula One Team Ltd* [2010] EWHC 2373 (QB) (Stadlen J) at para 502.

[31] *Attorney General v Blake* [2001] AC 268 (HL) obiter Lord Nicholls at 283.

[32] *Pell Frischmann Engineering Ltd v Bow Valley Iran Ltd* [2011] 1 WLR 2370 (PC) at para 48. See also *Experience Hendrix LLC v PPX Enterprises Inc* [2003] EWCA Civ 323 Peter Gibson LJ at para 56; *WWF v World Wrestling Federation Entertainment Inc* [2008] 1 WLR 445 (CA) Chadwick LJ at paras 41 and 58 and throughout; *Giedo Van der Garde BV v Force India Formula One Team Ltd* [2010] EWHC 2373 (QB) (Stadlen J) at paras 502 and 533; *Abbar v Saudi Economic & Development Co (SEDCO) Real Estate Ltd* [2013] EWHC 1414 (Ch) (David Richards J) at para 224.

[33] Note the comments of Dillon LJ in *Surrey County Council v Bredero Homes Ltd* [1993] 1 WLR 1361 (CA) at 1368: 'I find difficulty with that because in theory every time there is a breach of contract the injured party is deprived of his "bargaining power" to negotiate for a financial consideration a variation of the contract which would enable the party who wants to depart from its terms to do what he wants to do'.

[34] *Giedo Van der Garde BV v Force India Formula One Team Ltd* [2010] EWHC 2373 (QB) (Stadlen J) at para 505.

Practice, if not logic, seems to have confined the *Wrotham Park* award to negative covenant cases, especially restrictive covenants on land use and confidentiality clauses. As Arnold J summarised in a breach of confidence case:

> In recent years, however, the law has come to recognise that the problem posed by situations in which the Claimant cannot prove orthodox financial loss as a result of the breach of a negative contractual term (ie a term that restricts the Defendant's activities in some way) can be addressed by the award of what have variously been referred to 'Wrotham Park damages'.[35]

However, in the *Van der Garde* case, Stadlen J, obiter, confirmed that an award of *Wrotham Park* damages could be made for breach of a positive obligation, there the obligation to provide the time and facilities to enable the claimant to drive laps in a Formula One racing car around a track.[36] Certainly there does not seem any principled reason for confining awards to negative promise cases, although there is a need carefully to consider what restriction there might be.

In *Smith v Landstar Properties Inc*,[37] the Court of Appeal for British Columbia awarded *Wrotham Park* damages for breach of contract and tortious negligent misstatement where a commercial borrower had warranted that a loan would be secured. The fact of the security meant that the loan was less risky for the lender and so was lent at a lower interest rate than if unsecured. The loan in fact had not been secured, but the loan had been repaid in full in any case. The damages were quantified by the additional interest the lender claimant would have got if the loan had been expressly unsecured, even though the lender would in fact not have agreed to make an unsecured loan. Clearly this is not a case of a negative promise, but the decision seems right, save that this is a case where ordinary financial loss will sometimes result from a lack of security (just not in this case) and is provable,[38] and so arguably there should be no *Wrotham Park* damages award.[39]

D. Interaction with an Ordinary Loss Claim

The award has been said to be available where 'compensation which is the claimant's due cannot be measured (or cannot be measured solely) by reference to identifiable

---

[35] *Force India Formula One Team Ltd v 1 Malaysia Racing Team SDN BHD* [2012] EWHC 616 (Ch) (Arnold J) at para 383.

[36] *Giedo Van der Garde BV v Force India Formula One Team Ltd* [2010] EWHC 2373 (QB) (Stadlen J). The point was discussed at para 520–32 and 536.

[37] *Smith v Landstar Properties Inc* 2011 BCCA 44 (British Columbia CA).

[38] Where the loan is not repaid in full the financial loss will be the additional amount that would have been recovered had the security been in place: *ACC Bank plc v Johnston* [2011] IEHC 376 (Irish High Court); *AIB Group (UK) plc v Mark Redler & Co (a firm)* [2012] EWHC 35 (Ch) (HHJ Cooke). A further possible positive covenant fact pattern worth considering arose in the New York decision in *Chamberlain v Parker* 45 NY 569 (1871). The defendant promised to erect an oil well on land leased to the defendant, with no real chance of the claimant benefiting from that promise. Nominal damages only were awarded.

[39] See below section 22.3D.

financial loss'.[40] The question then arises as to how the award interacts with a financial loss claim.

The first point is that the hypothetical bargain award is an alternative to a more ordinary compensatory award,[41] and cannot ordinarily be awarded in addition to it (at least not for the same damage). However, it may be that proven financial loss forms one of the elements to be taken into account when determining what hypothetical bargain would have been struck.[42]

Secondly, and this follows, if a lost profit claim can be formulated and proven and is greater than the hypothetical bargain award then the lost profit claim is awarded instead (and not as well),[43] at least as regards the financial damage.

Thirdly, it must also be right that where loss is of a type that is financial but quantifiable at zero or a smaller sum than the hypothetical bargain measure would give, the hypothetical bargain measure will not be awarded, as it cannot 'be used to award a larger sum than a conventional calculation of loss provides'.[44] Likewise it has been observed that '*Wrotham Park* damages are only available ... where it is impossible to compute the loss or where compensatory damages would be inadequate' and so they have been refused where the claimant always maintained that it could prove its financial loss but ultimately was unable to do so (ie on the evidence the financial loss was zero).[45] Accordingly, in one case a financial loss had in principle been suffered and was capable of quantification, but the claimant had failed to lead evidence allowing the court to quantify that loss, and in the circumstances was not permitted a *Wrotham Park* award.[46]

The proper conclusion is that *Wrotham Park* damages amount to a presumption or proxy award where the claimant cannot prove greater financial or non-pecuniary loss and the defendant cannot prove that it is less (see further below in the next section).

---

[40] *WWF v World Wrestling Federation Entertainment Inc* [2008] 1 WLR 445 (CA) Chadwick LJ at para 59; *Abbar v Saudi Economic & Development Co (SEDCO) Real Estate Ltd* [2013] EWHC 1414 (Ch) (David Richards J) at paras 225–26.

[41] See eg *Giedo Van der Garde BV v Force India Formula One Team Ltd* [2010] EWHC 2373 (QB) (Stadlen J).

[42] *Gafford v Graham* [1999] 3 EGLR 75 (CA) Nourse LJ at 80.

[43] In the breach of confidence case of *Douglas v Hello! Ltd* [2003] EWHC 2629 (Ch) (Lindsay J) (award affirmed [2008] 1 AC 1 (HL) after [2006] QB 125 (CA)), relating to the wedding photographs of actors Michael Douglas and Catherine Zeta-Jones which had been published in *Hello* magazine although *OK!* magazine had been given an exclusive, the notional licence fee award was seen as an alternative to the conventional lost profit claim. In that case lost profits of over £1m were proven, and so the notional licence fee which was quantified at £125,000 was not awarded. The Court of Appeal disapproved the obiter licence fee award at *Douglas v Hello! Ltd (No 3)* [2006] QB 125 (CA) at paras 244–47, in part because the claimant could never have granted a licence having already given an exclusive licence to *OK!*, but this reasoning has been criticised in *Force India Formula One Team Ltd v 1 Malaysia Racing Team SDN BHD* [2012] EWHC 616 (Ch) (Arnold J) at para 417, and the Court of Appeal's decision as a whole was overturned on the confidence point: [2008] 1 AC 1 (HL).

[44] *BGC Capital Markets (Switzerland) LLC v Rees* [2011] EWHC 2009 (QB) (Sir Jack) at para 97.

[45] *Lighthouse Carwood Ltd v Luckett* [2007] EWHC 2866 (QB) (MacDuff QC) at para 58. Cf *The Trademark Licensing Co Ltd v Punch GmbH* [2012] EWCA Civ 985 at paras 34–35. But see the contrary obiter comments in *Giedo Van der Garde BV v Force India Formula One Team Ltd* [2010] EWHC 2373 (QB) (Stadlen J) at para 507, which must be doubted.

[46] *Abbar v Saudi Economic & Development Co (SEDCO) Real Estate Ltd* [2013] EWHC 1414 (Ch) (David Richards J) at para 225–27.

22.4 Basis of the Principles

As a compensatory award the *Wrotham Park* measure is not immediately easy to explain.[47] First, the promise breached is not a promise to warn the claimant and negotiate for a waiver, in which rare case, the claimant would have had the reasonable licence fee but for the wrong and so such a fee is a loss caused by the defendant. In the vast majority of cases the promise is simply not to do something or to do something.[48] Secondly, as we have seen, the award is made even where (as in *Wrotham Park* itself) the claimant would, if approached, not have agreed to waive the obligation for any amount of money, and quite possibly have obtained an injunction in advance of the breach of which the claimant had been warned. Thus as a matter of factual causation, it cannot be said that even if the defendant had approached the claimant the claimant would have ended up with the amount of the reasonable licence fee.[49] The truth is that but for the breach the right would not have been infringed, and it is therefore not correct as a matter of ordinary causation principles to say that the breach deprived the claimant of the right to a licence fee.

There is a particular camp of legal commentators and judges that sees this award as restitutionary, ie disgorgement.[50] This is because it does appear that the award is being measured not by any proven loss to the claimant, and the award does resemble an award of the profits made by the defendant. That explanation will not do, however. The award does not strip the defendant of its profits, but only awards a sum—usually significantly less than the profits—measured by the fee the defendant would have agreed to pay the claimant at the time of breach. This is naturally, as a matter of human psychology and business, related to the profit of the defendant, but only because the defendant would not pay more than the benefit it hopes to achieve. The judge must pay

> attention to the profits earned by the defendants, as it seems to me, not in order to strip the defendants of their unjust gains, but because of the obvious relationship between the profits earned by the defendants and the sum which the defendants would reasonably have been willing to pay to secure release from the covenant.[51]

Or as Millett LJ observed in the same decision, 'The amount of the profit which the defendant expected to make was a relevant factor in that assessment, but that

---

[47] It was described as a 'fiction' by Steyn LJ in *Surrey County Council v Bredero Homes Ltd* [1993] 1 WLR 1361 (CA) at 1369.

[48] There can be cases where the loss to the defendant is the lost opportunity to bargain with the defendant, eg business secrets cases such as *Seager v Copydex Ltd (No 2)* [1969] RPC 250 (CA) as discussed in *Dowson and Mason Ltd v Potter* [1986] 1 WLR 1419 (CA), where had the defendant not misused the secrets, it or others would have bought the information from the claimant (rather than the claimant merely using it itself). As explained in *Dowson and Mason Ltd v Potter* [1986] 1 WLR 1419 (CA), in such cases the reasonable licence fee award is therefore dependent upon determining whether the claimant in fact would have used or sold the information, whereas the general *Wrotham Park* award has no such requirement.

[49] A point made by Mance LJ in *Experience Hendrix LLC v PPX Enterprises Inc* [2003] EWCA Civ 323 at para 25.

[50] Eg C Rotherham, '"Wrotham Park Damages" and Accounts of Profits: Compensation or Restitution?' [2008] *LMCLQ* 24.

[51] *Jaggard v Sawyer* [1995] 1 WLR 269 (CA) Bingham MR at 281–82.

was all'.[52] If the defendant anticipates a very profitable business it may be willing to pay 25 per cent of those anticipated profits as a licence fee to the claimant and that would be the award even if the business was actually a disaster and earned less profit than the fee. Moreover, in revealing that this award is not restitutionary, it is important that the award is measured by reference to anticipated and not actual profits.

For these reasons the modern judicial understanding is that the award is compensatory.[53] The best view, in the opinion of this author, is that these awards reflect non-pecuniary loss.[54] As discussed above in relation to such loss,[55] one sensible measure of such loss, entirely orthodox as a matter of economics, is to ask how much the claimant values the infringed right, and to measure that by what the claimant would have accepted to give up the right, assuming (possibly contrary to reality) that the claimant would have done so. That is what the *Wrotham Park* award does. Thus Neuberger LJ has astutely explained the award as 'really a way of defining market value'.[56] Of course, to explain the award on this basis requires that non-pecuniary losses are available in a broader range of situations than is frequently recognised (eg that they can be awarded in some commercial cases), although the current legal principles and cases do in fact support such a view when correctly analysed.[57] It is then a matter of presuming in appropriate cases (eg those where the claimant has not laid out any expenditure such as could allow the presumption of breaking even to operate[58]) that the non-pecuniary loss is no less than the amount by which the claimant values the right in a hypothetical bargain for waiver, although either party may rebut that presumption.[59]

---

[52] Ibid at 291. Also *Giedo Van der Garde BV v Force India Formula One Team Ltd* [2010] EWHC 2373 (QB) (Stadlen J) at para 549.

[53] *Tito v Waddell (No 2)* [1977] Ch 106 (Megarry VC) at 335; *Jaggard v Sawyer* [1995] 1 WLR 269 (CA) Bingham MR at 281 and 283 and Millett LJ at 291; *Gafford v Graham* [1999] 3 EGLR 75 (CA) Nourse LJ at 80; *WWF v World Wrestling Federation Entertainment Inc* [2008] 1 WLR 445 (CA) Chadwick LJ at paras 29, 38–39, 47, 56–58; *Pell Frischmann Engineering Ltd v Bow Valley Iran Ltd* [2011] 1 WLR 2370 (PC) Lord Walker at paras 48, 50 and 60; *Jones v IOS (RUK) Ltd* [2012] EWHC 348 (Ch) (Hodge QC), obiter at paras 97; *Force India Formula One Team Ltd v 1 Malaysia Racing Team SDN BHD* [2012] EWHC 616 (Ch) (Arnold J) at para 386(1); *Abbar v Saudi Economic & Development Co (SEDCO) Real Estate Ltd* [2013] EWHC 1414 (Ch) (David Richards J) at para 224.

[54] Cf *Kemp v Sober* (1851) 61 ER 200 where anxiety damages were recognised in a case not wholly dissimilar to *Wrotham Park* of a neighbour breaching a covenant and running a business. And cf the comments of Mance LJ in *Experience Hendrix LLC v PPX Enterprises Inc* [2003] EWCA Civ 323 at para 26 that the award is compensatory but only if compensation is seen as going beyond actual financial loss.

[55] See above, text to chapter nineteen n 135 and chapter ten n 10.

[56] *Lunn Poly Ltd v Liverpool & Lancashire Properties Ltd* [2006] EWCA Civ 430 at para 19.

[57] See above in chapter nineteen, section 19.2B.

[58] See above in chapter eighteen, section 18.3.

[59] As explained above in section 22.2D.

23

Non-Compensatory Damages

Damages awards not based on compensation: nominal damages, account of profits/restitutionary damages, and punitive/exemplary damages.

23.1. Nominal Damages
23.2. Account of Profits/Restitutionary Damages
23.3. Punitive/Exemplary Damages

23.1 Nominal Damages

A claim for breach of contract (unlike a claim in the tort of negligence, for example) arises whether or not loss has been suffered; it is said to be 'actionable per se'. If no substantial damages are awarded, either because no loss recognised by law was suffered (eg there was no loss, or all loss was avoided or should have been avoided) or none was proven,[1] the claimant is still entitled to a judgment and to nominal damages (a nominal award of money) symbolically marking that judgment in its favour. In practice, this is likely to be a pyrrhic victory, as the claimant will often to be visited with liability for the costs of the litigation.[2]

23.2 Account of Profits/Restitutionary Damages

While the vast majority of contract damages awards are based upon compensation, ie seeking to counterbalance or undo a claimant's loss, there is an exceptional award known to the law of contract which requires disgorgement (ie surrender to the claimant) of the defendant's gain. Such an award, where made, may well end up putting a claimant in a *better* position than it would have been in but for the breach of contract and is certainly not based upon the position the claimant would have been in but for the breach, contrary to the compensatory rule from *Robinson v Harman* as discussed in the introduction chapter to this book; it all depends instead upon how much the defendant gained by breaching the contract.

---

[1] Cf the US Restatement (Second) of Contracts §346(2).
[2] Much depends upon the particular issues that were fought and won. See for example *Clack v Wrigleys Solicitors LLP* [2013] EWHC 413 (Ch) (Strauss QC).

A. Introduction to the Remedy in Other Contexts

(i) Restitution for Wrongs: Breach of Trust, Fiduciary Duty or Confidence, and Property Torts

This award is well-known in cases of breach of trust, breach of fiduciary duty or breach of confidence under the equitable remedy of 'account of profits'. Any profits (including bribes) made from such a breach of these equitable obligations must be given up.[3] The award is also available in cases of proprietary torts such as trespass, conversion and breach of trademark, but not other torts.[4] In all such cases of restitution for these wrongs, the remedy requires disgorgement of the benefit achieved from the breach.

In property tort cases, the usual measure of such benefit is the 'reasonable user' or 'wayleave' principle: the defendant used the defendant's property without asking and the benefit is often measured by the price that would have been paid as a licence fee had the parties instead negotiated such a fee in advance.[5]

(ii) Restitution for Unjust Enrichment

The remedy is also similar to the award of restitution for unjust enrichment, although in a case of unjust enrichment, the gain that is paid back to the claimant has actually been conferred by the claimant (for example under a mistaken payment), and so the restitution is a giving *back* or reversal of a *transfer* of benefit.

In a restitutionary damages award in contract, trusts or tort, which is properly characterised as an award of restitution for wrongs (rather than for unjust enrichment), the benefit arose out of a breach of the duty to the claimant but the benefit was not itself conferred by the claimant.[6]

---

[3] See for example *Reading v Attorney General* [1951] AC 507 (HL); *Boardman v Phipps* [1967] 2 AC 46 (HL).

[4] *Stoke-on-Trent City Council v W & J Wass Ltd* [1988] 1 WLR 1406 (CA); *Devenish Nutrition Ltd v Sanofi-Aventis SA (France)* [2009] Ch 390 (CA), where for this reason a claim for restitutionary damages was struck out in a case of compensation for the statutory action under Article 81 of the EC Treaty for acting in an anti-competitive cartel; also *Vercoe v Rutland Fund Management Ltd* [2010] EWHC 424 (Ch) (Sales J).

[5] See the summary of this award and the cases in which it is awarded in *Bocardo SA v Star Energy UK Onshore Ltd* [2011] 1 AC 380 (SC) Lord Clarke at paras 119–26, although in none of the opinions of their Lordships were the words 'restitution' or 'restitutionary damages' used. See further discussion of this type of award in the contract context in chapter twenty-two.

[6] Sometimes the distinction is made in contract cases between disgorgement of the gain made by the defendant and restitution of a benefit transferred to the defendant by the claimant. See eg *Esso Petroleum Co Ltd v Niad Ltd* [2001] EWHC 6 (Ch) (Morritt VC); *Denaro Ltd v Onyx Bar & Café (Cambridge) Ltd* [2011] NZHC 52 (NZ High Court) at paras 19–20.

B. Only Awarded in Exceptional Contract Cases

(i) Introduction[7]

In breach of trust and breach of fiduciary duty cases, an award of account of profits is available automatically as a matter of course, even where the breach was innocent.[8] This is justified by the need to deter breaches of these special close relationships of trust.[9]

The restitutionary damages award in breach of contract cases is very different, since most contracts are not relationships of trust and loyalty in the way that fiduciary and trust duties are, and so the breach of such contracts does not require deterrence. Indeed the general reluctance of the courts to award specific performance and the general focus on compensatory damages as the primary remedy means that as a rule even deliberate breach of contract is in a sense unobjectionable, although sounding in compensatory damages, and if a defendant can cover that compensation and still make a profit then good luck to it.[10]

(ii) Attorney General v Blake

This sets the scene for the origin of the contractual award of restitutionary damages, which was the truly exceptional contract case of *Attorney General v Blake*, which reached decision in the House of Lords in 2000[11] and which, as Mance LJ later observed, 'provides a new start in this area of law'.[12] Mr Blake was a Soviet spy who had worked under cover for 10 years in the British Secret Intelligence Service. After being caught and imprisoned for 42 years, he had in 1966 escaped from London's Wormwood Scrubs prison and his memoirs were published (entitled *No Other Choice*) in 1990 by a London publisher. By the date of trial, it was too late to obtain an injunction preventing publication,[13] and by the time of the House of Lords decision, the legal question had become one as to the remedy available for breach of

---

[7] See further J Edelman, *Gain-based Damages: Contract, Tort, Equity and Intellectual Property* (Oxford, Hart Publishing, 2002); J O'Sullivan, 'Reflections on the Role of Restitutionary Damages to Protect Contractual Expectations' in D Johnson and R Zimmermann (eds), *Unjustified Enrichment: Key Issues in Comparative Perspective* (Cambridge, CUP, 2002) 327; E McKendrick, 'Breach of Contract, Restitution for Wrongs, and Punishment' in A Burrows and E Peel (eds), *Commercial Remedies: Current Issues and Problems* (Oxford, OUP, 2003) 93.

[8] See for example *Boardman v Phipps* [1967] 2 AC 46 (HL).

[9] Although see the comments of Arden LJ in *Murad v Al Saraj* [2005] EWCA Civ 959, doubting whether deterrence justifies disgorgement in all cases of breach of fiduciary duty. In contrast, even in breach of confidence cases, the account of profits remedy is discretionary and not available as of right: *Walsh v Shanahan* [2013] EWCA Civ 411.

[10] In such a case a breach by the defendant is said to be an 'efficient breach', it being more efficient for the defendant to breach and pay compensation than to perform. This is a fundamental part of the thinking of many American economists, contract law scholars and judges. See above in chapter one, section 1.4A. See also the discussion of efficient breach in the restitutionary damages context by the Supreme Court of Canada in *Bank of America Canada v Mutual Trust Co* [2002] 2 SCR 601 (SC of Canada) at paras 31–32.

[11] *Attorney General v Blake* [2001] AC 268 (HL).

[12] *Experience Hendrix LLC v PPX Enterprises Inc* [2003] EWCA Civ 323 at para 16.

[13] The House of Lords confirmed that such an injunction or alternative remedy probably could have been obtained if sought early enough: Lord Hobhouse [2001] AC 268 at 289.

an undertaking in Mr Blake's 1944 employment contract not to disclose official information obtained during his employment,[14] and, in terms of realistic recovery, was a claim to attach the £90,000 debt owed by the publisher to Mr Blake.

Lord Hobhouse dissented, upholding the (at least until then) orthodox view that no disgorgement remedy was available for breach of contract, seeing it as an 'essentially punitive' award borne of the criminal history of the case which 'is a remedy based on proprietary principles when the necessary proprietary rights are absent', whereas contract damages are 'necessarily compensatory'.[15]

The majority, however, awarded what it called and is usually called an account of profits, although some would call it restitutionary damages.[16] Lord Nicholls explained that

> When, exceptionally, a just response to a breach of contract so requires, the court should be able to grant the discretionary remedy of requiring a defendant to account to the plaintiff for the benefits he has received from his breach of contract.[17]

The words 'exceptionally' and 'exceptional' were repeated.[18]

The House resisted providing guidance as to when the award would be granted. Lord Woolf MR in the Court of Appeal had suggested two categories in which such an award would be available,[19] both of which are often discussed in academic literature. One was cases of 'skimped performance' where the defendant skimps on the services promised. The other was where the claimant profited from doing the 'very thing' it had promised not to do. In the House of Lords Lord Nicholls disapproved Lord Woolf's categories,[20] as well as confirming that the breach being cynical and deliberate was not itself enough to justify such an award.[21]

---

[14] The information was, by the date of publication, no longer confidential information or damaging to the public interest, and (as was found at first instance and by the Court of Appeal) Mr Blake no longer owed a fiduciary duty to the Crown. The Court of Appeal made a freezing injunction on public law grounds but this was disapproved in the House of Lords ([2001] AC 268 at 289 and 295–96) because there was no likelihood of ever invoking permanent confiscation powers and it was unnecessary in the light of the House of Lords' findings as to the right to damages. The claim to contract damages was not pursued by the claimant until the House of Lords appeal, although it was suggested and discussed by the Court of Appeal (although at that stage the claimant declined the Court's invitation to make submissions on the point).

[15] Ibid at 295, 298 and 299.

[16] Lord Nicholls preferred to describe the award as an 'account of profits', which label has been adopted generally, eg in the Court of Appeal in *Experience Hendrix LLC v PPX Enterprises Inc* [2003] EWCA Civ 323 and *WWF v World Wrestling Federation Entertainment Inc* [2008] 1 WLR 445 (CA). The rival label of 'restitutionary damages' was used by Lord Woolf MR in the Court of Appeal in *Blake* [1998] Ch 439 (CA) but rejected by Lord Nicholls in the House of Lords [2001] AC 268 at 284 and 286, although Lord Steyn preferred it at 290–91. In *Pell Frischmann Engineering Ltd v Bow Valley Iran Ltd* [2011] 1 WLR 2370 (PC) Lord Walker at para 48 referred to 'an account of profits, alias restitutionary damages'.

[17] [2001] AC 268 at 284–85.

[18] Lord Nicholls ibid at 284, 285 (three times), 286; Lord Steyn at 292; also the discussion of Lord Hobhouse dissenting at 299.

[19] [1998] Ch 439 (CA) at 458–59.

[20] Lord Nicholls [2001] AC 268 at 286 and Lord Steyn at 291. Lord Nicholls thought at 286 that in skimped performance cases ordinary principles entitled the claimant to the difference in price between the services promised and those provided by analogy with goods cases. The true position is far from that simple (the result in goods cases is justified by the mitigation rule and the availability of a market replacement) and the problem is discussed in chapter two, section 2.2C. Lord Nicholls thought the second category unhelpfully wide.

[21] [2001] AC 268 at 286.

However, Lord Nicholls (with the support of a clear majority)[22] did say that the remedy would only be awarded where other remedies were 'inadequate' and that '[a] useful general guide, although not exhaustive, is whether the plaintiff had a legitimate interest in preventing the defendant's profit-making activity and, hence, in depriving him of his profit'.[23] As the Court of Appeal has subsequently pointed out, those are precisely the circumstances in which an injunction is likely to be granted.[24]

In *Blake* itself, the exceptional features (never likely to be repeated) were: that the breach of contract was also a crime; the Crown had a legitimate interest in preventing Blake profiting from the disclosure of official information while a member of the intelligence service and thereafter (Lord Nicholls referring to the 'special circumstances of the intelligence services'); that the undertaking was, although not fiduciary, 'closely akin to a fiduciary obligation'; and that it was of paramount importance that informers and members of the service have complete confidence in each other and therefore that such breaches of contract be deterred and such public servants have no financial incentive to breach.[25]

(iii) Distinguishing the Wrotham Park Hypothetical Bargain Award

In this context it is important to distinguish the *Wrotham Park* award for loss of a hypothetical bargain, by which the claimant is entitled to an award of the amount it would have accepted in order to agree (in advance) to the breach, which sum is often quantified as a fraction of the profits the defendant made or anticipated it would make from the breach. That award is discussed further in chapter twenty-two above, and is well-established as being (albeit somewhat abnormal in measure) a compensatory and not a restitutionary award.[26]

(iv) Commercial Contract Cases

The general approach in commercial contract cases is to refuse awards of accounts of profits or restitutionary damages. This was summarised in the arbitral decision of *The Sine Nomine* (the panel including Sir Christopher Staughton, formerly Staughton LJ):

> It is by no means uncommon for commercial contracts to be broken deliberately because a more profitable opportunity has arisen. Or the contract-breaker takes an over-generous view of his rights, knowing that the law may ultimately be against him. In such a case he may have little or nothing to lose by taking the chance; the downside at worst is that he will have to pay the costs of both sides. International commerce on a large scale is red in

---

[22] Lords Goff and Browne-Wilkinson agreed with Lord Nicholls without further comment, Lord Steyn also expressly approved Lord Nicholls' reasoning but added further comments of his own. Lord Hobhouse dissented.

[23] [2001] AC 268 at 285.

[24] *Experience Hendrix LLC v PPX Enterprises Inc* [2003] EWCA Civ 323 Mance LJ at para 35.

[25] Lord Nicholls [2001] AC 268 at 286–87 and Lord Steyn at 291–92 (who was particularly swayed by the obligation being akin to a fiduciary obligation). See also *Experience Hendrix LLC v PPX Enterprises Inc* [2003] EWCA Civ 323 Mance LJ at para 29.

[26] See below in chapter twenty-two, section 22.4.

tooth and claw. We do not say that the Respondents' action was either deliberate or cynical wrongdoing in this case; they had a respectable argument on liability, although a commercial judge refused their application for leave to appeal.

Our solution to the present problem is that there should not be an award of wrongful profits where both parties are dealing with a marketable commodity—the services of a ship in this case—for which a substitute can be found in the market place. In the ordinary way the damages which the claimant suffers by having to buy in at the market price will be equal to the profit which the wrongdoer makes by having his goods or his ships' services to sell at a higher price. It is in the nature of things unlikely that the wrongdoer will make a greater profit than that. And if he does, it is an adventitious benefit which he can keep. The commercial law of this country should not make moral judgments, or seek to punish contract-breakers; we do not, for example, award triple damages, as in the USA.[27]

Attempts to extend the *Blake* full account of profits award to cases of breach of a promise as to the density of housing on a development (ie the *Wrotham Park* situation) have been resisted,[28] as they have in the context of breach of a hedge fund investor introducer agreement.[29] In a pre-*Blake* decision of withdrawal of a vessel from a time charter by its owner, the idea of an account of profits was rejected without any difficulty by the judge.[30] The same result would be reached today, as is implicit from the citation of this decision by Lord Nicholls in *Blake* with no suggestion of disapproval.[31]

The circumstances in which the account of profits will apply were considered by the Court of Appeal in *Experience Hendrix LLC v PPX Enterprises Inc*.[32] That case concerned breach of a settlement agreement between Jimi Hendrix's estate and PPX by which breach the latter licensed to third parties the use of various Hendrix master recordings to PPX's profit. It was not disputed that it would be practically impossible for the claimant to show any lost profits.[33] Partly because the *Wrotham Park* award was available, the case was not regarded as sufficiently exceptional for an account of profits. There was no national security, no earlier breaches of relevance, and no relationship akin to a fiduciary relationship.[34] As Mance LJ observed:

Here, the breaches, though deliberate, took place in a commercial context. PPX, though knowingly and deliberately breaching its contract, acted as it did in the course of a business, to which it no doubt gave some expenditure of time and effort and probably the use of connections and some skill (although how much is evidently in issue, and is not a matter on which we can at this stage reach any view). An account of profits would involve a detailed assessment of such matters, which, as is very clear from *Blake*, should not lightly be ordered.[35]

---

[27] *AB Corp v CD Co (The Sine Nomine)* [2002] 1 Lloyd's Rep 805 at paras 9–10.
[28] *Lane v O'Brien Homes Ltd* [2004] EWHC 303 (QB) (Clarke J) at para 20.
[29] *Signet Partners Ltd v Signet Research and Advisory SA* [2007] EWHC 1263 (QB) (Burton J) at para 126.
[30] *Occidental Worldwide Investment Corp v Skibs A/S Avanti (The Siboen and The Sibotre)* [1976] 1 Lloyd's Rep 293 (Kerr J) at 337.
[31] [2001] AC 268 at 284.
[32] *Experience Hendrix LLC v PPX Enterprises Inc* [2003] EWCA Civ 323.
[33] See ibid at para 14.
[34] Ibid Mance LJ at paras 37 and 44.
[35] Ibid at para 44.

(a) *Esso Petroleum Co Ltd v Niad Ltd*

The high point of the awarding of an account of profits in commercial cases is the difficult High Court decision in *Esso Petroleum Co Ltd v Niad Ltd*, decided shortly after the House of Lords' decision in *Blake*.[36] The defendant owner of a petrol station, as part of its petrol supply agreement with the claimant supplier, entered into an agreement to adhere to the claimant's 'Pricewatch' scheme by which the claimant fixed the petrol prices the defendant could use (as part of a marketing campaign pressing Esso petrol as competitively priced) in exchange for which the defendant would be given a discount in the wholesale petrol price. The defendant obtained the price support but did not follow the scheme. The judgment only concerned liability and not quantum, and accordingly the approach to quantum was a little unclear. Morritt V-C in the High Court confirmed that to obtain contract damages in the ordinary way, Esso would have to show that it had lost sales as a result of the defendant's overcharging customers for the petrol, and that this would not be easy, as '[i]t is almost impossible to attribute lost sales to a breach by one out of several hundred dealers who operated Pricewatch',[37] although that issue was left over to the trial on quantum.

The judge also, however, confirmed that an account of profits was available (the amount to be determined at the trial on quantum). The reasoning for this was rather brief, and was that compensatory damages were inadequate, the breaches were repeated and knowing, and Esso had a legitimate interest in maintaining its pricing scheme and preventing Niad from profiting.[38] The quantum of the award was not clarified, but apparently was *not* the amount paid by Esso to Niad under the Pricewatch scheme.[39] The judge also confirmed that, in the alternative and somewhat surprisingly, a distinct restitutionary award for unjust enrichment was available to disgorge the amounts by which it was unjustly enriched by charging more than the prescribed pump prices, and indicated that this was in the judge's view the most appropriate remedy.[40]

Later case law explaining *Niad* has emphasised the difficulty of assessing lost profit in that case, thus rendering ordinary damages awards inadequate,[41] and, more usefully, the unusual feature that the profit made by Niad came in part as a transfer from Esso itself under the price control reductions.[42] As these cases confirm, restitutionary damages are usually refused in commercial cases, in favour of making compensatory awards.[43]

---

[36] *Esso Petroleum Co Ltd v Niad Ltd* [2001] EWHC 6 (Ch) (Morritt VC).
[37] See ibid at paras 56 and 63.
[38] Ibid at para 63.
[39] Ibid at para 57.
[40] Ibid at paras 57–58 and 64.
[41] Lewison J in *Devenish Nutrition Ltd v Sanofi-Aventis SA (France)* [2009] Ch 390 (CA) at para 90.
[42] *Experience Hendrix LLC v PPX Enterprises Inc* [2003] EWCA Civ 323 Mance LJ at para 38.
[43] In addition to the cases above, see eg *Ontario Inc v Select Restaurant Plaza Corp* 2006 CanLII 44266 (Ontario Superior Court) (wrongful eviction of restaurant business tenant).

C. The Future

Outside the situation in which there is a concurrent fiduciary duty, an account of profits is a contract remedy that (like specific performance) is only awarded where compensatory damages are deemed inadequate. There are two types of inadequacy worth distinguishing.

The first is inadequacy of compensation as a means of supporting the aims of contract law. Judges instinctively rebel against rules that allow a defendant cynically to breach a contract and to make a gain by it, although such an instinct should be resisted. Contract law is not concerned with morality but with bargains, and if no loss is suffered and performance remedies (specific performance, injunctions) are not available then there is nothing objectionable about the claimant having no further recourse. Nevertheless, it is in situations where the claimant is too late to obtain a specific remedy which would otherwise have been awarded that an account of profits is justified.

The second type of inadequacy is the inadequacy of compensatory damages as a means of giving compensation for the loss suffered. This type of inadequacy is not so much a resistance to finding compensation to be the sole aim of contract damages, as a criticism of the rules as they stand for not fully compensating for loss (eg because of an over-emphasis on financial loss against other types).

As the move towards expanding awards of compensation continues (including with awards of damages for non-pecuniary loss,[44] damages for loss suffered upon failure to confer a benefit on third parties, and damages for loss of a hypothetical bargain—the *Wrotham Park* measure), it is to be expected that, at least as regards this type of inadequacy, non-compensatory remedies such as an account of profits and specific performance will, by their own rules that are premised upon inadequacy of damages, be awarded in fewer and fewer situations.

Attorney General v Blake and *Esso v Niad* have not been followed by a flurry of awards of accounts of profits in contract cases, and it remains a very exceptional remedy.

23.3 Punitive/Exemplary Damages[45]

Awards of punitive or, as they are sometimes known, exemplary damages, are not designed to compensate; nor, unlike an account of profits/restitutionary damages, are they designed to force disgorgement of the defendant's gain. Rather, their purpose is to punish or make an example of the defendant. In the leading recent

---

[44] See chapter nineteen.

[45] See further NJ McBride, 'A Case for Awarding Punitive Damages in Response to Deliberate Breaches of Contract' (1995) 24 *Anglo-American L Rev* 369 and 'Punitive Damages' in *Wrongs and remedies in the Twenty-first Century* (Oxford, OUP, 1996) 175; J Swan, 'Punitive Damages for Breach of Contract: A Remedy in Search of a Justification' (2004) 29 *Queens LJ* 596; R Cunnington, 'Should Punitive Damages be Part of the Judicial Arsenal in Contract Cases?' (2006) 26 *Legal Studies* 369.

case on the recovery of punitive damages in tort, *Kuddus v Chief Constable of Leicestershire*,[46] Lord Scott observed that:

> The function of an award of damages in our civil justice system is to compensate the claimant for a wrong done to him. The wrong may consist of a breach of contract, or a tort, or an interference with some right of the claimant under public law. But whatever the wrong may consist of the award of damages should be compensatory in its intent. Measured by this fundamental principle of damages, an award of exemplary damages, the intention of which is not to compensate the victim of a wrong but to punish its perpetrator, is an anomaly.

Lord Scott was of the view that exemplary damages should not be awarded for any tort or breach of contract, and used the existence of restitutionary damages/the account of profits as part of his justification for this.[47] Such a blanket ban on such damages in contract cases can be found elsewhere.[48]

The majority declined to decide the point either way, it not having been argued and the appeal being from a strike out rather than a trial judgment, but did find that such damages might be awarded for the tort of misfeasance in public office, and that the determining factor would be the behaviour of the defendant (and not the precise cause of action under which the tortious claim was brought). As Lord Nicholls put it, the question should turn on whether there was 'conduct which was an outrageous disregard of the plaintiff's rights'.[49]

As far as contract cases are concerned, the general rule since the early twentieth-century House of Lords decision in the wrongful dismissal case of *Addis v Gramophone Co Ltd* has been that such damages are unavailable.[50] This was confirmed by the Court of Appeal, albeit without any real exploration, in two cases of contract damages by a tenant against a landlord,[51] and by Lord Scott in *Johnson v Unisys*.[52] The same rule applies in most of the Commonwealth.[53]

The rules on when recovery of such damages is possible in tort are relatively vague due to the absence of recent case law and the general approach taken in *Kuddus*, but there are two separate categories worth considering in which an award could possibly arise for breach of contract.[54]

A. Misuse of Executive Power

The first is where there is an extremely oppressive use of executive power.[55] It is not easy to answer the question as to whether an egregious breach of contract by a

---

[46] *Kuddus v Chief Constable of Leicestershire Constabulary* [2002] 2 AC 122 (HL).

[47] Ibid at paras 109–11 and 121.

[48] Eg the US Restatement (Second) of Contracts §352.

[49] [2002] 2 AC 122 at para 68.

[50] *Addis v Gramophone Co Ltd* [1909] AC 488 (HL).

[51] *Perera v Vandiyar* [1953] 1 WLR 672 (CA) at 677; *Kenny v Preen* [1963] 1 QB 499 (CA) at 513.

[52] *Johnson v Unisys Ltd* [2003] 1 AC 518 (HL) at para 15. Also *Abbar v Saudi Economic & Development Co (SEDCO) Real Estate Ltd* [2013] EWHC 1414 (Ch) (David Richards J) at para 232.

[53] *Paper Reclaim Ltd v Aotearoa International Ltd* [2006] 3 NZLR 188 (CA of New Zealand), where the Commonwealth authorities are summarised at paras 167–82.

[54] Reflecting the two categories identified by Lord Devlin in *Rookes v Barnard* [1964] AC 1129 (HL) at 1226.

[55] See Lord Hutton in *Kuddus* [2002] 2 AC 122 at para 75.

public authority might give rise to an award of exemplary damages. The argument that a state school, when interviewing for an internal promotion post, was acting in its private capacity and so an award could not be made by the tribunal in a discrimination case was rejected by the Court of Appeal in *City of Bradford Metropolitan Council v Arora*.[56] In Trinidad and Tobago, such an award was upheld in a case of egregious and threatening constructive dismissal by a state employer.[57]

In theory, therefore, it would seem that a public authority acting in an outrageous and abusive breach of contract might face an award of exemplary damages. It is difficult to imagine a case where this would happen (and where there would not also be a human rights claim, or tort claim for false imprisonment or the like).

B. Other Cases

The second category is the more general category of outrageous disregard of the claimant's rights, ie where there is no public authority element.[58]

There is Commonwealth and other Common Law authority for such awards. Most notably, although repeatedly emphasising the rarity of such an award,[59] the Canadian courts in practice take a more relaxed approach to such awards than the English courts. The Canadian Supreme Court has confirmed that punitive damages can be awarded in cases of wrongful dismissal to punish for the manner of dismissal.[60] In Canada such damages are also available in cases of an insurer's bad faith (and incorrect) refusal of an insurance claim,[61] and of a bank's appointment of a receiver without notice to the debtor.[62]

---

[56] *City of Bradford Metropolitan Council v Arora* [1991] 2 QB 507. Neill LJ noted, without doubting the position, that the first category was somewhat arbitrary in 'allowing such damages against a small local authority and refusing them against a powerful international company'.

[57] *Torres v Point Lisas Industrial Port Development Corp Ltd* (2007) 74 WIR 431 (Trinidad and Tobago CA).

[58] See the summary of the case law given by the Competition Appeal Tribunal in *2 Travel Group plc v Cardiff City Transport Services Ltd* [2012] CAT 19 at paras 461–77.

[59] Eg *Vorvis v Insurance Corp of British Columbia* [1989] 1 SCR 1085 (SC of Canada) and *Royal Bank of Canada v W Got & Associates Electric Ltd* [1999] 3 SCR 408 (SC of Canada) at para 29.

[60] *Vorvis v Insurance Corp of British Columbia* [1989] 1 SCR 1085 (SC of Canada) and *Wallace v United Grain Growers Ltd* [1997] 3 SCR 70 (SC of Canada). For some time such damages were awarded as part of the lost earnings award by increasing the reasonable notice period, but are now awarded by a separate award of punitive damages: *Honda Canada Inc v Keays* [2008] 2 SCR 362 (SC of Canada).

[61] *Whiten v Pilot Insurance Co* [2002] 1 SCR 595 (SC of Canada); *Fidler v Sun Life Assurance Co of Canada* [2006] 2 SCR 3 (SC of Canada).

[62] *Royal Bank of Canada v W Got & Associates Electric Ltd* [1999] 3 SCR 408 (SC of Canada). The Supreme Court was sceptical of such an award in that case but found that it fell within the judge's discretion and so did not allow the appeal against it.

24

Concurrent Claims

Claims in contract concurrent with other causes of action; claims in contract against more than one defendant.

24.1. Against the Same Defendant
24.2. Against Different Defendants

24.1 Against the Same Defendant

The broader questions of when a claimant can be concurrently liable in contract and tort, or contract and restitution/unjust enrichment, are beyond the scope of this book. Clearly where such concurrent liability does arise this impacts on damages in two respects.

First, it is important to understand the benefits of one cause of action over another in the damages context.[1] The remoteness test in the tort of negligence is more generous to the claimant than the contract test[2] and contributory negligence is generally available in negligence but not generally available in contract,[3] although where there is concurrent liability between a tortious and contractual breach of a duty of care contributory negligence will apply to both[4] and arguably the contract remoteness test will apply to both also.[5]

Secondly, it is important to understand the extent to which one award may prevent another, most particularly to avoid double recovery and because award under one cause of action removes the loss recoverable under another, as discussed in the remainder of this chapter.

Concurrent causes of action or the same cause of action may give rise to alternative remedies, such that the court cannot award both. In such situations the claimant must elect. As Lord Nicholls explains:

Faced with alternative and inconsistent remedies a plaintiff must choose, or elect, between them. He cannot have both. The basic principle governing when a plaintiff must make his choice is simple and clear. He is required to choose when, but not before, judgment is given in his favour and the judge is asked to make orders against the defendant. A plaintiff

---

[1] See further J Blom, 'Remedies in Tort and Contract: Where Is the Difference?' in J Berryman (ed), *Remedies: Issues and Perspectives* (Toronto, Carswell, 1991) 395.
[2] See above in chapter fourteen, section 14.3F(ii).
[3] See above in chapter fifteen, section 15.5.
[4] See above in chapter fifteen, section 15.5A.
[5] See above in chapter fourteen, section 14.5C.

is not required to make his choice when he launches his proceedings. He may claim one remedy initially, and then by amendment of his writ and his pleadings abandon that claim in favour of the other. He may claim both remedies, as alternatives. But he must make up his mind when judgment is being entered against the defendant. Court orders are intended to be obeyed. In the nature of things, therefore, the court should not make orders which would afford a plaintiff both of two alternative remedies.[6]

24.2 Against Different Defendants

A. Generally

It will often be the case that a claimant will have causes of action against more than one defendant in respect of the same loss, with one or more of those claims being in contract.

Bringing a claim against one defendant does not operate as a bar to bringing a claim against another defendant. However, the court may sometimes manage the litigation by requiring all claims to be brought at one time, and costs in successive actions may be disallowed if those actions should have been brought together with the earlier actions.[7]

Obtaining judgment against one claimant does not operate as a bar to bringing a claim and obtaining judgment against another defendant,[8] although in an unliquidated claim, such as for damages, the amount of that judgment will fix the amount of the claim in respect of that damage as against all defendants. Likewise, it may be appropriate to defer assessment of damages against a professional or misrepresentor until the claimant has had an opportunity to see whether judgment against a primary creditor will be easily satisfied.[9]

B. Double Recovery

Obtaining satisfaction of a judgment, ie actually receiving funds, will operate *pro tanto* to wipe out the loss, meaning that that part of the loss can no longer be claimed against another defendant (and the amount cannot be reopened in later litigation; in this sense the amount of the earlier judgment does apply between the claimant and the other defendants who were not party to or bound by that judgment). Thus, as Lord Nicholls has explained:

> Part satisfaction of a judgment against one person does not operate as a bar to the plaintiff thereafter bringing an action against another who is also liable, but it does operate to reduce

---

[6] See further *United Australia Ltd v Barclays Bank Ltd* [1994] AC 1 (HL) (damages for negligence and restitution for unjust enrichment).

[7] Section 4 of the Civil Liability (Contribution) Act 1978.

[8] Section 3 of the Civil Liability (Contribution) Act 1978, which applies to multiple causes of action for 'compensation' for the same 'damage'; *Isaacs & Sons v Salbstein* [1916] 2 KB 139 (CA).

[9] *Sibley v Grosvenor* (1916) 21 CLR 469 (HC of Australia); *Shuman v Coober Pedy Tours Pty Ltd* [1994] SASC 4401 (SC of South Australia) King CJ at para 29; *Marlborough District Council v Altimarloch Joint Venture Ltd* [2012] NZSC 11 (SC of New Zealand) Blanchard J at paras 73 ff.

the amount recoverable in the second action. However, once a plaintiff has fully recouped his loss, of necessity he cannot thereafter pursue any other remedy he might have and which he might have pursued earlier. Having recouped the whole of his loss, any further proceedings would lack a subject matter. This principle of full satisfaction prevents double recovery.[10]

This will apply unless the judgment makes it clear that it is only for part of the value of the claim.[11]

C. Joint and Several Liability

Where parties both make the same promise under a contract, they are each jointly liable.[12] They will not be severally liable unless the contract says so. Joint liability requires that all promisors are joined to an action, means that payment by any of them discharges the liability of the others, and means that death of a co-promisor merely drops that promisor out of the joint promise and does not pass any liability to the promisor's personal representatives. Joint and several liability does not require all parties to be joined, and amounts to a separate liability in each promisor that can pass to the promisor's estate, although it still entails that payment by one discharges the liability of all.

Judgment against one person jointly liable does not bar an action against another,[13] although there may be difficulty recovering costs in a successive action against a co-promisor.[14]

D. Contribution Claims between Defendants

All persons jointly or concurrently 'liable for the same damage' may recover from each other, under section 1 of the Civil Liability (Contribution) Act 1978, contribution in relation to any sum they have paid to the claimant, either at trial after being found liable, or under a settlement where they would have been found liable had the case against them been made out.[15]

(i) The 'Same Damage'

The various different persons must all be liable for the 'same damage',[16] and further must all be liable to pay 'compensation ... in respect of that damage (whatever the legal basis of his liability, whether tort, breach of contract, breach of trust or

---

[10] See the explanation in *Tang Man Sit v Capacious Investments Ltd* [1996] AC 514 (PC) Lord Nicholls at 522.

[11] *Jameson v Central Electricity Generating Board* [2000] 1 AC 455 (HL) Lord Hope at 474.

[12] Cf *Richard Adler v Soutos (Hellas) Maritimie Corp (The Argo Hellas)* [1984] 1 Lloyd's Rep 296 (Leggatt J).

[13] Section 3 Civil Liability (Contribution) Act 1978.

[14] Section 4 Civil Liability (Contribution) Act 1978.

[15] Section 1(4) Civil Liability (Contribution) Act 1978.

[16] Section 1(1) Civil Liability (Contribution) Act 1978.

otherwise)'.[17] Although there will not often be a problem in applying this test to joint contractors, difficulties may arise in determining whether two defendants liable under different contracts are liable for the same damage,[18] especially where one is a professional. One often-applied test is the mutual discharge test: if either defendant pays the claimant money towards its liability, will that reduce the other defendant's liability?[19] Accordingly, a negligent valuer and a borrower were not liable to a lender for the same damage (because payment by the valuer would not reduce the amount owed by the borrower).[20] On the other hand, a vendor who had breached warranties in a share purchase agreement and the buyer's accountants were liable for the same damage.[21]

(ii) The Amount of Contribution

The amount of contribution is fixed by the court's discretion under section 2 of the 1978 Act according to what is 'just and equitable', and can range from 0 to 100 per cent.[22] As in the case of a reduction in damages for contributory negligence,[23] the most important factors are causative potency and blameworthiness.[24]

E. Settlement against One Defendant

This also requires care when settling a claim against one defendant. If a compromise is made with one defendant (which will almost always be at less than the possible full value of the claim at trial) in full and final satisfaction of that defendant's liability and that debt is then satisfied by payment, that will, upon payment, discharge the liabilities of other defendants liable for the same damage, even though they are not party to the settlement agreement.[25] All will depend upon the terms of the settlement. If the terms of the settlement show that the parties have not treated the settlement as being for the full value of the claim, then the claim against others is not barred by satisfaction of the settlement.[26] The judge must construe the settlement to see that it compromises all the relevant causes of action, but, if it does, that is the

---

[17] Section 6(1) Civil Liability (Contribution) Act 1978.

[18] The leading case is *Royal Brompton Hospital NHS Trust v Hammond (No 3)* [2002] 1 WLR 1397 (HL).

[19] *Howkins & Harrison (a firm) v Tyler* [2001] PNLR 634 (CA) Scott V-C at 639–40; *Eastgate Group Ltd v Lindsey Morden Group Inc* [2002] 1 WLR 642 (CA); *Hurstwood Developments Ltd v Motor & General & Andersley & Co Insurance Services Ltd* [2001] EWCA Civ 1785.

[20] Ibid.

[21] *Eastgate Group Ltd v Lindsey Morden Group Inc* [2002] 1 WLR 642 (CA).

[22] Section 2(2) of the Civil Liability (Contribution) Act 1978. See further G Williams, *Joint Torts and Contributory Negligence* (London, Stevens & Sons, 1951).

[23] See above in chapter fifteen, section 15.5.

[24] *Fitzgerald v Lane* [1989] AC 328 (HL); *Dubai Aluminium Co Ltd v Salaam* [2003] 2 AC 366 (HL).

[25] *Jameson v Central Electricity Generating Board* [2000] 1 AC 455 (HL) (concurrent tortfeasors).

[26] Ibid Lord Hope at 474. This was obiter: in that case the settlement was held to extinguish the claim against the other tortfeasors.

end of matters; the claimant cannot pursue a concurrent defendant for more and also seek to re-open the amount of the settlement it made with one defendant.[27]

Although it is a matter of construction of the compromise agreement, it will usually only be payment of the settlement sum that is in satisfaction and extinction of the claim, and therefore only receipt of payment of the compromise amount (as it is with a judgment) that will discharge the loss and the right to claim against other defendants.[28]

---

[27] Ibid at 476.
[28] Ibid.

Index